D1639392

CASES AND STATUTES

ON THE

LAW OF EVIDENCE

WITH NOTES EXPLANATORY AND CONNECTIVE

PRESENTING A SYSTEMATIC VIEW OF THE WHOLE SUBJECT

BY

ERNEST COCKLE

Of Gray's Inn and the South-Eastern Circuit, Barrister-at-Law.

SEVENTH EDITION

BY

LEWIS FREDERICK STURGE

Of the Inner Temple, Barrister-at-Law.

LONDON:

SWEET & MAXWELL, LIMITED,

2 & 3 CHANCERY LANE. W.C.2

TORONTO, CANADA:
THE CARSWELL COMPANY, LTD.

AUSTRALIA:
THE LAW BOOK COMPANY OF AUSTRALASIA, PTY., LTD.

1946

(Printed in England)

First Edition	}	By Ernest Cockle	..	1907
Second Edition	}	By Ernest Cockle	..	1911
Third Edition	}	By Ernest Cockle	..	1915
Fourth Edition	..	By S. L. Phipson	.. ..	1925
Fifth Edition	..	By C. M. Cahn	.. ..	1932
Sixth Edition	..	By C. M. Cahn	.. ..	1938

PREFACE.

The development of the English law of evidence has undergone a change of emphasis in recent years, reflecting the altered procedure under which the great majority of civil cases are tried by a Judge sitting alone without a jury. The result has been that whereas formerly the most important topic was the admissibility of evidence, the present tendency is to place before the Judge all or most of the available evidence whether strictly admissible or not, and to concentrate most attention on problems relating to the burden of proof. Unlike the jury which gave a verdict without reasons, the modern judgment by a Judge sitting alone generally contains a reasoned justification for his findings of fact and this, in turn, is further analysed and criticised by appellate Courts. In consequence, there has been a large increase in the reported decisions dealing with questions of onus of proof. A considerable number (but by no means all) of those decisions have been included in the present edition, and it is hoped they will prove of assistance in understanding the law of to-day.

The passing into law of Lord Maugham's Evidence Act in 1938 introduced important changes in the law which will be found noted in their context, and it has been thought desirable to rewrite the notes dealing with Estoppel and the Interpretation of Documents.

The exigencies of the present time have necessitated the relegation of certain new matter to an Appendix, but it is anticipated that the usefulness of the book will not be seriously affected thereby. The present editor will feel amply rewarded if this edition in any way contributes to the rehabilitation in the legal profession of those who have been otherwise engaged during the past five years.

LEWIS F. STURGE.

4 Brick Court,
Temple.

December 4th, 1945.

PREFACE TO THE THIRD EDITION.

It is frequently said that a leading case book cannot be systematic. The present work represents a serious, and, it is believed, the first, attempt at system in such a matter. The method pursued may be shortly stated in detail.

1. Cases have been selected on all the main points of evidence. Such cases are, naturally, of various degrees of importance, and some may not be satisfactory expositions. But in each instance the case appearing to be the best available has been selected.

2. The principle laid down or explained in each case is stated in a newly-written headnote thereto.

3. The facts of each case, so far as they are essential to the point of evidence involved, are shortly stated.

4. The arguments of counsel are omitted, for one reason only—want of space.

5. All the most important portions of the judgments are given exactly as reported. It is believed that these include all that a busy practitioner or intelligent student would use in argument or study. The leading or vital passages of the judgments are emphasised by heavy type. The names of the judges constituting the Court are given, even when they do not appear in the original report.

6. With an eye to system, the cases have been arranged according to their subject and detail, and frequent notes, introducing cases of a class, or connecting and explaining individual cases, have been added.

7. Whenever a given case appears in several reports, that from which the judgments are taken is stated. In many cases,

where there is a difference between the reports, or one throws light upon another, judgments are taken from two or even three different reports.

8. A large collection of statutory provisions relating to evidence follows the cases, as a natural supplement to them. These are printed and noted in the same way as the cases.

9. All the Rules of the Supreme Court directly relating to evidence are also given.

10. The whole matter is summarised in a Table of Contents at the commencement of the book, an Index at the end, and two Appendices.

E. C.

8 New Court,
Lincoln's Inn, W.C.
July, 1915.

TABLE OF CONTENTS.

SYNOPSIS.

PART I.

CASES.

PAGE

MATTERS OF WHICH PROOF IS ALLOWED—*continued.*

(b) Facts Relevant to the Facts in Issue—*continued.*

(3) Statements made after the Transaction—*continued.*

PART II.

STATUTES.

PART III.

RULES OF THE SUPREME COURT.

APPENDICES.

TABLE OF BOOKS REFERRED TO.

Archbold. Criminal Evidence, 31st ed., 1943.
Best. Law of Evidence, 12th ed., 1922.
Phillipps. Law of Evidence, 10th ed., 1852.
Phipson. Law of Evidence, 8th ed., 1942.
Powell. Law of Evidence, 10th ed., 1921.
Roscoe, C. E. Criminal Evidence, 15th ed., 1928.
Roscoe, N. P. Evidence in Civil Actions, 20th ed., 1934.
Starkie. Law of Evidence, 4th ed., 1853.
Stephen. Digest of Evidence, 12th ed., 1936.
Taylor. Law of Evidence, 12th ed., 1931.
Thayer. Preliminary Treatise on Evidence, 1898.
Wills. Law of Evidence, 3rd ed., 1938.
Wills, C. E. Circumstantial Evidence, 7th ed., 1937.

TABLE OF CASES CITED IN JUDGMENTS AND NOTES.

[Leading Cases are printed in Capitals.]

TABLE OF STATUTES.

(*For Chronological Arrangement and Analysis see* ante, pp. xxvi—xlvi.)

CASES AND STATUTES
ON
THE LAW OF EVIDENCE.

PART I.

CASES ON EVIDENCE.

EVIDENCE GENERALLY.

The term "evidence" as used in law, or "judicial evidence", bears the same meaning as in popular language,—the means by which facts are made evident or established to the satisfaction of persons inquiring into them,—narrowed, however, by certain legal rules contrived to secure, as far as possible, its sufficiency and credibility; the result being that facts sufficient generally to satisfy or convince prudent persons of clear understanding may not be sufficient to fulfil the requirements of the law in matters arising for judicial determination.

It may be well to draw attention to the following

DEFINITIONS OF JUDICIAL EVIDENCE.

"That which demonstrates, makes clear, or ascertains the truth of the very fact or point in issue, either on the one side or on the other" (*Blackstone*, *Com.* III, 367).

"All the legal means, exclusive of mere argument, which tend to prove or disprove any matter of fact, the truth of which is submitted to judicial investigation" (*Taylor*, § 1).

"The *means* by which any alleged matter of fact, the truth of which is submitted to investigation, is established or disproved" (*Wills, Circ. Ev.*, 3).

"The evidence received by Courts of Justice in proof or disproof of *facts*, the existence of which comes in question before them" (*Best*, § 33).

"(1) Statements made by witnesses in Court under a legal sanction, in relation to matters of fact under enquiry; such statements are called oral evidence;

"(2) Documents produced for the inspection of the Court or Judge; such documents are called documentary evidence" (*Stephen*, Art. 1).

"The facts, testimony, and documents which may be legally received in order to prove or disprove the fact under enquiry" (*Phipson*, 1).

VARIETIES OF JUDICIAL EVIDENCE.

The following terms are used, but not uniformly, as descriptive of different varieties of evidence:—

Best Evidence.—This term is used to describe primary evidence as distinguished from secondary evidence (see *below*, and *post*, pp. 163, 345).

Conclusive Evidence.—Evidence of a fact which the Court must take as full proof of such fact and which excludes all evidence to disprove it (see *Stephen*, Art. 1). Such evidence is nearly always in cases of statutory provisions declaring particular evidence to be conclusive; unless the so-called conclusive or irrebuttable presumptions are considered as evidence (see *post*, p. 155).

Direct Evidence.—This term is used in two senses: as (*a*) Evidence of a fact actually in issue (as distinguished from circumstantial evidence); (*b*) Evidence of a fact actually perceived by a witness with one of his own senses, or of an opinion actually held by himself (as distinguished from hearsay evidence) (see *post*, pp. 58, 63, 163).

Circumstantial or Presumptive Evidence is evidence of a fact not actually in issue, but legally relevant to a fact in issue (*post*, p. 58).

Real Evidence.—Evidence supplied by material objects produced for the inspection of the Court, and not by information from a witness or document (*post*, p. 408).

Oral Evidence.—Evidence of a fact brought to the knowledge of the Court by the spoken statement of a qualified witness (see *post*, p. 268).

Documentary Evidence.—Evidence of a fact brought to the knowledge of the Court by inspection of a document produced to the Court (see *post*, p. 268).

Extrinsic Evidence.—This term is generally used as descriptive of oral or parol evidence when given in connection with written documents (see *below*, and *post*, p. 377).

Hearsay (or Second-hand) Evidence.—Evidence of a fact not actually perceived by a witness with one of his own senses, but proved by him to have been stated by another person (see *post*, p. 169).

Indirect Evidence.—Evidence which is not direct evidence in either of its two senses (see *above*). It means therefore (*a*) circumstantial evidence, or (*b*) hearsay evidence (see *above*).

Original and Derivative Evidence.—Best defines original evidence as "that which has an independent probative force of its own", and derivative (second-hand or secondary) evidence, as "that which derives its force from some other source" (§§ 29—30; see as to this distinction, *Phipson*, 3).

Parol Evidence.—This term is sometimes used as equivalent to oral evidence. It seems to be used chiefly as descriptive of the oral "extrinsic evidence" when given in connection with written documents (see *above*, and *post*, p. 377).

Pre-appointed Evidence.—Evidence declared by the law to be either a permissible, or a necessary and exclusive, mode of proof of a particular fact (see *Best*, § 31). This term is rarely used. It appears chiefly in connection with public documents (see *post*, p. 154).

Prima Facie Evidence.—Evidence of a fact which the Court must take as proof of such fact unless it is held disproved by further evidence. Such evidence appears frequently in cases of statutory provisions declaring particular evidence to be *prima facie* (see *post*, p. 155).

Primary Evidence.—Evidence which itself suggests that it is the best evidence, or, at least, does not itself suggest the existence of better evidence, and which the law therefore regards as being the most reliable, and requires to be produced if available, to the exclusion of certain less reliable evidence. The term is mainly of importance in connection with documents, of which the original or an admission of its contents is said to be primary, and must generally be produced. It may be identified with best evidence (see *above*), and is distinguished from secondary evidence (see *below*). The term is also, but rarely, applied to oral or parol evidence, of which direct evidence (see *above*) is said to be primary. But there does not appear to be any practical reason for so classifying oral evidence, as the existence of primary does not exclude the secondary evidence in such case (see *post*, p. 163).

Secondary Evidence.—Evidence which itself suggests the existence of better evidence, and which the law rejects if the better or primary evidence is available. The term is mainly of importance in connection with documents, a copy or verbal account whereof may not generally be given in evidence. It is distinguished from best evidence and primary evidence (see *above*). The term is also, but rarely, applied to oral or parol evidence, of which hearsay evidence (see *above*) is said to be secondary. But there does not appear to be any practical reason for so classifying oral evidence, as the existence of primary does not exclude the secondary evidence in such case (see *post*, p. 163). [As to the distinction between second-hand and secondary evidence, see *Best*, § 494; *Phipson*, 3.]

THE FUNCTIONS OF JUDGE AND JURY IN DEALING WITH EVIDENCE.

In the case of trial by jury, it is, in the first place, essential to distinguish the respective functions of the Judge and the jury, inasmuch as they both have to deal with the evidence tendered, but in different manner. **The Judge** has the general conduct of the proceedings, deciding questions of law and practice, including those relating to the production and admissibility of evidence. **The jury** find the facts, thus dealing with the credibility and weight of the evidence.

It is the **duty of the Judge** to instruct the jury in the rules of law and practice by which the evidence is to be weighed; for instance, he should advise them not to convict upon the uncorroborated evidence of an accomplice (see *post*, p. 157); he should explain to them the nature and effect of any presumptions applicable (see *post*, p. 23), or any rule of law rendering evidence either unnecessary (see *post*, p. 13), or of peculiar application (see *post*, p. 85). It is also his duty to withdraw the case from the jury if he decides there is no evidence fit to be left to them upon one or more issues at the trial. The Judge, in summing up the case to the jury, frequently comments upon the weight of the evidence.

With respect to the duty of the Judge thus to deal with the **weight of evidence** as opposed to a ruling that there is no evidence, there appears to be some difference of opinion. It is sometimes maintained that, when he has explained to the jury the matter in issue, together with the law and practice applicable, he is *functus officio* and should not comment on the facts. But this rule is certainly largely departed from in general practice and it is usually considered that temperate comment by the Judge on the facts may well be of material assistance to the jury, although any officious interference with the functions of the latter is not only improper on the part of the Judge, but frequently defeats its own purpose by inclining the jury against the Judge's opinion. As Lord Chancellor

Bacon said to Mr. Justice Hutton, when swearing in the latter as a Judge—"Draw your learning out of your books, not out of your brain. Mix well the freedom of your opinion with the reverence of the opinion of your fellows. Be a light to jurors to open their eyes, not a guide to lead them by the noses" (*Campbell's Chancellors*, II, 428).

Professor Thayer, dealing with the system in America, speaks of the notion, that a Judge has no right to indicate to the jury his own views of the facts, as one which would have amazed any English Judge "from the beginning down", remarking that "It is not too much to say of any period, in all English history, that it is impossible to conceive of trial by jury as existing there in a form which would withhold from the jury the assistance of the Court in dealing with the facts" (*Thayer, Pr. Tr. Ev.*, 188).

The general functions of the Judge have thus been shortly summarised:—

"The duty of a Judge presiding at a trial by jury is fourfold: first, he must decide all questions respecting the admissibility of evidence; secondly, he must instruct the jury in the rules of law, by which the evidence, when admitted, is to be weighed; thirdly, he must determine, as a legal question, whether there be any evidence fit to be submitted to the jury for their consideration; and lastly, he must explain and enforce those general principles of law that are applicable to the point at issue" (*Taylor*, § 23). These points are illustrated by the cases following.

METROPOLITAN RY. CO. v. JACKSON.

HOUSE OF LORDS. 1877.

L. R. 3 A. C. 193; 47 L. J. Q. B. 303; 37 L. T. 679; 26 W. R. 175.

Questions of law are for the Judge, questions of fact for the jury, to determine. Whether there is sufficient evidence to be left to the jury from which they may legally and properly infer the matter in issue is a question of law for the Judge; whether such evidence establishes the matter in issue is a question of fact for the jury.

In an action for damages caused by negligence, it was held that the Judge was to decide whether there was any evidence proper to be left to the jury of negligence causing the injury, and for the jury to say whether, and how far, such evidence was to be believed.

The following is from the Law Reports:—

LORD CAIRNS, L.C. . . . The Judge has a certain duty to discharge, and the jurors have another and a different duty. **The Judge has to say** whether any facts have been established by evidence from which negligence *may be* reasonably inferred; **the jurors have to say** whether, from those facts, when submitted to them, negligence *ought to be* inferred. It is, in my opinion, of the greatest importance in the administration of justice that **these separate functions should be maintained, and should be maintained distinct.** It would be a serious inroad on the province of the jury, if, in a case where there are facts from which negligence may reasonably be inferred, the Judge were to withdraw the case from the jury upon the ground that, in his opinion, negligence ought not to be inferred; and it would, on the other hand, place in the hands of the jurors a power which might be exercised in the most arbitrary manner, if they were at liberty to hold that negligence might be inferred from any state of facts whatever. . . .

LORD O'HAGAN. . . . Your Lordships have never held that, when negligence is alleged, any state of facts assumed to bear upon the issue can be made the subject of inference by jurors, although not really connected with the issue before them. The consequences of such a doctrine would be disastrous, and **it is of high importance that the authority of the Judge should restrain a latitude of decision** which might often in the result be very inconsistent with reason and justice. . . .

LORD BLACKBURN. . . . I think it has always been considered a **question of law to be determined by the Judge,** subject, of course, to review, **whether there is evidence which,** if it is believed, and the counter-evidence, if any, not believed, **would establish the facts** in controversy. It is for **the jury to say whether and how far the evidence is to be believed.** And if the facts, as to which evidence is given, are such that from them a farther inference of fact may legitimately be drawn, it is for the jury to say whether that inference is to be drawn or not. But it is for the Judge to determine, subject to review, as a matter of law, whether from those facts that farther inference may legitimately be drawn. . . .

LORD GORDON. . . . The duty of a Judge in such a case is an exceedingly delicate one, as **the line of division** between what is proper to be submitted to the jury, as necessary to support a charge of negligence in point of law, and what may be submitted to the jury as sufficient to support a charge of negligence in point of fact, **is often a very narrow one.** But I agree . . . that **there is in every case a preliminary question, which is one of law, namely, whether there is any evidence on which the jury could properly find the question** for the party on whom the onus of proof lies. If there is not, the Judge ought to withdraw the question from the jury, and direct a nonsuit if the onus is on the plaintiff, or direct a verdict for the plaintiff if the onus is on the defendant. . . .

Note.—The following matters have, amongst others, been held to be generally (but with exceptions) questions of fact for the jury to decide—actual knowledge, real intention, express malice, good faith, reasonable skill, reasonable time, due diligence, and negligence. As to libel, see *post*, p. 12.

Some matters are declared by statute to be questions of law or fact. *See* Marine Insurance Act, 1906, ss. 18, 20, 88, *post*, p. 486; Perjury Act, 1911, s. 1, *post*, p. 495.

Foreign law has to be proved as a fact by evidence, but questions as to the effect of the evidence given are decided by the Judge alone (see *post*, p. 18).

Where a contract is oral, wholly or partially, the question as to its terms is for the jury (*Bolckow* v. *Seymour*, 17 C. B. (N.S.) 107). As to written contracts, see *post*, p. 11.

BARTLETT v. SMITH.

EXCHEQUER. 1843.

12 L. J. Ex. 287; 7 Jur. 448; 11 M. & W. 483; 63 R. R. 664.

The admissibility of evidence, documentary or otherwise, is a question of law for the Judge; and, if its admissibility depend on the certain facts, the Judge should himself adjudicate upon such facts without submitting them to the jury.

It was objected by the defendant at the trial, that a bill of exchange with a foreign stamp could not be read, on the ground that it was drawn in this country. Evidence of that fact was tendered and refused at that stage, but was afterwards received as part of the defendant's case and submitted to the jury. It was held that the Judge ought to have received evidence of the place of drawing, in the first instance, to enable him to decide upon the admissibility of the bill, and that he ought not to have submitted the evidence to the jury.

The following is from the Law Journal:—

Lord Abinger, C.B. . . . **All facts, which are necessary to be proved with a view to the reception of evidence, are for the consideration of the Judge,** and he is to receive evidence respecting them for his own satisfaction. He might indeed, if he pleased, ask the opinion of the jury, but still the decision ought to be his own. **A Judge should receive evidence as to** the competency of a witness, or the sufficiency of a stamp, which is good upon the face of it, **and ought to determine these questions for himself,** instead of submitting them to the jury. . . .

Parke, B., and Alderson B., delivered judgment to the same effect and Rolfe, B., concurred.

Note.—Questions of admissibility, which the Judge decides, include such as—whether the fact offered in evidence is relevant (see *post*, p. 58), whether the witness is competent (see *post*, p. 269), whether a document comes from proper custody (see *post*, p. 373) or is properly stamped, whether a dying declaration (see *post*, p. 244) or confession (see *post*, p. 197) is admissible, and whether secondary evidence is admissible (see *post*, p. 345).

It may still be his duty so to decide even though it may involve his deciding himself the very same question as the jury will have to decide (*Doe* v. *Davies* (1847), 10 Q. B. 314).

The evidence of the accused may be received as to facts going to admissibility (*R.* v. *Cowell*, [1940] 2 K. B. 49, C. C. A.).

MORRELL v. FRITH.

EXCHEQUER. 1838.

3 M. & W. 402; 49 R. R. 659.

The construction of a document is generally a question of law for the Judge; but where extrinsic evidence is required, and allowed, to explain it, as where peculiar terms or expressions are used, such evidence is for the jury.

The question was, whether a certain letter was a sufficient acknowledgment in writing to take the case out of the Statute of Limitation. The Judge was of opinion that it was not sufficient; and, although requested by the plaintiff's counsel to leave the question to the jury, he declined to do so, and directed a nonsuit. On an application for a new trial, it was held that he was right.

Lord Abinger, C.B. . . . **One case in which the effect of a written document must be left to a jury, is, where it requires parol evidence to explain it,** as in the ordinary case of mercantile contracts in which peculiar terms and abbreviations are employed. So also, where a series of letters form part of the evidence in the cause, they must be left, with the rest of it, to the jury. **But where the question arises on the construction of one document only,** without reference to any extrinsic evidence to explain it, it is the safest course to adhere to the rule, that **the construction of written documents is a question of law for the Court.** The *intention of the parties* is a question for the jury, and, in some cases, in cases of libel for instance, the meaning of the document is part of that intention, and therefore must be submitted to the jury. But where a legal right is to be determined from the construction of a written document which either is unambiguous or of which the ambiguity arises only from the words themselves, that is a question to be decided by the Judge. . . .

PARKE, B. . . . **The construction of a doubtful instrument itself is not for the jury,** although the facts by which it may be explained are. . . .

ALDERSON, B. . . . Where it is a letter only, and there is no evidence beyond the written instrument itself, **the construction of it is for the Court only, and not for the jury. The case of mercantile documents is altogether different.** There the meaning of the words themselves is in question, being words that are used in a particular and technical sense; **it is as if the document were in a foreign language, and the truth or propriety of the translation were in question.**

BOLLAND, B., concurred.

Note.—The question of existence or non-existence of a document would be a question of fact for the jury. Cases on the admissibility of evidence to explain peculiar terms and ambiguities are given *post*, p. 396. The question whether a writing is sufficient acknowledgment to prevent a debt being statute-barred is for the Judge. So is the construction of policies of insurance, or foreign contracts (after proof of their meaning of words used), and of lost documents (after proof of their contents by secondary evidence), and the question whether an amount agreed to be paid is a penalty or liquidated damages. As to oral contracts, see *ante*, p. 9.

The case of libel deserves special notice. Prior to 1792, in prosecutions for libel, the general practice was for the jury to decide merely the question of publication, clearly one of fact; the Judge deciding whether the writing was defamatory or not. Although the defamatory meaning would appear strictly to be a question of law for the Judge, yet it was felt that the practice placed too much power in the hands of the Judge, and it caused much acrimonious discussion, which ultimately resulted in Fox's Libel Act of 1792 (32 Geo. 3, c. 60), providing that in criminal prosecutions for libel the jury shall, after direction by the Judge on the law, give a general verdict upon the whole matter; thus in effect construing the writing, if the Judge holds it to be capable of a defamatory meaning. This rule has now been applied to civil proceedings for libel (*Nevill* v. *Fine Arts Co.*, [1897] A. C. 68).

PROOF.

Before dealing with the matters requiring proof, and the mode of proving them, it is necessary to consider those matters which (*a*) do not require proof, or (*b*) are not allowed to be proved. Under the former head we have (1) matters judicially noticed, (2) matters presumed, and (3) matters admitted; under the latter head we have (1) matters which a party is estopped from alleging, (2) matters stated "without prejudice" and (3) matters which are irrelevant to the issue.

MATTERS OF WHICH PROOF IS NOT REQUIRED.

JUDICIAL NOTICE.

There are certain **matters which are considered too notorious to require proof: such matters are therefore** "judicially noticed", that is to say, the Judge takes notice of their existence and nature without requiring any evidence thereof. English Law is dealt with in the same way, as, although it may not be so notorious to the public generally, it is taken to be within the knowledge, or rather, in the "breast", of the Judge.

It is impossible to state completely the matters which the Court will judicially notice. Any matter of such common knowledge that it would be an insult to intelligence to require proof of it would probably be dealt with in this way. Sir James Stephen gives a list of twelve kinds of matters which would be judicially noticed, but it is obviously incomplete, and apparently without either classification or order (*Dig. Ev.*, Art. 58). Mr. Wills classifies the **matters under the three following heads** (*Wills*, 19):—

1. The Law and Practice of the Courts.

2. Public Acts and Matters connected with the Government of the Country.

3. Matters of Fact of Common and Certain Knowledge.

Cases are given below under each of these three heads.

Judicial Notice is required by Statute of many matters, among which may be mentioned the following:—

1. The signatures of the Judges of the Supreme Courts, appended to any judicial or official document (Evidence Act, 1845, s. 2, *post*, p. 438).

2. The seal of every county court on all summonses and other process of the Court (County Courts Act, 1934, s. 176, *post*, p. 535).

3. Every Act of Parliament passed after 1850, unless it is expressly provided to the contrary (Interpretation Act, 1889, s. 9, *post*, p. 472).

4. The signatures of officers of the High Court, and the official seal or stamp of the several offices of the High Court, appended to or impressed on any document made, issued or signed in proceedings for winding up companies (Companies Act, 1929, s. 289, *post*, p. 518).

5. The seal of every Court having jurisdiction in bankruptcy, and the signature of the Judge or Registrar of such Court (Bankruptcy Act, 1914, s. 142, *post*, p. 500).

By other Statutes the seals, etc., of various other Courts and Government Departments are directed to be judicially noticed.

I. THE LAW.

STOCKDALE v. HANSARD.

KING'S BENCH. 1839.

9 A. & E. 1; 8 L. J. Q. B. 294; 3 Jur. 905;
48 R. R. 326.

The English Courts will judicially notice the Law of England and Ireland, including the Law and Custom of Parliament, and the privileges and course of proceedings of each House of Parliament.

In an action for libel, the defence was publication by order of the House of Commons. It was held that the Court could determine whether the House of Commons had such privilege as would support the plea, and could judicially notice the nature and extent of parliamentary privilege as part of the law of the land.

The following is from Adolphus and Ellis:—

Lord Denman, C.J. . . . **It is said that the Courts of law** must be excluded from all interference with transactions in which the name of privilege has been mentioned, because they **have no means of informing themselves what these privileges are.** They are well known, it seems, to the two Houses, and to every member of them, as long as he continues a member; but the knowledge is as incommunicable as the privileges to all beyond that pale. It might be presumption to ask how **this knowledge may be obtained,** had not the Attorney-General read to us all he had to urge on the subject **from works accessible to all, and familiar to every man of education.** The argument here seems to run in a circle. The Courts cannot be entrusted with any matter connected with privilege, because they know nothing about privilege; and this ignorance must be perpetual, because the law has taken such matters out of their cognisance. . . . **Lord Holt** (see *R.* v. *Paty*, 2 Ld. Raym. 1114) **in terms denied this presumption of ignorance, and asserted the right and duty of the Courts to know the law of Parliament, because the law of the land** on which they are bound to decide. Other Judges, without directly asserting the proposition, have constantly acted upon it; and it was distinctly admitted by the Attorney-General in the course of his argument. . . .

Patteson, J. . . . It is further said that the Courts of law have no knowledge as to the *lex et consuetudo parliamenti,* and cannot therefore determine any question respecting it. And yet, at the same time, it is said that the *lex et consuetudo parliamenti* are part of the law of the land. And this Court is, in this very case, actually called upon by the defendants to pronounce judgment in their favour, upon the very ground that their act is justified by that very *lex et consuetudo parliamenti,* of which the Court is said to be invincibly ignorant, and to be bound to take the law from a resolution of one branch of the Parliament alone. . . . **There is nothing so mysterious in the law and custom of Parliament,** so far at least as the rest of the community not within its walls are concerned, **that this Court may not acquire a knowledge of it in the same manner as of any other branch of the law. . . .**

Littledale and Coleridge, JJ., concurred.

Note.—**The law judicially noticed** by the English Courts is that of **England** (including Wales) only; not that of the Channel Islands, nor of Scotland, except in the House of Lords, nor that of the Dominions, Colonies or India, except in the Privy Council, and, naturally, not that of foreign countries. Such laws can be proved by expert witnesses (see *post*, p. 131), or they may be ascertained under the British Law Ascertainment Act, 1859 (see *post*, p. 447) or the Foreign Law Ascertainment Act, 1861 (see *post*, p. 448). Scotch law is fundamentally different from English law.

The common law of England, except where varied by statute prevails in Ireland, but it is uncertain to what extent the English Courts would now take judicial notice of Irish law (see *Taylor*, § 5).

The law thus noticed includes both public and (since 1850) private **Acts of Parliament** (see *post*, p. 267), **general customs** and possibly some local customs of well-known extensive application; but, generally, local or particular customs must be proved.

If the Judge should happen not to bear in mind the particular law in question, he may refer to, or be referred to, authorities in order to direct his attention to the law in question, and to refresh his memory; but this is not "proving" the law.

BRANDAO v. BARNETT.

HOUSE OF LORDS. 1846.

12 C. & F. 787; 3 C. B. 519; 69 R. R. 204.

The Court will judicially notice all general customs, such as the custom of Banker's Lien, and other customs of the Law Merchant, when they have once been judicially ascertained and established.

In an action against bankers to recover certain exchequer bills, the defendants set up a general banker's lien by virtue of general custom. It was held that such custom should be judicially noticed.

The following is from Clark and Finnelly:—

LORD CAMPBELL. The first question that arises upon this record is, whether judicial notice is to be taken of the general lien of bankers on the securities of their customers in their hands? The exchequer bills, for which this action is brought, are found to be the property of the plaintiff, and the defendants rest their defence on their second plea, that they were not possessed, etc., relying on the lien claimed for the balance due to them from *Edward Burn*.

The usage of trade by which bankers are entitled to a general lien, is not found by the special verdict, and unless we are to take judicial notice of it, the plaintiff is at once entitled to judgment. But, my Lords, I am of opinion that **the general lien of bankers is part of the law merchant, and is to be judicially noticed**—like the negotiability of bills of exchange or the days of grace allowed for their payment. **When a general usage has been judicially ascertained and established, it becomes a part of the law merchant which Courts of Justice are bound to know and recognise.** Such has been the invariable understanding and practice in *Westminster Hall* for a great many years; there is no decision or *dictum* to the contrary, and justice could not be administered if evidence were required to be given *toties quoties* to support such usages, and issue might be joined upon them in each particular case. . . .

LORD LYNDHURST. . . . There is no question that, **by the law merchant, a banker has a lien** for his general balance on securities deposited with him. I consider this as part of the established law of the country, and that **the Courts will take judicial notice of it: it is not necessary that it should be pleaded, nor is it necessary that it should be given in evidence** in this particular instance. . . .

Note.—Care must be taken to distinguish "general" from "particular" customs, the latter not being judicially noticed, but requiring proof on each occasion. See note to previous case.

It appears, however, to be necessary, in practice, to prove a general custom once at least, so that it may become "judicially ascertained and established", as was said above. See *Moult* v. *Halliday*, [1898] 1 Q. B. 125, and *Edelstein* v. *Schuler*, [1902] 2 K. B. 144, as to proof of general customs.

Besides mercantile liens, the following general customs have, among others, been judicially noticed—the negotiability of instruments, the general practice of conveyancers, the custom or law of the road, customs of navigation, and market overt.

MOSTYN v. FABRIGAS.

KING'S BENCH. 1774.

1 COWPER 161.

The Court will not judicially notice the Laws of the Colonies or Foreign Countries. They must be proved as matters of fact.

In an action for assault and false imprisonment, alleged to have been committed in Minorca, then a British possession, by the governor thereof, a question arose as to the law of that island.

LORD MANSFIELD, C.J. . . . **The way of knowing foreign laws is by admitting them to be proved as facts,** and the Court must assist the jury in ascertaining what the law is. For instance, if there is a French settlement, the construction of which depends upon the custom of Paris, witnesses must be received to explain what the custom is; as evidence is received of customs in respect to trade. . . . **So in** the supreme resort before the King in Council, the Privy Council determines all **cases that arise in the plantations,** in Gibraltar or Minorca, in Jersey or Guernsey; and they inform themselves, by having the law stated to them. . . .

Note.—Foreign and Colonial Law is one of those matters of "science or art" upon which evidence of opinion may be given by experts. (See *Bristow* v. *Sequeville*, *post*, p. 131.) For the word "plantations" in the above case we may now read "colonies".

II. PUBLIC MATTERS.

DUFF DEVELOPMENT CO., LTD. v. GOVERNMENT OF KELANTAN.

HOUSE OF LORDS. 1924.

L. R. [1924] A. C. 797; 93 L. J. Ch. 343; 131 L. T. 676; 68 S. J. 559; 40 T. L. R. 566.

The Court will judicially notice Public, Constitutional, or International Matters, affecting the Government of Great Britain and its relations with other States, in order that the Court and the Executive may take the same view and act in unison in dealing with such matters. For such purpose the Court should inquire of the Executive and thereby acquire the information, and the information so received is conclusive.

The Government of Kelantan applied for an order to set aside an order obtained by the appellants to enforce an award on the ground that Kelantan was a sovereign independent State. The Secretary of State for the Colonies, in reply to an inquiry by the Master, wrote that Kelantan was an independent State and the Sultan the Sovereign Ruler thereof. *Held*, that this letter was conclusive.

The following is from the Law Reports:—

Viscount Cave. First, it was argued that the Government of Kelantan was not an independent sovereign State, so as to be entitled by international law to the immunity against legal process. . . . It has for some time been the **practice of our Courts,** when such a question is raised, **to take judicial notice of the sovereignty of a State, and** for that purpose (in case of any uncertainty) **to seek information from a Secretary of State;** and when information is so obtained the Court does not permit it to be questioned by the parties. . . .

In the present case the reply of the Secretary of State shows clearly that notwithstanding the engagements entered into by the Sultan of Kelantan with the British Government that Government continues to recognise the Sultan as a sovereign and independent ruler, and that His Majesty does not exercise or claim any rights of sovereignty or jurisdiction over that country. **If** after this definite statement **a different view were taken by a British Court, an undesirable conflict might arise;** and, in my opinion, it is the duty of the Court to accept the **statement of the Secretary of State** thus clearly and positively made as **conclusive** upon the point.

Viscount Finlay. It is settled law that **it is for the Court to take judicial cognisance of the status of any foreign Government.** If there can be any doubt on the matter **the practice is** for the Court **to receive information from the appropriate department of His Majesty's Government, and the information so received is conclusive.** . . . There are a great many matters of which the Court is bound to take judicial cognisance, and among them are all questions as to the status and boundaries of foreign powers. In all matters of which the Court takes judicial cognisance the Court may have recourse to any proper source of information. It has long been settled that on any question of the status of any foreign Power the proper course is that the Court should apply to His Majesty's Government, and that in any such matter it is bound to act on the information given to them through the proper department. Such information is not in the nature of evidence: it is a statement by the Sovereign of this country through one of his Ministers upon a matter which is peculiarly within his cognisance.

Lord Dunedin. If our Sovereign recognises and expresses the recognition through the mouth of his minister that another person is a sovereign, how could it be right for the Courts of our own Sovereign to proceed upon an examination of that person's supposed attributes to examine his claim and, refusing that claim, to deny to him the comity which their own sovereign had conceded?

Lord Sumner. **The status of foreign communities** and the identity of the high personages who are the chiefs of foreign States, are **matters of which the Courts of this country take judicial notice.** Instead of requiring proof to be furnished on these subjects by the litigants, they act on their own knowledge, or, if necessary, obtain the requisite information for themselves. I take it that in so doing the Courts are bound, as they would be on any other issue of fact raised before them, to act on the best evidence, and, if the question is whether some new State or some older State, whose sovereignty is not notorious, is a sovereign State or not, the **best evidence is a statement, which the Crown condescends to permit the** appropriate **Secretary of State to give** on its behalf. It is the prerogative of the Crown to recognise or to withhold recognition from States or chiefs of States, and to determine from time to time the status with which foreign Powers are to be deemed to be invested. This being so, a foreign ruler, whom the Crown recognises as a sovereign, is such a sovereign for the purposes of an English Court of law, and the best evidence of such recognition is the statement duly made with regard to it in His Majesty's name. Accordingly **where such a statement is forthcoming no other evidence is admissible** or needed.

LORD CARSON delivered a speech to the same effect.

Note.—This case has since been applied in *Engelke* v. *Musmann*, [1928] A. C. 433, where a statement to the Court by the Attorney-General that the defendant was a member of the staff of the German Ambassador was held to be conclusive. In *The Fagernes*, [1927] P. 311, the question arose whether a collision in the Bristol Channel occurred within the jurisdiction of the High Court; at the request of the Court of Appeal the Attorney-General stated that the Home Secretary instructed him to say that the spot where the collision occurred was not within the limits to which the territorial sovereignty of His Majesty extends. The Court by a majority held that this statement was conclusive.

It is said in *Taylor on Evidence*, § 18—"The Courts will judicially recognise the political constitution or frame of their own Government; its essential political agents or public officers sharing in its regular administration; and its essential and regular political operations and actions. . . . But they will not recognise private orders made at the council table, for these are 'matters of particular concernment . . .'; nor, it seems, any Orders of Council, even though they regard the Crown and the Government; nor the transactions on the journals of either House of Parliament".

See also the Foreign Jurisdiction Act, 1890, s. 4, *post*, p. 473.

III. MATTERS OF COMMON KNOWLEDGE.

R. v. LUFFE.

KING'S BENCH. 1807.

8 East 193; 9 R. R. 406.

The Court will judicially notice facts which must have happened according to the constant and invariable course of nature; matters of common knowledge.

The question arising as to the legitimacy of a child, and the fact appearing that the husband had not access to the wife until a fortnight before the birth, the Court took judicial notice of the fact that, according to the course of nature, he could not have been the father.

Lord Ellenborough, C.J. . . . Here, however, in nature, the fact may certainly be known that the husband, who had no access until within a fortnight of his wife's delivery, could not be the actual father of the child. **Where the thing cannot certainly be known, we must call in aid such probable evidence as can be resorted to,** and the intervention of a jury must, in all cases in which it is practicable, be had to decide thereupon; but where the question arises as it does here, and **where it may certainly be known from the invariable course of nature,** as in this case it may, that no birth could be occasioned and produced within those limits of time, **we may venture to lay down the rule plainly** and broadly, without any danger arising from the precedent. . . .

Upon the ground of improbability, however strong, I should not venture to proceed. No person, however, can raise a question, whether a fortnight's access of the husband, before the birth of a full grown child, can constitute in the course of nature the actual relation of father and child. . . . **The general presumption will prevail, except a case of plain natural impossibility is shewn. . . .** Without weakening, therefore, any established cases, or any legal presumption, applicable to the subject, we may without hesitation say, that a child born under these circumstances is a bastard. . . .

GROSE, J., and LE BLANC, J., delivered judgment to the same effect and LAWRENCE, J., concurred.

Note.—Other matters judicially noticed as matters of common knowledge are the course of time, the ordinary public fasts and festivals, the dates of legal sittings of the Court, the order of the months, the meaning of ordinary language, weights and measures, etc.

Where the alleged period of gestation is not so short as to be manifestly impossible the Court will hear experts and refer to medical text-books. If the evidence is indecisive and the Court is left in doubt the presumption of legitimacy (see *post*, p. 28) will prevail. See *Clark* v. *Clark*, [1939] P. 228.

McQUAKER v. GODDARD.

1940. See Appendix IV, *post*, p. 564.

PRESUMPTIONS.

In several cases the law itself presumes certain facts in favour of certain persons, who are thereby relieved from the burden of proof of such facts.

Presumptions, or conclusions drawn from certain facts, are **frequently stated to be of three kinds**—(1) Presumptions of fact; (2) Conclusive or irrebuttable presumptions of law; (3) Rebuttable presumptions of law. But, for the purposes of the law of evidence, **the first two may be disregarded.** A practical lawyer, when he speaks of a presumption, always means a rebuttable presumption. **Presumptions of fact** are nothing but the conclusions which the Court draws from any individual combination of facts in evidence before it, and are outside the law of evidence altogether. **Conclusive presumptions of law** may be, with advantage, considered as mere rules of substantive law, and not presumptions at all. For instance, it used to be said that it was a conclusive presumption that a child under seven cannot commit a crime. Is it not more proper to put it, as a rule of substantive law, that a person of such age is incapable of crime? (cf. *post*, p. 528).

Sir J. Stephen uses the term in the third sense only. He defines a presumption as "a rule of law that Courts and Judges shall draw a particular inference from a particular fact, or from particular evidence, unless and until the truth of such inference is disproved" (*Stephen*, 3).

Rebuttable presumptions or arbitrary conclusions of law can only be laid down by the law in **cases of certain well-defined, and generally frequent, combinations of fact.** In such cases the defined conclusion must be drawn until it is rebutted by other facts.

The place occupied by presumptions in the law of evidence may be said to be under the head of **Burden of Proof** (see p. 136 ff.). Generally speaking, some rebuttable presumption operates to place the general burden of proof on one party (*e.g.*, the presumption of innocence requires the prosecutor to begin in a criminal trial). As the trial proceeds, however, other presumptions may arise which have the effect of shifting the burden of proof. Presumptions are also of great importance in determining what conclusion the Court ought to arrive at in cases where, owing to lapse of time, death of material witnesses or other causes, the available evidence is scanty and incomplete. See *Wakelin* v. *L. & S. W. Ry. Co.* (1886), 12 App. Cas. 41; *Jones* v. *G. W. Ry. Co.* (1930), 144 L. T. 194.

It is practically **impossible to give any complete, or generally recognised, list of presumptions.** On no other question in the law of evidence does there appear to be such vagueness and difference of opinion. The cases given below illustrate five presumptions which may be said to be generally accepted by the authorities as actual presumptions of law. Beyond these there appears to be so little agreement among the authors of different works on evidence that there are not even two books giving the same list. **The main reason of this entire want of harmony seems to be this.** Presumptions appear to have developed in all cases from relevant facts. The relevant facts, as will appear later (see *post*, p. 58), are those from which the Court *may* draw a certain conclusion. Facts raising presumptions are those from which the Court *must* draw a certain conclusion, until it is rebutted. In every case, it appears, where there is now a presumption, or imperative conclusion, there was a time when the conclusion was optional, or, in other words, when the Court *might* draw the conclusion which now it *must* draw. There has been a **transition from relevancy to presumption.** The Court having repeatedly had before it the same combination of facts, and having drawn what may have been the natural or obvious conclusion from such facts, the rule of law was ultimately evolved that the usual and familiar conclusion *should* be drawn, for the sake of uniformity and convenience. Thus we have developed presumptions of law. **The difficulty is to ascertain when the boundary** between relevancy and presumption **has been passed.** Decisions and judicial statements are not always clear on the matter, partly because the word "presumption" is frequently used loosely as meaning a presumption of fact, and partly because the occasion for laying down the law definitely may not have occurred. These observations may be illustrated by the rule as to proof of marriage. It is clear that marriage *may* generally be proved by cohabitation and reputation (see *post*, p. 97). Such facts are clearly *relevant* to the fact of marriage, and some writers treat the question as one of relevancy merely. Others say there is a presumption of law in such a case, whilst some seek safety in putting the point under both heads. On the whole there seems to be no clear authority on this particular case.

There are certain well-recognised **presumptions respecting documents**; on which matter cases appear, *post*, pp. 372, 376.

Equitable Presumptions.

Courts of Equity have evolved several presumptions, the most noticeable being those relating to:—

1. **Ademption.** When a parent gives a legacy to a child, and afterwards gives him a "portion" or substantial sum for his "advancement", the presumption generally is that the legacy is "adeemed", wholly or partially, by the portion, and the child cannot take both. This is really a case of "satisfaction" (see *below*). Also, when two legacies are given to a stranger, of equal amount and for the same purpose or motive, there is a similar presumption.

2. **Performance.** When a person covenants to purchase and settle land, or to leave personalty by will, for a certain person, and he afterwards purchases land, and such land or personalty passes on his intestacy to such person, performance of the covenant is presumed.

3. **Satisfaction.** When a parent covenants to give a "portion" to a child, and afterwards leaves him a substantial legacy, satisfaction of the covenant is generally presumed. Also, a debt due to a creditor is generally presumed to be satisfied by a legacy equal to the debt.

4. **Trust.** When a person buys property and has it conveyed gratuitously to another person, the latter is generally presumed to be a trustee for the former.

Statutory Presumptions.

In many cases presumptions are declared by statutes; the following may be mentioned as examples of a practice, which has become very common in recent years:—

1. **Bills of Exchange Act, 1882,** ss. 27, 30, *post*, p. 466.
2. **Rights of Way Act, 1932,** s. 1, *post*, p. 520.
3. **Children and Young Persons Act, 1933,** ss. 4, 50, 99, *post*, p. 524.
4. **Law of Property Act, 1925,** s. 184, *post*, p. 505.

See further hereon, *post*, p. 155.

PRESUMPTION OF INNOCENCE.

WILLIAMS v. EAST INDIA CO.

KING'S BENCH. 1802.

3 East 192; 6 R. R. 589.

There is a presumption of innocence, not only on criminal charges, but in all cases where an allegation of criminality is made.

Where the plaintiff declared that the defendants, who had chartered his ship, put on board dangerous substances without due notice to the captain or any other person concerned in the navigation, it lay upon him to prove even such negative averment, as the law presumed innocence of such a criminal neglect of duty.

Lord Ellenborough, C.J. (*delivering the judgment of the Court, which then included* Grose, Lawrence, and Le Blanc, JJ.). . . . **Where any act is required to be done on the one part, so that the party neglecting it would be guilty of a criminal neglect of duty in not having done it, the law presumes the affirmative,** and throws the burden of proving the contrary, that is, in such case, of proving a negative, on the other side. . . . That **the declaration,** in imputing to the defendants the having wrongfully put on board a ship, without notice to those concerned in the management of the ship, an article of a highly dangerous combustible nature, **imputes to the defendants a criminal negligence,** cannot well be questioned. In order to make the putting on board wrongful, the defendants must be conversant of the dangerous quality of the article put on board ; and if being so, they yet gave no notice, considering the probable danger thereby occasioned to the lives of those on board, **it amounts to a species of delinquency in the persons so concerned in so putting such dangerous articles on board, for which they were criminally liable** and punishable as for a misdemeanour at least. . . .

Note.—The rule that an alteration in a deed is presumed to have been made before execution appears to be an illustration of the above presumption (see *post*, p. 376). There is also a presumption of innocence when a person accused of a crime is under fourteen, even after the act is proved. His guilty mind must also be shown.

There appears to be some doubt whether allegations of criminality in civil cases must be proved with as much strictness as in criminal proceedings. The weight of opinion seems to be that in many cases they need not be so strictly proved. See *Phipson*, 11; *Taylor*, § 112; *Stephen*, Art. 94; and *post*, p. 152.

PRESUMPTION OF LEGITIMACY.

BANBURY PEERAGE CASE.

HOUSE OF LORDS. 1811.

1 SIM. & ST. 153; 1 L. J. (O.S.) CH. 106; 24 R. R. 159.

There is a presumption that a child born during wedlock is legitimate.

In a claim of peerage the House of Lords requested the opinion of the Judges on certain questions.

The following is from Simons and Stuart:—

SIR JAMES MANSFIELD, C.J., stated the unanimous opinion of the Judges:—

"That **the presumption of legitimacy arising from the birth of a child during wedlock,** the husband and wife not being proved to be impotent, and having opportunities of access to each other, during the period in which a child could be begotten and born in the course of nature, **may be rebutted by circumstances** inducing a contrary presumption." . . .

"That, after proof given of such access of the husband and wife, by which, according to the laws of nature, he might be the father of a child, no evidence can be received except it tend to falsify the proof that such intercourse had taken place." . . .

"That in every case **where a child is born in lawful wedlock, the husband not being separated from his wife by a sentence of divorce,**

sexual intercourse is presumed to have taken place between the husband and wife, until that presumption is encountered by such evidence as proves, to the satisfaction of those who are to decide the question, that such sexual intercourse did not take place at any time, when by such intercourse, the husband could, according to the laws of nature, be the father of such child."

" That **the presumption of the legitimacy of a child born in lawful wedlock, the husband not being separated from his wife by a sentence of divorce, can only be legally resisted by evidence** of such facts or circumstances as are sufficient to prove, to the satisfaction of those who are to decide the question, **that no sexual intercourse did take place between the husband and wife, at any time, when, by such intercourse, the husband could, by the laws of nature, be the father of such child.** Where the legitimacy of a child, in such a case, is disputed, on the ground that the husband was not the father of such child, the question to be left to the jury is, whether the husband was the father of such child, and the evidence to prove that he was not the father must be of such facts and circumstances as are sufficient to prove to the satisfaction of a jury, that no sexual intercourse took place between the husband and the wife at any time, when, by such intercourse, the husband could, by the laws of nature, be the father of such child." . . .

Note.—The presumption of legitimacy is a very strong one. Formerly, indeed, in order to rebut it, it was necessary to show that the husband had been " beyond the four seas ", or out of the kingdom during the whole of the material period. This rule was relaxed to the extent shown above. Now, in addition to having no application when the parties are divorced, it has no application when they are living apart under a decree of judicial separation, an order of a Court of summary jurisdiction, or even, probably, under a voluntary deed of separation. See the cases quoted *post*, p. 330, as to the admissibility of the declarations of the parents to prove or disprove matrimonial access. As to what is the " material period ", see *Clark* v. *Clark*, [1939] P. 228, where the child was presumed legitimate in face of evidence that the earliest possible date of intercourse with the husband was 174 days prior to the birth.

PRESUMPTIONS OF CONTINUANCE, LIFE, AND DEATH.

There is a presumption of fact that things, circumstances, or positions, once proved to have existed in a certain state or condition at a certain date, continue to exist in such state or condition for a reasonable time. This presumption is applicable to the continuance of life, marriage, sanity, domicil, partnership, etc.

There is a presumption of law that a person who is proved not to have been heard of for seven years by those who would be likely to hear of him if living, is dead; but there is no presumption that he died at any particular time.

Note.—The presumption of continuance is clearly one of great practical importance. It is frequently quite impossible to prove, for instance, the existence of a certain thing in a certain state or condition at the particular moment in question. It is, in general, sufficient, with the aid of this presumption, to prove such existence and state at such an earlier time that, according to its nature, it may fairly be presumed to have lasted to the moment in question. Where, however, title to property depends on the survivorship of the claimant, this fact must be established by affirmative evidence and not by mere presumption (*infra*, 32).

R. v. LUMLEY.

CROWN CASES RESERVED. 1869.

L. R. 1 C. C. R. 196; 38 L. J. M. C. 86; 20 L. T. 454; 17 W. R. 685; 11 Cox C. C. 274.

On a trial for bigamy, it was proved that the prisoner, a woman, married A. in 1836, left him in 1843, and married another man in 1847. Nothing was heard of A. after the prisoner left him, nor was any evidence given of his age, but the Judge, holding that there was a presumption of *law* that A. was alive at the date of the second marriage, withdrew the case from the jury, in effect directing them to return a verdict of guilty. *Held*, that there was no presumption of *law* either in favour of, or against, the continuance of A.'s life up to 1847; but that it was a question for the jury as a matter of fact whether or not A. was alive at the date of the second marriage. Conviction quashed.

The following is from the Law Reports:—

LUSH, J. (*who delivered the judgment of the Court, consisting of five Judges*). . . . On an indictment for bigamy, it is incumbent on the prosecution to prove to the satisfaction of the jury that the husband or wife, as the case may be, was alive at the date of the second marriage. This is purely a question of fact. **The existence of the party at an antecedent date may, or may not, afford a reasonable inference that he is living at the subsequent date.** If, for example, it was proved that he was in good health on the day preceding the marriage, the inference would be strong, almost irresistible, that he was living on the latter day, and the jury would in all probability find that he was so. If, on the other hand, it were proved that he was then in a dying condition, and nothing further was proved, they would probably decline to draw that inference. Thus, the question is entirely for the jury. **The law makes no presumption either way.**

Note.—See further *In re Phené's Trusts, infra*; and for cases where the presumption of innocence conflicts with the presumption of continuance, *R.* v. *Willshire, post*, p. 37.

IN RE PHENÉ'S TRUSTS.

CHANCERY APPEALS. 1869.

L. R. 5 CH. APP. 139; 39 L. J. CH. 316;
22 L. T. 111; 18 W. R. 303.

A testator died in January, 1861, having bequeathed his residuary estate equally between his nephews and nieces. N., one of his nephews, born in 1829, had gone to America in 1853, and frequently written home till August, 1858, but nothing further was heard of him except that he was registered as a deserter from the American Navy in June, 1860. In 1868 he was advertised for in English and American papers, but without result, and the share which his representatives claimed was paid into Court under the Trustee Relief Act. The Vice-Chancellor (James), considering himself bound by previous decisions, from which, however, he dissented, decided that N. was to be presumed to have survived the testator, and so was entitled to his share. *Held*, on appeal, that N.'s survivorship had not been established, and that the claim failed.

The following is from the Law Reports:—

Sir G. M. Giffard, L.J. [after citing with approval the statement in *Nepean* v. *Doe*, 2 M. & W. 894, that "**where a person goes abroad, and is not heard of for seven years, the law presumes the fact that such person is dead, but not that he died at the beginning or the end of any particular period during those seven years**; and that if it be important to anyone to establish the precise time of such person's death, he must do so by evidence of some sort to be laid before the jury for that purpose, beyond the mere lapse of seven years since such person was last heard of"; but citing with disapproval certain other passages from that case to the effect that the *law* presumes that a person proved to be alive at a given time remains alive till the contrary is shown, continued]: Those passages are not essential to the conclusion arrived at, or sound in point of reasoning. The other parts of the same judgment go to prove that there is not, and ought not to be, any such presumption of *law*. . . . It is a general, well-founded rule that a person seeking to recover property must establish his title by affirmative proof . . . and to assert, as an exception to the rule, that the onus of proving death at any particular period, either within the seven years or otherwise, should be with the party alleging death at such particular period and not with the person to whose title that fact is essential, is not consistent with the authorities. . . . **The true proposition is, that those who found a right upon a person having survived a particular period must establish that fact affirmatively by evidence**; the evidence will, necessarily, differ in different cases, but sufficient evidence there must be, or the person asserting title will fail. . . . In my opinion the burden of proof is on N.'s representative and he has not proved affirmatively that N. survived the testator, a proof which I consider essential to his title.

Note.—It is frequently stated that this presumption of death only arises where the person in question "goes abroad", and is not heard of for seven years. It is true that in the above case the person had gone abroad, but the rule appears to be general, as stated. Indeed, the presumption of death must be stronger where the person has not gone abroad, as he is in such case more likely to be heard of, and the absence of news of him would still more strongly suggest his death.

It has been held that a person ought not to be presumed to be dead in consequence of seven years' absence, if the other circumstances of the case render it probable that he would not have been heard of (*Watson* v. *England*, 14 Sim. 28; *Bowden* v. *Henderson*, 2 Sm. & G. 360). So, it might be difficult to presume the death of an absconding thief, as it would be difficult to procure witnesses who were likely to hear from him.

It should be particularly noted that, in order **to raise this presumption, evidence must be given** that the person whose death is in question has not been heard of for seven years. It is not, as is thought sometimes, that the presumption of continuance of life comes to an end after seven years. If the only evidence were that a young person was alive and well eight years ago, the presumption would be that he was still alive. So, in the case of *R.* v. *Willshire* (*post*, p. 37), life was presumed to continue after eleven years. It has even been said that the presumption of life may continue for half a century (*Taylor*, § 200).

Three statutes which have given effect to seven years' absence should be noted, *viz.*, 18 & 19 Car. 2, c. 11, s. 2, providing that persons upon whose lives estates depend shall be accounted as naturally dead if they "remain beyond the seas or elsewhere absent themselves in this realm" for seven years; the Offences against the Person Act, 1861, s. 57, providing that the penalty of bigamy shall not extend to any person whose husband or wife "shall have been continually absent from such person" for seven years and "shall not have been known by such person to be living within that time"; and the Matrimonial Causes Act, 1937, s. 8, which provides that the Court may, on the application of one spouse, make a decree presuming the death of the other spouse and dissolving the marriage and, by sub-section (2), "in any such proceeding the fact that for a period of seven years or upwards the other party to the marriage has been continually absent from the petitioner and the petitioner has no reason to believe that the other party has been living within that time, shall be evidence that he or she is dead until the contrary is proved".

The Probate Court frequently presumes death after short absence, for the purpose of granting probate or letters of administration.

PRESUMPTION OF REGULARITY.

BERRYMAN v. WISE.

KING'S BENCH. 1791.

4 T. R. 366; 2 R. R 413.

There is a presumption that public and official acts and duties have been regularly and properly performed; and that persons acting as public officers, or in public capacities, have been regularly and properly appointed.

In an action by an attorney for words spoken of him in the way of his profession, it was held he need not prove that he was an attorney by his certificate or by a copy of the roll of attorneys; but that proof that he acted as such was sufficient.

The Court (*which then consisted of* Lord Kenyon, C.J., Buller, Ashhurst and Grose, JJ.) were of opinion that this was sufficient proof.

Buller, J., said that **in the case of all peace officers, justices of the peace, constables, etc., it was sufficient to prove that they acted** in those characters without producing their appointments. . . . Neither in actions for tithes is it necessary for the incumbent to prove presentation, institution and induction; proof that he received the tithes, and acted as the incumbent, is sufficient.

Note.—This presumption, which is of very wide application, is said to be based on principles of public policy, and upon the idea that a person is not likely to be in a position to act as a public officer unless he really were such. There is no such presumption concerning private offices (see *post*, p. 91), in which the course of business is merely a relevant fact from which a conclusion *may* be drawn. There are, however, certain statutory presumptions under the Companies Act, 1929, as to the regularity of proceedings of companies incorporated under that Act (see *post*, p. 516).

Among the other public officials to whom this rule has been applied may be mentioned—solicitors, commissioners for oaths, County Court Judges, Masters in Chancery, Post Office officials, churchwardens, vestry clerks, and Lords of the Treasury.

PRESUMPTION OF LAWFUL ORIGIN.

JOHNSON v. BARNES.

EXCHEQUER CHAMBER. 1873.

L. R. 8 C. P. 527; 42 L. J. C. P. 259; 29 L. T. 65.

There is a presumption that asserted rights exercised without interruption, for such a length of time that they may fairly be taken to have had a lawful origin, had such lawful origin.

Where the Corporation of a Borough had from time immemorial exercised exclusively a right of pasturage over certain lands, it was presumed that the Corporation was legally entitled to an exclusive right of pasturage over such lands, and not a mere right of common which could not, in the circumstances, have been legal, and this notwithstanding that the right had been described as a right of common in a long series of documents.

The following is from the Law Reports:—

KELLY, C.B. . . . **I think we are bound to presume a legal origin, if such be possible,** in favour of a right which appears, from the facts stated in the case, to have existed for many hundreds of years, **and that the inaccurate description of such a right in a series of conveyances cannot interfere with the presumption** which we should otherwise be entitled to make from the facts with relation to the enjoyment of the right. When we look to these facts, we find that the Corporation of Colchester has in fact exercised a right of pasturing an unlimited number of cattle or sheep on certain land around the walls of the town during a certain season of the year, except as to any part of the land under cultivation. . . . It seems to me manifest that what the Corporation have exercised from time immemorial is a right which, though frequently spoken of as a right of common, was, in fact, an exclusive right of pasturage. . . .

Then we come to what has been made one of the most important questions in the case, that is to say, supposing that the right actually exercised has always been in fact a right of exclusive pasturage, and has always been treated and dealt with as such, is the presumption which would naturally arise from the facts destroyed by the effect of a long and numerous series of documents in which the right is spoken of in expressions indicating a right in the nature of a right of common? I do not think we should be justified in giving this effect to the documents, if the result would be to set aside a right which has been so long exercised in fact. . . . It appears to me, therefore, on consideration of the whole of the facts and documents in this case, that **we are bound, in accordance with one of the best established principles of law, to presume a legal origin, if one were possible, in favour of a long and uninterrupted actual enjoyment of a right.**

MARTIN and CLEASBY, BB., and QUAIN and ARCHIBALD, JJ., concurred.

Note.—The most noticeable application of this presumption of legal origin occurs in the case of common law prescription. Strictly, a prescriptive right should have existed from "time immemorial", but when it was shown to have been actually exercised for a considerable number of years, according to circumstances, it was presumed to have existed from time immemorial, and thus to have had a legal origin, or to have been created by a "lost grant" since time immemorial. Without such presumption it would have been practically impossible to prove prescriptive rights. The Prescription Act, 1832, now simplifies the matter by laying down definite periods (*e.g.*, twenty years for easements, and thirty years for rights of common, etc.), for the acquirement of prescriptive rights in most cases.

The so-called "presumption of lost grant" was but an instance of the presumption of lawful origin in cases where such origin would properly be a "grant". Another illustration is afforded by the dedication of a highway. "If there has been a public uninterrupted user of a road for such a length of time as to satisfy the jury that the owner of the soil intended to dedicate it to the public, this is sufficient to prove the existence of a highway" (Williams, J., in *Dawes* v. *Hawkins*, 8 C. B. (N.S.) 848), and see now the Rights of Way Act, 1932, *post*, p. 520.

CONFLICTING PRESUMPTIONS.

R. v. WILLSHIRE.

CROWN CASES RESERVED. 1881.

L. R. 6 Q. B. D. 366; 50 L. J. M. C. 57; 44 L. T. 222; 29 W. R. 473; 45 J. P. 375; 14 Cox C. C. 541.

Where there are conflicting presumptions, they are to be dealt with in the same way as conflicting evidence, i.e., they must be left to the jury.

In a prosecution for bigamy, it appeared that the prisoner had gone through four marriage ceremonies with A, B, C and D, in 1864, 1868, 1879 and 1880 respectively. Having been convicted in 1868 of marrying B in the lifetime of A, he was now prosecuted for marrying D in the lifetime of C. In defence, the prisoner gave evidence of the previous conviction, thus proving that A, his real, or first, wife, was alive in 1868. The presumption then arose that her life continued to 1879, when the prisoner married C, and that therefore the marriage with C was void, and he had not committed bigamy by marrying D in the lifetime of C. On the other hand, there was a presumption of innocence as to the marriage with C, consequently a conflicting presumption of the real or first wife's death. It was held to be a question of fact for the jury whether she was alive or not.

The following is from the Law Journal:—

LORD COLERIDGE, C.J. . . . **This conflict of presumptions was sufficient to raise a question of fact for the jury to determine.** It was for the jury to decide whether the man told or acted a falsehood for the purpose of marrying in 1879, or whether his real wife was then dead. The learned Common Serjeant did not leave the question to the jury, but, on these conflicting presumptions, held that the burthen of proof was on the prisoner, who, besides showing the existence of the life in 1868, was bound to prove that it continued till 1879. There is no such rule of law. The prisoner was not bound to do more than set up the life in 1868, which would be presumed to continue, and it was then for the prosecution to show by evidence that that presumption was rebutted. . . .

LINDLEY, HAWKINS, LOPES and BOWEN, JJ., concurred.

Note.—As to the two presumptions which arose and were in conflict in this case, *viz.*, that of continuance, and that of innocence, see *ante*, pp. 30, 27.

ADMISSIONS.

Any matters which have been admitted for the purpose of the trial need not be proved. Admissions thus expressly made in the proceedings prior to or at the trial are sometimes called **formal or express** admissions, to distinguish them from those **informal or casual** statements made by a party against his interest, which may, at the trial, be proved by witnesses. Such "informal" admissions, as they may be called, are dealt with hereafter, as exceptions from the "hearsay" rule (see *post*, p. 169).

Formal or Express admissions may be made—

(*a*) On the Pleadings or otherwise in writing (see O. 32, r. 1, *post*, p. 538). Facts alleged in a pleading, if not denied, are taken to be admitted (see O. 19, r. 13, *post*, p. 537).

(*b*) On Notice to Admit facts or documents, served by one party on another (see O. 32, rr. 2, 4, *post*, p. 539).

(*c*) In Answers to Interrogatories administered by one party to another (see O. 31, r. 1, *post*, p. 537).

(*d*) By Solicitor or Counsel, in the exercise of his discretion, before or at trial.

It should, however, be noted here that express admissions are only allowed in civil cases. They are never allowed in **criminal cases,** unless a plea of "guilty" can be treated as such. It is otherwise as to informal admissions (see *post*, pp. 171, 175).

Details of admissions under heads (*a*), (*b*), and (*c*) should be sought in books on Procedure. See also O. 32, *post*, p. 539. The case following illustrates head (*d*).

SWINFEN v. LORD CHELMSFORD.

EXCHEQUER. 1860.

29 L. J. Ex. 382; 2 L. T. 406; 8 W. R. 545; 6 Jur. (n.s.) 1035; 5 H. & N. 890.

A barrister (or other advocate) may make any admission on behalf of his client which, in the honest exercise of his judgment, he thinks proper; but he has no authority on matters collateral to the suit.

The defendant, when Sir Frederick Thesiger, appeared for the plaintiff in a certain case, which he compromised. It was held that he was authorised to do so by virtue of his position.

The following is from the Law Journal:—

Pollock, C.B. (*delivering the judgment of the Court*, Pollock, C.B., Bramwell, Channell and Watson, BB.). . . . The conduct and control of the cause are left necessarily to counsel. If a party desires to retain the power of directing counsel how the suit shall be conducted, he must agree with some counsel willing to bind himself. . . . Although **counsel has complete authority over the suit, the mode of conducting it, and all that is incident to it,** such as withdrawing the record, withdrawing a juror, or calling a witness, or selecting such as in his discretion he thinks ought to be called, and other matters which properly belong to the suit, and the management and conduct of the trial, he has not, by virtue of his retainer in the suit, any power over matters that are collateral to it. . . .

Note.—The same rule would apply to a solicitor acting as an advocate.

MATTERS OF WHICH PROOF IS NOT ALLOWED.

ESTOPPEL.

The law in some cases estops or prevents a person from alleging certain facts, which then cannot be proved by him.

An estoppel, says Blackstone, "happens where a man hath done some act or executed some deed which estops or precludes him from averring anything to the contrary" (*Commentaries*, III, 308). Coke's explanation of it is that it is so called "because a man's owne act or acceptance stoppeth or closeth up his mouth to alleage or plead the truth" (*Coke on Littleton*, 352 a); for which reason it is said to be "odious" and to be construed strictly; but the better view appears to be that the reason is "to provide certain means by which a man may be concluded, not from saying the truth, but from saying that that which, by the intervention of himself or his, has once become accredited for truth, is false" (*Smith's Leading Cases*, 13th ed., II, 657). Sometimes an estoppel is spoken of as a "conclusive admission".

Estoppels are generally divided into three kinds:

1. **Estoppel by Record.** The rule that a person may not deny facts which have previously been decided against him by the judgment of a Court of Law, appears to be based on two maxims—*Interest reipublicæ ut sit finis litium*, and *Nemo debet bis vexari pro eadem causa.* It applies generally to judgments of all civil and criminal Courts, whether of record or not, and whether English or foreign, as regards matters which the Court had jurisdiction to decide directly between the parties. So it applies to judgments of county courts and Courts of summary jurisdiction, to judgments obtained in chambers, or by consent or default, if *final* and not merely interlocutory. It may even apply to judicial proceedings of domestic tribunals.

2. **Estoppel by Deed.** The rule that a party to a deed is not permitted to deny facts stated therein affords an illustration of the exaggerated importance of a "seal" in English law. There is no such estoppel in the case of ordinary signed documents; though a parol agreement may give rise to an estoppel on other grounds, *e.g.*, bailor and bailee.

3. **Estoppel by Conduct.** The rule that a person who has by his conduct or words caused another person to act in a certain manner cannot afterwards tell an inconsistent tale to the prejudice of such other person appears, on the other hand, to be based on sound common sense, good business and policy. It seems to have originated in equity, and is sometimes known as "equitable estoppel". The expression "estoppel *in pais*" seems to be falling into disuse. There would appear to be a fine future for this useful and elastic doctrine.

The cases appearing below illustrate and explain these three kinds of estoppel.

Estoppels are sometimes declared by Statute. Two noticeable provisions on this subject are the Bills of Exchange Act, 1882, s. 54 (*post*, p. 466), and the Partnership Act, 1890, s. 14 (*post*, p. 474).

I. ESTOPPEL BY RECORD.

THE DUCHESS OF KINGSTON'S CASE.

HOUSE OF LORDS. 1776.

20 Howell's State Trials 355, 537.

A person who was a party to legal proceedings in which judgment was given, or who claims under a person who was a party thereto, is estopped from denying the facts upon

which such judgment was based, if such judgment be pleaded as an estoppel.

But a judgment "in personam" does not estop persons who were neither parties nor privies thereto.

Nor are the parties or their privies estopped from denying matters which merely came collaterally into question in such legal proceedings, or which were only incidentally cognisable, or which might be inferred by argument from the judgment.

Any person against whom a judgment is offered in evidence may prove that it was obtained by fraud or collusion to which he was no party.

The Duchess of Kingston was indicted and tried in the House of Lords for bigamy, in marrying the Duke of Kingston in March, 1769, during the lifetime of her husband the Earl of Bristol. The Duchess pleaded that, in a suit for jactitation of marriage instituted by her against the Earl of Bristol, in the Ecclesiastical Court, namely, in the Consistory Court of the Bishop of London, it had been decreed and declared in February, 1769, that she was a spinster, and that the Earl of Bristol had wickedly and maliciously boasted and publicly asserted (though falsely) that they were joined and contracted together in matrimony; and he was admonished to desist from such boasting and asserting of such alleged marriage.

It was objected that such decree of the Ecclesiastical Court was not binding on the Crown, and did not estop the prosecution from proving that in fact there was a lawful marriage as alleged, at the date of such decree, on the grounds: (1) that the Crown was not a party to the proceedings in the Ecclesiastical Courts, and (2) that the decree was obtained by fraud or collusion of the parties to such proceedings.

It was ordered by the Lords that the following questions be put to the Judges, *viz.*:

1. Whether a sentence of the Spiritual Court against a marriage in a suit for jactitation of marriage is conclusive evidence so as to stop the counsel for the Crown from proving the said marriage in an indictment for polygamy?

2. Whether, admitting such sentence to be conclusive upon such

indictment, the counsel for the Crown may be admitted to avoid the effect of such sentence, by proving the same to have been obtained by fraud or collusion?

SIR WILLIAM DE GREY, C.J. (*delivering the unanimous opinion of the Judges*). . . . As a general principle, **a transaction between two parties, in judicial proceedings, ought not to be binding upon a third;** for it would be unjust to bind any person who could not be admitted to make a defence, or to examine witnesses, or to appeal from a judgment he might think erroneous; and therefore the **depositions** of witnesses in another cause in proof of a fact, the **verdict** of a jury finding the fact, and the **judgment** of the Court upon the facts found, **although evidence against the parties, and all claiming under them, are not, in general, to be used to the prejudice of strangers. . . .**

From the variety of cases relative to judgments being given in evidence in civil suits, **these two deductions seem to follow as generally true: first,** that the judgment of a Court of concurrent jurisdiction directly upon this point, is as a plea, a bar, or as evidence, conclusive, between the same parties, upon the same matter, directly in question in another Court; **secondly,** that the judgment of a Court of exclusive jurisdiction, directly upon the point, is, in like manner, conclusive upon the same matter, between the same parties, coming incidentally in question in another Court for a different purpose. **But neither the judgment of a concurrent or exclusive jurisdiction is evidence of any matter which came collaterally in question,** though within their jurisdiction, **nor of any matter incidentally cognisable, nor of any matter** to be inferred by argument from the judgment.

Upon the subject of marriage, the Spiritual Court has the sole and exclusive cognisance of questioning and deciding, directly, the legality of marriage; and of enforcing, specially, the rights and obligations respecting persons depending upon it; but the Temporal Courts have the sole cognisance of examining and deciding upon all temporal rights of property; and, so far as such rights are concerned, they have the inherent power of deciding incidentally, either upon the fact, or the legality of marriage, where they lie in the way to the decision of the proper objects of their jurisdiction. . . . So that the trial of marriage, either as to legality or fact, was not absolutely and from its nature, an object *alieni fori*. . . .

A sentence of nullity and a sentence in affirmation of a marriage have been received as conclusive evidence on a question of legitimacy arising incidentally upon a claim to a real estate. **A sentence in a case of jactitation has been received** upon a title in ejectment as evidence against a marriage, and, in like manner in personal actions immediately founded on a supposed marriage. . . . **But in all these cases the parties to the suits, or at least the parties against whom the evidence was received, were parties to the sentence and had acquiesced under it, or claimed under those who were parties and had acquiesced.**

But although the law stands thus with regard to civil suits, **proceedings in matters of crime, and especially of felony, fall under a different consideration,** first, because **the parties are not the same; for the King, in whom the trust of prosecuting public offences is vested,** and which is executed by his immediate orders, or in his name by some prosecutor, **is no party to such proceedings in the Ecclesiastical Court,** and cannot be admitted to defend, examine witnesses, in any manner intervene, or appeal; secondly, such doctrines would tend to give the Spiritual Courts, which are not permitted to exercise any judicial cognisance in matters of crime, an immediate influence in trials for offences, and to draw the decision from the course of the common law, to which it solely and peculiarly belongs. . . .

But if a direct sentence upon the identical question in a matrimonial cause should be admitted as evidence, . . . yet a cause of jactitation is of a different nature; it is ranked as a cause of defamation only. . . . **The sentence has only a negative and qualified effect, viz., " that the party has failed in his proof,** and that the libellant is free from all matrimonial contract, as far as yet appears " ; . . . so that, admitting the sentence in its full extent and import, it only proves that it did not yet appear that they were married, and not that they were not married at all. . . .

But if it was a direct and decisive sentence upon the point, and, as it stands, to be admitted as conclusive evidence upon the Court, and not to be impeached from within; **yet, like all other acts of the highest judicial authority, it is impeachable from without; although it is not permitted to show that the Court was mistaken, it may be shown that they were misled.**

Fraud is an extrinsic, collateral act; which vitiates the most

solemn proceedings of Courts of justice. Lord Coke says, it avoids all judicial acts, ecclesiastical or temporal. . . .

We are therefore unanimously of opinion:—

First, that a sentence in the Spiritual Court against a marriage in a suit of jactitation of marriage is not conclusive evidence so as to stop the counsel for the Crown from proving the marriage in an indictment for polygamy.

Secondly, admitting such sentence to be conclusive upon such indictment, the counsel for the Crown may be admitted to avoid the effect of such sentence by proving the same to have been obtained by fraud or collusion.

Note.—Judgments are of two kinds—*in Rem* and *in Personam.* The former comprise all judgments affecting the legal *status*, *e.g.*, a divorce decree or an adjudication in bankruptcy, and are conclusive against all persons, whether parties or strangers. Judgments *in personam* are all ordinary judgments between persons not affecting status. They bind only parties and privies as to the facts in issue. But all judgments are conclusive against all persons of their legal effect, as distinguished from the facts upon which they are based. That is to say, a judgment in favour of A against B for damages for negligence is proof against all the world that such judgment has been entered and between those parties, but there is no estoppel in the case of persons not parties to that judgment or their privies from disputing the facts on which it was based. See *Hollington* v. *Hewthorn*, [1943] 1 K. B. 597, C. A., *post*, p. 127. The estoppel may arise upon a judgment by default (see *Hoystead* v. *Taxation Commissioner*, [1926] A. C. 155, P. C.), or by consent (*Re South American and Mexican Co.*, [1895] 1 Ch. 37, C. A.). The judgment is only conclusive of what it actually decides and of matters necessarily implicit in the decision and actually raised before the tribunal by the pleadings (*Hoystead's Case*, (*supra*); *New Brunswick Ry. Co.* v. *British, etc., Corporation*, [1939] A. C. 1). A number of rather fine distinctions have been raised in the cases on this point (see, for example, *Davis* v. *Hedges* (1871), 6 Q. B. 687, distinguished in *Caird* v. *Moss* (1886), 33 Ch. D. 22, C. A.; and cf. *Humphries* v. *Humphries*, [1910] 2 K. B. 531, C. A.).

The position in the Divorce Court is peculiar. By section 6 (2) of the Matrimonial Causes Act, 1937, the Court *may* treat an order of the justices as sufficient proof of the facts on which it is based. The clear implication is that it is not bound to do so. It would seem that a decision of the Divorce Court between the same parties and on the same facts will supersede an order of the justices (see *Pratt* v. *Pratt* (1927), 137 L. T. 491), and there is no estoppel.

VOOGHT v. WINCH.

KING'S BENCH. 1819.

2 B. & Ald. 662; 21 R. R. 446.

A former judgment between the same parties on the same subject-matter will operate as an estoppel and be conclusive only when it is so pleaded, or there is no opportunity of so pleading it. Otherwise it is only a relevant fact from which the Court may draw a conclusion in favour of the person who tenders it as evidence.

In an action for diverting water from a stream, the defendant gave in evidence a judgment in a former action between the same parties for the same cause of action, and insisted that it operated as an estoppel. The Judge received it in evidence, but refused to nonsuit the plaintiff, the defendant having pleaded only "not guilty", and the plaintiff obtained a verdict. On motion to the Court for a nonsuit or new trial, a nonsuit was refused, but a new trial was granted on other grounds.

Abbott, C.J. . . . I am of opinion that **the verdict and judgment obtained for the defendant in the former action was not conclusive** evidence against the plaintiff upon the plea of not guilty. **It would indeed have been conclusive if pleaded in bar to the action by way of estoppel. In that case the plaintiff would not be allowed to discuss the case with the defendant, and for the second time to disturb and vex him by the agitation of the same question.** But the defendant has pleaded not guilty, and has thereby elected to submit his case to a jury. Now if the former verdict was proper to be received in evidence by the learned Judge, its effect must be left to the jury. If it were conclusive indeed, the learned Judge ought immediately to have nonsuited the plaintiff, or to have told the jury that they were bound, in point of law, to find a verdict for the defendant. It appears to me, however, that **the party, by not pleading the former judgment in bar, consents that the whole matter shall go to a jury,** and leaves it open to them to inquire into the same upon evidence, and they are to give their verdict upon the whole evidence then submitted to them. I am aware that in *Bird* v. *Randall* (3 Burr. 1353), Lord Mansfield is reported to have said that a former recovery need not be pleaded but will be a bar when given in evidence. I cannot, however, accede to that; for the very first thing I learnt in the study of the law was that a judgment recovered must be pleaded: that has so strongly engrafted itself on my mind as a general principle, that nothing I have heard in argument this day, has shaken it.

BAYLEY, J. . . . An action is here brought, as it is alleged, for the same cause in respect of which a former action had been brought, and in which a verdict was obtained by the defendant. Now **a defendant ought not, in point of law, to be twice vexed for the same cause of action; and he would have had a right, if he had thought fit, to have pleaded the former verdict by way of estoppel,** and thereby have shown that the plaintiff was not at liberty to try that question a second time, which had been tried before and decided against him. **Instead, however, of putting himself on that estoppel, he merely says, that he is not guilty** of the offence imputed to him; and, upon that issue, the jury are to try, not whether the plaintiff is estopped from trying the question, but whether the defendant be guilty or not. Upon that issue, the defendant may prove, that the act imputed was not done by him, and that another jury were of opinion that he was not guilty; and, for that purpose, **he may give in evidence the judgment in the former cause for the consideration of the second jury.** The question, however, for the second jury (when the defendant has chosen to plead the general issue) is, whether the defendant be guilty or not? and the question raised upon that issue, in an action on the case is, whether the plaintiff had or had not any cause of action at the time of the commencement of the suit? Now the judgment for the defendant in a former action for the same cause, does not necessarily prove that the plaintiff has no cause of action. It decides nothing unless by way of estoppel. In *Outram* v. *Morewood* (3 East 346), where this subject was very fully considered, Lord ELLENBOROUGH, C.J., in giving the judgment of the Court, takes this distinction, and states expressly that a former judgment, if properly pleaded by way of estoppel, would be conclusive, but if only offered in evidence it would not be so. For these reasons, I am of opinion, that, upon this issue, the judgment in the former verdict was evidence only to go to the jury.

HOLROYD, J. . . . **There were two modes, by either of which the defendant might defend himself.** There having been a former action, in which he had succeeded, **he might have alleged that he was not to be called upon to defend himself again for the same cause.** If he chooses to adopt that mode of defence, he must plead it in bar; and say that the other party is not at liberty to call upon him to answer again that which he had before called upon him to do, when a verdict was given in his favour. **If, however, he declines that mode of defence,** and submits to answer for the cause of action alleged, and defends himself by saying that the plaintiff has no ground of action; **he then leaves the question to the jury,** and they are to try, not whether there was a former action for the same cause, but whether the plaintiff has such a ground of action as he alleges in his present declaration. **A party may have matter which he may either give in evidence, or which, if pleaded, would be an estoppel;** but when he puts it to the jury to find what the fact was, it is inconsistent with the issue which he has joined, for him to say that the jury are estopped from going into the inquiry. He may, however, use the former verdict as evidence, and pregnant evidence, to guide the jury who are to try the second case, to a conclusion in his favour. But if, notwithstanding the prior verdict and judgment, the jury think the case is with the plaintiff, they are not estopped from finding the verdict accordingly. . . . In *Trevivan* v. *Lawrence* (Salk. 276) it was held, that if a party will not rely on the estoppel when he may, but takes issue on the fact, the jury shall not be bound by the estoppel, for they are to find the truth of the fact which is against him; and in *Buller's Nisi Prius*, it is laid down, that the jury cannot find anything against that which the parties have affirmed and admitted of record, though the truth is contrary; but in other cases, though the parties be estopped to say the truth, the jury are not; as in *Goddard's Case* (4 Coke 44), where the bond was dated nine months after the execution, and after the death of the obligor. I think, therefore, that **upon principle as well as upon authority, the former judgment was not conclusive** against the plaintiff upon this issue, and that the learned Judge, therefore, did right in receiving the evidence, and suffering the trial to proceed.

Note.—Apparently, estoppels either by record or by deed must be specially pleaded. There seems to be some doubt as to the necessity of pleading estoppels by conduct. For instance, *Taylor*, 8th ed., § 92, says there is no need to plead them; but *id.*, 12th ed., and *Odgers on Pleading*, 236, say they must always be pleaded, and this appears to be the modern practice.

II. ESTOPPEL BY DEED.

BOWMAN v. TAYLOR.

KING'S BENCH. 1834.

4 L. J. K. B. 58; 2 Ad. & E. 278; 4 N. & M. 264; 41 R. R. 437.

A person who is party to a deed, or instrument under seal, is estopped from denying its contents. So also are his privies.

The estoppel may extend to statements made even in recitals.

A deed, by which the plaintiff granted to the defendant a licence to use certain looms, recited that the plaintiff had invented certain improvements, etc., in power looms, and had obtained letters-patent and had caused a specification to be enrolled. It was held that the defendant was estopped from pleading that the plaintiff was not the inventor, that it was not a new invention, and that no specification had been enrolled.

The following is from the Law Journal:—

Lord Denman, C.J. . . . An estoppel operates because it concludeth a man to allege the truth by reason of the assertion of the party that that fact is true. **The doctrine, as laid down by Coke, that a recital doth not conclude, because it is no direct affirmation, is not supported by any authority.** If a party has by his deed directly asserted a specific fact, it is impossible to say that he shall not be precluded from disputing that fact, thus solemnly admitted by him on the face of his deed. . . .

Patteson, J. . . . The only authority which seems to press upon us is the authority of Lord Coke, but **there have been many cases in which a party has been estopped from disputing a recital.** But it is said that it will be found in these cases that the recitals are so bound up in and part of the deed as that they are the same as the deed itself. Try the present case by that test. **This recital is manifestly so clearly connected with the operative part of the deed as to be essentially part of the deed itself. . . .** The current of authorities is clearly in favour of the position, that the defendant in this case is estopped by the recital in the deed.

TAUNTON and WILLIAMS, JJ., concurred.

Note.—The present rule, that all statements in a deed of a material particular estop the parties, is doubtless based on the idea that they should be careful with regard to all the statements in a deed, even those which are merely introductory.

It may be, however, that the statement in question is in reality the statement of one party only. In such case it estops such party only (*Stroughill* v. *Buck*, 14 Q. B. 787). Nor will a party be estopped if the recital be included by a mistake, such mistake not being induced by that party (*Greer* v. *Kettle, Re Parent Trust, etc., Co., Ltd.*, [1939] 4 A. E. R. 396).

A mere receipt, for money or goods, does not amount to an estoppel. It is only *prima facie* evidence and is open to explanation. Even a receipt in a deed appears not to amount to an estoppel, generally, either at law or in equity, since the Judicature Act. Cf. Marine Insurance Act, 1906, s. 54, *post*, p. 487.

III. ESTOPPEL BY CONDUCT.

FREEMAN v. COOKE.

EXCHEQUER. 1848.

18 L. J. Ex. 114; 12 Jur. 777; 2 Ex. 654; 6 D. & L. 187; 76 R. R. 711.

A person who, by his words or conduct, "wilfully" causes another person to believe in the existence of a certain state of things, and induces him to act on that belief, so as to alter his position for the worse, is estopped from setting up against the latter person a different state of things as existing at the time in question.

This is so whatever such person's real intention was, if he so conducted himself that a reasonable man would take the representation to be true and believe that it was meant he should act upon it. Conduct by negligence or omission,

where there is a duty cast upon a person by usage of trade or otherwise to disclose the truth, may often have the same effect.

But there is no estoppel unless the words or conduct were intended to induce the other person so to act, or they were such that a reasonable man would act upon them; although he did as a fact act upon them to his prejudice.

The defendant was sheriff of Yorkshire, and his officer had seized certain goods under a writ of execution against Joseph and Benjamin Broadbent. Evidence was given that the goods belonged to William Broadbent, but that he, expecting an execution against himself, removed them to the house of his father, Joseph Broadbent; then again, anticipating a distress for rent on his father, Joseph, he removed them to the house of his brother, Benjamin Broadbent. When the sheriff's officer entered the house of Benjamin, William, supposing the writ to be against himself, gave him notice not to seize the goods as they were the property of Benjamin. The officer then produced his writ, which was against Benjamin. Then William said the goods belonged to another brother, and finally that they belonged to himself. The officer seized and sold the goods as the goods of Benjamin. William having become bankrupt, an action was brought by his assignees to recover the goods in question, and it was contended by the defendant that the statements of William operated as conclusive evidence, or an estoppel, that the property was not his. It was held that it was not so.

The following is from the Law Journal:—

PARKE, B. (*delivering the judgment of the Court,* PARKE, ALDERSON, ROLFE and PLATT, BB.). . . . The only question is whether it be an estoppel. It is contended that it was, upon the authority of **the rule laid down in Pickard v. Sears** (6 A. & E. 469). That rule **is, that** "where one by his words or conduct *wilfully* causes another to believe in the existence of a certain state of things, and induces him to act on that behalf, or to alter his own previous position, the former is concluded from averring against the latter a different state of things as existing at the time." . . . By the term "wilfully", however, in that rule, we must understand, if not that the party represents that to be true which he knows to be untrue, at least that he means his representation to be acted upon, and that it is acted upon accordingly; and **if, whatever a man's real meaning may be, he so conducts himself that a reasonable man would take the representation to be true, and believe that it was meant he should act upon it, and did act upon it as true, the party making the representation would be equally precluded from contesting its truth; and conduct by negligence or omission, when there is a duty cast upon a person by usage of trade or otherwise to disclose the truth, may often have the same effect**—as, for instance, a retiring partner omitting to inform the customers of the firm, in the usual mode, that the continuing partners were no longer authorised to act as his agents, is bound by all contracts made by them with third persons on the faith of their being authorised. . . .

It is not found that the bankrupt intended to induce the officers to seize the goods as those of Benjamin, and whatever intention he had on his first statement was done away with by an opposite statement before the seizure took place; nor can it be said that any reasonable man would have seized the goods on the faith of the bankrupt's representations taken all together. In truth, in most cases to which the doctrine in *Pickard* v. *Sears* is to be applied, the representation is such as to amount to the contract or licence of the party making it. Hence there is no pretence for saying it amounted to a licence, and a contract is out of the question.

Note.—The doctrine of estoppel by conduct may be applied generally to all cases in which a person seeks to give evidence in direct conflict with any of his previous deliberate acts or statements, by which he has naturally misled another person.

The representation either express or by conduct upon which it is sought to found an estoppel must normally be one of fact, not of law. But it seems that a statement of mixed fact and law may, in some cases, found an estoppel (see *Mansel-Lewis* v. *Lees* (1910), 102 L. T. 237; *De Tchihatchef* v. *Salerni Coupling, Ltd.*, [1932] 1 Ch. 330).

A person may by his conduct even be **estopped from pleading an Act of Parliament** or statutory defence. Thus, an employer was estopped from pleading that a workman had not taken proceedings under the Workmen's Compensation Act within the statutory period of six months, where he had led him to believe the claim was admitted (*Wright* v. *Bagnall*, [1900] 2 Q. B. 240); and a defendant might be estopped from pleading that money was paid in respect of a gaming debt, where he had led the plaintiff to believe it was not so (*Tatam* v. *Reeve*, [1893] 1 Q. B. 44).

But a person cannot by conduct or representation create a state of things which he is legally unable to create; he **cannot acquire**

capacity by estoppel. So, a corporation, infant, or married woman cannot be estopped from showing their respective legal incapacities.

"The truth is, that the Courts have been, for some time, favourable to the utility of the doctrine of estoppel, hostile to its technicality. Perceiving how essential it is to the quick and easy transaction of business, that one man should be able to put faith in the conduct and representations of his fellow, they have inclined to hold such conduct and such representations binding in cases where a mischief or injustice would be caused by treating their effect as revocable. At the same time, they have been unwilling to allow men to be entrapped by formal statements and admissions, which were perhaps looked upon as unimportant when made, and by which no one ever was deceived or induced to alter his position. Such estoppels are still, as formerly, considered *odious*" (*Smith's Leading Cases*, 13th ed., II, 812).

COVENTRY, SHEPPARD & CO. v. GREAT EASTERN RY.

1883. See Appendix IV, *post*, p. 565.

COOKE v. LOXLEY.

KING'S BENCH. 1792.

5 T. R. 4; 2 R. R. 521.

A tenant of land is estopped from disputing the title of the landlord by whom he was let into possession, or whom he has acknowledged by payment of rent.

In an action for use and occupation of land let to the defendant by the predecessor in title of the present plaintiff, to whom the defendant had also paid rent, the defendant offered evidence to the effect that the plaintiff had no title to the land. Lord Kenyon rejected the evidence, and, on an application for a new trial, his decision was upheld.

Lord Kenyon, C.J. Conforming to the uniform decisions in all the cases upon this subject, I ruled at the trial, and continue to entertain the same opinion, that in an action for use and occupation **it ought not to be permitted to a tenant, who occupies land by the licence of another, to call upon that other to show the title under which he let the land.** This is not a mere technical rule, but is founded in public convenience and policy. And the only question here is whether that rule shall still prevail; if it do, it applies equally strongly to the present case as to all others. Here the defendant, who occupied the land, did so by the permission of the plaintiff, and then refused to pay his rent under an idea that he might contest the plaintiff's right; but the plaintiff could not be supposed to come to trial prepared to meet such a defence and to make out his title; **such an action as the present does not involve the question of title. . . .**

Grose, J. It has been said that the rule of not giving in evidence *nil habuit in tenementis* in an action for use and occupation is a technical rule; but, in my opinion, **no rule is better founded in justice and policy than this.** The general rule is admitted that in such an action as this **the tenant cannot dispute the landlord's title**; and no exception to it has been shown applicable to this case.

Note.—This estoppel of a tenant is one of the most noticeable instances of estoppel by conduct. Similar cases of estoppel are those of bailees, licensees and agents, who cannot deny the title of the bailors, licensors or principals, after having acknowledged them by their dealings.

But the tenant is not estopped from showing that the title of his landlord has expired since the tenancy commenced, or that the land in question is not comprised in the lease. There is no inconsistency in holding the land and at the same time proving such matters.

Where the tenancy is by deed there might conceivably be also an estoppel by deed in the case of landlord and tenant.

STATEMENTS "WITHOUT PREJUDICE".

The second class of matters of which proof is not allowed consists of statements or admissions made "without prejudice". Such statements are invariably made **in the course of negotiations for settlement of disputes.** It is considered necessary to allow the parties to speak somewhat freely in attempting settlements, and to disclose their cases to each other to some extent. But it is clear that the necessary freedom of discussion could not well take place if all the statements or admissions made could be given in evidence after the negotiations for settlement had failed.

It is usual, and certainly **advisable, expressly to state** that the communications in question are made **without prejudice**; but it seems clear that the rule of exclusion would apply if it appeared from the circumstances that it was intended that the communications should not be used as evidence (see *Cory* v. *Bretton*, 4 C. & P. 462).

This matter is sometimes dealt with under the head of "Privilege" (see *post*, p. 321). But this seems scarcely correct. Privilege arises when a witness objects to disclose facts or documents; it is an advantage to the witness. In the case of statements made without prejudice, the law prohibits him from disclosing facts which he may wish to disclose. The rule is in favour of his opponent.

PADDOCK v. FORRESTER.

COMMON PLEAS. 1841.

3 Scott N. R. 715; 3 M. & G. 903; 67 R. R. 634.

Communications, admissions or other statements, written or oral, made by a party to an action, pending the dispute or action, and made expressly or impliedly "without prejudice", with the object of compromise or settlement, cannot be given in evidence against the person making them.

A letter written without prejudice protects from disclosure the whole of the correspondence of which it forms part.

A letter was written by one party "without prejudice". The reply thereto was not stated to have been so written. The latter was held inadmissible.

The following is from Scott:—

Tindal, C.J. **It is of great consequence that parties should be unfettered by correspondence** entered into upon the express understanding that it is to be **without prejudice.** And it would be hard indeed to hold that a letter which is stated to be written withou prejudice is admissible in evidence because the same terms are n adopted in the reply. **When used in the letter containing the offe the words "without prejudice" must cover the whole correspondenc**

COLTMAN, J. It is of the utmost importance that parties shoul have the opportunity of free communication without prejudice; an I should be sorry to hold anything that might be in the slightes degree calculated to embarrass or discourage the practice.

ERSKINE, J., concurred.

WALKER v. WILSHER.

COURT OF APPEAL. 1889.

L. R. 23 Q. B. D. 335; 58 L. J. Q. B. 501; 37 W. R. 723.

At the trial of an action, which resulted in a judgment by consen for an agreed sum, application was made to the Judge to depriv the plaintiff of his costs on the ground that, at an early stage of th proceedings, as appeared from letters, marked "without prejudice" which had passed between the parties, the case could have bee settled for the amount finally accepted. The letters, though objecte to, were received by the Judge as showing "good cause" fo depriving the plaintiff of his costs. The plaintiff appealed.

The following is from the Law Reports:—

LORD ESHER, M.R. . . . It is, I think, a good rule to say tha **nothing which is written or said without prejudice should be looke at without the consent of both parties,** otherwise the whole object o the limitation would be destroyed. I am therefore of opinion tha the learned Judge should not have taken these matters into con sideration in determining whether there was good cause, and as tha was all that was before him on the point, if that is excluded, i follows that there was no good cause, and that the plaintiff shoul not have been deprived of his costs.

LINDLEY, L.J. . . . What is the meaning of the words "withou prejudice"? I think they mean without prejudice to the position o the writer of the letter if the terms he proposes are not accepted. If the terms proposed in the letter are accepted, a complete contract is established, and the letter, although written without prejudice, operates to alter the old state of things and to establish a new one. A contract is constituted in respect of which relief by way of damages or specific performance would be given. . . . The case of *Williams* v. *Thomas* (2 Dr. & Sm. 29), is the only authority that I know of for the course taken by the learned Judge, and when we come to consider the principle on which it was decided, it does not convince me that a Judge is entitled to look at letters written without prejudice unless he has the consent of both parties to his so doing. No doubt there are cases where such letters may be taken into consideration, as was done the other day in a case in which a question of laches was raised. The fact that such letters have been written and the dates at which they were written may be regarded, and in so doing the rule to which I have adverted would not be infringed. The facts may, I think, be given in evidence, but the offer made and the mode in which that offer was dealt with—the material matters, that is to say, of the letters—must not be looked at without consent. I think, therefore, that there was no good cause for depriving the plaintiff of costs, and that the decision should be reversed.

BOWEN, L.J. . . . Negotiations which have taken place without prejudice may be material under circumstances which are not present here. The fact of such negotiations may perhaps in such circumstances be given in evidence, but the question whether what was said or done at such negotiations is admissible, is a very different one.

Appeal allowed.

Note.—Such communications are admissible for the purpose of proving independent admissions not concerning the matter in dispute (*Waldridge* v. *Kennison*, 1 Esp. 142). And a person cannot protect himself from liability for a communication, in itself involving legal liability, by expressly marking it "without prejudice". So, a threat made in such manner may be proved (*Kurtz* v. *Spence*, 57 L. J. Ch. 238).

RELEVANCY.

The third class of facts which a party is not allowed to prove consists of such facts as are irrelevant to the issue. It would be idle to attempt to discuss what matters are irrelevant; attention should be addressed to the question—what matters are relevant?

Evidence may be given of two sets of facts: (1) of facts in issue; (2) of facts relevant to the facts in issue. Evidence of (1) is generally known as **direct evidence,** that of (2) as **circumstantial evidence** (*ante*, pp. 2—3).

The facts in issue are those which are alleged by one party and denied by the other on the pleadings, in a civil case; or alleged in the indictment and denied by the plea of "not guilty", in a criminal case, so far as they are in either case material. There is, therefore, little difficulty in ascertaining what are the facts in issue.

The relevant facts are all other facts which are in the eye of the law so connected with or related to the facts in issue that they render the latter probable or improbable, or, roughly, throw light upon them. "Relevancy" may, indeed, be considered as synonymous with "connection", a word which frequently appears in discussions on the subject. Of course, both words must be taken in their legal meaning, which is generally restricted. Common sense, or logical, relevancy is, as a rule, wider than legal relevancy. A Judge might, in ordinary transactions, take one fact as evidence of another, and act upon it himself, when, in Court, he would rule that it was legally irrelevant. And he may exclude facts, although relevant, if they appear to him too remote to be really material to the issue (see *Stephen*, *Digest*, Appendix on "Relevance", pp. 231—240; *Phipson*, 47—50).

The limits of legal relevancy cannot be strictly stated, as the connection between facts varies infinitely in different cases. The cases below given show some of the chief rules.

In connection with relevancy, one general matter may be mentioned:—

It is sometimes asked—when can evidence be given of what was said or done behind the back of or in the absence of a party? As a general rule such evidence is not admissible, the maxim usually applied being, "*Res inter alios actae alteri nocere non debent*". But many instances of the admissibility of such evidence can be given.

It may be said generally, that acts done are more readily received than statements made in such circumstances.

Evidence of acts done in the absence of a party may be given in the following cases (*inter alia*):—

(1) When such acts, although not expressly connected with the fact in issue, are necessary to prove or show its nature or quality, provided such acts directly lead up to or explain such fact. So, on a charge of receiving stolen goods, the larceny may be proved; and on a charge of larceny, the deposit of the goods in a certain place, or the fact that a mark was put upon them may be proved (see *post*, p. 66).

(2) When such acts are expressly connected with the fact in issue, so as, in substance, to form the basis of such fact. So, if a contract were made with one person expressly on the same terms as a contract made with another person, such latter contract might be proved (see *post*, p. 106)

(3) When such acts are legally relevant to prove the actual fact in issue, as in the case of acts of possession to prove ownership (see *post*, p. 92), or cohabitation to prove marriage (see *post*, p. 97), or course of business to prove a business transaction (see *post*, p. 91).

(4) When such acts are admissible to corroborate, illustrate, or show the reason for, or ground of, evidence given, as in the case of experiments or examination of persons or things by experts in support of their opinions (see *post*, p. 131).

(5) When such acts tend to establish, or prove the nature of, any custom or usage (see *post*, p. 395).

Evidence of statements made in the absence of a party may be given in the following cases (*inter alia*):—

(1) When such statements are actually part of the transaction in issue (see *post*, p. 67).

(2) When such statements were made by a fellow-conspirator or by a person engaged in some joint transaction (see *post*, p. 82).

(3) When such statements amount to complaints in cases of rape and similar offences (see *post*, p. 83).

(4) When such statements were made by deceased persons under such circumstances that they amount to admissible declarations in course of duty (see *post*, p. 211); against interest (see *post*, p. 216); as to pedigree (see *post*, p. 223); as to public or general rights (see *post*, p. 233); as to cause of death (see *post*, p. 244); or as to contents of wills (see *post*, p. 250).

(5) When such statements are made in public documents (see *post*, p. 261).

Note.—With regard to the above five classes of statements, it should be observed that (1), (2), (3) are not in general evidence of the *truth* of the matters asserted; while (4) and (5) are, by exception to the hearsay rule, admissible as such evidence (*Phipson*, 5—6, 100, 212). Moreover, irrespective of this list, the particular *party* by whom a given statement is tendered may affect its admissibility. Thus, in an action by A against B, if A had written to B that a certain fact had happened, A might, at the trial, prove that statement to show that he gave B notice of such fact, though he could not tender it to show that the fact had actually happened. B, however, might use A's letter, not only for the former, but for the latter, purpose, because, when tendered against A, it would be receivable as an admission (*Id.*, 221, 227 *a*).

CIRCUMSTANTIAL EVIDENCE.

R. v. PALMER.

CENTRAL CRIMINAL COURT. 1856.

TRIAL OF WILLIAM PALMER; STEPHEN, HIST. OF CR. LAW, III, 389, AND GENERAL VIEW OF CR. LAW.

Evidence is admissible not only of the facts in issue, but also of other facts which render the facts in issue probable or improbable by reason of their connection with or relation to them. Facts so connected with the facts in issue are said to be "relevant facts", and they constitute what is known as "circumstantial evidence".

Thus, facts which supply a motive for an act, or constitute preparation for it, or conduct apparently influenced by the act, are relevant to the question whether such act was done by the person concerning whom such motive, preparation or conduct is proved.

In this trial for murder, the pecuniary embarrassment of the prisoner, his buying poison and attempting to avoid an inquest and other such facts (as appear below), were held to be revelant as circumstantial evidence.

The following is from the separate report published in 1856, *by J. Allen:—*

LORD CAMPBELL, C.J. (*in his charge to the jury*). . . . By the law and practice of some countries it is allowed, to raise a probability that the party accused has committed the offence which he has to answer, to show that he has committed other offences; with a view of showing that he is an immoral man, and not unlikely to commit other offences, whether of the same or of a different nature; but **the law of England** is different, and, presuming every man to be innocent until his guilt is established, it **allows his guilt to be established only by evidence directly connected with the charge** brought against him. . . .

But in a case of this kind **you cannot expect that witnesses should**

be called to state that they saw the deadly poison administered by the prisoner, or mixed up by the prisoner openly before them. **Circumstantial evidence as to that is all that can be reasonably expected;** and if there are a series of **circumstances leading to the conclusion of guilt,** then, gentlemen, a verdict of guilty may satisfactorily be pronounced. With respect to the alleged motive, **it is of great importance to see whether there was a motive for committing such a crime,** or whether there was not, or whether there was an improbability of its having been committed so strong as not to be overpowered by positive evidence. But, gentlemen, if there be any motive which can be assigned, I am bound to tell you that **the adequacy of that motive is of little importance.** We know from the experience of criminal Courts that atrocious crimes of this sort have been committed from very slight motives; not merely from malice or revenge, but to gain a small pecuniary advantage, and to drive off for a time pressing difficulties. . . .

I shall best discharge my duty by beginning with that part of the case that was first opened by the Attorney-General, respecting **the motive that the prisoner may have had for accomplishing the death** of Cook. Now I think that that arises out of **certain pecuniary transactions,** the nature of which has been most minutely laid before you. It appears that **the prisoner had borrowed large sums of money upon bills** of exchange, which he drew, and which purported to be accepted by his mother, a lady, it seems, of considerable wealth. **Those acceptances were forgeries. . . .** It had been expected by Palmer that he would have been able to meet those bills by the proceeds of a policy of insurance, which had been effected upon the life of his brother Walter . . .; but the Prince of Wales Insurance Office denied their liability upon that policy and refused to pay. **Thence arose a most pressing embarrassment**—payments were urgently required, and there was danger unless they were immediately paid that the law would be put in force, and that the system of forgeries which had been so long carried on would in all human probability be detected and brought to light. . . .

Then, gentlemen, comes the more direct evidence that the **prisoner at the bar, if you believe the witnesses, procured this very poison. . . .** For what purpose was that obtained? . . . You have no account of that poison. What was the intention with which it was purchased, and what was the application of it, you are to infer. . . .

Then, gentlemen, it is impossible that you should not **pay attention to the conduct of the prisoner** at the bar, and there are some instances of his conduct which you will say whether they belong to **what might be expected from an innocent or a guilty man.** He was **eager to have the body fastened down** in the coffin. Then, with regard to the betting-book, there is certainly evidence from which you may infer that he did **get possession of the betting-book,** that he abstracted it and concealed it. Then, gentlemen, you must not forget his conduct in **trying to bribe the postboy to overturn the carriage** in which the **jar was being conveyed, to be analysed in London, and from which** evidence might be obtained of his guilt. Again, you find him **tampering with the postmaster,** and procuring from the postmaster the opening of a letter from Dr. Taylor, who had been examining the contents of the jar, to Mr. Gardiner, the attorney employed on the part of Mr. Stevens. And then, gentlemen, you have **tampering with the coroner,** and trying to induce him to procure a verdict from the coroner's jury which would amount to an acquittal. . . .

Note.—Such facts as motive, preparation, subsequent conduct, opportunity, etc., referring to the circumstances and position of the party whose act is alleged, are the facts which are generally and specially referred to as "circumstantial" evidence. But this term is properly applicable to all evidence other than that of the facts in issue themselves. Evidence of such facts in issue is known as "direct" evidence. All evidence which is admissible merely as being relevant to the facts in issue is strictly "circumstantial" or "indirect".

"On a superficial view, direct and indirect or circumstantial, would appear to be *distinct* species of evidence; whereas, these words denote only the different modes in which those classes of evidentiary facts operate to produce conviction. Circumstantial evidence is of a nature identically the same with direct evidence; the distinction is that by DIRECT EVIDENCE is intended evidence which applies directly to the fact which forms the subject of inquiry, the *factum probandum*; CIRCUMSTANTIAL EVIDENCE is equally direct in its nature, but, as its name imports, it is direct evidence of a minor fact or facts of such a nature that the mind is led intuitively to the conviction that from it or them some other fact may be inferred. . . . The *evidence* of these facts is *direct*; the facts themselves are *indirect* and *circumstantial*" (*Wills, Circ. Ev.*, 7th ed., 17, 18).

The word "direct" is used in another sense. It is also opposed to "hearsay" in the law of evidence (see *post*, p. 163). The distinction between "direct" and "circumstantial" refers to the facts offered in evidence; that between "direct" and "hearsay" refers to the mode of proving such facts (see *ante*, pp. 2—3).

DOWLING v. DOWLING.

EXCHEQUER (IRELAND). 1860.

10 Irish C. L. R. 236.

Facts showing the circumstances and position of the parties whose conduct is in question are generally relevant to such conduct. So, evidence of opportunity is relevant to the question whether a certain act was done.

Circumstantial evidence is admissible not only in the absence of direct evidence, but also in aid of direct evidence.

The question being whether A lent money to B; evidence of the poverty of A about the time of the alleged loan, and for seven years previously, was held admissible as tending to disprove it, in support of the defendant's direct evidence that it had not been lent.

Pigot, C.B. . . . In my own experience, now of many years, it has been **the constant practice of Judges to receive such evidence** when offered, whether in a Court of law or a Court of equity, upon the question whether or not money was paid; especially where that question related to transactions of a remote period, to which it was difficult to apply other than circumstantial evidence. In such cases, **proof that a party was in such circumstances that he** *could not,* **has been received as evidence that he** *did not,* **pay the money in question. . . . Evidence of this nature is plainly admissible; for the simple reason, that it constitutes, or forms part of, circumstantial evidence,** from which the jury are entitled to form their judgment as to the fact of payment and as to the credibility of conflicting testimony. . . .

Here the evidence that was offered went back a distance of seven years; but **the object of showing the plaintiff's circumstances, seven years before, was to prove the position in life out of which he then emerged, and to show,** partly by his own statements, on his cross-examination, of his own intervening pursuits, and partly by the evidence of the defendant, **that he had not acquired property in the interval;** and that at the time when the loan was alleged to have been made he had not the means of making it. . . .

The circumstances of the parties, and the position in which they

stood when the matter the subject of controversy occurred, are, for the most part, proper subjects of evidence to be submitted to a jury, and the recent changes in the law, by which parties are enabled to swear for themselves, have rendered evidence of "surrounding circumstances" still more important than they were before. They often supply the only means of determining upon testimony at one side directly conflicting with the testimony at the other; and such was the testimony in the case now before us. . . .

Note.—A good deal of discussion has taken place as to the relative weight and reliability of direct and circumstantial evidence. The theory seems to be that the former is superior, as the latter is only a substitute for it. It is said also that there are only two chances of error in the case of direct evidence, namely (1) the mistake, and (2) the untruthfulness of witnesses; while there is a further danger in the case of circumstantial evidence, namely (3) the fallacious inference of the tribunal. On the other hand, it is said that circumstantial evidence has the advantage of presenting less opportunities for conspiracy and perjury. Many small unimportant facts are more difficult of fabrication, and less likely to be thought of beforehand, than single important facts nearer to the issue.

"Many writers of authority, both ancient and modern, have treated circumstantial evidence as inherently and of necessity of less value than direct evidence. . . . But, in truth, direct and circumstantial evidence ought not to be placed in contrast, since they are not mutually opposed; for evidence of a circumstantial and secondary nature can seldom, if ever, be justifiably resorted to, or carry conviction, except where direct evidence is unattainable or unreliable, or where the circumstantial evidence is used merely in confirmation of the direct. . . . Where the evidence is direct, and the testimony credible, belief is the immediate and necessary result; whereas, in cases of circumstantial evidence, processes of inference and deduction are essentially involved—frequently of a delicate and perplexing character—liable to numerous causes of fallacy" (*Wills*, *Circ. Ev.*, 7th ed., 36, 44, 45).

It will be observed from the above case that the "best evidence" rule (see *post*, p. 163) does not now exclude circumstantial in favour of direct evidence. They may be given together.

THE TRANSACTION. "RES GESTÆ."

R. v. ELLIS.

KING'S BENCH. 1826.

6 B. & C. 145.

Facts which are parts of the same transaction as the fact, or facts, in issue are in general admissible as forming parts of the "res gesta" or "res gestæ".

The prisoner being charged with stealing six shillings, marked money, from a till, evidence was allowed of the taking not only of that amount but also of other moneys taken at the same time.

Bayley, J. I think that **it was in the discretion of the Judge** to confine the prosecutor to the proof of one felony, or **to allow him** to give **evidence of other acts, which were all part of one entire transaction.** Generally speaking, it is not competent to a prosecutor to prove a man guilty of one felony, by proving him guilty of another unconnected felony; but **where several felonies are connected together, and form part of one entire transaction, then the one is evidence to show the character of the other.** Now all the evidence in this case tended to show that the prisoner was guilty of the felony charged in the indictment. **It went to show the history** of the till from the time when the marked money was put into it up to the time when it was found in the possession of the prisoner. I think, therefore, that the evidence was properly received.

Holroyd, J., concurred.

Note.—" A transaction is a group of facts so connected together as to be referred to by a single legal name, as a crime, a contract, a wrong, or any other subject of inquiry which may be in issue. Every fact which is part of the same transaction as the facts in issue is deemed to be relevant to the facts in issue, although it may not be actually in issue, and although if it were not part of the same transaction it might be excluded as hearsay" (*Stephen, Dig. Ev.*, Art. 3; *Phipson*, 51–79). Roughly a transaction may be described as any physical act, or series of connected physical acts, together with the words accompanying such act or acts.

R. v. BIRDSEYE.

BEDFORD ASSIZES. 1830.

4 C. & P. 386.

Acts are not part of the same transaction, unless they were done substantially at the same time, although they are similar in other respects.

The prisoner was charged with stealing pickled pork, a bowl, some knives and a loaf of bread. He went to the prosecutor's shop, took the pork and ran away with it. In about two minutes he returned, replaced the pork in a bowl which contained the knives, and took the lot away. About half an hour later he returned and took the loaf.

LITTLEDALE, J. This taking away the loaf cannot be given in evidence upon this indictment. I think that the prisoner's taking the pork, and returning in two minutes, and then running off with the bowl, must be taken as one continuing transaction, but I think that half an hour is too long a period to admit of that construction. The taking of the loaf, therefore, is a distinct offence.

Note.—See also *R.* v. *Rodley*, [1913] 3 K. B. 468, C. C. A., where on a charge of breaking and entering with intent to commit the felony of rape, evidence was held to have been wrongly admitted to the effect that on the same night about an hour later the prisoner had gone to a neighbouring farmhouse, climbed down the chimney into a woman's bedroom and there had connection with her consent.

THOMPSON v. TREVANION.

NISI PRIUS. 1693.

SKINNER 402.

A "transaction" consists both of the physical acts and the words accompanying such physical acts, whether spoken by the person doing such acts, the person to whom they were done or any other persons present. Such words are admissible in evidence as part of the transaction.

In a civil action for assault on the plaintiff's wife,

HOLT, C.J., allowed that what the wife said immediate upon the hurt received and **before that she had time to devise or contrive anything for her own advantage,** might be given in evidence.

Note.—The difficulty is to determine whether the words in question do really accompany the physical acts, or whether they are subsequent to such acts and are therefore mere "narrative" and inadmissible (see the next two cases).

The true test of admissibility of the spoken word seems to be indicated by HOLT, C.J., in the above case—did the speaker have time to contrive anything for his own advantage, or to invent a false tale? If sufficient time elapsed to allow the invention of a false tale, obviously the evidence would be unreliable. In the following case such time would scarcely appear to have elapsed, and yet the statement was rejected.

The case of *R.* v. *Fowkes* (*Stephen*, Art. 3 *n.*), shows how the statement of a third party may be admissible as part of the transaction, if he be actually present at the time.

R. v. BEDINGFIELD.

NORWICH ASSIZES. 1879.

14 Cox C. C. 341.

A statement, in order to be admissible in evidence as part of the transaction or "res gestæ", must strictly accompany, or be made at the same time as, the physical acts in question.

On a trial for murder, it appeared that the deceased, with her throat cut, came suddenly out of a room, in which she had left the prisoner, and that she said, immediately after coming out of the room, and shortly before she died, "Oh dear, Aunt, see what Bedingfield has done to me!" It was held that her statement was not admissible in evidence, either as a dying declaration, as it did not appear that she was in fear of death, or as *res gestæ*, as it was made after the transaction was complete.

COCKBURN, C.J., said it was not admissible. Anything, he said, **uttered by the deceased at the time the act was being done would be admissible,** as, for instance, if she had been heard to say something, as "Don't Harry!" But **here it was something stated by her after it was all over,** whatever it was, and after the act was completed. . . . The statement was not admissible as a dying declaration, because it did not appear that the woman was aware that she was dying. . . . Though she might have known it if she had had time for reflection, here that was not so, for at the time she made the statement **she had no time to consider and reflect that she was dying**; there is no evidence to show that she knew it, and I cannot presume it. There is nothing to show that she was under the sense of impending death, **so the statement is not admissible as a dying declaration.**

Note.—This case has been the subject of much discussion and criticism, and it certainly does not appear consistent with the next case, in which, apparently, a longer time elapsed between the act in question and the spoken words than in the present case. But the cases illustrate the difficulty in determining the limits of the transaction. Cases on such a subject are of little use. Each case must rest on its own facts.

For the rule under which dying declarations are admissible, see *post*, p. 244.

R. v. FOSTER.

OLD BAILEY. 1834.

6 C. & P. 325.

A statement may be part of the transaction, and admissible in evidence, although it followed the physical acts, and was indeed the last item of the transaction. It is a question, on the facts, whether it was made substantially at the same time.

The prisoner was charged with manslaughter by driving over deceased. A witness saw the vehicle drive by, but did not see the accident. He immediately afterwards went up to the deceased, who then made a statement as to the cause of the injury. Such statement was admitted in evidence.

Gurney, B. **What he said at the instant,** as to the cause of the accident, **is clearly admissible.**

Park, J. I am of opinion that his evidence ought to be received. It is the best possible testimony that, under the circumstances, can be adduced to show what it was that had knocked the deceased down. The case of *Aveson* v. *Lord Kinnaird*, [*post*, p. 72] in which I was counsel many years ago, bears strongly on this point.

PATTESON, J., concurred.

Note.—The words admitted in evidence as part of the transaction were spoken after the act of driving over the deceased was completed, and after the lapse of at least many seconds. But, assuming a statement is admissible as part of the *res gestae*, some doubt must remain as to what exactly is proved by it since it is not generally evidence of the truth of the matter stated. Opinion is at variance in England (see *Phipson*, 51) and the United States (*Wigmore*, ss. 1745 *et seq.*). The student is commended to the common-sense observations of Sir James Stephen upon *R.* v. *Fowkes*, reported in a note to Art. 3 of his Digest.

RAWSON v. HAIGH.

COMMON PLEAS. 1824.

2 BING. 99; 9 MOORE 217; 1 C. & P. 77.

A transaction may be a continuous one, extending over a long period. In such case any words or statements accompanying such continuous transaction at any time during its continuance are admissible as part of it.

The question was whether a debtor had absented himself from the realm "with the intent to hinder his creditors", and so brought himself within the Bankruptcy Act. Letters written during his absence, indicating such an intention, were held admissible in proof thereof.

The following is from Bingham:—

BEST, C.J. . . . When these letters are coupled with the fact of his running away in a hurry, would not the jury be warranted in finding that he went to avoid his creditors? If so, there has been a clear act of bankruptcy. But it has been urged, that the second and third letters, having been written subsequently to the act of departing the realm, were not admissible in evidence. I am clear that they were admissible. **The going abroad was of itself an equivocal act,** and where an act is equivocal, we must get at the motive with which it was committed. In ninety-nine cases out of a hundred, this can only be got at by the declarations of the party himself. . . . **The declarations, in order to be admissible, must be made, or the letters written, at the time of the act in question;** but it is sufficient if they are written at any time during the continuance of the act; **the departing the realm is a continuing act, and these letters were written during its continuance. . . .**

PARK, J. . . . I am satisfied that declarations made during departure and absence are admissible in evidence to show the motive of the departure. **It is impossible to tie down to time the rule as to the declarations; we must judge from all the circumstances of the case;** we need not go the length of saying, that a declaration made a month after the fact would of itself be admissible; but if, as in the present case, there are connecting circumstances, it may even at that time, form part of the whole *res gestæ*. . . . **The declarations, however, must be connected with the state of the party's mind at the time,** and in the present instance I think the connection sufficiently clear for the admission of the letters.

BURROUGH, J., concurred.

Note.—So on issues of domicil the declarations of a person who has lived abroad are admissible to show whether his intention was to remain there permanently or merely temporarily; though their weight may be very slight (*Bryce* v. *Bryce*, [1933] P. 83).

Other cases, such as *Rouch* v. *G. W. Ry.*, 1 Q. B. 51, and *Ridley* v. *Gyde*, 9 Bing. 349, have sometimes been cited for the proposition that the statements need not be strictly contemporaneous in order to be admissible; but they do not appear to show this, as the transactions were continuous and the statements were made during their continuance, although some time after the commencement of the continuous act. A good example is *Home* v. *Newman*, [1931] 2 Ch. 112, where, following a deposit of title deeds, a memorandum made no less than eighteen months after the act of depositing, but while the deposit still continued, was held admissible to explain the transaction as being a mortgage.

The Evidence Act, 1938 (*q.v.*) has radically altered the law where documentary matter is involved and the proceedings are civil and not criminal.

AVESON v. KINNAIRD.

KING'S BENCH. 1805.

6 EAST 188; 8 R. R. 455.

Statements made by a person respecting the state of his health or bodily feelings at a particular time are admissible as evidence of such state of health or feelings.

In an action upon a policy of insurance on the life of the plaintiff's wife, the question being whether the statement of the insured's good health, given at the time of effecting the policy, was false; the Court allowed evidence to be given by a friend to the effect that she had visited deceased at the time, and had been told by her that she was in a bad state of health.

LORD ELLENBOROUGH, C.J. . . . The question being, what was the state of her own health at a certain period, a witness has been received to relate that which has always been received from patients to explain, her own account of the cause of her being found in bed at an unseasonable hour with the appearance of being ill. She was questioned as to her bodily infirmity. She said it was of some duration, several days. . . . **What were the complaints, what the symptoms, what the conduct of the parties themselves at the time, are always received in evidence** upon such inquiries, and must be resorted to from the very nature of the thing. The substance of the whole conversation was that the wife had been ill at least from the 9th of November, when she was examined by the surgeon and certified to be in good health, down to the day when the conversation took place, and those appearances were exhibited to the witness; and in that view I think the evidence unexceptionable. . . . The admission, then, of the evidence in this case is free from any imputation of breaking in upon the confidence subsisting between man and wife; **the declaration was upon the subject of her own health at the time, which is a fact of which her own declaration is evidence;** and that, too, made unawares before she could contrive any answer for her own advantage and that of her husband, and therefore falling within the principle of the case in *Skinner* (*Thompson* v. *Trevanion*, *ante*, p. 67), which I have alluded to.

GROSE, J. . . . The question in the cause was concerning her state of health at the time of the insurance effected, and in order to ascertain that **it became material to inquire what the state of her health was** between the time of her first examination by the surgeon and the time when she was seen by the witness who conversed with her. The first question put the witness was, in what situation she found Mrs. Aveson when she called? The answer was, in bed. To that there could be no objection. The next question was, **why was she in bed? Now who could possibly give so good an account of that as the party herself?** It is not only good evidence, but the best evidence which the nature of the case afforded. . . .

LAWRENCE, J. . . . As to the general ground of objection to the evidence as hearsay, **it is in every day's experience in actions of assault that what a man has said of himself to his surgeon is evidence** to show what he suffered by reason of the assault. **The wife was found in bed at an unusual time; she complained of illness,** and naturally answered her friend's inquiries by **describing how long her health had been bad. . . .** If what she said to Susannah Lees were not evidence against her husband, then what she said to the surgeon could not be evidence for him; yet the testimony of the surgeon was brought forward by the plaintiff in order to show that the woman was an insurable life at the time. . . .

Note.—Although this decision has been generally considered correct, there seems to have been some difference of opinion as to the right ground of the admissibility of such evidence. It would appear to be but an instance of a statement accompanying a transaction or act, or being part of it, the act of living or being in a certain state of health, or, as the Judge put it, the act of being in bed at an unusual hour. See the reference to the above case by Park, J., in *R.* v. *Foster*, *ante*, p. 70.

R. v. GLOSTER.

CENTRAL CRIMINAL COURT. 1888.

16 Cox C. C. 471.

Upon a trial for murder by performing an illegal operation, it was proposed to ask a witness for the prosecution what the deceased had said as to her bodily condition, and what had been done to her.

CHARLES, J. The statement must be confined to contemporaneou symptoms, and nothing in the nature of a narrative is admissibl as to who caused them or how they were caused.

Note.—The statement was also rejected as a dying declaration since it was not shown to have been made when the declarant wa without hope of recovery (*post*, p. 244).

LLOYD v. POWELL DUFFRYN STEAM COAL CO., LTD.

HOUSE OF LORDS. 1914.

L. R. [1914] A. C. 733; 83 L. J. K. B. 1054; 11 L. T. 338; 30 T. L. R. 456; 58 S. J. 514.

In a claim under the Workmen's Compensation Act, 1906, by a posthumous illegitimate child as a dependant of its putative father evidence of statements by the deceased workman to the effect tha he was the father of the child and that he intended to marry th mother before the child was born was held admissible.

The following is from the Law Reports:—

EARL LOREBURN. . . . Now the evidence thus rejected consiste of statements made by the deceased in which he acknowledged th paternity of the child and promised to marry the mother before th child should be born. . . . In considering whether the evidenc was admissible or not the first question is, What were the issues Paternity was one issue. Whether the child was posthumous or ille gitimate or both is immaterial. I think the evidence was properly allowed on the issue of paternity. If paternity has been established the next issue is dependency. It is now clear that the existence o a legal duty upon the deceased workman to maintain wife or chil out of his earnings, where such duty exists, is not conclusive proo of dependency, but it is a strong element, and in my opinion may be of itself sufficient.

The evidence in question went to show that if the father ha not prematurely died this child would have been born legitimate and its father would have been legally bound to maintain it, which is a strong fact to prove dependency. Accordingly the evidence was, in my opinion, admissible upon that ground also. Further it went to show that the child would need, and would have received, its father's support. On that ground too I think it was admissible. . . .

LORD ATKINSON. . . . it necessarily follows, in my view, that if a man, with full knowledge of the pregnancy of a woman with whom he has had sexual intercourse, becomes, during her pregnancy, engaged to be married to her, the fact of that contract having been entered into, though not carried out, is a most powerful piece of evidence on both the issues of fact, namely, the dependency and the paternity of the child, because by the marriage a relation would be created from which the presumption of the legitimacy of the child would arise, and by reason of that legitimacy the legal liability of the father to support and maintain the child would result. If the contract should be terminated the fact that it was made would be evidence on the second issue. I further think that the mere proposal of marriage made by a man under such circumstances, whether accepted or not, would be admissible evidence, certainly on the issue of paternity, though possibly not on that of dependency. . . .

The proposal to marry and the acceptance of it may, of course, be made by word of mouth; but the making and the acceptance of it are acts, matters of conduct, and strong pieces of evidence on the issue of paternity, inasmuch as they show the character in which the parties regarded the child *en ventre sa mère*, and desired to treat it. The considerations which apply to a suit in which the issue of fact is the legitimacy of a child must obviously apply to a litigation like the present, in which one of the issues of fact is its paternity. In *Morris* v. *Davies* (5 Cl. & F. 163) the matter in issue was the legitimacy of a child born in wedlock. The statement of the deceased paramour of the mother to the effect that he objected to the child being brought up to a particular trade, and that he would clothe and provide for it, was admitted in evidence as proof of a matter of conduct, showing the character in which he regarded the child.

Again, in the case of the *Aylesford Peerage* (11 App. Cas. 1), where the question in issue was also the legitimacy of a child born in wedlock, the letters of both the mother of the child, Lady Aylesford, and of her paramour, both alive at the date of the hearing, were given in evidence as proofs of matters of conduct showing that they both regarded and treated this child as the offspring of their adulterous intercourse, and were, therefore, evidence to rebut the presumption of legitimacy.

It would appear to me, therefore, that on this question of paternity it is impossible to distinguish, on principle, the statements made by the deceased to Alice Lloyd, Mrs. Matilda Evans, and William Jones, from the statements contained in the letters received in evidence in the *Aylesford Case.* No doubt Alice Lloyd proved the paternity of the child, and her evidence was not impeached; the County Court Judge believed it; but of course that circumstance cannot make additional evidence on the same point inadmissible. **To treat the statements made by the deceased as** statements made by a deceased person against his pecuniary interest, and therefore, though **hearsay,** proof of the facts stated, **is wholly to mistake their true character and significance. This significance consists in the improbability that any man would make these statements, true or false, unless he believed himself to be the father of the child of whom Alice Lloyd was pregnant. . . .**

Lord Shaw of Dunfermline. . . . All the statements by the father, importing his knowledge of the condition of the mother, his intentions to set up a household, and the like, appear to me to be legitimate matter of proof on the point of paternity. In a question of status, I am of opinion that such statements, proved to have been made at the time and in the circumstances such as occurred in the present case, are part of the *res gestæ* equally with actual contracts entered into by the deceased or conduct apart from words, both of which contracts and conduct could undoubtedly have been proved. I agree with the view that statements made at the time are, in this question of status, similarly admissible evidence. . . .

Lord Moulton. . . . the argument before your Lordships was based on a wholly different ground, namely, that the state of mind of the deceased, so far as it bore on his acceptance of his position as the father of the child and his intention to fulfil his duties as such, was relevant to the issue of dependency, and that the **evidence in question was admissible as being proper to determine his state of mind.** I am of opinion, my Lords, that on this ground the evidence was admissible. It can scarcely be contested that the state of mind of the putative father and his intentions with regard to the child are matters relevant to the issue, whether there was a reasonable anticipation that he would support the child when born. It may be that an intention on his part so to do might be implied from the fact of his paternity and his recognition of it. But whether this be so or not, the attitude of mind of the putative father is that from which alone one can draw conclusions as to the greater or less probability of his supporting the child when born, and therefore evidence to prove that attitude of mind must be admissible if it be the proper evidence to establish such a fact. Now, it is well established in English jurisprudence, in accordance with the dictates of common sense, that **the words and acts of a person are admissible as evidence of his state of mind.** Indeed, they are the only possible evidence on such an issue. It was urged at the Bar that although the acts of the deceased might be put in evidence, his words might not. I fail to understand the distinction. Speaking is as much an act as doing.

It must be borne in mind that **there is nothing in the admission of such evidence which clashes with the rooted objection in our jurisprudence to the admission of hearsay evidence.** The testimony of the witnesses is to the act, *i.e.*, to the deceased speaking these words, and **it is the speaking of the words which is the matter that is put in evidence** and which possesses evidential value. The evidence is, therefore, not in any respect open to the objection that it is secondary or hearsay evidence. The connection between the conversation and the information as to paternity is so close that it is probable that the evidence would be admissible under the head of *res gestæ*, but its admissibility, on the grounds I have just mentioned, is so clear that it is not necessary to examine this further question. . . .

Note.—This case is a difficult one: clearly the fact that the deceased workman was engaged to be married to the mother and intended to support the child were relevant to the issues of paternity and dependency. The question in doubt was whether it was permissible to prove those facts by the statements of the deceased. Lord Moulton's argument is clear: the mere fact that the deceased *thought* that he was the father of the child and was minded to support it was in his view evidence of the child's dependence on him. The other law lords seem to have regarded the statements as evidence of treatment and within the *res gestæ* rule. It is somewhat hard to see how a mere statement of intention, apart from its truth, can be treatment of a child not yet born, or what exactly was the act which the words accompanied so as to bring them within the *res gestæ* rule. The case should be contrasted with *Gilbey* v. *G. W. Ry.* (102 L. T. 202) and *Amys* v. *Barton* ([1912] 1 K. B. 40), two other cases under the Workmen's Compensation Act, where statements made by the deceased workman as to the cause of the accident were rejected. How he *thought* the accident occurred could be no evidence of how in *fact* it happened (see *per* Lord Goddard in *Hollington* v. *Hewthorn*, [1943] 1 K. B. 587 at p. 595, *post*, p. 127).

WRIGHT v. DOE d. TATHAM.

HOUSE OF LORDS. 1838.

4 Bing. N. C. 489; 6 Scott 58; 5 C. & F. 670.

When the act or conduct of any person is in question, the contents of any documents, such as letters, upon which he has acted, or which qualify, illustrate or explain such act or conduct, are admissible as part of the transaction.

The question being as to the sanity of a deceased testator, Mr. Marsden, his conduct in indorsing, answering, and acting upon letters received by him from third persons would have been admissible and, such conduct having been proved, the contents of the letters would have been receivable as statements accompanying and explaining it.

But it was held that the mere fact that such letters were written to him was inadmissible as evidence of his sanity, although they were letters which would only be written to a person believed to be sane. Such facts would only show the writer's opinion of his sanity, and such opinion, being thus given out of Court, would be mere "hearsay".

The question being submitted by the House of Lords to the Judges, they gave their opinions separately.

The following is from Bingham:—

Coleridge, J. . . . I am now brought to the consideration of the third ground taken by the counsel for the defendant below; that these letters are admissible, because they accompany and explain acts done by Mr. Marsden; in other words, that there is evidence with respect to each of these letters that Mr. Marsden had done some act, which act would in itself be relevant to and admissible upon the point in issue, his competency, and **the act itself being admissible, whatever accompanies it and serves to explain his character, is relevant and admissible also.** The principle here applied is admitted on all hands to be correct. . . . **The only question therefore remaining is one of fact, whether there was any evidence of such act** by Mr. Marsden in regard to all or any one of these letters. . . . What is the evidence of these facts? None direct; and every circumstance stated is equally consistent with the assumption of competency or incompetency. . . . The facts then being consistent with either view of the case, he must fail whose duty it is affirmatively to establish either, and who relies on this for proof. . . .

WILLIAMS, J. . . . I think that all the three letters contained in the bill of exceptions are inadmissible. . . . **If upon the back of all or any of these letters, there had been any indorsement in the handwriting of Mr. Marsden, or if any act had been done by him avowedly in consequence of the contents, or any part of them, such letters or letter must of necessity be submitted to the jury with a view to ascertain how far such indorsement contained any material or appropriate comment,** or how far the act was consequent upon, or in accordance with, a fair and reasonable interpretation of the contents. . . .

The question then is, whether Mr. Marsden has in any manner identified himself with—if the expression be allowable—or in other words has **by any act, speech or writing, manifested an acquaintance with and knowledge of the contents of all or any of these letters.** If he has, such letter or letters must have been improperly rejected, otherwise not. . . . The foundation of my opinion is, that neither competency nor incompetency should be presumed, and that, therefore, the burthen was cast upon the defendant below, who tendered this piece of evidence, to give affirmatively some proof that the mind of Mr. Marsden had been exercised upon it, to make it admissible in a case where the only question was the actual state of that mind; and no such proof was given.

PATTESON, J. . . . **Every act of the party's life is relevant to the issue; of course, therefore, anything which he can be shown to have done in regard to any written document, being evidence, it follows**

that such written document must itself be received; otherwise the true character of the act which he has done in regard to it cannot be properly estimated, or the jury be enabled to judge how far that act is indicative of the state of his mind or not. In every case, therefore, the first point to be considered will be whether any act has in truth been done by the party in regard to the document proposed to be given in evidence. . . .

ALDERSON, B. . . . It is said that the letters are receivable as having been acted upon by the testator and as explanatory of his acts; and if that were the case, I should agree in the conclusion. **Every act of the testator is evidence, and if these are letters which qualify, or illustrate, or explain any act of his, they are receivable.** But then, the first step to be taken is to show some act of the testator, by clear evidence, for that is the foundation of the whole. Here, that step wholly fails; this is an attempt to raise a superstructure which has nothing to support it. **If the testator had made an indorsement on any one of them, the contents of the letter would have been receivable.** But why? Only for the purpose of showing that the indorsement was a rational act, not for the purpose of showing the opinion of the writer. If an answer to the letter had been sent by him, the letter is in like manner receivable to show the rationality of such answer. . . .

PARKE, B. . . . These letters are sufficiently proved to have been written and sent to the house of the deceased by persons now dead, and **they indicate the opinion of the writers that the alleged testator was a rational person and capable of doing acts of ordinary business.** But it is perfectly clear that in this case an opinion not given upon oath in a judicial inquiry between the parties is no evidence; for **the question is not what the capacity of the testator was reputed to be, but what it really was in point of fact**; and though the opinion of a witness upon oath, as to that fact, might be asked, it would only be a compendious mode of ascertaining the result of the actual observation of the witness, from acts done, as to the habits and demeanour of the deceased. . . .

Besides that, there is another ground, and the only other ground on which these letters are argued to be receivable in evidence, and that is, that there was proof in this case of acts done by the testator in reference to these letters, or at least one of them, which render the contents admissible by way of explanation of those acts. Those acts are the opening of two of the letters, and placing them in the supposed usual repository of the papers of the deceased, and the opening of the third one, and transmitting it to the attorney. . . .

The answer to this argument is,. that there is no direct proof whatever of these acts being done by the testator; and as to indirect proof, to infer that the testator did the acts is to assume the very fact to be proved. . . .

VAUGHAN, J. . . . If any acts on the part of the testator could be proved, either by letter or from other sources, all declarations and writings which tend to explain such acts, may be put in evidence. **The principle then upon which alone the letters can claim admission is the following: That where any facts are proper evidence upon an issue, all oral or written declarations which can explain such facts may be received in evidence. . . .**

LITTLEDALE, J. . . . If a party were alive and could be cross-examined he could be examined as to the ground of his belief of the competency. But **letters of this sort are much less likely to express the real sentiments of the writer than if written to a third person,** as it is not likely that the writer would in letters to the party himself indicate anything tending to a doubt of his incapacity. . . .

In a question of competence, where the party who alleges the competency is bound to prove it, **he must show that the person has done some act upon the manifestation of opinion,** which indicates that he understands the manifestation; if he does so, it is admissible in evidence, and the effect of it will be left to the jury. . . .

TINDAL, C.J. . . . **The question, therefore, with respect to the admissibility of the three letters comes to this: Is there any evidence** stated to us from which it can be inferred **that the contents** of these letters, or any of them, **were ever perused by the testator,** and by that means submitted to the exercise of his understanding and reasoning powers? or, Is there **any evidence of his doing any act with reference to them,** which may, according to the nature of such act, import the exercise of a larger or smaller extent of reasoning power?

GURNEY, B., BOSANQUET, J., BOLLAND, B., and PARK, J., also delivered opinions to the same effect.

R. v. BLAKE AND TYE.

KING'S BENCH. 1844.

13 L. J. M. C. 131; 8 Jur. 667; 6 Q. B. 126; 66 R. R. 311.

Acts and statements by one of several conspirators or joint offenders, or other persons engaged in any common transaction involving mutual legal responsibility, are parts of such common transaction and are evidence against the other party or parties thereto, as if they were done or made by him or them, so far as they were in the execution or furtherance of their common purpose, but not otherwise.

Blake was a "landing waiter" employed at the Custom House, and Tye was an agent for importers there. They were charged with conspiring to pass goods without paying full duty. Tye had made false entries in two books; in one book the entries were necessary in order to carry out the fraud, in the other book the entry was not thus necessary, but was for Tye's convenience only. The former were admissible against Blake, the latter were not.

The following is from the Law Journal:—

Lord Denman, C.J. . . . Upon **the first** point, the evidence was clearly receivable; **it was an entry made in the course of the transaction,** which could not have been proved by any other means. With regard to **the other** piece of evidence . . . full effect might have been given to the conspiracy without it. . . . **It is a mere statement of what this party was doing. . . .** A mere statement made by one conspirator, or an act that he may choose to do, which is not necessary to carry the conspiracy to its end, is not evidence to affect another. . . .

Coleridge, J. . . . **Acts or declarations are not receivable unless they tend to the advancement of the common object.** That assumes the object not to be then completed. If it has been accomplished, the act or statement is not receivable. **This was a mere statement as to the share of the plunder. . . .**

Patteson and Williams, JJ., concurred.

COMPLAINTS.

R. v. LILLYMAN.

CROWN CASES RESERVED. 1896.

L. R. [1896] 2 Q. B. 167; 65 L. J. M. C. 195; 74 L. T. 730; 44 W. R. 654; 60 J. P. 536.

Statements made after the transaction are generally irrelevant and inadmissible in favour of the person making them; but, in cases of rape and similar offences, the fact that a complaint was made by the prosecutrix shortly after the alleged occurrence, and the particulars of such complaint, may, so far as they relate to the charge, be given in evidence by the prosecution, not as evidence of the facts complained of, but as evidence of the consistency of the conduct of the prosecutrix with the story told by her in the witness-box, and as being inconsistent with her consent to that of which she complains.

On a charge of attempted rape and indecent assault the mistress of the prosecutrix, being a person to whom she would naturally complain, was allowed to state all that the prosecutrix told her, in the absence of the prisoner, very shortly after the commission of the act.

The following is from the Law Reports:—

HAWKINS, J. (*delivering the judgment of the Court,* LORD RUSSELL, C.J., POLLOCK, B., HAWKINS, CAVE and WILLS, JJ.). . . . It is necessary in the first place to have a clear understanding as to the principles upon which evidence of such a complaint, not on oath, nor made in the presence of the prisoner, nor forming part of the *res gestæ*, can be admitted. **It clearly is not admissible as evidence of the facts complained of**; those facts must therefore be established, if at all, upon oath by the prosecutrix or other credible witness, and, strictly speaking, **evidence of them ought to be given before evidence of the complaint is admitted. The complaint can only be**

used as evidence of the consistency of the conduct of the prosecutrix with the story told by her in the witness-box, and as being **inconsistent with her consent** to that of which she complains.

In every one of the old text-books, proof of complaint is treated as a most material element in the establishment of **a charge of rape or other kindred charge. . . .** It is too late, therefore, now to make serious objectión to the admissibility of evidence of the fact that a complaint was made, **provided it was made as speedily after the acts complained of as could reasonably be expected. . . .**

That **the general usage has been substantially to limit the evidence of the complaint to proof that the woman made a complaint** of something done to her, and that she mentioned in connection with it the name of a particular person, cannot be denied; but it is equally true that Judges of great experience have dissented from this limitation, and of those who have adopted the usage, none have ever carefully discussed or satisfactorily expressed the grounds upon which their views have been based. . . . When and for what reason the proof of the complaint was first limited to answers to such questions as these, "Did she make a complaint?" "Did she mention a name?" "Whose name?" etc., I have not been able to discover. . . .

After very careful consideration we have arrived at the conclusion that **we are bound by no authority to support the existing usage of limiting evidence of the complaint to the bare fact that a complaint was made,** and reason and good sense are against our doing so. The evidence is admissible only upon the ground that it was a complaint of that which is charged against the prisoner; **it can be legitimately used only for the purpose of enabling the jury to judge for themselves whether the conduct of the woman was consistent** with her testimony on oath given in the witness-box. . . . Is it to be left to the witness to whom the statement is made to determine and report to the jury whether what the woman said amounted to a real complaint? And **are the jury bound to accept the witness's interpretation of her words as binding upon them without having the whole statement before them,** and without having the power to require it to be disclosed to them, even though they may feel it essential to enable them to form a reliable opinion. . . . In reality, **affirmative answers to such stereotyped questions** as these, "Did the prosecutrix make a complaint" (a very leading question, by the way) "of something done to herself?" "Did she mention a name?" **amount to nothing to which any weight ought to be attached;** they tend rather to embarrass than to assist a thoughtful jury, for they are consistent either with there having been a complaint or no complaint of the prisoner's conduct. To limit the evidence of the complaint to such questions and answers is to ask the jury to draw important inferences from imperfect materials, perfect materials being at hand, and in the cognisance of the witness in the box. In our opinion, nothing ought unnecessarily to be left to speculation or surmise.

It has been sometimes urged that to allow the particulars of the complaint would be calculated to prejudice the interests of the accused and that the jury would be apt to treat the complaint as evidence of the facts complained of. Of course, if it were so left to the jury, they would naturally so treat it. But it never could be legally so left, and we think **it is the duty of the Judge to impress upon the jury in every case that they are not entitled to make use of the complaint as any evidence whatever of those facts,** or for any other purpose than that we have stated. With such direction we think the interests of an innocent accused would be more protected than they are under the present usage. For **when the whole statement is laid before the jury they are less likely to draw wrong and adverse inferences,** and may sometimes come to the conclusion that what the woman said amounted to no real complaint of any offence committed by the accused. . . .

R. v. OSBORNE.

CROWN CASES RESERVED. 1905.

L. R. [1905] 1 K. B. 551; 74 L. J. K. B. 311; 92 L. T. 393; 53 W. R. 494; 69 J. P. 189.

Evidence of complaints made in the absence of the accused, after the matter complained of, is only admissible in cases of rape and similar offences.

Such evidence is admissible, whether consent is or is not a material element in the charge, in order to show the consistency of the conduct of the prosecutrix with her evidence and so corroborate the latter.

But the complaint must be shown to have been made at the first opportunity which reasonably offered itself after the commission of the offence.

The fact that the complaint has been made in answer to a question does not of itself render it inadmissible; but it must not have been elicited by questions of a leading and inducing or intimidating character.

The Judge ought to inform the jury that the statement is not evidence of the facts complained of, and must not be regarded by them as other than corroboration of the evidence of the prosecutrix, or of the absence of consent.

On a charge of indecent assault on a girl aged twelve, evidence was given by another girl, Keziah Parkes, aged eleven, to the effect that she had left the prosecutrix with the prisoner shortly before the alleged offence, arranging to return soon. On her way back she met the prosecutrix running home, and said to her, "Why are you going home? Why did you not wait until we came back?" Her answer, incriminating the prisoner, was admitted in evidence as corroboration of her story.

The following is from the Law Reports:—

RIDLEY, J. (*delivering the judgment of the Court*, LORD ALVERSTONE, C.J., KENNEDY, RIDLEY, CHANNELL and PHILLIMORE, JJ.). . . . **It was contended for the prisoner that the evidence was inadmissible—first,** because the answer made by the girl was not a complaint, but a statement or conversation, having been made in answer to a question; and **secondly,** because, as Keziah Parkes was under the age of thirteen, her consent was not material to the charge.

As to the first point. . . . It appears to us that **the mere fact that the statement is made in answer to a question in such cases is not of itself sufficient to make it inadmissible as a complaint.** Questions of a suggestive or leading character will, indeed, have that effect, and will render it inadmissible; but **a question such as this,** put by the mother or other person, "What is the matter?" or "Why are you crying?" **will not do so.** These are natural questions which a person in charge will be likely to put. **On the other hand, if she were asked,** "Did So-and-so (naming the prisoner) assault you?" "Did he do this and that to you?" then the result would be different, and **the statement ought to be rejected.** In each case the decision on the character of the question put, as well as other circumstances, such as the relationship of the questioner to the complainant, must be left to the discretion of the presiding Judge. **If the circumstances indicate that but for the questioning there probably would have been no voluntary complaint, the answer is inadmissible.** If the question merely anticipates a statement which the complainant was about to make, it is not rendered inadmissible by the fact that the questioner happens to speak first. . . .

Upon the second point it was contended that, although under the decision of *R.* v. *Lillyman* (*ante*, p. 83), the particulars of a complaint made may in some circumstances be given in evidence on a charge of rape, that ruling does not extend to a charge of criminal knowledge or indecent assault where, as in the present case, consent is not legally material. . . .

By the judgment in *R.* v. *Lillyman* **it was decided that the complaint was admissible,** not as evidence of the facts complained of, nor as being a part of the *res gestæ* (which it was not), but "**as evidence of the consistency of the conduct of the prosecutrix** with the story told by her in the witness-box, **and as being inconsistent with her consent** to that of which she complains". (*Counsel for the prisoner*) argued upon this that the reasons so given were one only, and that the consistency of the complaint with the story given by the prosecutrix was material only so far as the latter alleged non-consent. If, however, that argument were sound, the words in question might have been omitted from the sentence, and it would have been sufficient to say that the complaint was admissible only and solely because it negatived consent. We think, however, if it were a question of the meaning of words, that the better construction of the judgment is that, while the Court dealt with the charge in question as involving in fact, though not in law, the question of consent on the part of the prosecutrix, yet the reasons given for admitting the complaint were two—first, that it was consistent with her story in the witness-box; and, secondly, that it was inconsistent with consent. . . . **It is not, therefore, because the charge itself involves proof of the absence of consent that the evidence is admissible;** on the contrary, the prosecutrix herself can make it evidence by deposing that she did not consent, when that is no part of the charge. In other words, **whether non-consent be legally a necessary part of the issue, or whether, on the other hand, it is what may be called a collateral issue of fact, the complaint becomes admissible.** But how does non-consent become a collateral issue of fact? The answer must be, in consequence of the story told by the prosecutrix in the witness-box. And the judgment treats the two cases on the same footing. If non-consent be a part of the story told by the prosecutrix, or if it be legally a part of the charge, in each case alike the complaint is admissible. But if that is so, does not the reasoning apply equally to other parts of the story and not merely to the part in which the prosecutrix has denied consent? If not, it seems illogical to allow, as the Court did allow, that the whole of the story may be given in evidence. The true result is, we think, that **while the decision in R. v. Lillyman is not strictly on all fours with the present case, yet the reasoning which it contains answers the questions now raised for decision.**

But, however that may be, it appears to us that, in accordance with principle, **such complaints are admissible, not merely as negativing consent, but because they are consistent with the story of the prosecutrix.** In all ordinary cases, indeed, the principle must be observed which rejects statements made by anyone in the prisoner's absence. Charges of this kind form an exceptional class, and in them such statements ought, under the proper safeguards, to be admitted. **Their consistency with the story told is, from the very nature of such cases, of special importance.** Did the woman make a complaint at once? If so, that is consistent with her story. Did she not do so? That is inconsistent. And in either case the matter is important for the jury. . . .

We are, at the same time, not insensible of the great importance of carefully observing the proper limits within which such evidence should be given. **It is only to cases of this kind that the authorities on which our judgment rests apply;** and our judgment also is to them restricted. It applies only where there is a complaint not elicited by questions of a leading and inducing or intimidating character, **and only when it is made at the first opportunity after the offence which reasonably offers itself.** Within such bounds we think the evidence should be put before the jury; **the Judge being careful to inform the jury that the statement is not evidence of the facts complained of, and must not be regarded by them, if believed, as other than corroborative** of the complainant's credibility, and, where consent is in issue, of the absence of consent.

R. v. CAMELLERI.

COURT OF CRIMINAL APPEAL. 1922.

L. R. [1922] 2 K. B. 122; 91 L. J. K. B. 671; 16 Cr. App. R. 162; 86 J. P. 135; 66 S. J. 667; 27 Cox C. C. 246.

On a charge against a male prisoner of gross indecency with a boy of fifteen the particulars of a complaint made by the boy to his parents, shortly after the offence, were admitted by the Judge, not as evidence of the facts complained of, but to show the consistency of his conduct with his testimony in the box. *Held*, that the evidence was rightly admitted.

The following is from the Law Reports:—

Lord Hewart, C.J. . . . Does the principle of *R.* v. *Osborne, sup.*, following *R.* v. *Lillyman, sup.*, apply to indecent assaults on males? . . . There are, it is true, historical reasons for allowing complaints of this character by females, but in view of the principle laid down in *R.* v. *Lillyman, sup.*, where no doubt the question of consent was material, and in *R.* v. *Osborne, sup.*, where no question of consent arose, it does not appear to us that at the present day the admissibility of evidence of this nature can depend upon the historical grounds upon which, in the first instance, in the case of female complainants, it was first admitted. It is true that in certain other cases, as, for example, *Beatty* v. *Cullingworth*, 60 J. P. 740, observations were made which appear to limit the class of cases in which complaints of the kind referred to are admissible, to indecent assaults upon women and girls. But when the facts of those cases are looked at, it is apparent that the **antithesis which the Judges had in their minds was not that between complaint by a female and complaint by a male person, but was the antithesis between sexual offences, on the one hand, and non-sexual offences, on the other.** So far as this country is concerned there is no authority which decides that the mere fact that the complainant is a male person renders the complaint or its particulars inadmissible. The question does not seem to have been considered by the High Court. In New Zealand, on the other hand, the fact and particulars of a complaint by a male person have been held admissible (*R.* v. *McNamara,* [1917] N. Z. L. R. 382). No doubt there is force in the suggestion that probably little attention would or should be paid to a complaint by an abandoned male person of mature years, but perhaps that observation goes rather to the weight than to the admissibility of the complaint. In this case, **where the complaint was by a young boy, we are of opinion that the Judge rightly admitted evidence of the fact and particulars of the complaint.** Hereafter, it may be that the limits of this matter may have to be considered. It is no part of the function of this Court to go beyond the facts of the case and lay down far-reaching principles.

Note.—The above decisions established the following points.—

1. That complaints are only admissible in "sexual" cases, which term is now held to include offences against males as well as females.
2. That both the *fact* and the *particulars* of the complaint are admissible.
3. That complaints are not evidence of the *truth* of the matters stated; but only (*a*) of the consistency of the complainant's conduct with the story she, or he, has told in the box, and (*b*) as negativing consent, where that fact is in issue.

COURSE OF BUSINESS.

HETHERINGTON v. KEMP.

NISI PRIUS. 1815.

4 CAMPBELL 193; 16 R. R. 773.

In an action on a bill of exchange, to prove notice of dishonour, the plaintiff testified that he wrote a letter to the defendant, to whom notice to produce had been given, stating that the bill had been dishonoured; that he put the letter on a table where, according to the usage of his office, letters for the post were always deposited; and that a porter carried them thence to the post. But the porter was not called, and no evidence was given of what became of the letter after it was put on the table.

LORD ELLENBOROUGH, C.J. You must go further. Some **evidence must be given that the letter was** taken from the table in the counting-house, and **put into the post-office.** Had you called the porter, and he had said that, although he had no recollection of the letter in question, he invariably carried to the post-office all the letters found upon the table, this might have done; but **I cannot hold this general evidence of the course of business in the plaintiff's counting-house to be sufficient.**

Note.—In modern cases less strictness has usually been exacted. Thus, to prove the copy of a letter, the original of which was alleged to have been posted to the plaintiff, but was not produced on notice, it was held sufficient for the defendant's clerk to testify that he had made the copy, and that though he did not remember posting the letter he had no doubt he would have done so in the ordinary course of business (*Trotter* v. *Maclean*, 13 Ch. D. 574, 580, *per* Fry, J.). As to public offices, see *ante*, p. 34.

POSSESSION OF PROPERTY.

ROBERTSON v. FRENCH.

KING'S BENCH. 1803.

4 EAST 130; 7 R. R. 535.

Possession of property, land or goods and chattels, and acts of ownership thereof, are evidence of ownership. Ownership or title need not generally be strictly proved by production of documents of title.

In an action on a policy of insurance on a ship and its cargo, evidence of the facts of possession and dealing with such ship as owners, was allowed as evidence of the plaintiffs' ownership, although the title of the plaintiffs actually depended on a deed, *i.e.*, a bill of sale.

LORD ELLENBOROUGH, C.J. (*delivering the judgment of the Court, which then included* GROSE, LAWRENCE and LE BLANC, JJ.). . . . As to the first point made in this case on the part of the defendant, *viz.*, that the ownership alleged was not sufficiently proved; **it was proved by the captain in the ordinary way, that the owners by whom, as such, he was appointed and employed, were the persons in whom the ownership is by the declaration averred to be.** And though it afterwards appeared by his answers on cross-examination, that the ownership was derived to those persons under a bill of sale executed by himself as attorney to one Lawrence Williams, the former owner, it did not on that account become necessary for the plaintiffs to produce that bill of sale, or the ship's register, or to give any further proof of such their property; **the mere fact of their possession as owners being sufficient prima facie evidence of ownership,** without the aid of any documentary proof or title deeds on the subject, until such further evidence should be rendered necessary in support of the *prima facie* case of ownership which they made, in consequence of the adduction of some contrary proof on the other side.

Note.—The fact of possession is clearly relevant to the fact of ownership, as the former undoubtedly renders the latter probable.

The person who possesses and acts as owner is generally the owner, at least as regards personal property.

The matter in question has been very clearly and concisely stated by a well-known and reliable author—"The acts of enjoyment from which the ownership of real property may be inferred are very various, as for instance, the cutting of timber, the repairing of fences or banks, the perambulation of boundaries of a manor or parish, the taking of wreck on the foreshore, and the granting to others of licences or leases under which possession is taken and held; also the receipts of rents from tenants of the property; for all these acts are fractions of that sum total of enjoyment which characterises *dominium*" (*Wills*, 60).

There is sometimes said to be a "presumption of ownership" in these cases. But there can scarcely be sufficient certainty of facts to create any recognised presumption of law. A presumption of fact may be drawn. See *ante*, p. 23.

DOE v. PENFOLD.

NISI PRIUS. 1838.

8 C. & P. 536.

Possession of land may be taken as sufficient "prima facie" evidence of seisin in fee simple.

In an action of ejectment, the only evidence to show the seisin of a person, in whom title was alleged, was that he was in possession of the whole of the property. This was held sufficient *prima facie* evidence.

PATTESON, J. **If he was in actual possession, that is evidence that he was seised in fee,** unless there be something to show that he had a less estate. I think that if nothing further be shown, it is, at least, **some evidence of a seisin in fee.**

Note.—This rule that the possessor of land is *prima facie* owner in fee simple is the basis of the law as to declarations against proprietary interest, as to which see *post*, p. 221.

JONES v. WILLIAMS.

EXCHEQUER. 1837.

2 M. & W. 326; 46 R. R. 611.

Acts of possession and enjoyment of land, as cutting timber, repairing hedges, granting leases, etc., may be evidence of ownership, not only of the particular piece or quantity of land with reference to which such acts are done, but also of other land so situated or connected therewith by locality or similarity that what is true as to the one piece of land is likely to be true of the other piece of land.

Acts and conduct of the plaintiff showing apparent ownership of a hedge and the bed of a river at a certain point were admitted as evidence of ownership thereof at a neighbouring point.

Lord Abinger, C.B. . . . **The plaintiff . . . was endeavouring to prove that upon both sides of the river**—on the same side with the land of the defendant—**he had exercised acts of ownership, such as repairing the hedge;** and therefore he claimed a right up to the hedge; and then **going further, he shows that the hedge continued a** visible line of demarcation without anything occurring to break its continuity—except that a cross hedge ran down to it, dividing the defendant's farm from his neighbour's land on the same side of the river—down to a considerable distance, **till it came opposite to** the extremity of **the plaintiff's land** on the other side. **From these facts the plaintiff purposes to show that it is all his;** and it appears to me that **the evidence ought to have been received,** in order to rebut the presumption that the middle of the river was to be considered as the boundary between two distinct closes. . . .

Parke, B. . . . **I think the evidence offered of acts in another part of one continuous hedge, and in the whole bed of the river, adjoining** the plaintiff's land, **were admissible in evidence,** on the ground that they are such acts as might reasonably lead to the inference that the entire hedge and bed of the river, and consequently the part in dispute, belonged to the plaintiff. **Ownership may be proved by proof of possession, and that can be shown only by acts of** njoyment of the land itself; but it is impossible, in the nature of hings, to confine the evidence to the very precise spot on which the lleged trespass may have been committed; **evidence may be given f acts done on other parts, provided there is such a common haracter of locality** between those parts and the spot in question as rould raise a reasonable inference in the minds of the jury that the lace in dispute belonged to the plaintiff if the other parts did. . . .

Bolland and Gurney, BB., concurred.

Note.—A similar case is *Doe* v. *Kemp*, 2 Bing. N. C. 102, in hich it was held that acts of ownership over certain strips of grass t the side of a highway were evidence of ownership of similar strips n the same highway at a considerable distance, but were not vidence of ownership of similar strips on other roads, although in he same manor. The matter must depend on the facts in each case.

R. v. LANGMEAD.

CROWN CASES RESERVED. 1864.

10 L. T. 350; 9 Cox C. C. 464; L. & C. 427.

ossession of property, proved to have been stolen recently, is evidence that the person in possession either stole it or received it knowing it to have been stolen.

The prisoner was indicted for (*a*) stealing, and (*b*) receiving eloniously, certain sheep, which were found in his possession a few lays after they had been stolen. The circumstances seemed to show hat he had not himself stolen them, and he gave no explanation f his possession. The jury, acting on this evidence of possession, ound him guilty of receiving. The Court for Crown Cases Reserved ffirmed the conviction.

The following is from Leigh and Cave:—

Byles, J. . . . There are three ways in which the prisoner may ave received these sheep with a guilty knowledge. . . . **The jury nay fairly have drawn any one of these conclusions from the facts efore them. Whether they were right or wrong in their conclusion**

is not a question for us. Where there has been a burglary, and some men and a woman are found in possession of the property stolen although the evidence may be the same against all, the jury almost universally find the men guilty of the burglary and the woman only of receiving; the consideration of her sex inclining their minds to the belief that she did not take any part in the burglary.

BLACKBURN, J. . . . **When it has been shown that property has been stolen, and has been found recently after its loss in the possession of the prisoner,** he is called upon to account for having it; and on his failing to do so, **the jury may very well infer** that his possession was dishonest, and **that he was either the thief or the receiver** according to the circumstances. If he had been seen near the place where the property was kept before it was stolen, they may fairly suppose **that he was the thief.** If other circumstances show that it is more than probable that he was not the thief, the presumption would be **that he was the receiver.** The jury should not convict the prisoner of receiving, unless they are satisfied that he is not the actual thief. . . .

MELLOR, J. In theory the jury ought to agree in their opinion; but in practice they often do not. Some think that the prisoner was the actual thief, and others that he was the receiver only. . . . It is clear that, whatever was the mode in which the jury in this case arrived at their verdict, **there was evidence from which they might safely have drawn either conclusion.**

POLLOCK, C.B., and MARTIN, B., concurred.

Note.—The substantial question in such cases is whether such possession of the property is so near in time to the stealing that it may fairly be concluded that the person in possession was connected with the offence. If such time had elapsed that, in all probability, the wrongdoer would have got rid of the property, possession thereof would rather show that the possessor had no connection with the crime. Much would depend on the nature of the property, the opportunity of getting rid of it, and other circumstances. Several cases illustrating the matter may be found in books on Criminal Law.

But such evidence is in any event only evidence on which the jury *may* convict the prisoner; they are not bound to do so in the absence of a convincing explanation by him. The onus of proving the prisoner's guilt in this as in all criminal cases remains on the prosecution (*R.* v. *Schama,* 84 L. J. K. B. 396; *Woolmington* v. *D. P. P.*, *post*, p. 140).

COHABITATION AND REPUTATION OF MARRIAGE.

DOE v. FLEMING.

COMMON PLEAS. 1827.

4 Bing. 266; 29 R. R. 562.

Marriage may usually be proved by evidence of cohabitation or general reputation, even when it is not supported by other evidence, and although the persons reputed to be married are still alive.

The plaintiff sought to recover certain premises as heir-at-law, and the only evidence of the marriage of his parents was the reputation of their having lived together as man and wife. This was held sufficient, although the father was still alive.

Park, J. **The general rule is, that reputation is sufficient evidence of marriage,** and a party who seeks to impugn a principle as well established ought, at least, to furnish cases in support of his position. As we have heard none, I see no reason for disturbing the verdict.

Best, C.J. The rule has never been doubted. It appeared on the trial that **the mother of the plaintiff was received into society as a respectable woman,** and under such circumstances improper conduct ought not to be presumed.

Note.—For the exceptions to this rule, see next case. As to whether there is a presumption in law of marriage, see *ante*, p. 25.

MORRIS v. MILLER.

KING'S BENCH. 1767.

4 Burrow 2057; 1 Wm. Blackstone 632.

In proceedings for bigamy, divorce, or damages for adultery the marriages or ceremonies alleged by the prosecution or petitioner and upon which the proceedings are based, cannot be proved by reputation. Strict evidence thereof must be given.

In an action for criminal conversation (damages for adultery), proof of "cohabitation, name, and reception by everybody as wife" was held insufficient.

The following is from Burrow:—

Lord Mansfield, C.J. (*delivering the judgment of the Court, which then included* Yates, Aston and Hewitt, JJ.). . . . We are all clearly of opinion that in this kind of action, an action for criminal conversation with the plaintiff's wife, **there must be evidence of a marriage in fact; acknowledgment, cohabitation, and reputation are not sufficient** to maintain this action.

But we do not at present define what may or may not be evidence of a marriage in fact.

This is a sort of criminal action; there is no other way of punishing this crime at common law.

It shall not depend upon the mere reputation of a marriage, which arises from the conduct or declarations of the plaintiff himself.

In prosecutions for bigamy, a marriage in fact must be proved.

No inconvenience can happen by this determination; but inconvenience might arise from a contrary determination, which might render persons liable to actions founded upon evidence made by the persons themselves who should bring the action.

The following is from Blackstone:—

Lord Mansfield, C.J. (*as above*). In these actions **there must be proof of a marriage in fact, as contrasted to cohabitation, and reputation** of marriage arising from thence. Perhaps, there need not be strict proof from the register, or by a person present; but strong evidence must be had of the fact; as by a person present at the wedding dinner, if the register be burnt, and the parson and clerk are dead.

This action is by way of punishment, therefore the Court never interfere as to the quantum of damages.

No proof, in such a case, shall arise from the parties' own act of cohabitation.

The case of bigamy is stronger than this. . . . **Except in these two cases, I know of none where reputation is not a good proof of marriage.**

Note.—Stephen says, "The facts that they cohabited and were treated by others as man and wife . . . are not sufficient to prove a marriage in a prosecution for bigamy", etc. (*Dig. Ev.*, Art. 54). But this seems to put it too broadly. The marriage and subsequent ceremony upon which the prosecution is based certainly cannot be so proved, but it may be that another marriage becomes material in such prosecution, and such marriage can certainly be proved by reputation, although it is proving a marriage "in a prosecution for bigamy". Thus, in the case of *R.* v. *Wilson*, 3 F. & F. 119, the prisoner pleaded that, when she went through the first ceremony alleged, the man was already married, and, therefore, the ceremony was void, and she had not committed bigamy. This marriage, so alleged by the prisoner, was allowed to be proved by reputation.

CONDUCT, CHARACTER, AND CONVICTION OF PARTIES.

It is most important to keep distinct **three entirely different matters** which are frequently confused, namely:—

(1) Conduct,
(2) Character,
(3) Convictions,

with reference to both parties and witnesses. As regards witnesses, these matters are considered *post*, p. 296.

It is also important to remember that as a general rule **cross-examination** as to conduct, character and previous convictions is allowed with a view to shaking the witness' credibility (see *post*, p. 296). But in such cases except as regards previous convictions the witness' answer must be accepted, and **evidence cannot be called in rebuttal.**

(1) CONDUCT.

The rules as to conduct on the occasion in question, as part of the transaction, have been dealt with *ante*, pp. 66, 67. It is proposed to consider in this place the cases in which evidence may be given of the conduct of the parties which is not part of the transaction.

The rules are mainly derived from cases, as will be shown by those given *post*, pp. 105—113. The position appears to be:—

(*a*) The evidence must be of **similar acts** of the party whose act is in question (see *post*, p. 107).

(*b*) It is, when admissible, **not evidence of the act** in question, unless directly connected therewith (see *post*, p. 105).

(*c*) It is admissible as **evidence of the state of mind** of the person when he did the act in question, after such act has been proved (see *post*, p. 107).

(*d*) It is so admissible in both **civil and criminal** cases (see *post*, p. 109).

(2) CHARACTER.

Evidence of character is admissible in the cases mentioned below:—

Civil Cases.

The character of the plaintiff:—

(1) In cases where **it is actually in issue,** as in actions for *defamation* (see *post*, p. 115).

(2) In cases where the amount of **damages may depend on it,** as in actions for *breach of promise* of marriage, *damages for adultery*, and *defamation* (see *post*, p. 120).

The character of the defendant:—

In no cases, apparently, except possibly to mitigate damages in actions for breach of promise of marriage.

The character of other persons:—

(1) In actions for **seduction,** evidence of the character of the *person seduced* may be given on the question of damages (see *post*, p. 116).

(2) In proceedings for **damages for adultery or for enticement** evidence of the character of the spouse enticed may be given on the question of damages (see *post*, p. 121).

Criminal Cases.

The character of the person prosecuting:—

In cases of **rape** and kindred offences, evidence of the character of the *prosecutrix* (see *post*, p. 124).

The character of the person charged:—

(1) **In all cases if he chooses** to introduce it by tendering evidence of his good character (see *post*, p. 121).

(2) On a charge of vagrancy, by the **Prevention of Crime Act, 1871,** s. 15, evidence of his *known charact[er] as proved* may be given to prove intent to commit felony (see *post*, p. 460).

(3) On a charge of being an habitual criminal, under the **Prevention of Crime Act, 1908,** evidence of his *character and repute* may be given on the question of dishonest or criminal life (see *post*, p. 493).

(4) On a charge of spying, etc., under the **Official Secrets Act, 1911,** evidence of his *known character as proved* may be given as evidence that his purpose was prejudicial to the safety or interests of the State (see *post*, p. 496).

(3) PREVIOUS CONVICTIONS.

The rules here are mainly statutory. The position appears to be:—

(*a*) The evidence must be of **actual conviction** of a crime (as to the mode of proof whereof, see *post*, p. 561).

(*b*) It is admissible as evidence **of various matters** in different cases, as stated below.

(*c*) It is admissible in both **civil and criminal** cases, as follows:—

In Civil Cases.

(1) If a **witness denies his conviction** when cross-examined as to that fact (Criminal Procedure Act, 1865, s. 6, which applies to civil as well as criminal proceedings, see *post*, p. 451).

(2) As evidence of the existence of a **public or general right** (see *post*, p. 236).

(3) In a few exceptional cases as evidence of commission of the crime by the person convicted, if he, or anyone claiming through him, is a party to the suit (see *post*, p. 125).

In Criminal Cases.

Before verdict, evidence of previous conviction of a person charged cannot generally be given (6 & 7 Will. 4, c. 111, see *post*, p. 433; 24 & 25 Vict. c. 96, s. 116, see *post*, p. 450; 34 & 35 Vict. c 112, s. 9, see *post*, p. 460), but it may be given in the following cases:—

(1) On any charge to which a **previous conviction is essential to the charge,** evidence of the *appropriate convictions* may be given in support of the charge (*e.g.*, 8 Edw. 7, c. 59, s. 10 (2), see *post*, p. 492).

(2) On any charge to which a **previous conviction is a defence,** *i.e.*, on a plea of *autrefois convict.*

(3) On a charge of **receiving stolen goods,** evidence of previous convictions for *fraud or dishonesty* within *five years* previous to the date of the offence charged may be given to prove guilty knowledge, *whether the person charged gives evidence of his good character or not* (Larceny Act, 1916, s. 43, see *post*, p. 501).

(4) In proceedings where the **indictment charges the accused with committing any offence after a previous conviction,** but only *if the person charged gives evidence of his good character* (Larceny Act, 1861, s. 116, see *post*, p. 450).

(5) Where the accused, *having rendered himself liable to such cross-examination*, **denies a previous conviction** put to him in cross-examination (Criminal Evidence Act, 1898, s. 1 (*f*), see *post*, p. 480; Criminal Procedure Act, 1865, s. 6, see *post*, p. 453).

The position summarised in (4) above was reached by a series of statutes, the Previous Conviction Act, 1836 (see *post*, p. 433), the Larceny Act, 1861, s. 116 (see *post*, p. 450), the Coinage Offences Act, 1861, s. 37 (since repealed), the Prevention of Crimes Act, 1871, ss. 9, 20 (see *post*, pp. 460, 461) and the decision in **Faulkner v. R.,** [1905] 2 K. B. 76, where it was held that the words "proceedings upon any indictment for committing any offence " in section 116 of the Larceny Act, 1861, were not confined to an indictment for any offence under that Act, but were wide enough to cover any offence at all charged on indictment, thus rendering, it would seem, all the other statutes on the subject superfluous.

In practice now evidence of the conviction would probably in any event be admissible under (5) above, but it is possible that the accused might give evidence of his good character by other witnesses, and not go into the witness-box himself, thus affording the prosecution no opportunity to invoke the procedure under (5).

After Verdict, information as to the character of the accused is always given, in order that the punishment may be properly adjusted to the offence. The mode in which such information is brought to the notice of the Court is not governed by the strict rules of evidence and it is customary to receive some hearsay material, *e.g.*, the character given a man by his employers or a soldier's army record (*R.* v. *Roche* (1944), 30 Cr. App. R. 29). The accused, however, may challenge the accuracy of what is said about him, in which case it is the duty of the presiding Judge, if he thinks the matter of sufficient importance, to direct formal proof of it by proper evidence. Otherwise he should ignore it, stating that he does so in passing sentence (*R.* v. *Campbell* (1911), 75 J. P. 16; 6 Cr. App. R. 131).

CONDUCT OF PARTIES ON OTHER OCCASIONS.

HOLLINGHAM v. HEAD.

COMMON PLEAS. 1858.

27 L. J. C. P. 241; 6 W. R. 442; 4 JUR. (N.S.) 379; 4 C. B. (N.S.) 388.

Conduct of the parties on other occasions, unconnected with the act or conduct in question, is generally irrelevant. The fact that a person has done a certain thing on other occasions is not relevant to the question whether he did it on the occasion in question.

The question being whether the plaintiff has sold guano to the defendant on certain special terms, the fact that he had sold guano to other persons on such terms was inadmissible in evidence.

The following is from the Law Journal:—

WILLES, J. . . . The question is, whether in an action for goods sold and delivered, it is competent for the defendant to show, by way of defence, that the plaintiff has entered into contracts with other persons in a particular form, for the purpose of inducing the jury to come to the conclusion that the contract sued upon was in that particular form, and so to defeat the action; and I am of opinion that it is not competent for the defendant to do so. . . .

It may be often difficult to decide upon the admissibility of evidence, where it is offered for the purpose of establishing probability, but **to be admissible it must at least afford a reasonable inference as to the principal matter in dispute. . . .** It appears to me that the evidence, which was proposed to be given in this case, would not have shown that it was probable that the plaintiff had made the contract, which the defendant contended he had made; for **I do not see how the fact that a man has once or more in his life acted in a particular way, makes it probable that he so acted on a given occasion.** The admission of such evidence would be fraught with the greatest inconvenience. **Where, indeed, the question is one of guilty knowledge or intent,** as in the case of uttering forged documents or base coin, **such evidence is admissible** as tending to establish a necessary ingredient of the crime. But if the evidence were admissible in this case, it would be difficult to say that in any case, where the question was whether or not goods had been sold upon credit, the defendant might not call evidence to prove that other persons had received credit from the plaintiff; or in an action for an assault, that the plaintiff might not prove that the defendant had assaulted other persons generally, or persons of a particular class.

To obviate the prejudice, the injustice, and the waste of time to which the admission of such evidence would lead, and bearing in mind the extent to which it might be carried, and that litigants are mortal, it is necessary not only to adhere to the rule, but to lay it down strictly. I think, therefore, **the fact that the plaintiff had entered into contracts of a particular kind with other persons on other occasions could not properly be admitted in evidence, where no custom of trade to make such contracts, and no connection between such and the one in question, was shown to exist. . . .**

BYLES, J. . . . As regards the question put to the plaintiff **on cross-examination, it may be that he might have been asked whether he had not made the same contract with other persons,** which the defendant contended he had made with him, for the purpose of testing his memory or his credit. **But such evidence, when offered as part of the defendant's case, was totally inadmissible.** To have admitted it would have been contrary to all principle, and to what has been the universal practice so long as I have known the profession.

WILLIAMS, J. . . . As to the evidence offered by the defendant, there can be no doubt whatever that that was inadmissible. **It would lead to the greatest inconvenience** if we were once to relax the rule, which requires the evidence to be confined to the points in issue, **by allowing other transactions to be inquired into. . . .**

Note.—It will be observed that the rule in the above case applies to "unconnected" conduct. If the conduct on another occasion were connected with that in question, as if it were part of the same transaction (see *ante*, p. 66), it then might be admissible. Or if, in the above case, the plaintiff had said he would supply guano to the defendant on the same terms as those made with the other persons in question, then, doubtless, his conduct in dealing with such persons would have been admissible.

HOLCOMBE v. HEWSON.

NISI PRIUS. 1810.

2 CAMP. 391.

The evidence to prove a particular transaction must generally be confined to the details of such transaction.

In an action by a brewer against a publican, on an agreement by the latter to take all his beer from the former, the question arose whether he had supplied bad beer. Evidence of certain other publicans that the plaintiff had supplied them with good beer was rejected.

LORD ELLENBOROUGH, C.J. This is *res inter alios acta.* We cannot here inquire into the quality of different beer furnished to different persons. **The plaintiff might deal well with one and not with the others.** Let him call some of those who frequented the defendant's house, and there drank the beer which he sent in, or let him give any other evidence of the quality of this beer; but I cannot admit witnesses to his general character and habits as a brewer.

Note.—If it had been shown that all the beer was of the same brewing and supplied at the same time, it is suggested that the evidence would have been admitted.

MAKIN v. ATTORNEY-GENERAL FOR NEW SOUTH WALES.

PRIVY COUNCIL. 1893.

L. R. [1894] A. C. 57; 63 L. J. P. C. 41; 69 L. T. 778.

Evidence is admissible of similar conduct by the accused on other occasions to show the intention with which the acts alleged to constitute the crime were done.

The prisoners were charged with the murder of an infant child which they had received from its mother for adoption on payment of a sum insufficient for its support, and whose body had been found buried in the garden of a house occupied by them. Evidence was held admissible that other children had been received by the prisoners on like terms and that other children's bodies had been found buried in a similar manner in the gardens of other houses occupied by the prisoners.

The following is from the Law Reports:—

LORD HERSCHELL, L.C. (*delivering the judgment of the Court, which consisted of* LORDS HERSCHELL, WATSON, HALSBURY, ASHBOURNE, MACNAGHTEN, MORRIS and SHAND). . . . The question which their Lordships had to determine was the admissibility of the evidence relating to the finding of other bodies, and to the fact that other children had been entrusted to the appellants.

In their Lordships' opinion the principles which must govern the decision of the case are clear, though the application of them is by no means free from difficulty. It is undoubtedly **not competent** for the prosecution **to adduce evidence tending to show that the accused has been guilty of criminal acts** other than those covered by the indictment, **for the purpose of leading to the conclusion that the accused** is a person **likely** from his criminal conduct or character **to have committed the offence** for which he is being tried. On the other hand, the mere fact that the evidence adduced tends to show **the commission of other crimes** does not render it inadmissible if it be relevant to an issue before the jury, and it **may be** so **relevant if it bears upon the question whether the acts alleged to constitute the crime** charged in the indictment **were designed or accidental, or to rebut a defence which would otherwise be open to the accused.** The statement of these general principles is easy, but it is obvious that it may often be very difficult to draw the line and to decide whether a particular piece of evidence is on the one side or the other. . . .

The leading authority relied on by the Crown was the case of *R.* v. *Geering* (18 L. J. (N.S.) M. C. 215), where on the trial of a prisoner for the murder of her husband by administering arsenic evidence was tendered, with the view of showing that two sons of the prisoner who had formed part of the same family, and for whom as well as for her husband the prisoner had cooked their food, had died of poison, the symptoms in all these cases being the same. The evidence was admitted by Pollock, C.B., who tried the case; he held that it was **admissible** inasmuch as **its tendency was to prove that the death of the husband was occasioned by arsenic, and was relevant to the question whether such taking was accidental or not. . . .**

After reviewing other authorities, the LORD CHANCELLOR *continued:* Under these circumstances their Lordships cannot see that it was irrelevant to the issue to be tried by the jury that several other infants had been received from their mothers on like representations, and upon payment of a sum inadequate for the support of the child for more than a very limited period, or that the bodies of infants had been found buried in a similar manner in the gardens of several houses occupied by the prisoners. . . .

Note.—The matter may be roughly stated thus: unconnected conduct on other occasions is never admissible to prove the *actus reus*, but is admissible to prove the *mens rea*, or other state of mind. The rule applies to both civil and criminal cases.

With regard to civil cases, *Hales* v. *Kerr*, [1908] 2 K. B. 601, is instructive. The plaintiff sued a barber in whose shop he alleged he had contracted barber's itch, owing to the defendant's negligence in using dirty materials. Evidence was allowed to be given by two other customers who had contracted such a complaint at the same shop, in order to show that the defendant's mode of carrying on business was dangerous.

With regard to criminal charges, in the case of *R.* v. *Bond*, [1906] 2 K. B. 389, Bray, J., summarised the law as follows:—

"A careful examination of the cases where evidence of this kind has been admitted shows that they may be grouped under three heads:—

"(1) Where the prosecution seeks to prove a system or course of conduct.

"(2) Where the prosecution seeks to rebut a suggestion on the part of the prisoner of accident or mistake.

"(3) Where the prosecution seeks to prove knowledge by the prisoner of some fact".

[This list, however, must not be taken as exhaustive: see *Phipson*, 147—172.]

R. v. RHODES.

CROWN CASES RESERVED. 1899.

L. R. [1899] 1 Q. B. 77; 68 L. J. Q. B. 83; 79 L. T. 360; 47 W. R. 121; 62 J. P. 774; 19 Cox C. C. 182.

Evidence of similar acts on other occasions is admissible to prove guilty knowledge or intention, or state of mind, even though such acts were subsequent to the transaction in question, if they show a connected, or entire, scheme or system of operations.

On a trial for obtaining eggs by false pretences, it was proved that the prisoner had falsely represented by advertisements that he was carrying on a *bona fide* dairyman's business. Evidence was admitted that, subsequently to the transaction in question, he had obtained eggs from other persons by similar advertisements.

The following is from the Law Journal:—

Lord Russell of Killowen, C.J. . . . It is plain that the prisoner was carrying on a single and entire scheme of fraud by means of one and the same sham business and sham advertisements. Had the transactions been disconnected and isolated, I should be by no means prepared to admit evidence of the later transactions upon a charge arising out of a former transaction. But here, where, so far from being isolated, **a plain connection between each of these transactions is afforded by the advertisement, which shows that the whole scheme was one entire fraud,** and that the business was an absolute sham, and that the method was the same in every case, and with the one view of defrauding the public, I am of opinion that the **evidence with regard to the prisoner's subsequent transactions was admissible. . . .**

Wills, J. . . . The charge here is that the prisoner falsely pretended he was carrying on a real business when he was carrying on a bogus business. How is this to be shown when a man has, as the prisoner had here, some of the apparatus of a regular business—that is to say, a real shop with his name over it—unless by showing that other like transactions have been carried on by the accused, and that **the transaction, the subject of the charge, was part of a system forming a single and entire scheme of fraud?** If these other transactions be prior in date to the one in question, there can be no doubt as to their admissibility in evidence. **What difference does it make whether they took place before or after, so long as they would fairly lead to the inference that the transaction on which the charge is based is part of a connected system of operation?** The difficulty here is the interval of time which elapsed; and if there had been no connecting link between the first and last transactions I agree that the evidence of the last transaction would have been inadmissible. . . . But here we find that **the same advertisement had been continued,** and that **its operation in the last case was precisely similar to its operation in the first.** This being so, in my judgment the evidence relating to the later transactions was properly left to the jury. As to this I can entertain no doubt.

Wright, J. . . . It was an essential part of the proof that it was a business of a bogus character to show its general nature, and the best evidence of this would be that it was carried on in the same manner for a considerable time, and **once the continuity of the business was shown, transactions after the date of the alleged particular crime were as relevant** in proof of its general character as transactions before that date. . . .

Bruce, J. . . . I cannot say that the evidence is not relevant, because I think it may have tended to show that the prisoner's business was a sham business. It seems to me, however, that **it had only a remote bearing upon the case, but that is an objection that relates to the weight of the evidence only,** and not to its admissibility.

Darling, J., concurred.

Note.—It is only in exceptional circumstances that evidence of similar acts subsequent to the act charged is admissible. It must be shown that there was a scheme or system of operations of which both the act charged and the subsequent act formed part. The above case is an example of the "long firm fraud" where the prisoners are charged with "obtaining money by falsely pretending that they were then carrying on a genuine business as —— etc." Proof of system is an essential ingredient of such offences. In *R.* v. *Fisher*, [1910] 1 K. B. 149, where a prisoner was charged with obtaining goods and credit by false pretences and other fraud, it was held that evidence should not have been admitted that on other occasions he had obtained goods from other persons by false pretences, as the acts were not, in the circumstances, sufficiently similar, Channell, J., saying, "Of course if the swindling charged was swindling by a particular method, the prosecution might prove similar acts of swindling". Cf. also *R.* v. *Boothby*, 24 Cr. App. R. 112.

R. v. RILEY.

CROWN CASES RESERVED. 1887.

L. R. 18 Q. B. D. 481; 56 L. J. M. C. 52; 56 L. T. 371; 35 W. R. 382; 16 Cox C. C. 191.

In prosecutions for rape, or assault with intent to commit rape, or indecent assault, evidence of similar conduct on other occasions between the prosecutrix and the prisoner is admissible, as being relevant to the issue.

On a charge of rape, the defence was consent of the prosecutrix. In cross-examination she denied previous voluntary acts of connection with the prisoner, and the Court rejected evidence offered by the prisoner to contradict her. The conviction was quashed on the ground that the evidence was admissible.

The following is from the Law Journal:—

LORD COLERIDGE, C.J. . . . The indictment charged the prisoner with an assault with intent to commit a rape upon a woman, and **the woman having denied previous voluntary connection with the accused, the prisoner proposed to show that she had had such connection with him. That evidence was rejected. It is clear that it was receivable.** It has been held again and again that if in such a case **evidence as to connection with persons other than the accused** is denied by the prosecutrix, evidence offered in contradiction **must be rejected.** There are good reasons, other than those suggested in argument, for rejecting such evidence. It would be very unfair and sometimes cruel to the prosecutrix to admit such evidence; but, in addition, it does not go to the point in issue. . . .

But rejection of evidence of previous voluntary connection with the prisoner is another matter, because **not only does such evidence**

render it more likely that the woman has consented, but it is a line of examination going to the very point in issue.

Upon principle and authority, I think that the evidence in question was receivable.

POLLOCK, B. I agree. **The only question is whether the evidence tendered was relevant to the issue.** If it was irrelevant as merely going to the woman's character, as in the case of evidence as to connection by the woman with other men, then it was properly rejected. In my opinion, **evidence as to her connection with the prisoner, whether of recent date or not, is clearly relevant to the issue.**

STEPHEN, J. I am of the same opinion, and have hardly anything to add. I think the weight of authority is decidedly in the direction in which this decision will place it. . . .

MATHEW and WILLS, JJ., concurred.

Note.—For other cases on special rules of evidence concerning rape, etc., see *ante*, p. 83, and *post*, pp. 124, 312.

CHARACTER OF PARTIES.

"Character" has at least two popular meanings—"disposition" and "reputation". The legal meaning of the term is **reputation,** at any rate so far as the Law of Evidence is concerned. A man of evil disposition who has secured a good reputation is entitled to the benefit of it in those cases where evidence of his good character is admissible, and *vice versa.*

It may be said, indeed, that a man's reputation is the best index to his real character or disposition, of which it would be very difficult to obtain any reliable evidence. And the law encourages a man to live in such a manner as to get a good reputation. The Prevention of Crime Act, 1908, uses the expression "character and repute" (see *post*, p. 493).

Character must be distinguished from conduct on other

occasions, with which it is sometimes confused. In order to show system and guilty knowledge, as we have seen (*ante*, p. 107), evidence of specific acts of conduct may be given. But a man concerning whom such specific acts are proved may still have a good character or reputation, which is not legally affected by evidence of specific acts, as character may be proved by evidence of general reputation only (see *post*, p. 121).

The cases in which evidence of character of the parties is admissible have been stated *ante*, p. 100.

The following cases illustrate the positions there referred to.

As to character of witnesses, see *post*, p. 296.

ATTORNEY-GENERAL v. BOWMAN.

NISI PRIUS. 1791.

2 B. & P. 532.

The character of the parties to a civil action is generally irrelevant and inadmissible.

Upon the trial of an information against the defendant for keeping false weights, and for offering to corrupt an officer, the defendant's counsel called a witness to character. His evidence was not admitted, as it was not a criminal prosecution, but only a penal action.

EYRE, C.B. **I cannot admit this evidence in a civil suit.** The offence imputed by the information is not in the shape of a crime. It would be contrary to the true line of distinction to admit it, which is this: that **in a direct prosecution for a crime, such evidence is admissible**; but where the prosecution is not directly for the crime but for the penalty, as in this information, it is not.

SCOTT v. SAMPSON.

QUEEN'S BENCH. 1882.

L. R. 8 Q. B. D. 491; 51 L. J. Q. B. 380; 46 L. T. 412; 30 W. R. 541; 46 J. P. 408.

In all actions or proceedings in which a plaintiff's character is actually in issue, as in actions for defamation, evidence of the plaintiff's character may be given. But evidence cannot be given of particular acts of misconduct by the plaintiff, nor evidence of rumours to the same effect as the matter complained of. Cross-examination as to particular acts is admissible solely as cross-examination to credit, but not in order to elicit evidence to mitigate damages.

This was an action for libel, the plaintiff, a journalist, alleging that the defendant had published words to the effect that he had obtained money under a threat of publishing facts injurious to the reputation of a certain lady, and systematically abused his position as a dramatic critic and journalist for the purpose of extorting money. The Judge at the trial refused to receive evidence of the plaintiff's character, of specific acts of misconduct, and also of rumours prior to the alleged libel to the same effect as the matters complained of. On an application for a new trial it was held that the evidence of character was admissible, but the other evidence was not admissible, but a new trial was refused on other grounds.

The following is from the Law Journal:—

MATHEW, J. . . . I have had the advantage of seeing the judgment which my brother Cave is about to deliver, and I agree with him in the conclusions at which he has arrived after a careful examination of the cases. . . .

CAVE, J. . . . These **decisions relate to** the admissibility—first, of evidence of **reputation;** secondly, evidence of **rumours** of and suspicions to the same effect as the defamatory matter complained of; and, thirdly, evidence of **particular facts** tending to show the character and disposition of the plaintiff. . . .

Speaking generally, **the law recognises in every man a right to have the estimation in which he stands in the opinion of others unaffected by false statements** to his discredit; and if such false statements are made without lawful excuse, and damage results to the person of whom they are made, he has a right of action. The damage, however, which he has sustained must depend almost entirely on the estimation in which he was previously held. **He complains of an injury to his reputation, and seeks to recover damages for that injury, and it seems most material that the jury who have to award those damages should know, if the fact is so, that he is a man of no reputation.** "To deny this would", as is observed in Starkie on Evidence, "be to decide that a man of the worst character is entitled to the same measure of damages with one of unsullied and unblemished reputation. A reputed thief would be placed on the same footing with the most honourable merchant, a virtuous woman with the most abandoned prostitute. To enable the jury to estimate the probable *quantum* of injury sustained, **a knowledge of the party's previous character is not only material, but seems to be absolutely essential."** . . .

As to the second head of evidence, or **evidence of rumours and suspicions** to the same effect as the defamatory matter complained of, it would seem that upon principle such evidence **is not admissible, as only indirectly tending to affect the plaintiff's reputation.** If these rumours and suspicions have, in fact, affected the plaintiff's reputation, that may be proved by general evidence of reputation. If they have not affected it, they are not relevant to the issue. . . . **Unlike evidence of general reputation, it is particularly difficult for the plaintiff to meet and rebut** such evidence; for all that those who know him best can say is that they have not heard anything of these rumours. Moreover, it may be that it is the defendant who himself has started them. . . .

As to the third head, or **evidence of facts and circumstances tending to show the disposition of the plaintiff, both principle and authority seem equally against its admission.** At the most it tends to prove not that the plaintiff has not, but that he ought not to have, a good reputation, and to admit evidence of this kind is, in effect, to throw upon the plaintiff the difficulty of showing a uniform propriety of conduct during his whole life. **It would give rise to interminable issues which would have but a very remote bearing on the question in dispute,** which is to what extent the reputation which he actually possesses has been damaged by the defamatory matter complained of. . . .

HOBBS v. TINLING & CO., LTD.

COURT OF APPEAL. 1929.

L. R. [1929] 2 K. B. 1; 98 L. J. K. B. 421;
141 L. T. 121; 73 S. J. 220; 45 T. L. R. 328.

In an action for libel the defendants did not plead justification, but gave notice under Order XXXVI, r. 37 (see *post*, p. 540), of their intention to give in evidence certain matters in mitigation of damages. The plaintiff at the trial gave evidence of good character, and was thereupon cross-examined as to specific incidents neither mentioned in the libel nor in the particulars given under Order XXXVI, r. 37. It was held that the cross-examination was admissible as to credit, but that, the incidents alleged being denied by the plaintiff, no evidence was admissible in rebuttal, and that the jury should have been directed (1) that his denials, even if unbelieved, afforded no evidence that the incidents had taken place, and (2) that the cross-examination was not admissible to mitigate damages.

The following is from the Law Reports:—

Scrutton, L.J. . . . The civil wrong of defamation by a published written or printed statement, commonly known as libel, is committed by any one who publishes such a statement expressed in such a way that it would be understood by reasonable people to injure appreciably the reputation of another amongst reasonable people acquainted with him. A plaintiff may recover general damages for such a statement without proving his actual reputation or any actual damage. . . . It follows that **a defendant may reduce the damages for libel by proving that the plaintiff had already a bad reputation. . . .**

Questions have, of course, arisen as to the circumstances under which evidence can be given to mitigate damages, and the judgment of Cave, J., concurred in by Mathew, J., in *Scott* v. *Sampson*, which carefully considered the authorities has, I think, been accepted as an accurate statement of the law. **The defendant may mitigate damages by giving evidence to prove that the plaintiff is a man of bad general reputation,** and the plaintiff may rebut it by "coming prepared with friends who have known him to prove that his reputation has been good ". On the other hand, **the defendant may not give evidence of rumours** at the time of publication to the same effect as the libel, **nor** may the defendant give evidence **of specific facts** and circumstances to show the disposition of the plaintiff, as distinct from general evidence that he has that reputation. If those specific facts are to the same effect as the libel, which he has not justified, he cannot justify under the plea of mitigation of damages. If those facts are different from the libel they do not prove actual reputation, which can be proved under the first head, but that he ought not to have such a reputation. . . .

In my opinion, **just as you cannot prove in chief specific instances of misconduct,** as distinguished from general reputation, whether involved in the libel or not, **in order to mitigate damages, so also you cannot achieve that purpose by cross-examination as to such specific instances.**

There is, however, another purpose for which cross-examination **as to specific instances** not involved in the libel can be used. When a witness has given evidence material to the issues in the case **you can cross-examine him** on matters not directly material to the case **in order to ask the jury to infer from his answers that he is not worthy of belief,** not a credible person, and therefore that they should not accept his answers on questions material to the case as true. This is cross-examination as to his credibility, commonly called cross-examination to credit. **But** as it is on matters not directly material to the case, **the party cross-examining is not allowed to call evidence in chief to contradict his answers.** To permit this would involve the Court in an interminable series of controversies not directly material to the case on alleged facts of which the witness had no notice when he came into Court, and which he or the party calling him might not be prepared without notice to meet. This rule, which has been established by cases in which the party cross-examining has desired to call rebutting evidence in chief, has been expressed in various ways. . . . But **this does not go to the extent** contended for by the appellant's counsel **that the jury must believe the answers given by the witness.** No case has been found where such a contention has been put forward, and if the jury, hearing the answers given by the witness, do not believe him they are entitled to do so, and to use the view thus obtained as to his credibility in rejecting answers given by him on matters material to the case. **But**

rejecting his denials, does not prove the fact he denies, of which there is, and can be, no other evidence. It only destroys his credibility in respect of other evidence. . . .

. . . the Lord Chief Justice gave a **wrong direction** when he ruled **that specific acts of misconduct,** not the subject of the libel, **might be given in evidence, by questions in cross-examination in mitigation of damages.**

GREER, L.J. . . . It seems to me convenient at this stage to state certain rules of law that have been established by the decisions. (1) It is **not permissible for a plaintiff to give evidence of particular facts** in support of his claim to have a good character, **nor** is it open **to a defendant to give evidence, or to cross-examine as to particular instances with the object of diminishing the damages:** . . . (2) On the other hand, if a plaintiff in chief gives evidence of any fact, and the defendant disputes that fact, the **defendant is entitled to cross-examine to credit, and** in particular **to cross-examine about details of misconduct, but** it has been laid down in a number of cases that the defendant **is bound to be content with the plaintiff's answers.** He cannot contradict them, but must be content to let them go to the jury as the only evidence on the matters involved in the cross-examination. . . .

In this case the plaintiff's counsel, in opening, gave an account of the plaintiff's life before the " Mr. A " case, and put him forward as, apart from the " Mr. A " case, a man of unblemished reputation, and the plaintiff adopted this view himself in his evidence. As the defendants entirely disagreed with this view of his character they were, by their counsel, entitled to cross-examine him to credit. His answers could only be used to remove the impression he had created that, apart from the instance mentioned, he was a man of unblemished character, but, under the circumstances, it would have been difficult for any jury to exclude from their consideration in estimating the damages any admission that he made in cross-examination, but the jury should have been told that they ought, as far as possible, to do so.

SANKEY, L.J. . . . Dealing with the **cross-examination of the plaintiff,** I am of opinion that it was **legitimate** in so far **as** it purports to be a **cross-examination as to credit,** but great care has to be taken to see that a jury appreciates, though it may be a difficult task for them, that answers given to such a cross-examination may **not** be **relevant upon the issue of mitigation of damages.** The law is beyond question. The decision in *Scott* v. *Sampson* states clearly the evidence that is admissible upon the issue of mitigation of damages.

Note.—It is perhaps unusual to find other cases, besides defamation, in which character is actually in issue. It might conceivably be so in applications to remove trustees or guardians, or in actions for wrongful dismissal on the ground of want of character.

VERRY v. WATKINS.

OXFORD CIRCUIT. 1836.

7 C. & P. 308.

In a few cases, where the amount of damages depends upon character, as in seduction and breach of promise of marriage, evidence may be given of the character of the woman seduced, or the female plaintiff, but upon the question of damages only.

In an action for seduction, the plaintiff's daughter was cross-examined with the object of showing that she was a girl of loose character. Evidence was also called for the defence showing her general bad character in respect of chastity and moral conduct.

Alderson, B. (to the jury). If you think that the defendant had such intercourse with the daughter of the plaintiff as caused him to be the father of the child to which she gave birth, your verdict must be for the plaintiff; and the case then comes to a **question of damages;** in which view, and **in which view alone, you will consider** what reliance you ought to place on **the evidence adduced** on the part of the defendant.

Note.—Stephen says: "In civil cases, the fact that a person's general reputation is bad, may, it seems, be given in evidence in reduction of damages" (*Dig. Ev.*, Art. 57). Stated in this general manner, it would suggest that a person's character could be given in vidence when he claimed damages for a breach of contract or a roken leg. It cannot be so. But in cases of seduction and breach f promise the woman's character for modesty, etc., may clearly be elevant as to the damage suffered. And it appears to be so onsidered in cases of damages for adultery. (See *Phipson,* 178).

R. v. ROWTON.

CROWN CASES RESERVED. 1865.

34 L. J. M. C. 57; 11 L. T. 745; 13 W. R. 436; 11 Jur. (n.s.) 325; 10 Cox C. C. 25; L. & C. 520.

A prisoner, or defendant in a criminal case, at his trial, can always give evidence of his good character. The prosecution may rebut such evidence by evidence of his bad character, although they cannot give evidence of his bad character as part of their case.

Evidence of character must not be evidence of particular facts, but must be evidence of general reputation only, having reference to the nature of the charge; not evidence of disposition.

On a trial for indecent assault, where the defendant had given evidence of his good character, a witness called by the prosecution to rebut such evidence was asked, "What is the defendant's general character for decency and morality of conduct?" The witness said, "I know nothing of the neighbourhood's opinion, because I was only a boy at school when I knew him; but my own opinion, and the opinion of my brothers, who were also pupils of his, is that his character is that of a man capable of the grossest indecency and the most flagrant immorality". It was held, by eleven Judges against two, that this answer was not admissible in evidence.

The following is from the Law Journal:—

Cockburn, C.J. . . . Two questions present themselves, the first, whether, **when evidence in favour of the character of the prisoner**

has been given on his behalf, evidence of his bad character can be adduced upon the part of the prosecution to rebut the evidence so given. I am clearly of opinion that such evidence may properly be received. It is true that, **probably in the experience of all of us, no occasion has presented itself when such evidence has been given** on the part of the prosecution. **That may be easily explained** by the circumstance that it seldom happens that evidence is called to the character of a prisoner when those who represent the prisoner are aware that the character will be liable to be rebutted. Notice is often given from a sense or spirit of fairness by the prosecuting counsel, that if any attempt is made to set up the character of the prisoner, against the facts adduced on the part of the prosecution, such attempt will be met either by a rigorous examination or rebutting evidence; but it seems to me when we come to consider whether such evidence is admissible, speaking logically and reasonably, it is impossible to come to any other than one conclusion. . . .

Assuming, then, that evidence was properly received to rebut the prior evidence of good character, adduced by the prisoner, the question still presents itself of whether the answer which was given to the question, which is perfectly legitimate in its character, was an answer which it was proper to leave to the jury? Now, in determining this, it becomes necessary, in the first instance, to consider **what is the meaning of evidence of character.** It is laid down in the books that a prisoner is entitled to give evidence as to his general character. What does that mean? **Does it mean evidence as to his reputation** amongst those to whom his conduct and position are known, **or does it mean evidence of disposition?** I think **it means evidence of reputation only. . . .** No one ever heard of a question put deliberately to a witness called on behalf of a prisoner as to the prisoner's disposition of mind; the way, and **the only way the law allows of your getting at the disposition and tendency of his mind, is by evidence as to his general character founded upon the knowledge of those who know anything about him and his general conduct.** Now, that is the sense in which I find the word "character" used and applied in all the books of the text-writers of authority upon the subject of evidence. . . .

No one pretends that, according to the present practice, examination can be made as to a specific fact, though every one would agree that evidence of one fact of honesty or dishonesty, as the case might be, would weigh infinitely more than the opinions of a man's friends or neighbours as to his general character. The truth is, **this part of our law is an anomaly.** Although, logically speaking, it is quite clear that an antecedent bad character would form quite as reasonable a ground for the presumption and probability of guilt, as previous good character lays the foundation for the presumption of innocence, yet **the prosecution cannot go into evidence as to the prisoner's bad character.** The allowing evidence of a prisoner's good character to be given has grown from a desire to administer the law with mercy, as far as possible. . . .

When we come to consider the question of what, in the strict interpretation of the law, is the limit of such evidence, I must say that, in my judgment, it must be restrained to this: **the evidence must be of the man's general reputation, and not the individual opinion of the witness. . . .** The witness who acknowledged that he knew nothing of the general character, and had no opportunity of knowing it in the sense of reputation, would not be allowed to give an opinion as to a man's character in the more limited sense of his disposition.

If that be the true doctrine on the subject of the admissibility of evidence to character in favour of the prisoner, the next question that presents itself is, **within what limits must the evidence be confined which is adduced in rebutting** evidence to meet the evidence which the prisoner has brought forward? I think that that evidence **must be of the same character and kept within the same limits;** that while the prisoner can give evidence of general good character, so the evidence called to rebut it must be evidence of the same general description, showing that the evidence which has been given to establish a good reputation on the one hand is not true, because the man's general reputation was bad.

Now, then, what is the answer in the present case? **The witness, it seems, disclaims all knowledge as to the general reputation of the accused; what he says is this:** "I know nothing of the neighbourhood's opinion." I take the witness in this expression to mean to say, "I know nothing of the opinion of those with whom the man has in the ordinary occupations of life been brought immediately into contact. I knew him, and so did two brothers of mine when we were at school, and in my opinion his *disposition*" (for in that sense the word "character" is used by the witness)—"in my opinion his disposition is such that he is capable of committing the class of offences with which he stands charged." I am strongly of opinion that **that answer was not admissible in evidence. . . . I take my stand on this:** I find it uniformly laid down in the books of authority that the **evidence to character must be evidence to general character in the sense of** *reputation*. . . .

POLLOCK, C.B., WILLIAMS, BLACKBURN, BYLES, KEATING, MELLOR and SHEE, JJ., and MARTIN, CHANNELL and PIGGOTT, BB., concurred; ERLE, C.J., and WILLES, J., dissented.

Note.—It is generally stated that evidence of a prisoner's good character is admissible, but evidence of his bad character is inadmissible, except in answer to evidence of his good character. But why cut up this rule into two parts It seems to be simply this—evidence of the prisoner's character, good or bad, is always admissible at the prisoner's option. Whenever his good character is admitted his bad character is admissible. [This statement may perhaps mislead. The option the prisoner has is to give, or withhold, evidence of his *good* character. If he elect (1) to give this, the prosecution then has the option of giving, or withholding, evidence of his *bad* character in rebuttal; if he elect (2) to withhold it, the prosecution's option does not arise, for there is nothing to rebut, and evidence of bad character (which here is only admissible *in* rebuttal) is consequently excluded. This is not quite adequately expressed by saying that "evidence of the prisoner's character, good *or bad*, is always admissible at the prisoner's option ".]

"Evidence of character must, of course, be applicable to the particular nature of the charge; to prove, for instance, that a party has borne a good character for humanity and kindness, can have no bearing in reference to a charge of dishonesty. The correct mode of inquiry is as to the *general* character of the accused " (*Wills, Circ. Ev.*, 7th ed., 285).

The rule in the above case only applies to criminal charges.

R. v. CLARKE.

NISI PRIUS. 1817.

2 STARKIE 241.

In prosecutions for rape, or assault with intent to commit rape or indecent assault, general evidence of the bad character of the prosecutrix may be given in defence, her character

in the circumstances, being considered, to some extent, in issue.

Upon an indictment for assault with intent to commit rape, it was proposed, on the part of the defendant, to call witnesses to impugn the character of the prosecutrix, both generally and particularly.

HOLROYD, J. **It is clear that no evidence can be received of particular facts,** and such evidence could not have been received, although the prosecutrix had been cross-examined as to those facts, because her answers upon those facts must have been taken as conclusive. With respect to such facts the case is clear. Then, **with respect to general evidence; such evidence, it has been held, is admissible in all cases where character is in issue,** and therefore the only question is, whether the character of the prosecutrix is involved in the present issue. **In the case of an indictment for a rape, evidence that a woman had a bad character previous to the supposed commission of the offence is admissible;** but the defendant cannot go into evidence of particular facts. This is the law upon an indictment for rape, and I am of opinion that the same principles apply to the case of an indictment for an assault with intent to commit a rape.

Note.—This seems to be the only case in which evidence is allowed of the character of the person prosecuting. The act here charged as a crime is, unlike most other criminal acts, one which may be consented to, and the character of the prosecutrix is material as to consent. See also *ante*, pp. 83 and 112, and *post*, p. 312.

CONVICTIONS OF PARTIES.

RE CRIPPEN.

PROBATE. 1911.

L. R. [1911] P. 108; 80 L. J. P. 47;
104 L. T. 224.

A conviction of a person is admissible in a subsequent civil proceeding only when the conviction itself is a relevant

circumstance, as distinct from the facts on which the conviction was founded.

Crippen was convicted of the murder of his wife and duly executed. An application by the sister of the murdered wife for administration of her estate was opposed by Crippen's executrix and legatee. The President (Sir Samuel Evans) held that the conviction was a "special circumstance" under the Court of Probate Act, 1857, s. 3, justifying him in refusing to allow the executrix to act.

Note.—The above gives the actual decision in *Crippen's Case* which is undoubtedly correct. But the case stood for many years as a somewhat doubtful authority for the proposition that the conviction could be some proof of the facts it recorded. *Crippen's Case* was followed in this regard, rather hesitatingly in *Partington* v. *Partington and Atkinson*, [1925] P. 34, and *O'Toole* v. *O'Toole* (1926), 42 T. L. R. 245. The Court of Appeal have now, while approving *Re Crippen* on its strict *ratio decidendi*, decisively rejected the doctrine that the conviction can be any proof in a civil case of the facts on which it proceeded (see *Hollington* v. *Hewthorn*, *infra*) and, in effect, overruled all three cases.

HOLLINGTON v. F. HEWTHORN & CO. and ANOTHER.

COURT OF APPEAL.

L. R. [1943] 1 K. B. 587; 112 L. J. K. B. 463; 169 L. T. 21; 59 T. L. R. 321.

In civil proceedings arising out of the collision of two vehicles, the fact that a party to such proceedings has been convicted of careless driving at the same time and place is inadmissible.

This was a running down action in which the plaintiff sued on behalf of the son's estate, the son having been fatally injured in the accident and there being no other direct evidence available to the plaintiff of what took place at the moment of collision. It was sought, in order to show a *prima facie* case of negligence, to put in evidence the conviction of one Poll, the second defendant, for careless driving at the same time and place under section 12 of the Road Traffic Act, 1930.

The following is from the Law Reports:—

GODDARD, L.J. Counsel for the plaintiff contends that, as he has to prove negligence as part of his case, he is entitled to put in the conviction, not as conclusive but as *prima facie* evidence that the defendant was driving negligently. He admits that he must prove by oral evidence that the defendant is the person who was convicted and also that he would in some manner have to identify the negligence of which the defendant was convicted with that which caused the accident. . . . **In truth the conviction is only proof that another Court considered that the defendant was guilty of careless driving.** . . . Just as a bystander may inform the Court of everything he saw but may not express an opinion on whether either or both parties were negligent, **so on the trial of the issue in the civil Court, the opinion of the criminal Court is legally irrelevant** . . . the Court trying the civil action can get no real guidance from the former proceedings without re-trying the criminal case. . . . We are of opinion that both on principle and authority the conviction was rightly rejected.

OPINION.

As a general rule, the fact that a witness has a certain opinion as to a fact in issue is not relevant to such fact. It is for the **Court to form opinions or draw inferences from the relevant facts** proved, and it is improper for a witness to express an opinion upon any fact as to which the Court itself can form **an** opinion.

"Vain would it be for the law to constitute the jury the triers of disputed facts, to reject derivative evidence when original proof is withheld, and to declare that a party is not to be prejudiced by the words or acts of others with whom he is unconnected, if tribunals might be swayed by opinions relative to those facts, expressed by persons who come before them in the character of witnesses. If the opinions thus offered are founded on no evidence, or on illegal evidence, they ought not to be listened to; if founded on legal evidence, that evidence ought to be laid before the jury, whom the law presumes to be at least as capable as the witnesses of drawing from them any inferences that justice may require " (*Best*, 424; see also *Stephen*, 12th ed., App., pp. 238—240).

But, of course, in those **matters on which the Court is not as capable as witnesses of drawing inferences,** *i.e.*, in matters which require special study or experience in order that a just opinion may be formed, such as **matters of science or art,** the rule of exclusion cannot prevail, and the **opinions of " experts "** must be received.

" The reasonable principle appears to be, that scientific witnesses shall be permitted to testify only to such matters of fact as have come within their own cognisance, or as they have acquired a knowledge of by their reading, and to such inferences from them, or from other facts provisionally assumed to be proved, as their particular studies and pursuits specially qualify them to draw; so that the jury may thus be furnished with the necessary scientific *criteria* for testing the accuracy of their conclusions, and enabled to form their own independent judgment by the application of those *criteria* to the facts established in evidence before them " (*Wills, Circ. Ev.*, 140).

Opinion evidence is by no means confined to " experts ". There have been many cases in which ordinary witnesses have been allowed to give their opinions in evidence, and they must frequently be allowed to do so. There are many matters on which it is naturally impossible for any witness to give positive evidence of facts which he observed. He must, if he says anything at all, speak as to his opinion of belief, on matters which are essentially matters of opinion or are so complex or indefinite that he can only form a general opinion upon them. **Thus, on questions of identity, handwriting, condition, age, appearance or resemblance** of persons or things; on the general character of the weather, or the general conduct of a business or of persons during a certain period, or the general character of a meeting alleged to be seditious, clearly only evidence of opinion can be given, and would in most cases be received.

Where opinion evidence is legally admissible, it must, in order to justify a Court in basing a finding of fact on it, amount to a coherent and rational inference pointing definitely to one conclusion and tending to negative any other conclusion inconsistent therewith. "Opinion" does not mean a mere surmise or guess, but the scientific or quasi-scientific conclusion of the experts drawn from facts proved to exist (see "Burden of Proof", *post*, p. 136).

HOLLINGTON v. F. HEWTHORN & CO. and ANOTHER.

COURT OF APPEAL.

L. R. [1943] 1 K. B. 587; 112 L. J. K. B. 463; 169 L. T. 21; 59 T. L. R. 321.

A witness may not (save in the exceptional cases mentioned *post*) give his opinion as to facts in issue or relevant facts. The fact that he has such an opinion is not relevant to such facts. It is for the Court to form opinions on the facts proved.

In this case (cited *ante*, p. 126, for another purpose) the plaintiff sought to recover damages for the death of his son alleged to be caused by the negligent driving of the defendant.

The following is from the Law Reports:—

GODDARD, L.J. It frequently happens that a bystander has a complete and full view of an accident. It is beyond question that **while he may inform the Court of everything that he saw he may not express any opinion on whether either or both of the parties were negligent.** The reason commonly assigned is that this is the precise question the Court has to decide, but, in truth it is **because his opinion is not relevant.** Any fact that he can prove is relevant but his opinion is not. The well-recognised exception in the case of scientific or expert witnesses depends on considerations which for present purposes are **immaterial.**

Note.—This principle is as old as any in our law of evidence and has constantly been reiterated. See the well-known judgment of Lord Mansfield in *Carter* v. *Boehm*, 3 Burrow 1905; 1 W. Bl. 593. The text of that case has been omitted in this edition as, though the principle remains, the particular application of it there laid down is no longer law (see *Scottish Shire Line* v. *London, etc., Insurance Co.*, [1912] 3 K. B. 70).

FOLKES v. CHADD.

KING'S BENCH. 1782.

3 DOUGLAS 157.

On certain matters, such as those of science or art, upon which the Court itself cannot form an opinion, special study, skill or experience being required for the purpose, "expert" witnesses may give evidence of their opinions.

The question arising whether a certain bank, erected for the purpose of preventing the sea overflowing certain meadows, contributed to the choking and decay of a certain harbour, the evidence of Mr. Smeaton, the celebrated engineer, of his opinion on the subject, was allowed.

LORD MANSFIELD, C.J. (*delivering the judgment of the Court, which then included* BULLER, ASHHURST and WILLES, JJ.). . . . The question is, to what has this decay been owing? The defendant says to this bank. Why? Because it prevents the back water. That is matter of opinion; **the whole case is a question of opinion, from facts agreed upon. Nobody can swear that it was the cause;** nobody thought that it would produce this mischief when the bank was erected. . . .

Mr. Smeaton is called. A confusion now arises from a misapplication of terms. It is objected that Mr. Smeaton is going to speak, not as to facts, but as to opinion. That opinion, however, is deduced from facts which are not disputed—the situation of banks, the course of tides and of winds, and the shifting of sands. His opinion deduced from all these facts, is, that, mathematically speaking, the bank may contribute to the mischief, but not sensibly. **Mr. Smeaton understands the construction of harbours, the causes of their destruction, and how remedied. In matters of science no**

other witnesses can be called. . . . I cannot believe that where the question is, whether a defect arises from a natural or an artificial cause, the opinions of men of science are not to be received. **Handwriting is proved every day by opinion;** and for false evidence on such questions a man may be indicted for perjury. . . .

Note.—The scope of opinion evidence by experts has been authoritatively described by the House of Lords as "the state of an art at a particular time and the meaning of any technical term used in connection therewith; whether any particular operation in connection with an art could be carried out and, generally, any explanation required as to facts of a scientific kind" (*per* Lord Tomlin in *British Celanese Ltd.* v. *Courtaulds Ltd.* (1935), 152 L. T. 537, at p. 543, in relation to patent cases). Matters commonly made the subject of such evidence include causes of death, insanity, effects of poison, genuineness of works of art, value of articles, genuineness of handwriting, proper navigation of vessels, meaning of trade terms, foreign law, etc. And in support of such opinion evidence the witness may prove experiments, inspection and other acts upon which he bases his opinion, although they were made or done in the absence of the party. See *R.* v. *Heseltine*, 12 Cox 404. In a trial for murder it was held that a medical witness, who had not seen the body, might be asked whether, in his opinion, assuming the facts described by another witness who had seen the body to be true, the wounds could have been self-inflicted (*R.* v. *Mason*, 76 J. P. 184).

BRISTOW v. SEQUEVILLE.

EXCHEQUER. 1850.

19 L. J. Ex. 289; 14 Jur. 674; 5 Ex. 275; 82 R. R. 664.

It is for the Judge to decide whether the skill of any proposed witness is sufficient to entitle him to be considered an "expert". A person whose knowledge of foreign law is derived solely from study without actual practice may be held incompetent to give evidence on such matter.

In order to prove the foreign law in force at Cologne, a witness was called, who stated that he was a jurisconsult and adviser to the Prussian consul in England; that he had studied law at the University of Leipzig, and knew from his studies there that the Code Napoléon was in force at Cologne. It was held that he was incompetent to prove the law of Cologne.

The following is from the Jurist:—

ALDERSON, B. If a man who has studied law in Saxony and never practised in Prussia be competent to prove the law of Prussia, why should not a Frenchman be competent to prove it? Or suppose I were to read in a book about the law of China, would the knowledge so acquired render my evidence admissible to prove the law of China? . . . Would the testimony of a man be receivable to prove the English law who had studied it abroad but never in England?

ROLFE, B. If you are right in your argument you need not have gone as far as Leipzig for a witness; the testimony of a man who should say, "I have been to Oxford and studied the German law there", would be receivable.

POLLOCK, C.B. Suppose a case depending on medical testimony, would the evidence of a man be receivable who had studied medicine at one of the universities, but never practised it?

The following is from the Law Journal:—

ALDERSON, B. If a man who has studied law in Saxony, and has never practised in Prussia, is a competent witness, why may not a Frenchman, who has studied the books relating to Chinese law, prove what the law of China is?

ROLFE, B. If this is sufficient, it would do to study the German law at Oxford.

POLLOCK, C.B., and PLATT, B., concurred in rejecting the evidence.

Note.—Foreign or Colonial law, which in our Courts is treated as a question of *fact*, is a subject upon which the opinion of experts is admissible, since competency to form an opinion thereon can only be acquired by a course of special study or experience. Although a question of fact, it is one which, by statute, is determinable by the Judge and not the jury (Administration of Justice Act, 1920, s. 15; *post*, p. 502; Judicature Act, 1925, s. 102; *post*, p. 507). As to the judicial notice of English law, see *ante*, p. 15.

The above case can scarcely be taken as laying down a definite rule that an expert witness must be a practitioner. No formal judgment is reported, the Judge's ideas being expressed in loose and indefinite questions. It may well be doubted whether the evidence of a learned jurisconsult or professor, who had never actually practised, would always be rejected. It would be strange that a young and comparatively inexperienced practitioner should be admitted as a witness in preference to a learned professor of high reputation. The Judge would probably consider the general qualification of the proposed witness, and would not rely solely upon the question of practice. The above case shows that the Judges were not satisfied with the particular witness.

The case seems to have been ignored in the later cases of *Wilson* v. *Wilson*, [1903] P. 157, and *Brailey* v. *Rhodesia, etc.*, [1910] 2 Ch. 95, in each of which the evidence of a person not practising in the particular country was admitted. As to the qualification of experts in handwriting, see *R.* v. *Silverlock*, *infra*, and *post*, p. 369.

R. v. SILVERLOCK.

CROWN CASES RESERVED. 1894.

L. R. [1894] 2 Q. B. 766; 63 L. J. M. C. 136; 72 L. T. 298; 18 Cox C. C. 104; 58 J. P. 788.

In order to prove by comparison with admittedly genuine letters that a certain advertisement was in the handwriting of the accused, the solicitor for the prosecution was, after objection, allowed to be called as "an expert". The solicitor testified that he had for the last ten years, and quite apart from his professional work, given considerable study and attention to handwriting, and especially to old parish registers and wills; that he had on several occasions professionally compared evidence in handwriting, but had never before given evidence as to handwriting; also that he had formed an opinion that the defendant was guilty before he began to compare the handwriting. The prisoner was convicted and appealed.

The following is from the Law Reports:—

Lord Russell of Killowen, C.J. . . . It is true that the witness who is called upon to give evidence founded on a comparison of handwritings must be *peritus*; he must be skilled in so doing; but we cannot say that he must have become *peritus* in the way of his business, or in any definite way. The question is, is he *peritus*? is he skilled? Has he an adequate knowledge? Looking at the matter

practically, if a witness is not skilled the Judge will tell the jury t
disregard his evidence. There is no decision which requires that th
evidence of a man who is skilled in comparing handwriting and ha
formed a reliable opinion from past experience, should be excludec
because his experience has not been gained in the way of his business
It is, however, really unnecessary to consider this point; for it seem
from the statement in the present case that the witness was not onl
peritus, but *peritus* in the way of his business. When once it i
determined that the evidence is admissible, the rest is merely a
question of its value or weight, and this is entirely a question fo
the jury, who will attach more or less weight to it according as the
believe the witness to be *peritus*.

Conviction affirmed.

Note.—The Criminal Procedure Act, 1865, s. 8; *post*, p. 453
contains statutory provision for the proof of handwriting both by th
evidence of non-experts and by the comparison of the disputed writin
with a proved genuine writing by the jury themselves.

The opinion of a non-expert has also been admitted as to the valu
of a thing (*R.* v. *Beckett*, 29 T. L. R. 332).

FRYER v. GATHERCOLE.

EXCHEQUER. 1849.

13 Jur. 542.

On matters with respect to which it is practically impossible for any witness to swear positively, ordinary or "non-expert" witnesses may give evidence of their opinions.

So, on questions of identification, condition, comparison o resemblance, of persons or things, a witness may speak as to his belief or opinion, when he cannot swear positively; although he has no special knowledge, skill o experience on such matters generally.

To prove the publication of a libellous pamphlet, a female witness
was called, who deposed to having received from the defendant a

copy of a pamphlet, of which she read some portions, and lent it to several persons in succession, who returned it to her, after which she wrote her name on it; and, although there was no mark by which she could identify it, she *believed* the copy produced to be the same but could not swear that it was. It was held that this was proper evidence of identification of the pamphlet.

POLLOCK, C.B. . . . The question resolves itself into a question of degree. **The witness could say no more than this: "I believe the copy of the pamphlet produced to be the same** with that which I received from the defendant, because when I lent that copy to other persons it was returned to me, and I had no reason to believe it otherwise when I last got it back. I then for certainty put my name to it." If the name had been written in the first instance no doubt could have arisen. . . . As has been truly argued, **there are many cases of identification where the law would be rendered ridiculous if positive certainty were required from witnesses. . . .** The evidence in this case was therefore properly received; any objection to it goes merely to its value.

ALDERSON B. . . . She said she read a portion—read several parts of it. She lends it to A B, he has it in his possession out of her sight, he returns her a similar book on the same subject, and **she believes it is the same copy.** It is open to contend that A B may have substituted another copy, and that that returned is not the same which was lent. The jury may judge how far that is probable or reasonable.

PARKE, B. (in course of argument). . . . **In the identification of person you compare** in your mind the man you have seen with the man you see at the trial. The **same rule belongs to every species of identification.**

THE BURDEN OF PROOF AND THE RIGHT TO BEGIN.

The term "burden of proof" is used in two senses. The result, unfortunately, is a certain amount of confusion in the language of the reports and text-books. The term "burden of proof" is used as regards (1) the whole case, (2) particular facts.

Note.—These terms are well established and have been retained here, though they hardly attain scientific precision. It may assist the student to understand the subject if it is explained that, in the practical administration of justice, the subject of "burden of proof" usually arises in one of three contexts: (a) at the Court of trial, to settle the question in a civil case which side is to begin; (b) either at the Court of trial or in some appellate Court, in discussing the question whether the evidence led is capable of satisfying the burden of proof which lies upon the party tendering it; (c) either at the Court of trial or on appeal in cases where from paucity of evidence (*e.g.*, in an accident case) there is not enough evidence to lead to any definite conclusion, the question arises which side must suffer for the inability of both to carry the matter to a definite result. The answer will then be, against the side on whom the burden of proof lies.

(1) *The General Burden of Proof.*

Before the Court can proceed to hear a case, it is, obviously, necessary to determine which party shall begin, or upon whom the burden of proof on the whole case lies.

In a criminal case there is generally no difficulty, as all the allegations are invariably made by the **prosecution,** on whom the general burden of proof invariably lies.

In a civil case, the pleadings must be looked at in order to settle the question. The plaintiff naturally, in his statement of claim, makes the first allegations. If the defendant, in his defence, pleads a *traverse*, or denial of an allegation made by the plaintiff, that puts it in issue and leaves the burden of proof upon the plaintiff. If the defendant pleads a *confession and avoidance*, admitting the plaintiff's allegation, but alleging further facts by way of defence, the matter in issue is not the plaintiff's allegation, but that of the defendant, if denied by the plaintiff, and the burden of proof is therefore upon the latter. But if there are several allegations, and the burden of proof of some is on one party and of others on the other party, *i.e.*, a **distribution of issues,** the general burden of proof is upon the plaintiff. This is so even if all the allegations of fact are admitted by the defendant, and the only question in issue is the amount of unliquidated damages. **The result is** that the general burden of proof is almost invariably upon the plaintiff.

The expression "right to begin", frequently used in this connection, merely refers to the same thing from another point of view, namely, that the "burden" of proof is compensated by the "right" to begin, and, generally, to the right to the last word.

(2) *The Particular Burden of Proof.*

It has been indicated above that the burden of proof of any particular fact in issue is **upon the party who alleges the affirmative of such fact.** It is only necessary to add, and to emphasise, that the *substance*, and not the mere *form*, of the pleading is to be considered. The position cannot be altered, nor can the Court be misled by the ingenious manipulation of language. Moreover, if the averment though negative in form amounts in substance to saying that the opposite party is guilty of some wrong or breach of duty, the burden will always lie on the party making such allegation, *e.g.*, if he alleges failure to perform a covenant, or prosecution without reasonable cause constituting the tort of malicious prosecution. Apart from this, in the case of some negative averments, by reason of their complexity or difficulty of proof, or by virtue of some statutory provision, the burden is cast upon the person denying the allegation, as will be seen below.

It should be borne in mind, generally, in considering burden of proof that the incidence of the burden or the moment when it shifts may be governed or closely affected by any relevant presumptions.

UPON WHOM THE BURDEN LIES.

AMOS v. HUGHES.

NISI PRIUS. 1835.

1 M. & Rob. 464.

The general burden of proof is upon the party who would be unsuccessful in the case if no evidence at all were given; and such party has the right to begin.

In an action for a breach of contract to emboss calico in a workmanlike manner, the defendant pleading that he had done the work properly, the question arose as to which party was entitled to begin; it was held that the plaintiff was.

Alderson, B., ruled that **the plaintiff was entitled.** He said, questions of this kind were not to be decided by simply ascertaining on which side the affirmative, in point of form, lay: **the proper test is, which party would be successful if no evidence at all were given?** Now here, supposing no evidence to be given on either side, **the defendant would be entitled** to the verdict, for it is not to be assumed that the work was badly executed; therefore **the onus lies on the plaintiff.**

PONTIFEX v. JOLLY.

1839. See *post*, p. 150.

MERCER v. W. HALL.

1845. See *post*, p. 149.

JOSEPH CONSTANTINE S.S. LINE v. IMPERIAL SMELTING CORPORATION.

1941. See Appendix IV, *post*, p. 566.

SOWARD v. LEGGATT.

NISI PRIUS. 1836.

7 C. & P. 613.

In determining which is the party affirming, it is not so much the grammatical language of the pleading which is to be considered as the substance and effect of it. The Judge should consider what is the real fact in issue, and who alleges the "affirmative in substance" thereof.

The plaintiff, being the landlord of the defendant, alleged that the latter "did not repair" the premises in question. The defendant pleaded that he "did well and sufficiently repair" the same. It was held that, notwithstanding that the defendant's pleading was the grammatical affirmative, the burden of proof was upon the plaintiff.

LORD ABINGER, C.B. Looking at these things according to common sense, **we should consider what is the substantive fact to be made out, and on whom it lies to make it out. It is not so much the form of the issue which ought to be considered, as the substance and effect of it.** In many cases, a party, by a little difference in the drawing of his pleadings, might make it either affirmative or negative, as he pleased. **The plaintiff here says,** "You did not repair"; **he might have said,** "You let the house become dilapidated". I shall endeavour by my own view to arrive at the substance of the issue, and I think in the present case that the plaintiff's counsel should begin.

Note.—The questions practically are—what is the matter in issue? who brought it into question? The party who did so must prove it. Moreover, if it were otherwise in doubt where the burden lay the test put forward in the previous cases would quickly solve it. The plaintiff accuses the defendant of a breach of covenant. "It is not to be assumed", as Baron Alderson says, that the defendant has done wrong by breaking his covenant, *i.e.*, the presumption of innocence operates in his favour and places the burden on the party alleging the breach of proving that it occurred.

WOOLMINGTON v. DIRECTOR OF PUBLIC PROSECUTIONS.

HOUSE OF LORDS. 1935.

[1935] A. C. 462; 104 L. J. K. B. 433; 153 L. T. 232; 51 T. L. R. 446; 25 Cr. App. R. 72; 30 Cox C. C. 234.

In a criminal case it is always the duty of the prosecution to prove the guilt of the accused beyond reasonable doubt. Subject to statutory exception and the defence of insanity, the Crown must prove every ingredient in the crime.

On a charge of murder the Judge directed the jury that once the Crown had proved the killing by the prisoner, it must be presumed to be murder and that it was for the prisoner to prove circumstances which would reduce the crime to manslaughter, or which would excuse the homicide as an accident. It was held that this was a misdirection and the conviction was quashed.

The following is from the Law Reports:—

Lord Sankey, L.C. (*after a review of the authorities*). . . . All that is meant is, that if it is proved that the conscious act of the prisoner killed a man and nothing else appears in the case, there is evidence upon which the jury may, not must, find him guilty of murder. It is difficult to conceive so bare and meagre a case, but that does not mean that the onus is not still on the prosecution.

If at any period of a trial it was permissible for the Judge to rule that the prosecution had established its case, and that the onus was shifted on the prisoner to prove that he was not guilty and that unless he discharged that onus the prosecution was entitled to succeed, it would be enabling the Judge in such a case to say that the jury must in law find the prisoner guilty and so make the Judge decide the case and not the jury, which is not the common law. It would be an entirely different case from those exceptional instances of special verdicts where a Judge asks the jury to find certain facts and directs them that on such facts the prosecution is entitled to succeed. Indeed, a consideration of such special verdicts shows that it is not till the end of the evidence that a verdict can properly be found and that at the end of the evidence it is not for the prisoner to establish his innocence, but for the prosecution to establish his guilt. Just as there is evidence on behalf of the prosecution so there may be evidence on behalf of the prisoner which may cause a doubt as to his guilt. In either case, he is entitled to the benefit of the doubt. But while the prosecution must prove the guilt of the prisoner, there is no such burden laid on the prisoner to prove his innocence and it is sufficient for him to raise a doubt as to his guilt; he is not bound to satisfy the jury of his innocence.

This is the real result of the perplexing case of *R.* v. *Schama* (84 L. J. K. B. 396), which lays down the same proposition, although perhaps in somewhat involved language. Juries are always told that, if conviction there is to be, the prosecution must prove the case beyond reasonable doubt. This statement cannot mean that in order to be acquitted the prisoner must "satisfy" the jury. This is the law as laid down in the Court of Criminal Appeal in *R.* v. *Davies* (29 T. L. R. 350), the headnote of which correctly states that where intent is an ingredient of a crime there is no onus on the defendant to prove that the act alleged was accidental. Throughout the web of the English criminal law **one golden thread is always to be seen,** that **it is the duty of the prosecution to prove the prisoner's guilt subject to** what I have already said as to **the defence of insanity and subject also to any statutory exception.** If, at the end of and on the whole of the case, there is a reasonable doubt, created by the evidence given by either the prosecution or the prisoner, as to whether the prisoner killed the deceased with a malicious intention, the prosecution has not made out the case and the prisoner is entitled to an acquittal. No matter what the charge or where the trial, the principle that the prosecution must prove the guilt of the prisoner is part of the common law of England and no attempt to whittle it down can be entertained. When dealing with a murder case the Crown must prove (*a*) death as the result of a voluntary act of the accused; and (*b*) malice of the accused. It may prove malice either expressly or by implication. For malice may be implied where death occurs as the result of a voluntary act of the accused which is (i) intentional; and (ii) unprovoked. When evidence of death and malice has been given (this is a question for the jury) the accused is entitled to show, by evidence or by examination of the circumstances adduced by the Crown that the act on his part which caused death was either unintentional or provoked. If the jury are either satisfied with this explanation or, upon a review of all the evidence, are left in reasonable doubt whether, even if his explanation be not accepted, the act was unintentional or provoked, the prisoner is entitled to be acquitted. It is not the law of England to say, as was said in the summing-up in the present case; "if the Crown satisfy you that this woman died at the prisoner's hands then he has to show that there are circumstances to be found in the evidence which has been given from the witness-box in this case which alleviate the crime so that it is only manslaughter or which excuse the homicide altogether by showing it was a pure accident". . . .

LORDS HEWART, ATKIN, TOMLIN and WRIGHT concurred.

Order of the Court of Criminal Appeal reversed and conviction quashed.

Note.—As stated in the text, the burden of proving insanity lies on the prisoner, but whether he discharges that burden falls to be judged in the same way as the burden in a civil case (*Sodeman* v. *R.*, [1936] 2 A. E. R. 1138, at p. 1140).

ABRATH v. NORTH EASTERN RY.

COURT OF APPEAL. 1883.

L. R. 11 Q. B. D. 440; 52 L. J. Q. B. 620; 49 L. T. 618; 32 W. R. 50; 47 J. P. 692.

The general burden of proof normally lies upon the plaintiff and this will be so even where it involves his proving a negative in the first instance.

Thus in an action for malicious prosecution, where the plaintiff alleges that the defendant instituted proceedings against him *without* reasonable and probable cause, the burden is on the plaintiff to prove, not only the prosecution, but also *prima facie*, the want of reasonable and probable cause. The burden may then shift to the defendant to show that he had such cause.

The following is from the Law Reports:—

BRETT, M.R. . . . **It seems to me that the propositions ought to be stated thus:** the plaintiff may give *prima facie* evidence which, unless it be answered either by contradictory evidence, or by the evidence of additional facts, ought to lead the jury to find the question in his favour: the defendant may give evidence either by contradicting the plaintiff's evidence or by proving other facts: the jury have to consider upon the evidence given upon both sides, whether they are satisfied in favour of the plaintiff with respect to the question which he calls upon them to answer; if they are, they must find for the plaintiff; but if upon consideration of the facts they come clearly to the opinion that the question ought to be answered against the plaintiff, they must find for the defendant. Then comes this difficulty—suppose that the jury, after considering the evidence, are left in real doubt as to which way they are to answer the question put to them on behalf of the plaintiff; in that case also the burden of proof lies upon the plaintiff; and if the defendant has been able, by the additional facts which he has adduced, to bring the minds of the whole jury to a real state of doubt, the plaintiff has failed to satisfy the burden of proof which lies upon him.

BOWEN, L.J. . . . Whenever litigation exists somebody must go on with it; the plaintiff is the first to begin; if he does nothing he fails; if he makes a *prima facie* case, and nothing is done to answer it, the defendant fails. **The test, therefore, as to the burden of proof or onus of proof, whichever term is used, is simply this: to ask oneself which party will be successful if no evidence is given, or if no more evidence is given** than has been given at a particular point of the case, for it is obvious that as the controversy involved in the litigation travels on, **the parties from moment to moment may reach points at which the onus of proof shifts,** and at which the tribunal will have to say that if the case stops there it must be decided in a particular manner. The test being such as I have stated, it is not a burden that goes on for ever resting on the shoulders of the person upon whom it is first cast. **As soon as he brings evidence which, until it is answered, rebuts the evidence against which he is contending, then the balance descends on the other side, and the burden rolls over until again there is evidence which once more turns the scale.** That being so, the question of onus of proof is only a rule for deciding on whom the obligation of going further, if he wishes to win, rests. **It is not a rule to enable the jury to decide on the value of conflicting evidence.** So soon as a conflict of evidence arises it ceases to be a question of onus of proof.

There is another point which must be cleared in order to make plain what I am about to say. **As causes are tried, the term "onus of proof" may be used in more ways than one. Sometimes** when a cause is tried the jury is left to find generally for either the plaintiff or the defendant, and it is in such a case essential that the Judge should tell the jury on whom the burden of making out the case rests, and when and at what period it shifts. Issues **again** may be left to the jury upon which they are to find generally for the plaintiff or the defendant, and they ought to be told on whom the burden of proof rests; and indeed it is to be observed that very often the burden of proof will be shifted within the scope of a particular issue by presumptions of law which have to be explained to the jury. But there is **another way** of conducting a trial at Nisi Prius, which is by asking certain definite questions of the jury. If there is a conflict of evidence as to these questions, it is unnecessary, except for the purpose of making plain what the Judge is doing, to explain to the jury about onus of proof, unless there are presumptions of law, such as, for instance, the presumption of consideration for a bill of exchange, or a presumption of consideration for a deed. And if the jury is asked by the Judge a plain question, as, for instance, whether they believe or disbelieve the principal witness called for the plaintiff, it is unnecessary to explain to them about the onus of proof, because the only answer which they have to give is "Yes" or "No", or else they cannot tell what to say. If the jury cannot make up their minds upon a question of that kind it is for the Judge to say which party is entitled to the verdict. I do not forget that there are canons which are useful to a Judge in commenting upon evidence and rules for determining the weight of conflicting evidence; but they are not the same as onus of proof.

Now in an action for malicious prosecution the plaintiff has the burden throughout of establishing that the circumstances of the prosecution were such that a Judge can see no reasonable or probable cause for instituting it. **In one sense this is the assertion of a negative,** and we have been pressed with the proposition that when a negative is to be made out the onus of proof shifts. That is not so. **If the assertion of a negative is an essential part of the plaintiff's case, the proof of the assertion still rests upon the plaintiff.** The terms "negative" and "affirmative" are after all relative and not absolute. In dealing with a question of negligence that term may be considered either as negative or affirmative according to the definition adopted in measuring the duty which is neglected. Wherever a person asserts affirmatively as part of his case that a certain state of facts is present or is absent, or that a particular thing is insufficient for a particular purpose, that is an averment which he is bound to prove positively. **It has been said that an exception exists in those cases where the facts lie peculiarly within the knowledge of the opposite party.** The counsel for the plaintiff have not gone the length of contending that in all those cases the onus shifts, and that the person within whose knowledge the truth peculiarly lies is bound to prove or disprove the matter in dispute. **I think a proposition of that kind cannot be maintained, and that the exceptions** supposed to be found amongst cases relating to the game laws **may be explained on special grounds. . . .**

The ground of our decision comes back to what was suggested, Who had to make good their point as to the proposition whether the defendants had taken reasonable and proper care to inform themselves of the true state of the case? **The defendants were not bound to make good anything. It was the plaintiff's duty to show the absence of reasonable care. . . .**

FRY, L.J., concurred.

Note.—It will be observed that in an action for malicious prosecution, the plaintiff makes two main allegations, (1) that the defendant prosecuted him, (2) that he had no reasonable cause for the prosecution; the first being affirmative and the second negative. The burden of proof of both of them is on the plaintiff.

A noticeable instance of the shifting of the burden of proof is afforded by the Bills of Exchange Act, 1882, s. 30 (2), see *post*, p. 466.

A negative averment must be distinguished from a contradiction of a positive averment, technically known as a "traverse". The former is part of the allegation which has, generally, to be proved by the party making it. The latter is an answer to the allegation of the opposite party, who must prove his allegation.

SCOTT v. LONDON DOCK COMPANY.

1865. See Appendix IV, *post*, p. 568.

R. v. TURNER.

KING'S BENCH. 1816.

5 M. & S. 206.

In some cases, if a negative averment is made by one party, and the facts involved are so numerous or complex or are so peculiarly within the knowledge of the other party that it is practically impossible for the party alleging to prove such negative, the burden of proof thereof may be on the party within whose knowledge such facts are, and not upon the party alleging.

So, in a prosecution against a carrier for having pheasants and hares in his possession without being qualified or authorised by law to do so; as there were ten different qualifications recognised by the game laws, and the prisoner knew which qualification, if any, he had, it was held that the burden of proof was upon him to show what qualification he had, notwithstanding that the absence of qualification was affirmatively alleged by the prosecution. Otherwise the prosecution would have been obliged to negative expressly the whole of the ten possible qualifications.

LORD ELLENBOROUGH, C.J. The question is, upon whom the *onus probandi* lies; whether it lies upon the person who affirms a qualification, to prove the affirmative, or upon the informer, who denies any qualification, to prove the negative. **There are, I think, about ten different heads of qualification** enumerated in the statute, to which the proof may be applied; **and, according to the argument** of to-day, every **person who lays an information of this sort is bound** to give satisfactory evidence before the magistrates **to negative** the defendant's qualification upon **each of those several heads.** The argument really comes to this, that **there would be a moral impossibility of ever convicting upon such an information.** If the informer should establish the negative of any part of these different qualifications that would be insufficient, because it would be said *non liquet*, but that the defendant may be qualified under the other. And does not then, common sense show, that **the burden of proof ought to be cast on the person who, by establishing any one of the qualifications,**

will be well defended? Is not the statute of Anne, in effect, a prohibition on every person to kill game, unless he brings himself within some one of the qualifications allowed by law; the proof of which is easy on the one side, but almost impossible on the other? . . .

BAYLEY, J. I have always understood it to be a general rule, that **if a negative averment be made by one party, which is peculiarly within the knowledge of the other, the party within whose knowledge it lies, and who asserts the affirmative, is to prove it,** and not he who avers the negative. And if we consider the reason of the thing in this particular case, we cannot but see that **it is next to impossible that the witness for the prosecution should be prepared to give any evidence of the defendant's want of qualification.** If, indeed, it is to be presumed that he must be acquainted with the defendant, and with his situation or habits in life, then he might give general evidence what those were; but if, as it is more probable, he is unacquainted with any of these matters, how is he to form any judgment whether he is qualified or not, from his appearance only? Therefore, if the law were to require that the witness should depose negatively to these things, it seems to me, that it might lead to the encouragement of much hardihood of swearing. The witness would have to depose to a multitude of facts; he must swear that the defendant has not an estate in his own or his wife's right of a certain value; that he is not the son and heir-apparent of an esquire, etc.; but how is it at all probable that a witness should be likely to depose with truth to such *minutiæ*? On the other hand, **there is no hardship in casting the burden of the affirmative proof on the defendant, because he must be presumed to know his own qualification,** and to be able to prove it. . . . But if the onus of proving the negative is to lie on the other party, it seems to me that it will be the cause of many offenders escaping conviction. I cannot help thinking, therefore, that the onus must lie on the defendant, and that **when the prosecutor has proved everything which, but for the defendant's being qualified, would subject the defendant to the penalty, he has done enough;** and the proof of qualification is to come in as matter of defence. . . .

HOLROYD, J. It is a general rule, that the affirmative is to be proved, and not the negative, unless under peculiar circumstances, where the general rule does not apply. Therefore, it must be shown, that this is a case which ought to form an exception to the general rule. Now **all the qualifications mentioned in the statute are peculiarly within the knowledge of the party qualified.** If he be entitled to any such estate as the statute requires, he may prove it by his title deeds, or by receipt of the rents and profits; or if he is son and heir-apparent, or servant to any lord or lady of a manor appointed to kill game, it will be a defence. All these qualifications are peculiarly within the knowledge of the party himself, whereas **the prosecutor has probably no means whatever of proving a disqualification. . . .**

Note.—The law on the subject-matter of this case is not free from doubt, and the above case has itself been criticised. If the negative averment be a simple one, as doing something " without consent of the owner ", the burden of proof would undoubtedly be upon the person so alleging, as he could easily satisfy it. But if the averment be complex, as in the above case, or difficult of proof, the matter is not so clear. In *Williams* v. *Russell* (1933), 149 L. T. 190, Talbot, J., stated that in his opinion, on a charge of using a motor vehicle without there being in force a policy of insurance complying with the Road Traffic Act, 1930, the onus was on the accused to prove possession of such a policy. In that case there was in fact some evidence given by the prosecution that the accused had not such a policy: it is submitted, in the light of *Woolmington* v. *D. P. P.* (*ante*, p. 140), that the prosecution must at least always first make out a *prima facie* case by showing from the surrounding circumstances that there is some ground for supposing that the accused is in default.

Some statutes expressly put upon the person charged the burden of proof of exemption, qualification, absence of fraudulent intent, and similar matters. The following may be mentioned:—

1. The Summary Jurisdiction Act, 1848, s. 14 (*post*, p. 440).
2. The Foreign Enlistment Act, 1870, ss. 8, 9.
3. The Summary Jurisdiction Act, 1879, s. 39 (*post*, p. 465).
4. The Explosive Substances Act, 1883, s. 4.
5. The Merchandise Marks Act, 1887, s. 2.
6. The Merchant Shipping Act, 1894, ss. 457, 697 (*post*, pp. 477, 479).
7. The Money-Lenders Act, 1900, s. 5.
8. The Bankruptcy Act, 1914, s. 154.
9. The Moneylenders Act, 1927, s. 10.
10. The Coinage Offences Act, 1936, ss. 7, 8, 9 and 10.
11. The Food and Drugs Act, 1938, ss. 4, 6, 83.

Many other examples might be given, there being a growing tendency to put such proof upon the person charged.

Also there are many statutes which declare that certain matters or positions are to be " presumed ", " deemed ", etc. These may be said also to affect the burden of proof (see *post*, p. 155).

MERCER v. WHALL.

QUEEN'S BENCH. 1845.

14 L. J. Q. B. 267; 9 Jur. 576; 5 Q. B. 447.

Whenever, on the pleadings, the plaintiff has to prove any of the facts in issue, or the damages which he claims are unliquidated, he has the right to begin, although the affirmative of all the other matters in issue is upon the other party.

In an action by an attorney's clerk for wrongful dismissal, the defendant pleaded that the plaintiff had been guilty of certain misconduct, for which he was dismissed. The plaintiff put in a replication *de injuria* (which put in issue the misconduct). It was held that the plaintiff was entitled to begin.

The following is from the Law Journal:—

Lord Denman, C.J. (*delivering the judgment of the Court, which then included* Patteson, Williams and Coleridge, JJ.). The natural course would seem to be, that **the plaintiff should bring his own cause of complaint before the Court and jury, in every case where he has anything to prove, either as to the facts necessary for his obtaining a verdict, or as to the amount of damage** to which he conceives the proof of such facts may entitle him. . . . It appears expedient that the plaintiff should begin, in order that the Judge, the jury, and the defendant himself, should know precisely how the claim is shaped. This disclosure may convince the defendant that the defence which he has pleaded cannot be established. . . . **If in an action for damages the damages are ascertained, and the plaintiff has a prima facie case** on which he must recover that known amount, and no more, unless the defendant proves what he has affirmed in pleading; **here is a satisfactory ground for the defendant's proceeding at once** to establish that fact. **But if the extent of damage is not ascertained, the plaintiff is the person to ascertain it,** and his doing so will have the good effect of making even the defence, in a vast majority of cases, much more easily understood for all who are interested with the decision. . . .

Note.—There is an acknowledged difficulty in cases where the proof of all the issues of a fact is upon the defendant, and that of the amount of damages is upon the plaintiff. Formerly the authorities were conflicting, but the above case seems to have settled the rule as stated.

PONTIFEX v. JOLLY.

NISI PRIUS. 1839.

9 C. & P. 202.

The right to begin is settled by the pleadings, and cannot be altered by any admissions made at the trial.

The plaintiff sued upon a bill of exchange. On the pleadings, acceptance and indorsement of the bill were denied. At the trial, Mr. Richards, for the defendant, said he would admit the acceptance and indorsement, and he proposed to open the case on the other pleas, the burden of which lay upon the defendant. He was not allowed to do so.

ALDERSON, B. I think Mr. Richards now admitting the acceptance and indorsement will not entitle him to begin. On this record the plaintiff is entitled to begin.

THE QUANTUM OF PROOF.

CIVIL AND CRIMINAL CASES.

The rules of law cannot, with advantage, deal generally and directly with the **quantity** or amount of evidence required in proof of any particular question, its **cogency** or its **weight.**

Note.—A distinction is to be drawn between two different questions in this connection, *viz*:—(a) given a certain body of evidence in support of a particular allegation, it will rest with the tribunal deciding questions of fact (whether Judge and jury or Judge alone or some other person or body of persons) to decide as **a question of fact** whether they feel satisfied by the proof offered and are prepared to make a finding of fact thereon; (b) when all the evidence in support of the allegation has been duly led, the opposite party may invite the Court of trial or an appellate Court to say that there is **"no evidence"** upon which a finding of fact in a certain sense, **could** be based and therefore **to say as a matter of law** that the state of the evidence being so and so, there is nothing fit for the jury, if any, to consider, and the Court **must**, as a matter of law, decide that the allegation in question is not proved. This topic is of crucial importance on the hearing of those appeals where only an error of law is subject to review (*e.g.*, appeals from county courts). If the appellate Court in such a case comes to the conclusion that though it might itself have come to a different decision on the evidence, yet there was evidence on which the Court below was entitled to act, it will not disturb the finding. In this sense there will be found constant references to the quantum of proof in the Law Reports.

On the other hand, where the Court trying an issue of fact has before it some evidence in support of each side of the issue, the English system of evidence is curiously free from rules of law requiring the Court to attach more weight or less weight to different types of evidence. This is the natural outcome of the jury system. Once seised of the issue the jury was left to its own common sense, the **law concerning itself mainly with** questions of **admissibility** of evidence and withdrawing the case from the jury when there is *no* evidence (see p. 8).

But it may be stated, as a clear proposition, that a **greater degree of conviction,** or a nearer approach to certainty, is **required to establish a criminal charge** than is required in a civil case.

The differences between civil and criminal cases, as regards evidence, may be shortly summarised thus:—

(1) **Stricter proof** is required to prove crimes than civil claims. They must be proved beyond all reasonable doubt. Corroboration is more frequently required as a matter of strict legal requirement, as in treason (see *post*, p. 156), and perjury (see *post*, p. 157). Also, it is frequently incumbent upon Judges, by the accepted practice, to direct juries that, though they may convict in certain cases upon uncorroborated evidence it would be "unsafe" to do so. Thus, in practice, the evidence of an accomplice is not sufficient to convict (see *post*, p. 158).

(2) A prisoner can always give evidence of his good **character,** which can be answered by evidence of his bad character (see *ante*, p. 121). In civil cases evidence of character is only admissible when it is in issue (see *ante*, p. 115), or when damages depend on it (see *ante*, p. 120).

(3) The rules as to the **evidence of the parties** themselves are somewhat different. In civil cases, the parties and their husbands and wives are generally both competent and compellable witnesses. In criminal cases, prisoners and their husbands and wives were, until 1898, generally incompetent. Now they are competent, but, with certain important exceptions, only with the prisoner's consent (Criminal Evidence Act, 1898, see *post*, pp. 273, 480).

(4) In civil trials the parties, by means of formal **admissions,** may render it unnecessary to adduce any evidence in proof of facts covered thereby. In criminal trials there is no "half-way house" between a plea of "guilty" which admits the truth of everything charged in the indictment and "not guilty" which puts everything in issue. In the latter case no admission or consent by the accused can avail to dispense with proof of every material fact.

(5) In criminal trials **confessions** are not admissible unless

they are proved to have been made voluntarily. There appears to be no analogous rule governing their admission in civil cases.

(6) **Depositions** of absent witnesses are more readily available in criminal than in civil cases (see *post*, p. 414), probably for the reason mentioned in (4), that there cannot in a criminal case be judgment by default or on admissions. On the other hand, the evidence of witnesses abroad is more available in civil cases (O. 37, r. 5, see *post*, p. 541).

(7) In civil proceedings **unstamped documents** cannot be given in evidence. In criminal proceedings they can be (see Stamp Act, 1891, s. 14, *post*, p. 475).

(8) In trials for homicide, **dying declarations** are admitted (see *post*, p. 244). In civil cases they never are.

(9) Generally, the **rules of evidence** may, by consent of the parties or order of the Court, be **relaxed** in civil cases (see for instance, O. 30, r. 2, *post*, p. 537; O. 32, rr. 1, 2, 4, *post*, pp. 538–9; O. 33, r. 3, *post*, p. 539; O. 37, rr. 1, 5, *post*, pp. 540, 541); but they cannot generally be so relaxed in criminal cases.

(10) In the event of **improper admission or rejection** of evidence, a judgment in a civil case cannot be set aside, and a new trial granted, unless the Court of Appeal is of opinion that "some substantial wrong or miscarriage has been thereby occasioned" (O. 39, r. 6, *post*, p. 545).

Formerly, it was held that a conviction in a criminal case, in such event, must be quashed. But now the Court of Criminal Appeal may dismiss an appeal if they consider that "no substantial miscarriage of justice has actually occurred" (Criminal Appeal Act, 1907, s. 4 (1), *post*, p. 489).

(11) In a prosecution, but not in a civil case, the unsworn evidence of a child must be corroborated.

COGENCY AND WEIGHT OF EVIDENCE.

Although, as we have seen, the law does not itself generally deal with cogency and weight of evidence, it may be useful to refer to certain matters which the Court would naturally consider in determining such questions. **As regards the witnesses and the reliance to be placed upon them,** the Court would obviously consider their (*a*) age, (*b*) apparent intelligence, (*c*) opportunities of observation, (*d*) memory, (*e*) interest or bias, (*f*) manner of answering questions, (*g*) confidence or nervousness, and such-like matters. **As regards the nature of the evidence** something may depend upon whether it is direct or circumstantial (see *ante*, p. 64); or upon whether it is oral, documentary or real (see *post*, p. 268). Moreover, certain **evidence, although legally admissible, may be practically worthless** (see *post*, pp. 161, 219), even to such an extent that the Judge might properly tell the jury to disregard it altogether, as, for example, the uncorroborated evidence of accomplices (see *post*, p. 158).

In some cases the sufficiency of evidence is dealt with by Statute; mainly in three ways, *viz.*, by providing that:—

(*a*) certain matters may be proved by specified or pre-appointed evidence.

(*b*) certain matters shall not be considered proved without corroborative evidence.

(*c*) certain matters may not be proved without written evidence.

It is proposed to consider these matters shortly. Further particulars can be ascertained by reference to the various provisions quoted.

PRE-APPOINTED EVIDENCE.

There would seem to be only two positions to be provided for; those in which certain matters are to be *prima facie* evidence, and those in which they are to be conclusive evidence. At least eight, if not more, **different expressions are used in this connection in various Statutes:—**

"Evidence".—Industrial Societies Act, 1893, s. 75

Merchant Shipping Act, 1894, ss. 64 (2), 239, 240, 691 (3), 695 (2), 719 (see *post*, p. 476); Friendly Societies Act, 1896, s. 100; Bankruptcy Act, 1914, ss. 137 (1), 138 (1), 139, 141 (see *post*, p. 499); Lead Paint Act, 1926, s. 5 (3); Companies Act, 1929, ss. 120 (2), 138 (see *post*, p. 516); Children and Young Persons Act, 1933, ss. 1 (5), (6), 100 (see *post*, p. 524).

"**Prima facie Evidence**".—Partnership Act, 1890, s. 2 (3) (see *post*, p. 473); Industrial Societies Act, 1893, s. 34; Companies Act, 1929, ss. 68, 102, 282 (see *post*, p. 516); Road Traffic Act, 1934, s. 33 (see *post*, p. 534).

"**Sufficient Evidence**".—Administration of Estates Act, 1925, s. 36 (7) (and see *Re Duce & Boots, etc., Chemists*, [1937] Ch. 642); Fertilisers and Feeding Stuffs Act, 1926, s. 22 (1); Companies Act, 1929, s. 15 (2); Rights of Way Act, 1932, s. 1 (3) (see *post*, p. 520).

"**Conclusive Evidence**".—Bankruptcy Act, 1914, ss. 137 (2), 143, 144 (2) (see *post*, p. 499); Companies Act, 1929, ss. 15 (1), 208 (1), 378 (2) (see *post*, p. 516); Local Government Act, 1933, s. 233 (see *post*, p. 532).

"**Presumed**".—Children and Young Persons Act, 1933, ss. 4 (2), 17, 99 (2); Food and Drugs Act, 1938, s. 33 (6) (see *post*, p. 524).

"**Raise a presumption unless the contrary is proved**".—Food and Drugs Act, 1938, s. 23 (1).

"**Deemed**".—Money-Lenders Act, 1900, s. 5; Official Secrets Act, 1911, s. 1 (2) (see *post*, p. 496); Criminal Law Amendment Act, 1912, s. 5 (2), (3); Bankruptcy Act, 1914, ss. 138 (2), 144 (1) (see *post*, p. 499); Companies Act, 1929, ss. 120 (3), 378 (1) (see *post*, p. 517); Children and Young Persons Act, 1933, ss. 1 (2), 6 (3), 17, 99 (1); Food and Drugs Act, 1938, s. 7 (see *post*, p. 524).

"**Unless the contrary is proved, be deemed**".—Food and Drugs Act, 1938, s. 3 (2).

CORROBORATIVE EVIDENCE.

With regard to the second class of statutory provisions respecting the quantity of proof required, those requiring corroboration, the result can be clearly and definitely stated. **The general rule is that the Court can act upon the uncorroborated evidence of a single witness** if satisfied with such evidence, and there appears to have been only one case in which the Judges themselves, without statutory provision, required corroboration, that is in prosecutions for perjury, for the obvious reason stated in 1716 by Holt, C.J., in the case of *R.* v. *Muscot*, 10 Mod. 192, where he said that the evidence for the prosecution must be "more numerous than the evidence given for the defendant; for else there is only oath against oath". This rule is now made statutory by the Perjury Act, 1911, s. 13 (see *post*, p. 495), the result being that corroboration is now legally required only by Statute, as follows.

Corroboration is required by Statute, as a matter of law, in the following cases:—

(1) Offences under the Act of Supremacy, 1558 (see *post*, p. 427).

(2) High Treason, by the Treason Acts, 1695 (see *post*, p. 429), and 1795 (see *post*, p. 431).

(3) Offences under the Blasphemy Act, 1697 (see *post*, p. 430).

(4) Personation at Elections, by the Parliamentary Registration Act, 1843 (see *post*, p. 434).

(5) Affiliation, by the Bastardy Acts, 1845 (see *post*, p. 437) and 1872 (see *post*, p. 461).

(6) Breach of Promise of Marriage, by the Evidence Further Amendment Act, 1869 (see *post*, p. 459).

(7) Removal of Paupers, by the Poor Law Act, 1930, s. 95 (6) (see *post*, p. 520).

(8) Offences under the Criminal Law Amendment Act, 1885 (see *post*, p. 469).

(9) Perjury and Subornation of Perjury, by the Perjury Act, 1911 (see *post*, p. 495).

(10) Generally, in all offences, the unsworn evidence of a child of tender years, given on behalf of the prosecution, must be corroborated, by the Children and Young Persons Act, 1933, s. 38 (see *post*, p. 527).

(11) Under the Road Traffic Act, 1934, s. 2 (3), a person shall not be convicted solely on the evidence of one witness who gives it as his opinion that the accused was exceeding the limit. This instance is included here, although it cannot in strictness be regarded as an ordinary case of statutory corroboration. The "opinion" of any witness on such a matter would be of questionable admissibility and it is submitted that the mere "opinion" of more than one witness would not justify a conviction. On the other hand, evidence of a single witness which is more than mere opinion, *e.g.*, of measurement and use of a stop watch, is sufficient (see *Russell* v. *Beesley*, [1937] 1 A. E. R. 527).

It should be observed that in the first **four cases** *two witnesses* are expressly required. In the other **six cases** *corroboration* only is required, which may be not only by a second witness, but in any other manner, as by conduct or admission (*Bessela* v. *Stern*, *post*, p. 172) or circumstances. **The kind of corroboration must depend upon the nature of the particular charge** (*R.* v. *Winkel*, 76 J. P. 191).

Corroboration is required by practice, as a matter of precaution, in the following cases:—

(1) In criminal cases, as regards the evidence of an accomplice on behalf of the prosecution (see *post*, p. 158).

(2) In civil cases, where a claim is made against the estate of a deceased person (see *post*, p. 161).

(3) In divorce cases, on behalf of the petitioner (see *post*, p. 162).

(4) In prosecutions for sexual offences. In some but not all of these corroboration will be required on the further ground that the other party is an accomplice.

WRITTEN EVIDENCE.

The Law not only, in many cases, requires certain transactions to be actually in writing, or created by writing; it also requires, by various Statutes, written evidence of certain transactions, which may actually be created verbally, and may legally exist prior to and independently of any writing (see, *e.g.*, Marine Insurance Act, 1906, s. 21, *post*, p. 487), although writing may be required to render them actionable. Transactions, such as assignments, requiring writing for their creation or existence appear to be quite outside the Law of Evidence.

Written evidence is required by the following Statutes (*inter alia*) for the matters specified in the particular sections referred to:—

(1) Statute of Frauds, 1677, s. 4 (see *post*, p. 429).

(2) Statute of Frauds Amendment Act, 1828, ss. 1, 6 (*post*, p. 433).

(3) Sale of Goods Act, 1893, s. 4 (see *post*, p. 475).

(4) Marine Insurance Act, 1906, s. 22 (see *post*, p. 487).

(5) Moneylenders Act, 1927, s. 6 (see *post*, p. 515).

R. v. BASKERVILLE.

COURT OF CRIMINAL APPEAL. 1916.

L. R. [1916] 2 K. B. 658; 86 L. J. K. B. 28; 115 L. T. 453; 60 S. J. 696.

It is a rule of practice, though not of strict law, that a person should not be convicted on the uncorroborated evidence of an accomplice. The Judge ought, therefore, to advise the jury not to convict on such evidence, although the jury may legally convict in spite of such advice.

The following is from the Law Reports:—

LORD READING, C.J. (*delivering the judgment of the Court*). There is no doubt that the uncorroborated evidence of an accomplice is admissible in law. . . . But **it has long been a rule of practice** at common law **for the Judge to warn the jury of the danger of convicting a prisoner on the uncorroborated testimony of an accomplice, and,** in the discretion of the Judge, **to advise them not to convict upon such evidence**; but the Judge should point out to the jury that it is within their legal province to convict upon such unconfirmed evidence. . . . This rule of practice has become virtually equivalent to a rule of law, and since the Court of Criminal Appeal Act came into operation this Court has held that, in the absence of such a warning by the Judge, the conviction must be quashed (*R.* v. *Tate*, [1908] 2 K. B. 680). If after the proper caution by the Judge the jury nevertheless convict the prisoner, this Court will not quash the conviction merely upon the ground that the accomplice's testimony was uncorroborated. . . . In considering whether or not the conviction should stand, this Court will review all the facts of the case, and will bear in mind that the jury had the opportunity of seeing and hearing the witnesses when giving their testimony. But **this Court,** in the exercise of its powers, **will quash a conviction even when the Judge has given to the jury the warning** or advice above mentioned **if this Court,** after considering all the circumstances of the case, **thinks the verdict unreasonable, or that it cannot be supported, having regard to the evidence** (Court of Criminal Appeal Act, 1907, s. 4 (1)). This jurisdiction gives larger powers to interfere with verdicts than had heretofore existed in criminal cases. In addition to the rule of practice above mentioned, there are, with regard to certain offences, statutory provisions that no person shall be convicted upon the evidence of one witness, unless such witness be corroborated in some material particular implicating the accused, *e.g.*, the Criminal Law Amendment Act, 1885, ss. 2—3. In these cases, the law is that the Judge, in the absence of such corroborative evidence, must stop the case at the close of the prosecution and direct the jury to acquit the accused. Where no such statutory provision is applicable to the offence charged, and the evidence for the prosecution consists of the uncorroborated testimony of an accomplice, the law is that the Judge should leave the case to the jury after giving them the caution already mentioned. . . . As to the nature and extent of the corroboration required . . . we have come to the conclusion that the better opinion of the law upon this point is that stated in *R.* v. *Stubbs*, Dears. C. C. 555, by Parke, B., namely, that the evidence of an accomplice must be confirmed not only as to the circumstances of the crime, but also as to the identity of the prisoner. The learned Baron does not mean that there must be confirmation of all the circumstances of the crime, that is unnecessary. It is sufficient if there is confirmation as to a material circumstance of the crime and of the identity of the prisoner. . . . The test applicable to determine the nature and extent of the corroboration is thus the same whether the case falls within the rule of practice at common law or within that class of offences for which corroboration is required by statute. . . . The corroboration need not be direct evidence that the accused committed the crime; it is sufficient if it is merely circumstantial evidence of his connection with the crime. . . . The question was discussed on the hearing of this appeal whether the evidence of an accomplice against two prisoners, corroborated as to one prisoner's participation in the crime, but not as to the other, can be regarded as corroboration with regard to both prisoners. We think the law is correctly stated by Alderson, B., in *R.* v. *Jenkins*, 1 Cox C. C. 177. The learned Baron said: **"Where there is one witness of bad character giving evidence against both prisoners, a confirmation of his testimony with regard to one, is no confirmation of his testimony as to the other."**

Note.—The distinction between corroboration required strictly by law, and that required as a matter of practice or prudence merely, should be specially noted. A conviction on uncorroborated evidence would, in the former case, be illegal, in the latter case, it is perfectly legal, although improper. Sir James Stephen's arrangement (*Dig. Ev.*, Art. 130), where the case of an accomplice is put with the cases where corroboration must be had, and is separated from the case of claims against estates of deceased persons, which stand on the same footing as the case of an accomplice (see next case), is misleading.

"Accomplices" are all those jointly concerned in a crime, either as principals or accessories.

"Corroboration by another accomplice, or even by several accomplices, does not suffice." Testimony by the wife of an accomplice requires corroboration, if the latter has himself given evidence; otherwise not (*R.* v. *Willis*, [1916] 1 K. B. 933, and see *R.* v. *Whitehead*, [1929] 1 K. B. 99).

RE HODGSON.

BECKETT v. RAMSDALE.

COURT OF APPEAL. 1885.

L. R. 31 Ch. D. 177; 55 L. J. Ch. 241; 54 L. T. 222; 34 W. R. 127.

A claim against the estate of a deceased person will not generally be allowed on the uncorroborated evidence of the claimant, although there is no rule of law against allowing it.

In an administration action, the evidence of a member of the plaintiff firm was held admissible without corroboration. But it was also considered that there actually was some corroboration.

The following is from the Law Journal:—

Sir J. Hannen. . . . It is said on behalf of the defendants that the evidence is not to be accepted by the Court because there is no corroboration of it, and that in the case of a conflict of evidence between living and dead persons there must be corroboration to establish a claim advanced by a living person against the estate of a dead person. We are of opinion that there is no rule of English law laying down such a proposition. **The statement of a living man is not to be disbelieved because there is no corroboration, but we must take into account the necessary absence through death of one of the parties** to the transaction, and in considering the statement of the survivor it is natural to look for corroboration in support of it; but if the evidence given by the living man does bring conviction to the tribunal which has to try the question, then **there is no rule of law which prevents that being acted upon. . . .**

Bowen and Fry, L.JJ., concurred.

Note.—" There is in England no rule of law precluding a claimant from recovering against the estate of a deceased person on his own testimony without corroboration; but the Court will always regard such evidence with jealous suspicion, and, it is said, will in general receive such corroboration, and in Ireland it has been said that there is a positive rule of law admitting of no exception, that a claim upon the assets of a deceased person cannot be allowed on the uncorroborated evidence of the claimant. In Scotland, the general rule is that the testimony of one witness is not full proof of any ground of action or defence whatever " (*Best*, 12th ed., § 621).

DIVORCE CASES.

CURTIS v. CURTIS.

DIVORCE. 1905.

21 T. L. R. 676.

The Divorce Court will not generally act upon the uncorroborated evidence of a petitioner. But it is only a rule of practice to require corroboration; there is no rule of law which prohibits the Court from acting on uncorroborated evidence if it is satisfied that the story told is true and that there is no collusion.

A wife petitioned for divorce, on account of cruelty, desertion and adultery. There was conflicting evidence, and the respondent denied or explained the facts adduced by the petitioner as corroboration of her evidence. The Judge was satisfied on the evidence and granted a decree.

BARGRAVE DEANE, J., said . . . **As a general rule the Court would not act upon the uncorroborated evidence of a petitioner, but there was no rule which prohibited it from so acting** if, on consideration of the whole of the materials before it, the Court was satisfied that the story put forward was a true one. . . . He did not believe the respondent's evidence, while he did believe that of the petitioner. . . .

Note.—A similar rule obtains in undefended cases: see *e.g.*, *Riches* v. *Riches*, 35 T. L. R. 141.

THE NATURE OF EVIDENCE REQUIRED.
DIRECT TESTIMONY.

A rule known as the "**Best evidence rule**", formerly of very wide application, still **excludes secondary evidence of documents** if the originals are available (see *post*, p. 345), but this seems to be **the only surviving application of the rule.** The term "Best Evidence" is sometimes, however, applied to what in this work is called "Real Evidence" (see *post*, p. 408 *et seq.*), that is to say, the actual production in Court of some physical object which is alleged to have been the subject-matter of, or to have played an important part in, the transaction under consideration, *e.g.*, the weapon used in an affray, or the article said to have been badly manufactured where, in an action for the price, this is the defence. But while the production in Court of such objects, if available, is obviously prudent and the subject of damaging comment if withheld, **it has never been a rule of our law under the "Best Evidence" or any other principle, that non-production of the article makes oral evidence concerning the same inadmissible** (see *post*, p. 412). That rule applies and **applies only** to documents (see *post*, p. 345).

The rule against "hearsay" evidence is also sometimes placed under the "Best evidence rule" This seems scarcely correct. The rule against hearsay is that such evidence is not legal evidence at all.

The rule respecting hearsay is clear and definite. It is, except in a few clearly defined cases, inadmissible, and direct testimony is generally the only permissible evidence. **The witness must have perceived the fact of which he speaks with one of his five senses;** he must not say that he heard of its existence from another person. Recent legislation (*viz.*, the Evidence Act, 1938, *q.v.*) has, however, introduced certain modifications of this rule.

For good general discussions of the "Best evidence rule", see *Best*, §§ 87—92; *Phipson*, 43—46; *Taylor*, §§ 391—427; *Thayer*, *Pr. Tr. Ev.*, 484—507.

STOBART v. DRYDEN.

EXCHEQUER. 1836.

5 L. J. Ex. 218; 1 M. & W. 615; 2 Gale 146;
1 Tyr. & Gr. 899; 46 R. R. 424.

Facts must, in general, be proved by the testimony of witnesses who actually perceived them, and not by the reported statements of unsworn persons.

The plaintiff sued the defendant on a mortgage deed. The defendant pleaded that the deed had been fraudulently altered by one of the attesting witnesses, who had since died. In support of this plea, the defendant called a witness to prove statements and letters made and written by the deceased attesting witness, tending to show that he had fraudulently altered the deed. It was held that the evidence was inadmissible.

The following is from Meeson and Welsby:—

Parke, B. (*delivering the judgment of the Court,* Lord Abinger, C.B., Parke, Bolland and Gurney, BB.). . . . **The general rule is, that hearsay evidence is not admissible as proof of a fact which has been stated by a third person.** This rule has been long established as a fundamental principle of the law of evidence; but certain **exceptions have also been recognised, some from very early times, upon the ground of necessity or convenience.** The simple question for us to decide is, whether such a declaration as this be one of the allowed exceptions to the general rule. . . . Is evidence of what the subscribing witness *has said* admissible?

It was contended on the argument that it was, and **that it formed an exception** to the general rule, and **on two grounds; one of them,** which I shall mention first, in order to dispose of it, was that, **as the plaintiff used the declaration of the subscribing witness,** evidenced by his signature, to prove the execution, **the defendant might** use any declaration of the same witness to disprove it. The **answer to this argument is,** that evidence of the handwriting in the attestation is not used as a declaration by the witness, but to show the fact that he put his name in that place and manner, in which in the ordinary course of business he would have done, if he had actually seen the deed executed. A statement of the attesting witness by parol, or written on any other document than that offered to be proved, would be inadmissible. The proof of actual attestation of the witness is, therefore, not the proof of a declaration, but of a fact.

The other ground, and the principal one, on which the most reliance was placed was, **that it was in the nature of a substitute for the loss of the benefit of the cross-examination** of the subscribing witness, if he had been alive and personally examined; by which, either the fact confessed would have been proved; or, if not, the witness would have been liable to be contradicted by proof of his admission: and it was contended that every declaration was admissible which might have been given in evidence to impeach the credit of the witness himself on his personal examination.

Let us inquire what the authorities are in support of this exception. If we should find them numerous, and of long standing, we should be bound to give effect to them, though we might doubt the policy of introducing such a departure from the established rule: if we find them few, and of comparatively recent origin, and not supported by the deliberate judgment of any Court, we ought not to sanction the introduction of such an exception, especially if its convenience and practical utility be of a doubtful nature. . . .

(*His Lordship here considered the authorities.*)

Such is the state of the authorities, which are very limited indeed in point of number . . . **it is impossible to say that there is any such weight or authority, however great our respect for the eminent Judges whose names have been mentioned, as to induce us to hold that this case is established and recognised as an exception from the great principle** of our law of evidence, that facts, the truth of which depends on parol evidence, are to be proved by testimony on oath.

If we had to determine the **question of the propriety of admitting the proposed evidence, on the ground of convenience,** apart from the consideration of the expediency of abiding by general rules, we should say that it was at the least **very doubtful whether, generally speaking, it would not cause greater mischief than advantage** in the investigation of truth. **An extreme case might occur,** as there seems to have done before Mr. Justice Heath, where the exclusion of evidence of a death-bed declaration would probably have been the **exclusion of one mode of discovering the truth.** The same may, perhaps, be said of all solemn assertions *in extremis* by deceased witnesses. **But, on the other hand,** if any declarations at any time from the mouth of subscribing witnesses who are dead are to be admitted in evidence (and you cannot stop short of that, for no one contends that the exception is to be confined to death-bed declarations, and if so confined, the evidence would be inadmissible in the present case), the result would be that the security of solemn instruments would be much impaired. **The rights of parties** under wills and deeds **would be liable to be affected at remote periods by loose declarations** of attesting witnesses, which those parties would have no opportunity of contradicting, or explaining by the evidence of the witnesses themselves. **The party impeaching the validity of the instrument would, it is true, have an equivalent for the loss of his power of cross-examination of the living witness; but the party supporting it would have none for the loss of his power of re-examination.** We cannot help feeling, therefore, that it is at least very doubtful whether the establishment of such an exception would be productive of any advantage: and when the great benefit to the administration of justice, of abiding by general rules and acting upon general principles, is taken into consideration, we feel no doubt but that **it would be inexpedient to sanction this additional exception to the established rule of evidence.**

Note.—Generally speaking, the only case in which evidence may be given of a statement made by a dying person is on a trial for homicide (see *post*, p. 244). Other cases may occur under the *res gestæ* rule, or in statements by testators, or in depositions under the Cr. L. Amdt. Act, 1867, s. 6, *post*, p. 454.

R. v. INHABITANTS OF ERISWELL.

KING'S BENCH. 1790.

3 T. R. (D. & E.) 707.

Subject to the exceptions enumerated post, pp. 169, 170, hearsay evidence is not admissible even though it be shown that the statement in question was made on oath and at a

former trial. The evidence must be given under oath administered at the trial.

Two justices of the peace took the evidence of a pauper as to his place of legal settlement, but made no order for his removal. About five years later, other justices made an order for his removal solely upon such evidence. The Court of Quarter Sessions confirmed such order. The Court of King's Bench, on appeal, was equally divided on the question, so the order stood. But the judgments against the admissibility of the evidence are generally approved as correct.

GROSE, J. . . . Is such evidence competent? Is it what is commonly called *hearsay evidence* of a fact? **Now it is a general rule that such evidence is not admissible, except in some few particular cases** where the exception (for aught we know) is as ancient as the rule. . . **No principle was stated to take this out of the general rule,** to show why hearsay evidence of the agreement should be permitted in this case any more than any other. But cases have been cited both to prove that this evidence was admissible as hearsay evidence, and as given upon oath before the magistrates. . . . An idea has prevailed that such hearsay evidence is sufficient; but I can make no difference between evidence necessary to prove an hiring, that is, an agreement to hire, and any other agreement; the law of evidence must be the same at the Quarter Sessions as in the Courts of *Westminster Hall*; and no one ever conceived that an agreement could be proved by a witness swearing that he heard another say that such an agreement was made.

Is the evidence better upon the ground that it was upon oath administered by two justices? Evidence, though upon oath, to affect an absent person, is incompetent, because he cannot cross-examine; as nothing can be more unjust than that a person should be bound by evidence which he is not permitted to hear.

But it may be said that it is in this case wise and discreet to depart from the general rule of evidence, and in this instance to admit hearsay evidence of a fact, or evidence on oath administered in the absence of the adverse party. I dread that rules of evidence shall ever depend upon the discretion of Judges; I wish to find the rule laid down, and to abide by it. **In this case I find the general rule; I find no decided authority that forms an exception to it;** and nothing but a clear uncontrovertible decision upon the point; and not the concession of counsel or the *obiter dictum* of a Judge, ought to form an exception to a general rule of law framed in wisdom by our ancestors, and adopted in every case except where the exception is as ancient as the rule. . . .

LORD KENYON, C.J. . . . **The evidence should be given under the sanction of an oath legally administered and in a judicial proceeding depending between the parties affected by it,** or those who stand in privity of estate or interest with them. . . . Examinations upon oath, except in the excepted cases, are of no avail unless they are made in a cause or proceeding depending between the parties to be affected by them, and where each has an opportunity of cross-examining the witness; **otherwise it is** *res inter alios acta,* **and not to be received. . . .**

BULLER and ASHHURST, JJ., dissented.

Note.—The two judgments from which extracts have been given are generally treated as correct expositions of the law. The two contrary judgments have been omitted as being generally discredited. In a later case (*R.* v. *Ferry Frystone,* 2 East 54) (1801), Lord Kenyon said—"The point upon which the Court were divided in opinion, in the case of *The King* v. *Eriswell,* has been since considered to be so clear against the admissibility of the evidence . . . that it was abandoned by the counsel at the bar in the case of *The King* v. *Nuneham Courtney,* 1 East 373, without argument".

It should be remembered that evidence may be taken out of Court by special order, before a commissioner or examiner (see *post,* p. 414).

HEARSAY EVIDENCE, WHEN ADMISSIBLE.

It will be observed that in the two last cases given, ference was made to **certain exceptions from the rule that arsay evidence is not admissible**. The law has, indeed, om early times allowed several exceptions, practically in ost cases on the ground of necessity, but it has invariably ken care that the exception shall be guarded by some curity which makes the evidence really reliable. We shall erefore find, **generally, there is** (1) some **special necessity** r the admission of such evidence, and (2) some **special arantee** of its credibility, to take the place of those inci- ntal to direct evidence, *viz.*, the oath and cross-examination.

Such special necessity for the admission of the hearsay idence is particularly noticeable in the case of the several stances of admissible **statements made by deceased persons, nerally called "declarations"**, hereinafter noticed. If such atements were not admitted, frequently most material idence, perhaps the only evidence on the subject, would be available, the only persons who could give direct evidence ing dead. But it will be noticed that in every case the w is careful to secure some guarantee of credibility, and nerally the rules for the admission of such evidence are rictly construed. The process has been carried a con- derable step further in the Evidence Act, 1938, but the regoing observations apply in the main to the innovations troduced by that Act (see *post*, p. 582).

The word "declaration" may suggest formality; but really e most informal statements, written or verbal, are generally lmissible, where the circumstances are otherwise proper.

The instances of admissible hearsay evidence at common w may be stated as follows:—

(1) Admissions.

(2) Confessions.

(3) Declarations in course of duty.

(4) Declarations against interest.

(5) Declarations as to pedigree.

(6) Declarations as to public and general rights.

(7) Declarations as to cause of death.

(8) Declarations as to contents of wills.

(9) Evidence given in former proceedings.

(10) Statements in public documents.

Mr. Taylor (§§ 658—667) gives as another exceptic statements in ancient documents, but it is not usual now treat these as hearsay (see *post*, p. 372).

The other branch of exceptions to the rule excluding hea say consists of those arising out of the Evidence Act, 193 which will be found in the section of this work dealing wit Statutes (see *post*, p. 582). In this connection it should appreciated: (1) that the Evidence Act, 1938, applies only **civil** proceedings; (2) that it only serves to admit **documenta** hearsay matter; but (3) it is in addition to, and does not der gate from, any ground of admissibility at common law.

(As to (8), *supra*, being treated as hearsay, see *pos* p. 254.)

It would appear that hearsay evidence may be render admissible by special order, on a summons for Direction See Order 30, r. 2, *post*, p. 537. The Evidence Act, 193 also contains provisions whereby the Court or Judge has discretion to admit hearsay matter in certain circumstanc (see *post*, p. 585).

ADMISSIONS.

Perhaps the most important instance of admissible hears is to be found in the case of "admissions", or **statemen made by either party to a suit against his interest,** as tendi either to the proof of his opponent's case or to the dispro of his own. At first sight admissions may not appear hearsay, but in reality, it is submitted, they are. For stance, a witness for the plaintiff, who may himself know thing of the facts, proves that the defendant told him mething which is against his case. This would appear to be early hearsay, although some writers do not treat it as such. *hipson*, *Stephen*, and *Wills* treat admissions and confessions hearsay; *Taylor*, *Powell* and *Best* do not.

The admissions here referred to are what may be called formal admissions, as distinguished from express or formal lmissions—those made for the purposes of the trial—dealt ith *ante*, p. 38, where an attempt has been made to explain e difference. Informal admissions, unlike formal admis- ons, may occur in criminal as well as in civil cases. In iminal cases they are usually treated under the general head "confessions" (see *post*, p. 197).

Informal admissions may be made in various ways, *e.g.*, by press statement, written or oral, by implied statement, by nduct, by silence; in various kinds of documents, such as ills, deeds, receipts, negotiable instruments, account books tradesmen and others, or on maps or plans. (See *Doe* v. *akin*, 7 C. & P. 481.)

Such admissions are admissible if made by—the parties emselves, whether real or nominal, their privies, persons intly interested with the parties, their agents, referees, rtners and others, according to circumstances. **They may made to** any person, generally, even a stranger, who may terwards be called as a witness; and, **as regards time,** if made the party himself, at any time; if by any representative, ring his right to represent or bind the party. A wife, less acting as her husband's agent, clearly has no authority bind him by admissions.

It should be observed that the above admissions are not nclusive, but only evidence, so that they can be explained rebutted by other evidence.

MALTBY v. CHRISTIE.

NISI PRIUS. 1795.

1 Esp. 340.

Statements made by either party to a suit tending to pro his opponent's case or disprove his own are admissib in evidence as admissions. Admissions need not be writing, or even in express words, or by way of expre statement. They may be gathered from a narrative descriptive words, or implied statement.

In an action brought against an auctioneer, to recover the procee of sale of goods belonging to one Durouveray, a bankrupt, t plaintiff (being the assignee of the bankrupt) put in evidence, as admission of the bankruptcy by the defendant, the catalogue of sa issued by him in which he described the goods as "the property Durouveray, a bankrupt".

Lord Kenyon, C.J., held, that this superseded the necessity going through the different steps, the defendant being there precluded from disputing the bankruptcy of Durouveray.

BESSELA v. STERN.

COURT OF APPEAL. 1877.

L. R. 2 C. P. D. 265; 46 L. J. C. P. 467; 37 L. T. 8 25 W. R. 561.

Silence or conduct may amount to an admission, when it natural to expect a reply or statement.

In an action for breach of promise of marriage, it was proved th the plaintiff said to the defendant, "You always promised to mar me, and you don't keep your word", and the defendant made no answer (beyond saying he would give her money to go away); his silence on the point was held to be an admission.

The following is from the Law Journal:—

COCKBURN, C.J. . . . If that conversation took place, no doubt **it is not conclusive; for a man might think it not worth while to contradict** the assertion of the promise and raise a dispute. On the other hand, it might be said he made no reply to the accusation, because he could not with truth deny it. . . .

BRAMWELL, L.J. . . . If in such a case it would not have been natural to deny it, it is no evidence of an admission that he does not. But, **if a denial is what one would naturally expect, it is strong evidence of an admission** and must be considered as corroboration of the claim set up.

BRETT, L.J. . . . **The question is, would it have been natural at the time when the woman made the statement, that the man should have contradicted it?** If so, the jury had a right to consider his not denying it evidence of the truth of what she said. . . .

Note.—The above case should be compared with the next case. See note thereto. It will be remembered that breach of promise of marriage is one of the cases in which corroboration is required (see *ante*, p. 157). The defendant's admission in the above case was held to be corroboration of the plaintiff's evidence.

WIEDEMANN v. WALPOLE.

COURT OF APPEAL. 1891.

L. R. [1891] 2 Q. B. 534; 60 L. J. Q. B. 762; 40 W. R. 114.

When the circumstances are such that a reply cannot naturally or reasonably be expected, the party's silence in face of a charge or assertion will not amount to an admission.

In an action for breach of promise of marriage, the fact that the defendant had not answered a letter written to him by the plaintiff, calling upon him to perform his promise of marriage, was held not to be any admission by him.

The following is from the Law Journal:—

LORD ESHER, M.R. . . . The letter could only be put in as some evidence of an admission of the truth of the statements contained in it. . . **There are no doubt mercantile and business cases in which it is the ordinary course of mankind to answer a letter** written upon a matter of business, and, if the letter were not answered, the Court would take notice of the ordinary course adopted by men of business —namely, to answer a letter where it is not intended to admit the truth of the statements contained in it; and if it were not answered, would take it as some evidence of the truth of the statements in it. **But that is not like the case of a letter charging a man with some offence or impropriety.** It could not be said that a man must answer such a letter at once, and that if he did not do so it must be taken as an admission that the statements are true. Life would not be bearable if a man had to answer such letters, and if it were to be taken as an admission of guilt if he did not do so. **It is the ordinary and wise practice of mankind not to answer such a letter,** because, if a man answered it, a correspondence would be entered into, and he would be lost. I have no doubt that the mere fact of not answering a letter containing a statement of a promise to marry is not an admission. . . .

BOWEN, L.J. . . . **It would be a monstrous thing if it were the law that the mere fact of a man not answering a letter** charging him with some offence, or making some claim against him, **would necessarily** and in all circumstances **be evidence of admission** of the truth of the charge or statement contained in the letter. There must be some limit placed upon such a proposition to make it consonant with common sense. **I think the limit to be placed upon it is,** that silence upon the receipt of a letter cannot be taken as evidence of admission of the truth of its contents, unless there are some circumstances in the case which would render it probable that the person receiving the letter, who dissented from the statements, would answer it and deny them. . . .

KAY, L.J. . . . **I decline to lay down any general rule.** There are certain business letters, the not answering of which by the persons who received them has been taken to be an admission by those persons of the truth of the statements contained in them. In other cases, **all the circumstances under which the letter was written and received must be looked at** in order to determine whether the omission to reply to it does fairly amount to an admission. . . .

Note.—This case appears to have been much misunderstood; and it has been treated in some text-books as laying down the broad rule that the omission to answer a letter is no admission (see *Best*, § 401; *Stephen*, Art. 121). But the case clearly does not lay down so broad a rule. It is plain from the judgments that the whole question depends upon whether it was natural to expect a reply or not. If it were, silence is an admission; if it were not, silence is no admission (see *Phipson*, 249). In the above case, the Court held it was not natural, in the circumstances, to expect a reply, therefore the silence was no admission. But the Judges all admitted that there might be cases in which silence to a letter would be an admission.

R. v. NORTON.

CROWN CASES RESERVED. 1910.

L. R. [1910] 2 K. B. 496; 79 L. J. K. B. 756; 102 L. T. 926; 74 J. P. 375; 26 T. L. R. 550.

Admissions made by a prisoner may be proved against him on a criminal charge. Such admissions may be made by his answer to, or words used in reply to, an accusation or statement made in his presence, or by his silence, conduct or demeanour when such statement is made, according to the circumstances.

But statements made in his presence are not, in themselves, evidence of the facts stated. They are admissible only as introductory to, or explanatory of, the accompanying words, conduct or demeanour of the prisoner at the time. Such conduct or demeanour may render such statement admissible even if the prisoner, in words, denies its truth.

On a charge of an offence against a girl under thirteen, the evidence in question was to the effect that, on being asked by the prisoner who had done the act, she said "You"; and, being asked by another person, she said "Stevie Norton", and pointed to the prisoner; that the prisoner said, "No, Madge, you are mistaken"; and then she said, "You have done it, Stephen Norton", and pointed to him again. According to one witness he then lifted his arms and said, "If I have done it I hope the Lord will strike me dead"; and according to another witness, "If you say so I might as well put my clothes on and go home". There was, therefore, nothing in his answers necessarily amounting to an admission of the girl's statements.

The evidence was admitted on the trial and the prisoner convicted. On appeal it was held that the evidence did not amount to an admission, and the conviction was quashed.

The following is from the Law Reports:—

PICKFORD, J. (*delivering the judgment of the Court*, LORD ALVERSTONE, C.J., PICKFORD and LORD COLERIDGE, JJ.). . . . As a general rule, statements as to the facts of a case under investigation are not evidence unless made by witnesses in the ordinary way, but to this rule there are exceptions. One is that **statements made in the presence of a prisoner upon an occasion on which he might reasonably be expected to make some observation, explanation, or denial are admissible under certain circumstances.** We think it is not strictly accurate, and may be misleading, to say that they are admissible in evidence against the prisoner, as such an expression may seem to imply that they are evidence of the facts stated in them and must be considered upon the footing of other evidence. **Such statements are, however, never evidence of the facts stated in them; they are admissible only as introductory to, or explanatory of, the answer given to them by the person in whose presence they are made.** Such answer may, of course, be given either by words or by conduct, *e.g.*, by remaining silent on an occasion which demanded an answer.

If the answer given amount to an admission of the statements or some part of them, they or that part become relevant as showing what facts are admitted; if the answer be not such an admission, the statements are irrelevant to the matter under consideration and should be disregarded. This seems to us to be correctly and shortly stated in *Taylor on Evidence*, § 814, p. 574: "The statements only become evidence when by such acceptance he makes them his own statements."

No objection was taken in this case to the admission of the statements in evidence, but as the prisoner may be tried again on an indictment on which that question may arise, we think it well to state in what cases such statements can be given in evidence. **We think that the contents of such statements should not be given in evidence unless the Judge is satisfied that there is evidence fit to be submitted to the jury that the prisoner by his answer to them, whether given by word or conduct, acknowledged the truth of the whole or part of them.** If there be no such evidence, then the contents of the statement should be excluded; if there be such evidence, then they should be admitted, and the question whether the prisoner's answer, by words or conduct, did or did not in fact amount to an acknowledgment of them left to the jury.

In trials of prisoners on indictment, in which the most numerous and important of these cases arise, **there is, as a rule, no difficulty in deciding whether there be such evidence or not, as the prisoner's answer appears upon the depositions,** and the chance that the evidence with regard to it may be different on the trial is so small that it may be disregarded. **When, however, the evidence of the prisoner's answer does not appear, there does not seem to be any practical difficulty in applying the rule above stated.** The fact of a statement having been made in the prisoner's presence may be given in evidence, but not the contents, and the question asked, what the prisoner said or did on such a statement being made. If his answer, given either by words or conduct, be such as to be evidence from which an acknowledgment may be inferred, then the contents of the statement may be given and the question of admission or not in fact left to the jury; if it be not evidence from which such an acknowledgment may be inferred, then the contents of the statements should be excluded. To allow the contents of such statements to be given before it is ascertained that there is evidence of their being acknowledged to be true must be most prejudicial to the prisoner, as, whatever directions be given to the jury, it is almost impossible for them to dismiss such evidence entirely from their minds. **It is perhaps too wide to say that in no case can the statements be given in evidence when they are denied by the prisoner,** as it is possible that a denial may be given under such circumstances and in such a manner as to constitute evidence from which an acknowledgment may be inferred; but, as above stated, we think they should be rejected unless there is some evidence of an acknowledgment of the truth. **Where they are admitted we think the following is the proper direction to be given to the jury:** That if they come to the conclusion that the prisoner had acknowledged the truth of the whole or any part of the facts stated they might take the statement, or so much of it as was acknowledged to be true (but no more), into consideration as evidence in the case generally, not because the statement standing alone afforded any evidence of the matter contained in it, but solely because of the prisoner's acknowledgment of its truth; but unless they found as a fact that there was such an acknowledgment they ought to disregard the statement altogether. . . .

Note.—This case should be read in conjunction with the following case of *R.* v. *Christie,* in which it was considered and explained.

The fact that the accused when cautioned and charged by the police (*R.* v. *Whitehead*, [1929] 1 K. B. 99) or at the hearing before the magistrates (*R.* v. *Naylor,* [1933] 1 K. B. 685) makes no denial does not amount to an admission. But although silence in such circumstances cannot be evidence so as to amount to corroboration in a case where corroboration is required by law or practice (see *ante,* p. 156), nevertheless the Judge may in a proper case, and with due fairness to the accused, comment on his silence and on the fact that he has reserved his defence, *e.g.*, an alibi, until the last possible moment, so depriving the police of any opportunity to verify it (*R.* v. *Littleboy,* [1934] 2 K. B. 408).

R. v. CHRISTIE.

HOUSE OF LORDS. 1914.

L. R. [1914] A. C. 545; 83 L. J. K. B. 1097; 111 L. T. 220; 30 T. L. R. 471; 10 Cr. App. R. 141.

A statement or accusation made to or in the presence of a prisoner may be evidence against him although he actually denied or repudiated it at the time, if by his conduct or demeanour he may be held to have admitted it or, apparently, if it be relevant otherwise to his conduct or demeanour at the time it was made, although it could

not be held admitted, either by words, conduct or demeanour.

But when a prisoner actually denies such statement or accusation, the Judge should, in the absence of special circumstances, intimate to the prosecution that such evidence, although legally admissible, has little value, and might prejudice the prisoner unfairly, and should, therefore, not be given against him.

Such evidence may be given in the first instance without proof of any words or acts of admission; it being left to the Judge to warn the jury to disregard it altogether if the subsequent evidence render it unreliable.

A statement made by a person, previous to the trial, cannot be taken as corroboration of the evidence he gives at the trial.

Christie was convicted of indecent assault on a small boy, who gave his evidence, without being sworn, under section 30 of the Children Act, 1908 (now replaced by section 38 of the Children and Young Persons Act, 1933, *post*, p. 527), describing the assault and identifying the prisoner, but he was not questioned as to previous identification, nor was he cross-examined. The boy's mother then gave evidence that, shortly after the act alleged, she and the boy went towards the prisoner, and the boy said "That is the man" and described the assault; and that Christie said "I am innocent". She was not cross-examined. The constable was then called and confirmed the mother's story, saying that the boy went up to Christie, touched him, and said "That is the man", describing the assault, and that Christie said "I am innocent". He was cross-examined, but his evidence on this point was not affected.

The Court of Criminal Appeal held, on the authority of *R.* v. *Norton* (*ante*, p. 175), that the boy's statement in Christie's presence was improperly admitted, as he had denied its truth, and they quashed the conviction. The House of Lords held:

1. That the first part of the boy's statement, but not the second describing the assault, was admissible as part of the act of identification.

2. That the second part was admissible, as made in the presence of the accused and in view of his demeanor; but that, in general,

where the evidence of a prisoner's assent to the truth of such statements is very slight, the Judge should exclude them.

3. That the second part was not admissible either as part of the *res gestæ*, or to corroborate the boy's testimony.

The order quashing the conviction was affirmed on the ground of want of such corroboration.

The following is from the Law Reports:—

VISCOUNT HALDANE, L.C. My Lords, I have had the advantage of considering the opinions which three of your Lordships are about to express. . . . **In the opinions about to be delivered** by Lord Atkinson, Lord Moulton, and Lord Reading the true view of **the law appears to me to be expressed. The only point on which I desire to guard myself is the admissibility of the statement in question as evidence of identification.** For the boy gave evidence at the trial, and if his evidence was required for the identification of the prisoner **that evidence ought, in my opinion, to have been his direct evidence in the witness-box** and not evidence of what he said elsewhere. . . . Had the boy, after he had identified the accused in the dock, been asked if he had identified the accused in the field as the man who assaulted him, and answered affirmatively, then that fact might also have been proved by the policeman and the mother who saw the identification. Its relevancy is to show that the boy was able to identify at the time and to exclude the idea that the identification of the prisoner in the dock was an afterthought or a mistake. But beyond the mere fact of such identification the examination ought not to have proceeded. **Subject to this observation I concur** in the judgments about to be delivered.

LORD ATKINSON. . . . **The Attorney-General contended that the entire statement of the boy was admissible on each of four separate grounds:—**

(1) As part of the **act of identification,** or as explanatory of it. (2) As a statement made in the **presence of the prisoner** in circumstances calling for some denial or explanation from him, the truth of which he admitted by his conduct and demeanour.

(3) As proof of the **consistency of the boy's conduct** before he was examined with his testimony at the trial.

(4) As part of the **res gestæ.**

Your Lordships intimated during the course of the argument that you would **not consider this third point.** It is, therefore, unnecessary to allude to it further.

Of course, it will suffice for the Attorney-General's purpose if the statement be admissible on any of these grounds. It is, I think, clear that the principle laid down in *R.* v. *Lillyman* (*ante*, p. 83), and in those cases which followed it, has no application to the present case. . . .

As to the first point, **it cannot, I think, be open to doubt that if the boy had said nothing more,** as he touched the sleeve of the coat of the accused, **than " That is the man ", the statement was so closely connected with the act** which it accompanied, expressing, indeed, as it did, in words little if anything more than would have been implied by the gesture simpliciter, **that it should have been admitted as part of the very act of identification itself. It is on the admissibility of the further statement made in answer to the question of the constable that the controversy arises.** On the whole, I am of opinion, though not without some doubt, that this statement only amplifies what is implied by the words " That is the man ", plus the act of touching him. . . .

I think that the entire statement was admissible on these grounds, even although the boy was not asked at the trial anything about the former identification. The boy had in his evidence at the trial distinctly identified the accused. If on another occasion he had in the presence of others identified him, then the evidence of these eye-witnesses is quite as truly primary evidence of what acts took place in their presence as would be the boy's evidence of what he did, and what expressions accompanied his act. . . .

As to the second ground, the rule of law undoubtedly is that a **statement made in the presence of an accused person,** even upon an occasion which would be expected reasonably to call for some explanation or denial from him, **is not evidence against him of the facts stated save so far as he accepts the statement,** so as to make it, in effect, his own. If he accepts the statement in part only, then to that extent alone does it become his statement. **He may accept the statement by word or conduct, action or demeanour,** and it is the function of the jury which tries the case to determine whether his words, action, conduct, or demeanour at the time when a statement was made amounts to an acceptance of it in whole or in part. **It by no means follows, I think, that a mere denial** by the accused of the facts mentioned in the statement **necessarily renders the statement inadmissible,** because he may deny the statement in such a manner and under such circumstances as may lead a jury to disbelieve him, and constitute evidence from which an acknowledgment may be inferred by them.

Of course, if at the end of the case the presiding Judge should be of opinion that **no evidence has been given upon which the jury could reasonably find that the accused had accepted the statement** so as to make it in whole or in part his own, **the Judge can instruct the jury to disregard the statement entirely.** It is said that, despite this direction, grave injustice might be done to the accused, inasmuch as the jury, having once heard the statement, could not, or would not, rid their mind of it. It is, therefore, in the application of the rule that the difficulty arises. **The question then is this: Is it to be taken as a rule of law that** such a statement is not to be admitted in evidence until a foundation has been laid for its admission by proof of facts from which, in the opinion of the presiding Judge, a jury might reasonably draw the inference that the accused had so accepted the statement as to make it in whole or in part his own, **or is it to be laid down that** the prosecutor is entitled to give the statement in evidence in the first instance, leaving it for the presiding Judge, in case no such evidence as the above-mentioned should be ultimately produced, to tell the jury to disregard the statement altogether?

In my view the former is not a rule of law, but it is, I think, a rule which, in the interest of justice, it might be most prudent and proper to follow as a rule of practice.

The course suggested by PICKFORD, J., in *R.* v. *Norton* (*ante*, p. 176), where workable, would be quite unobjectionable in itself as a rule of practice, and equally effective for the protection of the accused. . . .

The boy's statement was so separated by time and circumstances from the actual commission of the crime that it was not, I think, admissible as part of the res gestæ.

(*His Lordship here considered the cases, Thompson* v. *Trevanion* (*ante, p.* 67), *R.* v. *Bedingfield* (*ante, p.* 68), *R.* v. *Foster* (*ante, p.* 69), *etc.*).

Even, however, if the boy's statement was admissible in evidence, if properly dealt with, I think **the verdict should be quashed. The deputy chairman never properly explained** to the jury **that it is what**

he accused accepts as his own of the statement made in his presence **hat is evidence** against him, not the statement itself. **Again,** he **reated the evidence of the mother of the boy and the constable, as o what the boy said** and did on the occasion of the identification, **as orroboration of his testimony** at the trial, within the meaning of the 0th section of the Children Act of 1908. This is, of course, wholly rroneous. If the boy himself had been examined, either in chief r on cross-examination, and had detailed what took place at the dentification, this portion of his evidence could not be treated as orroboration of the other portion proving the charge. **He could not e his own corroborator. It can make no possible difference when thers tell what he did and said** on that occasion. Their evidence is o more " material corroborative evidence in support of his evidence t the trial implicating the accused " than his would be. . . .

My Lords, I have been requested by my noble and learned friend ORD PARKER to express his **concurrence in this judgment.**

LORD MOULTON. . . . I have great difficulty in seeing how this vidence is admissible on the ground that it is part of the evidence of dentification. **To prove identification of the prisoner by a person,** vho is, I shall assume, an adult, **it is necessary to call that person s a witness.** Identification is an act of the mind, and the primary vidence of what was passing in the mind of a man is his own estimony, where it can be obtained. **It would be very dangerous to llow evidence to be given of a man's words and actions, in order to how by this extrinsic evidence that he identified the prisoner,** if he as capable of being called as a witness and was not called to prove y direct evidence that he had thus identified him. Such a mode f proving identification would, in my opinion, be to use secondary vidence where primary evidence was obtainable, and this is contrary o the spirit of the English rules of evidence.

There remains the second ground, namely, that it is evidence of a tatement made in the presence of the accused, and of his behaviour n that occasion. Now, **in a civil action evidence may always be iven of any statement or communication made to the opposite party, rovided it is relevant to the issues. The same is true of any act or ehaviour of the party.** The sole limitation is that the matter thus iven in evidence must be relevant. I am of opinion that, **as a strict natter of law, there is no difference in this respect between the rules f evidence in our civil and in our criminal procedure. But there is**

a great difference in the practice. The law is so much on its guar against the accused being prejudiced by evidence which, thoug admissible, would probably have a prejudicial influence on the mind of the jury which would be out of proportion to its true evidentia value, that **there has grown up a practice of a very salutary nature under which the Judge intimates to the counsel for the prosecutio that he should not press for the admission** of evidence which woul be open to this objection, and such an intimation from the tribuna trying the case is usually sufficient to prevent the evidence bein pressed in all cases where the scruples of the tribunal in this respec are reasonable. Under the influence of this practice, which is base on an anxiety to secure for every one a fair trial, **there has grow up a custom of not admitting certain kinds of evidence which is s constantly followed that it almost amounts to a rule of procedure** It is alleged on the part of the respondent that an instance of this i the case of the accused being charged with the crime and denying it or not admitting it.

It is common ground that, if on such an occasion he admits it evidence can be given of the admission and of what passed on th occasion when it was made. It seems quite illogical that it shoul be admissible to prove that the accused was charged with the crim if his answer thereto was an admission, while it is not admissible t prove it when his answer has been a denial of the crime, and I canno agree that the admissibility or non-admissibility is decided as matter of law by any such artificial rule. Going back to firs principles as enunciated above, **the deciding question is** whether th evidence of the whole occurrence is relevant or not. **If the prisone admits the charge the evidence is obviously relevant. If he denies it it may or may not be relevant. For instance,** if he is charged with violent assault and denies that he committed it, that fact might b distinctly relevant if at the trial his defence was that he did commi the act, but that it was in self-defence. **The evidential value of th occurrence depends entirely on the behaviour of the prisoner,** for th fact that some one makes a statement to him subsequently to th commission of the crime cannot in itself have any value as evidenc for or against him. The only evidence for or against him is hi behaviour in response to the charge, but **I can see no justification fo laying down as a rule** of law that **any particular form of response** whether of a **positive or negative** character, is such that it cannot i some circumstances have an evidential value. I am, therefore, of opinion that **there is no rule of law that evidence cannot be given of the accused being charged with the offence and of his behaviour on hearing such charge where that behaviour amounts to a denial of his guilt.** This is said to have been laid down as a rule of law in *R.* v. *Norton*, and to have been followed by the Courts since that decision. If this be so, I think that the decision was wrong, but I am by no means convinced that it was intended in that case to lay down any such rule of law.

But while I am of opinion that there is no such rule of law, I am of opinion that **the evidential value of the behaviour of the accused where he denies the charge is very small** either for or against him, whereas the effect on the minds of the jury of his being publicly or repeatedly charged to his face with the crime might seriously prejudice the fairness of his trial. In my opinion, therefore, **a Judge would in most cases be acting in accordance with the best traditions** of our criminal procedure **if he exercised the influence which he rightly possesses** over the conduct of a prosecution in order **to prevent such evidence being given** in cases where it would have very little or no evidential value. Subject to these words of caution, I am of opinion that this appeal should be allowed upon this point, because we have to decide upon the admissibility as a matter of law, and so regarded I have no doubt that the evidence in question was rightly admitted.

I am, however, of opinion that the direction of the magistrates as to corroboration was wrong, and therefore, notwithstanding my opinion on the admissibility of the evidence, the conviction cannot stand.

Lord Reading. . . . As to the first ground. No objection was raised by Mr. Dickens, for the respondent, to the admission of the first part of the statement, namely, "That is the man". It implied that Christie was the man designated by the boy as the person who had committed the offence, and meant little, if anything more than the act of touching the sleeve of Christie or pointing to him. **The importance is as to the admission of the additional words, describing the various acts done by Christie. These were not necessary to complete the identification or to explain it. . . .** At the trial, and before the statement was admitted, the boy identified Christie in Court, and was not cross-examined. The additional statement was not required by the prosecution for the purpose of proving the act of identification by the boy. **The statement cannot, in my judgment, be admitted as evidence of the state of the boy's mind when in the act of identifying Christie,** as that would amount to allowing another person to give in evidence the boy's state of mind, when he was not asked, and had not said anything about it in his statement to the Court.

If the prosecution required the evidence as part of the act of identification it should have been given by the boy before the prosecution closed their case. In my judgment it would be a dangerous extension of the law regulating the admissibility of evidence if your Lordships were to allow proof of statements made, narrating or describing the events constituting the offence, on the ground that they form part of or explain the act of identification, more particularly when such evidence is not necessary to prove the act, and is not given by the person who made the statement. I have found no case in which any such statement has been admitted.

As to the second ground. **A statement made in the presence of one of the parties to a civil action may be given in evidence against him** if it is relevant to any of the matters in issue. **And equally such a statement made in the presence of the accused** may be given in evidence against him at his trial.

The principles of the laws of evidence are the same whether applied at civil or criminal trials, but they are not enforced with the same rigidity against a person accused of a criminal offence as against a party to a civil action. **There are exceptions to the law regulating the admissibility of evidence which apply only to criminal trials,** and which have acquired their force by the constant and invariable practice of Judges when presiding at criminal trials. **They are rules of prudence and discretion,** and have become so integral a part of the administration of the criminal law as almost to have acquired the full force of law. A familiar instance of such a practice is to be found in the direction of Judges to juries strongly warning them not to act upon the evidence of an accomplice unless it is corroborated. . . .

Such practice has found its place in the administration of the criminal law because Judges are aware from their experience that in order to ensure a fair trial for the accused, and to prevent the operation of indirect but not the less serious prejudice to his interests it is desirable in certain circumstances to relax the strict application of the law of evidence. **Nowadays, it is the constant practice for the Judge** who presides at the trial **to indicate his opinion** to counsel for the prosecution **that evidence which, although admissible in law, has little value** in its direct bearing upon the case, and might indirectly operate seriously to the prejudice of the accused, **should not be given** against him, and speaking generally counsel accepts the suggestion and does not press for the admission of the evidence unless he has good reason for it.

That there is danger that the accused may be indirectly prejudiced by the admission of such a statement as in this case is manifest, for however carefully the Judge may direct the jury, it is often difficult for them to exclude it altogether from their minds as evidence of the facts contained in the statement.

In general, such evidence can have little or no value in its direct bearing on the case **unless the accused,** upon hearing the statement, by conduct and demeanour, or by the answer made by him, or in certain circumstances by the refraining from an answer, **acknowledged the truth of the statement** either in whole or in part, or did or said something from which the jury could infer such an acknowledgment, for **if he acknowledged its truth, he accepted it as his own statement of the facts. If the accused denied** the truth of the statement when it was made, **and there was nothing in his conduct and demeanour** from which the jury, notwithstanding his denial, could infer that he acknowledged its truth in whole or in part, **the practice of the Judges has been to exclude it altogether.** In *R.* v. *Norton*, PICKFORD, J., in delivering the judgment of the Court of Criminal Appeal, said (see *ante*, p. 177): "If there be no such evidence" (that is of acknowledgment by the accused), "then the contents of the statement should be excluded; if there be such evidence, then they should be admitted". If it was intended to lay down rules of law to be applied whenever such a statement is tendered for admission, I think the judgment goes too far; they are valuable rules for the guidance of those presiding at trials of criminal cases when considering how the discretion of the Court, with regard to the admission of such evidence, should be exercised, but **it must not be assumed that the judgment in R. v. Norton exhausts all the circumstances which may have to be taken into consideration** by the Court when exercising its judicial discretion.

It might well be that the prosecution wished to give evidence

of such a statement in order to prove the conduct and demeanour of the accused when hearing the statement as a relevant fact in the particular case, notwithstanding that it did not amount either to an acknowledgment or some evidence of an acknowledgment of any part of the truth of the statement. I think it impossible to lay down any general rule to be applied to all such cases, save the principle of strict law to which I have referred.

Upon the whole, therefore, **I come to the conclusion that the rules formulated in R. v. Norton** and followed in this and other cases, must be restricted in their application as above indicated, and **cannot be regarded as strict rules of law** regulating the admissibility of such evidence.

I think, therefore, that this statement was in law admissible as evidence against Christie.

As to the fourth point. **The statement under review formed no part of the incidents constituting the offence.** It was not made whilst the offence was being committed or immediately thereafter. It took place after Christie had left the boy, and the mother had found him and taken him across the fields and had spoken to another man. **In my view it was not so immediately connected with the act of assault as to form part of the res gestæ. . . .**

Assuming that your Lordships were of opinion that the boy's statement was admissible, **this conviction, for other reasons, could not stand, and was properly quashed. . . .** By virtue of section 30 of the Children Act, 1908 (8 Edw. 7, c. 67), Christie could not be convicted unless the boy's testimony was "corroborated by some other material evidence in support thereof implicating the accused". **There was no sufficient direction, and there was misdirection to the jury of the requisites of corroboration** under this statute. Such direction as was given by the deputy chairman was erroneous, inasmuch as it treated the statement by the boy, given in evidence by the mother and the constable, as corroboration of the boy's evidence implicating the accused. This is manifestly wrong. It was for the deputy chairman to satisfy himself that there was evidence of corroboration fit to be submitted to the jury within the meaning of the statute, and then to direct them not to convict unless they accepted the evidence of corroboration. . . . I have been requested by Lord Dunedin to say that he **concurs in this judgment.**

MORIARTY v. L. C. & D. RY.

QUEEN'S BENCH. 1870.

L. R. 5 Q. B. 314; 39 L. J. Q. B. 109; 22 L. T. 163; 18 W. R. 625.

An admission may be by conduct only; and it may relate not only to specific facts, but even show that the party's whole case is bad.

Thus, where the plaintiff sued a railway company for personal injury, evidence was given that he had gone about suborning false witnesses who had not been present at the accident, and it was held that such conduct amounted to an admission that he had no case.

The following is from the Law Journal:—

COCKBURN, C.J. . . . Here, if you can show that a man has been suborning false testimony, and has endeavoured to have recourse to perjury, **it is strong to show that he knew perfectly well that his cause of action was an unrighteous one. . . .**

BLACKBURN, J. . . . **The jury should be cautioned against giving the evidence too much weight,** which they might possibly do, and directed that they were not to punish a man for giving false testimony by taking away his right of action, but only to see whether it shook their belief in his evidence. . . .

LUSH, J. . . . This species of evidence is receivable as an admission by the party that the case he is putting forward is not the true one. **It was an admission by conduct,** and receivable on that ground. . . .

WILLIAMS v. INNES.

KING'S BENCH. 1808.

1 CAMPBELL 364; 10 R. R. 702.

Admissions may be made by agents. If one party directs or requests another party to apply to any other person for information on a certain matter, such reference may constitute such other person an agent in such matter for such purpose.

In an action against executors, who pleaded that they had fully administered the estate, the plaintiff, in order to prove assets, put in a letter from the defendants, telling her that if she wanted further information concerning the affairs of the deceased she should apply to a Mr. Ross, and she proposed to give in evidence what he said on the matter. The evidence was held admissible.

LORD ELLENBOROUGH, C.J. If a man refers another upon any **particular business** to a third person, he is bound by what this third person says or does concerning it, as much as if that had been said or done by himself. This was agreed to be law by all the Judges on the trial of Mr. Hastings.

Note.—This case is generally quoted as an authority for the proposition stated, but the judgment is very short and general in its terms. It must, doubtless, be taken as applying only to cases of real " particular business ", not to every case of mere casual inquiry. In another case the same Judge said: " Wherever a party refers to the evidence of another, he is bound by it—and this is constantly good evidence " (*Daniel* v. *Pitt*, 1 Camp. 366).

KIRKSTALL BREWERY CO. v. FURNESS RY.

QUEEN'S BENCH. 1874.

L. R. 9 Q. B. 468; 43 L. J. Q. B. 142; 30 L. T. 783; 22 W. R. 876.

Whatever an agent or servant does or says, within the scope of his authority, express or implied, in carrying out the business in which he is employed binds his principal. An agent or servant may therefore bind his principal by admissions made within the scope of his authority or duty.

In an action against a railway company for loss of a parcel of money, statements made by the station-master to a police officer, tending to show theft thereof by one of the company's servants, were received as admissions against the company, the station-master being the proper agent to make such statements.

The following is from the Law Journal:—

COCKBURN, C.J. . . . I think it impossible to say that **a man who has the sole management** of a railway station, and **had authority to cause a person to be apprehended** if he had reasonable and probable cause to suppose that a felony had been committed, could not have **authority to give instructions to the police,** and could not make such communications as would be admissible in evidence just as if they were made by his principals.

QUAIN, J. . . . In putting the police in motion **he was acting within his duty, and within the scope of the authority** given to him. . . .

ARCHIBALD, J. . . . **Being in charge of the station** at the time a felony was committed, **it was his duty to put the police in motion.** That being so, I think that he was acting within the scope of his duty, that **he had power to bind the company,** and therefore that the evidence was admissible.

Note.—This appears to be scarcely a case of "course of employment", but of "scope of authority". The master may be responsible in tort for acts of his servant quite unauthorised by him, if done in the course of employment. But, in contract, and as regards admissions, the question appears to be one of authority. See *post*, p. 194.

A good example of admissions made by servants which are binding on their master occurs when there is a statutory duty on an employer to keep records: they are admissible against the employer whether they are in fact kept by the employer himself or by a servant (*Beer* v. *W. H. Clench* (*1930*) *Ltd.*, 53 T. L. R. 300).

G. W. RY. v. WILLIS.

COMMON PLEAS. 1865.

34 L. J. C. P. 195; 12 L. T. 349; 18 C. B. (N.S.) 748.

Statements made by agents or servants are not necessarily admissions against the principal, although they would have been admissions if made by the principal himself. Such statements, in order to bind the principal, must have been within the scope of the agent's authority, and made at the time of the transaction in question.

In an action against a railway company for not delivering cattle promptly, the plaintiff gave evidence of a conversation a week after the transaction between himself and the company's night inspector, who had charge of the night cattle trains at a certain station, in the course of which the night inspector said the cattle had been forgotten. It was held that this statement was not an admission against the company, as the n'ght inspector was a subordinate servant without authority to make such a statement, and also the statement was made some time after the transaction.

The following is from the Law Journal:—

ERLE, C.J. I am of opinion that this **night inspector is not** to be presumed to have been **authorised by the company to make admissions** on their behalf of things gone by. . . .

BYLES, KEATING and SMITH, JJ., concurred.

The following is from Common Bench Reports:—

ERLE, C.J. I am of opinion that this night inspector is **not to be presumed to have had authority** to make admissions relative to transactions gone by, so as to bind his employers. . . .

The following is from the Law Times:—

By the *Court*. There is no doubt **that** the night inspector had **no authority** to answer any inquiries. . . .

RE DEVALA PROVIDENT GOLD MINING CO.

CHANCERY. 1883.

L. R. 22 Ch. D. 593; 52 L. J. Ch. 434; 48 L. T. 259; 31 W. R. 425.

Summons by shareholder for removal of his name from the share register by reason of misrepresentation in the company's prospectus. The only evidence of the untruth of the representation was a statement made by the chairman in a speech to a meeting of the shareholders. It was claimed that the statement was material, that it was made by an agent of the company, and that the company themselves had put the report in evidence as a true report of what the chairman said. *Held*, that the statement was not admissible against the company.

The following is from the Law Reports:—

Fry, J. . . . **The only ground upon which,** in my view, **this statement could** possibly **be admitted would be that the chairman was the agent of the company,** and that he **was making the statement** in the course of a transaction with a third party in which he was acting as the agent of the company, and that it was **within the scope of his agency.** If that were so, the statement would be admissible against the company. It appears to me, however, that **it was not admissible, for it was made by the agent, not in a transaction between the company and a third party, but at a meeting of the company.** It is the case of an agent making a report to his own principal, and in my view when an agent is making a confidential report to his principal, **the report is not admissible evidence in favour of a third party.** It is said that the applicant was not a third party, but was a member of the company, and in that view the chairman was making the report to him as one of his principals. It does not appear to me that there is either principle or authority which justifies the use of a statement made by the common agent of two principals as evidence on behalf of one of the principals against the other.

PETO v. HAGUE.

NISI PRIUS. 1804.

5 Esp. 134.

Statements made by an agent about past transactions will not bind the principal as admissions. When the agent's authority to act in the particular matter has ceased, the principal cannot be affected by his subsequent statements.

The defendant was a coal-merchant who was sued for a penalty for selling short measure. A witness was proceeding to state what was said to him by one Peely, the defendant's manager, as to a sale about to take place. This was objected to, but was held admissible.

Lord Ellenborough, C.J., ruled that it was evidence; he said that Peely appeared to be the manager and conductor of the defendant's business; **what he might have said respecting a former sale** made by the defendant or on another occasion, **would not be evidence** to affect his master; but what he said **respecting a sale of coals, then about to take place,** and respecting the disposition of the coals then lying at the wharf, which were the object of sale, was **in the course of witness's employment** for the defendant, and **was evidence** to affect his master.

Note.—The Judge here uses the expression "course of employment", but it would appear that statements outside the scope of authority of an agent would not bind the principal although made in course of employment. But, to be within scope of authority, the statement must, apparently, be made in course of employment. See note, *ante*, p. 191.

WOOLWAY v. ROWE.

KING'S BENCH. 1834.

1 A. & E. 114; 3 L. J. K. B. 121; 3 N. & M. 849; 40 R. R. 264.

Admissions made by predecessors in title, or other persons in privity with a party, may be given in evidence against such party.

The statement of the plaintiff's father, the former owner of the plaintiff's land, that he had not the right claimed by the plaintiff in respect of it, was held admissible; although the father was living and in Court at the time.

The following is from Adolphus and Ellis:—

LORD DENMAN, C.J. (*delivering the judgment of the Court,* LORD DENMAN, C.J., LITTLEDALE, PARKE and PATTESON, JJ.). The first question raised in this case was, whether the **declarations of a person formerly interested in the estate** now the plaintiff's were admissible in evidence, when the party himself might have been called. We think they **were receivable, on the ground of identity of interest.** The fact of his being alive at the time of the trial, when perhaps his memory of facts was impaired, and when his interest was not the same, does not, in our opinion, affect the admissibility of those declarations which he formerly made on the subject of his own rights. . . .

The following is from the Law Journal:—

LORD DENMAN, C.J. (*as above*). . . . We are of opinion that these declarations are admissible against the plaintiff, **on the principle of identity of interest** between the plaintiff and the party making the declarations. . . .

Note.—As to "privies", see *ante*, p. 45, and cf. *Falcon* v. *Famous Players Film Co., Ltd.,* [1926] 1 K. B. 393; [1926] 2 K. B. 474.

R. v. SIMONS.

OXFORD CIRCUIT 1834.

6 C. & P. 540.

A statement made by a party to the proceedings to any person, even to his wife or himself, may be proved as an admission against him.

On a charge of arson it was proposed to call a witness to prove what the prisoner said to his wife on leaving the magistrates' room after committal.

ALDERSON, B. What a person is overheard saying to his wife, or even saying to himself, is evidence.

Note.—As to statements made to police constables, see *post*, p. 206.

SLATTERIE v. POOLEY.

EXCHEQUER. 1840.

6 M. & W. 664; 10 L. J. Ex. 8; 4 Jur. 1038; 1 Hurl. & Walm. 18; 55 R. R. 760.

Admissions are considered primary evidence against a party, and they are admissible to prove even the contents of written documents, without notice to produce, or accounting for the absence of, the originals.

The plaintiff sued upon a deed by which the defendant covenanted to indemnify him against all debts set out in a certain deed and schedule which itself was inadmissible as not being duly stamped. An oral admission of the defendant, that a debt in question in the action was the same as one mentioned in such schedule, was admitted.

The following is from the Law Journal:—

PARKE, B. . . . **The rule as to the production of the best evidence is not at all infringed.** It does not apply to the present case. That rule is founded on the supposition that a party is going to offer worse evidence than the nature of the case admits. But **what is said by a party to the suit is not open to that objection. . . .** We therefore think it is a sound rule that admissions made by a party to a suit may be received against him, although they relate to the contents of a written document.

LORD ABINGER, C.B., GURNEY, and ROLFE, BB., concurred.

The following is from Meeson and Welsby:—

PARKE, B. . . . the reason why such parol statements are admissible, without notice to produce, or accounting for the absence of the written instrument, is that **they are not open to the same objection which belongs to parol evidence from other sources, where the written evidence might have been produced**; for such evidence is excluded from the presumption of its untruth, arising from the very nature of the case, where better evidence is withheld; whereas **what a party himself admits to be true, may reasonably be presumed to be so.** The weight and value of such testimony is quite another question. . . . It is enough for the present purpose to say, that the evidence is admissible.

Note.—As to the rules concerning the "production of the best evidence", and notices to produce, see *post*, pp. 345, 355.

CONFESSIONS.

In criminal cases it may appear that the prisoner has admitted or confessed his guilt of the crime alleged. But, before such confession is put in evidence, **the prosecution must prove that such confession was free and voluntary,** as the following cases show. If objection to the admissibility of the confession is taken by the defence, evidence must be taken, if necessary (in the absence of the jury, if the trial be with a jury), and a ruling given upon that issue (*R* v. *Chadwick*, 24 Cr. App. R. 138).

Even when such a confession is admitted, it is not treated as conclusive. It is open to the prisoner to rebut or explain it.

"With respect to the effect of extra-judicial confessions or statements when received, the rule is clear that, unless otherwise directed by statute, no such confession or statement, whether plenary or not plenary, whether made before a justice of the peace or other tribunal having only an inquisitorial jurisdiction in the matter, or made by deed, or matter *in pais*, either amounts to an estoppel, or has any conclusive effect against an accused person, or is entitled to any weight beyond that which the jury in their conscience assign to it" (*Best*, § 552).

"Of the credit and effect due to a confessional statement the jury are the sole judges; they must consider the whole confession, together with all the other evidence of the case, and if it is inconsistent, improbable or incredible, or is contradicted or discredited by other evidence, or is the emanation of a weak or excited state of mind, they may exercise their discretion in rejecting it, either wholly or in part, whether the rejected part make for or against the prisoner" (*Wills, Circ. Ev.*, 7th ed., 133).

Confessions mean *informal* admissions of guilt whether made in or out of Court. A formal plea of "guilty" is a pleading (though an oral one) which acknowledges the truth of everything stated in the indictment with the result that there is no issue to try. Once a prisoner has pleaded "not guilty" and been given in charge to the jury a verdict must be taken unless the Court allows him to withdraw his plea and plead "guilty".

As to warning a prisoner before he gives evidence at his examination, see the Criminal Justice Act, 1925, s. 12, *post*, p. 510.

It should be noted that the Criminal Justice Act, 1925, s. 12, requires the magistrate, after taking the evidence for the prosecution, to warn the prisoner that he need not say anything in reply, that what he does say may be used in evidence at his trial, and that he has nothing to hope or fear from any promise or threat (see *post*, p. 510).

R. v. BALDRY.

CROWN CASES RESERVED. 1852.

2 DENISON 430; 21 L. J. M. C. 130; 16 JUR. 599; 5 COX C. C. 523.

In criminal cases a confession made by the prisoner can be given in evidence against him, if the prosecution show it was free and voluntary; not otherwise.

It will be held not to be free and voluntary if it were induced by any threat or promise made by a person in authority.

Any expressions suggesting that it would be "better" for the prisoner to tell the truth import a threat or promise.

On the part of the prosecution a police constable was called, whose evidence began thus: "I went to the prisoner's house on the 17th December. I saw the prisoner. Dr. Vincent, and Page, another constable, were with me. I told him what he was charged with. He made no reply, and sat with his face buried in his handkerchief. I believe he was crying. I said he need not say anything to criminate himself; what he did say would be taken down and used as evidence against him." It was held that such words did not amount to any threat or promise to induce the prisoner to confess; that it could have no tendency to induce him to say anything untrue; and that in spite of it if he did afterwards confess the confession must be considered voluntary and admissible.

The following is from Denison:—

POLLOCK, C.B. . . . **The ground for not receiving such evidence is that it would not be safe to receive a statement made under any influence or fear.** There is no presumption of law that it is false or that the law considers such statement cannot be relied upon; but such confessions are rejected because it is supposed that it would be dangerous to leave such evidence to the jury. **A simple caution to the accused to** *tell the truth* **if he says anything has been decided not to be sufficient to prevent the statement made being given in evidence;** and although it may be put that when a person is told to tell *the truth,* he may possibly understand that the only thing true is that he is guilty, that is not what we ought to understand. He is reminded that he need not say anything, but if he says anything let it be true. . . . **But where the admonition to speak the truth has been coupled with any expression importing that it would** *be better* **for him to do so, it has been held that the confession was not receivable,** the objectionable words being that *it would be better* to speak the truth, because they import that it would be better for him to say something. . . . **The true distinction between the present case and a case of that kind is,** that it is left to the prisoner a matter of perfect indifference whether he should open his mouth or not. . . .

The question now is, whether the words employed by the constable, "*he need not say anything to criminate himself; what he did say would be taken down and used as evidence against him*", **amount either to a promise or a threat.** We are not to torture this expression. . . . The words are to be taken in their obvious meaning. . . . It is proper that a prisoner should be cautioned not to criminate himself; but I think that what he says ought to be adduced either as evidence of his guilt, or as evidence in his favour. For these reasons I think that the Lord Chief Justice properly received the confession at the trial.

PARKE, B. . . . In order to render a confession admissible in evidence it must be perfectly voluntary; and there is no doubt that **any inducement in the nature of a promise or of a threat held out by a person in authority vitiates a confession.** The decisions to that effect have gone a long way; whether it would not have been better to have allowed the whole to go to the jury, it is now too late to inquire, but I think there has been too much tenderness towards prisoners in this matter. . . . The rule has been extended quite too far, and justice and common sense have too frequently been sacrificed at the shrine of mercy. . . .

ERLE, J. . . . I am of opinion that **when a confession is well proved it is the best evidence that can be produced**; and that unless it be clear that there was either a threat or a promise to induce it, it ought not to be excluded. . . .

WILLIAMS, J. . . . **What was said to the prisoner was nothing more than that what he said would not be kept secret,** but would be used in evidence; and it is an over-refinement to say that a statement made after such a caution was inadmissible.

Lord Campbell, C.J. . . . If there be any worldly advantage held out, or any harm threatened, the confession must be excluded. **The reason is, not that the law supposes that the statement will be false, but that the prisoner has made the confession under a bias,** and that, therefore, it would be better not to submit it to the jury. . . .

R. v. THOMPSON.

CROWN CASES RESERVED. 1893.

[1893] 2 Q. B. 12; 62 L. J. M. C. 93; 69 L. T. 22; 41 W. R. 525; 57 J. P. 313; 17 Cox C. C. 641.

The prisoner was convicted of embezzling the money of a company which employed him. It was proved that, on being taxed with the crime by the chairman of the company, he said, "Yes, I took the money", and afterwards made out a list of the sums and, with the help of his brother, paid back a part of them. The chairman admitted that before receiving the confession he had said to the prisoner's brother, "It will be the right thing for your brother to make a statement" or "to make a clean breast of it"; but he also said that at the time of the confession no promise or threat was made to the prisoner with regard to his prosecution, and there was no evidence that the chairman's statement had, in fact, been communicated to the prisoner prior to his confession. *Held,* that the confession was not admissible.

The following judgment, which was concurred in by four other Judges, is from the Law Reports:—

Cave, J. . . . By the law of England to be admissible a **confession must be free and voluntary.** If it proceeds from remorse and a desire to make reparation for the crime, it is admissible. **If it flows from hope or fear, excited by a person in authority, it is inadmissible. . . .** The material question consequently is whether the confession has been obtained by the influence of hope or fear; and the evidence to this point being in its nature preliminary, is addressed to **the Judge,** who **will require the prosecutor to show affirmatively, to his satisfaction, that the statement was not made under the influence of an improper**

inducement, and who, in the event of *any doubt subsisting on this head*, will reject the confession. . . . If these principles and the reasons for them are, as it seems impossible to doubt, well founded, they afford the magistrates a simple test by which the admissibility may be decided. They have to ask, is it proved affirmatively that the confession was free and voluntary—that is, was it preceded by any inducement to make a statement held out by a person in authority? If so, and the inducement has not clearly been removed before the statement was made, evidence of the statement was inadmissible. In the present case . . . there is, indeed, no evidence that any communication was made to the prisoner at all; but it seems to me that after the chairman's statement that he had spoken to the prisoner's brother about the desirability of the prisoner making a clean breast of it, with the expectation that what he said would be communicated to the prisoner, it was incumbent on the prosecution to prove whether any, and if so what, communication was actually made to the prisoner, before the magistrates could properly be satisfied that the confession was free and voluntary. The magistrates go on to say that they inferred that the details of the interview *would* be, by which I suppose they intended to say that they inferred they *were*, communicated to the prisoner, which seems to have been the right inference to draw under the circumstances. *Conviction quashed.*

R. v. JARVIS.

CROWN CASES RESERVED. 1867.

L. R. 1 C. C. R. 96; 37 L. J. M. C. 1; 16 W. R. 111.

A "threat or promise" must offer some temporal advantage or disadvantage connected with the result of the prosecution in order to render a confession involuntary.

Exhortations to confess on moral or religious grounds are not sufficient to exclude a confession.

One of a firm who employed the prisoner, having called him up into the private counting house of the firm, in the presence of another of the firm and two officers of police, said, "I think it is right that I should tell you that, besides being in the presence of my brother and myself, you are in the presence of two officers of the police: and I should advise you that, to any question that may be put to you, you will answer truthfully, so that if you have committed a fault you may not add to it by stating what is untrue"; and having shown a letter to him, which he denied having written, added, "Take care, we know more than you think we know". The prisoner thereupon made a confession, which was held admissible.

The following is from the Law Journal:—

KELLY, C.B. . . . The question is, do the words before us in substance and fairly considered import a threat of evil, or hold out a hope of benefit to the accused in case he should state the truth? . . . In the first place, **this appears to me to be advice given by a master to a servant,** and when he adds, "So that if you have committed a fault you may not add to it by stating what is untrue", **he appears to me to be giving further advice on moral grounds.** It is neither a threat that evil shall befall him, nor is it an inducement or holding out of advantage. . . .

As to **the words "you had better",** referred to in the argument, there are many cases in which those words have occurred, and they **seem to have acquired a sort of technical meaning,** that they hold out an inducement or threat **within the rule that excludes confessions** under such circumstances. It is sufficient to say that those words have not been used on this occasion; and that **the words used appear to me to import advice given on moral grounds,** and not to infringe upon the rule of law prohibiting a threat in these cases.

WILLES, J. I agree; but if it had appeared that the prisoner could have supposed the words meant **"you had better",** I think the case **would have been different.**

BRAMWELL, B., BYLES and LUSH, JJ., concurred.

Note.—If a magistrate were to tell a prisoner that if he did not confess he would get six months' longer sentence, a confession induced thereby would undoubtedly be inadmissible. But, if he told him he would go to Hell, that would not render it inadmissible, apparently. The latter threat might appear the worse, but it would scarcely have the same effect on the mind of the prisoner, who would for the moment be more troubled with his immediate difficulty of getting out of his present trouble, than with his affairs thereafter. Moreover, the magistrate has no jurisdiction with reference to the place mentioned in the latter threat. The prisoner therefore might naturally ignore it.

R. v. LLOYD.

OXFORD CIRCUIT. 1834.

6 C. & P. 393.

The offer of some merely collateral convenience, or temporal advantage unconnected with the result of the prosecution, or an appeal to a man's moral feelings, is not such an inducement as will render a confession inadmissible. The promise, or words, to have such effect, must have reference to the result of the prosecution; suggesting a more favourable determination of the proceedings.

The prisoner and his wife were both in custody for larceny, but in separate rooms. A person who was in the room where the former was in custody, said, "I hope you will tell, because Mrs. Gurner can ill afford to lose the money"; and the constable said, "If you will tell where the property is, you shall see your wife". A statement made afterwards by the prisoner was held admissible.

PATTESON, J. I think that **this is not such an inducement to confess as will exclude the evidence** of what the prisoner said. It amounts only to this, that if he would tell where the money was, he should see his wife.

Note.—"The cases on the subject of what is an illegal inducement to confess are very numerous, and far from consistent with each other; and there can be little doubt that the salutary rule which excludes confessions unlawfully obtained has been applied to the rejection of many not coming within its principle, although Judges are now less disposed than they formerly were to hold that the language used amounts to an inducement" (*Best*, § 551).

A few further illustrations, drawn from decided cases, may be useful.

The confession was rejected where the following expressions were used—

"Tell me where the things are, and I will be favourable to you." (*R.* v. *Thompson*, 1 Leach 291.)

"If you do not tell me all about it, I will send for a constable." (*R.* v. *Richards*, 5 C. & P. 318.)

"If you don't tell me, I will give you in charge of the police till you do tell me." (*R.* v. *Luckhurst*, 6 Cox 243.)

"If you don't tell, you may get yourself into trouble and it will be the worse for you." (*R.* v. *Coley*, 10 Cox 536.)

"You had better tell all you know." (*R.* v. *Kingston*, 4 C. & P. 387.)

"Speak the truth, it will be better for you if you do." (*R.* v. *Rose*, 78 L. T. 119.)

The confession was admitted where the following expressions were used—

"Don't run your soul into more sin, but tell the truth." (*R.* v. *Sleeman*, 6 Cox 245.)

"Be sure to tell the truth." (*R.* v. *Court*, 7 C. & P. 486.)

"I must know more about it." (*R.* v. *Reason*, 12 Cox 228.)

"You had better, as good boys, tell the truth." (*R.* v. *Reeve*, L. R. 1 C. C. 96.)

It would really appear to be rather a question of circumstances than of words, regard being had particularly to the position and authority of the person using the words.

R. v. GIBBONS.

OXFORD CIRCUIT. 1828.

1 C. & P. 97.

The term "person in authority", in connection with confessions by prisoners, includes the prosecutor, officers of justice, and other persons directly connected with the prosecution only.

On a charge of murder, Mr. Cozens, a surgeon, was called to prove certain confessions made by the prisoner to him. He objected to giving such evidence on the ground that, at the time of the statement, he was attending the prisoner as a surgeon.

PARK, J. That is no sufficient reason to prevent a disclosure for the purposes of justice.

The witness also said that he held out no threat or promise to the prisoner, but a woman present said that she had told the prisoner she had better tell all; and then the prisoner confessed to the witness.

PARK, J. (after consulting with HULLOCK, B.) laid down that, as no inducement had been held out by Mr. Cozens, to whom the confession was made; and **the only inducement had been held out** (as was alleged) **by a person having no sort of authority;** it must be presumed that the confession to Mr. Cozens was a free and voluntary confession. **If the promise had been held out by any person having any office or authority, as the prosecutor, constable, etc., the case would be different;** but here some person, having no authority of any sort, officiously says, You had better confess. No confession follows; but some time afterwards, to another person (the witness), the prisoner, without any inducement held out, confesses. They (the Judges) had not the least doubt that the present evidence was admissible.

Note.—The following have been held to be "persons in authority" —magistrates, even those not acting as such in the case, their clerks, coroners, police constables, warders and others having custody of the prisoners, searchers, prosecutors and their wives and attorneys. Masters and mistresses are only so considered if they are themselves prosecuting, or the charge is connected with the employment.

R. v. VOISIN.

COURT OF CRIMINAL APPEAL. 1918.

[1918] 1 K. B. 531; 87 L. J. K. B. 574; 118 L. T. 654; 13 CR. APP. R. 89; 34 T. L. R. 623; 26 COX C. C. 224.

The mere fact that the statement has been made in answer to a question by a police constable or that no caution has been administered is not sufficient to render it

inadmissible. The Judge may, however, in his discretion reject the statement on these grounds.

The body of a woman was found in a parcel together with a piece of paper on which were written the words " Bladie Belgiam ". The prisoner, who at the time was detained in custody for inquiries, but who had not yet been charged, after making a statement and without being cautioned, was asked by the police to write the words " Bloody Belgian ". He expressed his willingness and wrote " Bladie Belgiam ". It was held that the writing was admissible.

The following is from the Law Reports:—

A. T. LAWRENCE, J. (giving the judgment of the Court, consisting of himself and LUSH and SALTER, JJ.). . . . The alleged misreception of evidence relates to a paper writing containing the words " Bladie Belgiam ". . . . It was argued that that writing was inadmissible in evidence on the ground that it was obtained by the police without having first cautioned the prisoner and while he was in custody. A number of cases were called to our attention in which different views had been entertained by Judges as to when statements by prisoners should and when they should not be excluded from consideration by the jury. It is clear, and has been frequently held, that the duty of the Judge to exclude statements is one that must depend upon the particular circumstances of each case. The general principle is admirably stated by Lord Sumner in his judgment in the Privy Council in *Ibrahim* v. *R.*, [1914] A. C. 599, as follows : " It has long been established as a positive rule of English criminal law, that **no statement by an accused is admissible** in evidence against him **unless it is shown by the prosecution to have been a voluntary statement,** in the sense that it has not been obtained from him either by fear of prejudice or hope of advantage exercised or held out by a person in authority." The point of that passage is that the statement must be a voluntary statement; any statement which has been extorted by fear of prejudice or induced by hope of advantage held out by a person in authority is not admissible. As Lord Sumner points out, logically these considerations go to the value of the statement rather than to its admissibility. The question as to whether a person has been duly cautioned before the statement was made is one of the circumstances that must be taken into consideration, but this is a circumstance upon which a Judge should exercise his discretion. **It**

cannot be said as a matter of law that the absence of a caution makes the statement inadmissible; it may tend to show that the person was not upon his guard as to the importance of what he was saying or as to its bearing upon some charge of which he has not been informed. In this case the prisoner wrote these words quite voluntarily. The mere fact that the words were written at the request of police officers, or that he was being detained at Bow Street, does not make the writing inadmissible in evidence. Those facts do not tend to change the character of handwriting, nor do they explain the resemblance between his handwriting and that upon the label, or account for the same misspellings occurring in both. **There was nothing in the nature of a " trap "** or of the " manufacture of evidence " ; the identity of the deceased woman had not at this moment been established, and the police, though they were detaining the prisoner in custody for inquiries, had not then decided to charge him with this crime ; indeed, if the writing had turned out other than it did and other circumstances had not subsequently transpired, it is certain that he, like others who were similarly detained, would have been discharged. **It is desirable in the interests of the community that investigations into crime should not be cramped.** The Court is of opinion that they would be most unduly cramped if it were to be held that a writing voluntarily made under the circumstances here proved was inadmissible in evidence.

. . . We read that case (*i.e.*, *R.* v. *Best*, [1909] 1 K. B. 692) as deciding that **the mere fact that a statement is made in answer to a question put by a police constable is not in itself sufficient to make the statement inadmissible in law. It may be, and often is, a ground for the Judge in his discretion excluding the evidence;** but he should do so only if he thinks the statement was not a voluntary one in the sense above mentioned, or was an unguarded answer made under circumstances that rendered it unreliable, or unfair for some reason to be allowed in evidence against the prisoner. Even if we disagreed with the mode in which the Judge had in this case exercised his discretion, which we do not, we should not be entitled to overrule his decision on appeal. This was evidence admissible in law, and it could not be fairly inferred from the other circumstances that it was not voluntary.

In 1912 **the Judges,** at the request of the Home Secretary, **drew up some rules as guides for police officers. These rules have not**

the force of law; they are administrative directions the observance of which the police authorities should enforce upon their subordinates as tending to the fair administration of justice. It is important that they should do so, for **statements obtained from prisoners, contrary to the spirit of these rules, may be rejected as evidence** by the Judge presiding at the trial.

Note.—Statements are rarely admitted which are proved to have been obtained in contravention of the Judges' Rules (*post*, p. 550). Reference should be made to the interesting judgment of Lord Sumner in *Ibrahim* v. *R.* (cited *supra*) where he points out that this problem is of fairly modern growth with the rise of up-to-date police methods.

R. v. GOULD.

CENTRAL CRIMINAL COURT. 1840.

9 C. & P. 364.

Notwithstanding that a confession has been obtained by the threat or inducement of a person in authority, it seems that facts discovered in consequence thereof, and so much of such confession as distinctly relates to such facts, may be proved.

A prisoner, charged with burglary, made a statement to a policeman in some peculiar circumstances, which induced the prosecution, with the approbation of the Court, to decline offering it in evidence; but in consequence of the statement containing some allusion to a lantern, which was afterwards found in a particular place, the policeman was asked whether, in consequence of something which the prisoner had said, he made search for the lantern.

TINDAL, C.J., and PARKE, B., were both of opinion that the words used by the prisoner, with reference to the thing found, ought to be given in evidence, and the policeman accordingly stated that the

prisoner told him that he had thrown a lantern into a certain pond. The other parts of the statement were not given in evidence.

***Note.*—The rule as above stated is apparently considered correct now, although earlier cases are inconsistent with it. Such rule apparently gives the prisoner away altogether in such cases, notwithstanding that the confession was extorted.**

But the finding of articles, etc., in consequence of the confession certainly appears to render it trustworthy.

DECLARATIONS BY DECEASED PERSONS.

It has long been recognised that the exclusion of evidence of statements made by deceased persons would frequently lead to a defeat of justice. **In the six following instances** the law recognises that there is sufficient guarantee of the credibility of such hearsay statements to allow that they shall be **admitted as evidence:—**

1. Declarations in course of duty.
2. ,, against interest.
3. ,, as to pedigree.
4. ,, ,, public rights.
5. ,, ,, cause of death.
6. ,, ,, contents of wills.

For the principle underlying these exceptions, see the remarks of Jessel, M.R., *post*, p. 253.

The **Evidence Act, 1938,** has greatly increased the area of admissibility, but the Act is cumulative upon and expressly preserves the common law rules dealt with here.

It should be observed that, although the term "declaration" may suggest rather a formal statement, yet statements made in any manner are generally admissible.

The cases in which such declarations are admissible vary according to their nature, but it would appear that declarations in course of duty and against interest are admissible on any matter in issue whatever; those as to pedigree, only in pedigree cases (see *post*, p. 228); those as to public rights in cases of strictly public rights (see *post*, p. 235); those as to cause of death in cases of homicide (see *post*, p. 246); and those as to contents of wills in cases in which questions arise as to such contents (see *Phipson*, 271).

DECLARATIONS IN COURSE OF DUTY.

PRICE v. TORRINGTON.

NISI PRIUS. 1703.

1 SALKELD 285; 2 LD. RAYMOND 873; HOLT 300.

Statements made by a person in the regular course of his business or duty are admissible evidence, after his death, of the facts stated. Such statements are known as "declarations in the course of duty".

The following is from Lord Raymond:—

In *indebitatus assumpsit* for beer sold and delivered to the defendant, upon *non assumpsit* pleaded, at the trial at *Guildhall* before *Holt* chief justice, the evidence against the defendant was, that **the usual way of the plaintiff's trading was,** that the drayman came every night to the plaintiff's clerk, and gave account to him of all the beer that he had delivered that day; and an **entry was made of it in a book, which the drayman and clerk subscribed;** and that there was such an entry of —— barrels of beer delivered to the defendant, etc., and that **the drayman was dead,** and the subscription was proved to be of his writing.

HOLT, C.J., held this good evidence to charge the defendant.

The following is from Salkeld:—

The plaintiff, being a brewer, brought an action against the Earl of Torrington for beer sold and delivered, and the evidence given to charge the defendant was, that **the usual way of the plaintiff's dealing was** that the draymen came every night to the clerk of the brewhouse and gave him **an account** of the beer they had delivered out, which he **set down in a book kept for that purpose, to which the draymen set their hands**; and that **the drayman was dead,** but that this was his hand set to the book; and this was held good evidence of a delivery; otherwise of the shop-book itself, without more.

Note.—This is one of the earliest reported decisions on an evidence point. It will be noted that it implies already a fairly developed law about hearsay.

DOE d. PATTESHALL v. TURFORD.

KING'S BENCH. 1832.

3 B. & Ad. 890; 37 R. R. 581.

A declaration in the course of duty is admissible although the duty was only temporarily assumed by the person who made such declaration, if it be proved that there was in fact such a duty upon another person whose duty was thus assumed for the occasion.

In consequence of the absence of his clerk, a solicitor, named Patteshall, had on one occasion performed the clerk's duty for him, and served and indorsed a notice as his clerk would have done. The indorsement of service on such notice was admissible as evidence of service.

Lord Tenterden, C.J. . . . **I take it to be proved that the practice** in Messrs. Bellamy and Patteshall's office **was that any person who undertook to serve a notice to quit, indorsed** on the duplicate, at the time of the service, **the fact** of his having served the original. Notices to quit were usually served by the clerks, and not by the principals; but a principal might occasionally serve such a notice, and **we must assume that when a principal served the notice, he would do what he required his clerk to do.** Now, here it is proved that Patteshall took the notice with him when he went out, and that the indorsement on it is in his handwriting. Then **the indorsement, having been made in the discharge of his duty, was,** according to the authority cited, **admissible evidence** of the fact of the service of the original.

LITTLEDALE, J. . . . If the notice in question had been served by a deceased clerk, his indorsement on the duplicate, coupled with **proof of the practice of the office,** would have been sufficient evidence of the service. Then the next question is, whether Patteshall having served it himself, his indorsement is tantamount to a clerk's. I think it is; for **it must be assumed that he would do what he required his clerk to do. . . .**

PARKE, J. . . . The only question in the case is, whether the entry made by Mr. Patteshall was admissible in evidence, and I think it was, not on the ground that it was an entry against his own interest, but because the fact that such an entry was made at the time of his return from his journey was one of the chain of facts (there are many others) from which the delivery of the notice to quit might lawfully be inferred. . . . **It was proved to be the ordinary course of this office** that when notices to quit were served, indorsements like that in question were made; **and it is to be presumed that** Mr. Patteshall, **one of the principals, observed the rule of the office** as well as the clerks. . . .

TAUNTON, J. . . . A minute in writing like the present, made at the time when the fact it records took place, by a person since deceased, in the ordinary course of his business, corroborated by other circumstances which render it probable that that fact occurred, is admissible in evidence. . . .

Note.—But, although the duty may thus, apparently, be assumed for the occasion by a principal, it seems that a mere personal custom of a principal, to do a certain act and to record it, would not be sufficient. There must, it is said, be a *duty towards another person,* to do and to record the matter in question. See *Massey* v. *Allen*, 13 Ch. D. 558; *Simon* v. *Simon*, [1936] P. 17.

THE HENRY COXON.

ADMIRALTY. 1878.

L. R. 3 P. D. 156; 47 L. J. Adm. 83; 38 L. T. 819.

Declarations in the course of duty, in order to be admissible, must be contemporaneous, must be made by a person who has no interest to misrepresent, and must relate to his own acts only.

In an action against the owners of a ship for collision, entries made in the log book of a ship by the first mate, since deceased, were rejected on three grounds: (1) they were made two days after the occurrence recorded, whereas the "duty" was to make them immediately; (2) the first mate had an interest to misrepresent, so as to negative the idea of negligence of himself and the ship's crew; (3) the entries referred not only to his own acts, but to those of the crew, and such declarations are not admissible as to the acts of others.

The following is from the Law Journal:—

Sir Robert Phillimore, J. . . . Neither do I think that the entry can be considered as **contemporaneous**; also it was in the **interest** of the party who made it; and the authorities point to this, that when such evidence is admitted, it must relate to **acts done by the person who makes the entry and not by others,** but the mate must enter, not only the manœuvres on his own ship, but also the consequences of the manœuvres and navigation of the other ship. These different sets of facts are so inextricably mixed up that it is very difficult, if not impossible, to separate them. I therefore, **for these reasons, reject** this evidence. . . .

Note.—The case of *Mercer* v. *Denne*, [1904] 2 Ch. 534, 540-2, illustrates the point that the acts recorded must be those of the declarant and not of other persons.

With regard to log books, the provisions of the Merchant Shipping Act, 1894, ss. 239, 240, should be noticed (see *post*, p. 476). It will be observed that entries in the "official log" required thereby to be kept must be made "as soon as possible after the occurrence".

CHAMBERS v. BERNASCONI.

EXCHEQUER CHAMBER. 1834.

3 L. J. Ex. 373; 1 C. M. & R. 347; 4 Tyr. 531; 40 R. R. 604.

Declarations in the course of duty are evidence only of the precise facts which it was the writer's duty to state or record, and not of other matters which, though contained in the same statement, were merely collateral.

The question being whether A was arrested in a certain parish; a certificate by a deceased officer, stating the fact, time and place of the arrest, was held inadmissible, as to the place, it being his duty merely to record the fact and time, not the place of his arrest.

The following is from the Law Journal:—

Lord Denman, C.J. (*delivering the judgment of the Court*, Lord Denman and Tindal, C.JJ., Littledale, Taunton, Patteson, Parke, Gaselee and Bosanquet, JJ.). . . . We are all of opinion that, whatever effect may be due to an entry made in the course of any office reporting facts necessary to the performance of a duty, **the statement of other circumstances, however naturally they might be thought to find a place in the narrative, is no proof of those circumstances.** Admitting, then, for the sake of argument, that the entry tendered was evidence of the fact, and even of the day when the arrest was made (both which facts it might be necessary for the officer to make known to his principal), we are all clearly of opinion that **it is not admissible to prove in what particular spot** within the bailiwick the caption took place, **that circumstance being merely collateral** to the duty done.

Note.—It was shown in the above case to be the actual custom and practice of the officer to record the place of arrest, although it was not his strict duty to do so. This case has been much questioned. See, for instance, the observations in *Smith's Leading Cases*, 13th ed., II, 281. But, in the later case of *Smith* v. *Blakey*, L. R. 2 Q. B. 326, Blackburn, J., said—"It is an essential fact to render such an entry admissible, that not only it should have been made in the due discharge of the business about which the person is employed, but the duty must be to do the very thing to which the entry relates, and then to make a report or record of it."

With regard to declarations against interest a different rule as to the extent of the admissibility of the declaration has been laid down —the whole being admissible (see *post*, pp. 219-20).

R. v. BUCKLEY.

CHESTER ASSIZES. 1873.

13 Cox 293.

Declarations in the course of duty may be either written or oral.

The question being whether A murdered B, a policeman, at a certain time and place; a verbal report made by B in the course of his duty to his inspector, that he was about to go to that place at that time, in order to watch A's movements, was, by Lush, J., held admissible evidence to show that the prisoner and the deceased had met on that occasion.

DECLARATIONS AGAINST INTEREST.

1. PECUNIARY INTEREST.

HIGHAM v. RIDGWAY.

KING'S BENCH. 1808.

10 East 109; 10 R. R. 235.

Statements made by a person against his "pecuniary" interest are admissible evidence, after his death, not only of the facts against such interest, but also of all other

facts in the same statement. Such statements are known as "declarations against interest".

Any statement by a person tending to show that he owes money, or has received money owing to him, is considered to be against his interest in this sense.

An entry made by a deceased surgeon, who had delivered a woman of a child, of his having done so on a certain day, and referring to his ledger, in which he had made a charge for his attendance which was marked as "paid", was held evidence of the date of birth of such child; the word "paid" being held to be a statement against the pecuniary interest of the surgeon, as affording evidence against him if he had sued for his charges. All the facts stated in the same entry including those in the ledger to which it referred, which were considered part of the same entry, were held admissible in evidence.

LORD ELLENBOROUGH, C.J. . . . I think the evidence here was properly admitted, upon the broad principle on which receiver's books have been admitted; namely, that **the entry made was in prejudice of the party making it.** In the case of the receiver, he charges himself to account for so much to his employer. In this case **the party repelled by his entry a claim which he would otherwise have had upon the other for work performed,** and medicines furnished to the wife; and the period of her delivery is the time for which the former charge is made, the date of which is April 22; when it appears by other evidence that the man-midwife was in fact attending at the house of Wm. Fowden. If this entry had been produced when the party was making a claim for his attendance, it would have been evidence against him that his claim was satisfied. **It is idle to say that the word "paid" only shall be admitted in evidence, without the context, which explains to what it refers**; we must, therefore, look to the rest of the entry, to see what the demand was which he thereby admitted to be discharged. By the reference to the ledger, the entry there is virtually incorporated with and made a part of the other entry of which it is explanatory. . . . **The discharge** in the book in his own handwriting **repels the claim which he would otherwise have had** against the father from the rest of the evidence as it now appears. **Therefore, the entry made by the party was to his own immediate prejudice,** when he had not only no interest to make it, if it were not true, but he had an interest the other way, not to discharge a claim, which it appears from the evidence that he had. . . .

LE BLANC, J. **On inquiring into the truth of facts which happened a long time ago, the Courts have varied from the strict rules of evidence** applicable to facts of the same description happening in modern times, because of the difficulty or impossibility, by lapse of time, of proving those facts in the ordinary way by living witnesses. On this ground, **hearsay and reputation** (which latter is no other than the hearsay of those who may be supposed to have been acquainted with the fact, handed down from one to another) **have been admitted as evidence in particular cases.** On that principle stands the evidence, in cases of pedigree, of declarations of the family who are dead, or of monumental inscriptions, or of entries made by them in family Bibles. The like evidence has been admitted in other cases **where the Court were satisfied that the person whose written entry or hearsay was offered** in evidence, had no interest in falsifying the fact, but, on the contrary, **had an interest against his declaration or written entry;** as in the case of receiver's books. . . . Here the entries were made by a person who, so far from having any interest to make them, had an interest the other way; and such entries against the interest of the party making them are clearly evidence of the fact stated. . . .

BAYLEY, J. This is no officious entry made by one who had no concern in the transaction; he had no interest in making it; and as **he thereby discharged an individual against whom he would otherwise have had a claim,** I think the entry was evidence by all the authorities. . . . **If he had brought an action for his work,** and had received notice to produce his books, **this entry would have discharged the father.** Now, all the cases agree that a written entry, by which a man discharges another of a claim which he had against him, or charges himself with the debt of another, is evidence of the fact which he so admits against himself, there being no interest of his own to advance by such entry. . . .

GROSE, J., concurred.

Note.—It should be particularly observed that such statements, in order to be admissible, must be against "pecuniary" or "proprietary" interest. It is not sufficient, for instance, that the statement was made under circumstances which show that the person making it would be liable to a criminal prosecution (*Sussex Peerage*

Case, 11 C. & F. 108); although that would seem to be a case in which he would be liable to a pecuniary penalty, by way of fine, or to something admittedly worse, *i.e.*, imprisonment.

The entry in the above case must not be confounded with a declaration in "course of duty", as there was no duty towards another person to make such entry (see *ante*, p. 213).

The above case and the next one refer to pecuniary interest, the two subsequent cases to proprietary interest.

TAYLOR v. WITHAM.

CHANCERY. 1876.

L. R. 3 Ch. D. 605; 45 L. J. Ch. 798.

If any part of a statement by a deceased person is against such person's pecuniary interest, the whole statement is admissible, even such part thereof as prove to be actually in such person's interest. But though admissible, it may be of no weight as evidence.

The question being whether A (deceased) had lent money to B; an entry by A in his book, "B paid me three months' interest", followed by other entries connected therewith, and pointing to such a loan, was held admissible as evidence of the loan. The entry of such payment, by itself being against interest, was held to render admissible all the other entries, although the latter were actually for the declarant's interest.

The following is from the Law Reports:—

Jessel, M.R. . . . It is, no doubt, an established rule in the Courts of this country that **an entry against the interest of the man who made it is receivable in evidence after his death for all purposes.** . . . Of course, if you can prove *aliunde* that the man had a particular reason for making it, and that it was for his interest, you may destroy the value of the evidence altogether, but **the question of admissibility is not a question of value. The entry may be utterly worthless when you get it,** if you show any reason to believe that he had a motive for making it, and that though apparently against his interest, yet really it was for it; but that is a matter for subsequent consideration when you estimate the value of the testimony. . . .

Why should a man enter in his book **" Interest paid me ",** intending to make **an entry** for himself, and not against himself? Obviously the natural meaning of it is that it is **against himself.** " Interest " standing alone would not help him; but these entries appear to be **connected with two other entries:** " December 27. **Paid off £20 ";** that is, against his interest, but following that there is this, **" Left £1,980 ",** and that enables you to carry your eye to the connecting entry, which is, " January, 1872. J. Witham acknowledged **loan to this date £2,000 ",** and then y u see you connect the entries with the £1,980. No doubt, if admissible, it becomes very important evidence by reason of connecting it with the rest of the entry, but the entry itself is only an entry, " Interest paid me ". It would not, standing alone, have been evidence of a debt from any particular person independent of the connection, and it appears to me when a man puts **" Interest paid me ",** or **" Paid off £20 ",** it is *prima facie* **a clear entry against interest which ought to be admitted,** and I admit it on the general ground. But, independently of the general ground, there is proof that the £2,000 was paid to J. Witham, and there is proof that every one of these four sums of £20 was actually paid to the testator, so that here again we have this fact, that there are entries not standing alone, but connected with the facts proved. I have no hesitation in saying that it is not only admissible as evidence, but is evidence of a very material character.

Note.—This rule as to the admissibility of the whole declaration should be compared with the rule that, in the case of declarations in course of duty, only so much thereof as it was strictly the declarant's duty to state is legally admissible (see *ante*, p. 215).

There has been some conflict of opinion as to whether it is sufficient to show that the declaration is *prima facie* against interest, or whether it must be shown that it never could be made available for the declarant. Hamilton, L.J. (afterwards Lord Sumner) in *Lloyd* v. *Powell Duffryn Steam Coal Co.* ([1913] 2 K. B., at p. 137) expressed the view that the latter was the better opinion, but this has been questioned (see *Phipson*, p. 270); and in *Re Adams* ([1922] P. 240) a declaration which was *prima facie* against interest was admitted, and evidence was rejected that in the circumstances in which it was made it was in fact to the declarant's advantage.

It should also be noted that the above cases only deal with the question of *admissibility* of such evidence, not its *weight*, which is quite another matter.

2. PROPRIETARY INTEREST.

PEACEABLE v. WATSON.

COMMON PLEAS. 1811.

4 TAUNTON 16; 13 R. R. 552.

Statements made by a person against his "proprietary" interest are admissible evidence after his death.

Statements made by any one in possession of land tending to limit his interest therein to any less estate than a fee simple are admissible as declarations against his proprietary interest, possession being evidence of ownership in fee simple, until the contrary appears.

In an action of ejectment, in order to prove the seisin of a person through whom the plaintiff claimed, a witness was asked whether he had ever heard one Clarke (since deceased) say of whom he rented certain houses; but the identity of the houses was not established. Grose, J., rejected the evidence and nonsuited the plaintiff. A new trial was granted on the ground appearing below.

SIR J. MANSFIELD, C.J. The opinion of Grose, J., is unanswerable. The ground of the rejection is this. **Possession is** *prima facie* **evidence of seisin in fee simple; the declaration** of the possessor that he is tenant to another **makes most strongly, therefore, against his own interest,** and consequently is admissible, but it must be first shown that he was in possession of the premises for which the ejectment is brought. The learned Judge's report, however, seems to go further, and to intimate that he should have rejected the evidence of the declarations whether there had or had not been other evidence to identify the premises which Clarke held, as those that were sued for.

Note.—This rule is based on the rule that possession of land is evidence of ownership in fee simple (see *ante*, p. 92). Otherwise it would be impossible to say that any statement was against the occupier's proprietary interest. The statement of a deceased lord of a manor, as to the extent of the manor, was rejected in a suit between different parties on the ground that as he disclaimed part but affirmed title to some other part, there was nothing necessarily against his interest (*Crease* v. *Barrett*, 1 C. M. & R. 919). The essence of the matter is that the man in possession of a close is presumed the owner in fee simple till he is shown to have done or said something which rebuts that presumption. The principle affords no help where the declaration relates not to the quality of the estate but the area of the close.

PAPENDICK v. BRIDGWATER.

QUEEN'S BENCH. 1855.

24 L. J. Q. B. 289; 3 W. R. 490; 1 Jur. (n.s.) 657; 5 E. & B. 166.

A declaration against proprietary interest is admissible only against those persons who are privy to the estate of the person making it.

A declaration by a deceased tenant of a farm, to the effect that he was not entitled to common of pasture in respect of the farm, was held not to be admissible in evidence against the reversioner, his landlord.

The following is from the Law Journal:—

Lord Campbell, C.J. . . . **You cannot receive in evidence a declaration of a tenant which derogates from the title of the landlord. Such evidence, if receivable, would be most mischievous,** because a tenant might thus destroy a valuable easement or be enabled to impose a servitude.

Coleridge, J. . . . **Nothing, I think, would lead to greater inconvenience than that the landlord by loose declarations of his tenant should be ousted of his rights and burthened with a servitude. . . .**

Erle, J. . . . This does not come within any of the exceptions which were introduced for general convenience, such as entries made in discharge of legal duty, or in the course of business, nor, what is more apposite, declarations binding privies. . . . **This kind of evidence is of a most dangerous character, because, though** *prima facie* **it is against the interest of the declarant, it is easy to suggest** circumstances under which a tenant going out from one farm and coming into another might wish to burden the farm he was about to leave, with a view to benefit the latter, and be induced to make **a declaration** which, under the actual circumstances, was not against his interest at the moment, but **in furtherance of it.** I am, therefore, of opinion that we ought not to extend the exception to this case.

Note.—These cases as to declarations against proprietary interest should be compared with the case as to admissions by predecessors in title, *Woolway* v. *Rowe*, *ante*, p. 195.

DECLARATIONS AS TO PEDIGREE.

BERKELEY PEERAGE CASE.

HOUSE OF LORDS. 1811.

4 Campbell 401; 14 R. R. 782.

In "pedigree cases" the statements, oral or written, and conduct of deceased persons, who were related by blood or marriage with the family in question, if made "ante litem motam", are admissible to prove relationship, or family succession, or facts upon which such matters depend, such as births, marriages and deaths.

Entries in family Bibles, being looked on as family registers, to which the family have general access, are of special weight in this connection.

Such statements and conduct are known as "declarations as to pedigree".

In a claim before the Committee of Privileges of the House of Lords, the legitimacy of the claimant was disputed, the question being whether his parents were privately married before his birth. The Judges were summoned to give their opinions upon the following questions submitted to them by the Lords.

1. "Upon the trial of an ejectment respecting Black Acre, between A and B, in which it was necessary for A to prove that he was the legitimate son of J S, A after proving by other evidence that J S was his reputed father, offered to give in evidence *a deposition* made by J S in a cause in Chancery, instituted by A against C D, in order to perpetuate testimony to the alleged fact disputed by C D, that he was the legitimate son of J S, in which character he claimed an estate in remainder in White Acre, which was also claimed in remainder by C D. B, the defendant in the ejectment, did not claim Black Acre under either A or C D, the plaintiff and defendant in the Chancery suit.

"According to law, could the deposition of J S be received upon the trial of such ejectment, against B, as evidence of declarations of J S the alleged father in matters of pedigree?

2. "Upon the trial of an ejectment respecting Long Acre, between E and F, in which it was necessary for E to prove that he was the legitimate son of W, the said W being at that time dead, E after proving by other evidence that W was his reputed father, offered to give in evidence *an entry in a Bible* in which Bible W had made such entry in his own handwriting, that E was his eldest son, born in lawful wedlock from G, the wife of W, on the 1st day of May, 1778, and signed by W himself.

"Could such entry in such Bible be received to prove that E is the legitimate son of W, as evidence of the declaration of W in matter of pedigree?

3. "Upon the trial of an ejectment respecting Little Acre, between N. and P., in which it was necessary for N. to prove that he was the legitimate son of T., the said T. being at that time dead; N., after proving by other evidence that T. was his reputed father, offered to give in evidence *an entry in a Bible*, in which Bible T. had made such entry in his own handwriting that N. was his eldest son, born in lawful wedlock from J., the wife of T., on the 1st day of May, 1778, and signed by T. himself; and it was proved in evidence on the said trial that the said T. had declared: that he, T., had made such entry for the express purpose of establishing the legitimacy, and the time of the birth, of his eldest son N., in case the same

should be called in question, in any case or in any cause whatsoever, by any person, after the death of him the said T.

"Could such entry in such Bible be received, to prove that N. is the legitimate son of T., as evidence of the declaration of T. in matter of pedigree?"

In the opinion of the majority of the Judges, the deposition, referred to in the first question, was inadmissible, as it was made after the dispute had arisen, *post litem motam*, when the party making the same had an interest to misrepresent the facts.

In the unanimous opinion of the Judges, the entries in the Bibles, referred to in the second and third questions, were admissible, as they were made *ante litem motam*; the entry, however, referred to in the third question being liable to suspicion on account of the reason stated therein for the making of it. The Lords gave judgment accordingly.

Lord Eldon, L.C. . . . **There does seem a hardship in rejecting the declarations** of the late *Lord Berkeley* after the dispute had arisen; **for there was no way in which the claimant** as heir apparent to his **titles could have availed himself of his testimony. . . .** Upon the admissibility of this evidence, Judges have held different opinions, and it might appear remarkable that a declaration under no sanction was receivable, and a declaration upon oath was not. . . . **The previous existence of the dispute would be a sufficient ground to proceed upon.** I have known no instance in which declarations *post litem motam* have been received. . . . Therefore, although the authorities are at variance, **principle and practice unite in rejecting the evidence.**

I introduced *the Bible* into the second and third questions, as the book in which such entries are usually made. If the entry be the ordinary act of a man in the ordinary course of life, without interest or particular motive, this, as **the spontaneous effusion of his own mind, may be looked at without suspicion, and received without objection. Such is the contemporaneous entry in a family Bible, by a father, of the birth of a child.** But a doubt had been entertained upon this point, and it was fit that it should be solemnly decided. **I agree to the admissibility of similar entries in other books.** There is a great difference between the competency of evidence and the credit to which it is entitled.

LORD ELLENBOROUGH, C.J. I had conceived some doubts whether **this deposition could not be received as a declaration:** but the arguments of the learned Judges have convinced me that it is inadmissible. It is only the answer to particular interrogatories, and may be very different from the genuine reputation upon the subject. I agree with the Judges that **an entry made in a Bible** does not therefore become evidence; but I cannot say it is not greatly **strengthened by being found there, that being the ordinary register in families. . . .**

LORD REDESDALE. The circumstance of an entry being in **a family Bible, to which all the family have access,** gives it that solidity which it would not have if made in a book which remained in the exclusive possession of the father. Entries in family Bibles have therefore become **common evidence of pedigree** in this country; and in America, where there is no register of births or baptisms, hardly any other is known. **With regard to the main question of the admissibility of the deposition** as a declaration, one circumstance is in my mind decisive. In cases of reputation, the attorney takes down what old witnesses will prove, and it often happens that some of them afterwards die before the trial. But what was taken down from their mouths is never offered in evidence. And why? Because **declarations post litem motam are not receivable. . . .**

BUTLER v. MOUNTGARRETT.

HOUSE OF LORDS. 1859.

7 H. L. CASES 633; 115 R. R. 306.

A controversy in a family, though not at that moment the subject of a lawsuit, is sufficient to exclude evidence of declarations as to pedigree made at the time of such controversy, on the ground that they were not made "ante litem motam".

There was offered in evidence a letter written by one member of the family to another, stating that the writer said he knew of a certain alleged marriage, material to the issue. This letter itself showed that a dispute had then arisen with reference to such marriage. It was held inadmissible as evidence.

LORD CAMPBELL, L.C. . . . The question is this, whether there had been a marriage in *Scotland* between *Henry Butler* and *Mrs. Colebrooke.* It was to prove that there had been such a marriage that the letter was proposed to be given in evidence. Had there not been a controversy upon that subject before the letter was written? And at the time when the letter was written, did it not subsist?

It was for the Judge to say whether the letter was admissible or inadmissible, and in order to come to a right conclusion upon that question he was to **consider whether there was evidence of lis mota, independently of the letter.** And, **moreover, he was bound** to look at the letter, and to read it, and **to see from its contents whether it was admissible or not.** Without entering minutely into the evidence, I think that there was, independently of thé letter, evidence to show that **before the letter was written there had been a controversy in the Butler family** as to whether there had been this *Scotch* marriage or not. But the letter itself, I think, is quite conclusive on the subject, because the whole scope of it shows that there had been such a controversy. And it was in my opinion **a controversy which was likely to create a bias** one way or the other upon the mind of every member of the family. . . . It was a matter of great interest to them, as to which no doubt each might take one side or another; and, according to the established rules of the law of *England*, if there is such a controversy, it is supposed to create a bias upon the minds of those who make statements upon the subject, and **it renders hearsay evidence upon the subject inadmissible. . . .**

LORD BROUGHAM. . . . If the letter had been produced and tendered, and there had been nothing else in the cause to lead the learned Judge's mind to the conclusion of the existence of *lis mota* at the time, and if he had therefore admitted the letter, **the moment that letter was read, it would so clearly have proved that there was a lis mota at the time, that it must at once have been struck out of the evidence.**

LORD CRANWORTH. . . . **If the letter itself shows that at that time there was a lis mota, then the letter is inadmissible.** Now, upon the question whether this letter does show that or not, it appears to me that not only does it show that, but it shows nothing else. . . . It appears to me that to admit that letter would be directly at variance with the principle upon which this sort of evidence is received, and which is stated by Lord *Eldon* to be, that **such declarations are admitted upon the ground that they are the natural effusions of parties who must know the truth, "upon occasions when their minds stand in an even position without any temptation to exceed or to fall short of the truth".** As to every one of these propositions, the case here would fail. . . .

LORD CHELMSFORD. . . . The very commencement of the letter shows that the parties were entering into a consideration of the state of the family with reference to the devolution of the honours and the estates which were involved in the discussion. The writer of the letter says, "I think it fair and just to tell you what I know of the circumstances connected with Henry and Mrs. Colebrooke". Then **it was for the Judge to determine whether the letter itself, if there was no other evidence in the case, was not sufficient to establish the fact of there being a lis mota.** The learned Judge was of that opinion, and rejected the evidence. I think the learned Judge was perfectly justified in so doing. **I think the letter shows, in the strongest possible way, that there was a controversy existing. . . .**

LORD WENSLEYDALE concurred.

HAINES v. GUTHRIE.

QUEEN'S BENCH. 1884.

L. R. 13 Q. B. D. 818; 53 L. J. Q. B. 521; 51 L. T. 645; 33 W. R. 99; 48 J. P. 756.

A "pedigree case", in which evidence of declarations by deceased relations is admissible, must be one in which the question of pedigree or relationship is directly in issue. In such cases only, any fact upon which such

relationship depends may be so proved, e.g., the date of a birth.

In an action for goods sold, to which the defence of infancy was pleaded, the date of birth being thus in question, a declaration made by defendant's deceased father as to such date was not admissible, it not being a pedigree case. If it had been, then such fact could have been proved thus.

The following is from the Law Journal:—

Brett, M.R. . . . It is obvious that in this case the question of family is immaterial, that the question whose son the defendant was is immaterial, and so were all such questions as whether he was a legitimate or a natural son, an elder or a younger son, or as to what relation he occupied with regard to the rest of the family. **There was, therefore, no question which could be called a question of family;** the only question is, what was the date of the birth . . .?

This evidence is *prima facie* hearsay evidence, and the general rule of law is that hearsay evidence is not admissible; it is therefore sought to bring this case within some recognised exception to that rule. . . . The exception which applies to this case is that the evidence is admissible in cases where it is a question of pedigree. **Here there is no question as to pedigree, no question as to descent, none as to relationship, none as to the position of any person in any family**—all these questions are wholly immaterial—so that in this case no question of pedigree could arise, and therefore this case does not fall within the recognised exception to the general rule of evidence. . . .

Bowen, L.J. . . . **No question is raised as to the family of the defendant, or as to his position in that family;** the only question raised was as to the age of this particular individual.

Fry, L.J. . . . **The exception is confined to questions of pedigree, and no such question is raised in this case. . . .**

Note.—The evidence of the date of birth in this case was rejected merely on the ground that it was not a "pedigree case", *i.e.*, not a case in which a question of relationship was in issue. If it had been such a case, then the date of birth would have been a proper matter to prove in such manner.

"Matters of pedigree" are legitimacy, celibacy, intestacy, failure of issue and the like. The rule applies in petitions under the Legitimacy Act, 1926 (*Re Davy*, [1935] P. 1).

JOHNSON v. LAWSON.

COMMON PLEAS. 1824.

2 Bingham 86; 9 Moore 183; 27 R. R. 558.

Declarations as to pedigree must have been made by, or with the approval of, members of the family. If made by servants or intimate acquaintances, whatever their position or knowledge, they are not admissible, unless adopted by the family.

The question being, who was heir-at-law of one Henry Lidgbird, it was proposed to give in evidence declarations by a person, then deceased, who had been his housekeeper for twenty-four years. Such declarations were held inadmissible.

The following is from Bingham:—

Best, C.J. . . . As a general rule, hearsay is not admissible evidence, but to this general rule pedigree-causes form an exception, from the very nature of the case. **Facts must be spoken of which took place many years before the trial, and of these, traditional evidence is often the only evidence which can be obtained;** but evidence of that kind must be subject to limitation, otherwise it would be a source of great uncertainty, and the limitation hitherto pursued, namely, the **confining such evidence to the declarations of relations of the family, affords a rule at once certain and intelligible.** If the admissibility of such evidence were not so restrained, we should on every occasion, before the testimony could be admitted, have to enter upon a long inquiry as to the degree of intimacy or confidence that subsisted between the party and the deceased declarant. . . . If we look into the cases, we shall find that **the rule has always been confined to the declarations of kindred** . . . it has been carried as far as it can with safety, and we must not extend it farther.

Park, J. . . . It has been urged that great **confidence is often reposed in servants; but it is not confidence of this kind,** nor is it usual for a man to confer with his domestics on the situation of the various members of his family. My objection to the proposed evidence is, that if it were to be admitted, the practice would be so loose as to occasion great inconvenience; whereas, if the rule be confined to members of a family, the path to be pursued is clear and certain. . . .

Burrough, J. . . . This exception from the general rule, that hearsay shall not be admitted, must be construed strictly, and **the natural limits of it are the declarations of members of the family. If we go beyond, where are we to stop?** Is the declaration of a groom to be admitted? of a steward? of a chambermaid? of a nurse? may it be admitted if made a week after they have joined the family? and if not, at what time after? **We should have to try in every case the life and habits of the party who made the declaration,** and on account of this uncertainty such evidence must be excluded. . . .

Note.—It might well be that an old family servant had greater knowledge of the family affairs than a member of the family had; but it is considered that a servant would not have the same interest in keeping up a correct record of the family. Also, the admission of a servant's evidence would, as Burrough, J., said in the above case, involve the further inquiry as to the position and means of knowledge of the servant, after he was dead; not an easy matter.

DOE v. GRIFFIN.

KING'S BENCH. 1812.

15 East 293; 13 R. R. 474.

Declarations in pedigree cases are not confined to matters within the personal knowledge of the deceased relation or declarant. The matter stated may be mere family tradition or reputation, or hearsay upon hearsay, so long as it is confined to the statements and belief of deceased members of the family. Even a statement to the effect that there was absence of information in a family concerning one of its members would be admissible.

In an ejectment case the question arose whether a certain person had died without issue. Evidence by an elderly lady, one of the family, was admitted to the effect that the person in question "had many years before, when a young man, gone abroad, and according to the repute of the family, had afterwards died in the West Indies, and that she had never heard in the family of his having been married".

LORD ELLENBOROUGH, C.J. The evidence was sufficient to call upon the defendant to give *prima facie* evidence at least that Thomas was married; for what other evidence could the lessor be expected to produce that Thomas was not married, than that none of the family had ever heard that he was?

GOODRIGHT v. MOSS.

KING'S BENCH. 1777.

COWPER 591.

Declarations as to pedigree may be in any form, oral, written, carved on tombstones, inscribed on portraits, or on written or printed pedigrees, or even by conduct, as, for instance, by treating a child as legitimate or otherwise.

In an action of ejectment, the question was whether a certain person was the legitimate child of his parents. Declarations by his father and mother, then deceased, that he was born before marriage were held admissible.

LORD MANSFIELD, C.J. . . . The question is, whether the declarations of the father and mother in their lifetime can be admitted in evidence after their death? **Tradition is sufficient in point of pedigree; circumstances may be proved. For instance,** suppose from the hour of one child's birth to the death of its parent, it had always been **treated as illegitimate,** and another introduced and considered as the heir of the family; that would be good evidence. An entry in a father's **family Bible,** an inscription on a **tombstone,** a

pedigree hung up in the family mansion, are all good evidence. So the declarations of parents in their lifetime. . . .

Aston and Willes, JJ., concurred.

Note.—Inscriptions on tombstones, portraits, etc., would naturally be made by strangers, but with family approval, and would amount to declarations by relations.

The above case was thus commented on by Lord Eldon in *Whitelocke* v. *Baker*, 13 Ves. 514: "I accede to the doctrine of Lord Mansfield, as it has been stated from Cowper; but it must be understood, as it has been practised, and acted upon; and one word in that passage wants explanation. It was not the opinion of Lord Mansfield, or of any Judge, that tradition, generally, is evidence of pedigree; the tradition must be from persons having such a connection with the party to whom it relates that it is natural and likely, from their domestic habits and connections, that they are speaking the truth, and that they could not be mistaken.

DECLARATIONS AS TO PUBLIC AND GENERAL RIGHTS.

WEEKS v. SPARKE.

KING'S BENCH. 1813.

1 M. & S. 679; 14 R. R. 546.

In proof of public or general rights or customs, or matters of public or general interest, statements made by deceased persons of competent knowledge, as to the existence of such rights, etc., and as to the general reputation thereof in the neighbourhood, if made "ante litem motam", are admissible. Such statements are known as "declarations as to public and general rights".

So, on a question of prescriptive right of common, in which many persons had an interest, such evidence was allowed, on the ground that it was, in some degree, a public right. (But see note at end of this case.)

Lord Ellenborough, C.J. The admission of hearsay evidence upon all occasions, whether in matters of public or private right, is somewhat of an anomaly, and forms an exception to the general rules of evidence. **The question here is whether this is a case of a public or merely private right. . . .** I confess myself at a loss fully to understand upon what principle, even in matters of public right, reputation was ever deemed admissible evidence. It is said, indeed, that **upon questions of public right all are interested, and must be presumed conversant with them; and that is the distinction taken between public and private rights;** but I must confess I have not been able to see the force of the principle on which that distinction is founded so clearly as others have done, though I must admit its existence; and it has not been controverted in argument to-day, that **in the case of public rights reputation is to be received in evidence. . . .**

Reputation is in general weak evidence; and when it is admitted, it is the duty of the Judge to impress on the minds of the jury how little conclusive it ought to be, lest it should have more weight with them than it ought to have. . . .

Le Blanc, J. . . . The question arose upon a claim of a prescriptive right of common; such a right as the party alleged to have existed beyond the time of legal memory; and the question is how that right is to be proved. First, it is to be proved by acts of enjoyment within the period of living memory. And when that foundation is laid, then inasmuch **as there cannot be any witnesses to speak to acts of enjoyment beyond the time of living memory, evidence is to be admitted from old persons** (not any old persons, but persons who have been **conversant with the neighbourhood** where the waste lies over which the particular right of common is claimed), **of what they have heard other persons of the same neighbourhood, who are deceased, say respecting the right.** Thus far it is evidence as applicable to this prescriptive right, it being a prescription in which others are concerned as well as the person claiming it; because a right of common is to a certain degree a public right. And the only evidence of reputation which was received was that from persons connected with the district.

In the same manner in questions of pedigree, although they are not of a public nature, the evidence of what persons connected with the family have been heard to say, is received, as to the state of that family. **In like manner, also upon questions of boundary,** though the evidence of perambulations may be considered to a certain degree as evidence of an exercise of the right, yet it has been usual to go further and **admit the evidence of what old persons who are deceased have been heard to say on those occasions.**

The rule generally adopted upon questions either of prescription or custom is this, that after a foundation is once laid of the right by proving acts of ownership, then the evidence of reputation becomes admissible, **such evidence being confined to what old persons who were in a situation to know what these rights are, have been heard to say concerning them.** The issue here was on the prescriptive right of common, and the evidence admitted was as to a right derogatory to that prescriptive right; which must be governed by the same rules.

BAYLEY, J. . . . In cases of prescription, which must have **originated beyond the time of legal memory, and of which it is impossible to establish the claim by evidence of the grant, reputation seems to be admissible,** and therefore for that reason, when instances have been adduced to show the exercise of the right claimed, it is usual to admit it. . . . I take it that where the term " public right " is used, it does not mean public in the literal sense, but is synonymous with general; that is what concerns a multitude of persons. Now this is a general right exercised by a variety of persons, though not a public right of common.

DAMPIER, J. . . . **In public rights it is not disputed that reputation is admissible; and that it has been extended to other rights which cannot be strictly called public,** such as manors, parishes, and a modus, which comes the nearest to this case. That, strictly speaking, is a private right, but has been considered as public, as it regards the admissibility of this species of evidence, because it affects a large number of occupiers within a district. . . .

Note.—The above case is generally taken as the leading one, which first laid down the law clearly, although it has been disapproved of on the point whether the right in question was public or private (see the next case).

Although such evidence is not admissible as to *private* rights, it is admissible both as to *public* and as to *general* rights.

Public rights are those common to all the community, such as rights to use highways, ferries, and public fisheries.

General rights are those common to a considerable class of the community, such as parochial or manorial rights. The latter, however, may be private rights.

It was suggested (but not decided) in *Stoney* v. *Eastbourne R. D. C.*, [1927] 1 Ch. 367, that such declarations are admissible not only in suits which directly concern public or general rights but also where private rights are in question, but those rights are directly dependent upon or flow from public rights, *e.g.*, as in that case, where a breach of covenant for title is alleged because the land sold turns out to have a public right of way on it.

Such declarations may be made in any manner or form, as in oral statements, writings, deeds, depositions, maps, plans, books, presentments of Manorial Courts, or verdicts, judgments, orders or convictions of competent Courts, such as Quarter Sessions.

As to maps and plans, see *Hammond* v. *Bradstreet*, 10 Ex. 390; *Pipe* v. *Fulcher*, 28 L. J. Q. B. 12.

LORD DUNRAVEN v. LLEWELLYN.

EXCHEQUER CHAMBER. 1850.

19 L. J. Q. B. 388; 14 Jur. 1089; 15 Q. B. 791; 81 R. R. 809.

A public or general right, or matter of public or general interest, to be evidenced by reputation, or by declarations of deceased persons, must be one which is common to all persons interested, as to all the inhabitants of a particular manor. A right is not within the rule simply because it is enjoyed by many persons in their own individual capacities, such as a right of common enjoyed by several persons in the same manor in their individual capacities; or an aggregate of private rights.

Evidence of reputation, or declarations, is admissible although no actual enjoyment of the right be proved.

On a question between the lord of a manor and the owner of a freehold estate within the manor, whether a piece of land was part of the lord's waste or part of the defendant's land, after proof had been given that there were many lands held of the manor the tenants of which had always exercised rights of common on the waste of the manor, evidence was offered, on the part of the lord, of declarations of deceased tenants that the land was parcel of the waste. It was held that these declarations were not admissible in evidence, as there is no common law right for all tenants of a manor to have common on the waste of the manor, but that each tenant who has the right has it as an incident by law attached to his particular grant, and that the numerous private rights of common of the several tenants do not compose one public right so as to render evidence of reputation admissible. It was also held that evidence of actual enjoyment of a right need not be given in order to render evidence of reputation admissible.

The following is from the Law Journal:—

PARKE, B. (*delivering the judgment of the Court*, PARKE, ALDERSON and PLATT, BB., MAULE, CRESSWELL and TALFOURD, JJ.). . . . In the course of the argument we intimated our opinion that the **want of evidence of acts of enjoyment of the rights did not affect the admissibility of the evidence, but only its value when admitted.** We also stated that no objection could be made to the evidence, on the ground that it proceeded from persons who had not competent knowledge upon the subject, or from persons who were themselves interested in the question. The main inquiry was, whether this was a subject of a sufficiently public nature to justify the reception of hearsay evidence relating to it.

If this question had been one in which all the inhabitants of the manor, or all the tenants of it, or of a particular district of it, had been interested, reputation from any deceased inhabitant or tenant, or even deceased residents in the manor, would have been admissible, such residents having presumably a knowledge of such local customs; and if there had been a common law right for every tenant of the manor to have common on the wastes of a manor, reputation from any deceased tenant as to the extent of those wastes, and therefore as to any particular land being waste of the manor, would have been admissible. But . . . it is not to be understood that every tenant of a manor has by the common law such a right, but only that certain tenants have a right, not by prescription, but as a right by common law, incident to the grant. . . .

This right, therefore, is not a common right of all tenants, but

belongs only to each grantee of arable land by virtue of his individual grant, and is an incident thereto. . . . We are therefore of opinion that this case is precisely in the same situation as if evidence had been offered that there were many persons, tenants of the manor, who had separate prescriptive rights over the lord's wastes, and **reputation is not admissible in the case of such separate rights,** each being private and depending on each separate prescription, unless the proposition can be supported, that because there are many such rights, the rights have a public character, and the evidence therefore becomes admissible. We think this position cannot be maintained.

It is impossible to say in such a case where the dividing point is. What is the number of rights which is to cause their nature to be changed and to give them a public character? But it is said that **there are cases which have decided that where there are numerous private prescriptive rights, reputation is admissible,** and the case of *Weeks* v. *Sparke* (*ante*, p. 233) is relied upon as establishing that proposition. **The reasons given** by the different Judges in that case **would certainly not be satisfactory at this day. . . .**

We are of opinion, therefore, that the evidence of reputation offered in this case was, according to the well-established rule in the modern cases, inadmissible, as it is in reality in support of a mere private prescription, and **the number of these private rights does not make them to be of a public nature.**

Note.—Matters of public or general interest within the rule under discussion include among others—rights of highway, ferry, fishing, tolls, and landing places; boundaries of towns, parishes, counties, hamlets and manors; manorial, borough or district customs; and rights of common.

R. v. BLISS.

QUEEN'S BENCH. 1837.

7 A. & E. 550; 7 L. J. Q. B. 4; 2 N. & P. 464; W. W. & D. 624; 45 R. R. 757.

Declarations as to public or general rights must relate directly to the existence of the right itself, and not to particular facts which may support or negative it. The latter are liable to be misrepresented or misunderstood.

Thus, the question being whether a road was public or private, a statement made by a deceased resident that he had planted a tree to mark the boundary of the road, was inadmissible.

The following is from Neville and Perry:—

Lord Denman, C.J. . . . Is it then evidence of reputation? Everything which depends upon hearsay should be received with great caution. Hearsay evidence in matters of this sort was received by Lord *Ellenborough* in the first case with great reluctance. It is **only to be received as showing general reputation, and not as evidence of particular facts.** Here the hearsay evidence relates to a particular fact, and therefore is inadmissible. **The statement did not describe the road as public or private.**

Patteson, J. To determine whether it was receivable as evidence of reputation, it is necessary to see what was the issue. It was whether this was or was not a public road. **If the issue had been as to the boundary of a public road it might have been receivable in evidence,** but evidence of reputation as to boundary cannot be given in evidence where the question is whether the road is public or private. **If the witness had said this always was a public road as far as this place, it would have been receivable.** The statement is clearly not receivable as evidence of reputation. . . .

Williams, J. . . . **The declaration in this case related to a particular fact, and was not, therefore, admissible. . . .**

Coleridge, J. . . . No rule is more universal than that statements admissible in evidence on the ground that they are evidence of **reputation must relate to general matters and not to particular facts. . . .**

NEWCASTLE v. BROXTOWE.

KING'S BENCH. 1832.

4 B. & Ad. 273; 1 N. & M. 598.

Persons whose statements are receivable in evidence as declarations as to public and general rights must be shown to have been "competent declarants"; that is, they must have been so situated as to the place in question, by residence, duty or other connection that it may be concluded they had both the means and the motive for giving a true account of the matter.

In order to prove that a public building was within the hundred of Broxtowe, ancient orders made by justices at Quarter Sessions for the county, so describing it, were admissible without proof that such justices resided in the hundred or county, their competency being presumed from their office.

The following is from Neville and Manning:—

Parke, J. (*delivering the judgment of the Court,* Parke, Taunton and Patteson, JJ.). . . . These documents were admitted, not as orders upon matters over which the magistrates had jurisdiction, but *as evidence of reputation*; in that point of view we are of opinion that they were admissible. Four of them contain an express statement, the fifth an implied one, that the Castle (or the Brewhouse, or the Park of Nottingham, which belong to it) is within the wapentake or hundred of Broxtowe. **The statement is made by the justices of the peace assembled in Sessions who, though they were not proved to be resiants within the county or hundred, must from the nature of their offices alone be presumed to have sufficient acquaintance with the subject** to which these declarations relate; and the objection cannot prevail that they were made after a controversy upon that subject had arisen, because there appears to have been no dispute upon the particular question, whether the Castle and its precincts were in the hundred of Broxtowe. **These statements, therefore, fall within the established rule as to the admission of evidence of** *reputation*. . . .

Note.—It would appear, however, that all persons are strictly competent declarants as to public, as distinct from general, rights, as all persons are legally interested in them. But their declarations would be worthless, even if admissible, unless they were shown to have had competent knowledge.

MERCER v. DENNE.

COURT OF APPEAL. 1905.

L. R. [1905] 2 Ch. 538; 74 L. J. Ch. 71.

In an action to establish an immemorial custom for fishermen at Walmer to dry their nets on a plot of land owned by the defendant near the seashore, the defendant tendered the following documents as evidence of reputation: (1) *A Survey* made in 1616 of the reparations required to protect Walmer Castle from the sea, and estimates of the costs thereof; (2) *Depositions* taken in an Information brought by the Attorney-General in 1639 against persons who claimed to be entitled to the Manor of Walmer for destroying a bank between the sea and Walmer and thereby causing expense to the King; (3) *Old Maps and Plans* of the same locality prepared by the Board of Ordnance between 1641 and 1647. All these documents were produced from the War Office, and were tendered to show that the land in question was, at the various dates above mentioned, below high-water mark, so that the custom claimed could not have been immemorial. *Held,* affirming Farwell, J., that none of these documents was admissible.

The following is from the Law Reports:—

[As to No. 1.] Stirling, L.J. It does not appear by whom the survey was made, nor is there any evidence of the instructions given for it, beyond what appears from the document itself. . . . Now the action relates to the existence of a custom for the fishermen of Walmer to dry their nets on a particular plot of land, and the nature of the action is certainly such that evidence of reputation would be admissible. But what is the purpose for which it is sought to have this evidence admitted? The evidence does not in any way relate to the alleged custom, nor even to the plot of land over which the custom is said to be exercisable. It relates to the state of the foreshore adjoining the Castle of Walmer in the early part of the seventeenth century. The object is to establish that at that period the sea flowed twice a day over the *locus in quo*, the plot over which the custom is said to be exercisable, and it is said that, by establishing where the sea flowed at that time, . . . it will be shown that that plot of land was, at that time, subject to the flux and reflux of the sea, and therefore the custom must have arisen at a subsequent date, and consequently does not satisfy the requirements of the law as to period of time at which it began. In my opinion, that is not a matter of reputation. **It is laid down in all the cases that, when reputation is admissible, evidence of particular acts ought not to be allowed** (pp. 561, 564).

[As to No. 2.] VAUGHAN WILLIAMS, L.J. . . . These depositions showed that the sea then came up close to the Castle. . . . The parties to the present action are in no sense the successors of any party to that Information, and, therefore, if these depositions are admissible as against strangers to that proceeding, it can only be, as Farwell, J., said, if they relate to some subject-matter as to which evidence of reputation would be admissible. . . . In my judgment, both *Newcastle* v. *Broxtowe* (*supra*) and *Thomas* v. *Jenkins*, 6 A. & E. 525, go far to show that, as regards evidence of reputation, it is sufficient, when a question arises which is directly affected by the document tendered, if the subject-matter of the reputation is one in which the public is interested. Sometimes the word "public" means the public at large; sometimes it means a section of the public, such as the tenants of a manor, or the conventionary free tenants in the district of Cornwall mentioned in *Rowe* v. *Brenton*, 8 B. & C. 737. Therefore, if it had been shown that these depositions were made by persons to whom it was right to impute knowledge of these matters without any special proof, I should have thought that they might be admitted, not *qua* depositions, but as something written by the deponents in reference to a subject-matter of public interest. Therefore, in my view, **what we have to ask is, first, was the subject-matter dealt with** by that information **one of public interest?** Otherwise these depositions could not be admitted as evidence of reputation against strangers to the information. And the **second question is, were the deponents persons to whom we ought to impute such knowledge of the subject-matter as**

would render their statements evidence of reputation? In *Newcastle* v. *Broxtowe* the documents were orders of magistrates with regard to matters over which it was said they had no judicial jurisdiction, but the orders were made by the justices assembled in session, who, although they were not proved to be residents in the county or hundred, must, it was held, "from the nature and character of their offices, alone, be presumed to have sufficient acquaintance with the subject to which the declarations related". Were, then, these deponents persons to whom knowledge ought to be thus imputed so as to make their statements in their depositions admissible in the present action? In my opinion, they were not; and this being so, I think their depositions were not admissible (pp. 559—560).

Stirling, L.J. In my judgment, **these statements** (as to the flux and reflux of the sea at Walmer Castle) could only be admitted as evidence of reputation, and the matters to which they relate are, for the reasons I have already given with reference to the survey, not matters of reputation, but **are evidence with regard to particular facts** which it is intended to use, not for the purpose of establishing the custom or destroying it, but **from which, by way of inference, the custom is to be negatived.** I think, therefore, that on that ground these depositions are **inadmissible** (p. 567).

[As to No. 3.] Vaughan Williams, L.J. Farwell, J., thought that, so far as **these plans are evidence** at all, they are evidence **of particular facts and not of reputation.** I agree, and I think **they are not admissible in evidence** (pp. 560—561).

Stirling, L.J. For the reasons which I have already given with reference to the other documents, I think these plans are not admissible as evidence of reputation (pp. 567—568).

Note.—The surveys, maps and plans were also held not admissible as Public Documents, *post*, p. 264.

DYING DECLARATIONS.

R. v. JENKINS.

CROWN CASES RESERVED. 1869.

L. R. 1 C. C. R. 187; 38 L. J. M. C. 82; 20 L. T. 372; 17 W. R. 621; 11 Cox C. C. 250.

In trials of homicide, statements made by the deceased person, whose death is the subject of the charge, relating to the cause and circumstances of his death, are admissible in evidence, provided it is clearly proved by the party offering it in evidence that the deceased had at the time abandoned all hope of recovery. Such statements are known as "dying declarations".

The prisoner was charged with the murder of a woman, who, on her death-bed, accused him of the crime. A magistrate's clerk attended her to take down her statement, writing down that it was made "with no hope of my recovery". He then read it over to her, but, before she signed it, she desired the addition of the words "at present", so that the words read "with no hope at present of my recovery". It was held that such statement could not be received in evidence, as her objection to sign the statement without the words "at present" suggested some faint hope of recovery.

The following is from the Law Journal:—

KELLY, C.B. . . . I am of opinion that the result of the cases is, that **there must be an unqualified belief, without any hope of recovery, that the declarant is about to die.** According to the language of Eyre, C.B., every hope of this world must be gone. According to Tindal, C.J., any hope of recovery, however slight, must exclude the evidence. **Then the burden of proof lies entirely on the prosecution.** The Judge must be perfectly satisfied beyond a reasonable doubt that the declarant was under the belief that no hope of recovery existed. Now, **in the statement as it read at first**

it was " no hope of recovery "; then she herself desires the insertion of the important words " at present ". We have to consider the effect of those words under the circumstances under which they were uttered. For the prosecution **we were asked to give no importance to these words; but the woman must have had some meaning,** and, if so, we have to give effect to the meaning we think she had. It might have meant only that as the clerk had used the word "present" when he first put the question to her, she thought it more correct that the same form should be adhered to in the written statement. She may, however, have meant to say, not that she had absolutely no hope, but that at present she had not, but she hoped still that ultimately a change might come, and then she might recover. **We should have to solve the doubt, if we had any,** *in favorem vitæ* **in favour of the prisoner**; but we think the circumstances call upon us to give our decision in his favour.

BYLES, J. . . . **These dying declarations are to be received with scrupulous, I had almost said with superstitious, care.** The declarant is subject to no cross-examination. No oath need be administered. There can be no prosecution for perjury. There is always danger of mistake which cannot be corrected. **I think there should be the sense of danger of an almost immediate impending death.** Here the woman said, in effect, " I have no hope at present ". The clerk wrote it down **" I have no hope ". She said " That is not what I mean;** I mean I have no hope at present ". That merely means, If I don't get better soon, I shall not recover.

LUSH and BRETT, JJ., and CLEASBY, B., concurred.

Note.—The question in the above case apparently turned upon the woman's refusal to sign the statement without the words " at present ", although such words in themselves are apparently meaningless. If the statement had, in the first instance, been drawn up with such words it might well be argued that it would have been admissible.

In *R.* v. *Perry*, [1909] 2 K. B. 697 it was laid down that the real test is not that the person making the statement should believe that he was at the *immediate* point of death, but merely that he should have given up every hope of life (see *post*, p. 248)

R. v. MEAD.

KING'S BENCH. 1824.

2 B. & C. 605; 4 D. & R. 120; 26 R. R. 484.

A dying declaration is only admissible in trials for murder and manslaughter.

The defendant was convicted of perjury. A rule for a new trial was obtained by the Attorney-General, in opposition to which were tendered affidavits, stating a dying declaration of the prosecutor, James Law, who was shot by the defendant after conviction. Such declaration gave an account of the shooting and then proceeded to state certain facts material to the charge of perjury.

The following is from Barnewall and Cresswell:—

ABBOTT, C.J. (*delivering the judgment of the Court,* ABBOTT, C.J., BAYLEY, HOLROYD and BEST, JJ.). We are all of opinion that the evidence cannot be received. . . . Here the dying declaration of Law was for the purpose not of accusing, but of clearing himself. It therefore falls . . . within the general rule, that **evidence of this description is only admissible where the death of the deceased is the subject of the charge, and the circumstances of the death the subject of the dying declarations.**

Note.—This rule is also illustrated, as to a civil case, by *Stobart* v. *Dryden, ante,* p. 164.

R. v. WOODCOCK.

OLD BAILEY. 1789.

1 LEACH C. C. 500.

A dying declaration is admissible although the deceased did not expressly refer to his expectation of death. It is

sufficient if the circumstances show that he expected speedy death, and was without hope.

The prisoner was charged with the murder of his wife, whose statement was taken on oath by a magistrate. She died in about forty-eight hours afterwards. It was proved to be impossible from the first that she could live long, but that although she retained her senses to the last moment, and repeated the circumstances of the ill usage she had received, she never expressed any apprehension or seemed sensible of her approaching dissolution. The statement was held admissible.

EYRE, C.B. . . . The general principle on which this species of evidence is admitted is, that they are declarations made in extremity, **when the party is at the point of death, and when every hope of this world is gone; when every motive to falsehood is silenced,** and the mind is induced by the most powerful considerations to speak the truth; **a situation** so solemn and so awful is considered by law as **creating an obligation equal to that which is imposed by a positive oath** administered in a court of justice. But a difficulty also arises with respect to these declarations; for it has not appeared, **and it seems impossible to find out, whether the deceased herself apprehended that she was in such a state** of mortality as would inevitably oblige her soon to answer before her Maker for the truth or falsehood of her assertions. The several witnesses could give no satisfactory information as to the sentiments of her mind upon this subject. The surgeon said that she did not seem to be at all sensible of the danger of her situation, dreadful as it appeared to all around her, but lay, submitting quietly to her fate, without explaining whether she thought herself likely to live or die. Upon the whole of this difficulty, however, my judgment is, that inasmuch as **she was mortally wounded, and was in a condition which rendered almost immediate death inevitable;** as she was thought by every person about her to be dying, though it was difficult to get from her particular explanations as to what she thought of herself and her situation; **her declarations, made under these circumstances, ought to be considered by a jury as being made under the impression of her approaching dissolution;** for, resigned as she appeared to be, she must have felt the hand of death, and must have considered herself as a dying woman. She continued to repeat, rationally and uniformly, the facts which she had disclosed from the moment her senses had returned, until her tongue was no longer capable of performing its office. Declarations so made are certainly entitled to credit; they ought therefore to be received in evidence; **but the degree of credit to which they are entitled must always be a matter for** the sober consideration of **the jury,** under all the circumstances of the case. . . .

Note.—The case of *R.* v. *Bedingfield, ante*, p. 68, might be referred to in connection with the above case. It was there held that notwithstanding the dying condition of the woman, her statement was not admissible as a dying declaration.

R. v. PERRY.

COURT OF CRIMINAL APPEAL. 1909.

[1909] 2 K. B. 697; 78 L. J. M. C. 1034; 101 L. T. 127; 25 T. L. R. 676; 53 S. J. 810; 22 Cox C. C. 154.

If proof be given that the declarant's death was imminent and that he had abandoned all hope of living, it is not necessary to show that he believed his death would ensue immediately.

Appeal of Perry against her conviction for murder by means of an illegal operation performed on April 9. On April 14 the deceased had a miscarriage, and on the 16th, early in the morning, the deceased, in answer to her sister's question, "Maggie, what did you have that woman for?" replied, "Oh, Gert, I shall go. But keep this a secret. Let the worst come to the worst", adding a statement of what the prisoner had done to her. The deceased died the same evening. Lawrence, J., admitted the statement as a dying declaration.

The following is from the Law Reports:—

Lord Alverstone, C.J. . . . In *R.* v. *Peel*, 2 F. & F. 21, Willes, J., said: "It must be proved that the man was dying and there must be a settled hopeless expectation of death in the declarant." That sentence expresses in very clear and crisp language the rule which I have been trying to explain. In *R.* v. *Gloster*, 16 Cox C. C. 471, Charles, J., examining the cases, . . . said, " In the latest case of all, *R.* v. *Osman*, 15 Cox C. C. 1, Lush, L.J., lays down the principle in these terms: 'A dying declaration is admitted in evidence because it is presumed that no person who is immediately going into the presence of his Maker, will do so with a lie on his lips. But the person making the declaration must entertain a settled hopeless expectation of immediate death. If he thinks he will die to-morrow it will not do.' That is the judgment of Willes, J., with this addition, that Lush, L.J., inserts the word 'immediate' before 'death'. With the greatest deference I would prefer to adopt the language of Willes, J., and say that the declarant must be under a 'settled hopeless expectation of death'. 'Immediate death' must be construed in the sense of death impending, not on the instant, but within a very, very short distance indeed ". In other words, the **test is whether all hope of life has been abandoned so that the person making the statement thinks that death must follow.** I now propose to apply that principle to the present case. . . . If the expression " I shall go " is taken alone, it might mean " I shall die some day "; but, taking into consideration the whole sentence, we concur with Lawrence, J., that the statement was made by the deceased with the hopeless expectation of death.

Appeal dismissed.

Note.—If the above conditions are proved, the fact that the deceased subsequently entertained hope will not exclude the declaration (*R.* v. *Austin*, 8 Cr. App. R. 27).

R. v. PIKE.

SHROPSHIRE ASSIZES. 1829.

3 C. & P. 598.

A dying declaration is not admissible unless the declarant would have been competent as a witness, if living, and

was mentally capable of appreciating his condition. Thus, imbecility or tender age may exclude the declaration.

The prisoner being indicted for murder of a child aged four years, it was proposed to put in evidence, as a dying declaration, what the child said shortly before her death. It was held that it was inadmissible.

Park, J. We allow the declaration of persons *in articulo mortis* to be given in evidence, if it appear that the person making such declaration was then under the deep impression that he was soon to render an account to his Maker. Now, as this child was but four years old, **it is quite impossible that she,** however precocious her mind, **could have had that idea of a future state which is necessary** to make such a declaration admissible. . . .

Note.—As to the competency of deceased declarants generally, see *Phipson*, 267—8.

DECLARATIONS AS TO WILLS.

SUGDEN v. LORD ST. LEONARDS.

COURT OF APPEAL. 1876.

L. R. 1 P. D. 154; 45 L. J. P. 49; 34 L. T. 369: 24 W. R. 479.

When a question arises as to the contents, genuineness or identity of a will, whether existing, lost or destroyed, statements or declarations made by the testator concerning such will, either prior thereto, as to his testamentary intentions, or (perhaps) subsequent thereto, as to his testamentary acts, are admissible in proof thereof.

The will of Lord St. Leonards (the celebrated Lord Chancellor) was missing at his death, and was never found. A daughter of the deceased wrote out the contents of the will from memory, there being no draft or copy of it. The daughter had lived with the testator all her life; he had constantly consulted her about the will and explained its provisions to her, and she had from time to time assisted him to make and alter it. Her statement of the will was in some degree corroborated by other papers of the testator, and also by his verbal statements made after the execution of the will to his friends and relatives.

The Court held that such statements or declarations made by the testator, whether before or after the execution of the will, were admissible as evidence of its contents, and granted probate of the will as written down by the daughter.

The following is from the Law Journal:—

COCKBURN, C.J. . . . When the idea of the testator's having himself destroyed the will is done away with, the next question is, whether the will having been lost, secondary evidence can be given of its contents? Now that question is disposed of by the authority of the case of *Brown* v. *Brown* (8 E. & B. 876), which, as I think, has been recognised as perfectly sound. There Lord Campbell says, **" Parol evidence of the contents of a lost instrument may be received as much when it is a will as if it were any other document ",** and in that I, for one, most entirely concur. The consequence of a contrary ruling would be most mischievous. It would enable any person who desired, from some sinister motive, to frustrate the testamentary dispositions of a dead man. . . .

. . . The third question is, whether we have before us sufficient evidence of the contents of the will. This depends upon the evidence of Miss Sugden, and, I must say, upon her evidence alone, to this extent, that if we had not her evidence, all the other parol, and even the documentary evidence in the case, would not enable us to say that we had ascertained the contents of the will so as to give effect to it. . . .

The question presents itself whether the declarations of the testator can be received as secondary evidence of the contents of the lost will. No doubt, generally speaking, where secondary evidence is admissible, if oral, it must be given on oath; if documentary, it must be verified on oath. Nevertheless, **the declarations of deceased persons are, in several instances, admitted as exceptions to the general rule, when such persons had peculiar means of knowledge, and may be supposed to have been without motive** to speak otherwise than according to the truth. It is obvious that **a man who has made his will stands pre-eminently in that position.** He must be taken to know the contents of the will he has made. If he speaks of its provisions, he can have no motive for misrepresenting them, except in the rare instances in which a testator may have the intention of misleading by his statements respecting his will. Generally speaking, statements of this kind are honestly made, and this class of evidence may be put on the same footing with the declarations of members of a family in matters of pedigree, evidence not always to be relied upon, yet sufficiently so to make it worth admitting, leaving its effect to be judged of by those who have to decide the case. . . .

I entertain no doubt that prior instructions, or a draft authenticated by the testator, or verbal declarations of what he was about to do, though of course not conclusive evidence, are yet legally admissible as secondary evidence of the contents of a lost will. . . . **The question is simply one of the admissibility of secondary evidence, and has to be determined by the rules of evidence alone.** I am, therefore, decidedly of opinion that **all statements** or declarations, written or oral, made by a testator **prior to the execution** of the will **are admissible** as evidence of its contents. . . .

The admissibility of declarations made subsequently to the execution of the will **creates greater difficulties** by reason of a *dictum* of Lord Campbell and a decision of Lord Penzance. **In principle there appears to me to be no distinction.** The position of the testator is the same, both as respects peculiar knowledge and motive for speaking the truth, which can be no less than the motives which he has for making statements as to his intentions prior to the execution of the will. . . .

I am therefore of opinion that the various statem nts of Lord St. Leonards, whether before or after the execution of his will, are admissible to prove the contents of the will. . . .

JESSEL, M.R. . . . Can we admit, as a matter of course, secondary evidence in proof of a will? Now I should have thought there could be but one answer to that question. . . . The meaning of secondary evidence is to supply the loss by accident or otherwise of primary evidence. . . . **The whole theory of secondary evidence depends upon this,** that the primary evidence is lost, and that it is against justice that the accident of the loss should deprive a man of the rights to which he would otherwise be entitled. **I am at a loss to**

discover any reason whatever for distinguishing between the loss of a will and the loss of a deed. . . .

The next point, and one no doubt also of great importance, is what secondary evidence is admissible. In this particular instance there is the evidence of a person who had seen the will, and **the real point to be considered and decided is, whether that evidence can be confirmed or corroborated by declarations of the testator** made either to that witness or to other persons, and, if so, whether those declarations to be admissible in evidence must be limited to declarations **made at or before the execution of the will, or** may be extended to declarations **made after** the execution of the will. . . .

As a rule the declarations, whether in writing or oral, made by deceased persons, are in our law not admissible in evidence at all. But so inconvenient was the law upon this subject, so frequently has it shut out the only obtainable evidence, so frequently would it have caused a most crying and intolerable injustice, that **a large number of exceptions have been made** to the general rule. . . .

(*His Lordship here deals with the exceptions.*)

Now I take it that **the principle which underlies all these exceptions is the same.** In the **first** place, it must be a case in which it is difficult to obtain other evidence, for no doubt the ground for admitting the exceptions was that very difficulty. In the **next** place, the declarant must be disinterested; that is, disinterested in the sense that the declaration was not made in favour of his interest. And, **thirdly,** the declaration must be made before dispute or litigation, so that it was made without bias on account of the existence of dispute or litigation which the declarant might be supposed to favour. **Lastly,** and this appears to me one of the strongest reasons for admitting it, the declarant must have had peculiar knowledge—knowledge not possessed in ordinary cases.

Now you will find that all these reasons . . . exist in this case, that is the case of a testator declaring the contents of his will. Of course, as in the case of pedigree, **the Courts must be careful and cautious in admitting such evidence.** From its very nature it is evidence not open to the test of cross-examination, it is very often produced at second or third hand, and is therefore particularly liable to lose something of its colour in the course of transmission. It is so easily and so frequently fabricated that all Courts which dispose of such cases must be especially on their guard. **But that**

only goes to the question as to the weight to be attributed to the evidence when admitted; it does not go to the question of admitting the evidence itself, and I must say it appears to me that, having regard to the reasons and principles which have induced the tribunals of this country to admit exceptions in the other cases to which I have referred, we should be equally justified and equally bound to admit it in this case. . . .

I should, therefore, entirely concur with the Lord Chief Justice's conclusion that **this evidence would be admissible, not only as regards that portion which was anterior to the execution of the will, but also as regards that portion of it which is posterior to its execution. . . .**

JAMES and BAGGALLAY, L.JJ., concurred.

MELLISH, L.J., dissented as regarded the post-testamentary statements only.

Note.—It is very doubtful whether this case should be put under the head of "Hearsay". It might certainly be placed under the head of "Secondary Evidence" of documents (see *post*, p. 358). For a good discussion of the question see *Phipson*, 313—5. It should also be observed particularly that the admissibility of the evidence of the testator's post-testamentary statements has been seriously questioned (*Id.*; *Woodward* v. *Goulstone*, 11 App. Cas. 469; *Atkinson* v. *Morris*, [1897] P. 40; *Quick* v. *Quick*, 3 S. & T. 442; and see *Barkwell* v. *Barkwell*, *post*, p. 255).

IN THE GOODS OF RIPLEY.

PROBATE. 1858.

1 SW. & TR. 68; 6 W. R. 460; 4 JUR. (N.S.) 342.

Declarations or statements made by a testator are not admissible as evidence to prove the due execution of his will, or an interlineation or alteration.

In 1850, the deceased, when in India, sent to his brother, in England, a copy of his will, which did not contain testator's signature, names of witnesses or attestation clause. In 1857, the deceased sent to his brother a copy of a codicil, headed "Codicil No. 1, to my will, written at Delhi, 18th February, 1857". It bore the signatures of the testator and of two witnesses. A letter accompanying it referred to the will of 1850. After testator's death neither will nor codicil could be found. Probate of the same was refused.

The following is from the Jurist:—

SIR C. CRESSWELL. I have great difficulty as to the execution of these papers. **There is no doubt as to their contents; the only proof of the execution is the statement of the deceased himself. . . .** Upon principle, it seems to me, that there being no proof of the factum of the will, except the declaration of the supposed testator, the prayer must be refused. But as the circumstances of the case made me anxious to grant probate if possible, I have caused inquiries to be made whether any precedent could be found in the registry, but no such is forthcoming. There is a case at common law (*Doe* d. *Shallcross* v. *Palmer*, 16 Q. B. 747) which inclines the other way. **The Court there refused to admit declarations of a testator** made after the execution of a will, **as to an interlineation** it contained; *a fortiori* such declarations **could not be received as to the whole will.** I must therefore reject the motion.

BARKWELL v. BARKWELL.

PROBATE. 1927.

L. R. [1928] P. 91; 97 L. J. P. 53; 138 L. T. 526; 72 S. J. 69; 44 T. L. R. 207.

The following is from the Law Reports:—

LORD MERRIVALE, P. . . . **The question what declarations of a testator are admissible** in evidence **to establish testamentary dispositions** stands to-day where it was left by the statement of Lord Herschell, L.C., in the House of Lords in *Woodward* v. *Goulstone* (11 A. C. 469), upon consideration of a judgment of the Court of Appeal in relation to this matter in *Sugden* v. *Lord St. Leonards* (*ante*, p. 250), that is to say, it **remains a doubtful and difficult one.** So far as regards the admissibility of statements of a testator made before the execution of the will as to the contents of a will "in the making" *Sugden* v. *Lord St. Leonards* confirms numerous earlier decisions, and there is no uncertainty. The Court of Appeal in *Sugden* v. *Lord St. Leonards* held that certain statements made by the testator in that case after the execution of a will were admissible, and as matters stand—notwithstanding the doubts expressed in *Woodward* v. *Goulstone*—the judgment in *Sugden* v. *Lord St. Leonards* must be regarded here as having declared the law so far as it has been authoritatively declared.

As to the application of the rule which was considered in *Sugden* v. *Lord St. Leonards* two well-known principles are to be borne in mind. Inasmuch as the Wills Act, 1837, denies all effect to any will unless it shall be made in writing and executed in the prescribed manner, that statute plainly ought not to be evaded by the admission of parol statements made after the event to make out execution. Under the common law, however, which since 1857 has governed proceedings in this jurisdiction, a fact which is in issue may, subject to the provisions of the Wills Act, be proved by any kind of lawful evidence, provided it be the best available. **To exclude a subsequent statement of a testator as to the fact of execution of a will is one thing. To exclude, or to admit his statements as to the contents** of a writing no longer in being **is another.** It may be that the observance of this distinction will some day help in the decision of the vexed question what statements of the testator can be given in proof.

EVIDENCE IN FORMER PROCEEDINGS.

MAYOR OF DONCASTER v. DAY.

COMMON PLEAS. 1810.

3 TAUNTON 262; 12 R. R. 650.

When a witness, who gave evidence in a former proceeding between the same parties, or their privies, involving the same issue and subject to cross-examination, is dead, or

unable to attend, or to give reliable evidence at, the second trial (for certain recognised reasons), his evidence so given may be proved by any person who heard it.

A new trial having been granted, application was made that, if any of the witnesses, many of whom were very aged, should die or become unable to attend the second trial, their evidence given on the former occasion might be read at the next trial.

SIR J. MANSFIELD, C.J. You do not want a rule of Court for that purpose. **What a witness, since dead, has sworn upon a trial between the same parties, may, without any order of the Court, be given in evidence,** either **from the Judge's notes,** or **from notes** that have been taken **by any other person,** who will swear to their accuracy; or the former evidence may be proved by any person who will swear **from his memory** to its having been given.

HEATH, J., concurred.

Note.—Stephen also treats testimony given in former trials as hearsay evidence admissible by exception (Art. 33). This is, perhaps, a convenient course but it will be appreciated that such material is an attenuated type of "hearsay", for the security both of an oath and of cross-examination are here preserved, the only missing factor being the demeanour of the deponent.

The events in which such evidence is admissible are not quite clear. It certainly cannot be given unless the witness cannot, in the opinion of the Court, reasonably be expected to attend on the second occasion. If he be (1) dead, (2) permanently insane, or (3) kept out of the way by the adverse party, it seems the evidence is clearly admissible; but if he be (4) ill or (5) out of the jurisdiction, or (6) he cannot be found, then it would seem to be a question for the Court, having regard to the special circumstances.

No order is required to read such evidence (see O. 37, r. 3, *post*, p. 541), but the evidence when tendered will be admitted or rejected according to the common law principles above stated (*Printing, etc., Co.* v. *Drucker*, [1894] 2 Q. B. 801).

With regard to taking evidence before trial, see "Adduction of Evidence" (*post*, p. 414).

Evidence given at the trial may always be used in later proceedings of the same matter (O. 37, r. 25, *post*, p. 543).

LLANOVER v. HOMFRAY.

COURT OF APPEAL. 1881.

L. R. 19 Ch. D. 224; 30 W. R. 557.

Evidence given in former proceedings is admissible in subsequent proceedings although the parties in the subsequent proceedings are not personally the same, provided they are the privies of or claim through the former parties.

Thus, where in 1815 evidence was given in an action between manorial tenants and the lord of a manor as to a manorial right; and in 1881 another action was tried, as to the same right, between the manorial tenants and the lord of the manor of that time, none of whom were personally parties to the former suit, yet, as they were all "privies in estate" of the former parties, the evidence given in the former action, by witnesses since deceased, was admitted in the latter action.

The following is from the Law Reports:—

Jessel, M.R. . . . The question has been raised whether this evidence is admissible in the present suit. I must say that I have no doubt whatever that it is. **The previous suit was a suit by persons who were privies in estate with the present tenants**; they were not, indeed, owners of the same estate, but as the suit was on behalf of all the tenants it included the then owners of the estate now belonging to the Messrs. *Phillips*, **and on the other side there was a lord of the manor, who is now represented by the present lord of the manor.** Therefore it was a suit between persons privy in estate to the parties in the present action. **The issue in that suit was the same** as that in the present action, and the evidence in one is therefore admissible in the other. Why should the evidence not be admissible? **The lord had an opportunity of cross-examining,** and the evidence answers every condition of admissibility, the last condition being that **the witnesses must be dead or not producible, which, of course, is the case now** with these old witnesses. . . . If the witnesses were now alive, of course their evidence could not be read, but they must be called. There is, in my opinion, no more objection to reading this evidence than there is in any other case where the witnesses have been called and are dead. **If a witness gave evidence** at the trial of an action, **and a new trial was ordered,** then **if he were dead** at the time of the new trial **you would read his former evidence;** but if he were alive you could not do so, but would have to call him again.

Baggallay and Lush, L.JJ., concurred.

Note.—As to "privies", see *ante*, p. **45**.

MORGAN v. NICHOLL.

COMMON PLEAS. 1866.

L. R. 2 C. P. 117; 36 L. J. C. P. 86; 15 L. T. 184; 15 W. R. 110; 12 Jur. (n.s.) 963.

Evidence given in former proceedings is not admissible in subsequent proceedings merely on the ground that the parties in both proceedings claim in the same right. The parties must either be the same, or the later parties must claim under the former parties.

In 1856, A brought an action of ejectment against X, and in 1866, B, the father of A, brought a similar action against the same defendant, claiming the same property under the same title. The plaintiff in the later action was not allowed to read in evidence a shorthand writer's notes of the evidence given in the action of 1856, by a relation of the plaintiff, who gave evidence as to the pedigree, but who had since died.

The following is from the Law Journal:—

Erle, C.J. . . . **If that former trial had been in an action brought against the defendant by the present plaintiff, or anyone claiming under him, the evidence would have been admissible.** But the evidence ought not to be admissible against the defendant unless it would also have been admissible against the present plaintiff. In my opinion, the two plaintiffs, that is to say, **the plaintiff in the present action and the plaintiff in the former one, are perfect strangers.** On the former trial, the plaintiff, who was the son of the plaintiff in the present action, claimed under his father, in the belief that his father was dead; and on that trial this evidence of Henry Morgan was admitted. It turned out, however, that **the father** was not dead, and he has since brought this action, in which he **is a perfect stranger to the son, so far as this rule of law is concerned.** If the defendant had wanted to have used this evidence against the plaintiff in this action, he could not have done so; and therefore I think the evidence was not admissible for the plaintiff.

Willes, J. **The question is, whether the rule as to** the admissibility of evidence given by a witness on a former trial of the same matter in dispute, and between **the same parties or their privies, extends to the present case;** that is to say, whether all relations in blood are bound by or may take advantage of the rule, because **the only thing here connecting the present plaintiff with the plaintiff in the former action is the relationship** of blood, the present plaintiff being the father of the former plaintiff. The argument would be the same if the two plaintiffs had been cousins, which shows its absurdity. . . . **He is no privy to the plaintiff in the former action, since a father does not claim through his son. . . .** There has been no case in which the evidence has been admitted where the parties to the action were not parties to the former action, except they were persons who claimed under such former parties. . . .

Keating, J. . . . The defendant was party to the former action, but the plaintiff was not, nor was he claiming under the plaintiff in the former action. A son is obliged to claim through his father; but **the father does not claim through the son, and for the present purpose they are strangers.**

Byles, J., concurred.

STATEMENTS IN PUBLIC DOCUMENTS.

STURLA v. FRECCIA.

HOUSE OF LORDS. 1880.

L. R. 5 A. C. 623; 50 L. J. Ch. 86; 43 L. T. 209; 29 W. R. 217; 44 J. P. 212.

Entries or statements in "public documents", such as official books and registers, British or foreign, are evidence against every one, provided there was a legal duty to make such entries for public information or reference, and they were made in proper time by the proper officers, after proper inquiry.

Although foreign public documents are within the rule, yet the report of a committee appointed by a public department in a foreign State, though addressed to that department and acted on by the Government, was not admitted in the English Court as evidence of the facts stated therein; there being no evidence of any such legal duty to make either the entries therein, or any particular inquiries on which they were based, nor any evidence that such report was to be for public reference.

The following is from the Law Reports:—

Lord Selborne, L.C. . . . There is abundant proof that the report which contains the passage it is desired to use is an authentic public document of the Genoese Government, to which, so far as the good faith of those who made it is concerned, credit might be justly given on any occasion on which it might properly be used. But . . . **it does not appear that any particular rules were prescribed to them as to the kind of information which they should collect; still less as to the evidence which they were to require to substantiate such information. . . .** It appears to me to have been perfectly open to its members to receive any species of information, or hearsay or otherwise, to which they themselves at the moment thought credit could be given; and therefore, **I am unable to apply to them any analogy derived from the cases** of Courts, Commissioners, or other persons having a special duty or authority **under the English law** to make particular kinds of inquiries. . . .

LORD HATHERLEY. . . . When you come to look at the character of the document which is sought to be produced, what do you find? There are no original entries to be found in that document, but there appear to have been books kept, although we have not any very precise information about how they were kept, or whose duty it was to keep them, and the like. . . . **I do not think this comes near the case of the heralds' books, nor the commissions for making specific inquiries,** these specific inquiries falling plainly under the head of a discharge of a duty, which duty is discharged in the only proper manner in which it could be discharged; and, therefore, the law taking notice that such had been the course of investigation or inquiry and such had been the result of the due execution by the commission of that duty, gives credit to what the return states upon the matter. . . .

LORD BLACKBURN. . . . It is an established rule of law that public documents are admitted for certain purposes. What a public document is, within that sense, is of course the great point which we have now to consider. . . . **It should be a public inquiry, a public document, and made by a public officer.** I do not think that "public" there is to be taken in the sense of meaning the whole world. I think an entry in **the books of a manor** is public in the sense that it concerns all the people interested in the manor. And an entry probably in **a corporation book** concerning a corporate matter, or something in which all the corporation is concerned, would be "public" within that sense. But it must be a public document, and it must be made by a public officer. **I understand a public document there to mean a document that is made for the purpose of the public making use of it, and being able to refer to it. It is meant to be where there is a judicial, or quasi-judicial, duty to inquire,** as might be said to be the case with the bishop acting under the writs issued by the Crown. That may be said to be quasi-judicial. He is acting for the public when that is done; but I think the very object of it must be that it should be made for the purpose of being kept public, so that the persons concerned in it may have access to it afterwards. . . . Can the document in this case be said to come within that class of cases? I think it is impossible to look at it in that way. **There is not the slightest evidence, or the least**

circumstance, to lead me to the conclusion that it was even intended that this private and confidential report should be seen by anyone interested in it. It was meant for private information, to guide the discretion of the Government. It was not, like the bishop's return of the first-fruits, for the public information, to be kept in the office and to be seen by all in the diocese who might be concerned when there came to be any litigation.

LORD WATSON. . . . **It does not appear to me that the duty** cast upon the committee necessarily, or even by fair implication, **involved the necessity of making any quasi-judicial or strict inquiry** into the circumstances which they were about to report. . . . The sort of commission that was given here was one of a very roving description to find out every little circumstance, whatever it might be, wherever they could pick it up, and in whatever manner they could ascertain it. . . . I cannot conceive, when you take these circumstances into consideration along with the undoubted fact that **this was not made for the purpose of being recorded in a public register,** that it can have the authority of a public register. . . .

Note.—There are two special rules respecting "public documents"—

(1) Statements in them are evidence against everyone.

(2) They can always be proved by secondary evidence, *i.e.*, copies.

The first point only is in question here. The second is dealt with *post*, p. 363.

"The very gist of such documents", it has been well said, "is that they contain a statement of some matter of fact by a person duly authorized to make it, who is not, save in very exceptional cases, called as a witness. And the guarantee of their credibility consists in the public duty of the official who keeps them to ascertain the truth of the matters to be recorded, and to make accurate entries of them in the public interest for the purpose of reference" (*Wills*, 233). In connection with this matter, the presumption of regularity in public offices should be borne in mind (see *ante*, p. 34).

Among such "public documents" may be mentioned the following: Public Statutes, the London Gazette, Registers of births, marriages and deaths, and other public Registers, Surveys of Crown lands, maps, plans and charts attached to Inclosure Awards and public Inquisitions. As to the weight to be attached to various entries in public Registers, see *Re Stollery*, [1926] Ch. 284.

But ancient documents such as surveys, estimates and petitions of a private character, produced from the Record Office, which do not affect the King's property or revenues, are not public documents in the above sense. Nor are confidential plans or reports made to the

War Office, not intended as permanent records (*Mercer* v. *Denne*, [1905] 2 Ch. 238, cited on other points, *ante*, p. 241).

As regards maps and plans, it appears that they may be admissible in evidence, although they are not strictly public documents, if they are published maps or plans generally offered for sale to the public, as to matters of public notoriety, but not as to matters of private concern. Thus maps of Australia were admitted in the *Tichborne Case*, and of South Africa in the *Jameson Case*. As to the admissibility of maps and plans in other cases, see *Phipson*, 350–1, and cf. the Rights of Way Act, 1932, s. 3, *post*, p. 521.

R. v. SUTTON.

KING'S BENCH. 1816.

4 M. & S. 532.

Recitals in public Acts of Parliament are, like direct statements in public documents and State Papers, generally, "prima facie" evidence against every one.

Thus, to prove that certain organised outrages had occurred in various parts of England, recitals that such outrages had occurred, contained in a public Statute, and in a Royal Proclamation offering a reward for the discovery of the offenders, were held admissible.

LORD ELLENBOROUGH, C.J. . . . **Public Acts of Parliament are binding upon every subject, because every subject is, in judgment of law, privy to the making of them,** and therefore supposed to know them, and formerly the usage was for the sheriff to proclaim them at his county court and yet what every subject is supposed to know, and what the Judge is bound judicially to take notice of, it is said the jury cannot advert to; for if this evidence was inadmissible, it must be because the jury could not be charged with it.

Next as to the proclamation; I consider it as an act of State. The proclamation recites, that it had been represented to the Prince Regent, that a number of persons had committed **various acts of outrage** in the town, and in different parts of the county of Nottingham, etc.; and that the Prince Regent has thought it necessary to propound certain **rewards for the discovery and conviction**

of the persons concerned in such proceedings. The propounding of these rewards necessarily implies that such acts of outrage have actually been committed, for otherwise it would have been nugatory to propound them. I do not say that it was conclusive evidence of the fact that these outrages were committed; but **surely it was admissible** and, like other acts of State, to be laid before the jury. . . .

LE BLANC, J. . . . **This evidence consists of the King's proclamation, reciting** that it had been represented that **certain disturbances** caused by persons employed in the stocking manufactories had taken place in Nottingham and several parts of the county, and offering a reward for the discovery and apprehension of offenders. There are **likewise two Acts of Parliament reciting** in their preambles the existence of **these outrages,** and making provision in the body of them, the first, for the more exemplary punishment of persons committing these outrages; the second, for the better preserving the peace, by enforcing the duties of watching and warding. When the nature of these documents is considered, **is it possible to say that they were not admissible,** particularly as the libel refers to the conduct of the persons called *Luddites* in destroying frames in *Nottingham* and the neighbourhood, and compares that conduct with the conduct of the military in America? **Are not the documents material to show that these disturbances existed** in *Nottingham*, and existed to such a degree as to call for the interference of the Executive Government and the Legislature, to offer reward for their discovery, and to inflict a more exemplary punishment upon them, and to protect the peaceable inhabitants by compelling the observance of watch and ward? **Surely they were evidence for this purpose,** when the inquiry respected a libel of the description laid in the information, tending, as it is charged, to alienate the minds of the subjects from the King and Government, and to make them think that what had been condemned at Nottingham by the Government, was held laudable in America; when, according to the language of the libel, they were singing a new tune to an old song. **I cannot see therefore any ground on which these public instruments could be objected to as inadmissible.** They seem to me to go clearly to prove the facts which are alleged, because they show in what way the Executive Government and the Legislature acted upon them. . . .

BAYLEY, J. . . . **The proclamation sets forth,** that it had been represented to the Prince Regent that a number of persons, chiefly of those employed in the stocking manufactories, had actually committed **various acts of outrage**; it is therefore an assertion on the part of His Royal Highness, that such a representation had been made to him, and he proceeds to act upon it, by offering a reward for the discovery of the offenders. **This I think was evidence to this extent, and no farther,** that a representation was made to the Executive Government that such outrages existed, and that the Executive Government thought fit to act upon it; for they so far acted as to promulgate an Act of State upon it. . . .

The preambles to the two Acts of Parliament I think are still more free from objection than the proclamation, and they assume as facts that outrages did exist. **When we consider in what manner an Act of Parliament is passed,** and that it is a public proceeding in all its stages, and challenges public inquiry, and when passed is in contemplation of law the act of the whole body, **it seems to me that its recital must be taken as admissible evidence. . . .**

BRETT v. BEALES.

NISI PRIUS. 1829.

1 Moo. & M. 416; 34 R. R. 499.

Recitals or statements of fact in private Acts of Parliament are evidence only against the parties to them, even although they may be declared to be public for the purpose of proof.

A private Act, authorising the making and maintaining of a navigable canal, contained a recital that the Corporation of Cambridge were entitled to divers tolls. The plaintiff was the lessee of the tolls under the Corporation of Cambridge, and he brought the action to recover such tolls. In support of the claim it was proposed to read the said recital as evidence, it being urged that the Act was for this purpose to be treated as a public statute (in which case the recital would have been evidence), as it was provided "that this

Act should be deemed and taken to be a public Act, and shall be judicially taken notice of as such by all Judges, justices, and others, without being specially pleaded". It was held that the recital was not admissible in evidence.

LORD TENTERDEN, C.J. The point is quite new, and of great importance, as it will apply to so large a class of statutes. . . .

Two grounds have been laid for the admission of this evidence: the one, that the concluding clause renders it admissible as a public Act; the other, that even independently of this clause, it is so from its nature. The answer given to the first was that **the clause only applied to the forms of pleading, and did not vary the general nature and operation of the Act.** I was inclined to that opinion at the time, and my learned brothers agree with me in that impression. We also think that the second ground fails. It is said that the bill gives a power of levying a toll on all the King's subjects, and therefore the Act is public; the power given is not so extensive, it is only to levy toll on such as shall think fit to use the navigation. The ground, therefore, on which it is said the Act is public, and the evidence admissible, fails; and I cannot receive it.

Note.—It was customary, before the year 1850, to insert a clause in private Acts of Parliament declaring that the same should be deemed public and be judicially noticed. The effect of this clause was to dispense with the necessity, not only of pleading the Act specially, but of producing an examined copy, or a copy printed by the printer for the Crown; a public Act requiring neither to be specially pleaded nor proved. By 13 & 14 Vict. c. 21, it was enacted: "That every Act made after the commencement of this Act shall be deemed and taken to be a public Act, and shall be judicially taken notice of as such, unless the contrary be expressly provided and declared by such Act" (see *ante*, p. 16). This provision is now repealed by the Interpretation Act, 1889, 52 & 53 Vict. c. 63, which provides, by section 9, that every Act passed after 1850 "shall be a public Act and shall be judicially noticed as such, unless the contrary is expressly provided by the Act" (see *post*, p. 472).

THE MODE OF PROOF.

Three modes of proof are allowed by law:—

(1) Statements by Witnesses.

(2) Reading of Documents.

(3) Inspection of Things.

Three kinds of evidence consequently appear:—

(1) Oral or Parol Evidence.

(2) Documentary Evidence.

(3) Real Evidence.

It is proposed to deal with these several modes of proof and kinds of evidence in the order indicated.

Attention should be called to an important general rule laid down for use in the Supreme Court by O. 30, r. 2, to the effect that, **on the hearing of a Summons for Directions an order may be made** that any particular fact may be proved by affidavit, and that evidence of any fact shall be given by statement of information or belief, by production of documents or entries in books, or by copies or otherwise as directed (see *post*, p. 537). This rule does not appear to have been extensively used, except in the Commercial Court.

A similar provision exists in the Divorce Court (Mat. Causes Rules, 1944, r. 25 (1)), and is more extensively used.

ORAL EVIDENCE.

The general rule may be thus stated:—

The law requires oral evidence to be given—

(1) by legally competent witnesses;
(2) upon oath or affirmation;
(3) in regular course of examination;
(4) subject to contradiction as to facts;
(5) and to discredit as to veracity;
(6) and to privilege in refusing to answer.

The cases following are intended to illustrate successively these several features of the rule, and their exceptions or qualifications.

COMPETENCY OF WITNESSES.

Evidence must be given by legally competent witnesses. The normal man is competent, and presumed to be so. The law of competency is therefore practically **the law of incompetency,** consisting of rules of exclusion.

Formerly there were several grounds of exclusion of witnesses, the chief being (1) incompetency from **interest,** and (2) incompetency from **mental incapacity.** On the former ground, not only were parties themselves and their husbands and wives excluded, but also all persons who were *in pari jure* with either party, or otherwise substantially interested in the proceedings. Successive Statutes have abolished this kind of incompetency, leaving the fact of interest in the proceedings to affect credibility merely.

The change in the law of incompetency from interest was effected by the following steps:—

1833. The incompetency of persons *in pari jure* with the parties was abolished (3 & 4 Will. 4, c. 42).

1843. The Evidence Act provided that no person should be excluded by reason of incapacity from crime or interest, save the parties themselves or persons on whose behalf the action was brought or defended, and their husbands and wives (6 & 7 Vict. c. 85). See *post*, p. 436.

1846. The County Courts Act provided that parties and their wives might give evidence in the new county courts (9 & 10 Vict. c. 95).

1851. The Evidence Act made parties to all civil proceedings, and the persons on whose behalf they were instituted, competent and compellable to give evidence, except in breach of promise and adultery cases (14 & 15 Vict. c. 99). See *post*, p. 440.

1853. The Evidence Amendment Act made husbands and wives of parties, etc., to civil proceedings competent and compellable witnesses except in adultery cases (16 & 17 Vict. c. 83). See *post*, p. 443.

1869. The Evidence Further Amendment Act made parties in breach of promise and adultery cases, and their husbands and wives, competent witnesses (32 & 33 Vict. c. 68). See *post*, p. 459.

1882. The Married Women's Property Act made husbands and wives competent to give evidence against each other in proceedings under the Act for protection of the wife's separate property (45 & 46 Vict. c. 75). See *post*, p. 468.

1898. The Criminal Evidence Act made persons charged, and their husbands and wives, competent witnesses (61 & 62 Vict. c. 36). See *post*, p. 480.

Other Acts, from 1833 to 1909, have simplified oaths and substituted affirmations, etc., and may be said to have rendered many persons competent witnesses.

Mental incompetency is a question of degree only, as

appears from the cases given below. Stress is laid, in the older cases, upon the ability to understand the nature of an oath. The real question now is generally considered to be—is the witness mentally capable of understanding and giving an intelligible account of the matter in question?

The preceding observations refer to ordinary witnesses speaking to facts which any person may fairly be presumed to understand. There are some **cases in which competency must be proved** before evidence is admissible, as in the case of expert witnesses (see *ante*, p. 131), and deceased declarants (see *ante*, p. 240).

It appears that the **objection to competency of a witness may be taken at any time,** but should, of course, be taken as soon as there appears any doubt on the matter; before the witness is sworn, if possible. But even after a witness has been sworn and given his evidence the objection can be taken and his evidence struck out if untrustworthy (*R.* v. *Whitehead*, L. R. 1 C. C. R. 33; *Jacobs* v. *Layborn*, 11 M. & W. 685 (see *post*, p. 422)).

The question of competency is for the Judge to determine (see *ante*, p. 11). The preliminary examination of a proposed witness by the Judge used to be known as examination on the *voir dire*, a special form of oath being administered.

COMPELLABILITY OF WITNESSES.

It should be observed that "**competency**" **is not identical with** "**compellability**". A witness may be competent, but not compellable. It is said that Sovereigns and Ambassadors are competent but not compellable. Generally, however, persons who are competent are compellable also, to give evidence, although they may not be compellable to answer certain questions, being excused so far on the ground of privilege (see *post*, p. 321). But, apart from special privilege, there are a few cases where competency and compellability do not go together.

Thus, in **criminal proceedings,** the person charged is always competent, but not compellable (Criminal Evidence Act, 1898, ss. 1, 6, see *post*, p. 480). And the husband or wife of the person charged is generally not compellable though competent (see further below). In **civil proceedings** competence and compellability go hand in hand, with two possible exceptions. When Parliament, in 1851, abolished all disqualifications from interest and let in parties to give evidence, it was felt that in two cases, *viz.*, divorce proceedings based on adultery (*i.e.*, what we should now call judicial separation) and breach of promise actions the temptation to perjury was too great and these proceedings were expressly excepted. In 1869 Parliament decided that the exceptions were not justified and, by the Evidence Further Amendment Act, 1869, let in the parties and their spouses to give evidence in these two classes of case. But the Act said merely that they shall be " competent " and said nothing about compellability. In earlier editions of this work the author took the view that this meant what it said and no more, and that, accordingly, parties and their spouses in these two cases, alone of all civil actions, were not also compellable. The balance of learned opinion, however, is now against him (see *Phipson*, p. 445; *Wills*, p. 134, and the *obiter dictum* of Lopes, J., in *Tompkinson* v. *Nottingham Guardians*, (1878), 4 C. P. D. 350). The point is an open one and lengthy arguments can be adduced in support of either view, but the present editor, while in sympathy on the whole with the author's view, ventures to think the point too academic to justify further discussion. Having regard to the fact that in the anyhow unlikely event of one party to a divorce case based on adultery wanting to call the other spouse when he or she was unwilling, the privilege enjoyed by such spouse of refusing to answer questions about his or her adultery would deprive compellability, if it exists, of most of its value. It is perhaps to be regretted that, in framing the Judicature Act of 1925, opportunity was not taken in s. 198, which reproduces with slight alterations s. 3 of the Act of 1869, to set the above doubts at rest. The new section merely says " competent "

The question of husbands and wives of parties as witnesses, although partially dealt with above, is so important that it deserves separate treatment.

HUSBANDS AND WIVES AS WITNESSES.

The general rule of the common law, both in civil and in criminal proceedings, was that husbands and wives of parties thereto were *incompetent* to give evidence, either for or against them. In civil cases there appear to have been no exceptions at all. In criminal cases, however, there was **an exception** where either husband or wife charged the other with personal injury or violence. **Legislation on the matter appears to have produced the following result.**

(*a*) **In civil proceedings,** husbands and wives appear to have been rendered *competent* in every case, and *compellable* also, with the possible exception that they are not compellable in divorce proceedings *instituted in consequence of adultery* (though they are in other divorce proceedings), and they have a certain privilege as to answering questions about their own adultery. (Evidence Amendment Act 1853, ss. 1—2; Evidence Further Amendment Act, 1869, ss. 1, 3, now replaced by the Judicature Act, 1925, s. 198, see *post*, pp. 443, 508.)

(*b*) **In criminal proceedings,** husbands and wives of persons charged are always *competent* witnesses; but **generally, only**

on the application of the person charged. They are, however, competent witnesses **without the consent of the person charged in proceedings for the following matters:—**

(1) **Personal injury or violence** committed by the husband or wife to or against the wife or husband. (Common law, see *post*, pp. 279, 280; Criminal Evidence Act, 1898, s. 4 (2), see *post*, p. 481.)

(2) Non-repair of, or nuisance to, a highway, river, or bridge, or any other indictment or proceeding for the purpose of **enforcing civil rights only.** (Evidence Act, 1877, s. 1, see *post*, p. 462; Criminal Evidence Act, 1898, s. 6 (1), see *post*, p. 481.)

(3) Neglecting to maintain, or deserting, wife or family under the **Vagrancy Act, 1824.** (Criminal Evidence Act, 1898, s. 4 (1) and Schedule, see *post*, p. 481.)

(4) The following offences under the **Offences against the Person Act, 1861.** Rape (section 48), indecent assault (section 52), abduction of women and girls (sections 53—55).

(5) Protection or security of property of husband or wife of the person prosecuting, under the **Married Women's Property Act, 1882,** ss. 12 and 16. (Married Women's Property Act, 1884, s. 1, and Criminal Evidence Act, 1898, s. 4 (1) and Schedule, see *post*, pp. 469, 481.)

(6) Offences under the **Criminal Law Amendment Act, 1885.** (Criminal Evidence Act, 1898, s. 4 (1) and Schedule, see *post*, p. 481.)

(7) Offences under the **Vagrancy Act, 1898.** (Criminal Law Amendment Act, 1912, s. 7 (6), see *post*, p. 497.)

(8) Offences under the **Punishment of Incest Act, 1908.** (Section 4 (4), see *post*, p. 492.)

(9) **Bigamy.** (Criminal Justice Administration Act, 1914, s. 28 (3), see *post*, p. 498.)

(10) Offences under the **Infant Life (Preservation) Act, 1929.** (Section 2 (5), see *post*, p. 519.)

(11) **The Offences against Children and Young Persons** set out in the First Schedule to the Children and Young Persons Act, 1933. (Section 15, see *post*, pp. 526, 529.)

(12) **Allowing persons under eighteen to go abroad** for paid performances, etc., without a licence (Children and Young Persons Act, 1933, s. 26 (5), see *post*, p. 527).

(13) Offences under the **Unemployment Insurance Act, 1935.** (Section 89, see *post*, p. 535.)

And it is sometimes said:—

(14) **Treason.**—There is great doubt concerning this, as there is no statutory provision on the matter, nor apparently, any decision, and writers differ on the question. (See *Taylor*, § 1372; *Best*, 12th ed., § 178.) The better opinion appears to be against competency without consent.

Here again, as in connection with civil proceedings (see *ante*, p. 272), **doubt has arisen on the question of** *compellability*. There are obviously only two positions to be provided for, that in which the witness is " competent and compellable ", and that in which the witness is " competent but not compellable ", and if the Legislature had kept to the two expressions indicated there could have been no doubt. But the **expressions used by Statute** in the various cases mentioned above are as follows:—

(*a*) In case (2) **" admissible and compellable "** (see *post*, p. 462).

(*b*) In case (5) **" competent and admissible and compellable "** (see *post*, p. 469).

(*c*) In cases (3), (4), (6), (7), (8), (9), (10), (11), (12) and (13) **" may be called "** (see *post*, pp. 481, 497, 498, 527, 535).

In cases (1) and (14) there is no statutory provision.

Under heads (*a*) and (*b*) there was obviously no difficulty, the expressions being clear. But the expression **" may be called "** used in the Criminal Evidence Act, 1898, s. 4 (1) (see *post*, p. 481), **led to uncertainty,** and, as the ultimate decision showed, to a wrong view and practice. Contrasting such expression (which in itself would seem equivalent to "admissible" or "competent") with the expression "admissible and compellable", the former would appear to mean "not compellable"; contrasting it with the expression "competent but not compellable", it would appear to mean "compellable". The latter was the view generally taken, and the practice appears to have been to treat husbands and wives as compellable witnesses in cases under head (*c*), *supra*, until the House of Lords, in *Leach* v. *R.*, [1912] A. C. 305, decided that the expression **"may be called" does not make husbands and wives compellable witnesses** (overruling the Court of Criminal Appeal, see *post*, p. 282).

In cases (1) and (14) opinion has also been divided, but in case (1) the Court of Criminal Appeal has now finally laid down the rule that **husbands and wives are compellable as well as competent witnesses** (*post*, p. 280); in case (14) there has been no decision.

The result appears to be—

(*a*) In cases (1), (2) and (5), *supra*, husbands and wives are *competent and compellable* witnesses.

(*b*) In all the other cases, except (14), *supra*, husbands and wives are *competent* witnesses only.

(*c*) In case (14) it is *doubtful*.

R. v. BRASIER.

CROWN CASES RESERVED. 1779.

1 LEACH C. C. 199.

Mental competency to give evidence depends not upon age but upon understanding or intelligence. There is no fixed limit of age under which an infant is excluded as a witness.

The question having arisen, in a prosecution for assault, whether the evidence of a child under seven years of age was admissible, it was submitted to the twelve Judges, who held that, under the circumstances, it was not admissible, as the child did not have sufficient understanding of the nature of an oath, without which (at that time) evidence could not be given.

THE TWELVE JUDGES were unanimously of opinion: That no testimony whatever can be legally received except upon oath and that an infant, though under the age of seven years, may be sworn in a criminal prosecution, provided such infant appears, on strict examination by the Court, to possess a sufficient knowledge of the nature and consequences of an oath, for **there is no precise or fixed rule as to the time within which infants are excluded from giving evidence, but their admissibility depends upon the sense and reason they entertain of the danger and impiety of falsehood,** which is to be collected from their answers to questions propounded to them by the Court; but if they are found incompetent to take an oath their evidence cannot be received.

Note.—It is to be observed that the decision in the above case was based on the fact that the child appeared not to possess sufficient understanding of the nature and consequences of an oath. At the time of such decision **no evidence could be given without an oath. This is not now the case.** The Children and Young Persons Act, 1933, s. 38, provides that in all *criminal* proceedings if a **child of tender years** who is tendered as a witness does not, in the opinion of the Court, understand the nature of an oath, the evidence of such child must be received, though not given upon oath, if, in the opinion of the Court, such child is possessed of sufficient intelligence to justify the reception of the evidence, and understands the duty of speaking the truth.

The above rule, however, still applies in civil proceedings and in criminal proceedings in the case of persons other than those covered by the Children and Young Persons Act, 1933.

R. v. HILL.

CROWN CASES RESERVED. 1851.

20 L. J. M. C. 222; 2 DEN. C. C. 254.

Persons suffering from insanity are not necessarily incompetent as witnesses. Whether they are competent or not

depends on the character and extent of their insanity. A person insane on one matter can give evidence on matters not connected with his insanity, and which he is quite capable of understanding.

On a trial for manslaughter, evidence was given by one Donelly, who was a patient at a lunatic asylum. Before he was called as a witness, an attendant at the asylum stated—" Donelly labours under the delusion that he has a number of spirits about him which are continually talking to him; that is his only delusion ", and the medical superintendent at the asylum stated the same and added— " I believe him to be quite capable of giving an account of any transaction that happened before his eyes. I have always found him so. It is solely with reference to the delusion about the spirits that I attribute to him being a lunatic ". Other medical evidence was given to the effect that a man might have a delusion on one subject without its affecting his mind generally. The witness was held competent to prove the act of killing.

The following is from the Law Journal:—

LORD CAMPBELL, C.J. . . . If there be a delusion in the mind of a party tendered as a witness, **it is for the Judge to see whether the party tendered has a sense of religion and understands the nature and sanction of an oath**; and then if the Judge admits him as a witness, **it is for the jury to say what degree of credit is to be given to his testimony.** Various old authorities have been brought forward to show that a person *non compos mentis* is not a competent witness; but **the question is in what sense the expression** *non compos mentis* **is used.** If by that term is meant one who does not understand the sanction of an oath, of course he ought not to be admitted as a witness; but he may be *non compos* in another sense, and yet understand the sanction of an oath and be capable of giving material testimony. . . . **He had a clear apprehension of the obligation of an oath, and was capable of giving a trustworthy account** of any transaction which took place before his eyes, and he was perfectly rational upon all subjects except with respect to his particular delusion. . . .

COLERIDGE, J. . . . He appeared to be unusually well instructed in the nature and obligation of an oath, and *prima facie* therefore to be quite competent to give evidence proper for the consideration of the jury. **If his evidence had in the course of the trial been so tainted with insanity as to be unworthy of credit, it was the proper function of the jury to disregard it,** and not to act upon it.

TALFOURD, J. If the prisoner's counsel could maintain the proposition which he has laid down, that any human being who labours under a **delusion of the mind** is incompetent as a witness, there **would be most wide-spreading incompetency.** Martin **Luther,** it is said, believed that he had had a personal conflict with the Devil. The celebrated Dr. Samuel **Johnson** was convinced that he had heard his mother calling him in a supernatural manner. . . .

LORD CAMPBELL, C.J. The rule contended for would have excluded the evidence of **Socrates,** for he believed that he had a spirit always prompting him.

ALDERSON and PLATT, BB., concurred.

BENTLEY v. COOKE.

KING'S BENCH. 1784.

3 DOUGLAS 422.

At common law, the husband or wife of a party to the proceedings, civil or criminal, is incompetent to give evidence, either for or against such party; except on a charge of personal injury or violence, alleged to have been done or committed by the wife or husband of the complainant, in which case the latter can give evidence against the person charged.

Thus, in an action of assumpsit brought by a woman, her husband was held incompetent as a witness.

LORD MANSFIELD, C.J. **There never has been an instance** either in a civil or criminal case where the husband or wife has been permitted to be a witness for or against the other, **except in case of necessity,** and that necessity is not a general necessity, as where no other witness can be had, but a particular necessity, **as where, for instance, the wife would otherwise be exposed without remedy to personal injury.** I think the husband was not a competent witness.

WILLES, ASHHURST and BULLER, JJ., concurred.

R. v. LAPWORTH.

COURT OF CRIMINAL APPEAL. 1930.

L. R. [1931] 1 K. B. 117; 100 L. J. K. B. 52; 144 L. T. 126; 22 CR. APP. R. 87; 95 J. P. 2; 29 L. G. R. 61; 29 Cox C. C. 183; 74 S. J. 735; 47 T. L. R. 10.

The husband or wife of a person charged with inflicting personal injury upon such wife or husband is a competent and compellable witness for the Crown at common law.

On indictment against the husband for (1) attempting to strangle his wife with intent to murder her, (2) causing her grievous bodily harm with intent to do her some grievous bodily harm, (3) maliciously inflicting grievous bodily harm upon her, the wife was held a compellable witness for the Crown.

The following is from the Law Reports:—

AVORY, J. (*delivering the judgment of the Court,* AVORY, SWIFT, *and* ACTON, JJ.). **The question** that has been raised before us **is whether in a case charging personal violence as having been used by a wife to her husband or by a husband to his wife, the husband or wife, as the case may be, is not only a competent but a compellable witness for the prosecution. There is no doubt that at common law the husband or wife was always a competent witness in such a case,** and by the very nature of things it must have been so, for otherwise, where the assault was committed in secret by one spouse upon the other, there would be no means of proving it. Whatever the reason, we are satisfied that **at common law the wife was always a competent witness for the prosecution when the charge against her husband was one of having assaulted her. Once it is established that she is a competent witness, it follows that she is a compellable**

witness; that is to say that she, having made her complaint of, or independent evidence having been given of, an assault on her by her husband, and she having been summoned, as she may be, she is, like all other witnesses, bound to answer any questions put to her. In other words, she becomes a compellable witness.

It is said that there is no direct authority on this point. It does sometimes happen, where it has been recognised generally that a certain state of the law exists and where it has never been called in question, that there is no direct authority. I doubt whether this question has ever been raised before in this direct fashion so as to provide a decision. In everyday practice it has been assumed that if a wife so situated on coming into Court expresses a desire not to, or a reluctance to, give evidence for the Crown it is the duty of the Court, in order to ascertain the facts, to direct her to give evidence and, if necessary, to compel her to do so.

It has been suggested that in the case of *Leach* v. *R.* (*post*, p. 282) . . . the speeches of the Law Lords contained expressions which are inconsistent with the view of the law that I take. . . . But it must be borne in mind that the House of Lords in that case was dealing with the effect of a statute, section 4 of the Criminal Evidence Act, 1898 (*post*, p. 481), which had expressly authorised a wife or a husband to give evidence against their spouse in certain cases. . . . We are satisfied that **in the case of Leach v. R. the Law Lords had not present to their minds the case, which is now before this Court, where personal violence was alleged to have been done by a wife to her husband or by a husband to his wife,** and that they had no intention of including such a case in their observations.

R. v. PEARCE.

CENTRAL CRIMINAL COURT. 1840.

9 C. & P. 667.

Although the wife of a person charged with personal violence against her is a competent witness at common law, it is not indispensable that she should be called as a witness.

A man was charged with shooting at his wife with intent to

murder her. Counsel for the prisoner said he should not produce the prisoner's wife as a witness.

BOSANQUET, J. The charge is one of **personal violence** to the wife, she is, therefore, a **competent witness.** But it is **not indispensable** that she should be called.

LEACH v. R.

HOUSE OF LORDS. 1912.

L. R. [1912] A. C. 305; 81 L. J. K. B. 616; 106 L. T. 281; 22 Cox C. C. 721; 7 Cr. App. R. 157; 76 J. P. 203; 28 T. L. R. 289.

A distinction must be drawn between competency and compellability of witnesses. A wife, although rendered competent by Statute to give evidence against her husband in certain criminal proceedings, is not thereby made compellable to give such evidence, unless there is a clear and specified enactment to that effect.

The appellant Leach was tried under the Punishment of Incest Act, 1908, and convicted. His wife was called by the prosecution as a witness, although she raised the objection that she could not be compelled to give evidence against her husband. Pickford, J., held that she was a compellable witness under section 4 (1) of the Criminal Evidence Act, 1898 (see *post*, p. 481). This decision was upheld by the Court of Criminal Appeal, but was reversed by the House of Lords.

The following is from the Law Reports:—

EARL LOREBURN, L.C. . . . It is very desirable that in a certain class of cases justice should not be thwarted by the absence of the necessary evidence, but upon the other hand **it is a fundamental and old principle to which the law has looked, that you ought not to compel a wife to give evidence against her husband in matters of a criminal kind. . . .**

It is clear that this question must be governed by section 4 of the Criminal Evidence Act, 1898. . . .

(*His Lordship here read the section.*)

If it had not been for section 4 the wife could not have been allowed to give evidence, and the result of that was that the wife **could not have been compelled** to do so and was protected against compulsion. The difference between leave to give evidence and compulsion to give evidence is recognised in a series of Acts of Parliament. Does then section 4, which I have read, deprive the wife of this protection? **It is capable of being construed in different ways,** and it may hereafter lead, for all I know, to various other difficulties, but the present question is, does it deprive this woman of this protection? My Lords, **it says in effect that the wife can be allowed** to give evidence, even if her husband objects. **It does not say she must give evidence** against her own will. It seems to me that **we must have a definite change of the law in this respect, definitely stated in an Act of Parliament, before the right of this woman can be affected,** and therefore I consider this appeal ought to be allowed. . . .

Earl of Halsbury. . . . You must consider, when you are dealing with Acts of Parliament, and examining what the effect of your proposed construction is, whether or not you are dealing with something that it is possible the Legislature might either have passed by definite and specific enactment or have allowed to pass by some ambiguous inference.

Now, dealing with that question, I should have thought that it would occur not only to a lawyer, but to almost every Englishman, that a wife ought not to be allowed to be called against her husband, and that **those who are under the responsibility of passing Acts of Parliament would recognise a matter of that supreme importance as one to be dealt with specifically** and definitely and not to be left to inference.

I think that observation is true also for this reason that when you are dealing with a question of this kind **you cannot leave out of sight the different enactments that have been passed upon this subject with a sort of nomenclature of their own**; and speaking for myself, as an ordinary person, I should have asked, when it was proposed to call the wife against the husband, "Will you show me an Act of

Parliament that definitely says you may compel her to give evidence? because since the foundations of the common law it has been recognised that that is contrary to the course of the law". **If you want to alter the law which has lasted for centuries and which is almost ingrained in the English Constitution,** in the sense that everybody would say, "To call a wife against her husband is a thing that cannot be heard of", to suggest that that is to be dealt with by inference, and **that you should introduce a new system of law without any specific enactment of it, seems to me to be perfectly monstrous.**

The result is that I entirely concur with the judgment of the Lord Chancellor, and particularly with that part of it in which he said that such an alteration of the law as this ought to be by definite and certain language.

LORD ATKINSON. My Lords, I concur. **The principle** that a wife is not to be compelled to give evidence against her husband **is deep-seated in the common law** of this country, and I think if it is to be overturned **it must be overturned by a clear, definite, and positive enactment,** not by an ambiguous one such as the section relied upon in this case.

LORDS MACNAGHTEN, SHAW OF DUNFERMLINE and ROBSON, concurred.

Note.—In the case of *R.* v. *Acaster* (106 L. T. 384), decided in the Court of Criminal Appeal shortly after *Leach's Case*, it was held that the statement by the wife when called as a witness "I wish to shield my husband" was not equivalent to saying "I do not wish to give evidence". It might have meant "I wish to have an opportunity of giving evidence". Darling, J., said—"Speaking for myself, in future I shall feel bound to warn a wife, called as a witness by either the prosecution or defence, that she may object to give evidence if she does not wish to do so. There is no decision which makes this course binding, but it will probably be followed".

As to competency and compellability of husbands and wives as witnesses, see fully *ante*, p. 273. The leading case above would doubtless apply to a husband giving evidence against his wife.

SWEARING OF WITNESSES.

OATH OR AFFIRMATION.

Before a witness is permitted to give evidence, he must generally take an *oath* or make an *affirmation*, to the effect that his evidence shall be true. **In a few cases, however, unsworn statements** in the nature of evidence may be given, *e.g.*, **a child** of tender years may give unsworn evidence under certain conditions. (See Children and Young Persons Act, 1933, s. 38, *post*, p. 527.) A witness called merely to **produce a document** need not be sworn (*Taylor*, § 1429). And **a prisoner** may make an unsworn statement on the preliminary examination before the magistrate, and also at the trial itself. (See Criminal Justice Act, 1925, s. 12, *post*, p. 510; *Criminal* Evidence Act, 1898, s. 1 (*h*), *post*, p. 481.) For other cases, see *Phipson*, 446.

The oath is clearly a very ancient institution, by no means confined to the Christian, or any other religion, and it may be administered in any form recognised by the particular witness's religion. This is plainly shown by the celebrated leading case of *Omichund* v. *Barker*, *post*, p. 287. Certain statutes have since dealt with the matter, thus:—

The Oaths Act, 1838, recognising the principle laid down in the above case, provided that an oath should be binding if administered in the *form declared by the witness* to be binding. It was repealed in so far as it referred to witnesses by the Perjury Act, 1911, which contained a similar provision (see *post*, p. 495).

The Oaths Act, 1888, provides that any person may make an *affirmation* instead of taking an oath, if he states that—

(1) he has no religious belief; or

(2) an oath is contrary to his religious belief.

The same Act also provides that any person may be sworn in the Scotch manner, with *uplifted hand*, without kissing the book; and also that, if an oath has been duly administered, it shall not be affected by the fact that the person had no religious belief. See *post*, p. 471.

The Oaths Act, 1909, provides a new form of oath *without kissing the book.* See *post*, p. 494.

The Perjury Act, 1911, provides that, for the purposes of such Act, the *form is immaterial if accepted* without objection, or declared to be binding, by the witness. See *post*, p. 495.

The form of oath must obviously be of many kinds, according to the requirements of different religions. Thus, Protestants are sworn on the Evangelists, Jews on the Pentateuch, Mohammedans on the Koran, Hindoos on the Vedas or other sacred books, Parsees on the Zendavesta, and Chinese by breaking a saucer.

The Chinese form is thus described in *R.* v. *Entrehman*, C. & M. 248: "The prosecutor was then called, and on getting into the witness-box immediately knelt down, and a china saucer having been placed in his hand, he struck it against the brass rail in front of the box and broke it; the crier of the Court who swears the witnesses, then, by direction of the interpreter, administered the oath in these words, which were translated by the interpreter into the Chinese language:—'You shall tell the truth and the whole truth: the saucer is cracked, and if you do not tell the truth your soul will be cracked like the saucer.'"

As regards the oaths of **Christians** and **Jews** it will be observed that the Oaths Act, 1909, specifies the *New Testament* for the former and the *Old Testament* for the latter, and not the *Evangelists* and *Pentateuch* respectively, in accordance with the hitherto recognised principle. As, however, the specified books include the latter, it may be considered immaterial; except that the copies of the Evangelists and Pentateuch, without the remaining books of the Testaments, which have commonly been kept for use at many Courts, are no longer of use for the purpose.

It should be particularly observed that **affirmation is only**

allowed in two events, as specified in the Oaths Act, 1888, *supra.* It has been held that, where a witness desires to affirm, it is the duty of the Judge to examine the witness himself and ascertain that he objects to being sworn on the ground either that (*a*) he has no religious belief; or (*b*) an oath is contrary to his religious belief. A witness who states that he has religious belief cannot be allowed to affirm (*R.* v. *Moore*, 61 L. J. M. C. 80). And if a witness has no religious objection to an oath, but says that the ordinary forms do not bind him, and he cannot or will not state what form is binding upon him, it appears that his evidence cannot be given at all (*Nash* v. *Ali Khan*, 8 T. R. 444).

OMICHUND v. BARKER.

CHANCERY. 1744.

1 ATKYNS 21; WILLES 538; 1 WILSON 84.

Evidence must generally be given upon oath. The oath is not a peculiarly Christian ceremony, but "a religious function that mankind have universally established". The mode of administering an oath may, and should, be adapted to the special religious belief of the witness, it being in accordance with "the wisdom of all nations to administer such oaths as are agreeable to the notion of the person taking" the same. But religious belief of the witness is necessary for the taking of an oath.

Several persons, resident in the East Indies, and professing the Gentoo religion, having been examined on oath administered according to the ceremonies of their religion, under a commission issued by the Court of Chancery, it became a question whether such depositions could be read in evidence. Lord Chancellor Hardwicke, conceiving it to be a question of considerable importance, desired the assistance of the two Chief Justices and certain other Judges, who were unanimously of opinion that the depositions were admissible and should be read, and so the Lord Chancellor decided.

The following is from Atkyns:—

PARKER, C.B. . . . As to the *Gentoo* religion, it will appear from the best testimonies, that **persons of this religion do believe in God as the creator and governor of the world. . . .**

The books, cited by the defendant's counsel, to show jurors or witnesses must be sworn upon the Gospel, were *Bracton*, *Briton*, *Fleta*, *etc.* These authors prove no more than that the oaths are adapted to the natives of the kingdom. . . .

It is objected, that these witnesses do not swear by the true God, and for this purpose, the defendant's counsel cited *Deuteronomy* vi, 13 *and* 14 *vers. Thou shalt fear the Lord thy God, and serve Him, and shalt swear by His name. Ye shall not go after other gods, of the gods of the people which are round about you.*

Of the other side, *Jacob*, upon his covenant with *Laban*, *swore by the fear of his father Isaac* (*Gen.* xxxi, *v.* 53).

My answer is, this is not true in fact, for they do swear by the true God, the Creator of the world. . . .

It is plain that by the policy of all countries, oaths are to be administered to all persons according to their own opinion, and as it most affects their conscience, and laying the hand was originally borrowed from the Pagans.

It is said by defendant's counsel, that no new oath can be imposed without an Act of Parliament, and for this purpose several cases were cited.

My answer is. **This is no new oath. . . .**

WILLES, C.J. . . . If I was of the same opinion with Lord *Coke*, the consequence would be, that these depositions could not be read; but I am of opinion that some Infidels may under some circumstances be admitted as witnesses.

My Lord *Coke* is plainly of opinion, that *Jews* as well as Heathens were comprised under the same exclusion. . . .

Our Saviour and St. *Peter* have said, *God is no respecter of persons* (Acts x, v. 34).

Lord *Coke* is a very great lawyer, but our Saviour and St. *Peter* are in this respect much better authorities, than a person possessed with such narrow notions. . . .

There can be no evidence admitted without oath, it would be

absurd for him to swear according to the Christian oath, which he does not believe; and therefore, out of necessity, he must be allowed to swear according to his own notion of an oath. . . .

I cannot say I lay a great stress upon the authors which give an account of the *Gentoo* religion, because it must depend upon their veracity and private judgment; but I found my opinion upon the certificate, which says, the *Gentoos* **believe in a God as the Creator of the universe,** and that he is a rewarder of those who do well, and an avenger of those who do ill. . . .

LEE, C.J. I agree entirely with the opinion of Lord Chief Baron *Parker* and Lord Chief Justice *Willes*; that where it is returned by the certificate **the witness is of a religion, it is sufficient**; for the foundation of all religion is the belief of a God, though difficult to have a distinct idea of an infinite and incomprehensible Being as God is; yet mankind may have a relative idea of the being of a God, as dependent creatures upon Him.

An oath is a religious function that mankind have universally established. . . .

LORD HARDWICKE, L.C. My intention was to be certified whether these people believed the being of a God, and His providence. . . .

This objection being removed, the next question will be, whether the depositions ought to be read; which depends upon two things:

First, Whether it is a proper obligatory oath?

Secondly, Whether, on the special circumstances in this case, such evidence can be admitted according to the law of *England*? . . .

It is laid down by all writers that the outward act is not essential to the oath. . . .

All that is necessary appears in the present case: an external act was done to make it a corporal act. . . .

Suppose a Heathen, not an alien enemy, should bring an action at common law, and the defendant should bring a bill for an injunction, would anybody say that the plaintiff at law should not be admitted to put in an answer according to his own form of an oath? If otherwise, the injunction must be perpetual, and this would be a manifest denial of justice. . . .

This falls in exactly with what Lord *Stair*, *Puffendorf*, etc., say, that **it has been the wisdom of all nations to administer such oaths,**

as are agreeable to the notion of the person taking, and does not at all affect the conscience of the person administering, nor does it in any respect adopt such religion: it is not near so much a breaking in upon the rule of law, as admitting a person to be an evidence in his own cause. . . .

Upon the special circumstances of this case, I concur in opinion with my Lords the Judges, that **the depositions of these witnesses ought to be read as evidence** in this cause, and do therefore order that the objection be overruled, and the depositions read.

The following is from Wilson:—

It was held by the Lord Chancellor, assisted by Lord Chief Justice *Lee*, the Master of the Rolls, the Lord Chief Baron, and Justice *Burnett*, **that an infidel, pagan, idolater may be a witness, and that his deposition sworn according to the custom and manner of the country where he lives may be read in evidence**; so that at this day it seems to be settled, that infidelity of any kind doth not go to the competency of a witness. In the debate of this point, *Ryder*, the Attorney-General, cited the covenant between *Jacob* and *Laban*, *Genesis*, *cap.* xxxi, *vv.* 52, 53, where *Jacob* swore by the God of *Abraham*, and *Laban* swore by the God of *Nahor*. *Vide Psalm* 115, 106, *v.* 36.

The following is from Willes:—

WILLES, C.J. . . . I only give my opinion that such **infidels who believe a God and that he will punish them** if they swear falsely, in some cases and under some circumstances, **may and ought to be admitted as witnesses** in this, though a Christian country. And on the other hand, I am clearly of opinion that such **infidels** (if any such there be) **who either do not believe a God, or, if they do, do not think that he will either reward or punish** them in this world or in the next, **cannot be witnesses** in any case nor under any circumstances, for this plain reason: because an oath cannot possibly be any tie or obligation upon them. . . . **The oath was administered to the witnesses** in the same words as here in England, which fully answers the objection (if there was anything in it) that the form of the oath cannot be altered; and . . . after the oath was read and interpreted to them, **they touched the Bramin's hand or foot, the same being the usual and most solemn manner** in which oaths are administered to witnesses who profess the *Gentoo* religion . . . it being **their usual form,** is as much signifying their assent as kissing the book is here, where the party swearing likewise says nothing. . . . My opinion is that these depositions ought to be read in evidence.

EXAMINATION OF WITNESSES.

This comprises (1) Examination-in-chief; (2) Cross-examination; (3) Re-examination.

EXAMINATION-IN-CHIEF.

Two points should be noticed as to the questions permissible in examination-in-chief:—

(*a*) They must be on **facts strictly relevant.** They must not be as to the character or credibility of the witness.

(*b*) They must be **not leading questions.**

Note.—The phrase "leading question", which is constantly in use, is one of those expressions whose meaning is pretty plain in practice but singularly difficult to define in words. The gist of the matter is that the question must not be so framed that, with regard to the matter in dispute, it suggests the answer which the questioner hopes to receive. Nor must the question be couched in a way which assumes something to have occurred when the whole dispute is whether that thing occurred. Thus on a trial for assault where it is in dispute whether any assault ever took place a witness should not generally be asked, "Did you see the prisoner strike A", but preferably, "Were you walking down Green Street?" "Did something attract your attention?" The framing of questions so as to be clear to the witness without "leading" him is rightly regarded as one requiring great art and skill.

It may be said, shortly, that leading questions may be put in examination-in-chief, or re-examination, (*a*) on merely introductory matters, such as name or occupation of a witness, (*b*) on other matters not in dispute, (*c*) as to identification of persons or things, (*d*) to assist the memory of a witness or to lead his mind to the matter referred to, and for certain other necessary or unobjectionable purposes.

NICHOLLS v. DOWDING AND KEMP.

NISI PRIUS. 1815.

1 STARKIE 81.

Leading questions may not be put, in examination-in-chief, unless they are necessary to lead the mind of the witness to the subject of inquiry; or they are upon matters merely introductory or not in dispute. Questions suggesting the answer desired are inadmissible as "leading".

In order to prove that the defendants were partners, a witness was asked whether one of them had not interfered in the business of the other. The question was objected to as a leading one, but the Court allowed it to be put.

LORD ELLENBOROUGH, C.J. I wish that objections to questions as leading might be a little better considered before they are made. **It is necessary, to a certain extent, to lead the mind of the witness to the subject of inquiry.** If questions are asked to which the answer "Yes" or "No" would be conclusive, they would certainly be objectionable; but in general no objections are more frivolous than those which are made to questions as leading ones.

Note.—This prohibition on questions answerable by "Yes" or "No" must not be taken too literally. A question may be answerable by "Yes" or "No" without the slightest implication that "Yes" rather than "No" (or *vice versa*) is the hoped-for answer, in which case it is quite unobjectionable. Or again, it is a common and quite harmless trick of advocacy so to frame the question to your own witness as to invite him (as far as its form goes) to answer it in a way which would damage his case. The indignant "No" in answer consequently carries all the more weight. It must be remembered, too, that the inflection of the voice may render a proper question objectionable or *vice versa*. The topic almost defies analysis and the student must be guided by the underlying principle which is that your own witness must not be "prompted".

MAUGHAM v. HUBBARD.

KING'S BENCH. 1828.

6 L. J. (O.S.) K. B. 229; 8 B. & C. 14; 2 MAN & RY. 5; 32 R. R. 328.

A witness may refresh his memory by referring to any writing or document made by himself, at or so soon after the transaction in question that the Judge considers it was fresh in his memory at the time.

But it is not necessary that the witness should have any independent recollection of the fact recorded, if he is prepared to swear to it on seeing the writing or document.

Refreshing memory by inspecting a writing or document does not make it documentary evidence; so the fact that the same would be inadmissible in evidence as a document for want of a stamp is immaterial.

A witness, called to prove the receipt of a sum of money, was shown an acknowledgment of the receipt of the money signed by himself. On seeing it, he said he had no doubt that he had received it, although he had no recollection of the fact. It was held that this was sufficient parol evidence of the payment of the money, and that the written acknowledgment having been used to refresh the memory of the witness, and not as evidence of the payment, did not require any stamp.

The following is from Barnewall and Cresswell:—

LORD TENDERDEN, C.J. In order to make the paper itself evidence of the receipt of the money it ought to have been stamped. The consequence of its not having been stamped might be that the party who paid the money, in the event of the death of the person who received it, would lose his evidence of such payment. Here the witness, on seeing the entry signed by himself, said that he had no doubt that he had received the money. **The paper itself was not used as evidence of the receipt of the money, but only to enable the witness to refresh his memory**; and when he said that he had no doubt that he had received the money **there was sufficient parol evidence to prove the payment.**

BAYLEY, J. **Where a witness** called to prove the execution of a deed **sees his signature to the attestation, and says that he is, therefore, sure** that he saw the party execute the deed, that is a **sufficient proof** of the execution of the deed, **though the witness add that he has no recollection** of the fact of the execution of the deed.

Note.—The rule that an unstamped document, which would ordinarily require stamping, may be used merely for the purpose of refreshing memory was also adopted in *Birchall* v. *Bullough*, [1896] 1 Q. B. 325, despite the stricter wording of the Stamp Act, 1891, *post*, p. 475.

The opposite party is, naturally, always entitled to inspect any writing or document used to refresh memory, in order to check it, and to cross-examine upon it. But cross-examination does not make it documentary evidence, except so far as it refers to parts of the writing or document other than those used by the witness in refreshing his memory (*Gregory* v. *Tavernor*, 6 C. & P. 280). This appears to be in accordance with the rule that a party who calls for and inspects a document held by the other party is bound to put it in evidence if required to do so (see *Wharam* v. *Routledge*, *post*, p. 358).

Perhaps the commonest examples of writings used to refresh memory are entries in diaries, call-books, account-books, letter-books, and the like.

The position has now been radically altered by the Evidence Act, 1938.

BURROUGH v. MARTIN.

NISI PRIUS. 1809.

2 CAMPBELL 112; 11 R. R. 679.

A witness may refresh his memory not only from writings or documents in his own handwriting, but also from those made by other persons under his immediate observation when his recollection of the facts recorded was recent and fresh.

In an action on a charterparty, a witness was called to give an account of the voyage, and the log-book was laid before him for the purpose of refreshing his memory. Being asked whether he had written it himself, he said that he had not, but that from time to time he examined the entries in it while the events recorded were fresh in his recollection, and that he always found the entries accurate. He was allowed to refresh his memory from such book.

Lord Ellenborough, C.J. **If the witness looked at the log-book from time to time,** while the occurrences mentioned in it were recent and fresh in his recollection, **it is as good as if he had written the whole with his own hand.** This collation gave him an ample opportunity to ascertain the correctness of the entries, and he may therefore refer to these on the same principle that witnesses are allowed to refresh their memory by reading letters and other documents which they themselves have written.

R. v. LANGTON.

CROWN CASES RESERVED. 1877.

L. R. 2 Q. B. D. 296; 46 L. J. M. C. 136; 35 L. T. 527; 13 Cox C. C. 345.

The prisoner, a time-keeper at a colliery, was charged with obtaining money by falsifying the hours worked by, and amounts due to, certain workmen. To prove these particulars, the pay-clerk was called as a witness at the trial and allowed to refresh his memory by referring to the time-book, which, though kept by another clerk, was read out by the prisoner to the pay-clerk and verified by the latter as correct by reference to the book, when paying the amounts shown therein to be due. *Held*, that he was rightly allowed to do so.

The following is from the Law Reports:—

Cockburn, C.J. . . . If the witness had only seen the entries in the absence of the prisoner, the case might be different. There would then be obvious dangers in admitting such a use of the book, which do not exist in the present case. Here the entries were read aloud by the prisoner himself and seen by the witness at the time of reading and he made payments in accordance with them.

Note.—An expert witness may refresh his memory by reference to text-books, price-lists, or other such printed matter.

CROSS-EXAMINATION.

Two points should be noticed as to the questions permissible in cross-examination:

(*a*) They are **not confined to facts strictly relevant to the issue,** but may include others that are **relevant** merely **to the credibility** of the witness.

(*b*) They may be **leading questions.**

Moreover "**the rule against hearsay** applies to the proof of the relevant facts in the course of cross-examination just as much as to their proof by examination-in-chief. That is to say, a party is not entitled to prove his case merely by eliciting from his opponent's witness in cross-examination not his own knowledge on the subject, but what he has heard others say about it, but has not verified for himself" (*Wills*, 146).

In this place it is convenient to consider:—

CONDUCT, CHARACTER, AND CONVICTIONS OF WITNESSES.

The cases in which evidence may be given of the conduct, character and convictions of the parties themselves have been discussed *ante*, p. 100.

Similar matters concerning witnesses may sometimes be brought before the Court, chiefly by **cross-examination** of the witnesses themselves, but in some cases by the evidence of **other witnesses.**

The matter rests partly on decided cases, but mainly on Statute; the result appearing to be as follows:—

Cross-Examination.

(*a*) A party may always cross-examine his **opponent's** witness in order to test his **credibility**; questions being permissible as to his conduct on other occasions, his character and his previous convictions. See *post*, p. 299.

(*b*) A party may not cross-examine his **own witness,** unless the Judge allows him to do so on the ground that the witness is actually hostile, not merely adverse to him. It is also said that he may cross-examine his own witness when he has been compelled to call him. See *post*, p. 307.

(*c*) **A person charged** with an offence and giving evidence on his own behalf, cannot be cross-examined as to other offences or convictions, or as to his character, except in the cases specified in section 1 (*f*) of the Criminal Evidence Act, 1898. See *post*, pp. 302, 481.

Other Witnesses.

(*a*) A party cannot generally call witnesses to discredit his **opponent's witness,** when he has failed to shake him by cross-examination as to character; but he may do so in four cases. See *post*, p. 314.

(*b*) A party cannot in any case call witnesses to discredit his **own witness,** except that he may, by leave of the Judge, if his witness proves to be actually hostile, not merely adverse to him, call witnesses to prove that he has made previous statements inconsistent with his present testimony. See *post*, p. 317.

The above rules apply to witnesses generally, whether they are parties to the action or not.

WOOD v. MACKINSON.

NISI PRIUS. 1840.

2 M. & R. 273.

If a witness has been sworn, the opposite party is, in general, entitled to cross-examine him, even though he is not examined-in-chief.

But a party is not entitled to cross-examine a witness called

by mistake, if the mistake be discovered before any question is put to him.

The plaintiff's counsel called a witness, who was sworn in the usual way; but, before he had put any question to him, he said he had been misinstructed as to what the witness was able to prove, and he should not examine him at all. The defendant's counsel then claimed the right to cross-examine the witness. It was held that he had no right to do so.

COLERIDGE, J. . . . Upon the whole, it appears to me that the more satisfactory principle to lay down is this, that **if there really be a mistake,** whether on the part of counsel or officer, and that mistake be **discovered before the examination-in-chief has begun,** the adverse party ought not to have the right to take advantage of this mistake by cross-examining the witness. Here the learned counsel explains that there has been a mistake, which consists in this, that the witness is found not to be able to speak at all as to the transaction which was supposed to be within his knowledge. **This is, I think, such a mistake as entitles the party calling the witness to withdraw him without his being subject to cross-examination.** If, indeed, the witness had been able to give evidence of the transaction which he was called to prove, but the counsel had discovered that the witness, besides that transaction, knew other matters inconvenient to be disclosed, and therefore attempted to withdraw him, that would be a different case. I think the defendants have here no right to cross-examine the witness.

Note.—A witness who is only called to produce a document and is not sworn cannot be cross-examined (*Summers* v. *Moseley*, 1 Cr. M. & R. 96); nor can such a witness be cross-examined if he has been sworn unnecessarily (*Rush* v. *Smith*, 1 Cr. M. & R. 94). A witness called by the Judge himself cannot be cross-examined without the leave of the Judge.

PARKIN v. MOON.

NISI PRIUS. 1836.

7 C. & P. 408.

In cross-examination a witness may be examined by means of leading questions, as the presumption is that he is biased against the opposite party and will not be inclined to follow his lead. This is so, apparently, although the witness may actually appear to be favourable to the opposite party.

The plaintiff's counsel was cross-examining one of the defendant's witnesses (who, it seemed, was an unwilling witness for the defendant, but a willing one on the part of the plaintiff), by putting leading questions in the usual way. The defendant's counsel submitted that, in the circumstances, leading questions ought not to be allowed even on cross-examination. It was held that they were admissible

ALDERSON, B. I apprehend you may put a leading question to an unwilling witness on the examination-in-chief at the discretion of the Judge; but **you may always put a leading question in cross-examination whether a witness be unwilling or not.**

Note.—See O. 36, r. 38, *post*, p. 540.

BROWNE v. DUNN.

HOUSE OF LORDS. 1894.

6 THE REPORTS 67.

A witness may be cross-examined as to his credibility, but he should have his attention drawn to any facts with respect to which it is intended to impeach his credit by other witnesses so as to give him an opportunity of explanation, unless the evidence he gives is so incredible or romancing

that it is reasonable to let him leave the box without such questions being put.

In an action for libel certain witnesses were not cross-examined on a certain material matter. It was held that the jury could not be asked afterwards to disbelieve them.

LORD HERSCHELL, L.C. . . . **It seems to me to be absolutely essential to the proper conduct of a cause, where it is intended to suggest that a witness is not speaking the truth on a particular point, to direct his attention to the fact by some questions put in cross-examination** showing that that imputation is intended to be made, and not to take his evidence and pass it by as a matter altogether unchallenged, and then, when it is impossible for him to explain, as perhaps he might have been able to do if such questions had been put to him, the circumstances which it is suggested indicate that the story he tells ought not to be believed, to argue that he is a witness unworthy of credit. My Lords, I have always understood that **if you intend to impeach a witness you are bound, whilst he is in the box, to give him an opportunity of making any explanation** which is open to him; and, as it seems to me, that is not only a rule of professional practice in the conduct of a case, but is essential to fair play and fair dealing with witnesses. Sometimes reflections have been made upon excessive cross-examination of witnesses, and it has been complained of as undue; but it seems to me that **a cross-examination of a witness which errs in the direction of excess may be far more fair to him than to leave him without cross-examination, and afterwards to suggest that he is not a witness of truth,** I mean upon a point on which it is not otherwise perfectly clear that he has had full notice beforehand that there is an intention to impeach the credibility of the story which he is telling. Of course I do not deny for a moment that there are cases in which that notice has been so distinctly and unmistakably given, and the point upon which he is impeached, and is to be impeached, is so manifest, that it is not necessary to waste time in putting questions to him upon it. All I am saying is that **it will not do to impeach the credibility of a witness upon a matter on which he has not had any opportunity of giving an explanation** by reason of there having been no suggestion whatever in the course of the case that his story is not accepted. . . .

LORD HALSBURY. . . . With regard to the manner in which the

evidence was given in this case, I cannot too heartily express my concurrence with the Lord Chancellor as to the mode in which a trial should be conducted. To my mind **nothing would be more absolutely unjust than not to cross-examine witnesses upon evidence which they have given, so as to give them notice, and to give them an opportunity of explanation,** and an opportunity very often to defend their own character, and, not having given them such an opportunity, to ask the jury afterwards to disbelieve what they have said, although not one question has been directed either to their credit or to the accuracy of the facts they have deposed to. . . .

Lord Morris. . . . There is another point upon which I would wish to guard myself, namely, with respect to laying down any hard-and-fast rule as regards cross-examining a witness as a necessary preliminary to impeaching his credit. In this case, I am clearly of opinion that **the witnesses, having given their testimony, and not having been cross-examined,** having deposed to a state of facts which is quite reconcilable with the rest of the case, it was impossible for the plaintiff to ask the jury at the trial, and **it is impossible for him to ask any legal tribunal, to say that those witnesses are not to be credited. But I can quite understand a case in which** a story told by a witness may have been of so incredible and romancing a character that **the most effective cross-examination would be to ask him to leave the box.** I therefore wish it to be understood that I would not concur in ruling that it was necessary, in order to impeach a witness's credit, that you should take him through the story which he had told, giving him notice by the questions that you impeached his credit.

Lord Bowen concurred.

Note.—" This much counsel is bound to do, when cross-examining; he must put to each of his opponent's witnesses in turn, so much of his own case as concerns that particular witness or in which that witness had any share. Thus, if the plaintiff has deposed to a conversation with the defendant, it is the duty of the counsel for the defendant to indicate by his cross-examination how much of the plaintiff's version of the conversation he accepts, and how much he disputes, and to suggest what the defendant's version will be. If he ask no question as to it, he will be taken to accept the plaintiff's account in its entirety " (*Odgers, Pleading*, 327-8).

MAXWELL v. DIRECTOR OF PUBLIC PROSECUTIONS.

HOUSE OF LORDS. 1935.

[1935] A. C. 309; 103 L. J. K. B. 501; 151 L. T. 477; 50 T. L. R. 499; 24 Cr. App. R. 152; 30 Cox C. C. 160; 98 J. P. 387.

The cross-examination as to a prisoner's character allowed by the Criminal Evidence Act, 1898, s. 1, proviso (f) (see post, p. 480), is subject to the common law rule as to relevancy. The mere fact that a person has been charged with an offence and acquitted is not relevant to impeach his credibility as a witness.

The prisoner was charged with the manslaughter of a woman by performing an illegal operation on her. Having given evidence of good character, he was cross-examined as to a previous case in which a patient of his had died in suspicious circumstances and in which he had been prosecuted and acquitted. It was held that the questions were not admissible.

The following is from the Law Reports:—

VISCOUNT SANKEY, L.C. The question is whether it was permissible in the particular facts of the case, under the Criminal Evidence Act, 1898, s. 1, proviso (*f*), for the prosecution to ask the prisoner whether on a previous occasion he had been **charged** with a similar offence, the charge having been tried and having resulted in an **acquittal. . . .** It must first of all be stated that it has been admitted throughout that the **prisoner** in saying that he had lived a good, clean, moral life **had put his character in issue,** and had in the words of proviso (*f*) (ii) "given evidence of his good character". The first question here is, What consequences follow from that?

This involves the proper construction of section 1 (*f*) of that Act. We start with the hypothesis that the prisoner had given evidence of his good character. It will be remembered that it was not until the year 1854 that the parties to a civil case were entitled to give evidence on their own behalf. But a prisoner could not give evidence on his own behalf at his trial until the coming into operation of the Criminal Evidence Act, 1898, except in a few cases, of which the most important are those specified in certain sections of the Offences against the Person Act, 1861, the Law of Evidence Act, 1877, and the Criminal Law Amendment Act, 1885. When Parliament by the Act of 1898 effected a change in the general law and made the prisoner in every case a competent witness, it was in an evident difficulty, and it pursued the familiar English system of a compromise. It was clear that if you allowed a prisoner to go into the witness-box, it was impossible to allow him to be treated as an ordinary witness. Had that been permitted, a prisoner who went into the box to give evidence on oath could have been asked about any previous conviction, with the result that an old offender would seldom, if ever, have been acquitted. This would have offended against one of the most deeply rooted and jealously guarded principles of our criminal law, which, as stated in *Makin* v. *Attorney-General for New South Wales* (*ante*, p. 107), is that "it is undoubtedly not competent for the prosecution to adduce evidence tending to show that the accused has been guilty of criminal acts other than those covered by the indictment, for the purpose of leading to the conclusion that the accused is a person likely from his criminal conduct or character to have committed the offence for which he is being tried".

Some middle way, therefore, had to be discovered, and the result was that a certain amount of protection was accorded to a prisoner who gave evidence on his own behalf. As it has been expressed, he was presented with a shield and it was provided that he was not to be asked, and that, if he was asked, he should not be required to answer, any question tending to show that he had committed or been convicted of or been charged with any offence other than that wherewith he was then charged, or was a bad character. Apart, however, from this protection, he was placed in the position of an ordinary witness in an ordinary civil case. The laws of evidence were not otherwise altered by the Criminal Evidence Act, 1898, and the prisoner who was a witness in his own case could not be asked questions which were irrelevant or had nothing to do with the issue which the Court was endeavouring to decide. As has already been pointed out, the prisoner in the present case threw away his shield and, therefore, the learned counsel for the prosecution was entitled to ask him, and **he could be required to answer, any question tending to show that he had committed or been convicted of or been charged with an offence, but subject to the consideration that the question asked him must be one which was relevant and admissible in the case of an ordinary witness.** The Act does not in terms say that in any case a prisoner may be asked or required to answer questions falling within proviso (*f*), or impose any such affirmative or absolute burden upon him. I think this conclusion is confirmed by a study of the words of the statute. In section 1, proviso (*e*), it has been enacted that a witness may be cross-examined in respect of the offence charged, and cannot refuse to answer questions directly relevant to the offence on the ground that they tend to incriminate him: thus if he denies the offence, he may be cross-examined to refute the denial. These are matters directly relevant to the charge on which he is being tried. Proviso (*f*), however, is dealing with matters outside and not directly relevant to, the particular offence charged; such matters, to be admissible at all, must in general fall under two main classes: one is the class of evidence which goes to show not that the prisoner did the acts charged, but that, if he did these acts, he did them as part of a system or intentionally, so as to refute a defence that if he did them he did them innocently or inadvertently, as, for instance, in *Makin* v. *Attorney-General for New South Wales* (*ante*, p. 107), where the charge was one of murder; another illustration of such cases is *R.* v. *Bond* (*ante*, p. 109). This rule applies to cases where guilty knowledge or design or intention is of the essence of the offence.

The other main class is where it is sought to show that the prisoner is not a person to be believed on his oath, which is generally attempted by what is called cross-examination to credit. Closely allied with this latter type of question is the rule that, if the prisoner by himself or his witnesses seeks to give evidence of his own good character, for the purpose of showing that it is unlikely that he committed the offence charged, he raises by way of defence an issue as to his good character, so that he may fairly be cross-examined on that issue, just as any witness called by him to prove his good character may be cross-examined to show the contrary. All these matters are dealt with in proviso (*f*). The substantive part of that proviso is negative in form and as such is universal and is absolute unless the exceptions come into play. Then come the three exceptions: but it does not follow that when the absolute prohibition is superseded by a permission, that the permission is as absolute as the prohibition. When it is sought to justify a question it must not only be brought within the terms of the permission, but also must be capable of justification according to the general rules of evidence and in particular must satisfy the test of relevance. Exception (i) deals with the former of the two main classes of evidence referred to above, that is, evidence falling within the rule that where issues of intention or design are involved in the charge or defence, the prisoner may be asked questions relevant to these matters, even though he has himself raised no question of his good character. Exceptions (ii) and (iii) come into play where the prisoner by himself or his witnesses has put his character in issue, or has attacked the character of others. Dealing with exceptions (i) and (ii), it is clear that the test of relevance is wider in (ii) than in (i); in the latter, proof that the prisoner has committed or been convicted of some other offence can only be admitted if it goes to show that he was guilty of the offence charged. In the former (exception (ii)), **the questions permissible must be relevant to the issue of his own good character and if not so relevant cannot be admissible.** But it seems clear that the **mere fact of a charge cannot** in general **be evidence of bad character** or be regarded otherwise than as a misfortune. It seemed to be contended on behalf of the respondent that a charge was *per se* such evidence that the man charged, even though acquitted, must thereafter remain under a cloud, however innocent. I find it impossible to accept any such view. **The mere fact that a man has been charged with an offence is no proof that he committed the offence. Such a fact is, therefore, irrelevant**; it neither goes to show that the prisoner did the acts for which he is actually being tried nor does it go to his credibility as a witness. Such questions must, therefore, be excluded on the principle which is fundamental in the law of evidence as conceived in this country, especially in criminal cases, because, if allowed, they are likely to lead the minds of the jury astray into false issues; not merely do they tend to introduce suspicion as if it were evidence, but they tend to distract the jury from the true issue—namely, whether the prisoner in fact committed the offence on which he is actually standing his trial. It is of the utmost importance for a fair trial that the evidence should be *prima facie* limited to matters relating to the transaction which forms the subject of the indictment and that any departure from these matters should be strictly confined.

It does not result from this conclusion that the word "charged" in proviso (*f*) is otiose: it is clearly not so as regards the prohibition; and when the exceptions come into play there may still be cases in which a prisoner may be asked about a charge as a step in cross-examination leading to a question whether he was convicted on the charge, or in order to elicit some evidence as to statements made or evidence given by the prisoner in the course of the trial on a charge which failed, which tend to throw doubt on the evidence which he is actually giving, though cases of this last class must be rare and the cross-examination permissible only with great safeguards.

Again, a man charged with an offence against the person may perhaps be asked whether he had uttered threats against the person attacked because he was angry with him for bringing a charge which turned out to be unfounded. Other probabilities may be imagined. Thus, if a prisoner has been acquitted on a plea of *autrefois convict* such an acquittal might be relevant to his credit, though it would seem that what was in truth relevant to his credit was the previous conviction and not the fact that he was erroneously again charged with the same offence; again, it may be, though it is perhaps a remote supposition, that an acquittal of a prisoner charged with rape on the plea of consent may possibly be relevant to a prisoner's credit.

But these instances all involve the crucial test of relevance. And in general no question whether a prisoner has been convicted or charged or acquitted should be asked or, if asked, allowed by the Judge, who has a discretion under proviso (*f*), unless it helps to elucidate the particular issue which the jury is investigating, or goes to credibility, that is, tends to show that he is not to be believed on oath; indeed, the question whether a man has been convicted, charged or acquitted ought not to be admitted, even if it goes to credibility, if there is any risk of the jury being misled into thinking that it goes not to credibility but to the probability of his having committed the offence of which he is charged. I think that **it is impossible in the present case to say that the fact that the prisoner had been**

acquitted on a previous charge of murder or manslaughter, was relevant, or that it **tended** in the present case **to destroy his credibility as a witness.**

LORDS BLANESBURGH, ATKIN, THANKERTON and WRIGHT concurred. *Order of the Court of Criminal Appeal reversed.*

Note.—In *R.* v. *Waldman* (1934), 24 Cr. App. R. 204, the prisoner on a charge of receiving put his character in issue and was thereupon cross-examined on two previous cases, one of which resulted in a conviction and the other an acquittal. The C. C. A. held that this circumstance made the case distinguishable from *Maxwell's Case* and upheld the conviction. It should be observed that the section not only excuses the witness from answering. It also prohibits the question being put.

STIRLAND v. DIRECTOR OF PUBLIC PROSECUTIONS.

1944. See Appendix IV, *post*, p. 569.

PRICE v. MANNING.

COURT OF APPEAL. 1889.

L. R. 42 CH. D. 372; 58 L. J. CH. 649; 61 L. T. 537; 37 W. R. 785.

A party cannot generally cross-examine or discredit his own witness.

It is in the discretion of the Judge whether a party shall be permitted to cross-examine a witness whom he has called, even if the witness be a hostile litigant, as when one party calls the other party as a witness.

The plaintiff called the defendant as a witness to prove a point in his case. The defendant was cross-examined. On his re-examination the plaintiff's counsel put questions to him in the nature of cross-examination, treating him as a hostile witness. KAY, J., refused to allow this to be done.

The following is from the Law Journal:—

LOPES, L.J. Whether the witness called by one party is a litigant or non-litigant, **it is a matter of discretion in the presiding Judge whether the witness has shown himself so hostile** as to justify his cross-examination by the party calling him. **This rule applies in a case where an opponent is called as a witness. . . .**

Note.—It must be observed that the Judge can only allow a party to "cross-examine" his own witness. He cannot allow him to "discredit" generally a witness whom he has produced as a reliable person. This rule is now statutory by the Criminal Procedure Act, 1865, which applies to both civil and criminal cases (see *post*, p. 451, and *Stephen*, Art. 147).

R. v. HADWEN AND INGHAM.

1902. See Appendix IV, *post*, p. 571.

RE-EXAMINATION.

Two points should be noticed as to the questions permissible in re-examination:—

(*a*) They must be confined to **matters arising out of cross-examination.**

(*b*) They must be **not leading questions.**

PRINCE v. SAMO.

QUEEN'S BENCH. 1838.

7 L. J. Q. B. 123; 2 Jur. 323; 7 A. & E. 630; 3 N. & P. 139; 1 W. W. & H. 132; 45 R. R. 783.

Re-examination must be confined to matters arising out of, or explanatory of, the cross-examination. No new matter may be introduced without leave of the Judge.

So, proof by a witness, on cross-examination, of a statement made by him at a former time, does not authorise proof, on re-examination, of all that he said at the same time, but only of so much thereof as is connected with the statement proved on cross-examination.

The following is from the Law Journal:—

Lord Denman, C.J. (*delivering the judgment of the Court, which then included* Littledale, Patteson, Williams, and Coleridge,

JJ.). This was an action for a malicious arrest, on a false suggestion that money was lent by the defendant to the plaintiff, when it had, in fact, been given. **The plaintiff called** his attorney **as a witness;** he happened to be present at the trial of a prosecution for perjury, instituted by the plaintiff against a witness in the action wherein he had been arrested. **The defendant's counsel inquired of him in cross-examination** whether the plaintiff had not, on the trial for perjury, stated that he himself had been insolvent repeatedly, and remanded by the Court. This question was not objected to. **On his re-examination the same witness was asked** whether the plaintiff had not also on that occasion given an account of the circumstances out of which the arrest had arisen, and what that account was, for the purpose of laying before the jury proof that the arrest was without cause, or malicious, of both which facts there was scarcely any, if any, evidence whatever. The question, expressly confined to that purpose, was whether the plaintiff did not say, in his examination, that the money was given, and not lent. **To this question the defendant's counsel objected,** not on account of its leading form, but because the defendant, having proved one detached expression that fell from the plaintiff when a witness, does not make the whole of what he then said evidence in his own favour. My opinion was, that the witness might be asked as to everything said by the plaintiff, when he appeared on the trial of the indictment, that could in any way qualify or explain the statement as to which he had been cross-examined, but that he had no right to add any independent history of transactions wholly unconnected with it. **That a witness's statement of some one thing said by him, though drawn out by a cross-examination, does not permit the opposite party to add to it all that he may have uttered on the same occasion, was in effect decided** by seven out of eight Judges, whose opinion was taken **by the House of Lords,** in the progress of the bill of pains and penalties against Her Majesty Queen Caroline. **Lord Tenterden, in delivering that opinion, said:** "I think the counsel has a right, on re-examination, to ask all questions which may be proper to draw forth an explanation of the sense and meaning of the expressions used by the witness on cross-examination, if they be in themselves doubtful, and also of the motive by which the witness was induced to use those expressions; but I think he has no right to go further, and to introduce new matters not suited to the purpose of explaining either the expressions or the motives of the witness"; and as many things may pass in one and the same conversation, which do not relate to either, the learned Chief Justice declared the opinion of the Judges, that the witness could not be re-examined, even to the extent of all that might have passed relating to his becoming a witness, to which the statement proved had reference. . . .

Upon the whole, we think that it must be taken as settled that proof of a detached statement made by a witness at a former time, does not authorise proof by the party calling that witness, of all that he said at the same time, but only of so much as can be in some way connected with the statement proved. . . .

Note.—The Judge will, whenever he considers it proper or necessary, allow questions to be put although they may not arise out of the cross-examination. For instance, on important matters which have been overlooked. But in such case he will of course allow a further cross-examination on such questions. The Judge may, moreover, put further questions himself, or allow witnesses to be recalled.

In *R.* v. *Morrison*, 75 J. P. 272, the Court, in very special circumstances, even allowed the accused to call fresh evidence after counsel for the prosecution had commenced his final speech.

CONTRADICTION OF WITNESSES.

EWER v. AMBROSE.

KING'S BENCH. 1825.

3 B. & C. 746; 5 D. & R. 629.

If a witness gives evidence which is unfavourable to the party calling him, such party may contradict him by other witnesses, but he may not call general evidence to show that his own witness is not to be believed.

In an action for money had and received, the defence being that the defendant was jointly liable with a partner against whom judgment had been recovered, a witness was called by the defendant to prove the partnership, but he proved the contrary. It was held that the defendant could not discredit his own witness, but he could contradict him by other witnesses.

The following is from Barnewall and Cresswell:—

HOLROYD, J. I take the rule of law to be, that if a witness proves a case against the party calling him, the latter may show the truth by other witnesses. But it is undoubtedly true, that if a party calls a witness to prove a fact, **he cannot, when he finds the witness proves the contrary, give general evidence to show that that witness is not to be believed on his oath, but he may show by other evidence that he is mistaken** as to the fact which he is called to prove. . . .

LITTLEDALE, J. Where a witness is called by a party to prove his case, and he disproves that case, I think the party is still at liberty to prove his case by other witnesses. It would be a great hardship if the rule were otherwise, for **if a party had four witnesses upon whom he relied to prove his case, it would be very hard, that by calling first the one who happened to disprove it, he should be deprived of the testimony of the other three.** If he had called the three before the other who had disproved the case, it would have been a question for the jury upon the evidence whether they would give credit to the three or to the one. **The order in which the witnesses happen to be called ought not, therefore, to make any difference. . . .**

Note.—See also *Bradley* v. *Ricardo* (1831), 8 Bing. 57.

It is important to bear in mind the contrast between adducing evidence which conflicts with that given by the former witness where such evidence is relevant to the issue and contradicting a witness by other evidence where the subject matter is something not in itself relevant but merely going to credibility (see *Stephen*, Art. 147). The next case illustrates this point.

HARRIS v. TIPPETT.

NISI PRIUS. 1811.

2 CAMPBELL 637; 12 R. R. 767.

Although questions going to the character or credibility of a witness are admissible on cross-examination, yet if they be directed to matters collateral to the issue, the answers

must be accepted as conclusive, and other witnesses cannot be called to contradict him, except in a few cases.

A witness for the defendant, being asked in cross-examination whether he had not attempted to dissuade one of the plaintiff's witnesses from attending to give evidence, swore that he had not done so. The plaintiff's counsel then proposed to call back the other witness to contradict him. This was not allowed.

LAWRENCE, J. **Had this been a matter in issue, I would have allowed you to call witnesses to contradict** what the last witness has sworn, but it is entirely collateral, and you must take his answer. I will permit questions to be put to a witness as to any improper conduct of which he may have been guilty, for the purpose of trying his credit; **but when these questions are irrelevant to the issue on the record, you cannot call other witnesses to contradict the answer** he gives. No witness can be prepared to support his character as to particular facts, and such collateral inquiries would lead to endless confusion.

R. v. HOLMES.

CROWN CASES RESERVED. 1871.

L. R. 1 C. C. R. 334; 41 L. J. M. C. 12; 25 L. T. 669; 20 W. R. 122; 12 Cox C. C. 137.

In prosecutions for rape, or assault with intent to commit rape or indecent assault, the prosecutrix may be cross-examined as to particular acts of immorality with any persons. But, although as regards her acts committed with the prisoner himself, witnesses may be called to contradict her, if she denies them; it is otherwise as to her acts of immorality committed with other persons.

The prisoner was charged with indecent assault, which, from the evidence, appeared to amount to an attempt at rape. The defence was consent. The prosecutrix, in her cross-examination, was asked if she had had connexion with another man, and she denied it.

The man in question was then called to contradict her, but the Judge disallowed the evidence. The Court for Crown Cases Reserved affirmed the prisoner's conviction.

The following is from the Law Journal:—

KELLY, C.B. . . . On an indictment for rape, or for an attempt to commit a rape, or for an indecent assault, which, upon the circumstances of the case, amounts to an attempt to commit a rape, **a question put to the prosecutrix as to an act of connexion with a particular person, and denied by her, cannot be contradicted.** If a witness is cross-examined as to a collateral fact, the answer must be taken for better or worse, and the witness cannot be contradicted. If the question were admissible it might involve an inquiry into her whole life. . . . There is no doubt the prosecutrix may be asked **as to connexion with the prisoner on a prosecution for rape. There the fact has a direct bearing on the question** before the Court, which involves the fact of consent or non-consent on the part of the prosecutrix. . . .

BYLES, J. I concur. **I think the prosecutrix, on an indictment for rape, cannot be contradicted by men called to speak to connexion with her.** Rape may be committed on a prostitute; the evidence therefore is immaterial. . . .

PIGOTT, B. I am of the same opinion, because the prosecutrix in these cases might always have a number of persons spring upon her at the trial whose evidence she would be totally unprepared to meet.

LUSH, J. I am convinced that **this evidence is too remote** from the issue to be admissible. It has no bearing upon the particular charge, and was, therefore, properly rejected.

HANNEN, J. I think no distinction can be drawn between a charge of rape and an indecent assault, and that the same reasoning applies to both cases. . . . It would be impossible for the prosecutrix to be prepared to meet the cases which might be produced.

Note.—The above case merely decides that witnesses cannot be called to contradict the prosecutrix as to acts of immorality committed with persons other than the prisoner. It is an illustration of the rule stated in the previous case. The case of *R.* v. *Riley* (*ante*, p. 112) had decided that evidence could be called to contradict her as to other acts of immorality committed with the prisoner himself. Such evidence is admitted as relevant to consent, not as evidence of character; as such case shows.

EVIDENCE TO DISCREDIT WITNESSES.

The general rule is that a party is not allowed to call witnesses to prove facts which merely tend to discredit his opponent's witnesses, and are not otherwise relevant to the matters in issue. Such collateral inquiries are rejected on the grounds that they would unduly complicate and prolong trials without adequate reason, and that a man cannot be expected to defend all the acts of his life without notice. But there appear to be four generally recognised cases in which evidence to discredit is allowed.

Evidence to discredit a witness is admissible to prove:—

1. That he has made previous statements inconsistent with his present evidence. [This is not strictly an exception to the rule that an adversary's witnesses cannot be contradicted on matters that merely affect credit, for the previous statement must, in order to let in contradiction, be one "relative to the subject-matter of the case" (Criminal Procedure Act, 1865, s. 4; *post*, p. 452).]

2. That he is prejudiced or biased in favour of the party calling him, or is giving his evidence from some corrupt or indirect motive.

3. That he has such a general bad character for veracity that he is not to be believed on his oath.

4. That he has been convicted of a felony or misdemeanour.

Cases are here given on the first three points. The last was first laid down by the Common Law Procedure Act, 1854, s. 25, which is now repealed; but it is re-enacted, and applied to both civil and criminal cases, by the Criminal Procedure Act, 1865, which also makes statutory point (1) above. (See *post*, p. 451.)

ATTORNEY-GENERAL v. HITCHCOCK.

EXCHEQUER. 1847.

16 L. J. Ex. 259; 11 Jur. 478; 1 Ex. 91; 74 R. R. 592.

When a witness is asked in cross-examination if he has made a certain statement, which is material to the issue, and at variance with his evidence, and he denies that he made such a statement, witnesses may be called to prove that he did make such statement.

When a witness is cross-examined with the view of showing that he is biased, or giving his evidence from some corrupt or indirect motive, and he denies it, witnesses may be called to prove that he is biased; for instance, that he has been bribed to give evidence, or has offered a bribe to another witness, but not that a bribe has been offered to him and refused.

The defendant, a maltster, was charged on information with having used a cistern for the making of malt, without making an entry thereof, as required by Act of Parliament. A witness, having sworn that the cistern had been used, was asked if he had not said to one Cook that the Excise officers had offered him 20*l.* to say the cistern had been used; and he denied that he had made such statement. The defendant's counsel thereupon called Cook, and proposed to ask him whether the witness had told him so. The evidence was disallowed.

The following is from the Law Journal:—

Pollock, C.B. . . . The test of whether an inquiry is collateral or not is, whether the fact to be elicited is material to the issue. If it be, then the witness may be contradicted, or, as it is better put by my Brother Alderson, thus: **If you ask a witness whether he has not made a certain statement which would be material, and opposed to part of his testimony, you may then call witnesses to prove that he has made the statement,** and the jury are at liberty to believe either the one account or the other. . . . The statement which may be contradicted must be one which refers to matter that may be given in evidence, and if answered in one way would contradict part of the witness's testimony, and be material.

There is, however, a distinction between contradicting a witness in particulars stated by him, and those which have reference to his motives, temper, character, and feelings. . . . **A witness may be asked how he stands affected towards one of the parties;** and if his relation towards them is such as to prejudice his mind, and fill him with sentiments of revenge or other feelings of a similar kind, **and if he denies the fact, evidence may be given to show the state of his mind and feelings.** But these cases of the witness's connection with the parties in feelings and sentiments are not to be confounded with those other cases where the matter to be admissible in evidence must be connected with the question. . . .

In the present case it could not be proved that a bribe was offered to the witness and not accepted, for such a fact is clearly irrelevant to the matter in issue. **The offer of a bribe is a matter of no importance, if it be not accepted,** for it does not disparage the party to whom it is offered. . . .

ALDERSON, B. A witness may be asked a question, and if the answer tends to qualify another part of his testimony, evidence may be given in contradiction. So if the question relates not to what he has said, but to some fact material to the issue, the same rule prevails. . . . **The offer of a bribe by a witness to another, or the fact of a bribe having been accepted by him, tends to show that he is not impartial. . . .**

A witness, however, is not to be examined as to collateral facts. In many cases his doing a particular act is collateral. In such cases **his evidence as to the fact is to be received as final;** but no witness ought to be called on to prove his whole life; and if contradiction of his testimony were permitted, he ought to be allowed to support it by other evidence, and to prove his innocence; the result of which would be, that an endless amount of collateral issues would have to be tried. The convenient administration of justice, therefore requires that this course should not be adopted. If the witness has spoken falsely he may be indicted for perjury. **When the answer given is not material to the issue, public convenience requires that it be taken as decisive, and that no contradiction be allowed.** In the present case, the witness was asked whether he had been offered a bribe to say the cistern had been used. This was not material, nor did it qualify what had gone before, for his being offered a bribe did not show that he was not a fair and credible witness.

ROLFE, B. The rules of evidence are founded on abstract and practical consideration; and one principle is, that **you may contradict any part of the testimony that has been given, and which tends to support the issue.** Here the question was, whether the witness had ever said he had been offered a bribe; and if that may be contradicted, not by showing that he had received a bribe, but by showing that he had said he had been offered a bribe, there would be no end to the collateral inquiries that would arise. **The offer of a bribe, if rejected, has no bearing upon the credit of the witness.** In fact, it was offered in the present case merely for the purpose of discrediting other persons, and not to disparage the witness.

Note.—The rule as to calling evidence of previous inconsistent statements is now embodied in the Criminal Procedure Act, 1865, which applies to both civil and criminal cases, but it is provided by s. 4 that the witness's attention must first be called to the particular occasion (see *post*, p. 452). The other point in the above cases, as to bias or corrupt motive, is further illustrated by the case of *Thomas* v. *David*, *post*, p. 319.

GREENOUGH v. ECCLES.

COMMON PLEAS. 1859.

28 L. J. C. P. 160; 7 W. R. 341; 5 JUR. (N.S.) 766; 5 C. B. (N.S.) 786.

Although a party calling a witness may not discredit him generally, even if he proves "adverse" or "unfavourable", yet if he proves actually "hostile" he may under the Common Law Procedure Act, 1854 (now the Criminal Procedure Act, 1865), by leave of the Judge, give evidence that such witness has made previous inconsistent

statements. But he may not give general evidence of the bad character of a witness he himself produces.

The following is from the Law Journal:—

WILLIAMS, J. (*delivering the judgment of himself and* WILLES, J.). The question in this case is, whether in construing the terms of the 22nd section of the **Common Law Procedure Act, 1854,** "in case the witness shall prove adverse", the word "adverse" ought to be understood as meaning merely "unfavourable", or as meaning "hostile". . . . **The section lays down three rules as to the power of a party to discredit his own witness: First,** he shall not be allowed to impeach his credit by general evidence of his bad character. **Secondly,** he may contradict him by other evidence. **Thirdly,** he may prove that he has made at other times a statement inconsistent with his present testimony. These three rules appear to include the principal questions that have ever arisen on the subject. . . . The law relating to the first two of these rules was settled before the passing of the Act, while, as to the third, the authorities were conflicting.

The section requires the Judge to *form an opinion* that the witness is adverse, before the right to contradict or prove that he has made inconsistent statements is to be allowed to operate. **This is reasonable, and indeed necessary, if the word "adverse" means "hostile", but wholly unreasonable and unnecessary if it means "unfavourable".** On these grounds we think the preferable construction is, that **in case the witness** shall, in the opinion of the Judge, **prove "hostile", the party producing him may not only contradict him by other witnesses,** as he might heretofore have done, and may still do, if the witness is unfavourable, **but may also,** by leave of the Judge, **prove that he has made inconsistent statements. . . .**

Note.—S. 22 of the Common Law Procedure Act, 1854, which in the above case came before the Court for construction, provided:—

"A party producing a witness shall not be allowed to impeach his credit by general evidence of bad character, but he may, in case the witness shall, in the opinion of the Judge, prove *adverse*, contradict him by other evidence, or, by leave of the Judge, prove that he has made at other times a statement inconsistent with his present testimony".

In the above case the word "adverse" was held to mean "hostile" for the purposes of the section of the Act in question.

The above section is now repealed, but it is re-enacted *verbatim* by the Criminal Procedure Act, 1865, which applies to both civil and criminal cases (see *post*, p. 452).

Witnesses who *must* be called to prove attestation (see *post*, p. 371) are regarded as the Court's witnesses, and evidence of previous inconsistent statements by them is admissible, even though they are not hostile (*Coles* v. *Coles*, L. R. 1 P. & D. 70).

THOMAS v. DAVID.

NISI PRIUS. 1836.

7 C. & P. 350; 48 R. R. 794.

A witness may be cross-examined as to facts tending to show that he is prejudiced or biased in any way in favour of the party calling him, and if he denies such facts, witnesses may be called to contradict him.

In an action on a promissory note, one of the plaintiff's witnesses, who was his female servant, and who was one of the attesting witnesses to the defendant's signature of the promissory note, was asked, on cross-examination, whether she did not constantly sleep in the same bed with her master. She said that she did not. The defendant was allowed to call a witness to prove she did.

COLERIDGE, J. Is it not material to the issue, whether the principal witness who comes to support the plaintiff's case is his kept mistress? If the question had been, whether the witness had walked the streets as a common prostitute, I think that that would have been collateral to the issue, and that, had the witness denied such a charge, she could not have been contradicted; but here, **the question is, whether the witness had contracted such a relation with the plaintiff as might induce her the more readily to conspire with him** to support a forgery, just in the same way as if she had been asked if she was the sister or daughter of the plaintiff, and had denied that. I think that the contradiction is admissible.

Note.—See also *Att.-Gen.* v. *Hitchcock*, *ante*, p. 315.

R. v. BROWN.

CROWN CASES RESERVED. 1867.

L. R. 1 C. C. R. 70; 36 L. J. M. C. 59; 15 W. R. 795.

A party may call witnesses to swear that, in their opinion, based on their knowledge of the general character and reputation of a witness on the other side, he is not to be believed on his oath.

At the close of the case for the prosecution, the counsel for the defendants, after having called several witnesses to character, proposed to call witnesses to prove that they would not believe the witnesses for the prosecution on their oaths. The Court refused to receive such evidence, but stated a case for the Court for Crown Cases Reserved. The evidence was held admissible.

The following is from the Law Journal:—

KELLY, C.B. **It has been the practice to admit the evidence** rejected in this case **for centuries without dispute,** and we have personal knowledge of its existence during our time. So long a practice cannot be altered but by the Legislature.

MARTIN, B. **The practice has existed as long as I can remember** in my professional career.

BYLES and KEATING, JJ., concurred in testifying to the long existence of the practice.

The following is from the Law Reports:—

The Court, however, declined to hear any further argument on the subject, observing that all the text-writers were agreed that the evidence could be given, and that the practice was so ancient, and hitherto so undoubted, that it could not be altered now unless by the authority of the Legislature.

Note.—Notwithstanding the clear and emphatic language of the Judges in this case, there appears to be some question as to how far it can be relied on in practice. It certainly is not at all usual to call such evidence. But it seems clear that the evidence must relate to general reputation only and not to specific acts of misconduct.

As to proof of Previous Convictions, see *post*, p. 453.

MATTERS EXCLUDED BY PUBLIC POLICY OR PRIVILEGE.

Although a witness may, in general, be compelled to give evidence, he may still refuse to answer certain questions, or to produce certain documents, on well-recognised grounds of public policy or personal privilege.

The chief matters excluded by Public Policy are:—

(1) Affairs of State.

(2) Information for the detection of crime.

(3) Statements by parents bastardizing their offspring.

(4) Statements made "without prejudice" (see fully *ante*, pp. 54—57).

The chief matters protected by Privilege are:—

(1) That the answer to the question, or the production of the document, would tend to criminate the witness, or expose him to a criminal charge, penalty or forfeiture.

(2) That the answer or document would disclose confidential communications between client and legal adviser, or information obtained for the purposes of litigation.

(3) That the document relates solely to the title or case of the witness, if he be a party to the action.

(4) That the document is a document of title of the witness, if he be no party to the action.

(5) That the answer or document would disclose a communication made to the witness by his wife or her husband.

(6) That the answer would tend to show that the witness has been guilty of adultery.

Cases are given below on each of the above points excepting the fifth and sixth. The fifth is statutory, by the Evidence Amendment Act, 1853 (see *post*, p. 443), and the Criminal Evidence Act, 1898 (see *post*, p. 480). The sixth is also statutory, by the Judicature Act, 1925, s. 198 (see *post*, p. 508).

PUBLIC POLICY.

AFFAIRS OF STATE.

BEATSON v. SKENE.

EXCHEQUER. 1860.

29 L. J. Ex. 430; 2 L. T. 378; 8 W. R. 544; 6 Jur. (n.s.) 780; 5 H. & N. 838.

Documents and communications respecting matters of State are protected from disclosure, whenever it would be injurious to the public interests. The Judge will generally be guided in this matter by the opinion of the head of the department having the control of the document.

The plaintiff commanded a cavalry corps during the Crimean War. The defendant was a civil commissioner attached to such corps. General Vivian, who commanded in the district, directed Colonel Shirley to inquire into and report on the condition of the corps, referring him to the defendant for information. In a written communication from Colonel Shirley to the General were some defamatory observations concerning the plaintiff, the responsibility of which the defendant adopted, and the plaintiff sued him for slander. The rest of the facts appear from the judgment.

The following is from the Law Journal:—

Pollock, C.B. (*delivering the judgment of the Court*, Pollock, C.B., Martin, Bramwell and Wilde, BB.). . . . **It appeared that the Secretary of State for War,** Mr. Sidney Herbert, **had been subpœnaed** to produce certain letters written by the plaintiff to him, and also the minutes of a Court of Inquiry as to Colonel Shirley's conduct in writing the letters in question to General Vivian. Mr. Sidney Herbert attended at the trial, **but objected to produce the documents on the ground that his doing so would be injurious to the public service.** The learned Judge refused to compel their production on Mr. Sidney Herbert making this statement. . . .

We are all of opinion that it cannot be laid that all public documents of every sort, including treaties with foreign powers, and all the correspondence that may precede or accompany them, and all communications to the heads of departments, are to be produced and made public whenever a suitor in a court of justice thinks that his case requires such production. **It is manifest, we think, that there must be a limit to the duty or the power of compelling the production** of papers which are connected with acts of State.

We are of opinion that **if the production of a State paper would be injurious to the public service, the general public interest must be considered paramount** to the individual interest of a suitor in a court of justice; **and the question then arises, how is this to be determined?** .

It is manifest it must be determined either by the presiding Judge or by the responsible servant of the Crown in whose custody the paper is. **The Judge would be unable to determine it without ascertaining what the document was,** and why the publication of it would be injurious to the public service, an inquiry which cannot take place in private, and which, taking place in public, may do all the mischief which it is proposed to guard against. It appears to us, therefore, that **the question, whether the production of the document would be injurious to the public service, must be determined, not by the Judge, but by the head of the department** having the custody of the paper; and **if he is in attendance,** and states that in his opinion the production of that document would be injurious to the public service, we think the Judge ought not to compel the production of it. . . . **If the head of the department does not attend personally** to say that the production of the document will be injurious, but sends the document to be produced or not, as the Judge may think proper, or . . . where a subordinate is sent with the document, with instructions to object, but nothing more; **then, indeed, the case may be different, and the Judge may compel the production of it. . . .** Perhaps cases might arise where the matter would be so clear that the Judge might well ask for it in spite of some official scruples as to producing it; but this must be considered rather as an extreme case; and extreme cases throw very little light upon the practical rules of life. . . .

HENNESSY v. WRIGHT.

QUEEN'S BENCH DIVISION. 1888.

L. R. 21 Q. B. D. 509; 57 L. J. Q. B. 594.

In an action against a newspaper for libel in imputing that the plaintiff, the Governor of a Colony, had sent home garbled reports to the Colonial Secretary of certain official proceedings in the Colony, the defendant applied for discovery of copies, in the custody of the plaintiff, of various communications passing either between himself and the Colonial Secretary, or between himself and a Royal Commission appointed to inquire into the affairs of the Colony, or between such Commissioner and the Colonial Secretary. The plaintiff, in his affidavit, objected to produce these documents on grounds of public policy, stating that the Colonial Secretary (who, however, had not filed any affidavit) had directed him to that effect. *Held*, that the plaintiff was entitled to withhold production of the copies in question.

The following is from the Law Reports:—

Field, J. . . . It is not, and I suppose could not be, alleged that these copies are the joint property of the plaintiff and the Colonial Secretary. . . . A more important question remains. Accepting the other statements in the affidavit as to the circumstances under which the copies were prepared and the action taken by the Colonial Secretary as true, are the copies privileged? There are two aspects of this question. First, the publication of a State document may involve danger to the nation. If the confidential communications made by servants of the Crown to each other, by superiors to inferiors, or by inferiors to superiors, in the discharge of their duty to the Crown were liable to be made public in a Court of justice at the instance of any suitor who thought proper to say "fiat justitia ruat cælum", an order for discovery might involve the country in war. Secondly, the publication of a State document may be injurious to servants of the Crown as individuals. There would be an end of all freedom in their official communications, if they knew that any suitor could legally insist that any official communication, of no matter how secret a character, should be produced openly in a Court of justice. . . . Here, a servant of the Crown, who is himself a party to the communications, is plaintiff. But a servant of the Crown ought not to be placed at a disadvantage in comparison with other subjects, and the plaintiff will be placed at a serious disadvantage if he cannot defend his honour without the seal of secrecy being removed from his official communications. . . . These communications are State documents, and therefore the copies are also State documents and are *prima facie* as such privileged from production. . . . It is, however, argued that the copies are not privileged because there has been no sufficient claim of privilege by the Colonial Secretary. . . . The principal case relied on in support of this contention is *Beatson* v. *Skene* (*supra*). . . . It is clear, however, that this decision has no bearing on the present case. The judgment (there) refers not to a summons for discovery, at which the head of the department does not and need not attend, either personally or by deputy, and as regards which neither he nor anyone on his behalf is under any obligation to make an affidavit, but to a proceeding at *nisi prius*, at which the head of the department has both appeared and objected. I think, however, that there is authority for refusing production of these copies at this stage, apart from any intervention of the Colonial Secretary. . . . I say nothing as to what course should be taken at the trial.

WILLS, J. . . . In my judgment, if the Secretary of State's assurance be necessary in order to protect the documents from inspection, a mere statement such as is contained in the plaintiff's affidavit is quite insufficient. . . . The question, therefore, arises whether, in the absence of objection by the responsible minister of the Crown, it is the duty of the Judge in an application for discovery to prevent the disclosure of the contents of such documents as those now in question. . . . In my opinion, the present case is covered by authority. In *Anderson* v. *Hamilton*, 2 B. & B. 156, n., in an action against the Governor of Heligoland, a correspondence between Lord Liverpool and the defendant was produced by the Under-Secretary of State. He made no objection on behalf of the Government to its production; but, notwithstanding that fact, . . . Lord Ellenborough declined to allow "secrets of State to be taken out of the hands of His Majesty's confidential servants". . . . I think the cases show that no sound distinction can be drawn between the duty of the Judge when objection is taken by the responsible officer of the Crown, or by the party, or when, no objection being taken by anyone, it becomes apparent to him that a rule of public policy prevents the disclosure of the documents or information sought.

Note.—This case was followed in *Asiatic Petroleum Co.* v. *Anglo-Persian Oil Co.*, [1916] 1 K. B. 822.

Although generally in cases of privilege, other evidence may be given of the facts, yet in the case of State documents or matters the exclusion is absolute, so that no evidence thereof at all is admissible. Unlike other cases of privilege, this is not the privilege of any particular person (*Ankin* v. *L. & N. E. Ry.*, [1930] 1 K. B. 527).

The Court may accept the unsworn statement of a Minister, if it regards that as sufficient, or it may require an affidavit sworn by him, or it may require him to attend in person (*Robinson* v. *State of S. Australia* (*No.* 2), [1931] A. C. 704).

It seems to be clear that the protection *may* cover a whole class of documents (*Ankin* v. *L. & N. E. Ry.*, *supra*), but in *Spigelmann* v. *Hocker* (50 T. L. R. 87), Macnaghten, J., ruled that whereas the Court will accept as final the decision of a Head of Department that the production of a *particular* document would be against the public interest, where the Minister states that the document is one of a *class* of documents which it would be injurious to disclose, the Court will examine the document itself and form its own opinion. The cases are not easy to reconcile with one another; and in practice it depends very much on the opinion of the Court as to the real merits of the claim made, whether it is allowed or not.

INFORMATION FOR THE DETECTION OF CRIME.

MARKS v. BEYFUS.

COURT OF APPEAL. 1890.

L. R. 25 Q. B. D. 494; 59 L. J. Q. B. 479.

Prosecutions instituted by the Director of Public Prosecutions are public prosecutions, and the Director may refuse to disclose the names of his informants or the information that they have given him.

In an action against the defendants for maliciously conspiring to prosecute the plaintiff for fraud, upon the trial of which charge he had been acquitted, the plaintiff called the Director of Public Prosecutions as a witness, and asked him to give the names of his informants and to produce the statement on which he had acted in directing the prosecution. The witness declined, on grounds of public policy, and his objection was upheld by the Judge. The plaintiff appealed.

The following is from the Law Reports:—

LORD ESHER, M.R. . . . The ground taken on behalf of the Director of Public Prosecutions is that this was a public prosecution, ordered by the Government (or by an official equivalent to the Government) for what was considered to be a public object, and that therefore the information ought not, on grounds of public policy, to be disclosed. The question whether this was a public prosecution in this sense depends upon the true construction of the statutes by which the office of Director of Public Prosecutions was created. [After referring to 42 & 43 Vict. c. 20, s. 2, and the regulations thereunder, his Lordship continued:] This is language which seems to put the Director of Public Prosecutions in a different position from that of a private prosecutor; he is in the position which a person authorised by the Government in former days would have been in—that is to say, a prosecution instituted or conducted by him is a public as distinguished from a private prosecution. What, then, is the rule in the case of a public prosecution? In the case of *Attorney-General* v. *Briant*, 15 M. & W. 169, Pollock, C.B., says: **"The rule is, that in a public prosecution the witness cannot be asked such questions as will disclose the informer,** if he be a third person . . . and we think the principle of the rule applies where a witness is asked if he himself is the informer." Now **this rule was founded on grounds of public policy,** and if this was a public prosecution the rule attaches; I think it was a public prosecution and that the rule applies. I do not say it can never be departed from; **if** the Judge should be of opinion that the **disclosure** of the name of the informant **is necessary** or right in order **to show the prisoner's innocence,** then one public policy is in conflict with another **public policy,** and that **which says that an innocent man is not to be condemned** when his innocence can be proved, is the policy that **must prevail.** But, **except in that case,** this rule is not a matter of discretion; **it is a rule of law,** and as such should be applied by the Judge at the trial. The learned Judge was therefore perfectly right in declining to let the witness answer the questions.

Appeal dismissed.

STATEMENTS BASTARDIZING OFFSPRING.

RUSSELL v. RUSSELL.

HOUSE OF LORDS. 1924.

L. R. [1924] A. C. 687; 93 L. J. P. 97; 131 L. T. 482; 68 S. J. 682; 40 T. L. R. 713.

When a child has been born in wedlock, it is not competent for either husband or wife to give evidence of their non-access during marriage so as to bastardize such child. This rule is not confined to direct issues of legitimacy, but applies also to any case where the evidence tends to bastardize the issue of the marriage.

The following is from the Law Reports:—

EARL OF BIRKENHEAD. . . . The leading case on the subject, *Goodright's Case*, 2 Cowp. 591, was decided by Lord Mansfield in the year 1777. . . . This great Judge laid down the law with characteristic lucidity. . . . "**It is a rule** founded on decency, morality and policy **that the parents shall not be permitted to say, after marriage, that they had had no connection and therefore the offspring is spurious**; more especially the mother who is the offending party. . . ." We have not to ask whether we should ourselves have laid it down; still less to consider whether changed social conditions have undermined its authority. We find the rule living and authoritative. We find its application to legitimacy proceedings everywhere conceded. Our task, therefore, is to determine whether evidence inadmissible in such proceedings is admissible in divorce. . . . **The rule as laid down is not limited to any special class of case. It is absolutely general in the comprehensiveness of its expression.** It has no geographical qualification. It does not lay down that where husband and wife are present in the same bed; the same bedroom; the same house; or the same town the evidence must be rejected; but that it may, on the other hand, be received if the husband has (for instance) been absent from the country for twelve months before the birth of the child. It says, upon the contrary, that **such evidence shall not be given at all; and the reason given is that it would tend, if given, to bastardize the issue and to invade the very special sanctity inherent in the conjugal relation. . . .** Lord Mansfield was not concerned with the grossness or indecency of the subject-matter which the reception of such evidence might disclose. . . . No Court is contaminated by examining any facts, or reviewing any language, which the administration of justice requires. Judges must do their duty, sacrificing if necessary their delicacy in the process. What Lord Mansfield meant was that a deeply seated domestic and social policy rendered it unbecoming and indecorous that evidence should be received from such a source; upon such an issue; and with such a possible result. . . .

I find nowhere in any of the cases which were elaborately argued before us any authority for the suggested limitation. And by reference to what principle is such a distinction to be drawn? When we are told that a rule is founded on public policy, decency, and morality, it would seem natural to propose it in all cases to which it applies verbally. If, in an issue where the child himself is a party, it is against public policy to admit the evidence of a parent to prove the bastardy of that child, why should an entirely different policy permit such evidence in the case where the vital issue is still the legitimacy of the child, even though it be raised for a different purpose, and perhaps with secondary emphasis? . . . This evidence we are told is admissible in divorce; being therefore so received it bastardizes the child. But if and when the child, becoming of age, applies for his writ in this House, and proceedings follow, the evidence will not be admissible, and he will be pronounced legitimate. Equally, of course, if the child instituted proceedings to-morrow for a declaration of legitimacy, we should be afforded the agreeable prospect of holding judicially in 1924 that the child was illegitimate; and in 1925 that he was legitimate. Nothing but absolute necessity, founded upon decisions binding upon me, would drive me to a conclusion so ludicrous and incongruous. I find here no such necessity.

It is said that the view recommended above will revolutionise the practice of the Divorce Court. In such cases, the non-access can almost always be established *aliunde*. If it cannot be so proved, the practice of the Divorce Court must accommodate itself to the authority of the rule. If the inconvenience proves intolerable, the Legislature, if it thinks proper, may provide a remedy.

I have only now to consider whether section 3 of the Act of 1869 has affected the validity of the doctrine. . . . That section makes indeed the parties to any proceeding instituted in consequence of adultery, and the husbands and wives of such parties, competent to give evidence in such proceeding. What in effect does it make such persons competent to do? Plainly and only, I should have thought, to give such testimony as the law of evidence allowed at that date or, as afterwards modified, that law may allow. It did not, and it did not purport to, alter any existing rule of evidence except that which dealt with the actual competency to give evidence at all.

The conclusions, therefore, which I reach upon the whole matter are: firstly, that the rule as laid down by Lord Mansfield and other great Judges is a general rule to be applied, in the full generality of its scope, to all cases which it is wide enough to cover; secondly, that the Act of 1869 has not affected the rule in any way.

[So *held* by EARL OF BIRKENHEAD, VISCOUNT FINLAY and LORD DUNEDIN; LORD SUMNER and LORD CARSON dissenting.]

Note.—It should be carefully noted that what the rule prohibits is evidence of non-access. It does not shut out other statements tending to bastardize, as is pointed out in *Warren* v. *Warren*, [1925] P. 107; see also *Frampton* v. *Frampton*, [1941] P. 24. Hence, if a woman says that, at the time when her husband had access to her, she also had intercourse with another man and that the resultant offspring is the child of that other man, such statement is admissible and is not rendered inadmissible because of the statement of her belief that the child is a bastard. In any case, such statement by her alone would not bastardize the child.

This distinction between evidence of non-access and other statements bastardizing the child seems rather to have been lost sight of in *R.* v. *Carmichael*, [1940] 1 K. B. 630. Since *Russell* v. *Russell*, evidence of non-access may not be given by either spouse even when they are living apart under a decree of judicial separation, or a magistrate's separation order, or a deed of separation (*Ettenfield* v. *Ettenfield*, [1940] P. 96 C. A.). The rule does not apply when the child was still-born (*Holland* v. *Holland*, [1925] P. 101), nor on petitions for nullity on the ground of non-consummation either by the husband (*Farnham* v. *Farnham*, [1937] P. 49) or by the wife (*Burgess* v. *Burgess*, [1937] P. 60). Similarly, a husband may testify that he never had any intercourse with his wife *before* their narriage, and so may bastardize an alleged child of the marriage orn less than six months thereafter (*The Poulett Peerage*, [1903] A. C. 395). And statements and letters by the wife pointing to non-access may be admissible, not as direct evidence of illegitimacy, but as part of the *res gestæ*, *i.e.*, as part of a course of conduct from which adultery and illegitimacy may be inferred (*The Aylesford Peerage*, 11 App. Cas. 1).

PRIVILEGE.

CRIMINATING QUESTIONS AND DOCUMENTS.

R. v. BOYES.

QUEEN'S BENCH. 1861.

30 L. J. Q. B. 301; 5 L. T. 147; 7 Jur. 1158; 1 B. & S. 311.

A witness, whether a party or stranger, is not compellable to answer any question, or to produce any document, the tendency of which would be to expose the witness (or probably the wife or husband of the witness) to any criminal charge, or any penalty, or forfeiture reasonably likely to be brought, sued for, or enforced. But the danger to be apprehended must be real and appreciable, with reference to the ordinary operation of law in the ordinary course of things.

A witness had been pardoned under the Great Seal, and so could not be prosecuted in the ordinary way. It was no valid objection that he still remained liable to impeachment, to which a pardon is no bar (by the provision of the Act of Settlement).

The following is from the Law Journal:—

Cockburn, C.J. (*delivering the judgment of the Court,* Cockburn, C.J., Crompton, Hill and Blackburn, JJ.). . . . **The question** on which our opinion is now required **is, whether the enactment of the third section of the Act of Settlement,** that " no pardon under the Great Seal shall be pleadable to an impeachment by the Commons in Parliament ", **is a sufficient reason for holding that the privilege of the witness still existed** in this case, on the ground that the witness, though protected by the pardon against every other form of prosecution, might, possibly, be subject to parliamentary impeachment. . . . **It was contended that a bare possibility of legal peril was sufficient** to entitle a witness to protection; nay, further, that the witness was the sole judge as to whether his evidence would bring him into danger of the law, and that the statement of his belief to that effect, if not manifestly made *mala fide,* should be received as conclusive.

With the latter of these propositions we are altogether unable to concur. Upon a review of the authorities, we are clearly of opinion . . . that, to entitle a party called as a witness to the privilege of silence, **the Court must see, from the circumstances of the case and the nature of the evidence which the witness is called to give, that there is reasonable ground to apprehend danger to the witness** from his being compelled to answer. We, indeed, quite agree that if the fact of the witness being in danger be once made to appear, **great latitude should be allowed to him in judging for himself of the effect of any particular question,** there being no doubt . . . that a question, which might appear at first sight a very innocent one, might, by affording a link in a chain of evidence, become the means of bringing home an offence to the party answering. Subject to this reservation a Judge is, in our opinion, bound to insist on a witness answering, unless he is satisfied that the answer will tend to place the witness in peril. Further than this, we are of opinion that **the danger to be apprehended must be real and appreciable with reference to the ordinary operation of law in the ordinary course of things;** not a danger of an imaginary and unsubstantial character, having reference to some extraordinary and barely possible contingency, so improbable that no reasonable man would suffer it to influence his conduct. We think that a merely remote and naked possibility, out of the ordinary course of law, and such as no reasonable man would be affected by, should not be suffered to obstruct the administration of justice. **The object of the law is to afford to a party,** called upon to give evidence in a proceeding *inter alios,* **protection against being brought by**

means of his own evidence within the penalties of the law. But it would be to convert a salutary protection into a means of abuse if it were to be held that a mere imaginary possibility of danger, however remote and improbable, was sufficient to justify the withholding of evidence essential to the ends of justice.

Now, in the present case, **no one seriously supposes that the witness runs the slightest risk of an impeachment** by the House of Commons. . . . To suppose that such a proceeding would be applied to the case of this witness would be ridiculous. . . .

It appears to us, therefore, that the witness in this case was not, in a rational point of view, in the slightest real danger from the evidence he was called upon to give when protected from all legal proceedings and that **it was, therefore, the duty of the presiding Judge to compel him to answer. . . .**

Note.—It should be carefully noted that in the case of the common law privilege of refusing to answer criminating questions, it is perfectly lawful and proper for the question to be put and it is for the witness to claim his privilege if he thinks fit (*Boyle* v. *Wiseman* (1855), 10 Ex. 647; 24 L. J. Ex. 160). This is to be contrasted with the position of the accused under the Criminal Evidence Act, 1898 and of parties to divorce proceedings based on adultery (Judicature Act, 1925, s. 198) where the question ought not even to be asked.

Bankruptcy is not treated as criminal and the risk of proceedings confers no immunity (*Ex. p. Haes*, [1902] 1 K. B. 98, C. A.), nor is adultery (*Blunt* v. *Park Lane Hotel*, [1942] 2 K. B. 253).

Although, as a rule, a witness is not compelled to criminate himself, several statutes have provided that he shall, in certain specified proceedings, make full discovery and answer all questions, but it is generally provided that such evidence shall not afterwards be used against him. See, for instance, the Larceny Acts, 1861, ss. 29, 85 (*post*, p. 480), and 1916, s. 43 (*post*, p. 501); the Explosive Substances Act, 1883, s. 6; the Corrupt Practices Act, 1883, s. 59 (*post*, p. 468); the Merchandise Marks Act, 1887, s. 19; the Bankruptcy Act, 1914, s. 15 (*post*, p. 499); and the Companies Act, 1929, s. 216 (*post*, p. 518).

As regards questions tending to criminate husbands and wives of witnesses, there may be some doubt. Probably the privilege exists in such cases. See *Taylor*, § 1453; *Best*, § 126; *Stephen*, Art. 129.

PYE v. BUTTERFIELD.

QUEEN'S BENCH. 1864.

34 L. J. Q. B. 17; 13 W. R. 178; 11 Jur. 220;
5 B. & S. 829.

A witness may, on the ground of privilege, refuse to answer a question which tends to show he has done an act which would render him liable to forfeit property.

In an action of ejectment, the Court refused to compel the defendant to answer interrogatories where the answer would tend to show that he had incurred a forfeiture of his lease by reason of his having broken a covenant therein not to under-let the premises.

The following is from the Law Journal:—

Cockburn, C.J. . . . According to the authorities which have been cited and the expressions used by the text-writers who have written upon the subject, those rules are perfectly fixed and established, that **no man shall be compelled to give an answer which shall have an effect leading to the forfeiture of his estate. . . .**

Crompton, J. . . . It is a principle of the law of evidence which these Courts have always recognised as applicable to the examination of witnesses, and everything shows that they were averse to extending the power of discovery to cases of forfeiture. **From the earliest times the rule has been adopted in the Courts of Equity** with regard to discovery. . . .

Mellor, J., concurred.

Note.—It is only on this ground of forfeiture that a witness can object to answer a question tending to subject him to a civil suit. Otherwise there is no privilege. (See the Witnesses Act, 1806, *post*, p. 431.)

LEGAL PROFESSIONAL COMMUNICATIONS AND DOCUMENTS.

WHEELER v. LE MARCHANT.

CHANCERY. 1881.

L. R. 17 Ch. D. 675; 50 L. J. Ch. 793; 44 L. T. 632; 45 J. P. 728.

Communications made in professional confidence to counsel, solicitors and their clerks, may not be disclosed without consent of the client.

This privilege extends to communications, statements, reports, etc., made by other persons on behalf of the client to the legal adviser, if obtained by the latter for the purpose of litigation or other business, but not otherwise.

Communications made to any other persons than legal advisers, e.g., to medical attendants or advisers, or clergymen, are not privileged.

The Court ordered production of letters which had passed between the solicitors of the defendants and their surveyor, except such (if any) as the defendants should state by affidavit to have been prepared confidentially after dispute had arisen between the plaintiff and the defendants and for the purpose of obtaining information, evidence or legal advice with reference to litigation existing or contemplated between the parties to the action.

The following is from the Law Journal:—

Jessel, M.R. . . . **The principle is of a very limited character. It does not protect all confidential communications** which a man must necessarily make in order to obtain advice, even when necessary for the protection of his life or of his honour, to say nothing of his fortune. **There are many communications which must be made,** because without them the ordinary business of life cannot be carried on, **and yet they are not protected.** As I have said in the course of the argument, the communication made to a **medical man,** whose advice is sought by a patient . . . is not protected. Communications made to the **priest** in the confessional, on matters perhaps considered by the penitent to be more important even than the care of his life or his fortune, are not protected. Communications made to **a friend** with respect to matters of the most delicate nature, on which advice is sought with respect to a man's honour or reputation, are not protected. Therefore it must not be supposed that there is any principle which says that every confidential communication which, in order to carry on the ordinary business of life, must necessarily be made, is protected. The protection is of a very limited character. **It is a protection in this country restricted to the obtaining the assistance of lawyers, as regards the conduct of litigation or the rights of property.** It has never gone beyond the obtaining legal advice and assistance; and **all things reasonably necessary in the shape of communication to the legal advisers are protected** from production or discovery, in order that that legal advice may be obtained safely and sufficiently. . . .

The actual communication to the solicitor by the client is, of course, protected, and it is equally protected whether that communication is made **by the client** in person or **by an agent** on behalf of the client, and whether made **to the solicitor** in person or **to a clerk or subordinate** of the solicitor, who acts in his place and under his direction. Again, with the same view, **the evidence obtained by the solicitor, or by his direction, or at his instance, even if obtained by the client, is protected if obtained after litigation has been commenced or threatened,** or with a view to the defence or prosecution of such litigation. So, again, it does not matter whether the advice is obtained from the solicitor as to a dealing which is not the subject of litigation. **What is protected is the communication necessary to obtain legal advice.** It must be a communication made to the solicitor in that character and for that purpose.

But what we are asked to protect here is this: The solicitor being consulted in a matter as to which no dispute has arisen, thinks he would like to know some further facts before giving his advice, and **applies to a surveyor** to tell him what the state of a given property is, or information of that character, **and it is said that information** given in answer to such application **ought to be protected** because it is desired or required by the solicitor in order to enable him the better to give legal advice. It appears to me that **it is not only**

extending the rule beyond what has been previously laid down, but beyond what necessity warrants. . . . It is a rule invented and maintained only for the purpose of enabling a man to obtain legal advice with safety. . . .

BRETT, L.J. The proposition laid before us for approval is, that where one of the parties to an action has in his possession or control documents which passed between his solicitor and third parties, and which contain either information or advice, those documents are protected in his hands from inspection on the ground that they are documents which passed between the solicitor and the third party for the purpose of enabling the solicitor to give advice to his client, although **such information and advice was obtained** by the solicitor for that purpose at a time **when there was no litigation pending between the parties nor any litigation contemplated.** It seems to me that that proposition cannot be acceded to. It is beyond any rule which has ever been laid down by the Court, and it seems to me that **it is beyond the principle of the rules which have been laid down.** The rule as to the non-production of communications between solicitor and client is a rule which has been determined upon as a matter of general or public policy. **It is confined entirely to communications which take place with a view to obtaining legal advice from professional persons.** It is so confined in terms, it seems to me it is so confined in principle, and it does not extend to the suggested case. . . .

COTTON, L.J. . . . It is said communications between a client and his legal advisers, for obtaining legal advice, are privileged, and therefore any communication between the representatives of the client and the solicitor must also be privileged. That is a fallacious use of the word "representatives". If the representative is a person employed as **an agent on the part of the client to obtain the legal advice of the solicitor,** of course he stands in exactly the same position, as regards protection, as the client, and his communications with the solicitors stand **in the same position** as the communications of **the principal** with his solicitor. But these persons were not representatives in that sense. They were representatives in this sense, that they were employed on behalf of the clients, the defendants, to do certain work, but that work was not the communicating with the solicitors to obtain legal advice. So their communications cannot be protected on the ground that they are communications between the client by his representatives and the solicitor.

In fact, **the proposition of the defendant comes to this, that all communications between a solicitor and a third person, in the course of his advising his client, are to be protected.**

It was conceded that there was no case that went that length, and the question is, whether we ought, in fully developing the principle, with all reasonable consequences, to protect such documents. **Hitherto such documents have been protected only when they have been made in contemplation of some litigation,** or for the purpose of **giving advice or obtaining evidence** with reference to it. **And that is reasonable, because** then the solicitor is preparing for the defence, or for bringing the action, and all communications he makes for that purpose, and **the communications** made to him for the purpose of giving him the information **are, in fact, the brief** in the action, and ought to be protected. . . .

Note.—It should be noticed that **the privilege is that of the client,** who alone can waive it (*Wilson* v. *Rastall,* 4 T. R. 754).

Its extent is stated very clearly in *Wills,* 276, who says that the privilege **protects from disclosure two classes of communications.** A narrower one where no litigation is on foot or intended and a wider one where it is, *viz*:—

(i) All communications made by a client to his legal adviser whether solicitor or counsel (and including communications between solicitor and counsel) in his professional capacity for the purpose of procuring his legal advice to protect his interests:

(ii) All statements of fact or opinion (whether made by lawyers or not) which the legal adviser has procured with a view to the conduct on behalf of his client of litigation actually commenced or reasonably in prospect as well as communications under (i).

R. v. COX AND RAILTON.

CROWN CASES RESERVED. 1884.

L. R. 14 Q. B. D. 153; 54 L. J. M. C. 41; 52 L. T. 25; 33 W. R. 396; 49 J. P. 374; 15 Cox C. C. 611.

Privilege extends only to those communications between solicitor and client which are made in the legitimate course of professional employment of the solicitor.

Communications made in furtherance of any criminal or fraudulent purpose are not privileged.

The Court must in each case determine, upon the facts, whether the accused consulted his solicitor after the crime for the legitimate purpose of being defended, or before the crime for the purpose of being assisted in committing it.

So a solicitor was compelled to disclose what passed between the prisoners and himself on an occasion when they called to consult him with reference to drawing up a bill of sale which was alleged to be fraudulent.

The following is from the Law Reports:—

STEPHEN, J. (*delivering the judgment of the Court*, LORD COLERIDGE, C.J., HAWKINS, STEPHEN, WATKIN WILLIAMS, and MATHEW, JJ.). . . . The conduct of Mr. Goodman, the solicitor, appears to have been unobjectionable. He was consulted in the common course of business, and gave a proper opinion in good faith. The question therefore is, whether, **if a client applies to a legal adviser for advice intended to facilitate or to guide the client in the commission of a crime or fraud,** the legal adviser being ignorant of the purpose for which his advice is wanted, the communication between the two is privileged. We expressed our opinion at the end of the argument that **no such privilege** existed. If it did, the result would be that a man intending to commit treason or murder might safely take legal advice for the purpose of enabling himself to do so with impunity, and that the solicitor to whom the application was made would not be at liberty to give information against his client for the purpose of frustrating his criminal purpose. Consequences so monstrous reduce to an absurdity any principle or rule in which they are involved. . . .

(*His Lordship here considered the cases.*)

We were greatly pressed with the argument that, speaking practically, the admission of any such exception to the privilege of legal advisers as that it is not to extend to communications made in furtherance of any criminal or fraudulent purpose **would greatly diminish the value of that privilege. The privilege must, it was argued, be violated in order to ascertain whether it exists.** The secret must be told in order to see whether it ought to be kept. . . .

In each particular case **the Court must determine upon the facts** actually given in evidence, or proposed to be given in evidence, **whether it seems probable that the accused person may have consulted his legal adviser,** not after the commission of the crime **for the legitimate purpose of being defended,** but before the commission of the crime, for the purpose of being guided or helped in committing it. We are far from saying that the question whether the advice was taken before or after the offence will always be decisive as to the admissibility of such evidence. Courts must in every instance judge for themselves on the special facts of each particular case, just as they must judge whether a witness deserves to be examined on the supposition that he is hostile, or whether a dying declaration was made in the immediate prospect of death. . . . **Of course, the power in question ought to be used with the greatest care not to hamper prisoners** in making their defence, and not to enable unscrupulous persons to acquire knowledge to which they have no right, and every precaution should be taken against compelling unnecessary disclosures.

CALCRAFT v. GUEST.

COURT OF APPEAL. 1898.

[1898] 1 Q. B. 759; 67 L. J. Q. B. 505; 78 L. T. 283; 46 W. R. 420.

Secondary evidence of documents for which professional privilege has been claimed, may be given, if available by the opposite party.

In an action for trespass to a fishery, after judgment had been given for the plaintiff, the defendant discovered certain documents which had been used in a former action involving the same rights, but defended by a predecessor in title of the present plaintiff. The documents, which had been prepared for the purposes of the old action, included proofs of witnesses and rough notes of evidence used in the defence of the former action. The originals of these documents had been given up to the present plaintiff, after copies had been taken by the solicitors to the defendant, and on appeal in the present action the defendant claimed to use these copies in support of his case. It was contended by him that (1) as they had not been prepared for the purposes of the present action, they were not privileged; and (2) even if the originals were privileged, he was entitled to use the copies as secondary evidence thereof. *Held,* (1) that as the originals had been prepared for the purposes of the former action they retained their privilege in the present proceedings; but (2) that the copies were admissible as secondary evidence.

The following is from the Law Reports:—

LINDLEY, M.R. I take it that, as a general rule, one may say once privileged always privileged. I do not mean to say that privilege cannot be waived, but that the mere fact that documents used in a previous litigation are held and have not been destroyed, does not amount to a waiver of the privilege. I think that so far as regards professional privilege, *Minet* v. *Morgan* (L. R. 8 Ch. 361) covers these documents. Then comes the next question. It appears that **the appellant has obtained copies of some of these documents, and is in a position to give secondary evidence of them**; and the question is whether he is entitled to do that. That appears to me to be covered by the authority of *Lloyd* v. *Mostyn* (10 M. & W. 478), [where] Parke, B., said, "Where an attorney intrusted confidentially with a document communicates the contents, or suffers another to take a copy, surely the secondary evidence so obtained may be produced. Suppose the instrument were even stolen, and a correct copy taken, would it not be reasonable to admit it?" The matter dropped there; but the other members of the Court all concurred in that, which I take to be a distinct authority that **secondary evidence in a case of this kind may be received.**

RIGBY and VAUGHAN WILLIAMS, L.JJ., concurred.

DOCUMENTS RELATING SOLELY TO A PARTY'S OWN CASE.

MORRIS v. EDWARDS.

HOUSE OF LORDS. 1890.

L. R. 15 A. C. 309; 60 L. J. Q. B. 292; 63 L. T. 26.

A party to an action cannot be compelled to produce documents which he swears relate solely to his own title or case, and do not tend to prove or support that of his adversary.

In an action to recover land, the defendant swore, in an affidavit of documents, that the documents in question related solely to his own title and did not tend in any way to prove or to support the plaintiffs' title.

The following is from the Law Reports:—

LORD HALSBURY, L.C. . . . **The affidavit appears to be as plain as anything can be:** "I object to produce **the said documents** set forth in the first part of the second schedule hereto, on the ground that they **relate solely to my own title** to the freehold property in the statement of claim mentioned, **and do not in any way tend to prove or to support the title of the plaintiffs** or either of them." It appears to me that **it is absolutely hopeless to contend that there is any authority for going behind that statement. . . .** It would be absolutely destructive of anything like privilege of documents, because in every case you might controvert an affidavit and have an interrogatory as to whether or not the document might be seen, and the "privilege" would then be absolutely nugatory: the effect of it would be gone. For that plain and simple reason the Courts have always refused to enter into an inquiry of that sort. . . .

LORD HERSCHELL. . . . **The defendant,** in relation to those documents, **has stated on oath** that **they "do not in any way tend to prove or to support the title" of the plaintiffs,** and that they are deeds relating solely to his own title. . . . It appears to me that *prima facie* **this affidavit, according to the authorities, is absolutely sufficient. . . .** But assuming that there may be cases in which an interrogatory directed to a particular document would be admissible, there must be some special ground or reason shown why in the particular case the interrogatory ought to be permitted.

LORDS MACNAGHTEN, MORRIS and FIELD concurred.

Note.—It would appear from this case that, with respect to a party's documents, there is no real or substantial privilege, as he can only refuse production if he swears they will not help his opponent. It is otherwise with respect to a mere witness's documents. See next case.

DOCUMENTS OF TITLE OF A WITNESS.

PICKERING v. NOYES.

KING'S BENCH. 1823.

1 L. J. (o.s.) K. B. 110; 1 B. & C. 262; 2 D. & R. 386.

A person who is not a party to the action cannot be compelled to produce his title deeds, or other documents relating to his title to any property.

The Court, therefore, on the application of the defendant, in an action brought to try the title to land, refused to compel the plaintiff or his landlord to permit the defendant to inspect or take a copy of one of the landlord's title deeds to his estate.

The following is from the Law Journal:—

ABBOTT, C.J. . . . The present request is made, not in furtherance of a right, but with the intention of **looking into and examining another man's title to his estate. We should be much concerned if any authority could be found for such an application.** The Courts have gone quite far enough in these matters, but yet they have never made the order unless one party was clearly a trustee for the other.

It would work great injustice to compel a party to give a copy of his title-deeds. If he brings them into Court under the power of a *subpœna duces tecum*, no Judge would compel him to read them.

Bayley, Holroyd and Best, JJ., concurred.

COMMUNICATIONS BETWEEN HUSBAND AND WIFE.

It is now finally established that there is at common law no privilege protecting the disclosure of communications between husband and wife and that the only protection is that conferred by the Evidence Amendment Act, 1853, s. 3, *post*, p. 443, and the Criminal Evidence Act, 1898, s. 1 (d), *post*, p. 481.

SHENTON v. TYLER.

1939. See Appendix IV, *post*, p. 572.

QUESTIONS TENDING TO SHOW ADULTERY OF WITNESS.

See Evidence Further Amendment Act, 1869, s. 3, *post*, p. 459, and Judicature Act, 1925, s. 198, *post*, p. 508.

DOCUMENTARY EVIDENCE.

PRODUCTION OF DOCUMENTS.

When a party seeks to put in evidence the contents of a document, **the best evidence rule** (see *ante*, p. 163), lays down that he shall **produce the original,** the ordinary *primary evidence* thereof, unless his opponent has admitted the contents of the original: an admission being also considered primary evidence (see *ante*, p. 196). This rule is strongly illustrated by the first of the cases following. Other cases show that the rule only applies where the *contents* of the document are in question, and not merely its *existence*, or the *position* created by it.

But in certain cases, where the party is unable to get the original, *secondary evidence* of the document is allowed, *i.e.*, either a copy of the document or oral evidence of its contents. A " draft ", verified as correct, is really a copy.

Secondary evidence of the contents of a document is allowed:—

(1) When the original is in the possession or power of an opponent, who refuses or omits to produce it after notice to produce.

(2) When the original is in the possession of a stranger, not legally compellable to produce it, who refuses to do so when served with a *subpœna duces tecum.*

(3) When the original is lost or destroyed, and it is proved that proper search has been made for it.

(4) When the original cannot be brought to Court, either because it is physically impossible, or not legally allowed or required to be so brought, as in the case of " Public Documents "

Cases are given on each of these points.

PRIMARY EVIDENCE OF DOCUMENTS.

MACDONNELL v. EVANS.

COMMON PLEAS. 1852.

21 L. J. C. P. 141; 18 L. T. 241; 16 Jur. 103; 11 C. B. 930; 87 R. R. 818.

As regards documents, the best evidence in the possession or power of the party tendering it must be given. Generally, the best evidence of a document is the original document, which is "primary evidence" of its contents. Such original must be produced unless its absence is accounted for.

In an action on a bill of exchange, a witness, called by the plaintiff, was asked in cross-examination by the defendant's counsel, who produced a letter purporting to have been written by the witness: "Did you not write that letter in answer to a letter charging you with forgery?" The counsel for the plaintiff objected to the question on the ground that it was an attempt to get in evidence the contents of a written document without producing the document itself. It was held that the objection was a good one.

The following is from the Common Bench Reports:—

Jervis, C.J. . . . The rule of evidence which governs this case is applicable to all cases where witnesses are sworn to give evidence upon the trial of an issue. That rule is, that the **best evidence in the possession or power of the party must be produced.** What the best evidence is must depend upon circumstances. **Generally speaking, the original document is the best evidence; but circumstances may arise in which secondary evidence of the contents may be given.** In the present case, those circumstances do not exist. For anything that appeared, the defendant's counsel might have had the letter in his hand when he put the question. **It was sought to give secondary evidence of the contents of a letter, without in any way accounting for its absence,** or showing any attempt to obtain it. It is enough for us to decide upon the application of the general rule. The best evidence of the contents of the document was not tendered. . . .

MAULE, J. . . . It is a general rule . . . that, if you want to get at the contents of a written document, the proper way is, to produce it, if you can. That is a rule in which the common sense of mankind concurs. **If the paper is in the possession of the party who seeks to have the jury infer something from its contents, he should let them see it.** That is the general and ordinary rule; the contents can only be proved by the writing itself. **If the document does not exist, or the party seeking to show its contents cannot get at it, he is at liberty to give secondary evidence,** because in that case no better is to be had. An early writer (*Gilbert*) on the law of evidence states the rule to be, that **you shall not give evidence which shows that better is in existence.** That seems to me to be a reasonable way of dealing with the matter. Here, the very form of the question, "Did you not write that letter in answer to a letter containing so and so?" assumes that there is another letter in existence, the production of which would be the best proof of its contents. **There was nothing to show why that letter was not forthcoming.** Our decision does not, and need not, go further than that. . . .

CRESSWELL, J. . . . It is said here that the object of the question objected to was merely to test the accuracy of the witness's memory, to try his credit. But, shift it as you will, **it was a mere attempt to get in evidence of the contents of a written document, without putting in the document itself.** The jury were expected and intended to be induced to act upon the inference that the fact existed which that letter was assumed to state. **There was nothing to show that the defendant had not the letter in his possession or under his control at the time.** If the contents of an absent document may be repeated under pretence of testing the credit or the memory of a witness, it will always be in the power of parties to evade the rule which requires the best evidence to be produced, *viz.*, the instrument itself. The most mischievous consequences would, I conceive, result from such a relaxation of the rule.

WILLIAMS, J., concurred.

Note.—Among other kinds of primary evidence of a private document the chief are admissions (see *ante*, p. 38). "Duplicate originals", or copies executed by all parties, are primary evidence against all such parties. "Counterparts", or copies executed by certain parties only, are primary evidence against such parties only. In a few cases, copies of public documents are made primary evidence —*e.g.*, a probate copy of a will—by various statutes (see *Phipson*, 513—18; and as to what are "documents" within the rule, *id.* 513; and see *post*, pp. 352, 409).

R. v. ELWORTHY.

CROWN CASES RESERVED. 1867.

L. R. 1 C. C. R. 103; 37 L. J. M. C. 3; 17 L. T. 293; 16 W. R. 207; 10 Cox C. C. 579.

The original document must be produced whenever there is a question as to its contents or terms, unless for special reasons secondary evidence is allowed; for instance, where it is in the possession of the other party and notice to produce the original has been given to him.

But where its contents are not in question, the document being in the position of or treated as a chattel or piece of property merely, as where there are conflicting claims as to its possession, there is no legal obligation to produce or account for it.

A solicitor was indicted for perjury in having sworn there was no draft of a certain statutory declaration. No notice to produce this draft had been given to the accused in whose possession it was.

The materiality of the existence of such draft turned upon its contents and the fact of certain alterations having been made in it. It was held that secondary evidence of its contents was not admissible, as no notice to produce the original had been given, and the nature of the proceedings was not such as to operate as a notice to produce.

The following is from the Law Journal:—

KELLY, C.B. . . . **The exact contents of the draft, therefore, became essential** to the prosecution on the present indictment, because upon its contents depended the materiality or immateriality of the evidence on the former trial. The prosecution then gave evidence of the existence of the draft, that it came into the prisoner's hands and had not passed from him. Parol evidence of its contents was thereupon admitted, and **the question raised is, whether, in order to give parol evidence of the contents of that document, notice to produce it ought to have been given.** There is no doubt that, according to the general rule of evidence, such notice must have been given; but **it is contended that this case falls within those cases which have established an exception** to the rule, and made the secondary evidence here admissible without notice to produce the original. **For example,** it is said that **in trover for a deed** or other written document, parol **evidence might be given of the contents** of the document without notice to the defendant to produce it; **but the defendant there has notice by the nature of the action itself** and the description of the document in the declaration, without further notice that he is called upon to produce the document. He can therefore do so if he thinks fit. **We do not, however, think that that case is applicable here. . . .**

There was nothing on the indictment or the evidence to show that in order to sustain this prosecution, the prisoner was called upon to admit secondary evidence of this document being given against him. **If sufficient notice had been given to him, he might have produced it.** Speaking for myself, I think that the admissibility of secondary evidence, without the production of the best evidence or the document itself, ought not to be extended.

Bramwell, B. **If the question had been merely as to the existence of the draft, I should have been inclined to think the evidence admissible;** but the prosecution gave in evidence the contents to show that the prisoner's denial of its existence was wilful; therefore the contents and the alterations therein became material. I think that **parol testimony cannot be given of any existing written document without laying a proper foundation for it.** No exception to that rule is here applicable. The indictment did not give notice to the prisoner that he would be required to produce the original draft. . . .

Willes, Byles and Lush, JJ., concurred.

Note.—It is provided by the Merchant Shipping Act, 1894, s. 123, that a seaman may prove the contents of an agreement without producing or giving notice to produce the agreement. See *post,* p. 476.

R. v. HOLY TRINITY, HULL.

KING'S BENCH. 1827.

6 L. J. (o.s.) M. C. 24; 7 B. & C. 611; 1 Man. & Ry. 444; 31 R. R. 267.

Although a certain legal relation or position has been created by a written document, yet the mere fact of such relation or position may be proved by parol or secondary evidence, without production of the document.

The question was, whether a pauper had gained a settlement in a certain parish by the occupation of a tenement. Parol evidence was admitted to prove the mere fact of tenancy, although it had been created by a written document.

The following is from Barnewall and Cresswell:—

Bayley, J. The general rule is that the contents of a written document cannot be proved without producing it. **But although there may be a written instrument between a landlord and tenant defining the terms of the tenancy, the fact of the tenancy may be proved by parol** without proving the terms of it. It was unnecessary in this case to prove by the written instrument either the fact of tenancy or the value of the premises.

Littledale, J. **Payment of rent** as rent is evidence of tenancy, and **may be proved without producing** the written instrument.

Note.—Where it was necessary to prove the length of the tenancy as distinct from its mere existence, it was held that the lease must be produced (*Twyman* v. *Knowles*, 13 C. B. 222).

WHARAM v. ROUTLEDGE.

NISI PRIUS. 1805.

5 Espinasse 235; 8 R. R. 851.

A party who produces a document when called for on notice to produce may insist that it shall be put in evidence by

his opponent if the latter uses it or inspects it, provided it is relevant.

The defendant's counsel called for a certain book which was in the possession of the plaintiff. He was told he should have it, provided it was then to be received in evidence, but he required to see it first.

LORD ELLENBOROUGH, C.J. You cannot ask for a book of the opposite party and be determined upon the inspection of it whether you will use it or not. **If you call for it you make it evidence for** the other side if they think fit to use it. . . .

Note.—" The reason for this rule is, that it would give an unconscionable advantage to a party, to enable him to pry into the affairs of his adversary, without at the same time subjecting him to the risk of making whatever he inspects evidence for both parties " (*Taylor*, § 1817).

DOE v. HODGSON.

QUEEN'S BENCH. 1840.

9 L. J. Q. B. 327; 4 JUR. 1202; 12 A. & E. 135; 4 P. & D. 142; 2 MO. & ROB. 283; 54 R. R. 553.

A party who refuses to produce a document when called for on notice to produce, and so allows secondary evidence of its contents to be given, cannot afterwards use the original as evidence without the consent of the other party.

In an action of ejectment, the plaintiff relied on payment of rent by the defendant, whom he served with notice to produce receipts. Production was refused, and other evidence was given of payment. Defendant's counsel afterwards, as part of his case, put in the receipts as evidence. They were rejected by the Court.

The following is from Adolphus and Ellis:—

LORD DENMAN, C.J. (*delivering the judgment of the Court*, DENMAN, C.J., LITTLEDALE, PATTESON and WILLIAMS, JJ.). In this case the **question was, whether a party, who at the trial, had refused to produce a writing** which he possessed, and thereby had drawn the other party to give secondary evidence of its contents, **could afterwards produce it.** I thought, at the trial, that he could not; considering it to be the rule that, where he had the opportunity, and had declined to produce the writing, he could not afterwards bring forward its contents. Our opinion is, that that is the rule of practice; and that, when that refusal has taken place, **the party who had refused to produce the writing could not afterwards be at liberty to give it in evidence.**

Note.—The same rule has been applied to the refusal to produce things when called for by the opposite party, *e.g.*, a dog (*Lewis* v. *Hartley*, 7 C. & P. 405).

R. v. HUNT.

KING'S BENCH. 1820.

3 B. & Ald. 566; 22 R. R. 485.

The original writing must be produced, or its absence accounted for, only when it is really a "document". Parol evidence may be given of any other written or printed words, inscriptions, etc., without production or accounting for the originals.

On a charge of conspiracy, seditious meeting and riot, it appeared in evidence that there were various flags and banners, bearing inscriptions and devices of a seditious and inflammatory tendency, and that they were seized by the police officers on dispersion of the mob. On parol evidence of such inscriptions and devices being tendered, it was objected that the flags or banners ought to have been produced, or that notice should have been given to produce the originals. This objection was overruled, and the parol evidence was held admissible.

Abbott, C.J. . . . With respect to the last point, the reception of the evidence as to the inscriptions on the flags or banners, **I think it was not necessary either to produce the flags or to give notice to the defendants to produce them. The cases requiring the production of a writing itself will be found to apply to writings of a very different character.** There is no authority to show that in a criminal case ensigns, banners, or other things exhibited to public view, and of which the effect depends upon such public exhibition, must be produced or accounted for on the part either of the prosecutor or of the defendants. And in many instances the proof of such matters from eye-witnesses, speaking to what they saw on the occasion, has been received, and its competency was never, to my knowledge, called in question until the present time. Inscriptions used on such occasions are the public expression of the sentiments of those who bear and adopt them, and have rather the character of speeches than of writings. **If we were to hold that words inscribed on a banner so exhibited could not be proved without the production of the banner, I know not upon what reason a witness should be allowed to mention the colour of the banner or even to say that he saw a banner displayed, for the banner itself may be said to be the best possible evidence of its existence and its colour.** And if such parol proof may be received generally, the proof at this trial was properly received: notwithstanding the allegation that the things themselves, or some of them, were in the hands of a constable then at York; for, in the first place, this fact did not appear (if indeed it appeared at any time distinctly) until after the evidence was received; and, in the second place, if it had appeared distinctly at the time when the parol evidence was offered, still that particular fact would not affect the competency of the other proof, such other proof being competent upon general principles. **Its proper effect would only be to furnish matter of observation to the jury on the part of the defendants, that the prosecutor chose to offer only the fallible testimony of witnesses where he had it in his power to produce the infallible testimony of the things themselves. . . .**

BAYLEY, HOLROYD and BEST, JJ., concurred.

Note.—As to what are "documents", see *post*, p. 409.

SECONDARY EVIDENCE OF DOCUMENTS.

DWYER v. COLLINS.

EXCHEQUER. 1852.

21 L. J. Ex. 225; 16 Jur. 569; 7 Ex. 639; 86 R. R. 770.

Secondary evidence of a document is admissible when the original is in the possession of the opposite party, who refuses to produce it after a proper notice to produce has been served on him.

The object of a notice to produce is merely to give the other party sufficient opportunity to produce the document if he pleases, and not that he may have time to consider the terms of the document, and to prepare evidence or argument in support of or against it. Therefore, where the document is in Court at the time of the trial, a notice to produce it immediately is sufficient to render secondary evidence of its contents admissible if it be not produced.

In an action on a bill of exchange, the plaintiff's attorney, who was called by the defendant as a witness, admitted that he had the bill in Court but he declined to produce it. Secondary evidence of its contents was allowed.

The following is from the Law Journal:—

Parke, B. (*delivering the judgment of the Court,* Pollock, C.B., Parke, Platt and Martin, BB.). . . . The next question is, whether the bill being admitted to be in Court, parol evidence was admissible on its non-production by the attorney on demand, or whether previous notice to produce was necessary. **On principle the answer must depend on this: why the notice to produce is required. If it be** to give to the opponent notice that such a document would be used by the party to the cause, so **that the opponent may be enabled to**

prepare evidence to explain or confirm it, then, no doubt, **a notice at the trial,** although the document be in Court, **is too late; but if it be merely to enable the party to have the document in Court,** to produce it if he likes, and if he does not, to enable his opponent to give parol evidence,—if it be merely to exclude the argument that the opponent has not taken all reasonable means to procure the original, which he must do before he can be permitted to make use of secondary evidence, then **the demand of production at the trial is sufficient. . . .**

We think the plaintiff's alleged principle is not the true one on which the notice to produce is required, but that **it is merely to give sufficient opportunity to the opposite party to produce it if he pleases, and thereby to secure the best evidence** of its contents, and the request to produce it immediately is quite sufficient for that purpose if the document be in Court. . . .

Note.—It should be observed that one party to an action can always serve another party to the action with a *subpœna duces tecum* to produce a document in his possession, and thus compel him to produce the original, but he need not serve a *subpœna.* It may be that he has satisfactory secondary evidence of the document and does not require the original. But he cannot put in such secondary evidence without giving the other party the opportunity of producing the original if he wishes to do so. Such opportunity is afforded by serving the party holding the original with a mere *notice to produce* it. The party so served need not obey the notice and produce the original. As the document is to be put in evidence against himself, he may elect that secondary evidence thereof may be put in. If, therefore, he does not produce the original, the party serving the notice may avail himself of his secondary evidence. Naturally it is not so when the original is in the possession of a stranger, who cannot thus consent that secondary evidence shall be used against another person, a party to the action. The two cases following deal with such question.

Shortly, a *subpœna* is a writ, which must be obeyed. Its object is to *compel* production. A *notice to produce* is a mere invitation from one party to another. It cannot be used for a stranger to the action. It *invites* one party to produce the document and legally intimates to him that, if he does not do so, secondary evidence may be tendered against him. Its object is not to compel production, but to enable secondary evidence to be put in. See further, as to *subpœnas, post*, p. 418.

MILLS v. ODDY.

NISI PRIUS. 1834.

6 C. & P. 728; 40 R. R. 847.

Secondary evidence of a document is admissible when the original is in the hands of a stranger, or third person, who is, on the ground of privilege, not compellable by law to produce it, and who refuses to do so, either when summoned as a witness with a "subpœna duces tecum", or when sworn as a witness without a subpœna, if he admits that he has the document in Court.

In order to show the amount of ground-rent at which a certain house was held, a witness, not a party to the action, was called, having been subpœnaed to produce the lease. He said: "I am the principal clerk in the office of the Comptroller of the Bridge-house Estates. I have the counterpart of the lease of this house from the Corporation of the City of London to a person named Longmore. I decline producing it, as it is a title-deed of the Corporation. I am an attorney. The Comptroller of the Bridge-house Estates is the attorney and solicitor of the Corporation in all matters relating to the Bridge-house Estates."

It was held that production of the deed was rightfully refused, and therefore secondary evidence of its contents might be given.

Parke, B. **The attorney is not to produce his client's title-deeds, nor to disclose their contents**; and this witness is in fact in the same situation as the attorney. The Comptroller is the solicitor of the Corporation for this purpose, and this gentleman is the principal clerk in his Office. . . .

If you have any one who has seen this lease, who does not claim under it as one of his title-deeds, and who is not privileged as attorney or solicitor, he may give secondary evidence of its contents. **There is an impossibility of your producing it, as the person who has it cannot be compelled to produce it under his subpœna.**

Note.—As to privilege for title-deeds, see *ante*, p. 343. As to the differences between a *subpœna* and a *notice to produce*, and between parties and strangers, see note to previous case.

It is also said: "If a material document be in possession of a person who is beyond the jurisdiction of the Court and who consequently cannot be compelled to produce it, the party relying on it may give secondary evidence of its contents, provided he has informed the person outside the jurisdiction of the purpose for which the document is required, and done all in his power to procure the attendance of that person or the presence of that document at the trial" (*Powell*, 10th ed., 318—9; *Phipson*, 525—7, and cases cited).

R. v. INHABITANTS OF LLANFAETHLY.

QUEEN'S BENCH. 1853

23 L. J. M. C. 33; 2 W. R. 61; 17 Jur. 1123;
2 E. & B. 940; 2 C. L. R. 230.

Secondary evidence of a document is not admissible if a stranger or third person wrongfully refuses to produce the original after being served with a subpœna to do so, as such person can be compelled to produce the original.

A subpœna had been served on a witness to produce a rate-book, supposed to be in his possession. He did not attend, and the rate-book was not produced. It was held that parol evidence of rating was not admissible, the witness having improperly neglected to produce the book.

The following is from the Law Journal:—

Lord Campbell, C.J. . . . It has been held that if, under a *subpœna duces tecum*, the witness appears and stands on his privilege and refuses to produce the document, and the Judge admits the objection, secondary evidence is then admissible. But **here no privilege existed, and the witness would have been bound to produce** the rate-book, and would have been punishable for contempt if he had refused to do so. . . .

Erle, J. The appellants had the duty cast upon them of establishing the contents of the rate-book, and **they must therefore either produce it or account satisfactorily for its absence.** They have not done either of these things by serving the party who is supposed to have the rate-book, but who, in fact, had it not, with a subpœna to produce it. I am further of opinion that, **even if** they had served **the party in whose possession it really was,** to produce the book, and that party has **disobeyed the subpœna, secondary evidence of its contents would not have been admissible. . . .**

Note.—The law requires that a party shall do all that he can legally do to compel production of a document by a stranger before he puts in secondary evidence against an opponent. Otherwise secondary evidence of an unreliable character might be tendered against a party by collusion between his opponent and the stranger. If production can be compelled by *subpœna* it must be compelled. See note to the two previous cases.

BREWSTER v. SEWELL.

KING'S BENCH. 1820.

3 B. & Ald. 296; 22 R. R. 395.

Secondary evidence of a document is admissible when the original is lost or destroyed, but it must be shown that proper search has been made for it. What is proper search depends on the nature and value of the document. More careful search will be required for a valuable than for a useless document.

In 1813, a fire occurred at the plaintiff's premises, and the Insurance Co. paid the claim. A fresh policy was afterwards taken out by the plaintiff. In 1819 the plaintiff had occasion to give evidence concerning the earlier policy, but he could not produce the original. He produced evidence to the effect that search had been made in every place in which the document, if still in existence, would be likely to be found, but it could not be found; and that he had treated it as a worthless document after the new policy had been issued, and did not remember what had become of it. It was held that sufficient search for such an apparently useless document had been made to allow secondary evidence to be given.

Abbott, C.J. All evidence is to be considered with regard to the matter with respect to which it is produced. Now **it appears to be**

a very different thing, whether the subject of inquiry be **a useless paper,** which may reasonably be supposed to be lost, or whether it be **an important document** which the party might have an interest in keeping, and for the non-production of which no satisfactory reason is assigned. This is the case of a policy of insurance, by which a company undertook to indemnify the plaintiff against losses by fire. A fire took place, and a loss was paid. That having taken place, **the original policy became mere waste paper.** There was no reason to suppose that the policy could, at any future time, be called for, to answer any reasonable purpose whatever. . . . This being a case, therefore, **where the loss or destruction of the paper may almost be presumed, very slight evidence of its loss or destruction is sufficient. . . .**

The clerk of the plaintiff's attorney then went to the plaintiff's house, where the plaintiff himself showed him all his drawers and places where a person might reasonably be supposed to keep his papers; the clerk examines them all, searches a pile of papers, opens the iron chest, and, in short, he looks not only in every place which the plaintiff pointed out, but in every place which he thought, on his view of the premises, was likely to contain a paper of this description. **Upon such evidence, applied to such a paper, it does appear to me to be reasonable to presume that it was lost,** and that the legal presumption is, that it was absolutely lost.

Bayley, J. **There is a great distinction between useful and useless papers.** The presumption of law is that **a man will keep all those papers which are valuable to himself,** and which may, with any degree of probability, be of any future use to him. The presumption on the contrary is that **a man will not keep those papers which have entirely discharged their duty,** and which are never likely to be required for any purpose whatever. Under the circumstances of this case, and considering the lapse of time which has occurred, I should have thought that much less evidence would have been sufficient to entitle the party to give the secondary evidence.

Holroyd, J. **It appears that the document had for some time become wholly useless.** The contents of the paper, at least as far as particular terms of the policy were concerned, were perfectly immaterial. . . . **Now the reason why the law requires the original instrument to be produced is this,** that other evidence is not so satisfactory, where the original document is in the possession of the party, and where it is in his power to produce it or to get it produced, provided he gives notice. In either of these cases, if he does not produce it, or take the necessary steps to obtain its production, but resorts to other evidence, the fair presumption is, that the original document would not answer his purpose, and that it would differ from the secondary evidence which he gives with respect to the instrument itself. . . . It seems to me, therefore, that **this being a useless instrument, where the particular terms of the instrument are immaterial, the party cannot be presumed to have any improper purpose in resorting to secondary evidence.** Then, as to the search for the paper, I think, for the reasons stated by the Court, that sufficient was done to entitle the party to give secondary evidence.

BEST, J. It is very difficult to lay down any general rule as to **the degree of diligence necessary to be used in searching for an original document,** to entitle the party to give secondary evidence of its contents. **That must depend, in a great measure, upon the circumstances** of each particular case. **If a paper be of considerable value,** or if there be reason to suspect that the party not producing it has a strong interest which would induce him to withhold it, a very strict examination would properly be required; but **if a paper be utterly useless,** and the party could not have any interest in keeping it back, a much less strict search would be necessary to let in parol evidence of its contents. It seems to me, however, in this case, that sufficient diligence was used. . . .

Note.—Even if the document had been destroyed by the party tendering the secondary evidence under very suspicious circumstances, it would appear that the secondary evidence would be admissible, subject of course to strong criticism and discredit.

The cases of *Sugden* v. *St. Leonards*, *ante*, p. 250, and *Barkwell* v. *Barkwell*, *ante*, p. 255, might properly be placed under the present heading.

MORTIMER v. M'CALLAN.

EXCHEQUER. 1840.

4 JUR. 172; 6 M. & W. 58.

Secondary evidence of a document is admissible, where the original cannot be brought to Court; either because it

is physically impossible to bring the original, as in the case of writings on walls, tombstones and the like; or because the law does not allow, or require, the original to be brought to the Court, on grounds of public convenience, as in the case of public registers, and other "Public Documents", including the books of the Bank of England.

In order to prove acceptance of certain stock by the defendant, evidence was adduced that a person unknown to the clerk in the Bank of England came there with one Taylor, and made an entry of his acceptance of the stock, and a witness was then called, who proved that he had inspected the Bank books, and that the signature to the acceptance of the stock was in the defendant's handwriting. It was held that this evidence was admissible to prove the acceptance of the stock by the defendant, and that it was not necessary that the Bank books themselves should be produced—on the ground of public convenience.

The following is from Meeson and Welsby:—

LORD ABINGER, C.B. . . . **It has been established by a series of decisions,** the first of them I think by Lord *Mansfield*, **that the books of the Bank of England being of great concernment to the whole of the national creditors, the removal of them would be so inconvenient, that copies of them might be received in evidence.** It was founded upon the principle, that the public inconvenience, from the removal of documents of that sort, would justify the introduction of secondary evidence. **That principle has been adopted in a variety of cases, and has never been questioned since.** I know there have been attempts to apply it in cases where it was not applicable: the first was the case of *R.* v. *Lord George Gordon* (2 Doug. 590), where **copies of the journals of the House of Commons** were offered to be given in evidence, and supported on the ground of the above decision by Lord *Mansfield* as to the books of the Bank of England; but they **were rejected** by him on the trial, on the ground that no such inconvenience would attend the removal of the journals of the House of Commons, as any wishing to remove them could get the sanction of the Speaker to do so. . . . The next case that arose was with respect to **the books of the Customs and Excise.** It was formerly the practice to produce them, but after some consideration it was thought that the public inconvenience was so great, that it **has become every day'** **practice, in this and the other Courts, to allow copies of those book** to be received in evidence. That goes upon the general principl of not removing books of general concernment. **Then does not tha** **principle apply in all such cases? The public inconvenience in thi** **case is as great as in the case of any other books.** I think a case ha been aptly put by my brother *Alderson*, that **if a writing were on** **wall, might you not give evidence of the character of the handwriting** as probable evidence of who wrote it without producing the wall i Court? Suppose a man, instead of printing a libel in the usual way were to write it on the dead walls of the metropolis, is it to be sai that he cannot be punished, because you cannot produce the wall i Court? May you not, in such a case, prove his handwriting? . . .

I think it was competent evidence, for the purpose of proving th identity of the party who accepted this stock, to show that an entr in the books of the Bank of England was the handwriting of tha party. **The principle of law is, that where you cannot get the bes** **possible evidence, you must take the next best; and where the la** **was laid down that you cannot remove the document in which th** **writing is made, you are to be entitled to the next best evidence o** **it, by proving whose writing it was. . . .**

ALDERSON, B. . . . The Bank books are not capable of bein produced without so much public inconvenience, that the Court have directed them to remain in the Bank, and copies of them t be received in evidence for the purpose for which the books ar receivable. **Then, if they are not removable on the ground of publi** **inconvenience, that is upon the same footing in point of principle a** **in the case of that which is not removable by the physical nature o** **the thing itself.** Inscriptions upon **tombstones** or on a **wall** ar proved every day in this way for that reason. The **necessity** of th case in the one instance and in the other case the general publi **inconvenience** which would follow from the books being removed supplies **the reason of the rule. . . .**

GURNEY, B., concurred.

Note.—The *dictum* of Lord Abinger as to Journals of the Hous of Commons seems incorrect; copies were admitted in *R.* v. *Lord G Gordon* and other cases (*Phipson*, 542); and see now the Evidence Act, 1845, *post*, p. 437. The two special rules respecting "public documents" have been stated, *ante*, p. 263, where the former of such rules have been shortly explained. The latter rule, as to proof by secondary evidence, is here in question.

The reason for not requiring production of original public documents, and the consequent admission of secondary evidence—the inconvenience to the public—is obvious, and is emphasised in the above case.

A multitude of **statutory provisions** has been made for the proof of public documents of various kinds. These cannot be referred to here in detail, but an excellent summary of such provisions, in a tabular form, has been drawn up by Mr. *Wills* in his book on Evidence (Appendix A). The matter is also dealt with at length in *Taylor*, Pt. V, Ch. IV; *Phipson*, Ch. XLIII; and *Powell*, Book II, Ch. VI. Reference should be made to the above works for any special case. See also *post*, p. 560.

There are four chief methods of proof of public documents, i.e., by—

(1) **Examined Copies.** Copies proved by oral evidence to have been examined with, and to correspond with, the originals. The witness may either have examined the original himself with the copy, or have examined the copy while another person, not called as a witness, read from the original. All public documents may be proved in this manner, but certified or office copies are generally used when available. See *post*, p. 442.

(2) **Certified Copies.** Copies signed and certified as correct by officials having custody of the originals. They are allowed as evidence by various statutes, and are used chiefly to prove entries in registers, proceedings of corporations and companies, bye-laws and the like. See *post*, p. 442.

(3) **Office Copies.** Copies made by officials having custody of judicial documents, and sealed with the seal of the Court. They are the usual method of proving judicial documents, such as judgments, orders, affidavits and the like. See *post*, p. 541.

(4) **Government Printer's Copies.** Copies supplied by the Government Printer, King's Printer, or under the authority of the Stationery Office. They are the usual and proper method of proving Acts of Parliament, proclamations, orders, regulations, etc. See *post*, pp. 437, 455, 465, 488.

It will be observed that, in the above case, the books of the Bank of England were treated as public documents, as "being of great concernment to the whole of the national creditors". But the books of other banks were not so treated as public. The Bankers' Books Evidence Act, 1879, contains very important provisions with regard to banks generally. See *post*, p. 462.

DOE v. ROSS.

EXCHEQUER. 1840.

10 L. J. Ex. 201; 4 Jur. 321; 7 M. & W. 102; 8 D. P. C. 389.

There are, generally, no degrees of secondary evidence. When a party is at liberty to adduce secondary evidence, he may put in any description of the same he pleases.

Thus, although a party has a copy of a document, he may give oral evidence of it; subject of course to observation when more satisfactory evidence is thus withheld.

The following is from Meeson and Welsby:—

Lord Abinger, C.B. . . . Upon examination of the cases, and upon principle, we think **there are no degrees of secondary evidence.** The rule is, that if you cannot produce the original, you may give parol evidence of its contents. **If indeed the party giving such parol evidence appears to have better secondary evidence in his power, which he does not produce, that is a fact to go to the jury,** from which they might sometimes presume that the evidence kept back would be adverse to the party withholding it. But the law makes no distinction between one class of secondary evidence and another.

Parke, B. . . . There can be no doubt that an attested copy is more satisfactory, and therefore, in that sense, better evidence than mere parol testimony; but whether it excludes parol testimony is a very different thing. **The law does not permit a man to give evidence which from its very nature shows that there is better evidence within his reach,** which he does not produce. And, therefore, parol evidence of the contents of a deed, or other written instrument, cannot be given, without producing or accounting for the instrument itself. **But as soon as you have accounted for the original document, you may then give secondary evidence of its contents.** When parol evidence is then tendered, it does not appear from the nature of such evidence that there is any attested copy, or better species of secondary evidence behind. **We know of nothing but of the deed which is accounted for, and therefore the parol evidence is in itself**

unobjectionable. Does it then become inadmissible, if it be shown from other sources that a more satisfactory species of secondary evidence exists? I think it does not; and I have always understood the rule to be, that when a party is entitled to give secondary evidence at all he may give any species of secondary evidence within his power. . . .

ALDERSON, B. . . . **The objection must arise from the nature of the evidence itself.** If you produce a copy, which shows that there was an original, or if you give parol evidence of the contents of a deed, the evidence itself discloses the existence of the deed. But reverse the case,—**the existence of an original does not show the existence of any copy;** nor does parol evidence of the contents of a deed show the existence of anything except the deed itself. **If one species of secondary evidence is to exclude another, a party tendering parol evidence of a deed must account for all the secondary evidence that has existed.** He may know of nothing but the original, and the other side, at the trial, may defeat him by showing a copy, the existence of which he had no means of ascertaining. Fifty copies may be in existence unknown to him, and he would be bound to account for them all.

GURNEY, B., concurred.

Note.—*Phipson* states several exceptions to the rule that there are no degrees of secondary evidence, *e.g.*, public documents are only provable by oral evidence when the originals are lost and copies not obtainable; judicial documents are provable by office or other copies and not by parol; bankers' books by examined copies; and private documents requiring registration or enrolment, *e.g.*, bills of sale, by office copies 522, 527—43.

PROOF OF DOCUMENTS.

It is not sufficient merely to produce a document. It must generally be proved to have been signed, sealed, or otherwise executed by the persons whose document it purports to be, unless its due execution is admitted. But the matter is simplified by certain presumptions as to sealing, date, etc., as will appear in the cases following. The result of the first case given and the statute referred to in the note thereto appears to be that

Handwriting may be proved by:—

(1) **A witness who saw the actual document signed,** who may be either

(*a*) The person who signed, or

(*b*) An attesting witness, or

(*c*) Any person present.

(2) **A witness who** did not see the document in question signed, but who **gives his opinion** as to the signature, based on his acquaintance with the handwriting, obtained by

(*a*) Having seen the person in question write or sign on other occasions, or

(*b*) Having received documents purporting to be written or signed by him, or

(*c*) Having dealt with such documents in the ordinary course of business.

(3) **A witness who** neither saw the document in question signed, nor offers his opinion as to the signature, but who **swears to another signature** of the person in question, upon which comparison of the signatures may be made by

(*a*) Witnesses acquainted with the handwriting, or

(*b*) Expert witnesses, or

(*c*) The Court.

(4) **An admission** of the party against whom the document is offered in evidence.

It is also generally necessary, in civil cases, that the document should be **properly stamped.** See *post*, p. 474.

DOE v. SUCKERMORE.

KING'S BENCH. 1837.

7 L. J. K. B. 33; 5 A. & E. 703; 2 N. & P. 16; W. W. & D. 405; 44 R. R. 533.

Handwriting may be proved not only by the person who saw the particular document signed, but also by any person acquainted in any manner with the handwriting of the person said to have signed the document in question, e.g., by (a) having seen him write at any time, (b) having received documents purporting to be in his handwriting, or (c) having, in the ordinary course of business, observed or dealt with documents purporting to be in his handwriting.

In an action of ejectment, the signature of an attesting witness to a will was in dispute. He was called as a witness in the case and swore to his signature. He also admitted that two other signatures on other documents were his. An inspector of the Bank of England was called to prove that the signature to the will was not genuine. He stated that it was his duty at the Bank to compare signatures on powers of attorney and other documents, that he had never seen the attesting witness write, and that his only knowledge of his handwriting had been derived from comparison of the signatures produced in the case. It was held by Denman, C.J., and Williams, J., that his evidence was admissible, and by Patteson and Coleridge, JJ., that it was inadmissible.

The following is from the Law Journal:—

COLERIDGE, J. . . . **The rule as to the proof of handwriting, where the witness has not seen the party write the document in question, may be stated generally thus:** either the witness has seen the party write on some other occasion, or he has corresponded with him, and transactions have taken place between them, upon the faith that letters purporting to have been written or signed by him have been so written or signed. On either supposition, **the witness is supposed to have received into his mind an impression,** not so much of the manner in which the writer has formed the letters in the particular instances, as **of the general character of his handwriting;** and he is called on to speak as to the writing in question, by a reference to the standard so formed in his mind. It is obvious that **the weight of this evidence may vary in every conceivable degree;** but the principle appears to be sound. . . .

Williams, J. . . . That proof of handwriting is to be submitted to the consideration of the jury, like every other species of proof, I apprehend to be clear. From the highest degree of certainty, carrying with it perfect assurance and conviction, to the lowest degree of probability upon which it is found to be unsafe to act, it may be, and constantly is, so submitted. **From continued and habitual inspection, or correspondence, or both, carried on till the trial itself, down to a single instance, or knowledge twenty years old, evidence may be received.**

I am aware of no rule attempting to prescribe the quantity of knowledge which is requisite to enable a witness to speak to his belief; what degree of freshness and recency in the correspondence to admit, or what antiquity to exclude, may (as the reason of the thing would induce one to expect) in vain be looked for. . . .

Patteson, J. . . . **All evidence of handwriting, except where the witness sees the document written, is in its nature** *comparison.* It is the belief which a witness entertains upon comparing the writing in question with an exemplar in his mind derived from some previous knowledge. **That knowledge may have been acquired, either by seeing the party write,** in which case it will be stronger or weaker according to the number of times and the periods, and other circumstances under which the witness has seen the party write; but it will be sufficient knowledge to admit the evidence of the witness (however little weight may be attached to it in such cases), even if he has seen him write but once, and then merely signing his surname; **or the knowledge may have been acquired by the witness having seen letters or other documents professing to be the handwriting of the party,** and having afterwards communicated personally with the party upon the contents of those letters or documents, or having otherwise acted upon them by written answers, producing further correspondence, or acquiescence by the party in some matter to which they relate, or by the witness transacting with the party some business to which they relate, or by any other mode of communication between the party and the witness, which, in the ordinary course of the transactions of life, induces a reasonable presumption that the letters or documents were the handwriting of the party. . . .

LORD DENMAN, C.J. . . . He did not see him sign it; nor has he ever seen him write; but this is professedly immaterial, if he has had other adequate means of obtaining a knowledge of his hand. . . . **The clerk who constantly read the letters, the broker who was ever consulted upon them, is as competent to judge whether another signature is that of the writer of the letters, as the merchant to whom they were addressed.** The servant who has habitually carried letters addressed by me to others has an opportunity of obtaining a knowledge of my writing though he never saw me write, or received a letter from me. . . .

Note.—" The only evidence of handwriting which is entitled to be called direct is the evidence of a witness who proves that he himself wrote or signed the document in question, or that of a witness who proves that he saw the document written or signed. All other evidence of handwriting must rest in greater or less degree upon inferences drawn from the appearance of the writing in question or other circumstances " (*Wills, Circ. Ev.*, 7th ed., 241–2).

It should be noted that by Statute there is another way of proving handwriting. The Common Law Procedure Act, 1854, enacted:— " Comparison of a disputed writing with any writing proved to the satisfaction of the Judge to be genuine shall be permitted to be made by witnesses; and such writings and the evidence of witnesses respecting the same, may be submitted to the Court and jury as evidence of the genuineness, or otherwise, of the writing in dispute ". This is re-enacted and applied to both civil and criminal cases by the Criminal Procedure Act, 1865 (see *post*, p. 451).

An instructive case on this matter is *R.* v. *Silverlock*, *ante*, p. 133, in which a solicitor, who had given considerable study and attention to the question of handwriting, although he was not a professional expert, was held sufficiently skilled to give evidence as to comparison of handwriting.

RE SANDILANDS.

COMMON PLEAS. 1871.

L. R. 6 C. P. 411.

There is a presumption that a document signed and purporting to be a deed, and attested as such, was duly sealed and

delivered by the person who signed it, although no trace of a seal appears.

Thus a signed document, attested by witnesses and certified by Commissioners as a deed, was held sufficiently executed.

The following is from the Law Reports:—

BOVILL, C.J. . . . **To constitute a sealing, neither wax, nor wafer, nor a piece of paper, nor even an impression, is necessary.** Here is something attached to this deed which may have been intended for a seal, but which from its nature is incapable of retaining an impression. **Coupled with the attestation and the certificate,** I think we are justified in granting the application that the deed and other documents may be received and filed by the proper officer, pursuant to the Statute.

BYLES, J. **The sealing of a deed need not be by means of a seal; it may be done with the end of a ruler or anything else.** Nor is it necessary that wax should be used. **The attestation clause says that the deed was signed, sealed, and delivered** by the several parties; **and the certificate** of the two special commissioners says that the deed was produced before them, and that the married woman "acknowledged the same to be their respective acts and deeds". I think there was *prima facie* evidence that the deed was sealed.

MONTAGUE SMITH, J. Something was done with the intention of sealing the deed in question. I concur in granting this application, on the ground that **the attestation** is *prima facie* **evidence that the deed was sealed. . . .**

Note.—Although it is clear that a deed must be sealed, there was formerly some doubt as to whether it must also be signed. But signature is now made obligatory by the Law of Property Act, 1925, s. 73, *post*, p. 505.

ABBOT v. PLUMBE.

KING'S BENCH. 1779.

1 DOUGLAS 216.

When a document is (required by law to be) attested, one of the attesting witnesses must be called in order to prove it, if he be alive and capable of giving evidence.

This is so even if the person by whom the document was executed has admitted its execution by himself.

An action being brought by the assignees of a bankrupt, it became material to prove a debt due from the bankrupt under a bond executed by him and attested by an attorney living in Somersetshire (the proceedings being in London). The bond was produced, and a witness swore that the bankrupt had admitted its execution to him. It was held that this was not sufficient, and that the attesting witness must be called.

LORD MANSFIELD, C.J. To be sure, this is a captious objection, but **it is a technical rule that the subscribing witness must be produced,** and it cannot be dispensed with unless it appear that his attendance could not be procured. . . .

ASHHURST, J. If the evidence of the subscribing witness were to be dispensed with by this confession of the bankrupt, **the defendant would be deprived of the benefit of cross-examining him** concerning the time of the execution of the bond, which might be material.

BULLER, J. . . . It is necessary, to recover on a bond, to call the subscribing witness, unless some reason can be shown for his absence.

Note.—The above case is retained from earlier editions and a further case added, notwithstanding that by reason of the Evidence Act, 1938, the rule has lost its force, save only with regard to wills. The Act effects its purpose by providing for the general application of one branch of the old law (see *post*, p. 586) and it would not therefore be intelligible without some understanding of what that law was.

The Merchant Shipping Act, 1894, s. 694, provides that an attesting witness need not be called even where attestation is required by such Act (see *post*, p. 478).

As a rule, a document does not require "attestation", or the formal signing of the same by witnesses present at its execution. This is so even in the case of deeds, conveyances, leases, mortgages, etc. But attestation is sometimes required by statute in the case of specific documents, the most noticeable being wills and bills of sale.

A witness so called is the witness of the Court, and may be cross-examined by the party calling him on any part of his evidence tending to contravene due execution (*Oakes* v. *Uzzell*, [1932] P. 19). As to contradicting him by other evidence, see *ante*, p. 319.

NELSON v. WHITTALL.

1817. See Appendix IV, *post*, p. 574.

ANDERSON v. WESTON.

COMMON PLEAS. 1840.

9 L. J. C. P. 194; 6 Bingham (N. C.) 296.

There is a presumption that a document was made on the date which it bears.

A document thirty [now twenty] years old, i.e., a document dated thirty [twenty] years back, proves itself, if produced from "proper custody", as an "ancient document".

In an action on a bill of exchange, the date of the drawing and indorsement of the bill was material, but no evidence was given other than the date on the bill. Tindal, C.J., left it to the jury to find the date of the indorsement, and a verdict was found in favour of the plaintiff. On motion to enter a non-suit the verdict was upheld.

Bosanquet, J. (*delivering the judgment of the Court, which then included* Tindal, C.J., Park, Vaughan, Bosanquet and Coltman, JJ.). . . . The question is, what is the general rule of law on the subject, **where an instrument is proved to be in the handwriting of a party, and to bear a certain date**; whether that is evidence as to the time of making the instrument;—that it is not conclusive evidence is perfectly clear,—**the question is, whether it is not prima facie evidence. . . .**

Now when a deed is produced, and the execution of that deed is proved by the subscribing witness, or by accounting for the absence of the subscribing witness by death or otherwise, and proving the signature, and that deed bears a date, as far as my experience goes, **that date has uniformly been taken to be prima facie evidence that the deed was executed at the time when it purports to bear date.** It is the practice in cross-examination to inquire whether the deed was executed when it bears date, but I certainly never heard it contended that it was part of the proof of the person producing the instrument, not only to give evidence of the execution of the instrument, but **in the first instance, and before any evidence is offered to render doubtful the time** of making the instrument, that it was executed at the time it bears date.

This is the case not merely with respect to instruments binding on the person of the party in the cause, but also with respect to his title where a deed of conveyance comes from third parties.

But there is another case which may be put on the subject, which is a very strong one in proof of this being the general rule: that is this. It is a general rule that **an instrument thirty years old proves itself, provided it be produced from the proper custody**; if an instrument be produced from a custody where deeds of that description ought to be, then, if the instrument be thirty years old, there is no necessity for further proof.

What is the meaning of its being thirty years old? Parties are not called upon to prove that the deed has been in existence for thirty years; if **it bears date thirty years before the time of its production,** the course is, unless it be impeached, to receive that as proof of the instrument. . . .

Note.—The period is now reduced from thirty to twenty years (see the Evidence Act, 1938, s. 4, *post*, p. 587).

BISHOP OF MEATH v. MAYOR OF WINCHESTER.

HOUSE OF LORDS. 1836.

3 Bingham (N. C.) 183.

The rule that "ancient documents", or those thirty [now twenty] years old, "prove themselves", or, in other words,

are presumed to have been duly executed, applies only t those coming from "proper custody"; that is, not nece sarily from the strictly legal or most proper custody, bu from any custody consistent with their genuineness an legitimate origin, in which they might reasonably b expected to be found, if they are what they purport to be

Documents which had belonged to a deceased bishop by virtue c his office, and which were found among his private papers in posses sion of his family, were held to be produced from proper custody although the most proper custody of the same would have been i the hands of his successor, the bishop for the time being.

This case was brought to the House of Lords from the Excheque Chamber in Ireland by writ of error. Their Lordships put certai questions to the Judges, whose opinion was delivered by Tindal, C.J

TINDAL, C.J. . . . **These documents were found in a place i which, and under the care of persons with whom, papers of Bisho** *Dopping* **might naturally and reasonably be expected to be found** and that is precisely the custody which gives authenticity to docu ments found within it; for **it is not necessary that they should b found in the best and most proper place of deposit.** If document continue in such custody there never would be any question as t their authenticity; but it is when documents are found in othe than their proper place of deposit that the investigation commences whether it was reasonable and natural under the circumstances i the particular case, to expect that they should have been in the plac where they are actually found; for it is obvious that whilst **there ca be only one place of deposit strictly and absolutely proper, ther may be various and many that are reasonable and probable,** thoug differing in degree; some being more so, some less; and in those case **the proposition to be determined is,** whether the actual custody i so reasonably and probably to be accounted for that it impress the mind with the conviction that the instrument found in suc custody must be genuine. . . .

Note.—It has been held that in the following cases documents hav been produced from proper custody—expired leases produced by eithe lessor or lessee, a will produced by a tenant for life claiming under i a settlement produced by an equitable tenant for life claiming unde it, and family Bibles produced by members of the family.

PEARCE v. HOOPER.

COMMON PLEAS. 1810.

3 Taunton 60.

Although a document must generally be proved by evidence of its due execution, this is not so where the document is produced by an opponent who himself claims some interest under it.

The plaintiff sued the defendant for trespass to land. The defendant give notice to the plaintiff to produce, at the trial, the deeds under which he held the land. The plaintiff produced these, but he contended that the defendant must prove their due execution. The defendant contended that, since the deeds came from the hands of the plaintiff, under a notice to produce, and contained his title to the land, if he had any, further proof was unnecessary. It was held that the defendant need not prove execution.

Sir J. Mansfield, C.J. . . . **The mere possession of an instrument does not dispense with the necessity** which lies on the party calling for it, **of producing the attesting witness. . . . Supposing that** an heir-at-law is in possession of a will, and the devisee brings an ejectment, and calls on the heir to produce the will; there the heir claims, not under the will, but against the will, and it would be very hard that the will should be taken to be proved against him, because he produces it; **but that is very different from the case where a man is called on to produce the deed under which he holds an estate.** The [plaintiff] has no interest in the fee simple of the estate, if this deed does not convey it; consequently, **if he produces the deed under which he claims, shall it not be taken to be a good deed so far as relates to the execution, as against himself?**

Heath, Lawrence and Chambre, JJ., concurred.

In line 4 from the end of the judgment, the report says "defendant", an obvious misprint for "plaintiff".

DOE v. CATOMORE.

QUEEN'S BENCH. 1851.

20 L. J. Q. B. 364; 15 Jur. 728; 16 Q. B. 745; 83 R. R. 714.

An alteration, or erasure, in a deed, is presumed to have been made before execution; in a will, after execution.

In an action of ejectment, the plaintiff produced a lease in which there appeared an interlineation and erasure. The defendant contended that the interlineation and erasure rendered the lease void, unless it was shown by whom and when they were made. The Judge left it to the jury, who found they were made before execution of the lease. On application for a new trial it was held the Judge was right.

The following is from the Queen's Bench Reports:—

Lord Campbell, C.J. (*delivering the judgment of the Court,* Lord Campbell, C.J., Patteson, Wightman and Erle, JJ.). In this case the deed on which the plaintiff's title depended, when produced, appeared to have an interlineation and erasure in parts not material. Objection was made that the deed was void unless the plaintiff gave evidence to show when the alterations were made. The learned Judge left it to the jury to say whether the alterations were made before the execution of the deed; and it was found that they were.

In moving for a new trial it was contended that this question ought not to have been left to the jury without some evidence besides the deed itself. In Co. Lit. 225 b **it is said that** " of ancient time if the deed appeared to be rased or interlined in places material, the Judges adjudged upon their view the deed to be void. But the latter time the Judges have left that to the jurors to try whether the rasing or interlining were before the delivery." In a note, (1) [136], upon this passage in Hargrave and Butler's edition of " Coke upon Littleton " **it is laid down:** " 'Tis to be presumed, that an interlining, if the contrary is not proved, was made at the time of making the deed." This doctrine seems to us to rest upon principle. **A deed cannot be altered, after it is executed, without fraud or wrong. A testator may alter his will without fraud or wrong after**

it has been executed; and there is no ground for any presumption that the alteration was made before the will was executed.

We therefore think that the defendant has no right to complain of the course pursued by the learned Judge at the trial.

Note.—The Wills Act, 1837, s. 21, provides that no alteration in a will shall have any effect unless executed as a will.

ORAL (OR PAROL) EVIDENCE RESPECTING DOCUMENTS.

[The term "parol evidence" is loosely used in the present connection to mean any evidence, oral or otherwise, which is extrinsic to the document.]

It has been remarked by an eminent writer that "the admissibility of extrinsic parol testimony to affect written instruments is, perhaps, the most difficult branch of the law of evidence" (*Taylor*, § 1128).

The general rule can, indeed, be laid down in clear and definite terms—**parol evidence is not admissible to add to, vary, or contradict a written transaction**—but the application of the rule is beset with difficulties. The student may perhaps be induced to look with more sympathy on the muddle into which, on the whole, this branch of the law has fallen, if he appreciates the difficult task which has faced the Courts when working out the law as to construction of documents. On the one hand, they have had (and rightly so) a lively respect for the consideration that "matters in writing which finally import the certain truth of the agreement of the parties should not be controlled by the uncertain testimony of slippery memory" (*Countess of Rutland's Case*, 5 Coke·25 b); on the other hand, they have from time to time been faced with cases where strict and pedantic application of this rule would lead to grotesque injustice. It has not been easy to keep a middle course.

It is frequently said that there are several exceptions to the rule; but it is submitted (*see, however, the note on the next page*) that there is **no real exception** at all; no case in which parol evidence is admissible either to add to, vary, or contradict a written transaction.

The cases given below show that parol evidence can be used for the several purposes indicated, but it can scarcely be said that there is in such cases either addition to, or variation or contradiction of, a written transaction.

Parol evidence may be given to prove or explain :—

(1) The terms of any **oral transaction, although a writing exists** concerning it, if such writing be not the transaction itself, but a mere note, memorandum, receipt or the like.

(2) Fraud, mistake, illegality, incapacity, failure of consideration, or other matter showing that **the writing is not the valid transaction** it purports to be.

(3) Any collateral verbal **agreement on the same subject-matter,** consistent with the written transaction.

(4) Any collateral verbal **agreement suspending** the operation of the written transaction, or being a condition precedent thereto, so that the writing is not a presently operative transaction.

(5) Any subsequent verbal **agreement rescinding** or modifying the written transaction, so that the writing has ceased to be operative.

(6) Any **local or trade custom** or usage applicable to such written transaction, and not excluded thereby.

(7) The **subject-matter or persons** to which the written transaction applies; explaining latent, and (apparently) even patent ambiguities.

(8) The **meaning of words** having a special or unusual meaning, or, generally, the translation of a written transaction.

Cases are given below on each of these points.

[*Note.*—The author's statement, based apparently on *Taylor*, §§ 1135—50, that the rule "parol evidence is not admissible to add to, vary, or contradict a written transaction" has no real exceptions, is left as he wrote it. The present editor, however, ventures to think that the assertion is in truth indefensible and is really made from a misplaced feeling of loyalty to his subject which makes him reluctant to admit that a so-called rule has really broken down. The Courts have shown a fine record of earnest endeavour to do substantial justice over some hundreds of years in disputed will cases and the like and it seems more just to recognise that the process has been at the expense of logical consistency. No doubt, the question whether there are exceptions to a given rule depends largely on how the rule is expressed, but testing the author's own definition by his subsequent list of admissions, the statement in its present form appears difficult to support. Thus, to make it consistent with (2) and (4) of his list, it seems necessary to insert the words "valid" and "presently operative" before "written transaction". Again, in order to justify the admission of evidence of usage under (6), Mr. Cockle would have to contend that, here, there is no addition to the written transaction, so that the evidence is received not by way of exception to the rule, but independently of it. But it seems obvious that where proof of usage is received to annex an unexpressed term to a written contract there must be a parol addition to the written transaction, and in *Browne* v. *Byrne*, *post*, 393, this was so held; cf. *post*, 384 *n.* To make the author's rule conform to the law, therefore, it would require to be still further restricted to cases where the written transaction contains the *whole* of the contract between the parties. The same observations apply to evidence which contradicts the document. Where, for example, parol evidence is admitted to show that an absolute sale of property by deed was in fact only a loan on security, or that a testamentary bequest to a person "but not by way of trust" was, in fact, subject to a secret trust, it seems impossible to say that the written transaction is not thereby contradicted, and if so how can it be contended that the evidence is admitted independently of the rule and not by exception to it? To take another instance, not included in Mr. Cockle's list, suppose A and B have signed a written contract, and in an action between them B tenders evidence of a parol term inconsistent with the document. This would ordinarily be excluded because of that inconsistency. But suppose B's contract with A comes in question in an action between B and C, or C and D, and the inconsistent parol term is again tendered. It might well be admitted, because here the written transaction would be *inter alios* and not *inter partes.* But Mr. Cockle's rule gives no hint of such a distinction; it is a general rule excluding all contradiction. Surely, then, the admission of evidence contradicting a written transaction, if the transaction be *inter alios*, must form an exception to the rule as above stated and not stand outside it. It seems, therefore, either that the items in Mr. Cockle's list should be treated as exceptions to his rule, or that his rule should be restated with sufficient qualifications to prevent his list infringing it. The former, it is suggested, is the simpler and less confusing plan. But, however this may be, the important point for the student to remember is, that in certain well-defined cases, most of which are noticed by Mr. Cockle above, parol evidence is, for various reasons, admissible to affect written transactions, whether by exception to the rule or otherwise; while, in cases standing outside these, the exclusionary rule is strictly enforced. Headings (7) and (8), however, belong properly to the subject of Interpretation, and are not usually treated under the present rule. For a detailed examination of both topics, see *Phipson*, 564—649.]

MERES v. ANSELL.

COMMON PLEAS. 1771.

3 Wilson 275.

Parol evidence is not admissible to add to, vary, or contradict a written agreement, or any transaction in writing.

An agreement in writing had been made between the parties for the exchange of certain land, etc., no mention being made therein as to a certain piece of land in dispute. The defendant called evidence to show that it was at the same time verbally agreed that such other land was to be included in the agreement. On such evidence a verdict was found for the defendant. The Court granted a new trial on the ground that such evidence was inadmissible.

Per Curiam (*the Court at this date consisted of* De Grey, C.J., Blackstone, Nares and Gould, JJ.). **We are all clearly of opinion** that the verdict is wrong, and must be set aside; **that no parol evidence is admissible to disannul and substantially to vary a written agreement;** the *parol* evidence in the present case totally annuls and substantially alters and impugns the written agreement. Indeed in some cases of wills and deeds, where there are two *Johns* named or two *Blackacres* mentioned, **parol evidence may be admitted to explain which** *John* **or which** *Blackacre* **was meant and intended** by the will or deed. The rules of evidence are universally the same in Courts of law and Courts of equity. Suppose a bill in equity was to be brought by the defendant to have a specific performance of this agreement, the Court would not admit *parol* evidence.

You cannot depart from the writing, but may argue touching the operation thereof. If a man agrees in writing to sell *Blackacre* for £1,000, shall parol evidence be admitted that he intended *Whiteacre* should also pass? Certainly it shall not. . . .

Note.—There may be a substantial difficulty in deciding the preliminary question—is the "transaction" itself in writing? The rule applies only in such event, as the next case shows. Unless the law requires the transaction to be in writing, the formality of a writing would generally settle the question. But informal writings lead to doubt. They may be loosely drawn transactions, or mere notes, memoranda, receipts, etc.

ALLEN v. PINK.

EXCHEQUER. 1838.

4 M. & W. 140; 1 H. & H. 207; 7 L. J. (N.S.) Ex. 206; 51 R. R. 503.

Parol evidence of a verbal transaction is not excluded by the fact that a writing was made concerning or relating to it, unless such writing was in fact the transaction itself, and not merely a note or memorandum of it, or portion of the transaction.

The plaintiff bought of the defendant a horse, and received from him the following memorandum:—"Bought of G. Pink a horse for the sum of £7 2s. 6d. G. Pink." The horse having proved vicious, the plaintiff sued for the return of the price, and gave evidence of an oral warranty of the horse. It was held that such evidence was admissible, as the agreement itself had not been reduced into writing, the memorandum only referring to a portion of it.

The following is from Meeson and Welsby:—

Lord Abinger, C.B. . . . The general principle is quite true, that **if there has been a parol agreement, which is afterwards reduced** by the parties **into writing, that writing alone must be looked to** to ascertain the terms of the contract; **but the principle does not apply here;** there was no evidence of any agreement by the plaintiff that the whole contract should be reduced into writing by the defendant; the contract is first concluded by parol, and afterwards **the paper is drawn up,** which appears to have been meant **merely as a memorandum** of the transaction, or an informal receipt for the money, **not as containing the terms of the contract itself. . . .**

Bolland and Alderson, BB., concurred.

Note.—It is clear that the mere existence of a writing concerning an oral transaction cannot exclude proof by parol evidence. Otherwise, one party might exclude evidence of items of the transaction not to his liking by writing a letter, or giving some memorandum to the other party, containing merely the items favourable to himself.

DOBELL v. STEVENS.

KING'S BENCH. 1825.

3 L. J. (o.s.) K. B. 89; 3 B. & C. 623; 5 D. & R. 490; 27 R. R. 441.

Parol evidence is admissible to show that a writing is not really the valid transaction which it purports to be. Such evidence may therefore be given to prove fraud, mistake, illegality, incapacity, failure of consideration, or other matter affecting the validity of a writing as a document.

The plaintiff sued the defendant for damages for fraudulently misrepresenting the takings of a public-house sold to the plaintiff by the defendant. A written contract for the sale and an assignment of the lease of the premises were afterwards executed; but neither of such documents mentioned the alleged oral representation. Parol evidence of such representation was allowed to go to the jury, who found a verdict thereon for the plaintiff. On a motion for a new trial, the defendant urged that such parol evidence was inadmissible, as "the contract having been reduced into writing the parties must be bound by that, and cannot add to it by evidence of previous conversations". It was held that the evidence was rightly admitted.

The following is from Barnewall and Cresswell:—

ABBOTT, C.J. Whether any fraud or deceit had or had not been practised in this case was peculiarly a question for the jury; nor has any complaint been made against the mode in which that question was presented to their consideration. **If, then, this motion be sustainable at all, it must be sustainable on the ground that evidence of a fraudulent or deceitful representation could not be received, inasmuch as it was not noticed in the written agreement, or in the conveyance** which was afterwards executed by the parties. The case of *Lysney* v. *Selby* (2 Ld. Raym. 1118) is to the contrary of that position, and precisely analogous to the present case. That was an action against the defendant for falsely and fraudulently representing to the plaintiff that certain houses of his (defendant) were then demised at the yearly rent of £68, to which plaintiff giving credit, bought the houses for a large sum of money, to wit, etc., and an assignment was afterwards executed to him; whereas, in truth and in fact, the houses were at that time demised at the yearly rent of £52 10s., and no more. After verdict for the plaintiff a motion was made in arrest of judgment, on the ground that it did not appear that the assertion was made at the time of the sale. LORD HOLT says, "If the vendor gives in a particular of the rents, and the vendee says he will trust him, and inquire no further, but rely upon his particular, then if the particular be false an action will lie." Here the plaintiff did rely on the assertion of the defendant, and that was his inducement to make the purchase. **The representation was not of any matter or quality pertaining to the thing sold, and therefore likely to be mentioned in the conveyance, but was altogether collateral to it;** as was the rent in the case of *Lysney* v. *Selby*. That case appears to me to be exactly in point, **and the jury having found that that which was untruly represented was fraudulently and deceitfully represented, I think that we ought not to grant a rule for a new trial.**

BAYLEY, HOLROYD and LITTLEDALE, JJ., concurred.

Note.—The principle of this case may be taken **as applicable to any matter affecting the validity** of the document or transaction. So, with regard to mistake, it was said by Lord Hardwicke, as long back as 1749—"No doubt, but this Court has jurisdiction to relieve in respect of a plain mistake in contracts in writing as well as against fraud in contracts; so that if reduced into writing contrary to intent of the parties, on proper proof that would be rectified" (*Henkle* v. *Royal Ex. Ass. Co.*, 1 Ves. 317). And the matter was stated in wider terms by Baron Bramwell—"When the parties have recorded their contract in writing, the rule that they are not at liberty to alter or vary it, comes into effect. That which they put down is final as to what they mean; it is the binding record of the agreement. But they are always at liberty to show whether it is the binding record of the agreement. Suppose that the signature were made in the course of a dramatic representation, or suppose a printed form of agreement were used, and the witness, by mistake, signed his name in the space meant for the principal, and *vice versa*, would not the parties be at liberty to show the real state of the case?" (*Wake* v. *Harrop*, 7 Jur. 710). See also *Cowen* v. *Truefitt*, [1899] 2 Ch. 309; *Craddock* v. *Hunt*, [1923] 2 Ch. 136.

MORGAN v. GRIFFITH.

EXCHEQUER. 1871.

L. R. 6 Ex. 70; 40 L. J. Ex. 46; 23 L. T. 783.

Parol evidence is admissible to prove any collateral oral agreement as to any matter on which a document is silent, which is separate from it, not inconsistent with its terms, and might naturally be omitted therefrom.

The plaintiff took a lease of land from the defendant, reserving to the latter the sporting rights. Evidence was admitted of a collateral verbal agreement by which the defendant promised to destroy the rabbits if the plaintiff would sign the lease, although the lease was silent on the point.

The following is from the Law Reports:—

Kelly, C.B. . . . I think **the verbal agreement was entirely collateral to the lease,** and was founded on a good consideration. The plaintiff, unless the promise to destroy the rabbits had been given, would not have signed the lease, and a Court of equity would not have compelled him to do so, or only on the terms of the defendant performing his undertaking. . . .

Piggott, B. **The verbal agreement in this case, although it does affect the mode of enjoyment of the land demised, is, I think, purely collateral to the lease.** It was on the basis of its being performed that the lease was signed by the plaintiff, and **it does not appear to me to contain any terms which conflict with the written document.**

Note.—There is no rule that there shall only be one agreement upon any matter. There may be two (or more) if they can consistently stand together: and one may be written and the other oral. If proceedings are taken on the written agreement evidence may be given of the oral. This is not "adding to" the written agreement, although it may, at first sight, look like it. But see *Note, ante*, 378—9; and in *Malpas* v. *L. S. W. Ry.*, L. R. 1 C. P. 336, an oral extension of a written contract was admitted, although expressly held to be "an addition to it".

The above case was approved and followed in the next case given below; which may perhaps now be taken as the leading case on the matter.

It will be observed that in both cases the subject-matter of the oral undertaking was temporary and immediate; a matter which did not require to be dealt with amongst those permanent or continuous matters which are the subject of the covenants in the lease. Such covenants generally deal with matters to be periodically attended to during the tenancy, and it would, doubtless, be far more difficult to induce the Court to admit oral evidence of agreements concerning such matters, as it would be by no means natural to leave them to a collateral oral arrangement when there is a formal written transaction between the parties. On the other hand, it is most natural to omit from a lease an arrangement as to the immediate destruction of rabbits, or the condition of drains at the commencement of the tenancy.

DE LASSALLE v. GUILDFORD.

COURT OF APPEAL. 1901.

L. R. [1901] 2 K. B. 215; 70 L. J. K. B. 533; 84 L. T. 549; 49 W. R. 467.

The rule that parol evidence is admissible to prove matters collateral to a written transaction is applicable to the case of a warranty given by one of the parties to the other at the time of entering into such written transaction.

The plaintiff, being the tenant of the defendant of a certain house, sued for breach of warranty as to the condition of the drains. It appeared that the plaintiff raised the question as to the drains before he finally took the house, and he refused to hand over the counterpart lease and complete the transaction until the defendant assured him that the drains were in good order. The lease itself contained no reference to drains. The drains afterwards appeared to be out of order, and in consequence the plaintiff and his family suffered in health and he was put to expense. The jury found that there was a representation that the drains were in good order, but no fraud or breach of covenant, and assessed damages. The Judge gave judgment for the defendant on the ground that, if there were a warranty, it was not collateral to the lease. On appeal it was held that there was a collateral warranty and the plaintiff was entitled to judgment.

The following is from the Law Reports:—

A. L. SMITH, M.R. (*delivering the judgment of the Court,* A. L. SMITH, M.R., COLLINS and ROMER, L.JJ.). . . . **To create a warranty** no special form of words is necessary. **It must be a collateral undertaking** forming part of the contract by agreement of the parties express or implied, and must be given during the course of the dealing which leads to the bargain, and should then enter into the bargain as part of it. It was laid down by Buller, J., as long ago as 1789 in *Pasley* v. *Freeman*, 3 T. R. 51: "It was rightly held by Holt, C.J.", in *Crosse* v. *Gardner* (1688), Carth. 90, and *Medina* v. *Stoughton* (1699), Salk. 210, "and has been uniformly adopted ever since, that an affirmation at the time of sale is a warranty provided it appear on evidence to have been so intended." . . .

What is it the defendant asserts? I paraphrase **the evidence:** "You need have no certificate of a sanitary inspector—it is quite unnecessary; the drains are in perfect condition. I give you my word upon the subject. Will that satisfy you? If so, hand me over the counterpart." **What more deliberate and emphatic assertion of a fact could well be made** during the course of the dealing which led up to the counterpart lease being handed over to the defendant? . . .

The next question is, **Was the warranty collateral to the lease so that it might be given in evidence** and given effect to? It appears to me in this case clear that the lease did not cover the whole ground, and that it did not contain the whole of the contract between the parties. The lease is entirely silent about the drains, though there is a covenant that the lessee during the term should do the inside repairs, and the lessor the outside repairs, which would, I suppose, include the drains which happened to be inside or outside the house. **There is nothing in the lease as to the then condition of the drains**—*i.e.*, at the time of the taking of the lease, which was the vital point in hand. Then why is not the warranty collateral to anything which is to be found in the lease? The present contract or **warranty by the defendant was entirely independent of what was to happen during the tenancy.** It was what induced the tenancy, and it in no way affected the terms of the tenancy during the three years, which was all the lease dealt with. **The warranty in no way**

contradicts the lease, and without the warranty the lease never would have been executed. **Three cases were cited** in which parol collateral agreements outside leases had been allowed in evidence and given effect to by the Court, namely: *Morgan* v. *Griffith*, L. R. 6 Ex. 70 (*ante*, p. 384); *Erskine* v. *Adeane*, L. R. 8 Ch. 756, in this Court, and *Angell* v. *Duke*, L. R. 10 Q. B. 174 (*infra*). The first two cases related to parol agreements collateral to leases **as to keeping down rabbits,** and the last case to a parol collateral agreement **to do repairs** and to send in additional furniture. . . . In the rabbit cases the **agreements were held collateral to the leases,** and did not contradict the terms of the leases. It was argued by the learned counsel for the defendant that the collateral agreements in the rabbit cases were agreements that something should be done after the lease was taken, and that in the present case the agreement or warranty is that the drains were then in good order. This is true; but if in the rabbit cases the agreements were collateral and outside the leases, the leases not containing the whole terms and the collateral agreements not contradicting the leases, **I cannot see why the warranty in this case is not collateral also.** Then some cases were cited by the defendant's counsel to show that representations as to drains were never held to be warranties; but where examined I do not think they show this; for the representations in the cases cited were by no means such complete and emphatic statements of facts as were made in this case. And, indeed, upon principle why should there be any difference in the case of drains? . . . In my opinion, even if the jury had not found a warranty, **the true inference is that there was a warranty given in this case collateral to the lease,** and therefore the judgment entered for the defendant must be set aside, and judgment entered for the plaintiff. . . .

ANGELL v. DUKE.

QUEEN'S BENCH. 1875.

32 L. T. 320; 23 W. R. 548.

Where the whole of a contract between the parties is contained in a written document, no additional or conflicting oral terms may be proved; where the document does not

contain the whole of their contract, a collateral oral agreement is admissible.

The defendant let to the plaintiff, by written agreement, a house and the furniture therein. The plaintiff offered evidence of an oral agreement made at the same time to the effect that the defendant would send in additional furniture. It was held that such evidence was inadmissible, it being inconsistent with the written agreement.

The following is from the Law Times:—

COCKBURN, C.J. . . . **To allow the plaintiff to recover in this action would be to allow a parol agreement to conflict with a written agreement** afterwards entered into. I agree with the cases which have been cited to this extent, that **there may be instances of collateral parol agreements which would be admissible, but this is not the case here:** something passes between the parties during the course of the negotiations, but afterwards the plaintiff enters into a written agreement to take the house and the furniture in the house, which is specified. Having once executed that, without making the terms of the alleged parol agreement a part of it, he cannot afterwards set up the parol agreement.

BLACKBURN, J. It is a most important rule that **where there is a contract in writing it should not be added to if the written contract is intended to be the record of all the terms** agreed upon between the parties; where there is a collateral contract the written contract does not contain the whole of the terms. . . .

MELLOR and FIELD, JJ., concurred.

Note.—An important application of this principle is to be seen in *Humble* v. *Hunter* (1848), 12 Q. B. 310. There a third party set up the case that the plaintiff had acted as his agent and claimed his right as concealed principal of coming in to claim the benefit of his agent's contract. It was held that though he might otherwise do so he was precluded here by an evidence point, namely, by reason of there being a written contract in which the alleged "agent" was described as "owner" and that evidence was not admissible to contradict the word "owner" by showing that it really meant "agent". This case was distinguished in *Drughorn* v. *Red. Trans-Atlantic*, [1919] A. C. 203, where the word was "charterer".

PYM v. CAMPBELL.

QUEEN'S BENCH. 1856.

25 L. J. Q. B. 277; 27 L. T. 122; 4 W. R. 528; 2 Jur. (n.s.) 641; 6 E. & B. 370.

Parol evidence is admissible to prove any collateral oral agreement, to the effect that a document, apparently complete and operative on its face, should be conditional upon, and not operate until the happening of, a certain event, which has not occurred.

The defendants agreed in writing to buy of the plaintiff a certain invention. Evidence was tendered by the defendants to the effect that they declined to purchase unless one Abernethy, an engineer, approved of the machine, and that as Abernethy was absent, and one of the defendants could not conveniently return to sign the document after seeing him, it was expressly agreed orally that the written document was signed conditionally upon Abernethy's approval being obtained; and that Abernethy had disapproved of he machine. It was held that such evidence was admissible to show hat the written document was not operative.

The following is from the Law Journal:—

Erle, J. . . . **There was a paper signed by the parties, and there would be a very strong presumption that it contained all the terms** agreed upon, and if the jury had found that it was signed *animo contrahendi*, I am clearly of opinion that no evidence to vary it would be admissible. **But the matter goes a step farther here,** for the jury have found that **the parties, when they signed the paper, expressly said,** " We do not agree to the terms contained in it; we are prevented by the absence of a person whose judgment we desire to have from making up our minds definitely, and therefore, although we put our names to the paper we do so without making an agreement ". I grant that there may be danger in admitting such evidence, and that a jury ought to look very scrupulously at such a case; but if it is a true case, all that can be said about the danger of admitting parol evidence tells equally against the party seeking to set up as an agreement a document which was never intended so to operate. **The distinction is,** that the evidence is admitted not to vary or alter an actual agreement, but to show that the paper was not at the time an agreement.

CROMPTON, J. . . . If the parties really intended this agreement to operate from its date, no doubt it could not be varied by parol. But the jury have found that **no absolute agreement was ever intended to be made,** and they were justified in so finding. Therefore the parties never had an agreeing mind, but signed **the paper** for convenience, leaving it **to take effect or not according as Abernethy did or did not approve;** and there is nothing to prevent their so doing. . . .

LORD CAMPBELL, C.J. . . . It is well established that no alteration of a written instrument can be made by parol. But here **the evidence was not admitted to vary the written instrument, but to show that no agreement had been entered into;** and that evidence is found by the jury to be true. Before the paper was signed it was expressly declared by the defendants, and the plaintiff agreed, that the document was not to operate until the machine had been shown to Abernethy and he had approved of it. **The paper was signed at that time merely because one of the defendants had another engagement,** and could not conveniently go and see Abernethy and return and sign the paper, the plaintiff being contented with this; the signature, therefore, not being put for the purpose of binding the defendants, did not constitute an agreement. **By this evidence the plea denying the making of the agreement was proved.**

Note.—Another useful case is *Wallis* v. *Littell*, 11 C. B. (N.S.) 369, in which evidence was allowed of an oral arrangement that a written agreement for the sale of a lease should be conditional on the consent of the landlord. The Court said, "It is in analogy with the delivery of a deed as an escrow; it neither varies nor contradicts the writing, but suspends the commencement of the obligation". Thus, even a formal deed, fully executed, may be suspended in its operation by an oral agreement, as an "escrow".

In *Davis* v. *Jones*, 17 C. B. 625, it was held that parol evidence was admissible to show that a written contract, which was undated, was not intended to operate from its delivery, but from a future uncertain period.

GOSS v. LORD NUGENT.

KING'S BENCH. 1833.

2 L. J. K. B. 127; 5 B. & Ad. 58; 2 N. & M. 28; 39 R. R. 392.

Parol evidence is admissible to prove any subsequent oral agreement rescinding or altering the terms of a written document; unless writing is required by law to render the transaction in question enforceable, in which case such evidence cannot be given to alter the terms of such written document.

The plaintiff agreed to sell fourteen lots of freehold land to the defendant, by a written agreement, undertaking to make a good title to each lot; and he offered evidence of a subsequent oral agreement discharging him from the duty of making a good title to one of the lots. It was held that such evidence would have been admissible but for the Statute of Frauds, which requires writing in the case of any agreement relating to land.

The following is from Barnewall and Adolphus:—

Denman, C.J. (*delivering the judgment of the Court, which then included* Taunton, Littledale, Parke and Patteson, JJ.). By the general rules of the common law, **if there be a contract which has been reduced into writing, verbal evidence is not allowed to be given of what passed** between the parties, either **before the written instrument was made,** or during the time that it was in a state of preparation, so as to add to or subtract from, or in any manner to vary or qualify the written contract; but after the agreement has been reduced into writing, **it is competent to the parties, at any time before breach of it, by a new contract not in writing, either altogether to waive, dissolve, or annul the former agreements, or in any manner to add to, or subtract from, or vary or qualify the terms of it, and thus to make a new contract; which is to be proved,** partly by the written agreement, and **partly by the subsequent verbal terms** engrafted upon what will be thus left of the written agreement.

And if the present contract was not subject to the control of any

Act of Parliament, we think that it would have been competent for the parties, by word of mouth, to dispense with requiring a good title to be made to the lot in question, and that the action might be maintained.

But the Statute of Frauds has made certain regulations as to contracts for the sale of lands. . . .

We think the object of the Statute of Frauds was to exclude all oral evidence as to contracts for the sale of lands, and that any contract which is sought to be enforced must be proved by writing only. . . .

Note.—The provisions of the Statute of Frauds which relate to contracts for the sale of land have been repealed and re-enacted by the Law of Property Act, 1925, s. 40. The principle of the above case remains unaffected.

Although parol evidence cannot be given to *vary* a contract required by statute to be in writing, parol evidence is admissible of an agreement to *rescind* such a contract, and such rescission may be proved by giving evidence of a new agreement which, though unenforceable itself as not being in writing, may yet serve to rescind an enforceable contract. But " it is essential that there should have been made manifest the intention in any event of a complete extinction of the first and formal contract, and not merely the desire of an alteration, however sweeping, in terms which still leave it subsisting " (*per* Lord Haldane in *Morris* v. *Baron*, [1918] A. C., at p. 19).

The result in such a case is that there is no enforceable agreement at all between the parties, the first having been rescinded by the second and the second being unenforceable owing to non-compliance with the statutory requirements.

WIGGLESWORTH v. DALLISON.

KING'S BENCH. 1779.

DOUGLAS 201.

Parol evidence is admissible to prove any local custom of general application, in order that it may be applied to

the subject-matter and bind the parties to a written transaction, unless it is inconsistent with the writing.

In the case of an agricultural lease, evidence was allowed of a custom whereby, contrary to the general law, the tenant, on leaving at the end of his term, was allowed to take away his "way-going crop, that is to say, all the corn growing upon the said lands which hath before the expiration of such term been sown by such tenant upon any part of such lands"; although the lease was in writing and no mention was therein made of such custom.

LORD MANSFIELD, C.J. (*delivering the judgment of the Court, which then included* WILLES, ASHHURST and BULLER, JJ.). . . . **The custom is good.** It is just, for he who sows ought to reap, and it is for the benefit and encouragement of agriculture. It is, indeed, against the general rule of law concerning emblements, which are not allowed to tenants who know when their term is to cease, because it is held to be their fault or folly to have sown, when they knew their interest would expire before they could reap. But the custom of a particular place may rectify what otherwise would be imprudence or folly. The lease being by deed does not vary the case. **The custom does not alter or contradict the agreement in the lease; it only superadds a right which is consequential to the taking,** as a heriot may be due by custom, although not mentioned in the grant or lease.

Note.—Another important case is *Dashwood* v. *Magniac*, [1891] 3 Ch. 306, in which evidence of local usage as to waste and cutting of timber was held admissible on the construction of a will, the testator being taken to have framed his will with reference to such local usage.

BROWN v. BYRNE.

QUEEN'S BENCH. 1854.

23 L. J. Q. B. 313; 18 JUR. 700; 2 W. R. 471;
3 E. & B. 703; 2 C. L. R. 1599.

Parol evidence is admissible to prove any trade or mercantile custom or usage, either as to the obligations of the parties

in such transactions as that in question, or as to the meaning of words or terms used, in order that it may be applied to the subject-matter and bind the parties to a written transaction, unless it is inconsistent with the writing.

A bill of lading specified a certain amount as payable for freight. Parol evidence was offered of a custom whereby three months' credit or discount was allowed for freight. The evidence was held admissible.

The following is from the Law Journal:—

COLERIDGE, J. (*delivering the judgment of the Court*, COLERIDGE, WIGHTMAN, ERLE and CROMPTON, JJ.). . . . The principles on which this case is to be decided are perfectly clear; the difficulty lies in the application of them to the facts. **Mercantile contracts are very commonly framed in a language peculiar to merchants**; the intention of the parties, though perfectly well known to themselves, would often be defeated if this language were strictly construed according to its ordinary import in the world at large: **evidence, therefore, of mercantile custom and usage is admitted** in order to expound it and arrive at its true meaning. **Again, in all contracts, as to the subject-matter of which known usages prevail, parties are found to proceed with the tacit assumption of these usages**; they commonly reduce into writing the special particulars of their agreement but omit to specify these known usages, which are included, however, as of course, by mutual understanding: **evidence therefore of such incidents is receivable.** The contract in truth is partly express and in writing, partly implied or understood and unwritten. But, in these cases, a restriction is established on the soundest principle, that **the evidence received must not be of a particular which is repugnant to, or inconsistent with, the written contract.** Merely that it varies the apparent contract is not enough to exclude the evidence; for it is impossible to add any material incident to the written terms of a contract without altering its effect, more or less. **Neither, in the construction of a contract among merchants, tradesmen, or others, will the evidence be excluded because the words are in their ordinary meaning unambiguous**; for the principle of admission is, that words perfectly unambiguous in their ordinary meaning are used by the contractors in a different sense from that.

What words more plain than " a thousand ", " a week ", " a day "? Yet the cases are familiar in which " a thousand " has been held to mean twelve hundred, " a week " a week only during the theatrical season, " a day " a working day. **In such cases the evidence neither adds to, not qualifies nor contradicts the written contract; it only ascertains it, by expounding the language.** Here the contract is, to pay freight on delivery at a certain rate per pound: is it inconsistent with this to allege that, by the custom, the shipowner, on payment, is bound to allow three months' discount? We think not. . . . *Webb* v. *Plummer* (2 B. & Ald. 746) and *Hutton* v. *Warren* (1 M. & W. 466) are **cases which illustrate this principle. In the first** of these, by the custom of the country the outgoing tenant was bound to do certain acts, and entitled to receive certain compensation; but the lease which formed the written contract bound him to do the same acts in substance and specially provided for his payment as to some of them, omitting the others; and the Court held that the expression as to some excluded the implication as to the remainder, and that the language of the lease was equivalent to a stipulation that the lessor should pay for the things mentioned and no more. The custom therefore would have been repugnant to the contract. But **in the latter case,** in which the former was expressly recognised, the Court held that a specific provision, as to a matter *dehors* the custom, left the custom untouched and in full force. This latter case appears to us like the present: **the contract settles the right of freight; whether or not discount is to be allowed on the payment, it leaves open; and to that the usage applies. . . .**

Note.—**The cases in which evidence of custom or usage is receivable** may be summarised thus (*Phipson*, 101 *et seq.*):—

(1) To annex incidents to contracts and wills.

(2) To explain the meaning of peculiar or technical terms.

(3) To furnish standards of comparisons on questions of negligence, etc.

(4) To fix a party with knowledge or notice of the subject-matter of the usage.

(5) To rebut a fraudulent intent.

The methods of proof of such customs or usages may be stated thus:—

(1) By the direct evidence of witness (which must be positive and not amount to mere opinion).

(2) By a series of particular instances in which it has been acted upon.

(3) By proof of similar customs in the same or analogous trades in other localities.

(4) When ancient, by, *e.g.*, the declarations of deceased persons of competent knowledge, or other forms of reputation.

DOE v. NEEDS.

EXCHEQUER. 1836.

6 L. J. Ex. 59; 2 M. & W. 129; 46 R. R. 52.

Parol evidence is admissible to show the subject-matter to which, or the persons to whom, a written document applies or refers; and for such purpose to explain "latent" ambiguities. Such parol evidence may be of the surrounding circumstances, or in cases of equivocation of statements of intention made by parties to a document.

A will made various bequests to "George Gord the son of John Gord" and others to "George Gord the son of George Gord", but in one passage the testator wrote "George Gord the son of Gord" (presumably by inadvertence, there being as the Court points out no blank in front of "Gord"). There appeared by extrinsic evidence to be two persons answering such description, and evidence was allowed of the circumstances and of the testator's statements of intention to show which of the two persons he meant, notwithstanding that the fact that there were two such persons was also apparent on the face of the will itself.

The following is from Meeson and Welsby:—

PARKE, B. (*delivering the judgment of the Court*, BOLLAND, GURNEY, ALDERSON and PARKE, BB.). . . . **If upon the face of the devise, it had been uncertain** whether the devisor had selected a particular object of his bounty, **no evidence would have been admissible** to prove that he intended a gift to a certain individual: such would have been a case of *ambiguitas patens* within the meaning of **Lord Bacon's rule,** which ambiguity could not be holpen by averment; for to allow such evidence would be, with respect to that subject, to cause a parol will to operate as a written one; or, adopting the language of Lord Bacon, "to make that pass without writing which the law appointeth shall not pass but by writing". **But here, on the face of the devise, no such doubt arises.** There is no *blank* before the name of Gord the father, which might have occasioned a doubt whether the devisor had finally fixed on any *certain* person in his mind. The devisor has clearly selected a particular individual as the devisee. . . . Upon the **proof of extrinsic facts,** which is always **allowed in order to enable the Court to place itself in the situation of the devisor,** and to construe his will, it would have appeared that there were at the date of the will two persons, to each of whom the description would be equally applicable. . . . **The evidence of the declarations of the testator has not the effect of varying the instrument** in any way whatever; **it only enables the Court to** reject one of the subjects, or objects, to which the description in the will applies; and to **determine which of the two the devisor understood** to be signified by the description which he used in the will. . . . He is pointed out in the devise itself by a description which, so far as it goes, is perfectly correct. . . .

Note.—A **latent ambiguity** is one which does not appear from the words of the document itself, but is created or shown by extrinsic evidence. Obviously, similar evidence should be allowed to explain or remove it. A **patent ambiguity** is one apparent on the face of the document. The point of this not very satisfactory case is the absence of any blank in front of "Gord". If the testator had written "I give so and so to George Gord the son of Gord" the Court would have said that it was patent on the face of the instrument that the testator was in doubt which son he intended to favour and on such a point no evidence could be given, as the ambiguity was patent.

Two points arise in this type of case: (1) Is the doubt upon construction of such a kind that extrinsic evidence is admissible at all to help resolve the doubt (a difficult topic in which the lawyer is, to say the least, not assisted by having been burdened by Lord Bacon with a *damnosa hereditas* in the shape of the unworkable contrast between patent and latent ambiguity, as the above case shows)? (2) If extrinsic evidence is admissible, does the particular piece of evidence sought to be given fall on the permitted side of the line, that is, evidence of surrounding circumstances, or the prohibited side, that is, direct evidence of intention? The admissibility of **statements of intention,** as distinguished from that of surrounding circumstances, is a very difficult question, which cannot be here treated with the necessary detail. Sir James Stephen in a trenchant criticism of these over-subtle distinctions (*Digest*, pp. 209—213) makes the helpful observation that the law is unsatisfactory because it has wavered between two conflicting ideals, that of preserving the sanctity of the written word, and attempting to do justice to the testator's intention when it was manifest that he had not written what he intended; and see *Phipson*, 599, 639.

COLPOYS v. COLPOYS.

CHANCERY. 1822.

JACOB 451; 53 R. R. 42.

Parol evidence is admissible to explain even patent ambiguities, but only, it would seem, when they cannot be otherwise explained by construction of the context.

So, evidence of the nature and amount of a testator's property was held admissible to explain the meaning of certain bequests ambiguous in themselves.

SIR T. PLUMER, M.R. . . . I hope it will not be supposed that I dissent from the case of *Fonnereau* v. *Poyntz* (1 Bro. C. C. 472); nor that I agree to the opinion, that parol evidence is never to be let in, except in cases where there is a latent ambiguity. **The admission of extrinsic circumstances to govern the construction of a written instrument, is in all cases an exception to the general rule** of law, which excludes everything *dehors* the instrument. **It is only from necessity,** and then with great jealousy and caution, that Courts, either of law or equity, will suffer this rule to be departed from. **It must be the case of an ambiguity, which cannot otherwise be removed,** and which may by these means be clearly and satisfactorily explained. **This is always permitted in the case of a latent ambiguity,** which not appearing on the face of the instrument, but arising entirely from extrinsic circumstances, may always be removed by a reference to extrinsic circumstances.

In the case of a patent ambiguity, that is one appearing on the face of the instrument, as a general rule a reference to matter *dehors* the instrument is forbidden. **It must, if possible, be removed by construction,** and not by averment. **But in many cases this is impracticable;** where the terms used are wholly indefinite and equivocal, and carry on the face of them no certain or explicit meaning, and the instrument furnishes no materials by which the ambiguity thus arising can be removed: if in such cases the Court were to reject the only mode by which the meaning could be ascertained, *viz.*, the resort to extrinsic circumstances, the instrument must become inoperative and void. As a minor evil, **therefore,**

common sense, and the law of England (which are seldom at variance), warrant the departure from the general rule, and **call in the light of extrinsic evidence. The books are full of instances sanctioned by the highest authorities** both in law and equity. When the person or the thing is designated on the face of the instrument, by terms imperfect and equivocal, admitting either of no meaning at all by themselves, or of a variety of different meanings, referring tacitly or expressly for the ascertainment and completion of the meaning to extrinsic circumstances, **it has never been considered an objection to the reception of the evidence of those circumstances, that the ambiguity was patent,** manifested on the face of the instrument. When a legacy is given to a man by his surname, and the Christian name is not mentioned; is not that a patent ambiguity? Yet, it is decided, that evidence is admissible (*Price* v. *Page*, 4 Ves. 680). So where there is a gift of the testator's stock, that is ambiguous, it has different meanings when used by a farmer and a merchant. So with a bequest of jewels; if by a nobleman, it would pass all; but if by a jeweller, it would not pass those that he had in his shop. Thus, the same expression may vary in meaning according to the circumstances of the testator.

To show how mistaken the idea is, that extrinsic evidence is never to be received in cases of patent ambiguity, we may refer to a case in the House of Lords, unquestionably of that description, where the evidence was admitted. I mean the case of *Doe dem. Jersey* v. *Smith* (2 Brod. & Bing. 553). Mr. Justice *Bayley* thus states the principle upon which it was introduced: "The evidence here is not to produce a construction against the direct and natural meaning of the words; not to control a provision which was distinct and accurately described; *but because there is an ambiguity on the face of the instrument*; because an indefinite expression is used capable of being satisfied in more ways than one; and I look to the state of the property at the time, to the estate and interest the settlor had, and the situation in which she stood with regard to the property she was settling, to see whether that estate, or interest, or situation, would assist us in judging what was her meaning by that indefinite expression."

If it were necessary, **I could refer to many other instances of resorting to extrinsic matter in cases of patent ambiguity**; but this decision I ground upon the case of *Fonnereau* v. *Poyntz*.

Note.—**It is commonly stated that parol evidence is not admissible** to explain a "patent" ambiguity, or one appearing on the face of the document itself. But it is pointed out by a very well-known writer that this is not generally true, and that "the only patent ambiguity that is not open to explanation by extrinsic matter is one in which the nature of things is incapable of explanation". (*Phipson*, 589—90, where it is explained how the supposed rule arose out of a misapplication of Bacon's maxim referred to in the case of *Doe* v. *Needs*, *ante*, p. 396, and see the note to that case). See also a very full discussion of the matter in *Thayer*, 423, where it is said: "The maxim appears to have been wholly Bacon's own; it was well on towards two centuries before the profession took it up. . . . The *intuitus* of it, and the state of professional opinion to which it was addressed, may be appreciated if one observes the amazing pedantry of legal discussion in those days, in cases where the construction of writings was in question." **The correct rule appears** to have been thus stated in 1852, in the last edition of *Phillipps*, 391: "The result appears to be, with regard to an ambiguity apparent on the face of the instrument, that there is no peremptory rule of law, which, in all instances, should exclude the reception of extrinsic evidence; and that, although some descriptions are so uncertain as to be beyond the aid of extrinsic evidence, and incurable, others are capable of explanation, and when sufficiently explained, may admit of being carried into effect." But, as a recent treatise says, "where after the application of extrinsic evidence to determine the literal meaning of the words used, and of extrinsic evidence to determine in what secondary meaning, if any, they are employed, a patent ambiguity remains as to the person or thing intended, or as to what is to be done, the intention of the parties cannot be ascertained, or, as the rule is commonly expressed, the deed or clause is void for uncertainty" (*Norton on Deeds*, 2nd ed., 107—8. See also *Jarman on Wills*, 7th ed., I, 492).

It would certainly not be in accordance with common sense (as was indicated in the above case) if parol evidence were to be rejected where it could satisfactorily clear up an ambiguity, on the mere ground that it was patent. But **if the words used are so defective or ambiguous as to be meaningless,** and really incapable of being thus solved, they must fail (see *Baylis* v. *Att.-Gen.*, *post*, p. 403).

If, however, the words used are unambiguous, parol evidence cannot be allowed even of such matters as surrounding circumstances. *Higgins* v. *Dawson*, *infra*.

HIGGINS v. DAWSON.

HOUSE OF LORDS.

L. R. [1902] A. C. 1; 71 L. J. CH. 132.

A testator, after directing payment of his debts, funeral and testamentary expenses, and bequeathing a number of pecuniary legacies, gave "all the residue and remainder of the sum of £9,187 lent on mortgage to A, and £4,000 lent on mortgage to B, after payment of my debts, funeral and testamentary expenses", to certain persons, there being no general residuary gift. The question being whether the pecuniary legacies were to be paid out of the two mortgages, or only out of the general personal estate excluding the mortgages:—*Held*, that the latter construction was correct; and that, the words in inverted commas being unambiguous, evidence of the circumstances surrounding the testator at the date of the execution of the will (*viz.*, that if the legacies were to be paid out of the then general personal estate, without resorting to the mortgages, the legacies could not be paid in full) was not admissible to explain the words "residue and remainder" in the will.

The following is from the Law Reports:—

EARL OF HALSBURY, L.C. . . . Now, it has been said, and said very truly, that "residue" and "remainder" are relative terms; you cannot tell what they mean until you have found out in relation to what they are used. If, as Collins, L.J., says, these words had been left by themselves and without an exposition of what they were to be read in relation to, there would have been considerable justice in the suggestion that you might read them as applicable to the residue of the whole estate, after payment of its natural and just burdens. . . . But when I come to look at the will itself, I must construe them as they stand in the context, and in their grammatical meaning, and with reference to what is there said; and then, it seems to me, the problem is solved without the smallest difficulty. . . . The observations of very learned Judges have been quoted to show that you must read all the words in every instrument with reference to the circumstances under which they are uttered or written. In one sense that is quite true. **It is quite true that** where you are finding out persons or things—who are the persons designated by the will, and what are the things left by the will—you may find either the person or the thing by proper external evidence of what is referred to. . . . And here the odd thing is that the supposed ambiguous words which you are to construe are the words "residue and remainder", and yet, from first to last, the learned counsel have refused to refer to the words "residue and remainder" as they are used in the will. It is not "residue and remainder" absolutely, and that is the fallacy of the whole argument that has been addressed to your Lordships. It is the residue and remainder of a particular thing, and you cannot cut the phrase in two and pretend that it becomes ambiguous because you take one part of a phrase which is admittedly relative and treat it apart from the context in which it is, and the thing of which it purports to be the residue. And that is really the key to the whole matter. . . . Now, if I were to concede—what I certainly do not in this case, for I know nothing about it—that it is more probable that the testator would have treated the residue as being the residue of his whole estate, and not of this particular sum of which it is stated to be the residue, if he had had the facts and circumstances of his property before him; if I were to concede that, it would not help the present respondents, because, in the view I take, if you were to construe it with reference to any such question, **it would be making a new will for him,** and **not construing the will which he has made. . . . The language, therefore is to my mind absolutely unambiguous. . . .** I confess I am confirmed in the view which I entertain, by the 24th section of the Wills Act, that I am to construe this will as if the condition of things to which it refers was that immediately before the testator's death. I do not believe that for any such purpose as is now contended you have any right to go into the history of the testator's property and see when he came into possession of it.

LORD DAVEY. . . . No doubt the word "residue" is in itself a relative term; but in this case the **testator has himself told us the meaning in which he uses the word "residue",** and the subject-matter with reference to which the word "residue" is used, namely, it is to be the residue of the mortgage debts after the payment of the debts and funeral and testamentary expenses. Am I to change my opinion of the meaning of these words, which I think very plain, because I know that at the time when he made his will the mortgage debts formed the bulk of his property? I think not.

Note.—In *Re Hodgson* ([1936] Ch. 203) Farwell, J., stated the conditions in which evidence of surrounding circumstances can be given to construe the meaning of terms used in wills: "I think that it comes to this: the duty of the Court in the first place is to read the will itself. The Court is bound in the first instance to read it, giving the words used their primary and proper meaning. The Court is then entitled to look at the surrounding circumstances. If the surrounding circumstances are such that the words of the will, if construed in accordance with their primary meaning, are not apt to apply to any of the circumstances, then the Court is entitled, having regard to the surrounding circumstances, to see whether the language used is capable of some meaning other than its ordinary meaning, not for the purpose of giving effect to what the Court may think was the intention of the testator, but for the purpose of giving effect to what the intention of the testator is shown to be from the language used having regard to the surrounding circumstances. In other words, the Court is not entitled to disregard the language which the testator has used in order to give effect to what the Court may think to have been the intention, but the Court is entitled to say that the words which the testator has used were not intended to have their primary meaning if the surrounding circumstances are such as to lead inevitably to that conclusion."

In that case the testatrix's estate included both cash and National Savings certificates: by her will she bequeathed "my money" to two persons; there were no other legatees and she had no known relations. Evidence was admitted of the circumstances in which the testatrix had made her will in order to determine whether the word "money" could be given any other than its primary meaning. As the testatrix had money in the strict sense, it was held that "money" must be given its natural meaning, and that the National Savings certificates did not pass under the will.

BAYLIS v. ATTORNEY-GENERAL.

CHANCERY. 1741.

2 Atkyns 239.

Parol evidence is not admissible to supply total blanks in written documents, or to explain the meaning of words or

expressions so defective or ambiguous as to be meaningless in themselves, by showing what a party to such document intended to say.

A legacy was given to the ward of Bread Street, London, "according to Mr. —— his will". It was held that evidence could not be received to supply the blank.

LORD HARDWICKE, L.C. There are instances where **this Court has admitted parol evidence to ascertain the person** intended by the testator, where he has been **mentioned only by a nickname,** or where there have been two persons who have had the same Christian name and surname; **but I do not remember any case** where the Court has gone so far, as to allow parol evidence of the intention of a testator, **where there is only a blank. . . .**

Note.—A clear and sharp **distinction must be drawn** between a total blank, or an expression *incapable of any meaning* at all, and an expression which is *capable of two or more meanings*, *e.g.*, the "*Gord*" *Case* (*Doe* v. *Needs*, *ante*, p. 396). It is submitted that the former is not truly an *ambiguity*, but the latter is. If so, there seems to be no need at all to talk of or consider ambiguities in laying down the very obvious rule that **a person must make his own document complete,** and the Court will not do it for him, by speculating as to and supplying what he meant to say. So, in the case of *Hunt* v. *Hort*, 3 Br. C. C. 311, Thurlow considered that a bequest to "Lady ——" was equivalent to a total blank and that the name could not be supplied by parol evidence, and the same would doubtless be the case in a gift to "Mrs. ——". But in *Abbot* v. *Massie*, 3 Ves. 148, evidence was allowed to show the identity of "Mrs. G.", a partial or imperfect description; and in *Price* v. *Page*, 4 Ves. 680, to show who "—— Price" was. See *Phipson*, 599.

SMITH v. WILSON.

KING'S BENCH. 1832.

1 L. J. K. B. 194; 3 B. & AD. 728; 37 R. R. 536.

Parol evidence is admissible to interpret or translate a document or words or phrases therein, or to show that a word therein has been used with, and has acquired a special

and unusual meaning, in the locality or among the persons in question, with reference to the subject-matter; unless a definite meaning has been given to such word or term by statute.

In a lease it was provided that at the end of the term the tenant should leave not less than 10,000 rabbits on the premises, to be taken and paid for by the landlord, at the rate of £60 " per thousand ". It was held that evidence was admissible to show that the custom of that part of the country, in counting rabbits, was to allow six score to the hundred.

The following is from the Law Journal:—

Lord Tenterden, C.J. . . . I think that where in a deed, or in a declaration, or other pleading, a term is used, to which an Act of Parliament has given a definite meaning, the use of the term will be governed by the meaning given by the Act of Parliament. There is no Act of Parliament which provides that an hundred rabbits shall consist of five score to the hundred. **Then we must suppose that the parties to this deed used the word " thousand " with reference to the subject-matter, according to the meaning which it received in that part of the country.** I cannot say, then, that evidence to show what was the acceptation of the term " thousand ", with reference to this subject-matter ought not to have been received at all.

Parke, J. I am of the same opinion. I think the principle has been correctly laid down from the authorities, in the passage cited from Mr. Starkie's book—" Where terms are used which are known and understood by a particular class of persons, in a certain special and peculiar sense, **evidence to that effect is admissible, for the purpose of** *applying* **the instrument to its proper subject-matter."**

Littledale and Taunton, JJ., concurred.

Note.—It may be said that this is but a case of **translation of a document** according to legal language. As *foreign* language might be translated by verbal evidence, so might *local, technical, obsolete, trade, or family, language* be translated, it would appear. " There is no doubt that not only where the language of the instrument is such as the Court does not understand, it is competent to receive evidence of the proper meaning of that language, as when it is written in a foreign tongue; but it is also competent, where technical words or peculiar terms, or indeed any expressions are used, which at the time the instrument was written had acquired an appropriate meaning, either generally or by local usage, or amongst particular classes" (*Shore* v. *Wilson*, 9 C. & F. 555). In *De Beéche* v. *S. American Stores, Ltd.* ([1935] A. C., at p. 158), where evidence was admitted that the expression "payable in Chile in first class bills on London" had a special mercantile meaning in Chile, Lord Sankey, L.C., stated three conditions precedent to the admissibility of such evidence: "(1) the evidence must not conflict with a statutory definition; (2) the evidence must be of a usage common to the place in question; and (3) the evidence must expound and not contradict the terms of the contract."

See also the case of *Morrell* v. *Frith*, *ante*, p. 11, and cf. *Re How*, [1930] 1 Ch. 66.

KELL v. CHARMER.

CHANCERY. 1856.

23 BEAV. 195; 4 W. R. 787.

In order to interpret or ascertain the meaning of a written document, parol evidence may be given of the meaning or sense in which, not only words, but also signs, symbols, private marks, or nicknames, have been used. Such evidence may be given although the words, etc., the meaning of which is in question, appear to have been used with a particular meaning only by the person whose document is under construction; and not so used by any class of persons or in any locality.

A testator gave legacies by his will as follows: "I give and bequeath to my son William the sum of i. x. x.; to my son Robert Charles the sum of o. x. x.; to my daughter Harriet Emily the sum of ——; to my daughter Georgiana Five Hundred Pounds."

Evidence was given by the shopman of the testator to the effect that the testator had carried on the business of a jeweller, in the course of which he had used certain private marks or symbols to denote prices or sums of money, and that, according to such marks or symbols as used by him, i. x. x. means £100 and o. x. x. meant £200.

Sir John Romilly, M.R., held that such evidence was admissible to determine the amount of the first two legacies.

Note.—Parol, or extrinsic, evidence has been admitted to show the meaning of a great variety of expressions, and a number of the cases were summarised in former editions of this book. They deal, however, rather with the construction of the documents involved than with the question that alone concerns students of evidence, namely when and for what purposes extrinsic evidence is admissible to show the meaning of terms. It has been thought better now to omit them altogether.

The question of admissibility of evidence has also arisen concerning **Ademption and Repetition of Legacies.** The *equitable presumption* of "ademption" has been referred to, *ante*, p. 26. Parol evidence is generally admissible to *rebut* such presumption when it arises, but not to *raise* the presumption. So, if two legacies are given by different instruments, whether of the same amount or not, the rule of *construction* is that the legatee takes both, and evidence cannot be given to the contrary; unless the legacies are of the same amount and also the same motive is expressed for giving them, in which case there is a *presumption* that only one legacy is intended, and evidence may be given to rebut such presumption (*Hurst* v. *Beach*, 5 Mad. 351).

Extrinsic evidence is not admissible for the following purposes, among others:—

Filling up a total blank (*Baylis* v. *Att.-Gen.*, *ante*, p. 403).

Inserting a devise omitted by mistake (*Newburgh* v. *Newburgh*, 5 Mad. 364).

Proving what was intended by an unintelligible word (*Goblet* v. *Beechey*, 3 Sim. 24).

Changing the person described (*Delmare* v. *Robello*, 1 Ves. Jr. 412).

Reconciling conflicting clauses in a will (*Ulrich* v. *Litchfield*, 2 Atk. 372).

Construing a will with reference to instructions given for preparing it (*Goodinge* v. *Goodinge*, 1 Ves. Sen. 230).

Controlling a technical rule of verbal construction (*Lane* v. *Stanhope*, 6 T. R. 345).

Raising a presumption (*Rachfield* v. *Careless*, 2 P. W. 157).

Adding to, detracting from, or altering a will (*Herbert* v. *Reid*, 16 Ves. Jr. 481).

Proving intention, generally (*Doe* v. *Hiscocks*, 5 M. & W. 363).

(On this matter generally, reference should be made to the standard works, *Wigram on Extrinsic Evidence in Interpretation of Wills*, and *Hawkins on Construction of Wills.*)

REAL EVIDENCE.

It has been stated (*ante*, p. 268) that the third kind of evidence recognised by the English law is that known as "Real Evidence", or the evidence afforded by **production** of chattels or other physical objects for **inspection** by the Court.

The Court most naturally expects to see, and is invariably allowed to see, such things as **implements** with which an alleged crime is said to have been committed, **wounds** or other damage alleged to have been inflicted, young **persons** whose age is in question, **animals** alleged to be vicious, **writings** alleged to have been tampered with, **labels or devices** alleged to be an infringement, **the premises** in question in cases of obstruction of light, nuisance, or other injury, and the like.

Even the conduct and demeanour of a witness in the witness-box, from which the Court may draw conclusions, may be considered real evidence.

The necessity and reason for such evidence are indeed so obvious that there are few cases dealing with the matter, and even text-books on the law of evidence commonly neglect the subject. But, for the sake of completeness, it appears proper to refer shortly to the main features of such evidence. [For a detailed examination of this topic, see *Best*, 12th ed., §§ 28; 196—214; and App. A., pp. 593—606; *Taylor*, §§ 554—566; *Phipson*, 2—3, 5—6; *Powell*, Bk. II, Ch. X.] One of the most important points to be noticed is that dealt with in the second case given below—**production of chattels or physical objects is not legally requisite** in order to render parol evidence as to their nature admissible. Even if such production were easy, and manifestly the proper course, **non-production would only be matter of observation or comment.** This is so even although an important feature of the object in question consists of writing or words (*R.* v. *Hunt*, *ante*, p. 352), so long as it does not really amount to a " document ", in which case, as we have seen (*ante*, p. 348), parol evidence is not allowed without satisfactorily accounting for the original. It may indeed be a fine **question whether a particular physical object with words inscribed on it is a document** or not. On the one hand, objects without any words upon them may be documents, such as pieces of wood with notches only on them indicating the quantity of goods delivered, such as the " nick-sticks " referred to in Scott's Antiquary, Chapter XV, and the old Exchequer tallies indicating money paid in the same manner. On the other hand, flags, banners and the like with verbal inscriptions, or labels on bottles or packages, bearing descriptive words, would generally not be documents.

The well-known case of *Armory* v. *Delamirie* (1 Strange 504, *post*, p. 412), illustrates the **disadvantage of not producing an object when necessary.** There, a chimney-sweeper's boy sued a goldsmith for detaining a jewel which the latter had taken from a ring found by the former. As the jewel was not produced, when the question came as to the value of the jewel to be paid by the defendant, the evidence of several jewellers was taken as to the value of the best jewel to fit the socket, and such value was taken as the measure of the damages.

Real evidence generally requires some oral evidence to introduce it or to explain it, *e.g.*, to prove where the object was found, its condition, or the use to which it was put or to identify it.

There is danger in real evidence, especially with juries or persons inexperienced in judicial inquiries. Although, *prima facie*, such evidence is most satisfactory, being directly addressed to the senses of the tribunal, a jury may too readily draw conclusions from it. They may, in their natural horror or sympathy, excited by the sight of a bloody weapon or serious wound, too readily connect it with the prisoner charged, and lose sight of the necessity of establishing a clear connection, or showing that the object in question had actually been used as alleged. Readers of Dickens will remember how the country folk in "Barnaby Rudge" were satisfied that Queen Elizabeth had really stayed at the Maypole Inn, and had cuffed an unlucky page whilst standing on a mounting block, by merely being shown that there was such a mounting block outside the inn; and readers of the Bible will remember how the patriarch Jacob drew the hasty but erroneous conclusion that Joseph had been devoured by an evil beast, on the sight of his bloody coat of many colours. But when such evidence is strictly and **carefully dealt with** and properly applied, it may fairly be said to be **most reliable.**

Statutory recognition of real evidence appears in the provisions of the Children and Young Persons Act, 1933, s. 99 (see *post*, p. 528).

Inspection out of Court may also be had by special order, mainly under the provisions of the Juries Act, 1825 (see *post*, p. 432), and Order 50 of the Rules of the Supreme Court (see *post*, p. 545).

LINE v. TAYLOR.

HERTFORD ASSIZES. 1862.

3 FOSTER & FINLASON 731.

Evidence may be adduced by production in Court, for inspection by the Judge or jury, of physical objects, such as chattels, persons, animals, or objects with inscriptions or words thereon. Such evidence is known as "Real Evidence".

In an action for knowingly keeping a fierce and mischievous dog, which bit and wounded the plaintiff, the defendant's counsel proposed that the dog should be brought into Court, in charge of his keeper, to be inspected by the jury. Counsel for the plaintiff objected.

ERLE, C.J. "When I last went upon Circuit with the late lamented Lord Chief Justice Campbell, I recollect that, in a similar case, his Lordship allowed the dog to be brought into Court; I see no objection to it."

The dog was accordingly brought in, led by his keeper, with a chain. The jury had him brought up to them, and at their desire the keeper let go of him. They examined him, and appeared to be of opinion that, from the expression of his eyes and other indications, he was not of a vicious disposition.

ERLE, C.J. (to the jury), said they "**might judge partly from** their knowledge of dogs and **their own observance** of the animal in question".

R. v. FRANCIS.

CROWN CASES RESERVED. 1874.

L. R. 2 C. C. R. 128; 43 L. J. M. C. 97; 30 L. T. 503; 22 W. R. 663; 12 Cox C. C. 612.

Non-production of a chattel or physical object, which might conveniently be produced for inspection by the Court, does not render oral evidence respecting the same inadmissible. Such non-production is only a matter for observation or criticism; going merely to the weight, not to the admissibility, of the oral evidence.

The prisoner was indicted for false pretences, by having falsely represented a ring to be a diamond ring. In order to prove his guilty knowledge, evidence was admitted of attempts on other occasions to obtain money on a false ring, at Leicester. It was held that oral evidence of the nature of such ring was admissible although it was not produced in Court.

The following is from the Law Journal:—

LORD COLERIDGE, C.J. (*delivering the judgment of the Court*, LORD COLERIDGE, C.J., BLACKBURN and LUSH, JJ., PIGOTT and

CLEASBY, BB.). . . . It was objected that the evidence of what took place at Leicester was not properly received, because the cluster ring which he there attempted to pass was not produced in Court, and that the evidence of two witnesses who saw it, and swore to its being false, was not admissible. No doubt if there was not admissible evidence that this ring was false it ought not to have been left to the jury; but **though the non-production of the article may afford ground for observation** more or less weighty, according to circumstances, **it only goes to the weight, not to the admissibility, of the evidence,** and no question as to the weight of this evidence is now before us. Where the question is as to the effect of a written instrument, the instrument itself is primary evidence of its contents, and until it is produced, or the non-production is excused, no secondary evidence can be received. **But there is no case whatever deciding that, when the issue is as to the state of a chattel,** *e.g.*, the soundness of a horse, or the equality of the bulk of the goods to the sample, the production of the chattel is primary evidence, and **that no other evidence can be given till the chattel is produced** in Court for the inspection of the jury. The law of evidence is the same in criminal and civil suits.

Note.—See also *R.* v. *Hunt, ante,* p. 352.

HOCKING v. AHLQUIST BROTHERS, LTD.

1944. See Appendix IV, *post*, p. 575.

ARMORY v. DELAMIRIE.

KING'S BENCH. 1722.

1 STRANGE 505.

Non-production of a chattel or physical object, by a party who could produce it, or who has prevented himself from producing it, may induce the Court to discredit his evidence concerning it, and even to presume the strongest against him.

"The plaintiff being a chimney sweeper's boy found a jewel and carried it to the defendant's shop (who was a goldsmith) to know what it was, and delivered it into the hands of the apprentice, who, under pretence of weighing it, took out the stones, and calling to the master to let him know it came to three halfpence, the master offered the boy the money, who refused to take it, and insisted to have the thing again, whereupon the apprentice delivered him back the socket without the stones. And now in trover against the master these points were ruled" by

SIR JOHN PRATT, C.J. 1. That the finder of a jewel, though he does not by such finding acquire an absolute property or ownership, yet he has such a property as will enable him to keep it against all but the rightful owner, and consequently may maintain trover.

2. That the action will lay against the master, who gives a credit to his apprentice, and is answerable for his neglect.

3. **As to the value of the jewel,** several of the trade were examined to prove what a jewel of the finest water that would fit the socket would be worth; and the Chief Justice directed the jury, **that unless the defendant did produce** the jewel and show it not to be of the finest water, they should **presume the strongest against him,** and make the value of the best jewels the measure of their damages, which they accordingly did.

THE ADDUCTION OF EVIDENCE.

The proceedings, necessary or proper for the purpose of bringing evidence before the Court, would seem to be more appropriate for discussion in Books on the Procedure of the Courts. It may, however, be well to set out in this place some short account of the proceedings in ordinary civil and criminal cases, for adduction of evidence (i) before trial, (ii) at trial, and (iii) on appeal.

I. EVIDENCE BEFORE TRIAL.

(*a*) In Civil Cases.

In civil cases it is unusual to take evidence before trial. The witnesses must generally be "examined *viva voce* and in open Court" (O. 37, r. 1, *post*, p. 540). But various provisions are made for taking evidence before trial. **In the High Court evidence may be so taken by** the following methods.

1. **Affidavits.** These may be of the evidence generally, by agreement in writing between all parties; or of particular facts, by order of Court, under O. 30, r. 2, *post*, p. 537, and O. 37, r. 1, *post*, p. 540, and Mat. Causes Rules, 1944, r. 25, or in references under the Arbitration Act, 1934, s. 8 (1), and Schedule I, *post*, p. 533.

2. **Commissions.** Depositions may be taken by examination of witnesses before a commissioner or examiner, under O. 30, r. 2, *post*, p. 537, and O. 37, r. 1, *post*, p. 540, or before the Court, Judge, officer of the Court or any other person, at any place, under O. 37, r. 5, *post*, p. 541; or in references under the Arbitration Act, 1934, s. 8 (1), and

Schedule I, *post*, p. 533. Such order is generally made only in cases where the witness is abroad, or is unable to attend the trial owing to age, illness, or physical incapacity. Where the witness is abroad, the High Court has power to issue a commission, request or order to examine witnesses. The examination in England is generally taken before an examiner of the Court, or a practising lawyer. As to the procedure in such matters, see O. 37, rr. 7 *et seq.*, *post*, p. 541, and the Evidence by Commission Acts, 1843 and 1859, *post*, pp. 435, 446. As to the circumstances in which depositions in civil cases may be put in evidence at the trial, see O. 37, r. 18, *post*, p. 542.

3. **Letters of Request.** An order may be made for the issue of a "request" in lieu of a commission, under O. 37, r. 6A, *post*, p. 541. This process is used when the evidence is required of a witness resident in certain countries which object to the administration of an oath by anyone except their own officials, *e.g.*, Austria, Germany, Russia and Sweden. A request is also frequently issued to Colonial and Indian Courts. It is addressed to the tribunal of the other country asking the Judges thereof to order the evidence to be taken and remitted to the High Court.

4. **Interrogatories.** An order may be made for any party to deliver interrogatories in writing for examination of opposite parties, under O. 31, rr. 1, 2, *post*, p. 537. The answers by affidavit, may be put in evidence at the trial, as provided by O. 31, rr. 8, 24, *post*, p. 538.

5. **Perpetuation of Testimony.** Proceedings may be taken for perpetuating testimony in certain cases for use in a subsequent action, under O. 37, r. 35, *post*, p. 543.

As regards other civil Courts, reference should be made to books on the practice thereof.

(*b*) In Criminal Cases.

In cases of indictable offences depositions are always taken by the justices before whom a person is charged. This is generally under the provisions of the Indictable Offences Act, 1848, and the Criminal Justice Act, 1925. Several other provisions have also been made for taking depositions in criminal cases; and for the perpetuation of testimony. **The chief provisions are the following:—**

1. **The Indictable Offences Act, 1848,** by section 17, *post*, p. 438, provides for the taking of depositions on behalf of the *prosecution* in all cases of indictable offences.

2. **The Criminal Law Amendment Act, 1867,** by section 6, *post*, p. 454, provides for perpetuating the testimony of witnesses who are dangerously ill, and specifies the circumstances in which it may be given in evidence at the trial.

3. **The Coroners Act, 1887,** by section 4, *post*, p. 470, provides for the taking of depositions of all persons tendering evidence on *inquests* held before coroners. As to their admissibility in evidence in criminal trials, see *post*, p. 470, note.

4. **The Children and Young Persons Act, 1933,** by section 42, *post*, p. 527, provides for the taking of depositions in certain cases of *children* or young persons whose attendance before a Court would involve serious danger to life or health, and by section 43 specifies the circumstances in which they are admissible in evidence on trial, *post*, p. 528.

5. **The Criminal Justice Act, 1925,** by section 12 (replacing section 3 of the Criminal Law Amendment Act, 1867), *post*, p. 510, provides for the taking of depositions on behalf of the *accused* person, in all cases of indictable offences.

The duties of the justices in taking depositions, under the Acts of 1848 and 1925, *supra*, may be thus summarised. They must:—

1. Take the evidence of the witnesses for the prosecution, in the presence of the accused, allowing him to cross-examine and putting such evidence into writing, cause it to be read to the witnesses in the presence of the accused, and signed by them, and sign it themselves. (*Indictable Offences Act*, 1848,

s. 17, *post*, p. 438, and *Criminal Justice Act*, 1925, s. 12 (1) and (7), *post*, pp. 510, 512.)

2. Read the charge to the accused and explain its nature to him in ordinary language, inform him that he has the right to call witnesses and give evidence on his own behalf, and ask him whether he wishes to say anything in answer, warning him that he need not do so, but that what he says may be given in evidence on his trial, and giving him clearly to understand that he has nothing to hope from any promise of favour and nothing to fear from any threat which has been held out to him to induce him to make any admission or confession. (*Criminal Justice Act*, 1925, s. 12 (2) and (3), *post*, p. 510, replacing the Indictable Offences Act, 1848, s. 18.)

3. Take down in writing what he says in answer to the charge, read it over to him, sign it themselves, and cause him to sign it, if he so desires. (*Criminal Justice Act*, 1925, s. 12 (4), *post*, p. 510.)

4. Ask him whether he desires to give evidence on his own behalf and whether he desires to call witnesses, take down in writing any such evidence, cause it to be read to the witnesses in the presence of the accused and signed by them, and sign it themselves. (*Criminal Justice Act*, 1925, s. 12 (5) and (7), *post*, pp. 511, 512.)

It will be observed that the *prisoner's statement*, under para. 3 above, is unsworn, and is not strictly a deposition, but it is practically treated as part of the depositions and is read at the trial by the prosecution, whether it is in his favour or not. But it should be distinguished from the unsworn statement of the prisoner made at the trial itself, the right to make which is recognised and preserved by the Criminal Evidence Act, 1898, s. 1 (*h*), *post*, p. 481.

As to the circumstances in which depositions taken under these Acts may be put in evidence at the trial, see Criminal Justice Act, 1925, s. 13, *post*, p. 512.

II. EVIDENCE AT TRIAL.

(a) In Civil Cases.

A witness is generally brought to Court and called by the party desiring his evidence. A witness can only be called by consent of the parties in a civil case (*Re Enoch*, [1910] 1 K. B. 327), though it has always been the practice of Judges to ask further questions, if they see fit, of a witness in the box although neither side may have touched on the particular topic he raises. **The party against whom a witness is called may object that he is incompetent.** The objection should be made as soon as such incompetency appears; before he is sworn or examined on the *voir dire* if possible But the objection may be taken at any time; even after he has answered certain questions, the answers to which may be struck out and disregarded if he is held by the Judge to be incompetent (*Jacobs* v. *Layborn*, *post*, p. 422; *R.* v. *Whitehead*, L. R. 1 C. C. R. 33).

The attendance of witnesses is compelled, generally, by a writ of *subpœna ad testificandum*, if to give evidence merely, or *subpœna duces tecum*, if to produce documents, issued in the High Court, under the provisions of O. 37, rr. 26—34A, of the Rules of the Supreme Court, and in other Courts by various rules applicable thereto. If a person, who is not subpœnaed, happens to be in Court, he shall not be forced to be sworn against his will. But if he consents, the want of a subpœna is not material, and in a proper case, where the witness is recalcitrant the Court will wait for a subpœna to be issued (*Bacon's Abridgement*, tit. Evidence, sec. D). And if a person voluntarily submits to be sworn, it seems he is bound to answer all questions put to him on pain of attachment (see *dicta* in *R.* v. *Flavell* (1884), 14 Q. B. D. 366). As to trial by referee, see the Arbitration Act, 1889, s. 18 (*post*, p. 472), and O. 36, r. 49, *post*, p. 540. In the case of a *witness out of the* *jurisdiction* of the High Court, a *subpœna* in a special form must be issued under the Judicature Act, 1925, s. 49, *post*, p. 506. A *witness in prison* is generally brought up by a writ of *habeas corpus ad testificandum* or by a warrant or order of a Judge of the High Court, whose power extends to arbitrations (Arbitration Act, 1889, s. 18, *post*, p. 472). A County Court Judge may issue an order for the attendance of a prisoner before the county court (County Courts Act, 1934, s. 83, *post*, p. 534).

A party to an action may subpœna any person as a witness without leave, but the **Court can set aside** a *subpœna* issued improperly or being an abuse of the process of the Court (*R.* v. *Baines*, *post*, p. 420).

(*b*) In Criminal Cases.

As in a civil case, **a witness is generally brought to Court and called by the party** desiring his evidence, the prosecutor or the accused; not by the Court or any official. The **Judge** has, in a criminal case, however, a greater power of calling a witness not called otherwise, as he is charged with the public duty of inquiring into the offence, and cannot be restricted to the evidence or material which the parties choose to bring before the Court (*R.* v. *Harris*, *post*, p. 424). It appears also that a person who has not been subpœnaed as a witness, but who is present and is called for the prosecution or the defence, **cannot decline to give evidence in a criminal case** (*R.* v. *Sadler*, 4 C. & P. 218). The remarks made above as to objections to competency equally apply to criminal cases.

The attendance of witnesses is compelled, generally, by *recognisances*, whereby witnesses are bound over to appear at the trial by the justices who committed the accused for trial, under the Indictables Offences Act, 1848, s. 20, *post*, p. 439, and the Criminal Justice Act, 1925, ss. 12 and 13, *post*, p. 510. Other witnesses can be compelled to attend by *subpœna*, issued by the Clerk of Quarter Sessions or Assize, or from the Crown Office.

III. EVIDENCE ON APPEAL.

(*a*) In Civil Cases.

Evidence is brought before the **Court of Appeal** in accordance with the provisions of O. 58, rr. 4, 11, 13, *post*, p. 546; before the **Divisional Court,** on appeal from an inferior Court, in accordance with the provisions of O. 59, r. 8, *post*, p. 547.

There is now an official shorthand-writer for trials in the High Court and in most cases the evidence for the Court of Appeal consists of the transcript of his notes (see *post*, p. 546).

(*b*) In Criminal Cases.

Evidence is brought before the **Court of Criminal Appeal** in accordance with the provisions of the Criminal Appeal Act, 1907, ss. 8, 9, 16, *post*, p. 489.

R. v. BAINES.

KING'S BENCH. 1908.

L. R. [1909] 1 K. B. 258; 78 L. J. K. B. 119;
100 L. T. 78; 25 T. L. R. 79.

A party to legal proceedings may subpœna any person as a witness, without leave of the Court. But the Court has jurisdiction to interfere and set aside a subpœna where it is satisfied that its process is being used for indirect or improper objects or is being abused.

The defendant issued and served subpœnas commanding the Prime Minister, the Rt. Hon. H. H. Asquith, and the Home Secretary, the Rt. Hon. H. J. Gladstone, to attend and give evidence at the Leeds Assizes, on the trial of an indictment against him for breach of the peace and unlawful assembly. Mr. Asquith and Mr. Gladstone applied to the King's Bench Division for an order that the subpœnas served on them should be set aside on the ground that the issue thereof was an abuse of the process of the Court; supporting their application by affidavits to the effect (*inter alia*) that they were unable to give any relevant evidence, that they had so informed the defendant's solicitor, that no application had been made to either of them for any proof, and that they believed the subpœnas to have been issued, not with any *bona fide* belief that they could give any material evidence, but for purposes of vexation. The Court set aside the subpœnas.

The following is from the Law Reports:—

BIGHAM, J. . . . **There can be no doubt as to the jurisdiction of the Court to interfere where it is satisfied that its process is being used for indirect or improper objects.** It must not be supposed that the position which the applicants occupy affords them any privilege. They stand in the same position as any other of His Majesty's subjects. But the **Court has to inquire whether its process has been issued against them with the object and expectation on reasonable grounds of obtaining from them evidence which can be relevant.** What are the facts? (*His Lordship here considered the facts.*) I do not believe, as a matter of fact, that they saw or could have seen or that they heard or could have heard anything that can be material to the inquiry at Leeds. We have before us the affidavits of the applicants, in which **they both swear that they are wholly unable to give any evidence which can possibly be relevant** to any issue which may arise. I believe that to be true. Therefore it would be an idle waste of time and money to require them to go down to Leeds to give evidence. The applicants further say that no application has been made to them by the defendants for any proof of the evidence to be given by them. This statement satisfies me that **this process has not been issued for the simple and proper purpose of obtaining evidence,** but for a different and ulterior purpose, a purpose to which the process of the Court ought not to be applied. **It is sufficient to say, first,** that I am satisfied that neither of the applicants can give relevant evidence; **and, secondly,** that the process of the Court has not been issued for the purpose of obtaining relevant evidence, but for other reasons.

WALTON, J. I agree. There is no doubt that this Court has

jurisdiction to entertain this application. **There is no distinction on this point between civil and criminal proceedings. . . .** This case must not be taken as a precedent establishing any rule that a person can, by swearing that he can give no relevant evidence, get a subpœna set aside. Ministers of the Crown have no special privilege. But **these subpœnas are not bona fide required for the purpose of obtaining any evidence** that can be relevant. Our decision in no way interferes with the power of the Judge at the trial, if anything arises which leads him to think that the attendance of these gentlemen is necessary—although it is difficult to see how anything can arise to induce him to think so—to make an order for them to attend.

JACOBS v. LAYBORN.

EXCHEQUER. 1843.

11 M. & W. 685.

An objection to the competency of a witness may be taken whenever his incompetency appears. It may be taken even after he has been allowed to go into the witness-box, has been sworn, and has answered certain questions.

A witness was called on behalf of the defendant and allowed to answer several questions. The plaintiff's counsel then interposed and asked him whether he was not responsible for the costs of the defendant's attorney, and, on his answering in the affirmative, objected to him as incompetent (as the law then stood, he being an interested party). The defendant's counsel contended that the objection came too late, as the witness ought to have been examined on the "*voir dire*". The objection was overruled and the evidence received, the defendant obtaining a verdict. On an application for a new trial, the plaintiff's counsel contended that the practice was to allow such objection whenever the incompetency was discovered. This was held to be so, and a new trial was ordered.

Lord Abinger, C.B. . . . The plaintiff's counsel have furnished us with a proof of **the antiquity, at least, of the practice** contended for by them. They have shown that it has been recognised by the high authority of Lord *King* (see note, *post*) . . . and confirmed afterwards (*on the Trial of Lord Lovat,* 18 St. Tr. 596) by the opinion of Lord *Hardwicke*, one of the greatest Judges who ever presided in this country, not only on the law, but on the reason of the law. To this I can add the testimony of **my own experience,** which has been of more than forty years, that, **whenever a witness was discovered to be incompetent, the Judge always struck the evidence** which he had given out of his notes. I have known both Lord *Ellenborough* and Mr. Baron *Bayley* erase whole pages in this way; and it was not the practice to swear the witness on the *voir dire,* unless specially required by the party against whom he appeared. . . . In Courts of Equity, also, it is every day's practice to object to a witness as incompetent, whenever his incompetency appears. . . . **The reason of the practice rests on this ground,**—the law will not allow a verdict to stand which has been obtained on the evidence of a person whom the rules of law have declared incompetent to give evidence. Historians and others may receive all kinds of evidence of facts, hearsay as well as any other; but with juries it is otherwise, for the law (whether wisely or not it is unnecessary to discuss) excludes all testimony that it considers dangerous. . . . There is no statute which says that the incompetency of a witness must be determined by an examination on the *voir dire*; when a man is examined on the *voir dire,* the examination is only to satisfy the conscience of the Judge, the jury having nothing to do with it. Now a **witness may, on his examination on the voir dire, appear perfectly competent; and the circumstances showing him not to be so may appear afterwards.** Suppose, for instance, a man examined on the *voir dire* were, in answer to questions put to him, to swear distinctly that he had never been convicted of felony or perjury, he is then *prima facie* competent, and is sworn in chief; but while his examination is being proceeded with, the attorney for the party against whom he appears goes away, and fetches the record of his conviction—is not the opposite counsel to be permitted to question him anew as to that conviction? So, in any other case, **I do not see why counsel should be restrained from inquiring at any moment into the witness's competency;** and, if they see that he is swearing falsely, excluding his testimony if they can. A counsel who knows of an objection to the competency of a witness may very fairly say, "I will lie by, and see whether he will speak the truth; if he does not, I will exclude his evidence ". I see no hardship or injustice at all in that course. In short, there is ample authority to show that **the ancient, if not universal, practice has been to allow objections of this kind to be taken as was done in this case. . . .** I think, also, that there is much weight in the observation of my Brother *Rolfe*, that the **question of competency is not for the jury;** so that, in every case where any question is raised about it, there ought properly to be an inquiry made of the witness, who should be sworn " to make true answer to all such questions as the Court should demand of him "; in other words, that an **examination on the voir dire may be instituted at any period of the examination.** For the sake of convenience, it is the usual practice to swear him, in the first instance, to give his evidence in the cause, and the peculiar form of the oath administered on the *voir dire* arises from the circumstance, that the points to which the witness is about to be examined are not evidence in the cause. It may be very proper to interpolate that oath at any period of the examination of the witness that justice may require, and this consideration will reconcile all the difficulties which have been raised.

ROLFE, B., concurred.

Note.—The case referred to above as that in which Lord Chancellor King is said to have recognised the rule in question was *Needham* v. *Smith*, 2 Vern. 463, decided in 1704 by Lord Keeper Sir Nathan Wright, ten years before Lord King became a Judge.

Conviction for felony or perjury does not now, of course, render a witness incompetent, but goes only to credibility.

R. v. HARRIS.

COURT OF CRIMINAL APPEAL. 1927.

L. R. [1927] 2 K. B. 587; 96 L. J. K. B. 1069; 137 L. T. 535; 91 J. P. 152; 43 T. L. R. 774; 28 Cox C. C. 432; 20 Cr. App. R. 86.

A Judge at a criminal trial has the right to call a witness not called by either the prosecution or the defence, but after

the defence is closed he should only do so where a matter has been raised ex improviso on the part of the prisoner.

The appellant was tried together with four other persons before the Recorder of Liverpool. Two of the prisoners were charged with stealing and pleaded guilty; the appellant and the two other prisoners were charged with receiving and pleaded not guilty. After the appellant had given evidence denying guilty knowledge and had closed her case, the Recorder called one of the prisoners who had pleaded guilty but had not yet been sentenced, who gave evidence against the appellant, and she was duly convicted. It was held that in this particular case this course was irregular, and the conviction was quashed.

The following is from the Law Reports:—

AVORY, J. (*delivering the judgment of the Court,* LORD HEWART, C.J., AVORY and SALTER, JJ.). Two questions arise for our determination in this case. The first is whether the course taken by the Recorder in calling the prisoner Benton as a witness when the case for the defence had closed was in accordance with the well-recognised rule that governs proceedings at criminal trials. . . .

As to the first point, it has been clearly laid down by the Court of Appeal in *Re Enoch and Zaretsky, Bock & Co.* ([1910] 1 K. B. 327) that **in a civil suit the Judge has no right to call a witness not called by either party, unless** he does so **with the consent of both of the parties.** It also appears to be clearly established that **the rule does not apply to a criminal trial** where the liberty of a subject is at stake and where the sole object of the proceedings is to make certain that justice should be done as between the subject and the State. The cases of *R.* v. *Chapman* (8 C. & P. 558) and *R.* v. *Holden* (8 C. & P. 606) establish the proposition that the presiding Judge at a criminal trial has the right to call a witness not called by either the prosecution or the defence, and without the consent of either the prosecution or the defence, if in his opinion this course is necessary in the interests of justice. It is true that in none of the cases has any rule been laid down limiting the point in the proceedings at which the Judge may exercise that right. But it is obvious that injustice may be done to an accused person unless some limitation is put upon the exercise of that right, and for the purpose of this case we adopt the rule laid down by Tindal, C.J., in *R.* v.

Frost (4 St. Tr. (N.S.) 86, 386), where the Chief Justice said: "There is no doubt that the general rule is that where the Crown begins its case like a plaintiff in a civil suit, they cannot afterwards support their case by calling fresh witnesses, because they are met by certain evidence that contradicts it. They stand or fall by the evidence they have given. They must close their case before the defence begins; but if any matter arises *ex improviso,* which no human ingenuity can foresee, on the part of a defendant in a civil suit, or a prisoner in a criminal case, there seems to me no reason why that matter which so arose *ex improviso* may not be answered by contrary evidence on the part of the Crown." That rule applies only to a witness called by the Crown and on behalf of the Crown, but we think that the rule should also apply to a case where a witness is called in a criminal trial by the Judge after the case for the defence is closed, and that **the practice should be limited to a case where a matter arises ex improviso, which no human ingenuity can foresee, on the part of a prisoner,** otherwise injustice would ensue. As great a Judge as Bramwell, B., said, in *R.* v. *Haynes* (1 F. & F. 666), when it was proposed, after witnesses had been called for the defence and counsel had replied on behalf of the prosecution, to call another witness for the prosecution: "It is quite clear that counsel cannot call him, as the cases are closed; and if it were allowed, it would necessitate two more speeches. The only doubt I have is, whether I should examine him, as to which I will consult my brother Crompton." Having done so, he continued: "We are both of opinion that it is better to abide by the general rule, and that it would be inexpedient to allow this fresh evidence to be gone into after the close of the whole case."

(*The Judge then considered the particular facts of the case.*)

In the circumstances, without laying down that in no case can an additional witness be called by the Judge after the case for the defence has been closed, we are of opinion that in this particular case the course that was adopted was irregular, and was calculated to do injustice to the appellant Harris.

RE ENOCH AND ZARETSKY, BOCK & CO.'S ARBITRATION.

1910. See Appendix IV, *post*, p. 576.

PART II.

STATUTES ON EVIDENCE.

ACT OF SUPREMACY, 1558.

1 Eliz. c. 1.

21. **No person or persons shall be hereafter indicted** or arraigned for any offences made, ordained, revived, or adjudged by this Act, **unless there be two sufficient witnesses** or more to testify and declare the said offences whereof he shall be indicted or arraigned; and the said witnesses or so many of them as shall be living and within this realm at the time of the arraignment of such person so indicted, shall be brought forth in person, face to face before the party so arraigned, and there shall testify and declare what they can say against the party so arraigned, if he require the same.

Note.—This is one of the four cases in which two witnesses are required for corroboration. See hereon, *ante*, p. 156.

SHOP BOOK DEBTS ACT, 1609.

7 Jac. 1, c. 12.

Whereas divers men of trades and handicraftsmen keeping shop-books, **do demand debts of their customers upon their shopbooks** long time after the same hath been due, and when as they have supposed the particulars and certainty of the wares delivered to be forgotten, then either they themselves or their servants have inserted into their said shopbooks divers other wares supposed to be delivered to the same parties or to their use, which in truth never were delivered and this of purpose to increase by such undue means the said debt: And whereas divers of the said tradesmen and handicraftsmen **having received all the just debt due upon their said shopbooks,** do oftentimes leave the same books uncrossed or any way discharged, so as the debtors, their executors or administrators are often by suit of law enforced to pay the same debts again to the party that trusted the said wares or to his executors or administrators, unless he or they can produce sufficient proof by writing or witnesses of the said payment that may countervail the credit of the said shopbooks, which few or none can do in any long time after the said payment: Be it therefore enacted by the authorities of this present Parliament, that **no tradesman or handicraftsman** keeping a shopbook as is aforesaid, his or their executors or administrators, shall after the Feast of St. Michael the Archangel next coming, be allowed, admitted, or received **to give his shopbook in evidence in any action for any money due** for wares hereafter to be delivered or for work hereafter to be done, **above one year, before the same action brought,** except he or they, their executors or administrators shall have obtained or gotten a bill of debt or obligation of the debtor for the said debt, or shall have brought or pursued against the said debtor, his executors or administrators some action for the said debt, wares or work done, within one year next after the same wares delivered, money due for wares delivered, or work done.

Provided always, that this Act or any thing therein contained **shall not extend to any intercourse of traffic,** merchandizing, buying, selling, or other trading or dealing for wares delivered or to be delivered, money due or work done or to be done **between merchant and merchant, merchant and tradesman, or between tradesman and tradesman,** for anything directly falling within the circuit or compass of their mutual trades and merchandizes; but that for such things only they and every of them shall be in the case as if this Act had never been made; anything herein contained to the contrary thereof notwithstanding.

Note.—Although this Act appears to have been for a long time ignored in practice, it seems proper to include it here owing to its express recognition by the Statute Law Revision Act, 1863 (26 & 27 Vict. c. 125), which made the provision perpetual. It appears clear that at the time of the passing of the Statute such books were treated as admissible in evidence, a practice characterised by Mr. Best as "a violation of the rule, alike of law and common sense, that a man shall not be allowed to manufacture evidence for himself " (s. 503). For the history and explanation of this topic, see *Phipson*, 214.

For the cases in which shop books are otherwise available in evidence, see *post*, p. 552.

STATUTE OF FRAUDS, 1677.

29 Car. 2, c. 3.

4. **No action shall be brought whereby to** charge any executor or administrator upon any special promise to answer damages out of his own estate **or whereby to** charge the defendant upon any special promise to answer for the debt, default or miscarriages of another person **or to** charge any person upon any agreement made upon consideration of marriage *or upon any contract or sale of lands, tenements or hereditaments, or any interest in or concerning them* **or upon** any agreement that is not to be performed within the space of one year from the making thereof **unless** the agreement upon which such action shall be brought or some **memorandum or note thereof, shall be in writing and signed** by the party to be charged therewith or some other person thereunto by him lawfully authorised.

Note.—The words in italics in s. 4 of this Act have been repealed by the Law of Property Act, 1925. The Sale of Goods Act, 1893, s. 4, replaces s. 16 of this Act, *post*, p. 475. It should be noted that this section and also s. 16 (commonly cited as s. 17) of the Statute of Frauds (including the modern re-enactments thereof) merely require written *evidence* of a transaction which may itself be oral. It is therefore to be distinguished from enactments such as the Law of Property Act, 1925, s. 53, which make writing essential to the validity of the transaction itself.

TREASON ACT, 1695.

7 & 8 Will. 3, c. 3.

2. **No person** or persons whatsoever **shall be indicted, tried or attainted of high treason,** whereby any corruption of blood may or shall be made to any such offender or offenders, or to any the heir or heirs of any such offender or offenders or of misprision of such

treason **but by and upon the oaths and testimony of two lawful witnesses,** either both of them **to the same overt act or** one of them to one and the other of them to another overt act of **the same treason,** unless the party indicted and arraigned or tried shall willingly, without violence in open Court confess the same.

Note.—Treason is one of the four cases in which two witnesses are required for corroboration. See hereon, *ante*, p. 156.

BLASPHEMY ACT, 1697.

9 WILL. 3, c. 35.

If any person or persons having been educated in or at any time having made profession of the Christian religion within this realm **shall by writing, printing, teaching, or advised speaking deny** any one of the persons in the Holy Trinity to be God or shall assert or maintain there are more gods than one, or shall deny the Christian religion to be true, or the Holy Scriptures of the Old and New Testament to be of divine authority, **and shall upon indictment or information** in any of his Majesty's courts at Westminster, or at the assizes **be thereof lawfully convicted by the oath of two or more credible witnesses** such person or persons for the first offence shall be adjudged incapable and disabled in law to all intents and purposes whatsoever to have or enjoy any office or offices, employment or employments, ecclesiastical, civil, or military or any part in them or any profit or advantage appertaining to them or any of them. . . . (*Then follows a similar provision as to second convictions "as aforesaid".*)

Note.—This is one of the four cases in which two witnesses are required for corroboration. See hereon, *ante*, p. 156.

TREASON ACT, 1795.

36 Geo. 3, c. 7.

1. . . . **If any person** or persons whatsoever after the day of the passing of this Act, during the natural life of our most gracious sovereign lord the King (whom Almighty God preserve and bless with a long and prosperous reign), and until the end of the next session of Parliament after a demise of the Crown, shall, within the realm or without, **compass, imagine, invent, devise or intend death or destruction, or any bodily harm** tending to death or destruction, maim or wounding, imprisonment or restraint, **of the person of the same our sovereign lord the King,** his heirs and successors, . . . and such compassings, imaginations, inventions, devices or intentions, or any of them, shall express, utter or declare, by publishing any printing or writing, or by any overt act or deed, **being legally convicted thereof upon the oaths of two lawful and credible witnesses** upon trial, or otherwise convicted and attainted by due course of law, then every such person and persons so as aforesaid offending shall be deemed, declared and **adjudged to be a traitor** and traitors, and shall suffer pains of death, and also lose and forfeit as in cases of high treason.

Note.—Treason is one of the four cases in which two witnesses are required for corroboration. See hereon, *ante*, p. 156; and compare the Treason Act, 1695, *ante*, p. 429.

WITNESSES ACT, 1806.

46 Geo. 3, c. 37.

Whereas doubts have arisen whether a witness can by law refuse to answer a question relevant to the matter in issue, the answering of which has no tendency to accuse himself, or to expose him to any penalty or forfeiture, but the answering of which may establish, or tend to establish, that he owes a debt, or is otherwise subject to a civil suit at the instance of his Majesty, or of some other person or persons; be it therefore declared . . . that **a witness cannot by law**

refuse to answer a question relevant to the matter in issue, the answering of which has no tendency to accuse himself, or to expose him to penalty or forfeiture of any nature whatsoever, **by reason only or on the sole ground that** the answering of **such question may establish,** or tend to establish **that he owes a debt, or is otherwise subject to a civil suit,** either at the instance of his Majesty, or of any other person or persons

Note.—As to the privilege of refusing to answer criminating questions and as to what is a criminating matter, see *ante*, p. 331.

JURIES ACT, 1825.

6 Geo. 4, c. 50.

23. **Where in any case, either civil or criminal,** or on any penal statute, depending in any of the said courts of record at Westminster or in the counties palatine, or great sessions in Wales, **it shall appear** to any of the respective courts, or to any judge thereof in vacation, that it will be proper and **necessary that some of the jurors** who are to try the issues in such case **should have the view of the place** in question, in order to their better understanding the evidence that may be given upon the trial of such issues, in every such case such **court, or any judge** thereof in vacation, **may order** a rule to be drawn up, containing the usual terms. . . .

24. Where a view shall be allowed in any case, those **men who shall have had the view,** or such of them as shall appear upon the jury to try the issue, **shall be first sworn,** and so many only shall be added to the viewers who shall appear as shall after all defaulters and challenges allowed make up a full jury of twelve.

Note.—As to inspection of property, see *ante*, p. 408, and *post*, p. 545.

STATUTE OF FRAUDS AMENDMENT ACT, 1828.

9 Geo. 4, c. 14.

Lord Tenterden's Act.

1. . . . In Actions of Debt or upon the Case grounded upon any Simple Contract **no Acknowledgment or Promise** by Words only shall be deemed **sufficient Evidence** of a new or continuing Contract, whereby to take any Case out of the Operation of (*the Limitation Act*, 1623), or to deprive any Party of the Benefit thereof, **unless** such Acknowledgment or Promise shall be made or contained by or in **some Writing to be signed by the Party chargeable thereby. . . .**

3. **No Indorsement or Memorandum of any Payment** written or made . . . upon any Promissory Note, Bill of Exchange, or other Writing, **by or on Behalf of the Party to whom such Payment shall be made**, shall be deemed **sufficient Proof** of such Payment, so as to take the Case out of the Operation of (*the Limitation Act*, 1623).

6. **No action** shall be brought whereby to charge any Person upon or **by reason of any Representation** or Assurance made or given concerning or **relating to the Character, Conduct, Credit, Ability, Trade, or Dealings** of any other Person, to the Intent or Purpose that such other Person may obtain Credit, Money, or Goods upon, **unless** such Representation or Assurance be made **in Writing, signed** by the Party to be charged therewith.

Note.—The above statute is one of the few requiring written evidence. See hereon, *ante*, p. 158.

PREVIOUS CONVICTION ACT, 1836.

6 & 7 Will. 4, c. 111.

Whereas by an Act passed in the seventh and eighth years of the reign of King George the Fourth, intituled "An Act for further improving the administration of justice in criminal cases", provision is made for the more exemplary punishment of **offenders who shall**

commit any felony not punishable with death after a previous conviction for felony: And whereas since the passing of the said Act the practice has been on the trial of any person for any such subsequent felony to charge the jury to inquire at the same time concerning such previous conviction: And whereas doubts may be reasonably entertained whether such practice is consistent with a fair and impartial inquiry as regards the matter of such subsequent felony, and it is expedient that such practice should from henceforth be discontinued: Be it therefore enacted . . . **it shall not be lawful on the trial of any person for any such subsequent felony to charge the jury to inquire concerning such previous conviction until after they shall have inquired concerning such subsequent felony, and shall have found such person guilty of the same;** and whenever in any indictment such previous conviction shall be stated, the reading of such statement to the jury as part of the indictment shall be deferred until after such finding as aforesaid: **Provided nevertheless, that** if upon the trial of any person for any such subsequent felony as aforesaid **such person shall give evidence of his or her good character, it shall be lawful** for the prosecutor, in answer thereto, **to give evidence of the indictment and conviction of such person for the previous felony before such verdict of guilty** shall have been returned, and the jury shall inquire concerning such previous conviction for felony at the same time that they inquire concerning the subsequent felony.

Note.—The law as to evidence of previous convictions is summarised, *ante*, p. 102.

WILLS ACT, 1837, S. 9.

See Appendix IV, *post*, p. 577.

PARLIAMENTARY REGISTRATION ACT, 1843.

6 & 7 VICT. c. 18.

88. (*Dealing with Personation at Elections.*) **If on the hearing of the said charge** the said **two justices shall be satisfied, upon the evidence on oath of not less than two credible witnesses,** that the said person so brought before them has knowingly personated and

falsely assumed to vote in the name of some other person within the meaning of this Act, and is not in fact the person in whose name he voted, **then it shall be lawful for the said two justices to commit the said offender** to the gaol of the county, city, or borough within which the offence was committed, **to take his trial** according to law, and to bind over the witnesses in their respective recognizances to appear and give evidence on such trial as in the case of other misdemeanours.

Note.—This is one of the four cases in which two witnesses are required for corroboration. See hereon, *ante*, p. 156.

EVIDENCE BY COMMISSION ACT, 1843.

6 & 7 VICT. C. 82.

5. Whereas there are **at present no means of compelling the attendance of persons to be examined under any commission** for the examination of witnesses issued by the courts of law or equity in England or Ireland, or by the courts of law in Scotland, **to be executed in a part of the realm subject to different laws** from that in which such commissions are issued, and great inconvenience may arise by reason thereof: Be it therefore enacted, that **if any person, after being served with a written notice to attend** any commissioner or commissioners appointed to execute any such commission for the examination of witnesses as aforesaid (such notice being signed by the commissioner or commissioners, and specifying the time and place of attendance), **shall refuse or fail to appear** and be examined under such commission, such refusal or failure to appear shall be certified by such commissioner or commissioners, and **it shall thereupon be competent**, to or on behalf of any party suing out such commission, **to apply** to any of the superior courts of law in that part of the kingdom within which such commission is to be executed, or any one of the judges of such courts, **for a rule or order to compel** the person or persons so refusing or failing as aforesaid to appear before such commissioner or commissioners, and to be examined under such commission, **and it shall be lawful for the court or judge** to whom such application shall be made by rule or order **to command the attendance and examination** of any person to be named or the

production of any writings or documents to be mentioned in such rule or order.

7. Provided always, . . . that **no person shall be compelled to produce** under such rule or order any writing or other **document that he or she would not be compellable to produce at a trial,** nor to attend on more than two consecutive days, to be named in such rule or order.

Note.—This method of taking evidence is practically obsolete. The modern method is by an examiner or on letters of request under R. S. C., O. 37 (see *post*, p. 541).

EVIDENCE ACT, 1843.

6 & 7 Vict. c. 85.

Lord Denman's Act.

No person offered as a witness shall hereafter be excluded by reason of incapacity from crime or interest from giving evidence, either in person or by deposition, according to the practice of the court, on the trial of any issue joined, or of any matter or question or on any inquiry arising **in any suit, action or proceeding, civil or criminal,** in any court, or before any judge, jury, sheriff, coroner, magistrate, officer, or person having, by law or by consent of parties, authority to hear, receive, and examine evidence; but that **every person so offered may and shall be admitted to give evidence on oath, or solemn affirmation** in those cases wherein affirmation is by law receivable, **notwithstanding that such person may or shall have an interest in the matter** in question, or in the event of the trial of any issue, matter, question, or injury; or of the suit, action, or proceeding in which he is offered as a witness, and **notwithstanding that such person offered as a witness may have been previously convicted of any crime or offence.**

Note.—This Act abolished incompetency from crime or interest, but it further provided that it should not render the parties themselves or their husbands or wives competent witnesses. The parties and their husbands and wives were made competent by the Evidence Acts, 1851, 1853 and 1869. Persons charged with a criminal offence were not made competent till 1898 See *ante*, p. 270, and *post*, pp. 440, 443, 459 and 480.

BASTARDY ACT, 1845.

8 & 9 VICT. c. 10.

6. (*Dealing with Appeals to Quarter Sessions against Bastardy Orders.*) On the trial of any such appeal before any court of quarter sessions **the justices** therein assembled, or the recorder (as the case may be), **shall hear the evidence of the said mother,** and such other evidence as she may produce, and any evidence tendered on behalf of the appellant, and proceed to hear and determine the said appeal in other respects according to law, **but shall not confirm the order so appealed against unless the evidence of the said mother shall have been corroborated in some material particular by other testimony,** to the satisfaction of the said justices in quarter sessions assembled, or the said recorder.

Note.—This Act deals with appeals only. The Bastardy Laws Amendment Act, 1872, *post*, p. 461, requires corroboration also on original applications. As to corroboration generally, see *ante*, p. 156.

EVIDENCE ACT, 1845.

8 & 9 VICT. c. 113.

Lord Brougham's Act (*No.* 1).

1. . . . **Whenever** by any Act now in force or hereafter to be in force **any certificate, official or public document, or document or proceeding of any corporation** or joint stock or other company, **or any certified copy of any** document, bye-law, entry in any register or other book, or of any **other proceeding,** shall be **receivable in evidence** of any particular in any court of justice, or before any legal tribunal, or either House of Parliament, or any committee of either House, or in any judicial proceeding, **the same shall respectively be admitted in evidence, provided they respectively purport to be sealed or impressed** with a stamp, or sealed and signed, **or signed** alone, as required, or impressed with a stamp and signed, **as directed** by the respective Acts made or to be hereafter made, without any proof

of the seal or stamp, where a seal or stamp is necessary, or of the signature or of the official character of the person appearing to have signed the same, and **without any further proof** thereof, in every case in which the original record could have been received in evidence.

2. **All courts, judges,** justices, masters in chancery, masters of courts, commissioners judicially acting, and **other judicial officers, shall henceforth take judicial notice of the signature of any of the** equity or common law **judges of the superior courts** at Westminster, provided such signature be attached or appended to any decree, order, certificate, or other judicial or official document.

3. **All copies of private** and local and personal **Acts of Parliament** not public Acts, if purporting to be printed by the Queen's printers, and all copies of the **journals of either House of Parliament,** and of **royal proclamations,** purporting to be printed by the printers to the crown or by the printers to either House of Parliament, or by any or either of them, **shall be admitted as evidence** thereof by all courts, judges, justices, and others, **without any proof** being given that such copies were so printed.

Note.—**Ss. 1, 3.** As to proof of public documents, see *ante*, p. 361. **S. 2.** As to judicial notice, see *ante*, p. 14.

INDICTABLE OFFENCES ACT, 1848.

11 & 12 VICT. c. 42.

Jervis's Act.

17. **Where any person shall appear or be brought before any justice or justices of the peace, charged with any indictable offence,** whether committed in England or Wales, or upon the high seas, or on land beyond the sea, or whether such person appear voluntarily upon summons or have been apprehended, with or without warrant, or be in custody for the same or any other offence, **such justice or justices, before he or they shall commit** such accused person to prison for trial, or before he or they shall admit him to bail, **shall, in the presence of such accused person, who shall be at liberty to put questions to any witness produced against him, take the statement**

on oath or affirmation of those who shall know the facts and circumstances of the case, **and shall put the same into writing, and such depositions shall be read over to and signed respectively by the witnesses** who shall have been so examined, **and shall be signed also by the justice or justices** taking the same; and the justice or justices before whom any such witness shall appear to be examined as aforesaid shall, before such witness is examined, administer to such witness the usual oath or affirmation, which such justice or justices shall have full power and authority to do.

20. **It shall be lawful** for the justice or justices before whom any such witness shall be examined as aforesaid **to bind by recognizance the prosecutor and every such witness to appear** at the next court . . . at which the accused is to be tried, then and there **to prosecute,** or to prosecute and give evidence, **or to give evidence,** as the case may be, against the party accused, . . . and the several **recognizances so taken, together with the written information (if any), the depositions, the statement of the accused, and the recognizance of bail** (if any) in every such case, **shall be delivered** by the said justice or justices, or he or they shall cause the same to be delivered, **to the proper officer of the court in which the trial is to be had,** before or at the opening of the said court on the first day of the sitting thereof, or at such other time as the judge, recorder, or justice who is to preside in such court at the said trial, shall order and appoint: Provided always, that **if any such witness shall refuse to enter into or acknowledge such recognizance as aforesaid, it shall be lawful** for such justice or justices of the peace, by his or their warrant, to **commit him** to the common gaol or house of correction for the county, riding, division, liberty, city, borough, or place, in which the accused party is to be tried, there **to be imprisoned and safely kept until after the trial of such accused party.**

Note.—**S. 17.** The directions set out in this section must be strictly followed: it is not a compliance with the section for a witness to be taken through a statement which has been typed out beforehand and for him then to sign this statement (*R.* v. *Gee*, [1936] 2 K. B. 442).

As to the circumstances in which depositions can be read at the trial, see Criminal Justice Act, 1925, s. 13, *post*, p. 512.

The Criminal Justice Act, 1925, s. 12 (5), *post*, p. 511, makes provision for taking the depositions of the person charged with an indictable offence, and of witnesses on his behalf; the Criminal Law

Amendment Act, 1867, s. 6, *post*, p. 454, makes provision for taking the depositions of any persons dangerously ill, by way of "perpetuation of testimony", whether any person is already accused or not.

SUMMARY JURISDICTION ACT, 1848.

11 & 12 VICT. c. 43.

9. In all cases of informations for any offences or acts punishable upon summary conviction **any variance between** such **information** and the **evidence** adduced in support thereof **as to the time** at which such offence or act shall be alleged to have been committed **shall not be deemed material, if** it be proved that such information was in fact laid within the time limited by law for laying the same; and any variance between such information and the evidence adduced in support thereof **as to the parish or township** in which the offence or act shall be alleged to have been committed **shall not be deemed material, provided** that the offence or act be proved to have been committed within the jurisdiction of the justice or justices by whom such information shall be heard and determined; . . .

14. (*Dealing with Proceedings before Courts of Summary Jurisdiction.*) . . . **If the information or complaint** in any such case **shall negative any exemption, exception, proviso, or condition** in the statute on which the same shall be framed **it shall not be necessary** for the prosecutor or complainant in that behalf **to prove such negative,** but the defendant may prove the affirmative thereof in his defence, if he would have advantage of the same.

Note.—**S. 14.** This provision should be read in connection with s. 39 of the Summary Jurisdiction Act, 1879, *post*, p. 465. See also note, *ante*, p. 148.

EVIDENCE ACT, 1851.

14 & 15 VICT. c. 99.

Lord Brougham's Act (*No.* 2).

2. **On the trial of any issue** joined, or of any **matter or question, or on any inquiry** arising in any suit, action, or other proceeding

in any court of justice, or before any person having by law, or by consent of parties, authority to hear, receive, and examine evidence, **the parties** thereto, and the persons in whose behalf any such suit, action or other proceeding may be brought or defended, **shall, except as herein-after excepted, be competent and compellable to give evidence,** either *viva voce* or by deposition, according to the practice of the court, on behalf of either or any of the parties to the said suit, action, or other proceeding.

3. But **nothing herein contained shall render any person** who in any criminal proceeding is **charged with** the commission of **any** indictable **offence,** or any offence punishable on summary conviction, **competent or compellable to give evidence** for or against himself or herself, **or shall render any person compellable to answer any question tending to criminate himself** or herself, **or shall in any criminal proceeding render any husband** competent or compellable to give evidence for or against his wife, **or any wife competent or compellable** to give evidence for or against her husband.

4. *Nothing herein contained shall apply to any action, suit, proceeding, or bill in any court of common law, or in any ecclesiastical court, or in either House of Parliament, instituted in consequence of adultery, or to any action for breach of promise of marriage.*

7. **All proclamations, treaties, and other acts of state of** any **foreign state** or of any **British colony,** and all **judgments, decrees, orders, and other judicial proceedings** of any court of justice in any foreign state or in any British colony, and any **affidavits, pleadings, and other legal documents** filed or deposited in any such court, **may be proved** in any court of justice, or before any person having by law or by consent of parties authority to hear, receive, and examine evidence, either **by examined copies or by copies authenticated as herein-after mentioned;** that is to say, if the document sought to be proved be a proclamation, treaty, or other **act of state,** the authenticated copy to be admissible in evidence must purport to be sealed with the seal of the foreign state or British colony to which the original document belongs; and if the document sought to be proved be a judgment, decree, order, or other **judicial proceeding** of any foreign or colonial court, or an affidavit, pleading, or other legal document filed or deposited in any such court, the authenticated copy to be admissible in evidence must purport either to be sealed with the seal of the foreign or colonial court to which

the original document belongs, or, in the event of such court having no seal to be signed by the judge, or, if there be more than one judge, by any one of the judges of the said court; and such judge shall attach to his signature a statement in writing on the said copy that the court whereof he is a judge has no seal; but if any of the aforesaid authenticated copies shall purport to be sealed or signed as hereinbefore respectively directed, the same shall respectively be admitted in evidence in every case in which the original document could have been received in evidence **without any proof of the seal** where a seal is necessary, **or of the signature,** or of the truth of the statement attached thereto, where such signature and statement are necessary **or of the judicial character** of the person appearing to have made such signature and statement.

13. . . . Whenever in any proceeding whatever it may be necessary **to prove the trial and conviction or acquittal of any person** charged with any indictable offence, **it shall not be necessary to produce the record** of the conviction or acquittal of such person, or a copy thereof; but it shall be **sufficient that it be certified or purport to be certified under the hand of the clerk of the court or other officer** having the custody of the records of the court where such conviction or acquittal took place, or by the deputy of such clerk or other officer, that the paper produced is a copy of the record of the indictment, trial, conviction, and judgment or acquittal, as the case may be, omitting the formal parts thereof.

14. **Whenever any book or other document is of such a public nature as to be admissible in evidence on its mere production from the proper custody,** and no statute exists which renders its contents provable by means of a copy, **any copy thereof or extract therefrom shall be admissible in evidence** in any court of justice, or before any person now or hereafter having by law or by consent of parties authority to hear, receive, and examine evidence, **provided it be proved to be an examined copy or extract, or provided it purport to be signed and certified as a true copy or extract by the officer to whose custody the original is intrusted,** and which officer is hereby required to furnish such certified copy or extract to any person applying at a reasonable time for the same, upon payment of a reasonable sum for the same, not exceeding fourpence for every folio of ninety words.

16. **Every court, judge,** justice, officer, commissioner, arbitrator,

or other person, now or hereafter **having by law or by consent** of parties **authority to hear,** receive, and examine **evidence, is hereby empowered to administer an oath** to all such witnesses as are legally called before them respectively.

Note.—**S. 3.** As to the evidence of persons charged with criminal offences, and their husbands and wives, see now the Criminal Evidence Act, 1898, *post*, p. 480; and generally as to competency and compellability, *ante*, p. 269. As to criminating questions, see *ante*, p. 331.

S. 4. This was repealed by the Evidence Act, 1869, a new provision being made thereby. See *post*, p. 459.

Ss. 7, 13, 14. As to proof of public documents generally, see *ante*, p. 361.

EVIDENCE AMENDMENT ACT, 1853.

16 & 17 Vict. c. 83.

Lord Brougham's Act (No. 3).

1. **On the Trial of any Issue** joined, or of any **Matter or Question, or on any Inquiry** arising in any Suit, Action, or other Proceeding in any Court of Justice, or before any Person having by Law or by Consent of Parties Authority to hear, receive, and examine Evidence, the **Husbands and Wives of the Parties** thereto, and of the Persons in whose Behalf any such Suit, Action, or other Proceeding may be brought or instituted, or opposed or defended, **shall, except as herein-after excepted, be competent and compellable to give Evidence** either *viva voce* or by Deposition according to the Practice of the Court, on behalf of either or any of the Parties to the said Suit, Action, or other Proceeding.

2. **Nothing herein shall render any Husband** competent or compellable to give Evidence for or against his Wife, **or any Wife competent or compellable** to give Evidence for or against her Husband, **in any Criminal Proceeding** *or in any Proceeding instituted in consequence of Adultery.*

3. **No Husband** shall be compellable to disclose any Communication made to him by his Wife during the Marriage, **and no Wife**

shall be compellable to disclose any Communication made to her by her Husband **during the Marriage.**

Note.—**S. 1.** As to the evidence of husbands and wives generally, see *ante*, p. 273.

S. 2. As to criminal proceedings, see now the Criminal Evidence Act, 1898, *post*, p. 480. The words in italics were repealed by the Evidence Act, 1869, *post*, p. 459.

S. 3. As to the disclosure of matrimonial communications compare s. 1 (*d*) of the Criminal Evidence Act, 1898, *post*, p. 480.

FOREIGN TRIBUNALS EVIDENCE ACT, 1856.

19 & 20 Vict. c. 113.

Whereas it is expedient that facilities be afforded for taking evidence in Her Majesty's dominions in relation to civil and commercial matters pending before foreign tribunals: . . .

1. **Where,** upon an application for this purpose, it is made to appear to any court or judge having authority under this Act that **any court or tribunal of competent jurisdiction in a foreign country,** before which any civil or commercial matter is pending, **is desirous of obtaining the testimony** in relation to such matter **of any witness** or witnesses within the jurisdiction of such first-mentioned court, or of the court to which such judge belongs, or of such judge, **it shall be lawful** for such court or judge **to order the examination** upon oath, upon interrogatories or otherwise, before any person or persons named in such order, of such witness or witnesses accordingly; **and it shall be lawful** for the said court or judge, by the same order, or for such court or judge, or any other judge having authority under this Act, by any subsequent order, **to command the attendance of any person** to be named in such order, for the purpose of being examined, **or the production of any writings or other documents** to be mentioned in such order, **and to give all such directions** as to the time, place and manner of such examination, and all other matters connected therewith, **as may appear reasonable and just;** and any such order may be enforced in like manner as an order made by

such court or judge in a cause depending in such court or before such judge.

2. **A certificate under the hand of the** ambassador, minister, or other **diplomatic agent** of any foreign power, received as such by Her Majesty, or in case there be no such diplomatic agent, then of the consul-general **or consul of any such foreign power at London,** received and admitted as such by Her Majesty, **that any matter** in relation to which an application is made under this Act is a civil or commercial matter **pending before a court** or tribunal in the country of which he is the diplomatic agent or consul having jurisdiction in the matter so pending, **and that such court or tribunal is desirous** of obtaining the testimony of the witness or witnesses to whom the application relates, **shall be evidence** of the matters so certified; but where no such certificate is produced, other evidence to that effect shall be admissible.

3. It shall be lawful for every person authorised . . . to take all such examinations upon the oath of the witnesses, or affirmation in cases where affirmation is allowed by law instead of oath. . . .

5. Provided, that **every person examined** under any order made under this Act **shall have the like right to refuse to answer questions** tending to criminate himself, and other questions, which a witness in any cause pending in the court by which or by a judge whereof or before the judge by whom the order for examination was made would be entitled to; and that **no person shall be compelled to produce** under any such order as aforesaid any writing or other **document that he would not be compellable to produce at a trial of** such a cause.

6. Her Majesty's Superior Courts of Common Law at Westminster and in Dublin respectively, the Court of Session in Scotland, and any Supreme Court in any of Her Majesty's colonies or possessions abroad, and any judge of any such court, and every judge in any such colony or possession who by any Order of Her Majesty in Council may be appointed for this purpose, shall respectively be courts and judges having authority under this Act.

Note.—**S. 1.** As to attendance of witnesses generally, see *ante*, p. 418.

S. 5. As to privileged questions and documents generally, see *ante*, p. 321. A case on this section is *Eccles* v. *Louisville Ry.*, [1912] 1 K. B. 135.

EVIDENCE BY COMMISSION ACT, 1859.

22 VICT. C. 20.

Whereas it is expedient that facilities be afforded for taking evidence in or in relation to actions, suits, and proceedings pending before tribunals in Her Majesty's dominions in places in such dominions out of the jurisdiction of such tribunals: . . .

1. **Where** upon an application for this purpose it is made to appear to any court or judge having authority under this Act that **any court or tribunal of competent jurisdiction in Her Majesty's dominions has duly authorized,** by commission, order, or other process, **the obtaining the testimony** in or in relation to any action, suit, or proceeding pending in or before such court or tribunal **of any witness or witnesses out of the jurisdiction of such court or tribunal,** and within the jurisdiction of such first-mentioned court, or of the court to which such judge belongs, or of such judge, **it shall be lawful** for such court or judge **to order the examination** before the person or persons appointed, and in manner and form directed by such commission, order, or other process as aforesaid, of such witness or witnesses accordingly; **and it shall be lawful** for the said court or judge by the same order, or for such court or judge, or any other judge having authority under this Act, by any subsequent order, **to command the attendance of any person** to be named in such order for the purpose of being examined, **or the production of any writings or other documents** to be mentioned in such order, **and to give all such directions** as to the time, place, and manner of such examination, and all other matters connected therewith, **as may appear reasonable and just;** and any such order may be enforced, and any disobedience thereof punished, in like manner as in case of an order made by such court or judge in a cause depending in such court or before such judge.

4. Provided, that **every person examined** under any such commission, order, or other process as aforesaid, **shall have the like right to refuse to answer questions** tending to criminate himself, and other questions which a witness in any cause pending in the court by which, or by a judge whereof, or before the judge by whom the order for examination was made, would be entitled to; and that **no person shall be compelled to produce** under any such order as

aforesaid any writing or other **document that he would not be compellable to produce at a trial** of such a cause.

5. Her Majesty's Superior Courts of Common Law at Westminster and in Dublin respectively, the Court of Session in Scotland, and any Supreme Court in any of Her Majesty's colonies or possessions abroad, and any judge of any such court, and every judge in any such colony or possession, who by any order of Her Majesty in Council, may be appointed for this purpose shall respectively be courts and judges having authority under this Act.

Note.—**S. 1.** As to attendance of witnesses generally, see *ante*, p. 418.

S. 4. As to privileged questions and documents generally, see *ante*, p. 321.

BRITISH LAW ASCERTAINMENT ACT, 1859.

22 & 23 Vict. c. 63.

1. **If in any action depending in any court within Her Majesty's dominions,** it shall be the opinion of such court, that **it is necessary or expedient** for the proper disposal of such action **to ascertain the law applicable** to the facts of the case as administered **in any other part of Her Majesty's dominions** on any point on which the law of such other part of Her Majesty's dominions is different from that in which the court is situate, **it shall be competent** to the court in which such action may depend **to direct a case to be prepared** setting forth the facts, as these may be ascertained by verdict of a jury or other mode competent, or may be agreed upon by the parties, or settled by such person or persons as may have been appointed by the court for that purpose in the event of the parties not agreeing; **and upon such case being approved of by such court or a judge thereof, they shall settle the questions** of law arising out of the same on which they desire to have the opinion of another court, **and shall pronounce an order remitting the same, together with the case, to the court** in such other part of Her Majesty's dominions, being one of the superior courts thereof, **whose opinion is desired** upon the law administered by them as applicable to the facts set forth in such

case, and **desiring them to pronounce their opinion** on the questions submitted to them in the terms of the Act; **and it shall be competent to any of the parties to the action to present a petition to the court** whose opinion is to be obtained, praying such last-mentioned court to hear parties or their counsel, and **to pronounce their opinion** thereon in terms of this Act, or to pronounce their opinion without hearing parties or counsel; **and the court** to which such petition shall be presented **shall, if they think fit, appoint an early day** for hearing parties or their counsel on such case, **and shall thereafter pronounce their opinion** upon the questions of law as administered by them which are submitted to them by the court; and in order to their pronouncing such opinion they shall be entitled to take such further procedure thereupon as to them shall seem proper.

2. Upon such opinion being pronounced, **a copy thereof, certified by an officer** of such court, shall be given to each of the parties to the action by whom the same shall be required, and **shall be deemed and held to contain a correct record of such opinion.**

3. (*Opinion to be applied by the court making the remit, etc.*)

4. (*Her Majesty in Council or House of Lords on appeal may adopt or reject opinion.*)

5. (*Interpretation of terms.*)

Note.—**S. 1.** As to proof of Colonial Law generally, see *ante*, p. 18.

S. 2. As to proof of judicial proceedings, see *ante*, p. 363.

FOREIGN LAW ASCERTAINMENT ACT, 1861.

24 & 25 VICT. c. 11.

Whereas an Act was passed in the twenty-second and twenty-third years of Her Majesty's reign, intituled "An Act to afford facilities for the more certain ascertainment of the law administered in one part of Her Majesty's dominions when pleaded in the courts of another part thereof": And whereas it is expedient to afford the like facilities for the better ascertainment, in similar circumstances, of the law of any foreign country or state with the Government of which Her Majesty may be pleased to enter into a convention for the purpose of mutually ascertaining the law of such foreign country or state when pleaded in actions depending in any courts within Her Majesty's dominions and the law as administered in any part of Her Majesty's dominions when pleaded in actions depending in the courts of such foreign country or state: . . .

1. **If, in any action depending in any of the Superior Courts within Her Majesty's dominions,** it shall be the opinion of such court that **it is necessary or expedient,** for the disposal of such action, **to ascertain the law applicable** to the facts of the case as administered **in any foreign state or country with the Government of which Her Majesty shall have entered into such convention** as aforesaid, **it shall be competent** to the court in which such action may depend **to direct a case to be prepared** setting forth the facts as these may be ascertained by verdict of jury or other mode competent, or as may be agreed upon by the parties, or settled by such person or persons as may have been appointed by the court for that purpose in the event of the parties not agreeing; **and upon such case being approved of by such court or a judge thereof, such court or judge shall settle the question** of law arising out of the same on which they desire to have the opinion of another court, **and shall pronounce an order remitting the same, together with the case, to such superior Court** in such foreign state or country **as shall be agreed** upon in said convention, **whose opinion is desired** upon the law administered by such foreign court as applicable to the facts set forth in such case, and **requesting them to pronounce their opinion** on the questions submitted to them; and upon such opinion being pronounced, **a copy thereof, certified by an officer** of such court, **shall be deemed and held to contain a correct record of such opinion.**

2. (*Copy of opinion to be lodged in court in which action depends. Court to apply opinion to the facts set forth in the case, etc. Remitter of case back to foreign court.*)

3. (*Courts in Her Majesty's dominions shall pronounce opinion on case remitted by a foreign court.*)

4. (*Interpretation of terms.*)

Note.—**S. 1.** As to proof of foreign law generally, see *post*, p. 562. As to proof of judicial proceedings, see *ante*, p. 351.

LARCENY ACT, 1861.

24 & 25 Vict. c. 96.

29. (*Dealing with Larceny of Deeds and Wills, etc.*) **No person shall be liable to be convicted of any of the felonies in this and the last preceding section** mentioned, by any evidence whatever, in respect of any act done by him, **if he** shall at any time previously to his being charged with such offence have **first disclosed** such act, on oath, **in consequence of any compulsory process of any court** of law or equity in any action, suit, or proceeding which shall have been *bona fide* instituted by any party aggrieved, or if he shall have first disclosed the same in any compulsory examination or deposition before any court upon the hearing of any matter in bankruptcy or insolvency.

85. (*Dealing with Frauds by Bankers, Agents, etc.*) **Nothing in** any of the last **ten preceding sections** of this Act contained **shall enable or entitle any person to refuse to make a full and complete discovery** by answer to any bill in equity, or to answer any question or interrogatory in any civil proceeding in any court, or upon the hearing of any matter in bankruptcy or insolvency; **and no person shall be liable to be convicted of any of the misdemeanours in any of the said sections mentioned** by any evidence whatever in respect of any act done by him, **if he** shall at any time previously to his being charged with such offence have **first disclosed** such act on oath, **in consequence of any compulsory process of any court** of law or equity, in any action, suit, or proceeding which shall have been *bona fide* instituted by any party aggrieved *or if he shall have first disclosed the same in any compulsory examination or deposition before any court upon the hearing of any matter in bankruptcy or insolvency.*

116. . . . the proceedings upon any indictment for committing any offence after a previous conviction or convictions shall be as follows; (that is to say,) **the offender shall, in the first instance, be arraigned upon** so much only of the indictment as charges **the subsequent offence,** and if he plead not guilty, or if the court order a plea of not guilty to be entered on his behalf, the jury shall be charged, in the first instance, to inquire concerning such subsequent offence only; **and if** they find him **guilty,** or if on arraignment he

plead guilty, **he shall then, and not before, be asked whether he had been previously convicted,** as alleged in the indictment; and if he answer that he had been so previously convicted, the court may proceed to sentence him accordingly; **but if he deny** that he had been so previously convicted, or **stand mute** of malice, or will not answer directly to such question, **the jury shall then be charged to inquire concerning such previous conviction** or convictions, and in such case it shall not be necessary to swear the jury again but the oath already taken by them shall for all purposes be deemed to extend to such last-mentioned inquiry: **Provided, that if** upon the trial of any person for any such subsequent offence **such person shall give evidence of his good character, it shall be lawful** for the prosecutor, in answer thereto, **to give evidence of the conviction** of such person for the previous offence or offences **before such verdict of guilty** shall be returned, and the jury shall inquire concerning such previous conviction or convictions at the same time that they inquire concerning such subsequent offence.

Note.—**Ss. 29, 85.** These sections afford instances of the cases in which a witness is compelled to answer criminating questions but is protected from subsequent prosecution for the offences disclosed. Other instances are given, *ante*, p. 333. S. 85 (of which the last four lines are repealed) should be read with the Bankruptcy Act, 1914, *post*, p. 499, and the Larceny Act, 1916, s. 43, *post*, p. 501.

S. 116. It has been held that this section applies to all proceedings where the offender is charged in the indictment with committing an offence after a previous conviction, and is not limited to proceedings for offences under this Act (*Faulkner* v. *R.*, [1905] 2 K. B. 76; see *ante*, p. 102, where the whole law as to proof of previous convictions is summarised).

CRIMINAL PROCEDURE ACT, 1865.

28 & 29 VICT. c. 18.

1. The Provisions of **Sections from Three to Eight, inclusive, of this Act shall apply to all Courts of Judicature, as well Criminal as all others,** and to all Persons having, by law or by Consent of Parties, Authority to hear, receive, and examine Evidence.

2. **If any Prisoner or Prisoners,** Defendant or Defendants, shall **be defended by Counsel,** but not otherwise, it shall be the Duty of

the presiding **Judge, at the Close of the Case for the Prosecution, to ask** the Counsel for each Prisoner or Defendant so defended by Counsel **whether he or they intend to adduce Evidence, and in the event of none of them thereupon announcing his Intention** to adduce Evidence, the **Counsel for the Prosecution** shall be **allowed to address the Jury a Second Time** in support of his Case, for the Purpose of **summing up the Evidence** against such Prisoner or Prisoners, or Defendant or Defendants; **and** upon every Trial for Felony or Misdemeanour, **whether the Prisoners** or Defendants, or any of them, shall be **defended by Counsel or not,** each and **every such Prisoner** or Defendant, or his or their Counsel respectively, **shall be allowed** if he or they shall think fit, **to open his or their Case** or Cases respectively; and after the Conclusion of such Opening or of all such Openings, if more than One, such Prisoner or Prisoners, or Defendant or Defendants, or their Counsel, shall be entitled **to examine such Witnesses** as he or they may think fit, **and when all the Evidence is concluded to sum up the Evidence** respectively; and the Right of Reply, and Practice and Course of Proceedings, save as hereby altered, shall be as at present.

3. **A Party producing a Witness shall not be allowed to impeach his Credit by general Evidence** of bad character, **but he may, in case the Witness shall,** in the Opinion of the Judge, **prove adverse** (*see note*, p. 454), **contradict him by other Evidence, or, by Leave** of the Judge, **prove that he has made** at other Times a **Statement inconsistent** with his present Testimony; **but before such** last-mentioned **Proof** can be given **the Circumstances** of the supposed Statement, sufficient to designate the particular Occasion, **must be mentioned to the Witness,** and he must be asked whether or not he has made such Statement.

4. **If a Witness, upon Cross-examination as to a former Statement made by him** relative to the Subject Matter of the Indictment or Proceeding, **and inconsistent** with his present Testimony, **does not distinctly admit** that he has made such Statement, **Proof may be** given that he did in fact make it; **but before such Proof** can be given **the Circumstances** of the supposed Statement, sufficient to designate the particular Occasion, **must be mentioned to the Witness,** and he must be asked whether or not he has made such Statement.

5. **A witness may be cross-examined as to previous Statements** made by him **in Writing** or reduced into Writing relative to the

Subject Matter of the Indictment or Proceeding, **without such Writing being shown to him; but if it is intended to contradict such Witness by the Writing, his Attention must, before such** contradictory **Proof** can be given, **be called to those Parts of the writing** which are to be used for the Purpose of so contradicting him: Provided always, that it shall be competent for the Judge, at any Time during the Trial, to require the Production of the Writing for his Inspection, and he may thereupon make such Use of it for the Purposes of the Trial as he may think fit.

6. **A Witness may be questioned as to whether he has been convicted** of any Felony or Misdemeanour, **and** upon being so questioned, **if he either denies or does not admit** the Fact, or refuses to answer, **it shall be lawful** for the cross-examining Party **to prove such Conviction**; and a Certificate containing the Substance and Effect only (omitting the formal Part) of the Indictment and Conviction for such Offence, purporting to be signed by the Clerk of the Court or other Officer having the custody of the Records of the Court where the Offender was convicted, or by the Deputy of such Clerk or Officer (for which Certificate a Fee of Five Shillings and no more shall be demanded or taken), shall, upon Proof of the Identity of the Person, be sufficient Evidence of the said Conviction, without Proof of the Signature or official Character of the Person appearing to have signed the same.

7. **It shall not be necessary to prove by the attesting Witness any instrument to the Validity of which Attestation is not requisite,** and such Instrument may be proved as if there had been no attesting Witness thereto.

8. **Comparison of a disputed Writing with any Writing proved** to the Satisfaction of the Judge to be **genuine shall be permitted** to be made **by Witnesses; and such Writings, and the Evidence** of Witnesses respecting the same, **may be submitted** to the Court and Jury **as Evidence** of the Genuineness or otherwise of the Writing in dispute.

Note.—**S. 1.** It should be particularly noted that, notwithstanding its inconsistent title, the Act applies to *civil* cases.

S. 2. The right of the prosecution to a second speech, by way of "summing up" the evidence, depends upon the prisoner being defended by counsel. The right of the prosecution to a second speech, by way of "reply", to the case of the prisoner, depends upon the prisoner adducing evidence, by witnesses or documents.

Ss. 3-5. S. 3, "adverse" means "hostile" (*Greenhough* v. *Eccles* (1859), 5 C. B. (N.S.) 268). See as to evidence to discredit witnesses, *ante*, p. 314; as to previous inconsistent statements by an opponent's witness, *ante*, p. 315, and by a party's own witness, *ante*, p. 317.

Ss. 4-5. See Appendix IV, *post*, p. 578.

S. 6. It appears that such conviction may be proved, although it is wholly irrelevant to the issue (*Ward* v. *Sinfield*, 49 L. J. C. P. 696).

S. 7. See *ante*, p. 371, and Evidence Act, 1938, s. 3, *post*, p. 586.

S. 8. As to who are permitted to testify as "experts" in handwriting, see *R.* v. *Silverlock*, *ante*, p. 133.

CRIMINAL LAW AMENDMENT ACT, 1867.

30 & 31 VICT. C. 35.

Russell Gurney's Act.

6. Whereas it may happen that **a person dangerously ill,** and unable to travel, may be **able to give material and important information** relating to an indictable offence, or to a person accused thereof, . . . and it is desirable in the interests of truth and justice that means should be provided **for perpetuating such testimony,** and for rendering the same available in the event of the death of the person giving the same: Therefore, **whenever it shall be made to appear to the satisfaction of any justice of the peace that any person dangerously ill,** and in the opinion of some registered medical practitioner not likely to recover from such illness, **is able and willing to give material information relating to any indictable offence,** or relating to any person accused of any such offence, . . . **it shall be lawful for the said justice to take in writing the statement on oath or affirmation of such person** so being ill, and such justice shall thereupon subscribe the same, and shall add thereto by way of caption a statement of his reason for taking the same, and of the day and place when and where the same was taken, and of the names of the persons (if any) present at the taking thereof, **and, if the same shall relate to any indictable offence for which any accused person is already committed or bailed to appear for trial, shall transmit the same** with the said addition **to the proper officer** of the

court for trial at which such accused person shall have been so committed or bailed; **and in all other cases he shall transmit the same to the clerk of the peace** of the county, division, city or borough in which he shall have taken the same, who is hereby required to preserve the same, and file it of record; **and if afterwards, upon the trial** of any offender or offence to which the same may relate, **the person who made the same statement shall be proved to be dead, or** if it shall be proved that **there is no reasonable probability that such person will ever be able to travel or to give evidence, it shall be lawful to read such statement in evidence,** either for or against the accused, without further proof thereof, if the same purports to be signed by the justice by or before whom it purports to be taken, and **provided it be proved** to the satisfaction of the court **that reasonable notice of the intention to take such statement has been served upon the person** (whether prosecutor or accused) **against whom it is proposed to be read in evidence, and that such person,** or his counsel or attorney, **had or might have had,** if he had chosen to be present, **full opportunity of cross-examining** the deceased person who made the same.

Note.—**S. 6.** The object of this provision is to enable depositions to be taken in *criminal* cases by way of "perpetuation of testimony", of persons dangerously ill, whether any person is actually accused of the offence in question or not. As to perpetuation of testimony in *civil* cases, see Order 37, r. 35, *post*, p. 543.

DOCUMENTARY EVIDENCE ACT, 1868.

31 & 32 Vict. c. 37.

2. **Prima facie evidence of any proclamation, order, or regulation issued** before or after the passing of this Act **by Her Majesty, or by the Privy Council, also** of any proclamation, order, or regulation issued before or after the passing of this Act **by or under the authority of any such department** of the Government or officer as is **mentioned in** the first column of the **schedule** hereto, **may be given** in all courts of justice, and in all legal proceedings whatsoever, **in all or any of the modes hereinafter mentioned**; that is to say:—

(1) By the production of **a copy of the Gazette** purporting to contain such proclamation, order or regulation.

(2) By the production of **a copy** of such proclamation, order, or regulation, **purporting to be printed by the Government printer,** or, where the question arises in a court in any British colony or possession, of a copy purporting to be printed under the authority of the legislature of such British colony or possession.

(3) By the production, in the case of any proclamation, order, or regulation issued by Her Majesty or by the Privy Council, of **a copy or extract purporting to be certified to be true by the clerk of the Privy Council,** or by any one of the lords or others of the Privy Council, and, in the case of any proclamation, order, or regulation issued by or under the authority of any of the said departments or officers, by the production of **a copy or extract purporting to be certified to be true by the person or persons specified in the second column** of the said schedule in connection with such department or officer.

Any copy or extract made in pursuance of this Act may be in print or in writing, or partly in print and partly in writing.

No proof shall be required of the handwriting or official position of any person certifying, in pursuance of this Act, to the truth of any copy of an extract from any proclamation, order, or regulation.

3. Subject to any law that may be from time to time made by the legislature of any British colony or possession, this Act shall be in force in every such colony and possession.

6. The provisions of this Act shall be deemed to be in addition to, and not in derogation of, any powers of proving documents given by any existing statute, or existing at common law.

SCHEDULE AS AMENDED BY LATER ENACTMENTS.

COLUMN 1. Name of Department or Officer.	COLUMN 2. Name of Certifying Officers.
The Commissioners of the Treasury.	Any Commissioner, Secretary, or Assistant Secretary of the Treasury.
The Commissioners for executing the office of Lord High Admiral.	Any of the Commissioners for executing the office of Lord High Admiral or either of the Secretaries to the said Commissioners.

SCHEDULE—*continued.*

COLUMN 1. Name of Department or Officer.	COLUMN 2. Name of Certifying Officers.
Secretaries of State.	Any Secretary or Under-Secretary of State.
Committee of Privy Council for Trade.	Any member of the Committee of Privy Council for Trade, or any Secretary or Assistant Secretary of the said Committee.
Board of Education (*a*).	Any member of the Board of Education Department, or any Secretary or Assistant Secretary.
Ministry of Agriculture (*b*).	The Minister, or Secretary, or any person authorised by the Minister to act on behalf of the Secretary.
Department of Agriculture and Technical Instruction, Ireland (*c*).	Member, or Secretary, or person authorised to act on behalf of the Secretary.
Postmaster-General (*d*).	The Director-General or Deputy Director-General or any Assistant Secretary.
Army Council (*e*).	Two members of the Army Council, or the Secretary to the Army Council, or any person authorised by the Army Council to act on their behalf.
Local Government Board for Ireland (*f*).	Commissioner of the Local Government Board for Ireland, or a Secretary or Assistant Secretary of the Board.
Ministry of Pensions (*g*).	The Minister, or Secretary, or any person authorised by the Minister to act on his behalf.

(*a*) 33 & 34 Vict. c. 75, s. 83; 62 & 63 Vict. c. 33, s. 2 (1).
(*b*) 58 & 59 Vict. c. 9, s. 1; 9 & 10 Geo. 5, c. 91, s. 1.
(*c*) 62 & 63 Vict. c. 50, s. 21 (3).
(*d*) 8 Edw. 7, c. 48, s. 36; 25 & 26 Geo. 5, c. 15, s. 12 (3).
(*e*) 5 & 6 Geo. 5, c. 94, s. 5.
(*f*) 5 & 6 Geo. 5, c. 94, s. 5.
(*g*) 6 & 7 Geo. 5, c. 65, s. 6 (5).

SCHEDULE—*continued.*

COLUMN 1. Name of Department or Officer.	COLUMN 2. Name of Certifying Officers.
Ministry of Labour (*h*).	The Minister, or Secretary, or any person authorised by the Minister to act on his behalf.
Ministry of Transport (*i*).	The Minister, or Secretary, or any person authorised by the Minister to act on his behalf.
Air Council (*k*).	The President, or a Secretary, or a person authorised by the Minister.
Ministry of Health (*l*).	The Minister, or Secretary, or any person authorised by the Minister to act on his behalf.
Forestry Commissioners (*m*).	The Chairman or any other Commissioner or the Secretary or person authorised to act on behalf of the Secretary.
Commissioners of Works (*n*).	Any Commissioner, or the Secretary or any person authorised to act on behalf of the Secretary.
Scottish Departments (Health, Agriculture and Pensions) (*o*).	The Secretary, or any officer of the Department authorised by the Secretary.
Wheat Commission (*p*).	Any two members of the Commission.
National Health Insurance Joint Committee (*q*).	Chairman or other member or the Secretary, or any person authorised to act on behalf of the Secretary, of the Committee.

(*h*) 6 & 7 Geo. 5, c. 68, s. 11 (4).
(*i*) 6 & 7 Geo. 5, c. 68, s. 11 (4).
(*k*) 7 & 8 Geo. 5, c. 51, s. 10 (5).
(*l*) 9 & 10 Geo. 5, c. 21, s. 7 (5).
(*m*) 9 & 10 Geo. 5, c. 58, s. 2 (5).
(*n*) 16 & 17 Geo. 5, c. 36, s. 2 (4); 21 & 22 Geo. 5, c. 16, ss. 12, 15 (4)
(*o*) 18 & 19 Geo. 5, c. 34, s. 1 (5) (e).
(*p*) 22 & 23 Geo. 5, c. 24, s. 5 (5).
(*q*) 26 Geo. 5 & 1 Edw 8, c. 32, s. 160 (6).

SCHEDULE—*continued.*

COLUMN 1. Name of Department or Officer.	COLUMN 2. Name of Certifying Officers.
Tithe Redemption Commission and Board of Inland Revenue (for the purposes of the Tithe Act) (*r*).	Any person authorised to act on behalf of the Commission or the Board.
Crown Lands Commissioners (*s*)	The Commissioners or any person authorised to act on behalf of the Commissioners.

Note.—**S. 2 (2).** As to who are now Government printers, etc., see Documentary Evidence Act, 1882, *post*, p. 465.
Schedule. See also Appendix IV, *post*, p. 578.

EVIDENCE FURTHER AMENDMENT ACT, 1869.

32 & 33 VICT. c. 68.

1. (*Repeals*; *see* Appendix IV, *post*, p. 579.)

2. **The parties to any action for breach of promise of marriage shall be competent to give evidence** in such action: **Provided** always, that **no plaintiff** in any action for breach of promise of marriage **shall recover a verdict unless** his or her testimony shall be **corroborated by some other material evidence** in support of such promise.

3. **The parties to any proceedings instituted in consequence of adultery, and the husbands and wives of such parties, shall be competent to give evidence** in such proceeding: **Provided** that **no witness** in any proceeding, whether a party to a suit or not, **shall be liable to be asked or be bound to answer any question tending to show that he or she has been guilty of adultery, unless such witness shall have** already **given evidence** in the same proceeding **in disproof** of his or her alleged adultery.

Note.—**S. 2.** As to the effect of this section, see *ante*, p. 272. As to corroboration generally, see *ante*, p. 156.

(*r*) 26 Geo. 5 & 1 Edw. 8, c. 43, s. 42 (2).
(*s*) 26 Geo. 5 & 1 Edw. 8, c. 47, s. 6 (4).

S. 3. In so far as it relates to the High Court, this section has been repealed by the Judicature Act, 1925, which re-enacts it by s. 198, *post*, p. 508. See the note to that section.

PREVENTION OF CRIMES ACT, 1871.

34 & 35 Vict. c. 112.

9. **The rules** contained in the one hundred and sixteenth section of (*the Larceny Act*, 1861: 24 *&* 25 *Vict. c.* 96), . . . **in relation to** the form of, and the proceedings upon an indictment for any offence punishable under that Act committed after **previous conviction,** shall, with the necessary variations, **apply to** any indictment for committing **a crime as defined by this Act** after previous conviction for a crime, whether the crime charged in such indictment or the crime to which such previous conviction relates be or be not punishable under the said Act. . . .

15. (*Dealing with Proceedings under section* 4 *of the Vagrancy Act*, 1824.) . . . In proving the intent to commit a felony it shall not be necessary to show that **the person suspected** was guilty of any particular act or acts tending to show his purpose or intent, and he **may be convicted if** from the circumstances of the case, and **from his known character as proved** to the justice of the peace or court before whom or which he is brought, **it appears** to such justice or court **that his intent was to commit a felony. . . .**

18. **A previous conviction may be proved** in any legal proceeding whatever against any person **by producing a record or extract** of such conviction, **and by giving proof of the identity** of the person against whom the conviction is sought to be proved with the person appearing in the record or extract of conviction to have been convicted.

A record or extract of a conviction shall in the case of an indictable offence consist of a certificate containing the substance and effect only (omitting the formal part of the indictment and conviction), and **purporting to be signed by the clerk of the court or other officer having the custody of the records** of the court by which such conviction was made, or purporting to be signed by the deputy of such clerk or officer; **and in the case of a summary**

conviction shall consist of a copy of such conviction **purporting to be signed by any justice** of the peace having jurisdiction over the offence in respect of which such conviction was made, **or to be signed by the proper officer** of the court by which such conviction was made, **or by the clerk or other officer** of any court to which such conviction has been returned.

A record or extract of any conviction made in pursuance of this section **shall be admissible in evidence without proof of the signature or official character** of the person appearing to have signed the same.

20. **The expression "crime" means,** in England and Ireland, any felony, or the offence of uttering false or counterfeit coin, or of possessing counterfeit gold or silver coin, or the offence of obtaining goods or money by false pretences, or the offence of conspiracy to defraud or any misdemeanour under the fifty-eighth section of the Act passed in the session of the twenty-fourth and twenty-fifth years of the reign of Her present Majesty, chapter ninety-six. . . .

Note.—**S. 9.** The section of the Larceny Act referred to is set out *ante*, p. 450. As to evidence of previous convictions, see *ante*, p. 102. The expression "crime" for the purposes of this section is defined by s. 20 above.

S. 18. This should be read in connection with s. 28 (1) of the Criminal Justice Administration Act, 1914, see *post*, p. 497, and s. 22 of the Summary Jurisdiction Act, 1879, see *post*, p. 464. As to proof of convictions generally, see *post*, p. 102.

S. 20. The Act referred to in this section is the Larceny Act, 1861, and the misdemeanour in question is being armed with intent to break and enter any house in the night.

BASTARDY LAWS AMENDMENT ACT, 1872.

35 & 36 Vict. c. 65.

4. (*Dealing with Summonses in Petty Sessions by Women for Bastardy Orders.*) The justices in such petty session shall hear the evidence of such woman and such other evidence as she may produce, and shall also hear any evidence tendered by or on behalf of the person alleged to be the father, and **if the evidence of the mother be corroborated** in some material particular by other evidence to the

satisfaction of the said **justices,** they **may adjudge the man to be the putative father** of such bastard child.

Note.—This Act deals with original applications only. The Bastardy Act, 1845, *ante*, p. 437, requires corroboration also on appeals. As to corroboration generally, see *ante*, p. 156.

EVIDENCE ACT, 1877.

40 & 41 VICT. C. 14.

1. **On the trial of any indictment or other proceeding** for the non-repair of any public highway or bridge, or for a nuisance to any public highway, river, or bridge, and of any other indictment or proceeding **instituted for the purpose of trying or enforcing a civil right only, every defendant** to such indictment or proceeding, **and the wife or husband of any such defendant, shall be admissible witnesses and compellable** to give evidence.

Note.—As to the evidence of husband and wives generally, see *ante*, p. 273; where it will be observed that, when a wife or husband is by statute made a *competent witness* in criminal cases, she or he is not generally rendered *compellable* also.

BANKERS' BOOKS EVIDENCE ACT, 1879.

42 VICT. C. 11.

3. Subject to the provisions of this Act, **a copy of any entry in a banker's book shall in all legal proceedings be received as prima facie evidence** of such entry, and of the matters, transactions, and accounts therein recorded.

4. **A copy of an entry** in a banker's book **shall not be received** in evidence under this Act **unless it be first proved** that the book was at the time of the making of the entry **one of the ordinary books of the bank,** and that the entry was made in the usual and **ordinary**

course of business, and that the book is in **the custody or control of the bank.**

Such proof may be given by a partner or officer of the bank, and may be given orally or by an affidavit sworn before any commissioner or person authorised to take affidavits.

5. **A copy of an entry** in a banker's book **shall not be received** in evidence under this Act **unless it be further proved** that the copy has been **examined with the original entry and is correct.**

Such proof shall be given **by some person** who has examined the copy with the original entry, and may be given either orally or by an affidavit sworn before any commissioner or person authorised to take affidavits.

6. A banker or officer of a **bank shall not, in any legal proceeding to which the bank is not a party, be compellable to produce any banker's book** the contents of which can be proved under this Act, or to appear as a witness to prove the matters, transactions, and accounts therein recorded, **unless by order of a judge made for special cause.**

7. **On the application of any party** to a legal proceeding a **court or judge may order** that such party be at **liberty to inspect and take copies of any entries in a banker's book** for any of the purposes of such proceedings. An order under this section may be made either with or without summoning the bank or any other party, and shall be served on the bank three clear days before the same is to be obeyed, unless the court or judge otherwise directs.

9. In this Act the expressions **"bank" and "bankers" mean** any person, persons, partnership, or company carrying on the business of bankers and having duly made a return to the Commissioners of Inland Revenue, and also any savings bank certified under the Acts relating to savings banks, and also any post office savings bank.

Expressions in this Act relating to **"bankers' books" include** ledgers, day books, cash books, account books, and all other books used in the ordinary business of the bank.

Note.—Books of the Bank of England seem to have been treated as "public documents" at Common Law; and production thereof was excused, secondary evidence being admissible. But books of other banks were not so treated. See note, *ante*, p. 363.

S. 3. An inquiry before a disciplinary committee of the Law Society is a legal proceeding within the meaning of this Act (Solicitors Act, 1936, s. 14).

S. 5. The words "some person" are not limited to a partner or officer of a bank; they include any person who has examined the copy (*R.* v. *Albutt*, 75 J. P. 112).

S. 7. A magistrate before whom criminal proceedings are pending is a "court" within this section (*R.* v. *Kinghorn*, [1908] 2 K. B. 949).

SUMMARY JURISDICTION ACT, 1879.

42 & 43 VICT. c. 49.

22.—(1) **The clerk of every court of summary jurisdiction shall keep a register** of the minutes or memorandums of all the **convictions** and **orders** of such court, and of such other **proceedings** as are directed by a rule under this Act to be registered, and shall keep the same with such particulars and in such form as may be from time to time directed by a rule under this Act.

(2) **Such register, and also any extract** from such register **certified by the clerk** of the court keeping the same to be a true extract, **shall be prima facie evidence** of the matters entered therein for the purpose of informing a court of summary jurisdiction acting for the same county borough or place as the court whose convictions, orders, and proceedings are entered in the register; *but nothing in this section shall dispense with the legal proof of a previous conviction for an offence when required to be proved against a person charged with another offence.*

(4) **The entries** relating to each minute, memorandum, or proceeding **shall be either entered or signed by the justice** or one of the justices constituting the court by or before whom the conviction or order or proceeding referred to in the minute or memorandum was made or had, **except that** when a court of summary jurisdiction is not a petty sessional court a return signed as aforesaid, and made and entered in the register in manner provided by a rule under this Act, shall suffice.

31.—(1) Subject to the provisions of this section, **where a person is authorised** by or under any Act, including any local Act, **to appeal** to a court of general or quarter sessions against a conviction, sentence, order, determination or other decision of a court of summary jurisdiction, the following provisions shall apply:—

(ix) **the clerk of the peace shall send** to the clerk to the court by whom the decision appealed against was given, **for entry in his register, a memorandum of the decision** of quarter sessions, and if the appeal was an appeal against a conviction or sentence or against an order, shall endorse a like memorandum on the conviction or order, as the case may be, and whenever any copy or certificate of the conviction or order is made, **a copy of the memorandum** shall be added thereto and **shall be sufficient evidence** of the decision of quarter sessions in every case where the copy or certificate would be sufficient evidence of the conviction or order.

39.—(2) (*Dealing with Proceedings before Courts of Summary Jurisdiction.*) **Any exception, exemption, proviso, excuse, or qualification,** whether it does or does not accompany in the same section the description of the offence in the Act, order, bye-law, regulation, or other document creating the offence, **may be proved by the defendant, but** need not be specified or negatived in the information or complaint, and, if so specified or negatived, **no proof** in relation to the matter so specified or negatived **shall be required on the part of the informant or complainant.**

Note.—**Ss. 22, 31.** As to proof of convictions and judicial proceedings generally, see *post*, p. 561. The clause in italics at the end of s. 22 (2) has been repealed by the Criminal Justice Administration Act, 1914, *post*, p. 497. S. 31, as set out above, was substituted for the original s. 31 by the Summary Jurisdiction (Appeals) Act, 1933, s. 1.

S. 39 (2). This provision should be read in connection with s. 14 of the Summary Jurisdiction Act, 1848, *ante*, p. 440. See also note, *ante*, p. 148.

DOCUMENTARY EVIDENCE ACT, 1882.

45 VICT. c. 9.

2. **Where any enactment,** whether passed before or after the passing of this Act, **provides that a copy of any** Act of Parliament, proclamation, order, regulation, rule, warrant, circular, list, gazette, or **document shall be** conclusive evidence, or be **evidence, or have any other effect, when purporting to be printed by the Government printer,** or the Queen's printer, or a printer authorised by Her

Majesty, **or otherwise under Her Majesty's authority,** whatever may be the precise expression used, **such copy shall** also be conclusive evidence, or evidence, or **have the said effect** (as the case may be) **if it purports to be printed under** the superintendence or **authority of Her Majesty's Stationery Office.**

Note.—As to proof of public documents generally, see *ante*, p. 363.

BILLS OF EXCHANGE ACT, 1882.

45 & 46 VICT. c. 61.

PART II.—BILLS OF EXCHANGE.

9.—(2) Where the sum payable is expressed in words and also in figures, and there is a discrepancy between the two, **the sum denoted by the words is the amount payable.**

27.—(2) **Where value** has at any time been **given for a bill the holder is deemed to be a holder for value as regards** the acceptor and all parties to the bill who became **parties prior** to such time.

(3) **Where the holder of a bill has a lien** on it, arising either from contract or by implication of law, **he is deemed to be a holder for value to the extent** of the sum for which he has a lien.

30.—(1) **Every party whose signature appears on a bill** is *prima facie* **deemed** to have become a **party thereto for value.**

(2) **Every holder of a bill is prima facie deemed to be a holder in due course; but if** in an action on a bill it is admitted or proved that the acceptance, issue, or subsequent negotiation of the bill is affected with **fraud, duress, or force and fear, or illegality, the burden of proof is shifted,** unless and until the holder proves that, subsequent to the alleged fraud or illegality, value has in good faith been given for the bill.

Liabilities of Parties.

54. **The acceptor** of a bill, by accepting it— . . .

(2) **Is precluded from denying** to a holder in due course:—

(*a*) The existence of the drawer, the genuineness of his

signature, and his capacity and authority to draw the bill;

(*b*) In the case of a bill payable to drawer's order, the then capacity of the drawer to indorse, but not the genuineness or validity of his indorsement;

(*c*) In the case of a bill payable to the order of a third person, the existence of the payee and his then capacity to indorse, but not the genuineness or validity of his indorsement.

55.—(1) **The drawer** of a bill, by drawing it— . . .

(*b*) **Is precluded from denying** to a holder in due course the existence of the payee and his then capacity to indorse.

(2) **The indorser** of a bill, by indorsing it— . . .

(*b*) **Is precluded from denying** to a holder in due course the genuineness and regularity in all respect of the drawer's signature and all previous indorsements;

(*c*) **Is precluded from denying** to his immediate or a subsequent indorsee that the bill was at the time of his indorsement a valid and subsisting bill, and that he had then a good title thereto. . . .

PART IV.—PROMISSORY NOTES.

89.—(1) Subject to the provisions in this part, and, except as by this section provided, the **provisions of this Act** relating to bills of exchange **apply, with the necessary modifications, to promissory notes.**

Note.—**S. 9 (2).** This expresses the rule laid down in *Saunderson* v. *Piper*, 5 Bing. N. C. 425. See *ante*, p. 397.

Ss. 27 (2), (3), 30 (1), (2). Consideration is here, contrary to the general rule, presumed, and the burden of proof consequently shifted. It may be proved that no consideration was given. The term "holder in due course" is defined by s. 29.

Ss. 54, 55. These sections afford instances of statutory *estoppel*, as to which see *ante*, p. 41.

S. 89 (1). There appear to be no provisions of the Act preventing the full application of the above sections to promissory notes.

MARRIED WOMEN'S PROPERTY ACT, 1882.

45 & 46 Vict. c. 75.

12. **Every woman,** whether married before or after this Act, **shall have** in her own name against all persons whomsoever, including her husband, the same **civil remedies, and also** (subject, as regards her husband, to the proviso hereinafter contained) the same remedies and redress by way of **criminal** proceedings, **for the protection and security of her own separate property,** as if such property belonged to her as a *feme sole*, but, except as aforesaid, no husband or wife shall be entitled to sue the other for a tort . . . **and in any proceeding under this section a husband or wife shall be competent to give evidence against each other,** any statute or rule of law to the contrary notwithstanding. . . .

16. **A wife** doing any act with respect to any property of her husband, which, if done by the husband with respect to property of the wife, would make the husband liable to criminal proceedings by the wife under this Act, **shall in like manner be liable to criminal proceedings by her husband.**

Note.—**S. 12.** Criminal proceedings under this section afford one of the instances in which husband or wife can give evidence without consent of wife or husband. See *ante*, p. 274.

S. 16. This section did not enable a husband to give evidence in criminal proceedings against his wife, although s. 12 expressly allowed both husband and wife to give evidence in proceedings by wife against husband. This is now altered by the Act of 1884, which also renders both husband and wife *compellable* witnesses (*post*, p. 469); and, as to competency and compellability of husbands and wives as witnesses, *ante*, p. 273.

CORRUPT PRACTICES PREVENTION ACT, 1883.

46 & 47 Vict. c. 51.

59.—(1) A person who is called as a **witness** respecting an election before any election court **shall not be excused from answering any question** relating to any offence at or connected with such election,

on the ground that the answer thereto may criminate or tend to criminate himself **or on the ground of privilege;**

Provided that—

(*a*) **A witness who answers truly** all questions which he is required by the election court to answer shall be **entitled to receive a certificate of indemnity** under the hand of a member of the court stating that such witness has so answered: and

(*b*) **An answer** by a person to a question put by or before any election court **shall not,** except in the case of any criminal proceeding for perjury in respect of such evidence, **be in any proceeding, civil or criminal, admissible in evidence against him.**

Note.—This is an instance of the cases in which a witness is compelled to answer criminating questions, but is protected from subsequent proceedings thereon. See note, *ante*, p. 333.

MARRIED WOMEN'S PROPERTY ACT, 1884.

47 & 48 VICT. c. 14.

1. **In any such criminal proceeding against a husband or wife** as is authorized by the Married Women's Property Act, 1882, the **husband and wife respectively shall be competent and admissible witnesses, and,** except when defendant, **compellable** to give evidence.

Note.—See the provisions of the Act of 1882, *ante*, p. 468; and, as to competency and compellability of husbands and wives as witnesses, *ante*, p. 273.

CRIMINAL LAW AMENDMENT ACT, 1885.

48 & 49 VICT. c. 69.

2. (*Providing Penalties for Procuration of Girls, etc.*) **No person shall be convicted** of any offence under this section **upon the evidence of one witness, unless** such witness be **corroborated** in some material particular by evidence implicating the accused.

3. (*Providing Penalties for Threatening, Intimidating, and*

Administering Drugs, etc., to Girls, etc., for Purposes of Prostitution, etc.) **No person shall be convicted** of an offence under this section **upon the evidence of one witness only, unless** such witness be **corroborated** in some material particular by evidence implicating the accused.

Note.—As to corroboration generally, see *ante*, p. 156.

CORONERS ACT, 1887.

50 & 51 VICT. c. 71.

4.—(1) The coroner *and jury* shall, at the first sitting of the inquest, *view the body, and the coroner shall* **examine on oath touching the death all persons who tender their evidence respecting** the facts and all persons having knowledge of the facts whom he thinks it expedient to examine.

(2) **It shall be the duty of the coroner in a case of murder or manslaughter to put into writing the statement on oath of those who know the facts** and circumstances of the case, or so much of such statement as is material, **and any such deposition shall be signed by the witness and also by the coroner.**

5.—(3) **The coroner shall deliver the inquisition, deposition, and recognizances, with a certificate** under his hand that the same have been taken before him, **to the proper officer of the court** in which the trial is to be, before or at the opening of the court.

Note.—The words in italics have been repealed by the Coroners Act, 1926.

It will be observed that neither this Act nor the Coroners Act, 1926, nor the rules made under s. 25 thereof contain any provisions as to the circumstances in which the depositions are admissible in evidence at the trial. In this respect it differs from the Acts relating to examining justices (Indictable Offences Act, 1848, s. 17, *ante*, p. 438, and Criminal Justice Act, 1925, ss. 12 and 13, *post*, p. 511), and the Children and Young Persons Act, 1933, s. 43 (*post*, p. 528).

It was held in *R.* v. *Butcher*, 64 J. P. 808, that depositions taken before coroners are on the same footing as those taken before justices. But, in *R.* v. *Cowle*, 71 J. P. 152, it was held that they were not governed by the Acts relating to examining justices, and they were held admissible if (*a*) they were signed by the deponent and coroner; (*b*) the accused had opportunity of cross-examination, and (*c*) the deponent is dead. And in *R.* v. *Marriott,* 75 J. P. 288, it was held that a deposition of the prisoner could be proved by any person present at the inquest who could prove the coroner's handwriting and that the deposition was read over to the prisoner, and signed by the deponent. See also *R.* v. *Black,* 74 J. P. 71.

OATHS ACT, 1888.

51 & 52 VICT. c. 46.

1. **Every person upon objecting to be sworn, and stating,** as the ground of such objection, either **that he has no religious belief, or that the taking of an oath is contrary to his religious belief,** shall be **permitted to make his solemn affirmation** instead of taking an oath in all places and for all purposes where an oath is or shall be required by law, **which affirmation shall be of the same force and effect as if he had taken the oath;** *and if any person making such affirmation shall wilfully, falsely, and corruptly affirm any matter or thing which, if deposed on oath, would have amounted to wilful and corrupt perjury, he shall be liable to prosecution, indictment, sentence, and punishment in all respects as if he had committed wilful and corrupt perjury.*

2. Every such affirmation shall be as follows:

"I, A.B., do solemnly, sincerely, and truly declare and affirm", and then proceed with the words of the oath prescribed by law, omitting any words of imprecation or calling to witness.

3. Where an oath has been duly administered and taken, the fact that the person to whom the same was administered had, at the time of taking such oath, no religious belief, shall not for any purpose affect the validity of such oath.

5. **If any person** to whom an oath is administered **desires to swear with uplifted hand,** in the form and manner in which an oath is usually administered in Scotland, **he shall be permitted to do so,** and the oath shall be administered to him in such form and manner without further question.

Note.—**S. 1.** The words in italics were repealed by the Perjury Act, 1911; cf. s. 15 of that Act (*post,* p. 495). This Act should be read in connection with that Act and the Oaths Act, 1909 (*post,* p. 495). As to oaths generally, see *ante,* p. 285.

ARBITRATION ACT, 1889.

52 & 53 VICT. C. 49.

8. Any party to a submission may sue out a writ of *subpœna ad testificandum* or a writ of *subpœna duces tecum*, but no person shall be compelled under any such writ to produce any document which he could not be compelled to produce on the trial of an action.

18.—(1) The Court or a judge may order that a writ of *subpœna ad testificandum* or of *subpœna duces tecum* shall issue to compel the attendance before an official or special referee, or before any arbitrator or umpire, of a witness wherever he may be within the United Kingdom.

(2) The Court or a judge may also order that a writ of *habeas corpus ad testificandum* shall issue to bring up a prisoner for examination before an official or special referee, or before any arbitrator or umpire.

27. In this Act, unless the contrary intention appears—

"Submission" mean a written agreement to submit present or future differences to arbitration, whether an arbitrator is named therein or not.

Note.—As to subpœnas, see *ante*, p. 418. As to privileged documents, see *ante*, p. 321.

INTERPRETATION ACT, 1889.

52 & 53 VICT. C. 63.

9. **Every Act** passed after the year one thousand eight hundred and fifty, whether before or after the commencement of this Act, shall be a public Act and **shall be judicially noticed** as such, unless the contrary is expressly provided by the Act.

20. In this Act and in every other Act whether passed before or after the commencement of this Act, **expressions referring to writing** shall, unless the contrary intention appears, be **construed**

as including references to printing, lithography, photography, and **other modes of representing or reproducing words** in a visible form.

Note.—**S. 9.** As to judicial notice of Acts of Parliament, see *ante*, pp. 16, 267.

FOREIGN JURISDICTION ACT, 1890.

53 & 54 VICT. c. 37.

4.—(1) **If in any proceeding,** civil or criminal, in a court in Her Majesty's dominions, or held under the authority of Her Majesty **any question arises as to** the existence or extent of **any jurisdiction of Her Majesty in a foreign country, a Secretary of State shall,** on the application of the court, **send** to the court within a reasonable time his **decision on the question,** and his decision shall for the purposes of the proceeding be final.

(2) **The court shall send to the Secretary of State,** in a document under the seal of the court, or signed by a judge of the court, **questions framed so as properly to raise the question, and sufficient answers to those questions shall be returned by the Secretary of State** to the court, and those answers shall, on production thereof, be conclusive evidence of the matters therein contained.

Note.—A similar procedure is appropriate when questions arise as to the status of foreign governments. See note, *ante*, p. 21.

PARTNERSHIP ACT, 1890.

53 & 54 VICT. c. 39.

2.—(3) The receipt by a person of a **share of the profits of a business is prima facie evidence** that he is a partner in the business **but** the receipt of such a share, or of a payment contingent on or varying with the profits of a business, **does not of itself make** him **a partner** in the business; **and in particular . . .** (*such receipt by creditors, servants, agents, widows or children of deceased partners, lenders, and vendors of goodwill does not make such persons partners*).

14.—(1) **Every one who by words** spoken or written **or by conduct represents himself, or** who knowingly **suffers himself to be represented, as a partner** in a particular firm, **is liable** as a partner **to any one who has on the faith of any such representation given credit** to the firm whether the representation has or has not been made or communicated to the person so giving credit by or with the knowledge of the apparent partner making the representation or suffering it to be made.

(2) **Provided** that where after a partner's death the partnership business is continued in the old firm-name, the continued use of that name or of the deceased partner's name as part thereof shall not of itself make his executors or administrators estate or effects liable for any partnership debts contracted after his death.

15. **An admission or representation made by any partner** concerning the partnership affairs, and in the ordinary course of its business, **is evidence against the firm.**

Note.—**S. 2 (3).** As to statutory *prima facie* evidence, see *ante*, p. 155.

S. 14. This section affords an instance of *statutory estoppel*, as to which see *ante*, p. 41.

S. 15. As to admissions by partners and agents, see *ante*, pp. 171, 190.

The above provisions are made applicable to Limited Partnerships by the Limited Partnerships Act, 1907, s. 7, see *post*, p. 491.

STAMP ACT, 1891.

54 & 55 Vict. c. 39.

Adjudication Stamps.

12.—(5) Every instrument stamped with the particular stamp denoting either that it is not chargeable with any duty, or is duly stamped, shall be admissible in evidence, and available for all purposes notwithstanding any objection relating to duty.

Production of Instruments in Evidence.

14.—(1) **Upon the production of an instrument** chargeable with any duty as evidence in any court of civil judicature in any part of the United Kingdom, or before any arbitrator or referee, **notice shall be taken** by the judge, arbitrator or referee **of any omission or insufficiency of the stamp** thereon, **and if** the instrument is **one which may legally be stamped after** the execution thereof, **it may, on payment** to the officer of the court whose duty it is to read the instrument, or to the arbitrator or referee, of the amount of unpaid duty, and the penalty payable on stamping the same, and of a further sum of one pound, **be receivable in evidence,** saving all just exceptions on other grounds.

(4) **Save as aforesaid, an instrument** executed in any part of the United Kingdom, or relating, wheresoever executed, to any property situate, or to any matter or thing done or to be done, in any part of the United Kingdom, **shall not, except in criminal proceedings, be given in evidence, or be available for any purpose whatever, unless it is duly stamped** in accordance with the law in force at the time when it was first executed.

Note.—As to production and proof of documents, see *ante*, pp. 345, 365. In spite of the strict wording of s. 14 (4) it has been held that such instruments may be used to refresh memory, see *ante*, p. 294.

SALE OF GOODS ACT, 1893.

56 & 57 VICT. c. 71.

4.—(1) **A contract for the sale of any goods of the value of ten pounds** or upwards **shall not be enforceable** by action unless the buyer shall accept part of the goods so sold, and actually receive the same, or give something in earnest to bind the contract, or in part payment, or **unless** some **note or memorandum in writing** of the contract be made and signed by the party to be charged or his agent in that behalf.

Note.—This sub-section re-enacts with slight variations s. 16 (commonly cited as s. 17) of the Statute of Frauds (*ante*, p. 429). The variations are that the words "enforceable by action" are substituted for "allowed to be good", and the word "value" is substituted for "price". This is one of the few cases in which written evidence is required. As to written evidence generally, see *ante*, p. 158. See further Appendix IV, *post*, p. 579.

MERCHANT SHIPPING ACT, 1894.

57 & 58 VICT. c. 60.

PART I.

REGISTRY.

64.—(2) **The following documents shall be admissible in evidence** in manner provided by this Act, namely:—

(*a*) Any register book under this Part of this Act on its production from the custody of the registrar or other person having the lawful custody thereof;

(*b*) A certificate of registry under this Act purporting to be signed by the registrar or other proper officer;

(*c*) An endorsement on a certificate of registry purporting to be signed by the registrar or other proper officer;

(*d*) Every declaration made in pursuance of this Part of this Act in respect of a British ship.

A copy or transcript of the register of British ships kept by the Registrar-General of Shipping and Seamen under the direction of the Board of Trade **shall be admissible in evidence** in manner provided by this Act, and have the same effect to all intents as the original register of which it is a copy or transcript.

PART II.

MASTERS AND SEAMEN.

123. In any legal or other proceeding **a seaman may bring forward evidence to prove the contents of any agreement** with the crew or otherwise to support his case, **without producing,** or giving notice to produce **the agreement** or any copy thereof.

239. **An official log shall be kept in every ship** (except ships employed exclusively in trading between ports on the coasts of Scotland) in the appropriate form for that ship approved by the Board of Trade.

(4) **An entry required by this Act** in an official log book **shall be made as soon as possible after the occurrence** to which it relates, and if not made on the same day as that occurrence shall be made and dated so as to show the date of the occurrence, and of the entry

respecting it; and if made in respect of an occurrance happening before the arrival of the ship at her final port of discharge shall not be made more than twenty-four hours after that arrival.

(5) **Every entry** in the official log book **shall be signed** by the master, and by the mate, or some other of the crew, and also (*by the surgeon, mate and other persons in special cases*).

(6) **Every entry** made in an official log book in manner provided by this Act **shall be admissible in evidence.**

240. **The master** of a ship for which an official log is required **shall enter or cause to be entered** in the official log book **the following matters**; (that is to say) (*here follows a list of matters, e.g., convictions, offences, conduct, character, illnesses, injuries, marriages, wages, collisions, etc.*). (*By* s. 254 *births and deaths must be entered.*)

457.—(1) **If any person sends** or attempts to send, or is party to sending or attempting to send a British **ship to sea in such an unseaworthy state that the life of any person is likely to be thereby endangered,** he shall in respect of each offence be **guilty of a misdemeanour, unless he proves either that** he used all reasonable means to insure her being sent to sea in a seaworthy state, **or that** her going to sea in such an unseaworthy state was, under the circumstances, reasonable and justifiable, and for the purposes of giving that proof he may give evidence in the same manner as any other witness.

(2) **If the master of a British ship knowingly takes the same to sea** in such an unseaworthy state that the life of any person is likely to be thereby endangered, he shall in respect of each offence be **guilty of a misdemeanour, unless he proves that** her going to sea in such an unseaworthy state was, under the circumstances, reasonable and justifiable, and for the purpose of giving such proof he may give evidence in the same manner as any other witness.

PART XIII.

LEGAL PROCEEDINGS.

691.—(1) **Whenever in the course of any legal proceeding** instituted in any part of Her Majesty's dominions before any judge or magistrate, or before any person authorised by law or by consent of parties to receive evidence, **the testimony of any witness is required** in relation to the subject matter of that proceeding, **then**

upon due proof, if the proceeding is instituted in the United Kingdom, **that the witness cannot be found** in that kingdom, or if in any British possession, that he cannot be found in that possession, **any deposition** that the witness may have previously made on oath in relation to the same subject matter before any justice or magistrate in Her Majesty's dominions, or any British consular officer elsewhere, **shall be admissible in evidence, provided that:—**

(*a*) if the deposition was made in the United Kingdom, it shall not be admissible in any proceeding instituted in the United Kingdom; and

(*b*) if the deposition was made in any British possession, it shall not be admissible in any proceeding instituted in that British possession; and

(*c*) if the proceeding is criminal it shall not be admissible, unless it was made in the presence of the person accused.

(2) **A deposition so made shall be authenticated** by the signature of the judge, magistrate, or consular officer before whom it is made; and the judge, magistrate, or consular officer shall certify if the fact is so, that the accused was present at the taking thereof.

(3) **It shall not be necessary in any case to prove the signature or official character** of the person appearing to have signed any such deposition, and in any criminal proceeding a certificate under this section shall, unless the contrary is proved, be sufficient evidence of the accused having been present in manner thereby certified.

(4) Nothing herein contained shall affect any case in which depositions taken in any proceeding are rendered admissible in evidence by any Act of Parliament, or by any Act or ordinance of the legislature of any colony, so far as regards that colony, or interfere with the power of any colonial legislature to make those depositions admissible in evidence, or to interfere with the practice of any court in which depositions not authenticated as hereinbefore mentioned are admissible.

694. **Where any document is required** by this Act to be executed in the presence of, or **to be attested** by any witness or witnesses, that document **may be proved** by the evidence of any person who is able to bear witness to the requisite facts **without calling the attesting witness** or the attesting witnesses or any of them.

695.—(1) **Where a document is by this Act declared to be admissible in evidence, such document** shall, on its production from the proper custody, be admissible in evidence in any court or before any person having by law or consent of parties authority to receive evidence, and, subject to all just exceptions, **shall be evidence of the matters stated therein** in pursuance of this Act or by any officer in pursuance of his duties as such officer.

(2) **A copy** of any such document or extract therefrom shall also be so admissible in **evidence if proved to be an examined copy or extract, or if it purports to be signed and certified** as a true copy or extract by the officer to whose custody the original document was entrusted. . . . (*here follow provisions for supplying copies and extracts on payment therefor*).

697. **Any exception, exemption, proviso, excuse, or qualification** in relation to any offence under this Act, whether it does or does not accompany in the same section the description of the offence, **may be proved by the defendant,** but need not be specified or negatived in any information or complaint, and, if so specified or negatived, **no proof** in relation to the matter so specified or negatived shall be **required on the part of the informant or complainant.**

719. **All documents purporting to be made, issued, or written by or under the direction of the Board of Trade,** and to be sealed with the seal of the Board, or to be signed by their secretary, or one of their assistant secretaries, or, if a certificate, by one of the officers of the Marine Department, shall be **admissible in evidence** in manner provided by this Act.

Note.—**S. 64.** This should be read in connection with s. 695, *supra*.

S. 123. As to the general rule concerning production of original documents, see *ante*, p. 345.

Ss. 239, 240. As to entries in log books, etc., in the course of duty generally, see *ante*, p. 214.

S. 457. This is one of the cases in which the burden of proof is put upon the person charged. See hereon generally, *ante*, p. 148.

S. 691. See also the Workmen's Compensation Act, 1925, s. 38 (1) (d), *post*, p. 509. As to depositions generally, see *ante*, p. 415.

S. 694. As to calling attesting witnesses generally, see *ante*, p. 371.

S. 695. See also the Workmen's Compensation Act, 1925, s. 38 (1) (d), *post*, p. 509. As to proof of documents generally, see *ante*, pp. 363, 365.

S. 697. This is one of the cases in which the burden of proof is put upon the person charged. See hereon generally, *ante*, p. 148.

CRIMINAL EVIDENCE ACT, 1898.

61 & 62 VICT. c. 36.

This is the Act which abolished the common law rule that an accused person was not competent to give evidence in his own behalf. In view of the important and somewhat complicated character of the provisions it is thought more convenient to annotate it by sections.

1. **Every person charged** with an offence, **and the wife or husband,** as the case may be, of the person so charged, shall be a **competent witness for** the **defence at every stage** of the proceedings, whether the person so charged is charged solely or jointly with any other person. **Provided** as follows:

Note.—It will be observed that this section provides only that the person charged and the wife and husband may be called for the *defence*. S. 4 provides that in certain cases the wife or husband may also be called for the *prosecution*. See hereon generally, *ante*, p. 273.

It is the duty of the Judge to inform a prisoner of his right to give evidence, and his neglect to do so will render the conviction invalid unless no substantial miscarriage of justice has occurred (*R.* v. *Villars,* 20 Cr. App. R. 150). Although the Act says the person charged shall be a competent witness "for the defence at every stage" of the proceedings, he cannot give evidence in mitigation of sentence after he has pleaded guilty. The phrase "stage of the proceedings" is not applicable to the period between the plea of guilty and sentence (*R.* v. *Hodgkinson,* 64 J. P. 808). But he can give evidence both on the preliminary proceedings before the magistrate and at the trial by the petty jury.

A person charged jointly with another is "a competent witness for the defence", so he may give evidence, not only on behalf of himself, but also on behalf of his fellow-prisoner (*R.* v. *McDonald,* 73 J. P. 490).

(*a*) A **person so charged shall not be called** as a witness in pursuance of this Act **except upon his own application:**

Note.—If a person charged has chosen to give evidence before the magistrate, it can be put in against him at the trial, although he then chooses not to give evidence (*R.* v. *Bird,* 79 L. T. 359).

(*b*) The **failure** of any person charged with an offence, or of the wife or husband, as the case may be, of the person so charged, **to give evidence** shall **not** be made the **subject of any comment** by the prosecution:

Note.—Although the prosecution may not comment on failure to give evidence, the Judge may do so. The right to do so rests solely on his discretion; its exercise depends upon the circumstance of each case, and no general rule can be laid down (*R.* v. *Rhodes*, [1899] 1 Q. B. 77). And the prosecution may comment on any evidence given by the person charged (*R.* v. *Gardner*, [1899] 1 Q. B. 150).

(*c*) The **wife or husband** of the person charged **shall not,** save as in this Act mentioned, **be called** as a witness in pursuance of this Act **except upon the application of the person so charged:**

Note.—See *post*, s. 4.

(*d*) **Nothing in this Act shall make a husband** compellable to disclose any communication made to him by his wife during the marriage, **or a wife compellable to disclose any communication made** to her by her husband **during the marriage:**

Note.—A similar provision as to such privileged communications in civil cases is contained in the Evidence Amendment Act, 1853, s. 3, *ante*, p. 443. No privilege exists at common law (*ante*, p. 344).

(*e*) A **person charged** and being a witness in pursuance of this Act **may be asked any question** in cross-examination notwithstanding that it would tend **to criminate him as to the offence charged:**

Note.—If the question asked actually tends to show the offence charged, it cannot be objected to on the ground that it tends to show that the person charged has committed another offence, or is of bad character (*R.* v. *Chitson*, [1909] 2 K. B. 945). It is to be observed that not only is the answer privileged but the mere asking of the question is prohibited If a person charged does not give evidence on his own behalf, but does so on behalf of a fellow-prisoner, he can be cross-examined in order to show that he himself is guilty of the offence charged (*R.* v. *Rowland*, [1910] 1 K. B. 458), and if he says nothing in the witness box, except that he is guilty, he may be cross-examined so as to incriminate another prisoner jointly charged with him (*R.* v. *Paul*, [1920] 2 K. B. 183).

(*f*) A **person charged** and called as a witness in pursuance of this Act **shall not be asked,** and if asked shall not be required to answer any **question tending to show that he has committed or been convicted of or been charged with any offence other than that** wherewith he is then charged, **or is of bad character, unless—**

Note.—Despite the words "convicted of or being charged with any offence" the person charged cannot, save in quite exceptional circumstances, be cross-examined as to charges of which he has been acquitted, nor as to a mere accusation which does not result in a prosecution (*Maxwell* v. *D. P. P.*, *ante*, p. 302; *Stirland* v. *D. P. P.*, [1944] A. C. 315. See, however, *R.* v. *Waldman* (1934), 24 Cr. App. R. 204). As this Act applies to all criminal proceedings (s. 6), a person charged cannot be asked the questions mentioned in this section even in a case in which he is allowed to give evidence under any other statute which renders him a competent witness (*Charnock* v. *Merchant*, [1900] 1 Q. B. 474). But the Court will not, as a matter of course, quash a conviction on the ground that a prisoner has been improperly asked and has answered such question, if it appears that his counsel allowed the question to be answered without objection (*R.* v. *Bridgwater*, [1905] 1 K. B. 131). And where a man was charged with assault before a Court of summary jurisdiction, and a question improperly put to him as to his previous conviction was disallowed, but the solicitor for the prosecution stated that he had a certified copy of the conviction; the justices having convicted, stating that the above incident was entirely ignored by them; it was held by a Divisional Court that the conviction was valid (*Barker* v. *Arnold*, [1911] 2 K. B. 120).

In considering whether a question tends to show that a person charged has committed another offence, it must be judged by the light of the other questions put to him. Any questions which would reasonably lead the jury to believe that it is being imputed that he has committed another offence tend to show that he has committed the same. The object of the enactment is that, except in the specified cases, it should not be suggested to the jury by means of questions put to the person charged that he has committed another offence. Where a question of this nature is improperly put, it is the duty of the Judge not to wait for counsel to object, but to stop the question himself; and if by mischance the question is put, it was held to be the duty of the Judge to direct the jury to disregard it, and not to let it influence them (*R.* v. *Ellis*, [1910] 2 K. B. 746). But it has been held that a Judge may use his discretion whether it would not be against a defendant's interest to warn the jury against the effect of an inadmissible question improperly put and disallowed (*R.* v. *Cohen*, 10 Cr. App. R. 91). And the Judge has a discretion, with which the Court of Appeal is slow to interfere, whether he will allow cross-examination as to the character of the accused under this section (*R.* v. *Watson*, 8 Cr. App. R. 249).

[**1 (f)**] (i) the proof that he has committed or been convicted of such **other offence is admissible evidence to show** that he is guilty of the **offence** wherewith he is then **charged**; or

Note.—This appears to be a restatement of s. 1 (*e*). So, where a prisoner was charged with an offence against a girl under sixteen, he was allowed to be cross-examined as to his relations with another girl, and his statements made to the prosecutrix in relation thereto, as such evidence tended to show the credibility of the story of the prosecutrix, and was some evidence that he had committed the offence against her (*R.* v. *Chitson*, [1909] 2 K. B. 945). So, also, evidence of such other offence might be admissible evidence to show the offence charged under the head of "similar conduct" on other occasions (see *ante*, p. 107), or as being part of the same "transaction" (see *ante*, p. 66).

[1 (f)] (ii) **he has** personally or by his advocate **asked questions** of the witnesses for the prosecution with a view **to establish his own good character,** or has **given evidence of his good character, or** the nature or conduct of the **defence is such as to involve imputations on** the character of the **prosecutor or the witnesses for the prosecution;** or

Note.—The provision with regard to a person charged asking questions or giving evidence as to his good character is intended to apply where witnesses to his character are called, or where evidence thereof is sought to be elicited from witnesses for the prosecution (see *ante*, p. 121). It does not apply to mere assertions of innocence, or repudiation of guilt, by the person charged, nor to reasons given by him for such assertions or repudiation (*R.* v. *Ellis*, [1910] 2 K. B. 746). But evidence by a prisoner that he has been earning an honest living for a considerable time is evidence of his good character within the section (*R.* v. *Baker*, 7 Cr. App. R. 252).

The provision with regard to the defence involving imputations on the character of the prisoner, etc., must receive its ordinary and natural interpretation, and must not be qualified by adding or inserting the words "unnecessarily" or "unjustifiably" or "for purposes other than that of developing the defence", or other similar words. So, where prisoner's counsel cross-examined witnesses to show it was they who committed the offence charged, it was held that the conduct or nature of the defence involved imputations on their character within the section (*R.* v. *Hudson*, [1912] 2 K. B. 464).

Where a person charged, in reply to a question put to him in cross-examination as to the truth of a statement made by the prosecutor, said, "It is a lie, and he is a liar", it was held that this did not "involve imputations on the character of the prosecutor" within the meaning of the Act (*R.* v. *Rouse*, [1904] 1 K. B. 184). And a statement by a prisoner that a constable, who was giving evidence against him, was telling lies, was not such an imputation on the constable's character (*R.* v. *Grout*, 26 T. L. R. 60). A mere denial of the truth of the evidence given for the prosecution, or setting up a defence inconsistent with the truth of the statements made by the witnesses for the prosecution, does not thus involve such imputations. It is merely "developing the defence" (*R.* v. *Bridgwater*, [1905] 1 K. B. 131).

Nor is a statement that a police officer used unnecessary violence in arresting a prisoner; nor the suggestion that a prosecutor is an habitual drunkard; nor is a statement made before the magistrate that the evidence of the prosecution is concocted, put in by the prosecution at the trial, but not made the basis of the defence, an imputation within the section (*R.* v. *Westfall*, 7 Cr. App. R. 176), but a defence setting up that a witness had invented a story out of malice towards the prisoner is (*R.* v. *Dunkley*, [1927] 1 K. B. 323).

Where a prisoner alleged, in his evidence, that his identification at the police-station was not reliable, as the persons brought to identify him had been coached for the purpose by a police officer who was called as a witness, saying, "it was not an honest case, but a got-up affair", it was held that such evidence was not part of the "nature or conduct of the defence", yet questions as to previous convictions were inadmissible (*R.* v. *Preston*, [1909] 1 K. B. 568).

But if answers given by a person charged are not "necessary for the conduct of the defence", and they involve imputations on the character of a witness for the prosecution, he brings himself within the provisions of the Act, and can be cross-examined as to other offences (*R.* v. *Jones*, 74 J. P. 30).

So, it is an imputation within the section to suggest that a witness for the prosecution, tendered as an accomplice, and a person of bad character, has committed a crime other than that he has admitted (*R.* v. *Cohen*, 10 Cr. App. R. 91). And evidence by a prisoner that a witness for the prosecution had himself committed the offence charged was held to involve an imputation on the character of such witness (*R.* v. *Marshall*, 63 J. P. 36). But where a person is tried for rape, and gives evidence to the effect that the prosecutrix consented to the act, it is now settled that it does not amount to an imputation on her character within the Act (*R.* v. *Biggin*, [1920] 1 K. B. 217).

[**1 (f)**] (iii) **he has given evidence against any other person charged** with the same offence:

Note.—Where a prisoner gives evidence, and in doing so incriminates another prisoner jointly indicted with him, the latter is entitled to cross-examine the former (*R.* v. *Hadwen*, [1902] 1 K. B. 882; see *post*, Appendix IV); but not as to character or previous convictions, unless they are jointly indicted for the *same* offence (*R.* v. *Roberts*, 52 T. L. P. 234).

(*g*) **Every person called as a witness in pursuance of this Act shall, unless otherwise ordered by the court, give his evidence from the witness box or other place from which the other witnesses give their evidence:**

Note.—The prisoner's "unsworn statement" (see *ante*, p. 417), if any, is made from the dock.

(*h*) Nothing in this Act shall affect the provisions of section eighteen of the Indictable Offences Act, 1848, or any right of the person charged to make a statement without being sworn.

Note.—S. 18 of the Indictable Offences Act, 1848, is now replaced by s. 12 of the Criminal Justice Act, 1925, *post*, p. 510.

2. **Where the only witness to the facts** of the case called by the defence **is the person charged,** he shall be **called** as a witness **immediately after** the close of the **evidence for the prosecution.**

Note.—Where the person charged calls other witnesses to the facts (not merely as to his character), his own evidence is given, together with the evidence of his other witnesses, after he or his counsel has opened his defence, and in any order desired (*Phipson*, 43-4).

3. In cases where the right of reply depends upon the question whether evidence has been called for the defence, **the fact that the person charged has been called** as a witness **shall not of itself confer** on the prosecution the **right of reply.**

Note.—As to the right of reply, see *id.*, and *ante*, pp. 451–2. If the person charged calls his or her consort as a witness, the prosecution has a right of reply.

4.—(1) **The wife or husband of a person charged with an offence** under any enactment mentioned **in the schedule** to this Act **may be called** as a witness either **for the prosecution or defence** and **without the consent** of the person charged.

Note.—The schedule referred to is printed as amended by subsequent enactments. The cases in which the husband or wife of a person charged can give evidence without consent of the person charged are summarised *ante*, p. 274. A spouse rendered competent by virtue of s. 4 (1) is **not** compellable (*Leach* v. *R.*, [1912] A. C. 305, *ante*, p. 276, and see *R.* v. *Acaster*, *ante*, p. 284).

(2) Nothing in this Act shall affect a case where the wife or husband of a person charged with an offence may at common law be called as a witness without the consent of that person.

Note.—See hereon, *ante*, p. 274. A spouse who is competent at common law **is also compellable** (*R.* v. *Lapworth*, [1931] 1 K. B. 117.

5. (*Application of Act to Scotland.*)

6.—(1) This Act shall apply to all criminal proceedings, notwithstanding any enactment in force at the commencement of this Act, except that nothing in this Act shall affect the Evidence Act, 1877.

Note.—Including summary proceedings (see *Charnock* v. *Merchant*, *ante*, p. 484). See also the Evidence Act, 1877, *ante*, p. 462.

SCHEDULE.

ENACTMENTS REFERRED TO.

Session and Chapter.	Short Title.	Enactments referred to.
5 Geo. 4, c. 83.	The Vagrancy Act, 1824.	The enactment punishing a man for neglecting to maintain or deserting his wife or any of his family.
24 & 25 Vict. c. 100.	The Offences against the Person Act, 1861.	Sections forty-eight to fifty-five.
45 & 46 Vict. c. 75.	The Married Women's Property Act, 1882.	Section twelve and section sixteen.
48 & 49 Vict. c. 69.	The Criminal Law Amendment Act, 1885.	The whole Act.

ENACTMENTS SINCE ADDED.

Session and Chapter.	Short Title.	Enactments referred to.
8 Edw. 7, c. 45.	The Punishment of Incest Act, 1908.	The whole Act (see *post*, p. 492).
3 & 4 Geo. 5, c. 28.	The Mental Deficiency Act, 1913.	Section 56 (see *post*, p. 497).
19 & 20 Geo. 5, c. 34.	The Infant Life (Preservation) Act, 1929.	The whole Act (see *post*, p. 519).
23 Geo. 5, c. 12.	The Children and Young Persons Act, 1933.	The offences mentioned in the First Schedule to the Act (see *post*, p. 529).

Note.—**Schedule.** The offences of procuring and living on immoral earnings (Vagrancy Act, 1898) are, by the Criminal Law Amendment Act, 1912, put on the same footing but without in terms referring to this Act.

MARINE INSURANCE ACT, 1906.

6 EDW. 7, C. 41.

Disclosure and Representations.

18.—(4) Whether any particular **circumstance**, which is not disclosed, be **material** or not is, in each case, a **question of fact.**

20.—(7) Whether a particular **representation** be **material** or not is, in each case, a **question of fact.**

21. **A contract of marine insurance is deemed to be concluded** when the proposal of the assured is accepted by the insurer, **whether the policy** be then **issued or not**; and for the purpose of showing when the proposal was accepted, **reference may be made to the slip** or covering note or other customary memorandum of the contract, **although it be unstamped.**

The Policy.

22. Subject to the provisions of any statute, a contract of marine insurance is **inadmissible in evidence unless it is embodied in a marine policy** in accordance with this Act. The policy may be executed and issued either at the time when the contract is concluded, or afterwards.

23. (*What policy must specify.*)

24.—(1) **A marine policy must be signed** by or on behalf of the insurer, provided that in the case of a corporation the corporate seal may be sufficient, but nothing in this section shall be construed as requiring the subscription of a corporation to be under seal.

(2) Where a policy is subscribed by or on behalf of two or more insurers, **each subscription,** unless the contrary be expressed, **constitutes a distinct contract** with the assured.

The Premium.

54. **Where** a marine policy effected on behalf of the assured by a **broker acknowledges the receipt of the premium,** such acknowledgment is, in the absence of fraud, **conclusive as between the insurer and the assured,** but not as between the insurer and broker.

Supplemental.

88. Where by this Act any reference is made to reasonable time, reasonable premium, or reasonable diligence, the question **what is reasonable is a question of fact.**

89. Where there is a duly stamped policy, **reference may be made,** as heretofore, **to the slip** or covering note, in any legal proceeding.

Note.—**Ss. 18 (4), 20 (7).** As to the mode of dealing with questions of fact, see *ante*, pp. 6, 8; and for the various facts and representations which are "material", see s. 18 (1), (2), (3), and s. 20 (1), (2), (3), (4).

S. 21. As to the necessity generally of stamping a document before producing it in evidence, see *ante*, p. 153, and s. 14 of the Stamp Act, 1891, *ante*, p. 475.

Ss. 22—24. These provisions are among the few requiring written evidence (see *ante*, p. 158). Any other contract of insurance may apparently be oral, without any policy or written evidence of any kind.

S. 54. As to the general effect of a receipt, see *ante*, p. 50.

S. 88. Questions of "reasonable" time, diligence, and the like, are generally treated as questions of fact, and thus for the jury, if any, to decide, see *ante*; p. 9.

S. 89. Compare s. 21, and note thereto, *supra*.

EVIDENCE (COLONIAL STATUTES) ACT, 1907.

7 Edw. 7, c. 16.

1.—(1) **Copies of Acts, ordinances, and statutes** passed (whether before or after the passing of this Act) by the Legislature of any British possession, and of **orders, regulations, and other instruments** issued or made, whether before or after the passing of this Act, under the authority of any such Act, ordinance, or statute, if **purporting to be printed by the Government printer, shall be received in evidence** by all courts of justice in the United Kingdom without any proof being given that the copies were so printed.

(3) In this Act—

The expression "**Government printer**" **means,** as respects any British possession, the printer purporting to be the printer authorised to print the Acts, ordinances, or statutes of the Legislature of that possession, or otherwise to be the Government printer of that possession:

The expression "**British possession**" **means** any part of His Majesty's dominions exclusive of the United Kingdom, and, where parts of these dominions are under both a central and a local Legislature, shall include both all parts under the central Legislature and each part under a local Legislature.

Note.—As to proof of public documents generally, see *ante*, p. 363.

CRIMINAL APPEAL ACT, 1907.

7 EDW. 7, c. 23.

3. A person convicted on indictment may appeal under this Act to the Court of Criminal Appeal. . . .

4.—(1) The Court of Criminal Appeal on any such appeal against conviction **shall allow the appeal if they think that the verdict** of the jury should be set aside on the ground that it is **unreasonable** or **cannot be supported having regard to the evidence,** or that the judgment of the court before whom the appellant was convicted should be set aside on the ground of a **wrong decision of any question of law or** that on any ground there was a **miscarriage of justice,** and in any other case shall dismiss the appeal:

Provided that the **court may,** notwithstanding that they are of opinion that the point raised in the appeal might be decided in favour of the appellant, **dismiss the appeal if** they consider that **no substantial miscarriage of justice** has actually occurred.

5.—(2) **Where an appellant has been convicted of an offence and the jury could on the indictment have found him guilty of some other offence,** and on the finding of the jury it appears to the Court of Criminal Appeal that the jury must have been satisfied of facts which proved him guilty of that other offence, the **court may,** instead of allowing or dismissing the appeal, **substitute** for the verdict found by the jury **a verdict of guilty of that other offence,** and pass such sentence in substitution for the sentence passed at the trial as may be warranted in law for that other offence, not being a sentence of greater severity.

8. **The judge or chairman of any court** before whom a person is convicted **shall, in the case of an appeal** under this Act against the conviction or against the sentence, or in the case of an application for leave to appeal under this Act, **furnish** to the registrar, in accordance with rules of court, **his notes** of the trial; and shall also furnish to the Registrar in accordance with rules of court **a report giving his opinion** upon the case or upon any point arising in the case.

9. For the purposes of this Act, the **Court of Criminal Appeal may,** if they think it necessary or expedient in the interest of justice,—

(*a*) **order the production of any document, exhibit, or other thing** connected with the proceedings, the production of which appears to them necessary for the determination of the case; and

(*b*) if they think fit **order any witnesses** who would have been compellable witnesses at the trial **to attend and be examined** before the court, whether they were or were not called at the trial, **or order the examination** of any such witnesses to be conducted in manner provided by rules of court **before any judge** of the court or before any officer of the court or justice of the peace **or other person** appointed by the court for the purpose, and allow the admission of any depositions so taken as evidence before the court; and

(*c*) if they think fit **receive the evidence,** if tendered, **of any witness** (including the appellant) who is a **competent but not compellable** witness, and, if the appellant makes an application for the purpose, of the **husband or wife** of the appellant, in cases where the evidence of the husband or wife could not have been given at the trial except on such an application; and

(*d*) **where any question** arising on the appeal **involves prolonged examination** of documents or accounts, or any **scientific or local investigation,** which cannot in the opinion of the court conveniently be conducted before the court, **order the reference of the question** in manner provided by rules of court for inquiry and report to a special commissioner appointed by the court, and act upon the report of any such commissioner so far as they think fit to adopt it; and

(*e*) **appoint any person with special expert knowledge** to act as **assessor** to the court in any case where it appears to the court that such special knowledge is required for the proper determination of the case;

and exercise in relation to the proceedings of the court any other **powers which may** for the time being **be exercised** by the court of appeal on appeals **in civil matters,** and issue any warrants necessary for enforcing the orders or sentences of the court: Provided that in no case shall any sentence be increased by reason of or in consideration of any evidence that was not given at the trial.

16. **Shorthand notes shall be taken,** of the proceedings at the trial of any person on indictment who, if convicted, is entitled or may be

authorised to appeal under this Act, and on any appeal or application for leave to appeal **a transcript** of the notes or any part thereof **shall be made if the registrar so directs, and furnished to the registrar** for the use of the Court of Criminal Appeal or any judge thereof: Provided that a transcript shall be furnished to any party interested upon the payment of such charges as the Treasury may fix.

Note.—**S. 4.** It will be observed that the Court *shall* allow the appeal, not only where the verdict cannot be supported by the evidence, but also where it is *unreasonable*; and not only where the decision is wrong in *law*, but also where *on any ground* there is a *miscarriage of justice*. So, a conviction upon the uncorroborated evidence of an accomplice was quashed, although corroboration is not in such case required by law (*R.* v. *Tate*, [1908] 2 K. B. 680; see *ante*, p. 158). As to the proviso, see *R.* v. *Murray*, 9 Cr. App. R. 248.

LIMITED PARTNERSHIPS ACT, 1907.

7 Edw. 7, c. 24.

5. **Every limited partnership must be registered** as such in accordance with the provisions of this Act, or **in default thereof it shall be deemed to be a general partnership,** and every limited partner shall be deemed to be a general partner.

6.—(1) **A limited partner** shall not take part in the management of the partnership business, and **shall not have power to bind the firm.**

7. Subject to the provisions of this Act, the Partnership Act, 1890, and the rules of equity and of common law applicable to partnerships, except so far as they are inconsistent with the express provisions of the last-mentioned Act, shall apply to limited partnerships.

8. (*Manner and particulars of registration.*)

16.—(1) Any person may inspect the statements filed by the registrar in the register offices . . . and **any person may require a certificate of the registration** of any limited partnership, or a copy of or extract from any registered statement, to be certified by the registrar (*on payment of certain fees*). . . .

(2) **A certificate of registration, or a copy of or extract** from any

statement registered under this Act, if **duly certified,** to be a true copy under the hand of the registrar or one of the assistant registrars (whom it shall not be necessary to prove to be the registrar or assistant registrar) **shall, in all legal proceedings,** civil or criminal, and in all cases whatsoever **be received in evidence.**

Note.—This Act must be read in connection with the sections of the Partnership Act, 1890, set out *ante*, p. 473. It would appear that ss. 2 (3) and 14 (1) of such Act cannot apply to limited partners, who must comply with certain formalities in order to be considered as such (see s. 4 of the Act of 1907). Nor can s. 15 of the Act of 1890 apply, apparently, in face of s. 6 (1) of the Act of 1907.

PUNISHMENT OF INCEST ACT, 1908.

8 Edw. 7, c. 45.

4.—(4) Section 4 of the Criminal Evidence Act, 1898, shall have effect as if this Act were included in the schedule to that Act.

Note.—The schedule in question appears *ante*, p. 482. A noticeable case on this Act is *R.* v. *Ball*, [1911] A. C. 47.

PREVENTION OF CRIME ACT, 1908.

8 Edw. 7, c. 59.

PART II.

DETENTION OF HABITUAL CRIMINALS.

10.—(2) **A person shall not be found to be a habitual criminal unless the jury finds on evidence:—**

(*a*) that since attaining the age of sixteen years he has at least **three times previously** to the conviction of the crime charged in the said indictment been **convicted of a crime,** whether any such previous conviction was before or after the passing of this Act, and that he is **leading persistently a dishonest or criminal life;** or (*b*) that he has on such a previous conviction been **found to be a habitual criminal and sentenced** to preventive detention.

(4) In the proceedings on the indictment **the offender shall in the first instance be arraigned on** so much only of the indictment as charges **the crime, and if** on arraignment he pleads guilty or is found **guilty** by the jury, **the jury shall,** unless he pleads guilty to being a habitual criminal, be charged to **inquire whether he is a habitual criminal,** and in that case it shall not be necessary to swear the jury again:

Provided that a charge of being a habitual criminal **shall not be inserted** in an indictment—

(*a*) **without the consent** of the Director of Public Prosecutions; and

(*b*) **unless not less than seven days' notice** has been given **to the proper officer** of the court by which the offender is to be tried, **and to the offender,** that it is intended to insert such a charge;

and the notice to the offender **shall specify the previous convictions and the other grounds** upon which it is intended to found the charge.

(5) Without prejudice to any right of the accused to tender evidence as to his character and repute, **evidence of character and repute may,** if the Court thinks fit, **be admitted** as evidence on the question whether the accused is or is not leading persistently a dishonest or criminal life.

(6) For the purposes of this section the expression " crime " has the same meaning as in the Prevention of Crimes Act, 1871, and the definition of " crime " in that Act, set out in the schedule to this Act, shall apply accordingly.

Note.—**S. 10 (2).** The burden of proof that a person is a *habitual criminal* is upon the prosecution (*R.* v. *Young*, 9 Cr. App. R. 185; *R.* v. *Stewart*, 74 J. P. 246).

S. 10 (2) (a). As to the person charged being of the *age of sixteen*, there must be evidence before the Court that he was of such age at the date of the first alleged conviction. If the jury cannot act upon their view as to his age, it may be proved by a prison official deposing that his age, as stated in the calendar, was so stated from information given by the accused himself (*R.* v. *Turner*, [1910] 1 K. B. 346).

S. 10 (4) (a). It is necessary to prove the *consent of the Director of Public Prosecutions*, if it is challenged by the accused; if, however, such consent is not challenged, it will be presumed (*R.* v.

Waller, [1910] 1 K. B. 364). For the mode of proof, see Criminal Justice Act, 1925, s. 34, *post*, p. 514.

S. 10 (4) (b). It is not necessary that the *notice to the proper officer* of the Court should be proved by calling such officer; but it was held that it must be proved either by the officer or clerk of the Court or by the person who gave the notice (*R.* v. *Turner*, [1910] 1 K. B. 346). It has, however, since been held that there is a presumption that the notice has been given, and the onus is on the prisoner of showing it has not been given (*R.* v. *Westwood*, 8 Cr. App. R. 273).

S. 10 (5). As to evidence of character generally in criminal cases, see *ante*, pp. 100, 121.

S. 10 (6). The Act of 1871 is set out *ante*, p. 461, the definition referred to being in s. 20 thereof.

OATHS ACT, 1909.

9 Edw. 7, c. 39.

2.—(1) **Any oath may be administered and taken in the form and manner following:—**

The person taking the oath shall **hold the New Testament, or,** in the case of a Jew, **the Old Testament,** in his uplifted hand, and shall say or repeat after the officer administering the oath **the words** "I swear by Almighty God that . . .", followed by the words of the oath prescribed by law.

(2) The officer shall (unless the person about to take the oath voluntarily objects thereto, or is physically incapable of so taking the oath) administer the oath in the form and manner aforesaid without question:

Provided that, in the case of a person who is neither a Christian nor a Jew, the oath shall be administered in any manner which is now lawful.

3. In this Act the word "officer" shall mean and include any and every person duly authorised to administer oaths.

Note.—This Act should be read in connection with the Oaths Act, 1888, *ante*, p. 471. It will be observed that the "New Testament" and "Old Testament" are mentioned in the above Act, not the "Gospels" and "Pentateuch", upon which Christians and Jews have hitherto been sworn. See *ante*, p. 286.

PERJURY ACT, 1911.

1 & 2 GEO. 5, c. 6.

1.—(6) The question **whether a statement** on which perjury is assigned **was material is a question of law** to be determined by the court of trial.

13. **A person shall not be liable to be convicted of** any offence against this Act, or of any offence declared by any other Act to be **perjury or subornation of perjury,** or to be punishable as perjury or subornation of perjury **solely upon the evidence of one witness** as to the falsity of any statement alleged to be false.

14. On a prosecution—

(*a*) for perjury alleged to have been committed on the trial of an indictment for felony or misdemeanour; or

(*b*) for procuring or suborning the commission of perjury on any such trial,

the fact of the **former trial shall be sufficiently proved by** the production of a **certificate** containing the substance and effect (omitting the formal parts) of the indictment and trial **purporting to be signed** by the clerk of the court, or other person having the custody of the records of the court where the indictment was tried, or by the deputy of that clerk or other person, **without proof of the signature or official character** of the clerk or person appearing to have signed the certificate.

15.—(1) For the purposes of this Act **the forms and ceremonies used in administering an oath are immaterial,** if the court or person before whom the oath is taken has power to administer an oath for the purpose of verifying the statement in question, and **if the oath has been administered in a form** and with ceremonies **which the person** taking the oath **has accepted** without objection, **or has declared to be binding** on him.

(2) In this Act—

The expression "oath" in the case of persons for the time being allowed by law to affirm or declare instead of swearing, includes "affirmation" and "declaration", and the expression "swear" in the like case includes "affirm" and "declare" . . .

Note.—**S. 1 (6).** As to the respective functions of Judge and jury in deciding questions of law and fact, see *ante*, p. 6.

S. 13. As to corroboration generally, see *ante*, p. 156.

S. 14. As to the proof of convictions and judicial proceedings generally, see *post*, p. 561.

S. 15. As to the forms and ceremonies of oaths, see *ante*, pp. 285—291.

OFFICIAL SECRETS ACT, 1911.

1 & 2 Geo. 5, c. 28.

1.—(1) (*Penalties for Spying.*)

(2) On a prosecution under this section, it shall not be necessary to show that **the accused person** was guilty of any particular act tending to show a purpose prejudicial to the safety or interests of the State, and, notwithstanding that no such act is proved against him, he **may be convicted if, from the circumstances** of the case, or **his conduct, or** his known **character** as proved, **it appears that his purpose was** a purpose **prejudicial to** the safety or interests of **the State; and** if any **sketch, plan, model, article, note, document, or information** relating to or used in any prohibited place within the meaning of this Act, or anything in such a place, [or any secret official code word or pass word] is made, obtained, [collected, recorded, published] or communicated by any person other than a person acting under lawful authority, it **shall be deemed to have been** made, obtained, [collected, recorded, published] or communicated **for a purpose prejudicial** to the safety or interests of the State unless the contrary is proved.

Note.—The words in brackets were added by the Official Secrets Act, 1920.

As to evidence of conduct and character of accused persons generally, see *ante*, p. 100. As to matters being "deemed" to be, as against accused persons, see *ante*, p. 155.

CRIMINAL LAW AMENDMENT ACT, 1912.

2 & 3 Geo. 5, c. 20.

7.—(6) (*Dealing with offences under the Vagrancy Act*, 1898, *and the Immoral Traffic* (*Scotland*) *Act*, 1902.) **The wife or husband of a person charged** with an offence under either of the said Acts **may be called as a witness** either for the prosecution or defence and **without the consent of the person charged,** but nothing in this provision shall affect a case where the wife or husband of a person charged with an offence may at common law be called as a witness without the consent of that person.

Note.—The section does not in terms refer to the Criminal Evidence Act, 1898, Schedule, but presumably on the analogy of *Leach* v. *R.* (*ante*, p. 276), the witness is competent but not compellable.

MENTAL DEFICIENCY ACT, 1913.

3 & 4 Geo. 5, c. 28.

56.—(6) (*Dealing with protection of defectives from acts of sexual immorality, procuration, etc.*) Section four of the Criminal Evidence Act, 1898, shall have effect as if this section of this Act were included in the Schedule to that Act.

Note.—The schedule in question appears *ante*, p. 482.

CRIMINAL JUSTICE ADMINISTRATION ACT, 1914.

4 & 5 Geo. 5, c. 58.

28.—(1) **The record or extract by which a conviction may be proved** under section eighteen of the Prevention of Crimes Act, 1871, **may in the case of a summary conviction consist of a copy of the minute or memorandum** of the conviction entered in the register required to be kept under section twenty-two of the Summary Jurisdiction Act, 1879, **purporting to be signed by the clerk** of the court by whom the register is kept.

(3) **The wife or husband of a person charged with bigamy may be called as a witness** either for the prosecution or defence and **without the consent of the person charged.**

(4) **In any proceedings before a court of summary jurisdiction to enforce the payment of a sum of money adjudged** by that or any other court of summary jurisdiction to be paid by one person to another person, then—

(*a*) if the person to whom the sum is ordered to be paid was an officer of a court of summary jurisdiction, the production of a **certificate purporting to be signed by that officer** that the sum has not been paid to him; and

(*b*) in any other case the production of a **statutory declaration** to a like effect **purporting to be made by the person** to whom the sum is ordered to be paid;

shall be evidence of the facts therein stated, unless the court requires such officer or other person to be called as a witness.

29. The provisions of section 16 of the Indictable Offences Act, 1848, section 7 of the Summary Jurisdiction Act, 1849, and section 36 of the Summary Jurisdiction Act, 1879, enabling a justice to issue a summons to any witness to attend to give evidence before a Court of Summary Jurisdiction shall be deemed to include the power to summon and require a witness to produce to such Court, books, plans, papers, documents, articles, goods and things likely to be material evidence on the hearing of any charge, information, or complaint, and the provisions of those sections relating to the neglect or refusal of a witness, without just excuse, to attend to give evidence, or to be sworn, or to give evidence, shall apply accordingly.

Note.—**S. 28 (1).** The sections of the Acts referred to are set out *ante*, pp. 460, 464. As to proof of convictions generally, see *post*, p. 561.

S. 28 (3). As to competency and compellability of husbands and wives generally as witnesses, see *ante*, p. 273.

S. 28 (4). As to proof of judicial proceedings generally, see *post*, p. 562.

S. 29. This section gives to justices a much-needed power to order production of material documents and articles. It has been extended by the Criminal Justice Act, 1925, s. 31 (4), so as to authorise the issue of process to any person in England or Wales.

BANKRUPTCY ACT, 1914.

4 & 5 Geo. 5, c. 59.

Public Examination of Debtor.

15.—(1) **Where the court makes a receiving order, it shall,** save as in this Act provided, **hold a public sitting,** on a day to be appointed by the court, **for the examination of the debtor,** and the debtor shall attend thereat, and shall be examined as to his conduct, dealings, and property.

(7) **The court may put such questions** to the debtor as it may think expedient.

(8) **The debtor shall** be examined upon oath, and it shall be his duty to **answer all such questions** as the court may put or allow to be put to him. Such **notes of the examination** as the court thinks proper **shall be taken** down in writing, and shall be read over either to or by the debtor and signed by him, **and may thereafter,** save as in this Act provided, **be used in evidence against him;** they shall also be open to the inspection of any creditor at all reasonable times.

Procedure.

109.—(5) Subject to general rules, the **court may in any matter take** the whole or any part of the **evidence** either **viva voce,** or by **interrogatories,** or, out of the United Kingdom, by **commission.**

Evidence.

137.—(1) **A copy of the London Gazette** containing any notice inserted therein in pursuance of this Act, **shall be evidence** of the facts stated in the notice.

(2) **The production of a copy of the London Gazette** containing any notice of a receiving order, or of an order adjudging a debtor bankrupt **shall be conclusive evidence** in all legal proceedings of the order having been duly made, and of its date.

138.—(1) **A minute of proceedings at a meeting of creditors** under this Act, signed at the same or the next ensuing meeting, by a person describing himself as, or appearing to be, chairman of the meeting at which the minute is signed, **shall be received in evidence** without further proof.

(2) Until the contrary is proved, **every meeting** of creditors in respect of the proceedings whereof a minute has been so signed shall be **deemed to have been duly convened** and held, **and all resolutions** passed **or proceedings** had thereat to have been **duly passed or had.**

139. **Any petition** or copy of a petition in bankruptcy, any **order or certificate** or copy of an order or certificate made by any court having jurisdiction in bankruptcy, **any instrument** or copy of an instrument, **affidavit, or document** made or used in the course of any bankruptcy proceedings or other proceedings had under the Act, shall, **if it appears to be sealed** with the seal of any court having jurisdiction in bankruptcy, **or purports to be signed** by any judge thereof, **or is certified** as a true copy by any registrar thereof, be **receivable in evidence** in all legal proceedings whatever.

140. (*Swearing of Affidavits.*)

141. **In the case of the death** of the debtor or his wife, or **of a witness** whose evidence has been received by any court in any proceeding under this Act, **the deposition** of the person so deceased, purporting to be sealed with the seal of the court, or a copy thereof purporting to be so sealed, **shall be admitted as evidence** of the matters therein deposed to.

142. **Every court** having jurisdiction in bankruptcy under this Act **shall have a seal** describing the court in such manner as may be directed by order of the Lord Chancellor, and **judicial notice shall be taken** of the seal, and of the signature of the judge or registrar of any such court, in all legal proceedings.

143. **A certificate** of the Board of Trade **that a person has been appointed trustee** under this Act shall be **conclusive evidence** of his appointment.

144.—(1) **All documents purporting to be** orders or certificates made or **issued by the Board of Trade, and to be sealed** with the seal of the Board, **or to be signed** by a secretary or assistant secretary of the Board, or any person authorised in that behalf by the President of the Board, **shall be received in evidence,** and deemed to be such orders or certificates without further proof unless the contrary is shown.

(2) **A certificate signed by the President** of the Board of Trade that any order made, certificate issued, or act done, is the order, certificate, or act of the Board of Trade **shall be conclusive evidence** of the fact so certified.

Bankruptcy Offences.

166. **A statement or admission made by any person in any compulsory examination or deposition** before any court on the hearing of any matter in bankruptcy **shall not be admissible** as evidence **against that person** in any proceedings **in respect of any of the misdemeanours referred to** in section eighty-five of the Larceny Act, 1861 (which section relates to frauds by agents, bankers and factors).

Note.—**S. 15 (7), (8).** There appear to be two cases in which a person is compelled to answer criminating questions, the answers to which may afterwards be used in evidence against him, *viz.*, in an examination under this section, as to which a limited protection is provided by s. 166, and in an examination of a promoter, director or other person under s. 216 of the Companies Act, 1929 (*post*, p. 518), as to which there is no protection.

Ss. 137—144. The variety of expressions used is noticeable—"evidence", "conclusive evidence", "received in evidence", "receivable in evidence", "admitted as evidence", and "deemed to be". See hereon, *ante*, p. 154. As to judicial notice, see *ante*, p. 13.

S. 166. This must be read in connection with s. 15, *supra*.

LARCENY ACT, 1916.

6 & 7 Geo. 5, c. 50.

43.—(1) Whenever **any person** is being **proceeded against for receiving** any property, knowing it to have been stolen, or for having in his possession stolen property, **for the purpose of proving guilty knowledge** there may be given in **evidence** at any stage of the proceedings—

(*a*) **the fact that other property stolen within the period of twelve months preceding the date of the offence charged was found or had been in his possession;**

(*b*) **the fact that within the five years preceding the date of the offence charged he was convicted of any offence involving fraud or dishonesty.**

This last-mentioned fact may not be proved unless—

(i) Seven days' notice in writing has been given to the

offender that proof of such previous conviction is intended to be given;

(ii) Evidence has been given that the property in respect of which the offender is being tried was found or had been in his possession.

(2) **No person shall be liable to be convicted** of any offence against sections six, seven, sub-section (1), twenty, twenty-one, and twenty-two of this Act **upon any evidence whatever** in respect of any act done by him, **if** at any time previously to his being charged with such offence **he has first disclosed** such act on oath, **in consequence of any compulsory process of any court** of law or equity, in any action, suit, or proceeding which has been bona fide instituted by any person aggrieved.

(3) In any proceedings in respect of any offence against sections six, seven, sub-section (1), twenty, twenty-one, and twenty-two of this Act, a statement or admission made by any person in any compulsory examination or deposition before any court on the hearing of any matter in bankruptcy shall not be admissible in evidence against that person.

Note.—**Sub-s. (1)** of this section repeals, but substantially re-enacts, s. 19 of the Prevention of Crimes Act, 1871, except that the date from which the twelve months and five years respectively are to run is now declared to be "the date of the offence charged" (and not, as was formerly contended, the date of the commencement of the proceedings).

It is commonly understood that the offence of receiving stolen goods, knowing them to have been stolen, is particularly difficult of proof, so far as regards the guilty knowledge. The above provisions were designed to facilitate the proof of such knowledge.

Sub-ss. (2) and **(3).** The effect of these sub-sections is dealt with *ante*, p. 451.

ADMINISTRATION OF JUSTICE ACT, 1920.

10 & 11 GEO. 5, C. 81.

15. **Where** for the purpose of disposing of any action or other matter which is being tried by a judge with a jury in any court in England or Wales it is **necessary to ascertain the law of any other**

country which is applicable to the facts of the case, **any question as to the effect of the evidence given with respect to that law shall,** instead of being submitted to the jury, **be decided by the judge alone.**

Note.—Cf. the Judicature Act, 1925, s. 102, which Act repeals this Act so far as it relates to the High Court.

TRIBUNALS OF INQUIRY (EVIDENCE) ACT, 1921.

11 Geo. 5, c. 7.

1.—(1) **Where it has been resolved** (whether before or after the commencement of this Act) **by both Houses of Parliament that it is expedient that a tribunal be established for inquiring into a definite matter** described in the Resolution as **of urgent public importance,** and in pursuance of the Resolution a tribunal is appointed for the purpose either by His Majesty or a Secretary of State, **the instrument by which the tribunal is appointed** or any instrument supplemental thereto **may provide that this Act shall apply,** and in such case the **tribunal shall have all such powers, rights, and privileges as are vested in the High Court,** or in Scotland the Court of Session, or a judge of either such court, on the occasion of an action **in respect of the following matters:—**

(*a*) The enforcing the attendance of witnesses and examining them on oath, affirmation, or otherwise;

(*b*) The compelling the production of documents;

(*c*) Subject to rules of court, the issuing of a commission or request to examine witnesses abroad;

and a summons signed by one or more of the members of the tribunal may be substituted for and shall be equivalent to any formal process capable of being issued in any action for enforcing the attendance of witnesses and compelling the production of documents.

(2) If any person—

(*a*) on being duly summoned as a witness before a tribunal makes default in attending; or

(*b*) being in attendance as a witness refuses to take an oath legally required by the tribunal to be taken, or to produce any document in his power or control legally required by the tribunal to be produced by him, or to answer any question to which the tribunal may legally require an answer; or

(*c*) does any other thing which would, if the tribunal had been a court of law having power to commit for contempt, have been contempt of that court;

the chairman of the tribunal may certify the offence of that person under his hand to the High Court, or in Scotland the Court of Session, and the court may thereupon inquire into the alleged offence and after hearing any witnesses who may be produced against or on behalf of the person charged with the offence, and after hearing any statement that may be offered in defence, punish or take steps for the punishment of that person in like manner as if he had been guilty of contempt of the court.

(3) A witness before any such tribunal shall be entitled to the same immunities and privileges as if he were a witness before the High Court or the Court of Session.

2. A tribunal to which this Act is so applied as aforesaid—

(*a*) shall not refuse to allow the public or any portion of the public to be present at any of the proceedings of the tribunal unless in the opinion of the tribunal it is in the public interest expedient so to do for reasons connected with the subject matter of the inquiry or the nature of the evidence to be given; and

(*b*) shall have power to authorise the representation before them of any person appearing to them to be interested to be by counsel or solicitor or otherwise, or to refuse to allow such representation.

Note.—This Act has since been applied to the Coal Mines Reorganisation Commission (Coal Mines Act, 1930, s. 12 (2)), Inquiries under the Public Works Facilities Act, 1930 (s. 1 (6)), the Agricultural Marketing Reorganisation Commissions (Agricultural Marketing Act, 1931, s. 15 (5)), the Sea-Fish Commission (Sea Fishing Industry Act, 1933, s. 5 (5)), and the committee appointed under s. 2 (3) of the Wheat Act, 1932 (Wheat Act, 1932, s. 12 (1) (*e*)).

LAW OF PROPERTY ACT, 1925.

15 Geo. 5, c. 20.

73.—(1) **Where an individual executes a deed, he shall either sign or place his mark upon the same and sealing alone shall not be deemed sufficient.**

(2) This section applies only to deeds executed after the commencement of this Act.

74.—(1) In favour of a purchaser a deed shall be deemed to have been duly executed by a corporation aggregate if its seal be affixed thereto in the presence of and attested by its clerk, secretary or other permanent officer or his deputy, and a member of the board of directors, council or other governing body of the corporation, and where a seal purporting to be the seal of a corporation has been affixed to a deed, attested by persons purporting to be persons holding such offices as aforesaid, the deed shall be deemed to have been executed in accordance with the requirements of this section, and to have taken effect accordingly.

(4) Where a corporation aggregate is authorized under a power of attorney or under any statutory or other power to convey any interest in property in the name or on behalf of any other person (including another corporation), an officer appointed for that purpose by the board of directors, council or other governing body of the corporation by resolution or otherwise, may execute the deed or other instrument in the name of such other person; and where an instrument appears to be executed by an officer so appointed, then in favour of a purchaser the instrument shall be deemed to have been executed by an officer duly authorized.

(5) The foregoing provisions of this section apply to transactions wherever effected, but only to deeds and instruments executed after the commencement of this Act, except that, in the case of powers or appointments of an agent or officer, they apply whether the power was conferred or the appointment was made before or after the commencement of this Act or by this Act.

184. In all cases **where,** after the commencement of this Act, **two or more persons have died in circumstances rendering it uncertain which of them survived the other or others,** such deaths shall (subject to any order of the court), **for all purposes affecting the title to**

property, be presumed to have occurred in order of seniority, and accordingly **the younger shall be deemed to have survived the elder.**

Note.—**S. 73.** As to what constitutes a sealing, see *ante*, p. 369. **S. 184.** Prior to the passing of this Act, there was no presumption of survivorship; if the evidence was not sufficient to establish the survival of any individual, the law treated it as a matter incapable of determination (*Wing* v. *Angrave*, 30 L. J. Ch. 65). Persons who die in a common calamity are called "commorientes". See *Hickman* v. *Peacey*, [1945] Appendix IV, *post*, p. 580.

SUPREME COURT OF JUDICATURE (CONSOLIDATION) ACT, 1925.

15 & 16 Geo. 5, c. 49.

PART II.

JURISDICTION AND LAW.

49.—(1) **If any cause or matter in the High Court** (including a cause or matter referred to an official or special referee or arbitrator under the provisions of this Act relating to inquiries and trials by referees) **it appears** to the court or a judge that it is **proper to compel the personal attendance at any trial of a witness who may not be within the jurisdiction** of the court, **it shall be lawful** for the court or a judge, if in the discretion of the court or a judge it seems fit so to do, **to order** that **a writ of subpœna** ad testificandum or writ of subpœna duces tecum shall issue **in special form** commanding the witness to attend the trial wherever he shall be within the United Kingdom, **and the service of any such writ in any part of the United Kingdom shall be as valid and effectual** to all intents and purposes as if it had been served within the jurisdiction of the High Court.

(2) Every such writ shall have at its foot a statement to the effect that it is issued by the special order of the court or a judge as the case may be, and no such writ shall issue without such a special order.

(3) (*Witness making default to be punished.*)

(4) (*But not unless sufficient expenses tendered.*)

(5) **Nothing herein contained shall alter or affect:—**

(*a*) **the power** of the High Court **to issue a commission** for the examination of witnesses out of the jurisdiction of the court in any case in which, notwithstanding this section, the court thinks fit to issue such a commission; **or**

(*b*) **the admissibility of any evidence** at any trial where such evidence is now by law receivable on the ground of any witness being beyond the jurisdiction of the court, and the admissibility of any such evidence shall be determined as if this section and any enactment reproduced by this section had not passed.

Note.—**S. 49.** This section re-enacts with slight verbal alterations the Attendance of Witnesses Act, 1854, which is repealed by this Act. As to attendance of witnesses generally, see *ante*, p. 414.

PART IV.

GENERAL PROVISIONS AS TO TRIAL AND PROCEDURE.

85.—(1) In every district registry there shall be used such seal as the Lord Chancellor from time to time directs.

(2) The seal of the district registry shall be impressed on every writ and other document issued out of or filed in that registry, and **all writs and documents, and all exemplifications and copies thereof. purporting to be sealed with the seal of a district registry, shall be received in evidence** in all parts of the United Kingdom without further proof.

99.—(1) **Rules of Court may be made** under this Act for the following purposes:—

(*i*) **For regulating the means by which particular facts may be proved, and the mode in which evidence thereof may be given,** in any proceedings or on any application in connection with or at any stage of any proceedings.

102. **Where** for the purpose of disposing of any action or other matter which is being tried in the High Court by a judge with a jury it is **necessary to ascertain the law of any other country** which is applicable to the facts of the case, **any question as to the effect**

of the evidence given with respect to that law shall, instead of being submitted to the jury, **be decided by the judge alone.**

Note.—**S. 102.** Cf. the Administration of Justice Act, 1920, s. 15 (*ante*, p. 502, and note thereto).

PART VII.

PROBATE CAUSES AND MATTERS.

174.—(1) In the principal probate registry and in every district probate registry there shall be used such seal [or seals] as the President of the Probate Division may from time to time direct.

(2) **All probates, letters of administration, orders and other instruments and copies thereof and all exemplifications purporting to be sealed with any such seal as aforesaid shall be received in evidence** in all parts of the United Kingdom without further proof.

Note.—**S. 174.** The words in brackets were added by the Administration of Justice Act, 1932, s. 4.

PART VIII.

MATRIMONIAL CAUSES AND MATTERS.

198. **The parties to any proceedings instituted in consequence of adultery and the husbands and wives of the parties shall be competent to give evidence** in the proceedings, **but no witness** in any such proceedings, whether a party thereto or not, **shall be liable to be asked or be bound to answer any question tending to show that he or she has been guilty of adultery unless he or she has** already **given evidence** in the same proceedings **in disproof** of the alleged adultery.

200.—(1) The seal of the court to be used in respect of its jurisdiction in matrimonial causes and matters shall be such as the Lord Chancellor may from time to time direct.

(2) **All decrees and orders of the court, or copies thereof,** made in pursuance of the said jurisdiction **shall, if purporting to be**

sealed with the said seal, be received in evidence in all parts of the United Kingdom without further proof.

Note.—**S. 198.** S. 198 re-enacts with slight verbal alterations s. 3 of the Evidence Further Amendment Act, 1869 (*ante*, p. 459), which is repealed by this Act so far as it relates to the High Court. Under the Act of 1869 it was held that if a party denied in examination-in-chief one charge of adultery contained in the pleadings, he could be cross-examined on all the charges contained in the pleadings (*Brown* v. *Brown*, L. R. 3 P. & D. 198; *Allen* v. *Allen*, [1894] P., at p. 254); but under the Act of 1925 cross-examination may only be directed to the specific act of adultery which has been denied by the party in examination-in-chief (*Morton* v. *Morton*, [1937] P. 151).

The protection given by s. 198 is strictly confined to "proceedings instituted in consequence of adultery"; it does not apply to proceedings instituted to establish the status of a child (*Evans* v. *Evans*, [1904] P. 378; *Nottingham* v. *Tomkinson*, L. R. 4 C. P. D. 343), nor to an intervention by the King's Proctor to rescind a decree *nisi* on the ground of condonation (*Sneyd* v. *Sneyd*, 42 T. L. R. 106).

As to the competency and compellability of husbands and wives as witnesses generally, see *ante*, pp. 273 *et seq*.

WORKMEN'S COMPENSATION ACT, 1925.

15 & 16 Geo. 5, c. 84.

35.—(1) (*d*) **Where an injured master, seaman or apprentice is discharged or left behind** in a British possession or in a foreign country, **depositions** respecting the circumstances and nature of the injury **may be taken** by any judge or magistrate in the British possession, and by any British consular officer in the foreign country, and if so taken shall be transmitted by the person by whom they are taken to the Board of Trade, and **such depositions or certified copies thereof shall** in any proceedings for enforcing the claim **be admissible in evidence** as provided by sections 691 and 695 of the Merchant Shipping Act, 1894, and those sections shall apply accordingly.

Note.—Ss. 691 and 695 of the Merchant Shipping Act, 1894, are set out *ante*, pp. 477, 478.

CRIMINAL JUSTICE ACT, 1925.

15 & 16 Geo. 5, c. 86.

PART II.

JURISDICTION AND PROCEDURE.

12.—(1) **Where any person is charged before examining justices with an indictable offence, the justices shall,** as soon as may be after the examination of each witness for the prosecution has been concluded, **cause the deposition of that witness to be read to him in the presence and hearing of the accused, and shall cause him to sign the deposition, and shall forthwith bind him over to attend the trial** in manner directed by section twenty of the Indictable Offences Act, 1848, as amended by this Act.

(2) **Immediately after the last witness for the prosecution has been bound over** to attend the trial, the examining **justices shall read the charge to the accused and explain the nature thereof to him in ordinary language, and inform him that he has the right to call witnesses and,** if he so desires, **to give evidence on his own behalf.**

After so doing the examining **justices shall then address to him the following words** or words to the like effect—

"Do you wish to say anything in answer to the charge? You are not obliged to say anything unless you desire to do so, but whatever you say will be taken down in writing and may be given in evidence upon your trial."

(3) **Before the accused makes any statement** in answer to the charge, the examining **justices shall state to him and give him clearly to understand that he has nothing to hope from any promise of favour and nothing to fear from any threat** which may have been held out to him to induce him to make any admission or confession of his guilt, but that whatsoever he then says may be given in evidence on his trial notwithstanding the promise or threat.

(4) **Whatever the accused states in answer to the charge, shall be taken down** in manner shown in a form to be prescribed . . . **and shall be read over to the accused, and signed by the examining justices** and also, if he so desires, by him, **and shall be transmitted**

to the court of trial with the depositions of the witnesses in manner provided in section twenty of the said Act.

On the trial the statement of the accused taken down as aforesaid, and whether signed by him or not, **may be given in evidence** without further proof thereof, unless it is proved that the examining justices purporting to sign the statement did not in fact sign it.

(5) **Immediately after complying with the requirements of this section relating to the statement of the accused,** and whether the accused has or has not made a statement, the examining **justices shall ask the accused whether he desires to give evidence on his own behalf and whether he desires to call witnesses.**

If the accused in answer to the question **states that he wishes to give evidence but not to call witnesses, the justices shall** proceed to **take forthwith the evidence of the accused,** and after the conclusion of the evidence of the accused his counsel or solicitor shall be heard on his behalf if he so desires.

If the accused in answer to the question **states that he desires to give evidence on his own behalf and to call witnesses,** or to call witnesses only, the **justices shall** proceed to **take** either forthwith, or, if a speech is to be made by counsel or solicitor on behalf of the accused, after the conclusion of that speech, **the evidence of the accused,** if he desires to give evidence himself, **and of any witness called by him** who knows anything relating to the facts and circumstances of the case or anything tending to prove the innocence of the accused.

All statements made by the accused and all evidence given by him or any such witness as aforesaid (not being a witness merely to the character of the accused) under this subsection **shall be taken down in writing and shall be transmitted to the court of trial,** together with the depositions of the witnesses for the prosecution, and the provisions of subsection (1) of this section shall apply in the case of witnesses for the defence as they apply in the case of witnesses for the prosecution, except that the justices shall not bind over to attend the trial any witness who is a witness merely to the character of the accused.

(6) **Nothing contained in this section shall prevent the prosecutor in any case from giving in evidence at the trial any admission or confession or other statement of the accused** made at any time which is by law admissible as evidence against the accused.

(7) The depositions taken in connection with any charge for an indictable offence shall be signed by the justices before whom they are taken in such manner as may be directed by rules made under this Act, and where any such charge is enquired into by two or more examining justices, the deposition of a witness or the statement of the accused shall for all purposes be deemed to be sufficiently signed if signed by any one of those justices.

(8) **The examining justices shall,** notwithstanding anything in the Indictable Offences Act, 1848, **before determining whether they will or will not commit an accused person for trial, take into consideration his statement or any such evidence as is given** in pursuance of this section **by him or his witnesses.**

13.—(1) **Where any person charged before examining justices with an indictable offence is committed for trial and it appears to the justices,** after taking into account anything which may be said with reference thereto by the accused or the prosecutor, **that the attendance at the trial of any witness who has been examined before them is unnecessary** by reason of anything contained in any statement by the accused, or of the accused having pleaded guilty to the charge or of the evidence of the witness being merely of a formal nature, **the justices shall,** if the witness has not already been bound over, **bind him over to attend the trial conditionally** upon notice given to him and not otherwise, or shall, if the witness has already been bound over, direct that he shall be treated as having been bound over to attend only conditionally as aforesaid, and shall transmit to the court of trial a statement in writing of the names, addresses and occupations of the witnesses who are, or who are to be treated as having been bound over to attend the trial conditionally.

(2) Where a witness has been, or is to be treated as having been bound over conditionally to attend the trial, the prosecutor or the person committed for trial may give notice at any time before the opening of the assizes or quarter sessions to the clerk to the examining justices and at any time thereafter to the clerk of assize or the clerk of the peace, as the case may be, that he desires the witness to attend at the trial, and any such clerk to whom any such notice is given shall forthwith notify the witness that he is required so to attend in pursuance of his recognizance.

The examining justices shall on committing the accused for trial inform him of his right to require the attendance at the trial of any such witness as aforesaid, and of the steps which he must take for the purpose of enforcing such attendance.

(3) **Where any person has been committed for trial for any offence, the deposition of any person taken before the examining justices may, if the conditions hereinafter set out are satisfied, without further proof be read as evidence on the trial of that person,** whether for that offence or for any other offence arising out of the same transaction, or set of circumstances, as that offence.

The conditions hereinbefore referred to are the following:—

(*a*) **The deposition must be the deposition either of a witness whose attendance at the trial is stated to be unnecessary in accordance with the provisions of this section, or of a witness who is proved at the trial** by the oath of a credible witness **to be dead or insane, or so ill as not to be able to travel, or to be kept out of the way by means of the procurement of the accused or on his behalf:**

(*b*) **It must be proved at the trial,** either by a certificate purporting to be signed by the justice before whom the deposition purports to have been taken or by the clerk to the examining justices, or by the oath of a credible witness, **that the deposition was taken in the presence of the accused and that the accused or his counsel or solicitor had full opportunity of cross-examining the witness:**

(*c*) **The deposition must purport to be signed by the justice before whom it purports to have been taken:**

Provided that the provisions of this subsection shall not have effect in any case in which it is proved—

(i) That the deposition, or, where the proof required by paragraph (*b*) of this subsection is given by means of a certificate, that the certificate, was not in fact signed by the justice by whom it purports to have been signed; or

(ii) Where the deposition is the deposition of a witness whose attendance at the trial is stated to be unnecessary as aforesaid, that the witness has been duly notified that he is required to attend the trial.

(4) A witness whose attendance at the trial is stated to be unnecessary in accordance with the provisions of this section shall not be required to attend before the grand jury, and his deposition may be read as evidence before the grand jury.

(5) Any documents or articles produced in evidence before the examining justices by any witness whose attendance at the trial is stated to be unnecessary in accordance with the provisions of this section and marked as exhibits shall, subject to the provisions of section five of the Prosecution of Offences Act, 1879 (which relates to delivery of documents to the Director of Public Prosecutions), and unless in any particular case the justices otherwise order, be retained by the justices and forwarded with the depositions to the court of trial.

34. **Any document purporting to be the fiat, order or consent of the Attorney-General, the Solicitor-General, the Director of Public Prosecutions,** *the Postmaster-General* **or the Board of Control** respectively, **for or to the institution of any criminal proceedings** or the institution of criminal proceedings in any particular form, **and to be signed by the Attorney-General, the Solicitor-General, the Director of Public Prosecutions or an Assistant Director of Public Prosecutions,** *the Postmaster-General* **or a Commissioner or the Secretary of the Board of Control,** as the case may be, **shall be admissible as prima facie evidence without further proof.**

PART IV.

MISCELLANEOUS AND GENERAL.

47. **Any presumption of law that an offence committed by a wife in the presence of her husband is committed under the coercion of the husband is hereby abolished,** but on a charge against a wife for any offence other than treason or murder it shall be a good defence to prove that the offence was committed in the presence of, and under the coercion of, the husband.

Note.—**S. 12.** This section replaces s. 18 of the Indictable Offences Act, 1848, and s. 3 of the Criminal Law Amendment Act, 1867, which sections are repealed by this Act. It should be read in conjunction with ss. 17 and 20 of the Indictable Offences Act, 1848 (*ante*, p. 438).

S. 13. This section, which incorporates the latter part of s. 17 of the Indictable Offences Act, 1848 (repealed by this Act), for the first time gives justices the power to bind over witnesses conditionally, and sets out clearly all the circumstances in which depositions may be read at the trial. In *R.* v. *Scaife* (20 L. J. M. C. 229) it was held that if procurement of absence be shown, and there are several prisoners, the deposition is evidence against those only who are proved to have procured such absence.

The Criminal Law Amendment Act, 1867, s. 6, makes provision for taking the depositions of any persons dangerously ill, by way of "perpetuation of testimony", whether any person is already accused or not. See *ante*, p. 454.

S. 34. The words in italics were repealed by the Post Office (Amendment) Act, 1935, which makes a similar provision for proof of the Postmaster-General's consent (see *post*, p. 535).

MONEYLENDERS ACT, 1927.

17 & 18 Geo. 5, c. 21.

6.—(1) **No contract for the repayment by a borrower of money lent to him** or to any agent on his behalf **by a moneylender** after the commencement of this Act **or for the payment by him of interest on money so lent and no security given by the borrower** or by any such agent as aforesaid **in respect of any such contract shall be enforceable, unless a note or memorandum in writing of the contract be made and signed personally by the borrower,** and unless a copy thereof be delivered or sent to the borrower within seven days of the making of the contract; and no such contract or security shall be enforceable if it is proved that the note or memorandum aforesaid was not signed by the borrower before the money was lent or before the security was given as the case may be.

(2) **The note or memorandum aforesaid shall contain all the terms of the contract,** and in particular shall show the date on which the loan is made, the amount of the principal of the loan, and, either the interest charged on the loan expressed in terms of a rate per cent. per annum, or the rate per cent. per annum represented by the interest charged as calculated in accordance with the provisions of the First Schedule to this Act.

Note.—This is one of the few cases in which written evidence of a contract is required (see *ante*, p. 158).

COMPANIES ACT, 1929.

19 & 20 Geo. 5, c. 23.

PART I.

INCORPORATION OF COMPANIES AND MATTERS INCIDENTAL THERETO.

15.—(1) **A certificate of incorporation** given by the registrar in respect of any association shall be **conclusive evidence that** all the requirements of this Act in respect of registration and of matters precedent and incidental thereto have been complied with, and that the association is a company authorized to be registered and duly registered under this Act.

PART II.

SHARE CAPITAL AND DEBENTURES.

68. **A certificate,** under the common seal of the company, specifying any **shares** held by any member, shall be **prima facie evidence** of the title of the member to the shares.

PART III.

REGISTRATION OF CHARGES.

82.—(2) The registrar shall give **a certificate** under his hand **of the registration of any charge** registered in pursuance of this Part of this Act, stating the amount thereby secured, and the certificate shall be **conclusive evidence** that the requirements of this Part of this Act as to registration have been complied with.

PART IV.

MANAGEMENT AND ADMINISTRATION.

94.—(3) The registrar of companies shall, on the delivery to him of the said statutory declaration, and, in the case of a company which is required by this section to deliver a statement in lieu of prospectus, of such a statement, certify that the **company is entitled**

to commence business, and that **certificate** shall be **conclusive evidence** that the company is so entitled.

102. **The register** of members shall be **prima facie evidence** of any matters by this Act directed or authorised to be inserted therein.

120.—(1) Every company shall cause minutes of all proceedings of general meetings, and where there are directors or managers, of all proceedings at meetings of its directors or of its managers, to be entered in books kept for that purpose.

(2) Any such **minute if purporting to be signed** by the chairman of the meeting at which the proceedings were had, or by the chairman of the next succeeding meeting, shall be **evidence** of the proceedings.

(3) **Where minutes** have been made in accordance with the provisions of this section of the proceedings **at any general meeting** of the company or meeting of directors or managers, then, until the contrary is proved, **the meeting** shall be **deemed to have been duly held** and convened, **and all proceedings** had thereat to have been duly had, **and all appointments** of directors, managers, or liquidators, shall be **deemed to be valid.**

138. **A copy of the report of any inspectors** appointed under this Act, authenticated by the seal of the company whose affairs they have investigated, shall be admissible in any legal proceeding **as evidence of the opinion of the inspectors** in relation to any matter contained in the report.

PART V.

WINDING UP.

208.—(1) **An order made by the court on a contributory** shall, subject to any right of appeal, be **conclusive evidence** that the money, if any, thereby appearing to be due or ordered to be paid is due.

214.—(1) (*Power to summon any person to give information, etc.*)

(2) **The court may examine him** on oath concerning the matters aforesaid, either by word of mouth or on written interrogatories, and may reduce his answers to writing and require him to sign them.

(3) **The court may require him to produce** any books and papers in his custody or power relating to the company. . . .

216.—(1) (*Power to order public examination of promoters, directors, etc.*)

(4) **The court may put such questions** to the person examined as the court thinks fit.

(5) **The person examined** shall be examined on oath, and **shall answer all such questions** as the court may put or allow to be put to him.

(7) **Notes of the examination shall be taken** down in writing, and shall be read over to or by, and signed by, the person examined, **and may thereafter be used in evidence against him,** and shall be open to the inspection of any creditor or contributory at all reasonable times.

282. Where a company is being wound up, **all books and papers** of the company and of the liquidators shall, as between the contributories of the company, be **prima facie evidence** of the truth of all matters purporting to be therein recorded.

289. In all proceedings under this Part of this Act, all **courts, judges, and persons judicially acting, and all officers,** judicial or ministerial, of any court, or employed in enforcing the process of any court, **shall take judicial notice of the signature** of any officer of the High Court . . . and also of the official **seal or stamp** of the several offices of the High Court . . . **appended to or impressed on any document** made, issued, or signed under the provisions of this Part of this Act, or any official copy thereof.

PART XIII.

MISCELLANEOUS.

369. Where proceedings are instituted under this Act against any person by the Director of Public Prosecutions or by or on behalf of the Lord Advocate, **nothing in this Act shall** be taken to **require any** person who has acted as **solicitor for the defendant to disclose any privileged communication** made to him in that capacity.

378.—(1) **All documents purporting to be orders or certificates** made or issued **by the Board of Trade** for the purposes of this Act and to be sealed with the seal of the Board, or to be signed by a secretary or assistant secretary of the Board, or any person authorised in that behalf by the President of the Board, **shall be received**

in evidence and deemed to be such orders or certificates without further proof; unless the contrary is shown.

(2) **A certificate signed by the President** of the Board of Trade that any order made, certificate issued, or act done, is the order, certificate, or act of the Board, shall be **conclusive evidence** of the fact so certified.

Note.—It will be observed that certain matters are by the above sections made "evidence", "*prima facie* evidence", or "conclusive evidence", or they are "deemed" to be or have been. It is not always easy to ascertain the precise meaning of several expressions used when there are only two positions to be provided for. See hereon, *ante*, p. 154.

S. 120. Loose leaves fastened together in two covers in such a way that leaves can easily be removed or substituted are not a book within the meaning of this section (*Hearts of Oak Assurance Co.* v. *Flower*, [1936] Ch. 76).

S. 216 (5), (7). There appear to be two cases in which a person is compelled to answer criminating questions, the answers to which may afterwards be used in evidence against him, *viz.*, in an examination under this section, and, to a limited extent, under the Bankruptcy Act, 1914 (see ss. 15, 166, *ante*, pp. 499, 501). See generally as to criminating questions, *ante*, p. 331.

S. 289. As to judicial notice generally, see *ante*, p. 13.

S. 369. As to solicitors' privilege generally, see *ante*, pp. 321, 335-40.

INFANT LIFE (PRESERVATION) ACT, 1929.

19 & 20 Geo. 5, c. 34.

2.—(5) Section four of the Criminal Evidence Act, 1898, shall have effect as if this Act were included in the Schedule to that Act.

Note.—The schedule in question appears *ante*, p. 482.

POOR LAW ACT, 1930.

20 Geo. 5, c. 17.

95. Proviso (*b*). **A removal order in respect of a settlement** alleged to have been acquired by residence **shall not be made** upon the evidence of the person to be removed **without such corroboration** as the justices think sufficient.

Note.—This section replaces a similar provision formerly contained in the Divided Parishes Act, 1876. As to corroboration generally, see *ante*, p. 156.

ROAD TRAFFIC ACT, 1930.

(*See Appendix IV*, post, *p.* 580.)

RIGHTS OF WAY ACT, 1932.

22 & 23 Geo. 5, c. 45.

1.—(1) **Where a way,** not being of such a character that user thereof by the public could not give rise at common law to any presumption of dedication, upon or over any land **has been** actually **enjoyed by the public** as of right and without interruption **for a** full period of **twenty years, such way shall be deemed to have been dedicated as a highway unless there is sufficient evidence that there was no intention** during that period to dedicate such way, or unless during such period of twenty years there was not at any time any person in possession of such land capable of dedicating such way.

(2) **Where any such way has been enjoyed** as aforesaid **for a** full period of **forty years, such way shall be deemed conclusively to have been dedicated as a highway unless there is sufficient evidence that there was no intention** during that period to dedicate such way.

(3) **A notice** by the owner of the land over which any such way passes inconsistent with the dedication of the way as a highway, placed before or after and maintained after the commencement of this Act in such a manner as to be visible to those using the way, **shall, in the absence of proof of a contrary intention, be sufficient evidence** to negative the intention to dedicate such way as a highway,

and where a notice has been placed in the manner provided in this subsection and is subsequently torn down or defaced, **notice in writing** by the owner of the land to the council of the county and of the borough or urban or rural district council in which the way is situate that the way is not dedicated to the public **shall, in the absence of proof of a contrary intention be sufficient evidence** to negative the intention of the owner of the land to dedicate such way as a highway.

(4) (*a*) (*Right of owner of land to deposit with local authority map and statement.*)

(*b*) In any case in which a deposit under paragraph (*a*) of this subsection has been made, **statutory declarations** made by the owner aforesaid or by his successors in title and lodged by him or them with the councils aforesaid at any time prior to the expiration of six years from the date of such deposit or prior to the expiration of six years from the date on which any previous declarations were lodged under this paragraph to the effect that no additional ways (other than any specifically indicated in such declaration) over the lands delineated on the said map have been dedicated to the public since the date of such deposit or since the date of the lodgment of such previous declarations (as the case may be) **shall in the absence of proof of a contrary intention be sufficient evidence** to negative the intention of the owner or his successors in title to dedicate any such additional ways as highways.

2.—(2) Nothing in this Act shall operate to prevent the dedication of a way as a highway being **presumed** on proof of user for any less period than twenty years or to prevent the dedication of a way as a highway being **presumed** or approved under any circumstances under which it can be **presumed** or proved at the time of the passing of this Act.

3. **Any court** or other tribunal **shall,** before determining (*a*) whether a way upon or over any land has or has not been dedicated as a highway, or (*b*) the date upon which such dedication, if any, took place, **take into consideration any map, plan or history** of the locality or other relevant document that is tendered in evidence, and such weight shall be given thereto as the court or tribunal consider justified by the circumstances, including the antiquity of the tendered document, the status of the person or persons by whom it was made or compiled, its purpose, and the custody in which it has been kept and from which it is produced.

EVIDENCE (FOREIGN, DOMINION AND COLONIAL DOCUMENTS) ACT, 1933.

23 Geo. 5, c. 4.

1.—(1) If, upon consideration of a report from the Lord Chancellor and a Secretary of State, His Majesty in Council is satisfied with respect to any country that, having regard to the law of that country as to the recognition therein of public registers of the United Kingdom as authentic records and as to the proof of the contents of such registers and other matters by means of duly authenticated certificates issued by public officers in the United Kingdom, it is desirable in the interests of reciprocity to make with respect to public registers of that country and certificates issued by public officers therein such an Order as is hereinafter mentioned, it shall be lawful for His Majesty in Council to make such an Order accordingly.

(2) An **Order in Council** made under this section **may provide that** in all parts of the United Kingdom—

(*a*) a **register** of the country to which the Order relates, being such a register as is specified in the Order, **shall be deemed to be a public register** kept under the authority of the law of that country and recognised by the courts thereof as an authentic record, and to be a **document of such a public nature as to be admissible as evidence** of the matters regularly recorded therein;

(*b*) such **matters** as may be specified in the Order shall, if **recorded in such a register,** be **deemed,** until the contrary is proved, to **be regularly recorded** therein;

(*c*) subject to any conditions specified in the Order and to any requirements of rules of court a document purporting to be issued in the country to which the Order relates as an **official copy** of an entry in such a register as is so specified, and **purporting to be authenticated** as such in the manner specified in the Order as appropriate in the case of such a register, **shall,** without evidence as to the custody of the register or of inability to produce it and without any further or other proof, **be received as evidence** that the register contains such an entry;

(*d*) subject as aforesaid a certificate purporting to be given in the country to which the Order relates as an **official**

certificate of any such class as is specified in the Order, and purporting to be signed by the officer, and to be authenticated in the manner, specified in the Order as appropriate in the case of a certificate of that class, **shall be received as evidence of the facts stated in the certificate**;

(e) no official document issued in the country to which the Order relates as proof of any matters for the proof of which provision is made by the Order shall, if otherwise admissible in evidence, be inadmissible by reason only that it is not authenticated by the process known as legalisation.

(3) **Official books of record** preserved in a central registry and containing entries copied from original registers may, if those entries were **copied** by officials **in the course of** their **duty** themselves **be treated** for the purposes of this section **as registers.**

(4) In this section the expression " country " means a Dominion, the Isle of Man, any of the Channel Islands, a British colony or protectorate, a foreign country, a colony or protectorate of a foreign country, or any mandated territory:

Provided that where a part of a country is under both a local and a central legislature, an Order under this section may be made as well with respect to that part, as with respect to all the parts under that central legislature.

(5) His Majesty in Council may vary or revoke any Order previously made under this section.

2. In all parts of the United Kingdom **entries made,** whether before or after the commencement of the British Nationality and Status of Aliens Act, 1914, **in any register** kept in accordance with instructions of the Secretary of State **by an officer in the diplomatic or consular service** of His Majesty for the registration of the **births and deaths of British subjects** born or dying out of His Majesty's dominions may be proved by such copies, certified in such manner, as may be directed by the Secretary of State, and the **copies of any such entries shall be evidence** of any matters authorised by any instruction of the Secretary of State to be inserted in the register.

3. This Act may be cited as the Evidence (Foreign, Dominion and Colonial Documents) Act, 1933.

Note.—The powers granted by s. 1 of this Act have been exercised in respect of certain registers and certificates of Belgium and France (S. R. & O., 1933, No. 383, and 1937, No. 575).

CHILDREN AND YOUNG PERSONS ACT, 1933.

23 Geo. 5, c. 12.

PART I.

PREVENTION OF CRUELTY AND EXPOSURE TO MORAL AND PHYSICAL DANGER.

1.—(1) (*Providing penalties for cruelty to persons under sixteen.*)

(2) For the purposes of this section—

(*a*) **a parent or other person legally liable to maintain** a child or young person shall be **deemed to have neglected** him in a manner likely to cause injury to his health **if he has failed to provide** adequate food, clothing, medical aid or lodging for him, **or if,** having been unable otherwise to provide such food, clothing, medical aid or lodging, **he has failed to take steps to procure** it to be provided under the Acts relating to the relief of the poor;

(*b*) **where it is proved that the death of an infant** under three years of age **was caused by suffocation** (not being suffocation caused by disease or the presence of any foreign body in the throat or air passages of the infant) while the infant was in **bed with some other person** who has attained the age **of sixteen** years, **that other person shall, if** he was, when he went to bed, **under the influence of drink, be deemed to have neglected** the infant in a manner likely to cause injury to its health.

(6) . . .

(*a*) **a person shall be deemed to be** directly or indirectly **interested in a sum of money if** he has any share in or any benefit from the payment of that money, notwithstanding that he may not be a person to whom it is legally payable; and

(*b*) **a copy of a policy of insurance,** certified to be a true copy by an officer or agent of the insurance company granting the policy, **shall be evidence** that the child or young person therein stated to be insured has in fact been so insured, and that the person in whose favour the policy has been granted is the person to whom the money thereby insured is legally payable.

2.—(1) (*Providing penalties for causing seduction or prostitution of girl under sixteen.*)

(2) For the purposes of this section **a person shall be deemed to have caused** or encouraged the seduction, unlawful carnal knowledge, or prostitution of, or the commission of an indecent assault upon, a girl who has been seduced, unlawfully carnally known, or indecently assaulted, or who has become a prostitute, **if he has knowingly allowed** her to consort with, or to enter or continue in the employment of, any prostitute or person of known immoral character.

4.—(1) (*Providing penalties for allowing persons under sixteen to beg, etc.*)

(2) **If a person having the custody, charge, or care** of a child or young person **is charged** with an offence under this section, **and it is proved that** the child or young person was in any street, premises, or place for any such purpose as aforesaid, **and that** the person charged allowed the child or young person to be in the street, premises, or place, **he shall be presumed to have allowed** him to be in the street, premises or place for that purpose unless the contrary is proved.

(3) **If any person while singing,** playing, performing or offering anything for sale in a street or public place **has with him a child** who has been lent or hired out to him, **the child shall,** for the purposes of this section, **be deemed** to be in that street or place for the purpose of inducing the giving of alms.

6.—(1) (*Providing penalties for allowing children in bars of licensed premises.*)

(3) If a child is found in the bar of any licensed premises during the permitted hours, the **holder of the licence shall be deemed to have committed an offence** under this section **unless he shows that** he had used due diligence to prevent the child from being admitted to the bar or that the child had apparently attained the age of fourteen years.

14.—(3) A person shall not be summarily convicted of an offence mentioned in the First Schedule to this Act, unless the offence was wholly or partly committed within six months before the information was laid; but, subject as aforesaid, **evidence may be taken of acts** constituting, or contributing to constitute, the offence, and **committed at any previous time.**

15. As respects proceedings against any person for any of the offences mentioned in the **First Schedule to this Act, the Criminal Evidence Act, 1898,** shall apply as if the Schedule to that Act included references to those offences.

17. For the purposes of this Part of this Act—

Any person who is the **parent or legal guardian of a child or young person or** who is **legally liable to maintain him shall be presumed to have the** custody of him, and as between father and mother the father shall not be deemed to have ceased to have the custody of him by reason only that he has deserted, or otherwise does not reside with, the mother and the child or young person;

Any person to whose charge a child or young person is committed by any person who has the custody of him **shall be presumed to have charge** of the child or young person;

Any other person having actual possession or control of a child or young person **shall be presumed to have the care** of him.

PART II.

EMPLOYMENT.

26.—(1) (*Providing penalties for allowing persons under eighteen to go abroad for paid performances etc., without a licence.*)

(2) **Where,** in proceedings under this section against a person, **it is proved that** he caused, procured, or allowed a person under the age of eighteen years to go abroad **and that** that person has while abroad been singing, playing, performing, or being exhibited, for profit, the **defendant shall be presumed to have caused, procured, or allowed** him to go abroad for that purpose, unless the contrary is proved: . . .

(4) In any such proceedings as aforesaid, **a report of any British consular officer and any deposition made on oath before a British consular officer** and authenticated by the signature of that officer, respecting the observance or non-observance of any of the conditions or restrictions contained in a licence granted under the last foregoing section **shall, upon proof that** the consular officer, or deponent, cannot

be found in the United Kingdom, **be admissible in evidence, and it shall not be necessary** to prove the signature or official character of the person appearing to have signed any such report or deposition.

(5) **The wife or husband** of a person charged with an offence under this section **may be called as a witness** either for the prosecution or defence, and **without the consent** of the person charged.

PART III.

PROTECTION OF CHILDREN AND YOUNG PERSONS IN RELATION TO CRIMINAL AND SUMMARY PROCEEDINGS.

38.—(1) Where, **in any proceedings against any person for any offence, any child** of tender years called as a witness does not in the opinion of the court understand the nature of an oath, **his evidence may be received, though not given upon oath, if,** in the opinion of the court, **he is possessed of sufficient intelligence** to justify the reception of the evidence, and understands the duty of speaking the truth; **and his evidence,** though not given on oath, but otherwise taken and reduced into writing in accordance with the provisions of section seventeen of the Indictable Offences Act, 1848, or of this Part of this Act, **shall be deemed to be a deposition** within the meaning of that section and that Part respectively:

Provided that where evidence admitted by virtue of this section is given on behalf of the prosecution **the accused shall not be liable to be convicted** of the offence **unless that evidence is corroborated** by some other material evidence in support thereof implicating him.

(2) **If any child** whose evidence is received as aforesaid **wilfully gives false evidence** in such circumstances that he would, if the evidence had been given on oath, have been guilty of perjury, **he shall be liable** on summary conviction to be dealt with as if he had been summarily convicted of an indictable offence punishable in the case of an adult with imprisonment.

42.—(1) **Where a justice of the peace is satisfied** by the evidence of a duly qualified medical practitioner **that the attendance before a court of any child or young person** in respect of whom any of the offences mentioned in the First Schedule to this Act is alleged to have been committed **would involve serious danger** to his life or health, **the justice may take in writing the deposition of the child or young person** on oath, and shall thereupon subscribe the deposition and add thereto a statement of his reason for taking it and of the day when and place where it was taken, and of the names of the persons (if any) present at the taking thereof.

43. **Where**, in any proceedings in respect of any of the offences mentioned in the First Schedule to this Act, **the court is satisfied** by the evidence of a duly qualified medical practitioner **that the attendance before the court of any child or young person** in respect of whom the offence is alleged to have been committed **would involve serious danger** to his life or health, **any deposition of the child or young person** taken under the Indictable Offences Act, 1848, or this Part of this Act, **shall be admissible in evidence** either for or against the accused person without further proof thereof if it purports to be signed by the justice by or before whom it purports to be taken:

Provided that the deposition shall not be admissible in evidence against the accused person unless **it is proved that reasonable notice** of the intention to take the deposition **has been served** upon him and that he or his counsel or solicitor had, or might have had if he had chosen to be present, an opportunity of cross-examining the child or young person making the deposition.

50. **It shall be conclusively presumed that no child under** the age of **eight years can be guilty of any offence.**

61.—(1) (*Definition of "in need of care or protection".*)

(2) For the purposes of this section, **the fact that a child or young person is found destitute,** or is found wandering without any settled place of abode and without visible means of subsistence, or is found begging or receiving alms (whether or not there is any pretence of singing, playing, performing or offering anything for sale), or is found loitering for the purpose of so begging or receiving alms, **shall** (without prejudice to the generality of the provisions of paragraph (*a*) of the last foregoing subsection) **be evidence that he is exposed to moral danger.**

PART VI.

SUPPLEMENTAL.

99.—(1) **Where a person,** whether charged with an offence or not, **is brought before any court** otherwise than for the purpose of giving evidence, **and it appears** to the court **that he is a child or young person, the court shall** make due inquiry as to the age of that person, and for that purpose shall **take such evidence as may be forthcoming** at the hearing of the case, but an order or judgment of the court shall not be invalidated by any subsequent proof that the age of that person has not been correctly stated to the court, **and the age presumed or declared by the court** to be the age of the person so brought before it **shall, for the purposes of this Act, be deemed to be the true age** of that person, and, where it appears to the court that the person so brought before it has attained the age of seventeen years, that person shall for the purposes of this Act be deemed not to be a child or young person.

(2) **Where in any charge or indictment** for any offence under this Act or any of the offences mentioned in the First Schedule to this Act, **except** an offence under the Criminal Law Amendment Act, 1885, **it is alleged that the person** by or in respect of whom the offence was committed was a child or young person or **was under or had attained any specified age, and he appears to the court to have been** at the date of the commission of the alleged offence a child or young person, or to have been under or to have attained the specified age, as the case may be, **he shall** for the purposes of this Act **be presumed** at that date **to have been** a child or young person or to have been under or to have attained that age, as the case may be, unless the contrary is proved.

100. In any proceedings under this Act a **copy of an entry in the wages book of any employer of labour, or** if no wages book be kept **a written statement signed** by the employer or by any responsible person in his employ, **shall be evidence that the wages** therein entered or stated as having been paid to any person, **have in fact been so paid.**

FIRST SCHEDULE.

OFFENCES AGAINST CHILDREN AND YOUNG PERSONS, WITH RESPECT TO WHICH SPECIAL PROVISIONS OF THIS ACT APPLY.

The murder or manslaughter of a child or young person.

Infanticide.

Any offence under sections 27, 55 or 56 of the Offences against the Person Act, 1861, and any offence against a child or young person under sections 5, 42, 43, 52 or 62 of that Act, or under the Criminal Law Amendment Act, 1885.

Any offence under the Punishment of Incest Act, 1908, in respect of a child or young person.

Any offence under sections 1, 2, 3, 4, 11 or 23 of this Act.

Any other offence involving bodily injury to a child or young person.

Note.—**Ss. 1, 2, 4, 17 and 26.** As to persons charged being "presumed" or "deemed" to have committed offences, see *ante*, p. 155.

S. 14. As to the general rules concerning evidence of conduct on other occasions, see *ante*, pp. 100, 105.

S. 15. The schedule to the Act in question appears *ante*, p. 482.

S. 26 (5). As to the competency and compellability of husbands and wives as witnesses generally, see *ante*, p. 273.

S. 38. As appears from this section, a child of tender years can now give unsworn evidence in all *criminal* cases; but his evidence must be corroborated before the accused is liable to be convicted. One child, whose evidence requires corroboration, cannot be corroborated by the unsworn testimony of another child which itself requires corroboration (*R.* v. *Manser*, 25 Cr. App. R. 18).

Ss. 42, 43. As to depositions generally, see *ante*, p. 415.

S. 50. As to presumptions generally, see *ante*, pp. 23 *et seq.*

S. 99. Compare this section with a similar provision in s. 266 of the Public Health (London) Act, 1936, *post*, p. 536.

Schedule. S. 27 of the Offences against the Person Act, 1861, relates to the abandonment or exposure of children, s. 55 to their abduction, and s. 56 to child-stealing.

S. 5 relates to manslaughter, s. 42 to common assault, s. 43 to aggravated assault, s. 52 to indecent assault upon females, and s. 62 to indecent assault upon males.

S. 1 of this Act relates to cruelty to persons under sixteen, s. 2 to the seduction or prostitution of girls under sixteen, s. 3 to allowing persons under sixteen to be in brothels, s. 4 to allowing such persons to be used for begging, s. 11 to exposing children under seven to the risk of burning, and s. 23 to the taking part by persons under sixteen in dangerous performances.

RENT AND MORTGAGE INTEREST RESTRICTIONS (AMENDMENT) ACT, 1933.

23 & 24 Geo. 5, c. 32.

3.—(2) **A certificate** of the housing authority for the area in which the said dwelling-house is situated, certifying **that the authority will**

provide suitable alternative accommodation for the tenant by a date specified in the certificate, **shall be conclusive evidence** that suitable alternative accommodation will be available for him by that date.

(3) **Where no such certificate** as aforesaid **is produced** to the court, **accommodation shall be deemed to be suitable if it consists** either—

(*a*) of a dwelling-house to which the principal Acts apply; or

(*b*) of premises to be let as a separate dwelling on terms which will, in the opinion of the court, afford to the tenant security of tenure reasonably equivalent to the security afforded by the principal Acts in the case of a dwelling-house to which those Acts apply,

and is, in the opinion of the court, reasonably suitable to the needs of the tenant and his family as regards proximity to place of work, and either—

(i) similar as regards rental and extent to the accommodation afforded by dwelling-houses provided in the neighbourhood by any housing authority for persons whose needs as regards extent are, in the opinion of the court, similar to those of the tenant and his family; or

(ii) otherwise reasonably suitable to the means of the tenant and to the needs of the tenant and his family as regards extent and character.

(4) For the purposes of the last foregoing subsection **any certificate of a housing authority stating**—

(*a*) the extent of the accommodation afforded by dwelling-houses provided by it to meet the needs of tenants with families of such number as may be specified in the certificate; and

(*b*) the amount of the rent charged by it for dwelling-houses affording accommodation of that extent,

shall be conclusive evidence of the facts so stated.

(5) **Any document purporting to be a certificate** of a housing authority named therein issued for the purposes of this section and to be signed by the clerk to that authority **shall be received in evidence and be deemed to be such a certificate** without further proof unless the contrary is shown.

LOCAL GOVERNMENT ACT, 1933.

23 & 24 Geo. 5, c. 51.

233.—(1) Any sum which is certified by a district auditor to be due and has become payable shall, on complaint made or action taken by or under the direction of the district auditor, be recoverable either summarily or otherwise as a civil debt.

(2) In any proceedings for the recovery of such a sum, **a certificate signed by a district auditor shall be conclusive evidence of the facts certified,** and **a certificate signed by the treasurer** of the authority concerned **or other officer** whose duty it is to keep the accounts **that the sum certified to be due has not been paid to him shall be conclusive evidence of non-payment, unless it is proved** that the sum certified to be due has been paid since the date of the certificate.

Unless the contrary is proved, **a certificate purporting to be signed** by a district auditor, or by the treasurer of the authority or other officer whose duty it is to keep the accounts, **shall be deemed to have been signed** by such auditor, treasurer or other officer, as the case may be.

252. The production of **a printed copy of a byelaw** purporting to be made by a local authority, **upon which is endorsed a certificate purporting to be signed** by the clerk of the authority *stating*—

(*a*) that the byelaw was made by the authority;

(*b*) that the copy is a true copy of the byelaw;

(*c*) that on a specified date the byelaw was confirmed by the authority named in the certificate or, as the case may require, was sent to the Secretary of State and has not been disallowed;

(*d*) the date, if any, fixed by the confirming authority for the coming into operation of the byelaw;

shall be prima facie evidence of the facts stated in the certificate, and without proof of the handwriting or official position of any person purporting to sign a certificate in pursuance of this section.

ARBITRATION ACT, 1934.

24 & 25 Geo. 5, c. 14.

8.—(1) The Court shall have, for the purpose of and in relation to a reference, the same power of making orders in respect of any of the matters set out in the First Schedule to this Act as it has for the purpose of and in relation to an action or matter in the Court: . . .

FIRST SCHEDULE.

MATTERS IN RESPECT OF WHICH THE COURT MAY MAKE ORDERS.

(2) Discovery of documents and interrogatories:

(3) The giving of evidence by affidavit:

(4) Examination on oath of any witness before an officer of the Court or any other person, and the issue of a commission or request for the examination of a witness out of the jurisdiction:

(7) The detention, preservation or inspection of any property or thing which is the subject of the reference or as to which any question may arise therein, and authorising for any of the purposes aforesaid any persons to enter upon or into any land or building in the possession of any party to the reference, or authorising any samples to be taken or any observation to be made or experiment to be tried which may be necessary or expedient for the purpose of obtaining full information or evidence.

Note.—The jurisdiction conferred on the Court by this section may be exercised by a Judge in chambers or a Master of the King's Bench Division (Rules of the Supreme Court, Order 54, rr. 11A and 12). As to the Court's powers, see *ante*, pp. 414, 418-9.

ROAD TRAFFIC ACT, 1934.

24 & 25 Geo. 5, c. 50.

33.—(2) **Particulars of a conviction endorsed on a licence** to drive a motor vehicle granted under Part I of the principal Act may be produced as **prima facie evidence of the conviction.**

Note.—The principal Act is the Road Traffic Act, 1930. As to proof of convictions in ordinary cases, see *post*, p. 561.

COUNTY COURTS ACT, 1934.

24 & 25 Geo. 5, c. 53.

23.—(1) **The registrar for every district shall keep or cause to be kept such records** of and in relation to proceedings in the court for that district as the Lord Chancellor may by regulations prescribe.

(2) **Any entry in a book or other document required** by the said regulations to be kept for the purposes of this section, **or a copy thereof purporting to be signed and certified as a true copy by the registrar, shall** at all times without further proof **be admitted in any court or place whatsoever as evidence** of the entry and of the proceeding referred to thereby and of the regularity of that proceeding.

82.—(1) The **High Court shall,** on application made in manner prescribed by rules of the Supreme Court, **have the same power to issue a commission, request or order to examine witnesses abroad for** the purpose of proceedings in **a county court** as it has for the purpose of an action or matter in the High Court.

83.—(1) **In any proceedings** pending **before a county court, the judge may,** if he thinks fit, upon application on affidavit by any party, **issue an order** under his hand **for bringing up before the court any person** (hereafter in this section referred to as a "prisoner") **confined in any place under any sentence** or under commitment for trial or otherwise, to be examined as a witness in the proceedings: . . .

175.—(1) **Where any summons** or other process **issued from a county court is served by the bailiff** of any court, **the service may**

be proved by endorsement on a copy of the summons or process under the hand of that bailiff showing the fact and mode of the service.

176.—(1) **All summonses** issuing out of a county court, **and all such other documents** so issuing as may be prescribed, **shall be sealed** or stamped with the seal of the court.

(2) **All such summonses and other documents purporting to be sealed** as aforesaid **shall,** in England, **be received in evidence** without further proof thereof.

Note.—**S. 23.** As to proof of judicial proceedings generally, see *post*, p. 562.

S. 82. As to the powers of the High Court, see *ante*, pp. 414-5.

S. 83. As to bringing up a prisoner before the High Court, *see ante*, p. 419.

UNEMPLOYMENT INSURANCE ACT, 1935.

25 Geo. 5, c. 8.

89.—(1) **The wife or husband of a person charged** with an offence under this Act **may be called as a witness** either for the prosecution or defence and **without the consent of the person charged.**

Note.—As to competency and compellability of husbands and wives as witnesses generally, see *ante*, p. 273.

POST OFFICE (AMENDMENT) ACT, 1935.

25 Geo. 5, c. 15.

11.—(6) Where the consent or order of the Postmaster-General is required to or for any prosecution, **an instrument purporting to be executed by an officer of the Post Office** duly authorised in that behalf by or under this Act **and stating that the prosecution has been consented to or ordered by the Postmaster-General shall be sufficient evidence of that fact,** unless the contrary is shown.

Note.—Cf. a similar provision in the Criminal Justice Act, 1925, s. 34 (*ante*, p. 515).

MONEY PAYMENTS (JUSTICES PROCEDURE) ACT, 1935.

25 & 26 Geo. 5, c. 46.

12. **A statement in writing** to the effect **that wages of any amount have been paid** to a person during any period, **purporting to be signed by or on behalf of his employer, shall be prima facie evidence of the facts therein stated in any proceedings** taken before justices of the peace—

(*a*) **for the enforcement** of the payment by the person to whom the wages are stated to have been paid **of a sum adjudged to be paid by a** conviction or order of a **court of summary jurisdiction ;**

(*b*) **on any application** made by or against that person for the making of an order in any matter of **bastardy** or an order enforceable as an affiliation order, or for the enforcement, variation, revocation, discharge or revival of any such order ; or

(*c*) **for the enforcement** of the payment by that person of any sum or sums to which he has been **rated or assessed.**

PUBLIC HEALTH (LONDON) ACT, 1936.

26 Geo. 5 & 1 Edw. 8, c. 50.

PART XIII.

CHILD LIFE PROTECTION.

266. **Where,** in proceedings for an offence under this Part of this Act, it is alleged that the person in respect of whom the alleged offence was committed was under, or had attained, any specified age, and **it appears to the court that,** at the date of the commission of the alleged offence, **the said person was under, or had attained, the specified age,** as the case may be, **he shall,** for the purposes of this Part of this Act, **be deemed** at that date **to have been under, or to have attained, that age,** as the case may be, unless the contrary is proved.

Note.—Compare a similar provision in the Children and Young Persons Act, 1933, s. 99 (*ante*, p. 529).

For further Statutes on Evidence, see Appendix IV, *post*, **p. 577, ff.**

PART III.

RULES OF THE SUPREME COURT, 1883, RELATING TO EVIDENCE.

ORDER XIX.

Pleading Generally.

13. Every allegation of fact in any pleading, not being a petition or summons, if not denied specifically or by necessary implication, or stated to be not admitted in the pleading of the opposite party, shall be taken to be admitted, except as against an infant, lunatic, or person of unsound mind not so found by inquisition.

25. Neither party need in any pleading allege any matter of fact which the law presumes in his favour or as to which the burden of proof lies upon the other side, unless the same has first been specifically denied (*e.g.*, consideration for a bill of exchange where the plaintiff sues only on the bill, and not for the consideration as a substantive ground of claim).

ORDER XXX.

Summons for Directions.

2.—(1) Upon the hearing of the summons the powers of the court or a judge shall include those specified in this rule.

(2) The court or a judge may—

(*a*) make such order as may be just with respect to any of the following matters, that is to say, discovery and inspection of documents, interrogatories, inspections of real or personal property, and admissions of fact or of documents;

(*c*) subject to paragraph (3) of this rule, order that any particular fact or facts may be proved by affidavit, or that the affidavit of any witness may be read at the trial on such conditions as the court or judge may think reasonable, or that any witness whose attendance in court ought for some sufficient cause to be dispensed with, be examined before a Commissioner or Examiner;

(*d*) order that evidence of any particular fact or facts, to be specified in the order, shall be given at the trial by statement on oath of information and belief, or by production of documents or entries in books, or by copies of documents or entries or otherwise as the court or judge may direct;

(*e*) order that no more than a specified number of expert witnesses may be called;

and may revoke or vary any such order.

(3) Where it appears to the court or judge that any party **reasonably** desires the production of a witness for cross-examination, and that such witness can be produced, an order shall not be made authorising the evidence of such witness to be given by affidavit, but the expenses of such witness at the trial shall be specially reserved.

Note.—The word "reasonably" which was substituted for "bona fide" by the Rules Committee in 1937, and confirmed by the Evidence Act, 1938, s. 5, effects an important alteration of the law, in that the former absolute right to cross-examine the deponent is abolished, and the Judge now has an absolute discretion in the matter.

ORDER XXXI.

Discovery and Inspection.

1. In any cause or matter the plaintiff or defendant by leave of the court or a judge may deliver interrogatories in writing for the examination of the opposite parties, or any one or more of such parties, and such interrogatories when delivered shall have a note at the foot thereof, stating which of such interrogatories each of such persons is required to answer: Provided that interrogatories which do not relate to any matters in question in the cause or matter shall be deemed irrelevant, notwithstanding that they might be admissible on the oral cross-examination of a witness.

2. A copy of the interrogatories proposed to be delivered shall be delivered with the summons or notice of application for leave to deliver them, at least two clear days before the hearing thereof (unless in any case the court or judge shall think fit to dispense with this requirement) and the particular interrogatories sought to be delivered shall be submitted to and considered by the court or judge. In deciding upon such application, the court or judge shall take into account any offer, which may be made by the party sought to be interrogated, to deliver particulars, or to make admissions, or to produce documents relating to any matter in question, and leave shall be given as to such only of the interrogatories as shall be considered necessary either for disposing fairly of the cause or matter or for saving costs.

8. Interrogatories shall be answered by affidavit to be filed within ten days, or within such other time as a judge may allow.

19a.—(1) Where inspection of any business books is applied for, the court or a judge may, if they or he shall think fit, instead of ordering inspection of the original books, order a copy of any entries therein to be furnished and verified by the affidavit of some person who has examined the copy with the original entries, and such affidavit shall state whether or not there are in the original book any and what erasures, interlineations, or alterations. Provided that, notwithstanding that such copy has been supplied, the court or a judge may order inspection of the book from which the copy was made.

24. Any party may, at the trial of a cause, matter, or issue, use in evidence any one or more of the answers or any part of an answer of the opposite party to interrogatories without putting in the others or the whole of such answer: Provided always, that in such case the judge may look at the whole of the answers, and if he shall be of opinion that any others of them are so connected with those put in that the last-mentioned answers ought not to be used without them, he may direct them to be put in.

ORDER XXXII.

Admissions.

1. Any party to a cause or matter may give notice, by his pleading, or otherwise in writing, that he admits the truth of the whole or any part of the case of any other party.

2.—(1) Either party may by notice in writing at any time not later than nine days before the day for which the notice of trial has been given call upon any other party to admit any document, saving all just exceptions, and if the other party desires to challenge the authenticity of the document, he shall within six days after service of such notice, give notice that he does not admit the document and requires it to be proved at the trial.

(2) If such other party refuses or neglects to give notice of non-admission within the time prescribed in the last preceding paragraph, he shall be deemed to have admitted the document, unless the court or a judge otherwise orders.

4. Any party may, by notice in writing, at any time not later than nine days before the day for which notice of trial has been given, call on any other party to admit, for the purposes of the cause, matter, or issue only, any specific fact or facts mentioned in such notice. . . . Provided that any admission made in pursuance of such notice is to be deemed to be made only for the purposes of the particular cause, matter, or issue, and not as an admission to be used against the party on any other occasion or in favour of any person other than the party giving the notice; provided also, that the court or a judge may at any time allow any party to amend

or withdraw any admission so made on such terms as may be just.

7. An affidavit of the solicitor or his clerk, of the due signature of any admissions made in pursuance of any notice to admit documents or facts, shall be sufficient evidence of such admissions, if evidence thereof be required.

ORDER XXXIII.

Issues, Inquiries, and Accounts.

3. The court or a judge may, either by the judgment or order directing an account to be taken or by any subsequent order, give special directions with regard to the mode in which the account is to be taken or vouched, and in particular may direct that in taking the account, the books of account in which the accounts in question have been kept shall be taken as *prima facie* evidence of the truth of the matters therein contained, with liberty to the parties interested to take such objections thereto as they may be advised.

ORDER XXXVI.

Trial.

VII. *Proceedings at Trial.*

31. If, when a trial is called on, the plaintiff appears, and the defendant does not appear, then the plaintiff may prove his claim, so far as the burden of proof lies upon him.

32. If, when a trial is called on, the defendant appears, and the plaintiff does not appear, the defendant, if he has no counter-claim, shall be entitled to judgment dismissing the action, but if he has a counter-claim, then he may prove such counter-claim so far as the burden of proof lies upon him.

36. Upon a trial with a jury, the addresses to the jury shall be regulated as follows: the party who begins, or his counsel, shall be allowed at the close of his case, if his opponent does not announce any intention to adduce evidence, to address the jury a second time for the purpose of summing up the evidence, and the opposite party, or his counsel, shall be allowed to open his case, and also to sum up the evidence, if any, and the right to reply shall be the same as heretofore.

37. In actions for libel or slander, in which the defendant does not by his defence assert the truth of the statement complained of, the defendant shall not be entitled on the trial to give evidence in chief, with a view to mitigation of damages, as to the circumstances under which the libel or slander was published, or as to the character of the plaintiff, without the leave of the judge, unless seven days at

least before the trial he furnishes particulars to the plaintiff of the matters as to which he intends to give evidence.

38. The judge may in all cases disallow any questions put in cross-examination of any party or other witness which may appear to him to be vexatious, and not relevant to any matter proper to be inquired into in the cause or matter.

49. Subject to any order to be made by the court or judge ordering the same, evidence shall be taken at any trial before a referee, and the attendance of witnesses may be enforced by *subpœna*, and every such trial shall be conducted in the same manner, as nearly as circumstances will admit, as trials are conducted before a judge.

IX. *Writ of Inquiry and Reference as to Damages.*

56. The provisions of Rules . . . 36 and 37 of this Order, shall, with the necessary modifications, apply to an inquiry, pursuant to a writ of inquiry.

ORDER XXXVII.

I. Evidence Generally.

1. In the absence of any agreement in writing between the solicitors of all parties, and subject to these Rules, the witnesses at the trial of any action or at any assessment of damages shall be examined *viva voce* and in open court: Provided that the judge at the trial may . . . exercise the powers conferred by Order XXX, Rule 2 (2) (*a*), (*c*), (*d*), (*e*), (*g*) and (*h*), subject, however, to the provisions of paragraph (3) of that Rule.

3. An order to read evidence taken in another cause or matter shall not be necessary, but such evidence may, saving all just exceptions, be read on *ex parte* applications by leave of the court or a judge, to be obtained at the time of making any such application and in any other case upon the party desiring to use such evidence giving two days' previous notice to the other parties of his intention to read such evidence.

4. Office copies of all writs, records, pleadings, and documents filed in the High Court of Justice shall be admissible in evidence in all causes and matters and between all persons or parties, to the same extent as the original would be admissible.

II. Examination of Witnesses.

5. The court or a judge may, in any cause or matter where it shall appear necessary for the purposes of justice, make any order for the examination upon oath before the court or judge or any officer

of the court, or any other person, and at any place, of any witness or person, and may empower any party to any such cause or matter to give such deposition in evidence therein on such terms, if any, as the court or a judge may direct.

6A. If in any case the court or a judge shall so order, there shall be issued a request to examine witnesses in lieu of a commission.

7. The court or a judge may in any cause or matter at any stage of the proceedings order the attendance of any person for the purpose of producing any writings or other documents named in the order which the court or judge may think fit to be produced: Provided that no person shall be compelled to produce under any such order any writing or other document which he could not be compelled to produce at the hearing or trial.

10. Where any witness or person is ordered to be examined before any officer of the court, or before any person appointed for the purpose, the person taking the examination shall be furnished by the party on whose application the order was made with a copy of the writ and pleadings, if any, or with a copy of the documents necessary to inform the person taking the examination of the questions at issue between the parties.

11. The examination shall take place in the presence of the parties, their counsel, solicitors, or agents, and the witnesses shall be subject to cross-examination and re-examination.

12. The depositions taken before an officer of the court, or before any other person appointed to take the examination, shall be taken down in writing by or in the presence of the examiner, not ordinarily by question and answer, but so as to represent as nearly as may be the statement of the witness, and when completed shall be read over to the witness and signed by him in the presence of the parties, or such of them as may think fit to attend. If the witness shall refuse to sign the depositions, the examiner shall sign the same. The examiner may put down any particular question or answer if there should appear any special reason for doing so, and may put any question to the witness as to the meaning of any answer, or as to any matter arising in the course of the examination. Any questions which may be objected to shall be taken down by the examiner in the depositions, and he shall state his opinion thereon to the counsel, solicitors, or parties, and shall refer to such statement in the depositions, but he shall not have power to decide upon the materiality or relevancy of any question

14. If any witness shall object to any question which may be put to him before an examiner, the question so put, and the objection of the witness thereto, shall be taken down by the examiner, and

transmitted by him to the Central Office to be there filed, and the validity of the objection shall be decided by the court or a judge.

16. When the examination of any witness before any examiner shall have been concluded, the original depositions, authenticated by the signature of the examiner, shall be transmitted by him to the Central Office, and there filed.

18. Except where by this Order otherwise provided, or directed by the court or a judge, no deposition shall be given in evidence at the hearing or trial of the cause or matter without the consent of the party against whom the same may be offered, unless the court or judge is satisfied that the deponent is dead, or beyond the jurisdiction of the court, or unable from sickness or other infirmity to attend the hearing or trial, in any of which cases the depositions certified under the hand of the person taking the examination shall be admissible in evidence saving all just exceptions without proof of the signature to such certificate.

19. Any officer of the court, or other person directed to take the examination of any witness or person, or any person nominated or appointed to take the examination of any witness or person pursuant to the provisions of any convention now made or which may hereafter be made with any foreign country, may administer oaths.

20. Any party in any cause or matter may by *subpœna ad testificandum* or *duces tecum* require the attendance of any witness before an officer of the court, or other person appointed to take the examination, for the purpose of using his evidence upon any proceeding in the cause or matter in like manner as such witness would be bound to attend and be examined at the hearing or trial; and any party or witness having made an affidavit to be used or which shall be used on any proceeding in the cause or matter shall be bound on being served with such *subpœna* to attend before such officer or person for cross-examination.

21. Evidence taken subsequently to the hearing or trial of any cause or matter shall be taken as nearly as may be in the same manner as evidence taken at or with a view to a trial.

22. The practice with reference to the examination, cross-examination, and re-examination of witnesses at a trial shall extend and be applicable to evidence taken in any cause or matter at any stage.

23. The practice of the court with respect to evidence at a trial, when applied to evidence to be taken before an officer of the court or other person in any cause or matter after the hearing or trial, shall be subject to any special directions which may be given in any case.

24. No affidavit or deposition filed or made before issue joined in any cause or matter shall without special leave of the court or a

judge be received at the hearing or trial thereof, unless within one month after issue joined, or within such longer time as may be allowed by special leave of the court or a judge, notice in writing shall have been given by the party intending to use the same to the opposite party of his intention in that behalf.

25. All evidence taken at the hearing or trial of any cause or matter may be used in any subsequent proceedings in the same cause or matter.

IV. Perpetuating Testimony.

35. Any person who would under the circumstances alleged by him to exist become entitled, upon the happening of any future event, to any honour, title, dignity, or office, or to any estate or interest in any property, real or personal, the right or claim to which cannot by him be brought to trial before the happening of such event, may commence an action to perpetuate any testimony, which may be material for establishing such right or claim.

ORDER XXXVIII.

I. Affidavits and Depositions.

1. Upon any motion, petition, or summons evidence may be given by affidavit; but the court or a judge may, on the application of either party, order the attendance for cross-examination of the person making any such affidavit.

3. Affidavits shall be confined to such facts as the witness is able of his own knowledge to prove. . . . Provided that on interlocutory proceedings or with leave under Order XXX, rule 2 (see *ante*, p. 537), an affidavit may contain statements of information and belief, with the sources and grounds thereof.

21. All affidavits which have been previously made and read in court upon any proceeding in a cause or matter may be used before the judge in chambers.

28. When the evidence is taken by affidavit, any party desiring to cross-examine a deponent who has made an affidavit filed on behalf of the opposite party may serve upon the party by whom such affidavit has been filed, a notice in writing, requiring the production of the deponent for cross-examination at the trial, such notice to be served at any time before the expiration of fourteen days next after the end of the time allowed for filing affidavits in reply, or within such time as in any case the court or a judge may specially appoint;

and unless such deponent is produced accordingly, his affidavit shall not be used as evidence unless by the special leave of the court or a judge. . . .

ORDER XXXIX.

New Trial.

6. A new trial shall not be granted on the ground of misdirection or of the improper admission or rejection of evidence, or because the verdict of the jury was not taken upon a question which the judge at the trial was not asked to leave to them, unless in the opinion of the Court of Appeal some substantial wrong or miscarriage has been thereby occasioned; and if it appears to the Court of Appeal that such wrong or miscarriage affects part only of the matter in controversy, or some or one only of the parties, the Court of Appeal may give final judgment as to part thereof, or as to some or one only of the parties, and direct a new trial as to the other part only or as to the other party or parties.

ORDER L.

Interlocutory Orders.

3. It shall be lawful for the court or a judge, upon the application of any party to a cause or matter, and upon such terms as may be just, to make any order for the detention, preservation, or inspection of any property or thing, being the subject of such cause or matter, or as to which any question may arise therein, and for all or any of the purposes aforesaid, to authorise any persons to enter upon or into any land or building in the possession of any party to such cause or matter, and for all or any of the purposes aforesaid to authorise any samples to be taken, or any observation to be made or experiment to be tried, which may be necessary or expedient for the purpose of obtaining full information or evidence.

4. It shall be lawful for any judge, by whom any cause or matter may be heard or tried with or without a jury, or before whom any cause or matter may be brought by way of appeal, to inspect any property or thing concerning which any question may arise therein.

5. The provisions of rule 3 of this order shall apply to inspection by a jury, and in such case the court or a judge may make all such orders upon the sheriff or other person as may be necessary to procure the attendance of a special or common jury at such time and place, and in such manner as they or he may think fit.

ORDER LV.

Chambers in the Chancery Division

IV.— *Assistance of Experts.*

19. The judge in chambers may, in such way as he thinks fit, obtain the assistance of accountants, merchants, engineers, actuaries, and other scientific persons the better to enable any matter at once to be determined, and he may act upon the certificate of any such person.

ORDER LVIII.

Appeals to the Court of Appeal.

4. The Court of Appeal shall have all the powers and duties as to amendment and otherwise of the High Court, together with full discretionary power to receive further evidence upon questions of fact, such evidence to be either by oral examination in court, by affidavit, or by deposition taken before an examiner or commissioner. Such further evidence may be given without special leave upon interlocutory applications, or in any case as to matters which have occurred after the date of the decision from which the appeal is brought. Upon appeals from a judgment after trial or hearing of any cause or matter upon the merits, such further evidence (save as to matters subsequent as aforesaid) shall be admitted on special grounds only, and not without special leave of the court. The Court of Appeal shall have power to draw inferences of fact and to give any judgment and make any order which ought to have been made, and to make such further or other order as the case may require. The powers aforesaid may be exercised by the said court, notwithstanding that the notice of appeal may be that part only of the decision may be reversed or varied, and such powers may also be exercised in favour of all or any of the respondents or parties, although such respondents or parties may not have appealed from or complained of the decision. . . .

11. When any question of fact is involved in an appeal, the evidence taken in the court below bearing on such question shall, subject to any special order, be brought before the Court of Appeal as follows :—

(a) As to any evidence taken by affidavit, by the production of printed copies of such of the affidavits as have been printed, and office copies of such of them as have not been printed ;

(*b*) As to any evidence given orally—
(i) where the judge has intimated that in the event of an appeal his note will be sufficient, by a copy of the judge's note; and
(ii) in any other case by a copy of the transcript of the official shorthand note or by such other means as the Court of Appeal shall direct.

Note.—The rule was altered in 1940 consequent upon the institution of the official shorthand writer.

13. If, upon the hearing of an appeal, a question arise as to the ruling or direction of the judge to a jury or assessors, the court shall have regard to verified notes or other evidence, and to such other materials as the court may deem expedient.

ORDER LIX.

Divisional Courts.

7. On any motion by way of appeal from an inferior court, the court to which any such appeal may be brought shall have power to draw all inferences of fact which might have been drawn in the court below, and to give any judgment and make any order which ought to have been made. No such motion shall succeed on the ground merely of misdirection or improper reception or rejection of evidence, unless, in the opinion of the court, substantial wrong or miscarriage has been thereby occasioned in the court below.

8. On any motion by way of appeal from an inferior court, the court to which any such appeal may be brought shall have power, if the notes of the judge of such inferior court are not produced, to hear and determine such appeal upon any other evidence or statement of what occurred before such judge which the court may deem sufficient.

ORDER LXI.

Central Office.

7. All copies, certificates, and other documents appearing to be sealed with a seal of the Central Office shall be presumed to be office copies or certificates or other documents issued from the Central Office, and if duly stamped may be received in evidence, and no signature or other formality, except the sealing with a seal of the Central Office, shall be required for the authentication of any such copy, certificate, or other document.

APPENDICES.

I. The Judges' Rules.

II. Table of Admissibility.

III. Modes of Proof of Particular Matters.

IV. Supplementary Matters.

APPENDIX NUMBER I.

THE JUDGES' RULES.

1. When a police officer is endeavouring to discover the author of a crime there is no objection to his putting questions in respect thereof to any person or persons, whether suspected or not, from whom he thinks that useful information can be obtained.

2. Whenever a police officer has made up his mind to charge a person with a crime, he should first caution such person before asking any question or any further questions, as the case may be.

3. Persons in custody should not be questioned without the usual caution being first administered.

4. If the prisoner wishes to volunteer any statement, the usual caution should be administered. It is desirable that the last two words ("against you") of such caution should be omitted, and that the caution should end with the words "be given in evidence".

5. The caution to be administered to a prisoner, when he is formally charged, should therefore be in the following words: "*Do you wish to say anything in answer to the charge? You are not obliged to say anything unless you wish to do so, but whatever you say will be taken down in writing and may be given in evidence.*" Care should be taken to avoid any suggestion that his answers can only be used in evidence *against* him, as this may prevent an innocent person making a statement which might assist to clear him of the charge.

6. A statement made by a prisoner before there is time to caution him is not rendered inadmissible in evidence merely by reason of no caution having been given, but in such a case he should be cautioned as soon as possible.

7. A prisoner making a voluntary statement must not be cross-examined, and no questions should be put to him about it except for the purpose of removing ambiguity in what he has actually said. For instance, if he has mentioned an hour without saying whether it was morning or evening, or has given a day of the week and day

of the month which do not agree, or has not made it clear to what individual or what place he intended to refer in some part of his statement, he may be questioned sufficiently to clear up the point.

8. When two or more persons are charged with the same offence and statements are taken separately from the persons charged, the police should not read these statements to the other persons charged, but each of such persons should be furnished by the police with a copy of such statements and nothing should be said or done by the police to invite a reply. If the person charged desires to make a statement in reply, the usual caution should be administered.

9. Any statement made in accordance with the above rules should, whenever possible, be taken down in writing and signed by the person making it after it has been read to him and he has been invited to make any corrections he may wish.

Note.—These Rules are printed here for convenience, but it should be appreciated that though frequently mentioned in trials they are in strictness administrative only and cannot alter the law (see *ante*, p. 209).

APPENDIX

TABLE OF

(The figures in brackets re

MATTERS ADMISSIBLE.	FOR PURPOSES SPECIFIED.
Absence for seven years ..	To raise presumption of death of absent person.
Do.	To prove death of *cestui que vie* .. ..
Do.	To rebut charge of bigamy .. .. ..
Admission	To prove facts admitted .. .. ..
Books, generally	As admission .. ..
Do.	As declaration against interest .. ..
Books, log	As declaration in course of duty .. ..
Do.	As evidence of matter stated in pursuance of Merchant Shipping Act, 1894.
Books, tradesmen's ..	As declaration in course of duty .. ..
Do.	As evidence of goods delivered or work done, under Shop Book Debts Act, 1609.
Books, public	To prove statements therein .. .. ..
Books, wages	To prove wages paid .. .. ..
Character of plaintiff ..	To prove or disprove fact in issue .. ..
Do.	To regulate damages
Do.	Do. .. ..
Character of person seduced	Do. .. ..
Character of prisoner ..	To support or rebut charge .. .. ..
Do.	To prove intent to commit felony .. ..

BER II.

ISSIBILITY.

pages of this book.)

IN CASES SPECIFIED.	UNDER CONDITIONS SPECIFIED.
enerally	If witness likely to have heard from absent person (30).
Recovery of land	No conditions (33).
Bigamy	Do. (33).
Generally	Do. (170).
Do.	Do. (171).
Do.	See "Declarations against Interest" (216).
Do.	See "Declarations in course of duty" (214).
Do.	If made in official log in accordance with Merchant Shipping Act, 1894 (476).
Do.	See "Declarations in course of duty" (211).
n action by shopkeeper ..	If made within one year, unless action between tradesman and tradesman (427).
Generally	No conditions (261).
Proceedings under Children and Young Persons Act, 1933.	Do. (529).
Where plaintiff's character in issue, *e.g.*, defamation.	Do. (101, 115).
Where character material to damages, *e.g.*, breach of promise, defamation where truth not pleaded.	No conditions, except 7 days' notice in defamation (101, 117, 540).
Damages for adultery ..	No conditions (101, 120).
Seduction	Do. (101, 120).
Criminal	If prisoner introduces the evidence (101, 121).
Vagrancy	No conditions (102, 460).

MATTERS ADMISSIBLE.	FOR PURPOSES SPECIFIED.
Character of prisoner ..	To prove leading persistently dishonest criminal life.
Do.	To prove purpose prejudicial to State
Character of prosecutrix ..	To rebut charge .. .. ..
Character of wife	To regulate damages .. .. ..
Character of witness ..	To discredit witness .. .. ..
Circumstances of person ..	To prove or disprove act .. ..
Cohabitation	To prove marriage .. .. ..
Complaints	To corroborate prosecutor .. ..
Conduct	To prove act alleged .. .. ..
Do.	Do. .. ..
Do.	To prove state of mind .. ..
Do.	As admission .. ..
Do.	As estoppel .. ..
Do.	As declaration .. ..
Confession	To prove crime .. ..
Conviction	As declaration of public or general right
Conviction of plaintiff ..	To prove commission of crime .. ..
Conviction of prisoner :—	
(*a*) Of any crime ..	To prove plea of *autrefois convict* ..
Do.	To prove essential part of charge ..
Do.	To adjust sentence .. .. ..
Do.	To rebut evidence of prisoner's good characte
(*b*) Of fraud or dishonesty	To show guilty knowledge .. ..
Conviction of witness ..	To discredit witness .. .. ..
Course of business or duty ..	To prove act done in private office ..
Do.	To raise presumption of act done in publi office.
Custom	To attach obligations to contracting partie explain terms, etc.
Declaration as to cause of death.	To prove circumstances of declarant's deat
Declaration in course of duty	To prove facts stated strictly in accordanc with duty.
Declaration against pecuniary interest.	To prove any facts stated in declaration .
Declaration against proprietary interest.	To prove facts stated against such interes

IN CASES SPECIFIED.	UNDER CONDITIONS SPECIFIED.
Habitual criminality ..	No conditions (102, 493).
pying	Do. (102, 496).
Rape and assaults on females	Do. (101, 124).
Damages for adultery ..	Do. (101, 120).
Generally	If such witness called by opponent (320).
Do.	No conditions (64).
Do.	Do. (97).
Rape and similar offences ..	After prosecutor's evidence of facts (83).
Generally	If part of same transaction (66).
Do.	If connected with act alleged (61, 106).
Do.	If similar, or part of system (107).
Do.	If subsequent to act alleged (61, 189).
Do.	If intended or likely to induce person to act (50).
Pedigree cases	On proof of relationship and death of declarant (232).
Criminal	On proof that it was free and voluntary (197).
Where public or general right in question.	On proof of competency of Court (236, 240).
Civil	If person convicted or any claiming through him is party to suit (102, 125).
Criminal	On proof of identity of charges (103).
Do.	No conditions (103, 492).
Do.	After verdict of guilty (104).
Any offence	If prisoner gives evidence of good character and indictment charges previous conviction for felony (103, 450).
Receiving stolen goods ..	After proof of receiving, and such conviction within 5 years (103, 501).
Generally	If witness denies conviction (314, 451).
Do.	No conditions (91).
Do.	Do. (34).
Do.	If custom general as regards subject-matter (392, 395).
Homicide of declarant ..	On proof of (*a*) declarant's expectation of death at time, (*b*) declarant's death (244).
Generally	On proof of (*a*) declarant's duty to third person to do act and state fact as appears, (*b*) absence of any interest to misrepresent, (*c*) declarant's death (211).
Do.	On proof of (*a*) declarant's apparently conflicting pecuniary interest, (*b*) declarant's death (216).
Where question as to interest in land.	On proof of (*a*) declarant's possession of land, (*b*) declarant's death (221).

MATTERS ADMISSIBLE.	FOR PURPOSES SPECIFIED.
Declaration as to pedigree	To prove relationship, or any fact on whi[ch] it depends.
Declaration as to public or general right.	To prove actual right itself .. ..
Declaration as to will ..	To prove validity or contents of will
Document, copy of	To prove contents or terms of original
Document, parol evidence of	Do. .. ..
Document, original of ..	To prove contents or terms .. ..
Judgments	To raise estoppel of parties thereto or the[ir] privies.
Do.	As evidence against parties thereto or the[ir] privies.
Long use or enjoyment ..	To prove lawful origin .. ..
Maps and plans, private ..	As admission .. ..
Do.	As declaration of public or general right
Maps and plans, public ..	To prove matters of public or general intere[st]
Motive	To prove act alleged .. .. ..
Opinion	To explain matters of science or art
Do.	To prove matters which cannot be sworn [to] positively.
Opportunity	To prove act alleged .. .. ..
Physical objects	To show their nature, qualities, etc.
Possession of property ..	To prove ownership .. .. ..
Do.	To prove larceny by, or guilty knowledge o[f] possessor.

IN CASES SPECIFIED.	UNDER CONDITIONS SPECIFIED.
Pedigree cases	On proof of (*a*) declarant's relationship to family, (*b*) declaration before dispute arose, (*c*) declarant's death (223).
Where public or general right in question.	On proof of (*a*) declarant's competency to make declaration, (*b*) declarant's death (233).
Where validity or contents of will in issue.	On proof of (*a*) declarant's identity with testator, (*b*) declarant's death (250).
Generally	On proof of (*a*) notice to opponent to produce original, or *subpœna* to stranger to produce original, and lawful refusal to produce, or loss or destruction of original, or physical or legal impossibility to produce original, (*b*) correctness of copy, (*c*) proper execution (345, 354).
Do.	Do. do. do.
Do.	On proof of (*a*) proper execution, or (*b*) production from proper custody if 30 years old (365, 372).
Do.	If pleaded as estoppel (41).
Do.	No conditions (46).
Do.	Do. (35).
Do.	If prepared by party against whom put in evidence, or his privies (171).
Where public or general right in question.	On proof of maker's competency as declarant (236).
Generally	If really a public document (264, 521).
Do.	No conditions (61).
Do.	On proof of competency of witness as expert (128, 130).
Do.	No conditions (128, 134).
Generally	No conditions (64).
Do.	On proof of identity (408).
Do.	No conditions (92).
Larceny or receiving stolen goods.	On proof that the goods were recently stolen (95).

MATTERS ADMISSIBLE.	FOR PURPOSES SPECIFIED.
Possession of property ..	To prove guilty knowledge of larceny of other goods.
Prejudice of witness	To discredit witness .. ..
Preparation	To prove act alleged .. ..
Proclamations, etc.	To prove statements therein .. .. ..
Public documents generally	Do. .. ..
Reputation	To prove marriage .. ..
Do.	As declaration in pedigree .. .. ..
Do.	As declaration of public or general right ..
Statements of party ..	To prove act alleged .. ..
Do.	As admission .. ..
Statements of prosecutor ..	To corroborate prosecutor .. .. ..
Statements of witness ..	To discredit witness .. ..
Statutes, public	To prove statements therein .. .. ..
Statutes, private	Do. .. ..
Do.	As declaration of public or general right ..
Things	To show their nature, qualities, etc. ..
Usages	To attach obligations to contracting parties, explain terms, etc.

IN CASES SPECIFIED.	UNDER CONDITIONS SPECIFIED.
Receiving stolen goods ..	On proof that the goods were stolen within previous 12 months (501).
Generally	If witness denies it on cross-examination (314, 319).
Do.	No conditions (61).
Do.	Do. (264).
Do.	Do. (261).
Do.	Do. (97).
Pedigree cases	On proof of reputation in family before dispute arose (231).
Where public or general right in question.	On proof of reputation in neighbourhood before dispute arose (233).
Generally	If part of same transaction (67).
Do.	If subsequent to act alleged (61, 170).
Rape and similar offences	After prosecutor's evidence of facts (83).
Generally	If witness does not admit making statement, and his attention is drawn to the circumstances; and, in case of party's own witness, leave of Judge is obtained (314, 317).
Do.	No conditions (264).
Do.	If against parties thereto, or their privies (266).
Where public or general right in question.	No conditions (236).
Generally	On proof of identity (408).
Do.	If usage general as regards subject-matter (392, 395).

APPENDIX NUMBER III.

MODES OF PROOF OF PARTICULAR MATTERS.

(The figures in brackets refer to the pages of this book.)

1. **Acquittal.**—Copy of record, purporting to be certified by clerk or officer having custody of records (442).

2. **Administration, Letters of.**—Original, or exemplification or copy, purporting to be sealed with seal of Probate Court (508).

3. **Age of Person.**—1. Evidence of birth (*see below*, 8). 2. Inspection (408, 528-9, 536).

4. **Arrangement, Deed of.**—Copy or extract, purporting to be office copy or extract (Deeds of Arrangement Act, 1914, s. 25).

5. **Bankers' Books.**—Copy of entry, proved to be correct examined copy of entry made in ordinary course of business in ordinary book of bank under its control (462-3).

6. **Bankruptcy Matters.**—1. Copy of *London Gazette*—as to receiving order, adjudication, or anything stated in any notice inserted therein, *e.g.*, annulment, discharge, composition, release or removal of trustee (499). 2. Certificate of Board of Trade—as to appointment of trustee or facts certified thereby (500). 3. Minute signed by apparent chairman of meeting—as to proceedings thereat (499). 4. Deposition, or copy thereof, purporting to be sealed with seal of Court—as to matters deposed to (500). 5. Original or copy, appearing to be sealed with seal of Court or to be signed by Judge or certified by registrar—as to petitions, orders, certificates, affidavits or other documents (500).

7. **Bill of Sale.**—Copy of bill of sale and affidavit, purporting to be office copy thereof (Bills of Sale Act, 1878, s. 16).

8. **Birth.** — 1. Evidence of person present at event (217). 2. Declaration by deceased person (216, 223). 3. Certificate under the Births and Deaths Registration Acts, 1836 and 1874, or other statute. 4. Entry in official log book of birth at sea (477).

9. **Bye-law.**—Printed copy purporting to be made by the local authority endorsed with a certificate purporting to be signed by the clerk to the authority (532).

10. **Colonial Act of State.**—Copy, purporting to be sealed with seal of colony (441).

11. **Colonial Judicial Proceeding.**—Copy, purporting to be sealed with seal of Colonial Court, or signed by Judge of such Court (441).

12. **Colonial Law.**—1. Evidence of expert (132). 2. Case stated and remitted by Court (447).

13. **Colonial Statute.**—1. Copy, with certificate of clerk or proper officer of legislative body that it is a true copy, attached thereto (Colonial Laws Validity Act, 1865). 2. Copy, purporting to be printed by Government printer of colony (488).

14. **Company Matters.**—1. Certificate of registrar—as to incorporation, registration of charges or right to commence business (516). 2. Certificate under common seal—as to title to shares or stock (516). 3. Certificate of President of Board of Trade—as to orders, etc., of Board of Trade (519). 4. Order of Court—as to money due from contributory (517). 5. Register of members—as to matters authorised to be inserted therein (517). 6. Minutes signed by apparent chairman of meeting—as to proceedings thereat (517). 7. Copy of report of inspectors, authenticated by seal of company—as to opinion of inspectors (517). 8. Books and papers of company—as to matters recorded, between contributories in winding-up (518).

15. **Conviction.**—1. Copy of record, or certificate purporting to be certified, or signed, by clerk or officer having custody of records—as to indictable offences (442, 453, 460). 2. Copy of conviction, purporting to be signed by justice of peace, clerk or proper officer; or extract from register of Court, certified by clerk; or copy of minute or memorandum in register, purporting to be signed by clerk—as to summary convictions (460-1, 465, 497). 3. Endorsement on driving licence in case of motoring offences (534).

16. **Corporation Books.**—Mode specified by particular statute, if any, *i.e.*, generally by copy sealed with common seal of corporation; otherwise, apparently, by verified original, or examined or certified copy of entry of public nature, or verified original of entry of private nature (437, 442).

17. **County Court Proceedings.**—Entry in Court book, or copy signed and certified by registrar; or summons, etc., purporting to be sealed with seal of Court (534).

18. **Custom.**—1. Evidence of its actual existence, by witnesses acquainted with subject-matter (392). 2. Evidence of particular instances of its exercise (395). 3. Evidence of similar customs in

analogous trades, connected localities, etc. (396). 4. Declaration by deceased person (233).

19. **Death.**—1. Evidence of person who saw occurrence or body (30). 2. Declaration by deceased person (223). 3. Evidence of absence for seven years (30). 4. Certificate under the Births and Deaths Registration Acts, 1836 and 1874, or other statute. 5. Entry in official log book of death at sea (477).

20. **Foreign Act of State.**—Copy, purporting to be sealed with seal of foreign State (441).

21. **Foreign Judicial Proceeding.**—Copy, purporting to be sealed with seal of foreign Court, or signed by Judge of such Court (441).

22. **Foreign Law.**—1. Evidence of expert (132). 2. Case stated and remitted by Court (448).

23. **Government Orders, etc.**—Copy, purporting to be printed by Government printers, etc., or certified by specified officials; or copy of *Gazette* (437, 455, 465, 488).

24. **Handwriting.**—1. Evidence of witness who saw the act of writing or signing (366). 2. Opinion evidence of witness acquainted with the handwriting (367). 3. Comparison with other handwriting (369, 453).

25. **High Court Proceedings.**—Office copy, appearing to be sealed with seal of Central Office (541, 547).

26. **Intestacy.**—1. Declaration by deceased person (229). 2. Letters of administration (*see above*, 2).

27. **Judgment.**—*See above*, 11 (Colonial), 17 (County Court), 21 (Foreign), *and* 25 (High Court).

28. **Judicial Proceedings.**—(*See above*, 1, 6, 11, 15, 17, 21, 25, *and below*, 39).

29. **Legitimacy.**—1. Proof of birth during marriage of mother (28). 2. Declaration by deceased person (223).

30. **Marriage.**—1. Evidence of person present at ceremony (98). 2. Declaration by deceased person (223). 3. Cohabitation and reputation (97). 4. Certificate under the Births and Deaths Registration Act, 1836, or other statute. 5. Entry in official log book of marriage at sea (477).

31. **Naturalization.**—Original certificate or copy, certified by Secretary of State or person authorised by him (British Nationality and Status of Aliens Act, 1914, s. 21).

32. **Ownership.**—1. Production and proof of documents of title (92). 2. Possession or acts of ownership of the actual property (92). 3. Possession or acts of ownership of connected property (94). 4. Declaration by deceased person (223, 233).

33. **Partnership, Limited.**—Certificate of registration, or copy or extract, certified by registrar or assistant registrar (491).

34. **Relationship.**—1. Proof of facts under heads 8, 19 *and* 30, *above.* 2. Declaration by deceased person (223).

35. **Shipping, Merchant.**—1. Original register book, certificate of registry or endorsement thereon, declaration, official log book or document of Board of Trade, properly signed or sealed and produced from proper custody—as to matters stated therein by any officer in pursuance of his duties (476-9). 2. Copy of or extract from admissible documents, proved to be examined or purporting to be signed and certified as true copy or extract by officer with custody of original (479). 3. Deposition, signed by Judge, magistrate or consular officer, if witness cannot be found in United Kingdom (478).

36. **Signature.**—*See above,* 24.

37. **Statute, Private.**—Copy, purporting to be printed by King's printers, or under authority of Stationery Office (437, 465), unless passed after 1850, when no proof is required (472).

38. **Title.**—*See above,* 32.

39. **Trial.**—On prosecution for perjury—certificate of substance and effect of former trial, purporting to be signed by clerk or person having custody of records (495).

40. **Usage.**—*See above,* 18.

41. **Will.**—1. Of personal estate—probate, letters of administration with will annexed, exemplification, or copy, purporting to be sealed with seal of Probate Court (508). 2. Of real estate—if testator died after 1897, same as of personal estate; if before 1898, production of will, and proof by attesting witness if living (371), unless will thirty years old, and produced from proper custody (372).

APPENDIX NUMBER IV

SUPPLEMENTARY MATTERS.

PROOF—JUDICIAL NOTICE.

MATTERS OF COMMON KNOWLEDGE.

(*See* ante, *pp.* 22—23.)

McQUAKER v. GODDARD.

COURT OF APPEAL. 1940.

[1940] 1 K. B. 68.

No evidence need be given of facts which are judicially noticed, but the Judge may require books of reference to be cited to him, or may of his own motion consult such books.

In this case the plaintiff while visiting the defendant's zoological gardens was bitten by a camel. The question was whether the camel was a domestic or a wild animal for purposes of the law relating to liability for animals.

The following is from the Law Reports:—

Clauson, L.J. . . . I should like to add a word as to the part taken in the matter by the "evidence" (*the word is placed in inverted commas as it is clear in the context that the learned Judge considers it a misnomer in this connection*) given as to the facts of nature regarding camels. That "evidence" is not, it must be understood, in the ordinary sense evidence bearing upon an issue of fact. In my view the exact position is this. The Judge takes judicial notice of the ordinary course of nature, and in this particular case . . . in regard to the position of camels among other animals. (*The Judge then cited with approval Art.* 62 *of Stephen.*) "No evidence of any fact of which the Court will take judicial notice need be given by the party alleging its existence; but **the Judge upon being called upon to take judicial notice thereof** may, if he is unacquainted with such fact, **refer to any person or to any document or book of reference** for his satisfaction in relation thereto, or may refuse to take judicial notice thereof unless and until the party calling upon him to take such notice produces any such book of reference." From that statement it appears that the document or book of reference only enshrines the knowledge of those who are acquainted with the particular branch of natural phenomena.

Note.—The dividing line between the class of facts judicially noticed and those which require evidence to establish them is obscure, as is also the difference between the position of a person referred to by the Judge as described above, and one giving evidence proper. In *Turner* v. *Coates*, [1917] 1 K. B. 670, evidence in the strict sense seems to have been given regarding the habits of colts.

MATTERS OF WHICH PROOF IS NOT ALLOWED.

Estoppel by Conduct.

(*See* ante, *p.* 53.)

COVENTRY, SHEPPARD & CO. v. GREAT EASTERN RY. CO.

COURT OF APPEAL. 1883.

L. R. 11 Q. B. D. 776; 52 L. J. Q. B. 694; 49 L. T. 641.

A railway company negligently issued two delivery orders, not purporting to be duplicates, in respect of one consignment of wheat whereby a fraudulent person was enabled to obtain two advances of money as on two separate consignments. They were held to be estopped by their negligence from disputing that there were two consignments.

The following is from the Law Reports:—

BRETT, M.R. This judgment must be affirmed. It can be upheld only on the ground of estoppel, that is, that the defendants were prevented by their own conduct from relying upon the fact that there were not two parcels of goods . . . the negligence of the defendants was to the prejudice of the plaintiffs and allowed the fraud to be perpetrated upon them. It seems to me, therefore, that the defendants are estopped as against the plaintiffs, their negligence having been the immediate cause of the advance.

Note.—See also *London Joint-Stock Bank* v. *Macmillan* ([1918] A. C. 777), a case of banker and customer.

THE BURDEN OF PROOF.

UPON WHOM THE BURDEN LIES.

(*See* ante, *p.* 138.)

JOSEPH CONSTANTINE STEAMSHIP LINE, LTD. v IMPERIAL SMELTING CORPORATION, LTD., THE KINGSWOOD.

HOUSE OF LORDS. 1942.

L. R. [1942] A. C. 154; 110 L. J. K. B. 433; 165 L. T. 27; 57 T. L. R. 485.

The burden of proof, whether general or particular, lies normally upon the party who affirms and not upon the party who denies. Any departure from this rule must be justified by strong reasons.

A ship on charter was damaged by the explosion of her boiler while in harbour and before she sailed, with the result that she was unable to commence her voyage. The charterers claimed damages from the owners of the ship, whose defence was that the impossibility of performance resulting from the explosion amounted to frustration and they were not liable. The charterers contended that frustration did not arise unless the shipowners proved affirmatively that the explosion was not attributable to any default or negligence of theirs. In reply, the shipowners said that having proved that the explosion disabled the vessel, the defence of frustration protected them unless the charterers showed affirmatively some default which would deprive the shipowners of the benefit of this defence. There were at least three possible hypotheses which would account for the disaster, and the arbitrator came to the conclusion that the evidence did not warrant his finding which of these actually did cause it, nor was he able to find affirmatively that the shipowners' negligence or that of their servants did *not* cause the accident. In the circumstances, therefore, the decision turned on which side carried the burden of proof. The House of Lords held that it lay upon the charterers to establish affirmatively that there had been such negligence or default as would vitiate the defence of frustration, and that they had failed to discharge this burden.

The following is from the Law Reports:—

VISCOUNT MAUGHAM. . . . I think the burden of proof in any particular case depends on the circumstances under which the claim arises. **In general, the rule which applies is " Ei qui affirmat non ei qui negat incumbit probatio ".** It is an ancient rule founded on considerations of good sense and it should not be departed from without strong reasons. The position as to proof of non-responsibility for the event in such a case as the present is not very different from the position of a plaintiff in an action for negligence, where contributory negligence on his part is alleged. In such a case the plaintiff must prove that there was some negligent act or omission on the part of the defendant which caused or materially contributed to the injury, but it is for the defendant to prove affirmatively if he so contends that there was contributory negligence on the part of the person injured, though here again the onus may easily be shifted. . . . If I am right . . . that the onus of establishing absence of default did not rest on the shipowners, the mere possibility of default on their part is not sufficient to disentitle them to rely on the principle of frustration. (*The House therefore restored the judgment of the Court of trial to the effect that the shipowners' defence of frustration was good.*)

SCOTT v. LONDON DOCK CO.

EXCHEQUER CHAMBER. 1865.

34 L. J. Ex. 220; 2 H. & C. 596; 13 L. T. 148; 159 E. R. 665.

The mere proof that an accident happened may amount to prima facie evidence of negligence, and shift the burden to the defendant to prove that he was not negligent, but this rule only applies where the circumstances were under the control of the defendant, and the accident was one which would not normally occur with proper management.

The plaintiff, a customs officer, visited the defendants in the course of his duty when some bags of sugar fell on him from a crane fixed over the doorway and injured him.

The following is from the Law Journal Reports:—

ERLE, C.J. The majority of the Court have come to the following conclusion: that there must be reasonable evidence of negligence; that where the thing is solely under the management of the defendant or his servants and the accident is such as in the ordinary course of things does not happen to those who have the management . . . and use proper care, it affords reasonable evidence, **in the absence of explanation by the defendants,** that the accident arose from want of care.

Note.—This is the well-known principle of *res ipsa loquitur*. It is essential that the defendant had sole control of the thing (see *Britannia Hygienic Laundry* v. *Thorneycroft* (1925), 95 L. J. K. B. 237).

ORAL EVIDENCE.

Cross-Examination.

(*See* ante, *p.* 307.)

STIRLAND v. DIRECTOR OF PUBLIC PROSECUTIONS.

HOUSE OF LORDS. 1944.

L. R. [1944] A. C. 315; 113 L. J. K. B. 394; 171 L. T. 79; 60 T. L. R. 461.

The words "been charged with any offence" mean "brought before a criminal court" and do not extend to mere accusations which have not led to a prosecution. On the other hand, a prisoner who has made statements intended to show his good record may be cross-examined on the details of those statements to impeach his accuracy or veracity. The Judge has a discretion to exclude questions on this line which may be unduly prejudicial.

The prisoner was accused of forgery and gave evidence of his own good character and, in particular, of his good record with a previous employer. He also called a witness to say he had never been "charged" before. He was then cross-examined as to whether that employer had suspected and questioned him about a suggested forgery. *Held*, the question was improper and should have been disallowed, but that no miscarriage of justice had occurred.

The following is from the Law Reports:—

Lord Simon, L.C. . . . When the appellant denied that he had ever been "charged", he may fairly be understood to use the word in the sense it bears in the statute, and to mean that he had never previously been brought before a criminal Court. Questions as to whether his former employer had suspected him of forgery were not therefore any challenge to the veracity of what he had said. . . .

It is most undesirable that the rules which should govern cross-examination to credit of an accused person in the witness box should be complicated by refined distinctions . . . the following propositions seem to cover the ground. (I am omitting the rule which admits evidence tending to prove other offences where this evidence is relevant . . . as helping to negative accident or establish system, intent or the like.)

(1) The accused in the witness box may not be asked any question "tending to show that he had committed or been convicted of or been charged with any offence other than that wherewith he is then charged or is a bad character" unless one or other of the three conditions laid down in s. 1 (*f*) of the Act of 1898 is fulfilled.

(2) He may, however, be cross-examined as to any of the evidence he has given in chief, including statements as to his own good record, with a view to **testing his veracity** or accuracy or to showing he is not to be believed on his oath.

(3) An accused who puts his character in issue must be regarded as putting the **whole of his past record** in issue. He cannot assert his good character in certain respects without exposing himself to enquiry as to the rest of his record so far as this tends to disprove a claim for good character.

(4) An accused is not to be regarded as depriving himself of the protection of the section because the proper conduct of his defence necessitates the making of injurious reflections on the prosecutor or his witnesses.

(5) It is no disproof of good character that a man has been **suspected or accused** of a previous crime. Such questions as "Were you suspected?" or "Were you accused?" are inadmissible because they are **irrelevant** to the issue of character and can only be asked if the accused has sworn **expressly** to the contrary.

(6) The fact that a question put to the accused is irrelevant is in itself no reason for quashing a conviction, though it should have been disallowed by the Judge. . . .

Note.—The above report lays down a set of important and valuable general rules, but the actual *ratio decidendi* of the particular case is not altogether easy to follow. The accused said he was a loyal and faithful servant of his former employer, and that he was never suspected. In cross-examination the first question was why he had left that employer, and the answer was that he had literary interests outside his work which his employers did not like, and also the prospect of other employment. This would seem, *prima facie*, to invite and authorise cross-examination under rule (2) laid down above.

Cross-Examination.

(*See* ante, *p.* 308.)

R. v. HADWEN AND INGHAM.

CROWN CASES RESERVED. 1902.

L. R. [1902] 1 K. B. 882.

Where one of two prisoners jointly indicted gives evidence under s. 1 of the Criminal Evidence Act, 1898, and in so doing incriminates the other prisoner the latter is entitled to cross-examine him.

The two prisoners who had been partners in business were accused of certain bankruptcy offences. They were indicted and tried together but represented by separate counsel. Each prisoner gave evidence exculpating himself and accusing his late partner. The trial Judge refused to allow cross-examination of each accused by the other's counsel, but stated a case for the Court.

The following is from the Law Reports:—

Lord Alverstone, C.J. . . . I come to the conclusion therefore, both on principle and on the analogy of the decisions before the Act, that a prisoner who has **given evidence incriminating his fellow-prisoner** has, in the words of the Act, given evidence against another person charged with the same offence and that in these circumstances **cross-examination of the other prisoner ought to be allowed.**

Wright (R. S.), J. The only question is whether the evidence of one co-defendant given in self-defence is evidence which is legally admissible to inculpate the other defendant, because if it is, it necessarily follows that the latter should be allowed to cross-examine. I can find nothing in the Act except section 1 (*f*) (iii) which tends to abrogate the ordinary common law rule—see *R.* v. *Payne* (1872), L. R. 1 C. C. 349 and *Allen* v. *Allen*, [1894] P. 248 at p. 253, that evidence of one defendant cannot on a criminal trial be received as evidence either for or against another defendant, the reason being that otherwise one defendant would be tempted to exculpate himself at the expense of his co-defendant. I have had some doubt whether clause (*f*) (iii) does get over the difficulty, but I think it can be construed as dealing with evidence given by one prisoner not only in his own defence but also with the object of making a case against the other prisoner. If that is so, and I am not disposed to decide otherwise, it follows that there may be cross-examination of one prisoner by the other.

Note.—Such cross-examination must be directed to relevant matters and not to character or previous convictions unless both prisoners are charged with the *same* offence (*R.* v. *Roberts* (1935), 52 T. L. R. 234).

PRIVILEGE.

Communications Between Husband and Wife.

(*See* ante, *p.* 344.)

SHENTON v. TYLER.

COURT OF APPEAL. 1939.

L. R. [1939] Ch. 620; 108 L. J. Ch. 256; 160 L. T. 315; 55 T. L. R. 522.

In this case it was sought to administer interrogatories to a widow as to what had passed between her late husband and herself. It was held (a) that there is no privilege at common law for communications between husband and wife, and (b) that the statutory privilege under s. 3 of the Evidence Amendment Act, 1853, does not extend to widows or divorced persons.

The following is from the Law Reports:—

Lord Greene, M.R. . . . It is necessary at the outset to distinguish four rules of evidence . . . (1) the rule which existed at common law that neither a party nor the spouse of a party was a competent witness; (2) the rule at common law that a party was not a compellable witness against himself (*the rule is now different, see p.* 308); (3) the rule at common law that a spouse was not a competent witness against his or her spouse . . . like the first rule, this was a rule affecting competence and extended to the whole of the evidence which the witness might be able to give, whether it related to marital communications or not . . . (4) which is the rule now in question, . . . a rule not of competence or admissibility but of privilege which protects marital communications as such. The question whether this privilege existed at common law or is the creature of statute is at the heart of the present controversy. (*The Master of the Rolls then reviewed the course of the statutory reforms which made parties and their spouses usually competent and compellable*) . . . it was argued on behalf of the respondent that there existed and there still exists at common law, independently of s. 3 of the Act of 1853, a rule of privilege protecting communications between husband and wife during marriage, and that this privilege continues to exist notwithstanding that the marriage has come to an end through death or dissolution. The appellant, on the other hand, contends that no such privilege ever existed at common law, and that the only rule of privilege is that enacted by s. 3 of the Act of 1853, and that that section is by its language confined to a subsisting marriage. . . . It is important to appreciate that the alleged common law rule on which the respondent relies is admittedly a rule of privilege and does not make the evidence inadmissible. It is not suggested that the Court would refuse to hear evidence of a marital communication if the privilege were waived. (*The Master of the Rolls then reviewed a series of text-books beginning with Duncombe's Tryals per Pais,* 1666, *and ending with Cockle's Cases and Statutes on Evidence, and referred to numerous authorities and particularly to the* dicta *of Maule, J., in* O'Connor *v.* Marjoribanks (1842), 4 Man. & G. 435, *and of Erle, J., in* Stapleton *v.* Croft (1852), 18 Q. B. 367). . . . From this review of the English text-books and the observations of Maule, J., and Erle, J., I conclude that the alleged common law rule of privilege protecting marital communications as such never existed . . . If my view is right, that the only rule that exists is that contained in s. 3 of the Act of 1853, it remains to consider whether under that section on its true construction, the privilege continues to exist after the marriage has come to an end. In my opinion it does not. . . . No principle of construction . . . entitles me to read into the section a reference to widows, widowers or divorced persons.

DOCUMENTARY EVIDENCE.

PROOF OF DOCUMENTS.

(*See* ante, *p.* 371.)

NELSON v. WHITTALL.

KING'S BENCH. 1817.

1 B. & ALD. 19; 106 E. R. 8.

If the attesting witness is dead, proof of his handwriting, together with some evidence to connect the maker with the instrument purporting to be executed in his name, is sufficient. It is not essential to prove the handwriting of the maker.

This was an action by the indorsee of a promissory note against the maker, there being one attesting witness of the note. The only evidence was that of the plaintiff, who proved that the attesting witness was dead, identified his handwriting and testified that the defendant was present when the attesting witness had prepared the note. No evidence was given of the defendant's handwriting

The following is from Barnewall & Alderson's Reports:—

BAYLEY, J. It is laid down in Mr. Phillips' treatise on Evidence that **proof of the handwriting of the attesting witness is in all cases sufficient** (*that is, of course, where it is proved as it was in this case that the attesting witness is dead*). The difficulty I have always felt is that that proof alone does not connect the defendant with the note. . . . In this case, however, there is **evidence sufficient to connect the defendant with the note**; for he was present in the room when it was prepared.

Note.—The Evidence Act, 1938, s. 3 (see *post*, p. 586), provides that any instrument to the validity of which attestation is legally requisite may be proved as if the attesting witnesses were all dead.

REAL EVIDENCE.

(*See* ante, *p.* 412.)

HOCKING v. AHLQUIST BROTHERS, LTD.

KING'S BENCH DIVISION. 1944.

L. R. [1944] 1 K. B. 120; 113 L. J. K. B. 65; 170 L. T. 3; 60 T. L. R. 722.

There is no rule or principle of law that real evidence is best evidence in any sense which compels production of a chattel or renders it the only admissible evidence.

The defendants were accused of infringing certain statutory regulations which during scarcity of materials in war-time imposed restrictions in the method of making garments. The offending garments were not produced at the trial, and it was argued on behalf of the accused that evidence could therefore not be given by witnesses who had inspected them. The Court, on a case stated, decided that this argument was erroneous.

The following is from the Law Reports:—

VISCOUNT CALDECOTE, C.J. . . . We have had an interesting discussion on the history of the supposed rule that the best evidence must always be produced. . . . **The suggested rule is recent in the history of our law as compared with the rule of law regarding the proof of documents,** which dates from a much earlier time. (*His Lordship then cited with approval* R. *v.* Francis, ante, *p.* 411.) . . . In my judgment it is much too late, even if it was ever possible, **to suppose that evidence of the nature of chattels cannot be given by witnesses who have seen them and speak to their condition.** To suppose that all the articles about which issues are raised in a great variety of cases ought to be produced in Court would lead to consequences which would show how impossible the suggested rule would be in practice.

ADDUCTION OF EVIDENCE.

(*See* ante, *p.* 426.)

RE ENOCH AND ZARETSKY, BOCK & CO.'S ARBITRATION.

COURT OF APPEAL. 1910.

L. R. [1910] 1 K. B. 327; 79 L. J. K. B. 363; 101 L. T. 801.

In civil cases the Judge cannot call a witness without the parties' consent.

An arbitrator called a witness without the consent of the parties. *Held*, that an arbitrator is in the same position as a Judge in this matter, and that neither has any right to call witnesses against the will of the parties.

The following is from the Law Reports:—

FLETCHER MOULTON, L.J. . . . There may in some cases be a person whom it would be desirable to have before the Court; but neither party wishes to take the responsibility of vouching his personal credibility, or admitting that he is fit to be called as a witness. In such cases the Judge may relieve the parties by letting him go into the box as the witness of neither party; and, of course, if the answers are immaterial he may refuse to allow cross-examination. But the *dictum* [*in Coulson* v. *Disborough*, [1894] 2 Q. B. 316] does not lay down, and in my opinion it certainly is not the law, that a Judge, or any person in a judicial position such as an arbitrator, has any power himself to call a witness to fact against the will of either of the parties.

STATUTES ON EVIDENCE.

(*See* ante, *p.* 434.)

WILLS ACT, 1837.

1 VICT. c. 26.

S. 9. . . . no will shall be valid unless it shall be in writing and executed in manner hereinafter mentioned; (that is to say,) it shall be signed at the foot or end thereof by the testator, or by some other person in his presence and by his direction; and such signature shall be made or acknowledged by the testator in the presence of two or more witnesses present at the same time, and such witnesses shall attest and shall subscribe the will in the presence of the testator, but no form of attestation shall be necessary.

Note.—The above section lays down requisites for the validity of wills and therefore belongs properly to substantive law and not the law of evidence. But it is included for convenience in this edition, having regard to the express exception made by the Evidence Act, 1938, s. 3, as to the proof of wills.

(*See* ante, *p.* 454.)

CRIMINAL PROCEDURE ACT, 1865.

4. If a Witness, upon Cross-examination as to a former Statement made by him relative to the Subject Matter of the Indictment or Proceeding, and inconsistent with his present Testimony, does not distinctly admit that he has made such Statement, Proof may be given that he did in fact make it; but before such Proof can be given the Circumstances of the supposed Statement, sufficient to designate the particular Occasion, must be mentioned to the Witness, and he must be asked whether or not he has made such Statement.

5. A witness may be cross-examined as to previous Statements made by him in **Writing** or reduced into Writing relative to the Subject Matter of the Indictment or Proceeding without such Writing being shown to him: but if it is intended to contradict such Witness by the Writing, his Attention must, before such contradictory Proof can be given, be called to those Parts of the

writing which are to be used for the Purpose of so contradicting him: Provided always, that it shall be competent for the Judge, at any Time during the Trial, to require the Production of the Writing for his Inspection, and he may thereupon make such Use of it for the Purposes of the Trial as he may think fit.

Note.—**Ss. 4–5.** Superficially these two sections appear so similar as to be redundant. In fact, however, they differ widely both in origin and purpose. S. 4 is probably only declaratory of the common law under which inconsistent statements (oral or written) formed one of the exceptions to the rule that in matters going only to credit you must take the answer and cannot lead evidence of your own to contradict him. It will be noticed that s. 4 is not limited to written statements. In contrast, s. 5 makes a big change in the common law by getting rid of the rule that you could not cross-examine on a document without first putting it in and proving it yourself, a requirement which might seriously hamper effective cross-examination and give a clue to a dishonest witness (see *North Australian Territory Co.* v. *Goldsborough*, [1893] 2 Ch. 381 (C. A.)).

(*See* ante, *p.* 459.)

The following additions have been made to the **Schedule** to the **Documentary Evidence Act, 1868.**

COLUMN 1.	COLUMN 2.
Ministry of Supply (*t*).	Minister, Secretary, or person authorised by Minister.
Any Minister appointed under the Ministers of the Crown (Emergency Appointments) Act, 1939 (*u*).	Minister, Secretary, or person authorised by Minister.
Minister of Works (*x*).	Minister, Secretary, or person authorised by Minister.
Minister of Town and Country Planning (*y*).	Minister, Secretary, or person authorised by Minister.

(*t*) 2 & 3 Geo. 6, c. 38, s. 15 (4).
(*u*) 2 & 3 Geo. 6, c. 77, s. 4 (4).
(*x*) 5 & 6 Geo. 6, c. 23, s. 5 (4).
(*y*) 6 & 7 Geo. 6, c. 5, s. 5 (4).

(*See* ante, *p.* 459.)

EVIDENCE FURTHER AMENDMENT ACT, 1869.

32 & 33 Vict. c. 68.

S. 1. The 4th section of c. 99 of the Statutes . . . 14 & 15 Vict. and so much of the 2nd section of "The Evidence Amendment Act, 1853" as is contained in the words "or in any proceeding instituted in consequence of adultery" are hereby repealed.

Note.—S. 1 of the above Act repeals s. 4 of the Evidence Act, 1851, and the words in the Evidence Amendment Act, 1853, "or in any proceeding initiated in consequence of adultery". The effect of these two repeals is to get rid of the exception made at the time of the great reform which let in parties to civil suits to give evidence in their own behalf but expressly retained the old law in regard to proceedings based on adultery.

(*See* ante, *p.* 475.)

The following is an additional note on **s. 4** of the **Sale of Goods Act, 1893.**

It has given rise to more litigation in the course of its history than perhaps any other section of any Act. It would be beyond the scope of this work to enumerate the decisions, but the following salient points should be noted: (1) the memorandum must set out the whole bargain as agreed by the parties and must name or identify the parties (see *Archer* v. *Baynes*, 20 L. J. Ex. 54; 5 Ex. 625; 82 R. R. 792). It need not set out terms implied by law where none were expressly agreed, *e.g.*, the implied term of reasonable price (*Hoadley* v. *McLaine*, 10 Bing. 482; 3 L. J. C. P. 162); (2) it need not be contained in one document, but if the documents do not bear on their face some reference to one another, parol evidence is generally inadmissible to connect them (*Long* v. *Millar*, L. R. 4 C. P. D. 450; 48 L. J. C. P. 596, C.A.); (3) the memorandum need not be contemporaneous with the contract, but it must be in existence before action brought (*Lucas* v. *Dixon* (1889), 22 Q. B. D. 357, C. A.); (4) it may be addressed to a third party (*Gibson* v. *Holland* (1865), L. R. 1 C. P. 1); (5) the memorandum may still be effective although its purpose is to repudiate the bargain, provided it admits its making (*Buxton* v. *Rust* (1872), L. R. 7 Ex. 279). A full treatment will be found in *Benjamin on Sale*.

(*See* ante, *p.* 506.)

Add the following note to the note to **s. 184** of the **Law of Property Act, 1925.**

The problem is not as simple as it looks and indeed the section, which is not very happily worded, has given rise to a most violent conflict of judicial opinion. In the case of a shipwreck, for example, the probability is that the victims die many hours and days apart; but where, as in the late war, deaths occurred during enemy air raids, and it was sought to apply the section, acute difficulties arose. Firstly, what do you mean by "died"? If a number of bodies were blown to fragments in a tenth of a second what bodily process taking place within that fraction of time can you specify such that its cessation marks the difference between life and no-life? Secondly, and arising out of this, there being on this reasoning a possibility and even a probability of deaths being so contemporaneous as to be indistinguishable from simultaneity, does the wording of the section cover this contingency? The House of Lords, overruling the Court of Appeal by a majority has held that it does (*Hickman* v. *Peacey* (1945), 173 L. T. 89, reversing the C. A., *sub nom. Re Grosvenor*, [1944] Ch. 138; 113 L. J. Ch. 113; 60 T. L. R. 124). The decision puts an end to many metaphysical subtleties and renders the section normally applicable to any sudden calamity. But the opinions in the above cited case well repay study.

(*See* ante, *p.* 521.)

ROAD TRAFFIC ACT, 1930.

20 & 21 Geo. 5, c. 43.

S. 10 (3). A person charged under this section with the offence of driving a motor vehicle . . . at a speed greater than the maximum allowed . . . shall not be liable to be convicted of the offence solely on the evidence of one witness to the effect that in the **opinion** of the witness the person charged was driving the vehicle at such greater speed.

Note.—This is not quite the ordinary case of corroboration since one witness quite uncorroborated can support a conviction if he goes to work properly, that is to say, he must give evidence of measuring a distance and keeping observation by timing with a watch (*Russell* v. *Beesley*, [1937] 1 A. E. R. 527; 53 T. L. R. 298). The prosecution have the choice of proceeding as above; or of adducing corroborative evidence in the ordinary way, but if they do so the corroborative evidence must relate to observations made at the same time (*Brighty* v. *Pearson*, [1938] 4 A. E. R. 127; 102 J. P. 522).

TRADE MARKS ACT, 1938.

1 & 2 Geo. 6, c. 22.

46. In all legal proceedings relating to a registered trade mark (including applications under section 32 of this Act) the fact that a person is registered as proprietor of the trade mark shall be prima facie evidence of the validity of the original registration of the trade mark and of all subsequent assignments and transmissions thereof.

47. In any legal proceeding in which the validity of the registration of a registered trade mark comes into question and is decided in favour of the proprietor of the trade mark the Court may certify to that effect . . . (*and the holder of the certificate may penalise in costs anyone opposing him in the Courts thereafter*).

49. In any action or proceeding relating to a trade mark or trade name the tribunal shall admit evidence of the usages of the trade concerned and of any relevant trade mark or trade name or get-up legitimately used by other persons.

55. In any proceeding under this Act before the Board of Trade or the Registrar the evidence shall be given by statutory declaration . . . but the tribunal may take evidence viva voce. . . .

56.—(1) All documents purporting to be orders made by the Board of Trade and to be sealed with the seal of the Board or to be signed by a secretary or an under-secretary or an assistant secretary of the Board or by any person authorised in that behalf by the President of the Board shall be received in evidence and shall be deemed to be such orders without further proof unless the contrary is shown.

(2) A certificate signed by the President of the Board of Trade that any order made or act done is the order or act of the Board shall be conclusive evidence of the fact so certified.

57.—(1) A printed or written copy of any entry in the register, purporting to be certified by the Registrar and sealed with the seal of the Patent Office, shall be admitted in evidence in all courts, and in all proceedings, without further proof or production of the original.

(2) Any person requiring such a certified copy as aforesaid shall be entitled to obtain it on payment of the prescribed fee.

58. (*Registrar's certificate to be prima facie evidence of acts done or not done by him.*)

EVIDENCE ACT, 1938.

1 & 2 Geo. 6, c. 28.

S. 1.—(1) In any **civil** proceedings where direct oral evidence of a fact would be admissible, **any statement made by a person in a document** and tending to establish that fact shall, on production of the **original** document, **be admissible** as evidence of that fact. . . .

Note.—S. 1 of this Act is by far the most important section in it. Although limited to **civil** proceedings and to **documentary** evidence, it contains provisions which, within those limits, effect a fundamental change in the law of evidence. The innovations, arranged in order of the extent of their departure from the common law, are three: (1) the previous written statements of a person who is called as a witness are themselves promoted from mere "notes to refresh memory" as they were at common law—and not always allowable even in that limited role—to the status of substantive evidence in themselves, co-ordinate with his oral testimony; (2) hearsay is admitted in the shape of the written statements of a person who had personal knowledge of the matters stated but who is not called as a witness at all, either because he cannot be produced, *e.g.*, being dead or not to be found, or because the Court, in the exercise of a discretion vested in it by the Act, excuses his being called, *e.g.*, on the grounds of delay or expense; (3) a so-to-speak double degree of hearsay, whereby not only is the document received in evidence in lieu of the witness, but the statements in it are themselves made by the maker from hearsay, that is from information supplied him by other persons who had personal knowledge of the matter stated, and which it is his duty to collect and record. The resultant position resembles the common law as to public documents (see *ante*, p. 261). On the other hand, the Court is given an overriding discretion to shut out the evidence where the trial is with a jury.

. . . if the following conditions are satisfied, that is to say—

(i) if the maker of the statement either—

(*a*) had **personal knowledge** of the matters dealt with by the statement; **or**

(*b*) where the document in question is or forms part of a record purporting to be a **continuous record,** made the statement (in so far as the matters dealt with thereby are not within his personal knowledge) in the performance of a duty to record information supplied to him by a person who had, or might reasonably be supposed to have, personal knowledge of those matters; **and**

(ii) if the maker of the statement is **called as a witness** in the proceedings: . . .

Note.—It will be observed that the conditions of qualification for admissibility which relate to the maker's means of knowledge are alternative and it is sufficient if one or the other is satisfied, but the second condition, *viz.*, that the maker must be called is governed by "and", that is to say, it is a condition which must be complied with, whichever type of document of the two mentioned in the first condition it is sought to admit. As will appear, however, this second condition is much mitigated by extensive dispensatory provisions, including a general discretion vested in the Court to excuse the calling of the witness.

Provided that the condition that the maker of the statement shall be called as a witness need not be satisfied if he is **dead,** or **unfit** by reason of his bodily or mental condition to attend as a witness, or if he is **beyond the seas** and it is **not reasonably practicable to secure his attendance,** or if **all reasonable efforts to find him have been made without success. . . .**

Note.—It will be seen that these four dispensatory conditions are all absolute and as of right; but inasmuch as all of them, except the first (the witness being dead), are matters of degree, the Judge in practice has a considerable discretion. See *Infields Ltd.* v. *Rosen* ([1939] 1 A. E. R. 121).

(2) In any **civil** proceedings, the court may at any stage of the proceedings, if having regard to all the circumstances of the case it is satisfied that **undue delay or expense** would otherwise be caused, order that such a statement as is mentioned in subsection (1) of this section shall be admissible as evidence or may,

without any such order having been made, admit such a statement in evidence—

(*a*) notwithstanding that the maker of the statement is available but is not called as a witness;

(*b*) notwithstanding that the original document is not produced, if in lieu thereof there is produced a copy of the original document or of the material part thereof certified to be a true copy in such manner as may be specified in the order or as the court may approve, as the case may be.

Note.—This is a further radical departure from the common law with respect to private documents and resembles the existing position in the case of public documents. It will be noticed, however, that unlike the statutes which render admissible copies of public documents this Act does not use the phrase "purporting to be certified", the effect of which is to dispense with the need of calling the certifying officer, but merely "certified", which of itself would entail the necessity of such proof; but inasmuch as the certification is to be in such manner as the Court may approve or specify, presumably it could specify or approve the mere production of a purported signature without calling the person who made it.

With regard to dispensing with the calling of the maker of the statement though available, a rather obvious example is to be found in *Bagg* v. *London Graving Dock Co., Ltd.*, [1943] 1 K. B. 291.

(3) Nothing in this section shall render admissible as evidence any statement made by a person interested at a time when proceedings were pending or anticipated involving a dispute as to any fact which the statement might tend to establish.

Note.—This provision is analogous to the common law rule excluding statements *post litem motam* in pedigree cases. It will be noticed that the statement is wholly shut out, in contrast to s. 2 (1) of the Act, where in estimating the weight of such evidence regard is to be had to "any incentive to conceal or misrepresent facts", that is to say, the statement is admissible and the Court will judge of its weight. Having regard to these two contrasted provisions and to the interpretation put upon "interest" in the cases relating to competence at common law (see *ante*, p. 269) it is submitted that "person interested", which primarily means the parties and their privies, is not an extensive class. But that it cannot be regarded very narrowly is now settled by the decision in *Plomien Fuel Economiser Co.* v. *National Marketing Co.*, [1941] 1 Ch. 248, where an employee of the plaintiffs whose importance to the company and his expectation of advancement (though no necessary and immediate certainty thereof) were bound up with the plaintiffs' success in the action, was held to be "interested", and his statement inadmissible under the section, *sed quære?* It does not appear from the Report that the Court's attention was called to s. 2 (1) or to any of the cases on incompetence from interest at common law (see Wills, 1st ed., p. 85). Those cases show that "interest" meant not the mere hope or fear of gain or loss, but a certainty contingent only on the result of the action.

For an obvious example of a statement *post litem motam* and therefore excluded, see *Robinson* v. *Stern*, [1939] 2 K. B. 260.

(4) For the purposes of this section, a statement in a document shall not be deemed to have been made by a person unless the document or the material part thereof was **written, made** or **produced** by him with his own hand, or was **signed or initialled** by him or otherwise recognised by him in writing as one for the accuracy of which he is responsible.

Note.—This is an important provision which excludes statements made by the agent of the maker and prevents a statement being admitted as the statement of the person who dictated it, or in whose presence it was made, unless such person make some written mark upon it. On the other hand, there need be nothing in the appearance of a document to identify it with its maker. Thus, a piece of typescript looks much the same whoever executes it (unlike handwriting), but the "maker" is the person who actually tapped the keys, together, of course, with the other persons, if any, who made themselves "makers" by placing some written mark on the paper.

(5) For the purpose of deciding whether or not a statement is admissible as evidence by virtue of the foregoing provisions, the court may draw any reasonable inference from the form or contents of the document in which the statement is contained, or from any other circumstance, and may, in deciding whether or not a person is fit to attend as a witness, act on a certificate purporting to be the certificate of a registered medical practitioner, and **where the proceedings are with a jury, the court may in its discretion reject the statement** notwithstanding that the requirements of this section are satisfied with respect thereto, if for any reason it appears to it to be inexpedient in the interests of justice that the statement should be admitted.

Note.—"Other circumstances" are presumably provable by oral evidence, and, it is submitted, may be adduced both by the party tendering the statement to induce the Court to admit it, and by his opponent to induce the Court to reject it. With regard to the credibility of such statement when admitted, it is submitted on the analogy of the common law as to declarations and depositions (see *Stephen*, Art. 149) that an opponent would be entitled to prove, in order to damage the credibility of the maker of the statement, any of those matters as to which, the maker being called as a witness, if he denied them in cross-examination, evidence thereof could have been led to contradict him, *e.g.*, a previous inconsistent statement or previous conviction (see *ante*, p. 452–3).

S. 2.—(1) In estimating the weight, if any, to be attached to a statement rendered admissible as evidence by this Act regard shall be had to all the circumstances from which any inference can reasonably be drawn as to the accuracy or otherwise of the statement, and in particular to the question whether or not the statement was made contemporaneously with the occurrence or existence of the facts stated, and to the question whether or not the maker of the statement had any incentive to conceal or misrepresent facts.

(2) For the purpose of any rule of law or practice requiring evidence to be corroborated or regulating the manner in which uncorrobated (*sic—an obvious misprint*) evidence is to be treated a statement rendered admissible as evidence by this Act shall not be treated as corroboration of evidence given by the maker of the statement.

Note.—This section, which in the main consists of commonsense directions which would occur to any Judge of experience, seems to contemplate and authorise the giving of oral evidence of the circumstances surrounding the making of the statement if these are material to its weight.

S. 3. Subject as hereinafter provided, in any proceeding, whether **civil or criminal,** an instrument to the validity of which attestation **is requisite** may, instead of being proved by an attesting witness, be proved in the manner in which it might be proved if **no attesting witness were alive:**

Provided that nothing in this section shall apply to the proof of wills or other testamentary documents.

Note.—This section goes far to complete the extinction of a troublesome piece of archaic formalism. As long ago as 1865 the Criminal Procedure Act (28 & 29 Vict. c. 18, s. 7, see *ante*, p. 453) enacted that a document which was in fact attested, though legally it need not have been, might be proved as an ordinary document. The present section deals with documents that *do* require attestation.

The mode of proof where the witness is dead is to prove his handwriting and either prove the handwriting of the party purporting to have executed the document (*Stephen*, Art. 69) or give some other evidence to connect him with the document (see *ante*, p. 574). It will be noted that this section and the one following apply also to criminal proceedings. As to the proof of wills, see *ante*, p. 577.

S. 4. In any proceedings, whether **civil or criminal,** there shall, in the case of a document proved, or purporting, to be not less than **twenty** years old, be made any presumption which immediately before the commencement of this Act would have been made in the case of a document of like character proved, or purporting, to be not less than thirty years old.

Note.—That is to say, documents now acquire in twenty years, instead of thirty as at common law, the status and privileges of "ancient documents" (see *ante*, p. 372).

S. 5. It is hereby declared that section ninety-nine of the Supreme Court of Judicature (Consolidation) Act, 1925, and section ninety-nine of the County Courts Act, 1934 (which relate to the making of rules of court) authorise the making of rules of court providing for orders being made at any stage of any proceedings directing that specified facts may be proved at the trial by affidavit with or without the attendance of the deponent for cross-examination, notwithstanding that a party desires his attendance for cross-examination and that he can be produced for that purpose.

Note.—This section is intended to allay doubts which had arisen when, in 1937, the Rules of the Supreme Court were altered (O. 30, r. 2 (3) and O. 37, r. 1) by taking away the hitherto absolute right of objecting to a witness giving his evidence on affidavit if he were available to come and give evidence in person. The altered rules give the Court a discretion in the matter and evidence on affidavit may be ordered notwithstanding that the witness could be produced in Court. It was suggested that it was *ultra vires* the Rules Committee to make this alteration and, accordingly, the Act gives statutory confirmation to the new rule.

S. 6 (1). In this Act—

"Document" includes books, maps, plans, drawings and photographs;

"Statement" includes any representation of fact, whether made in words or otherwise;

"Proceedings" includes arbitrations and references, and "Court" shall be construed accordingly.

(2) Nothing in this Act shall—

(*a*) prejudice the admissibility of any evidence which would apart from the provisions of this Act be admissible; or

(*b*) enable any documentary evidence to be given as to any declaration relating to a matter of pedigree, if that declaration would not have been admissible as evidence if this Act had not passed.

Note.—The Act preserves and is cumulative upon all the common law rules by which, in certain cases, hearsay may be admitted, *e.g.*, public documents, declarations by deceased persons, etc. (see *ante*, p. 210, ff).

S. 7 (2). This Act shall not extend to Scotland or Northern Ireland.

PHARMACY AND MEDICINES ACT, 1941.

4 & 5 Geo. 6, c. 42.

S. 13 (2). In any proceedings for a contravention of any of the provisions of the last two preceding sections a document purporting to be a certificate signed by a public analyst within the meaning of the Food and Drugs Act, 1938, or a person appointed by the Secretary of State to make analyses for the purpose of the principal Act, and stating the result of an analysis made by him, shall be admissible as evidence of the matters stated therein, but any party to the proceedings may require the person by whom the analysis was made to be called as a witness.

SOLICITORS ACT, 1941.

4 & 5 Geo. 6, c. 46.

S. 16 (3). Every order made by the Disciplinary Committee under this section shall be prefaced by a statement of their findings in relation to the facts of the case and shall be signed by the Chairman of the Committee or by a member of the Committee authorised by the Committee to sign the same and any document purporting to be an order so signed shall be received in evidence in any criminal proceedings or in any proceedings under this section or under the disciplinary enactments and be deemed to be such an order without further proof unless the contrary is shown.

MINISTER OF WORKS AND PLANNING ACT, 1942.

5 & 6 Geo. 6, c. 23.

S. 5 (4). The Documentary Evidence Act, 1868, as amended by the Documentary Evidence Act, 1882, shall apply to the Minister as if his name were included in the first column of the Schedule to the first-mentioned Act, and as if he or a secretary of the Ministry of Works and Planning or any person authorised by him to act on his behalf were mentioned in the second column of that Schedule, and as if the regulations referred to in that Act included any document issued by the Minister.

Note.—The name and functions of this Ministry have been somewhat modified by the Ministry of Town and Country Planning Act, 1943, s. 7, but the substance of the above enactment remains, omitting, however, the word "planning" wherever it occurs.

MINISTER OF TOWN AND COUNTRY PLANNING ACT, 1943.

6 & 7 Geo. 6, c. 5.

S. 5 (4). The Documentary Evidence Act, 1868, shall apply to the Minister as if his name were included in the first column of the Schedule to that Act, and as if he or a secretary of the Ministry or any person authorised by him to act on his behalf were mentioned in the second column of that Schedule, and as if the regulations referred to in that Act included any document issued by the Minister.

CATERING WAGES ACT, 1943.

6 & 7 Geo. 6, c. 24.

S. 12 (1) and (2). (*Providing that where an employer is prosecuted in respect of an offence committed by his servant, the servant also is liable to prosecution, and giving the employer the right to insist on his servant being made a co-defendant at his own trial and making it a defence for the employer to show that he used due diligence to secure observance of the Act*).

(3) Where a defendant seeks to avail himself of the provisions of sub-section (2) of this section:—

(*a*) the prosecution, as well as the person whom the defendant charges with the offence, shall have the right to cross-examine him if he gives evidence and any witnesses called by him in support of his pleas and to call rebutting evidence.

Note.—It is submitted that this provision is quite superfluous and that the normal rules applicable to such a case lead to exactly the same result. Unfortunately modern legislation is all too frequently drafted apparently in ignorance of the law of evidence and therefore cluttered up with special provisions and exceptions most of which are quite needless.

INDEX.

(*Reference should also be made to Appendices I and II.*)

Printed in Great Britain by
The Berkshire Printing Co. Ltd., Reading